The Cornwallis Papers

The Campaigns of 1780 and 1781

in

The Southern Theatre of the American Revolutionary War

Volume I

Arranged and edited by

Ian Saberton

The Naval & Military Press Ltd

Published by
The Naval & Military Press Ltd

Unit 10 Ridgewood Industrial Park,
Uckfield, East Sussex,
TN22 5QE England

Tel: +44 (0) 1825 749494
Fax: +44 (0) 1825 765701

www.naval-military-press.com
www.military-genealogy.com
www.militarymaproom.com

Documents hitherto unpublished © Crown copyright 2010

Documents previously published in which Crown copyright subsists
© Crown copyright

Introductory chapters, footnotes and other editorial matter © Ian Saberton 2010

The right of Ian Saberton to be identified as author of the introductory chapters, footnotes and other editorial matter in this work has been asserted in accordance with sections 77 and 78 of the UK Copyright, Designs and Patents Act 1988

ISBN Volume I   9781845747923
ISBN Volume II   9781845747916
ISBN Volume III 9781845747909
ISBN Volume IV   9781845747893
ISBN Volume V   9781845747886
ISBN Volume VI   9781845747879

Printed and bound in Great Britain by
CPI Antony Rowe, Chippenham and Eastbourne

In memory of my parents, Andrew and Rhoda

"This work makes a very valuable contribution to our understanding of the American War, of the British Army, and of the politics of counterinsurgency. It is an outstanding feat of scholarship.

"The introductory chapters are exemplary. I find edited papers that lack this comment rather irritating, for the reader, who often has little idea of the path ahead, has to pick his or her way through the documents, uncertain whether a foot will come to rest on a cow-pat or not. The footnotes, which are models of their kind, contribute substantially to our knowledge of the period.

"These are the papers of someone who played an extraordinarily important role at a crucial period in the history of two great nations. I could scarcely envisage any that are more significant."

Professor Richard Holmes

CONTENTS

Preface		ix
Acknowledgements		xi
Editorial method		xiii

PART ONE
THE SIEGE OF CHARLESTOWN
1st April to 12th May 1780

1.	Introduction to the rest of Part One	3
2.	Correspondence between Cornwallis and Clinton	9
3.	Miscellaneous papers	23

PART TWO
CONSOLIDATION OF BRITISH AUTHORITY IN SOUTH CAROLINA
13th May to 25th June 1780

4.	Introduction to the rest of Part Two	31
5.	Correspondence between Cornwallis and Clinton or Arbuthnot	43
6.	Correspondence between Cornwallis and Balfour	72
7.	Correspondence between Cornwallis and Ferguson	99
8.	Correspondence between Cornwallis and Innes	110
9.	Other correspondence etc	
	1 – Between Cornwallis and Paterson	121
	2 – Rawdon to Cornwallis	128
	3 – Between Cornwallis and McArthur	130
	4 – Between Cornwallis and Turnbull	138
	5 – Paroles	144

PART THREE
INCIPIENT UNREST – REVOLUTIONARY FORCES FROM THE NORTH
26th June to 15th August 1780

10.	Introduction to the rest of Part Three	149
11.	Correspondence between Cornwallis and Clinton or Arbuthnot	159
12.	Correspondence between Cornwallis and Rawdon	182
13.	Correspondence with Ninety Six and Augusta	
	1 – Between Cornwallis and Balfour or Cruger	235
	2 – Between Cornwallis and Innes	265
	3 – Between Cornwallis and Brown or Wright Jr	270
14.	Correspondence between Cornwallis and Ferguson	285
15.	Correspondence between Cornwallis and Wemyss	304
16.	Correspondence with Savannah or St Augustine	
	1 – Between Cornwallis and Clarke	328
	2 – Between Cornwallis and Sir James Wright	344
	3 – Between Cornwallis and Tonyn or Glasier	354
17.	Miscellaneous letters etc	
	1 – From sundry British officers	361
	2 – Between Cornwallis and Governor Martin	368
	3 – From Simpson	372
	4 – Other papers	373
Index		379

Preface

The part played by the British in the American Revolutionary War has been much misunderstood over the years. In due course the tide of history would flow against the concept of empires, but for the time being, and indeed until the Statute of Westminster, the unity of the British Empire was for many an inspirational cause, supported, in the present case, not only to a preponderant degree by the British but also by the numerous American loyalists, especially in the south. With hindsight it is easy to castigate them for their support of a cause which would eventually prove outdated, but at the time it was by no means clear that they were mistaken or that prosecuting the war was ill advised. *Tempora mutantur et nos mutamur in illis.*

In view of the numberless inaccuracies published about the war it is most important to present the Cornwallis Papers in an accurate, balanced and dispassionate way. To this end the editor has written an introductory chapter to each Part. Yet it is so very difficult to be accurate, balanced and dispassionate about a conflict in which political passions were so polarised and views so warped by them. Inevitably, it is the perspective from which the Papers are viewed which will to a degree determine whether the editor is seen to have squared the circle.

The Papers open the door to re-evaluating certain aspects of the war. The introductory chapters very briefly provide pointers. They also address certain important considerations that have long gone by default, together with others that are equally pertinent to placing the Papers in context.

As we shall see, neither the British nor the revolutionaries came out of the war in the south smelling of roses. Both were to blame for the uncommon savagery with which it was waged.

IAN SABERTON *Kensington*
1st May 2010 *London*

Acknowledgements

The editor would like to thank the staff of the UK National Archives, the British Library, the Libraries of the Universities of London and Sheffield, and the Hessisches Staatsarchiv, Marburg, for courteously dealing with his various requests for assistance.

He is particularly indebted to Terry W Lipscomb for contributing information involved in the preparation of those footnotes in which reference is made to him. Terry, sometime Editor of the South Carolina Colonial Records, is an established authority on the war in South Carolina. Thanks are also due to others mentioned in the footnotes, who, apart from Todd W Braisted, publisher of *The On-Line Institute for Advanced Loyalist Studies,* are sadly too numerous to name. Charles B Baxley, publisher of the on-line *Southern Campaigns of the American Revolution,* has been most helpful in passing on various queries to colleagues for answer.

Last but not least, the editor is indebted to his parents, Andrew and Rhoda, without whose encouragement this work would not have been completed.

Editorial method

Comprehensiveness

The Cornwallis Papers relating to the southern theatre of the American Revolutionary War form part of the series PRO 30/11/- in the UK National Archives. They are published in their entirety apart from the following omissions:

- duplicates, triplicates, and quadruplicates of papers published in this or later volumes, subject to any material differences highlighted in footnotes;

- the odd, extremely isolated paper listed below or in later volumes.

Arrangement of papers

The Papers have been compartmentalised into chapters so that they may deal separately with New York, London, etc and with the officers in command of the various posts, etc. Letters within each chapter from Cornwallis are in date order but those received by him are not necessarily so but rather in the order in which he received them. Both sets are interleaved so that the correspondence is always in the correct sequence and so that at any given point in time it is possible to be aware of Cornwallis's thinking and of the information available to him. Compartmentalisation and the correct sequencing of papers avoid the major problem with papers listed entirely in chronological order, which is that it is necessary to be constantly flipping through them to find the precursor or follow-up to the paper one is reading.

Heading of papers

Apart from stating the date and, in the case of letters, the addresser and addressee, the heading of each paper contains two forms of reference adjacent to the right margin.

The first indicates in an abbreviated way the location of the paper in the series PRO 30/11/-. For example, '4(65)' means folio 65 in the file PRO 30/11/4.

The second uses one of the following abbreviations to describe the kind of paper involved:

C   Copy
CS   Copy signed
AC   Autograph copy
ACS   Autograph copy signed

D   Document
DS   Document signed
AD   Autograph document
ADS   Autograph document signed

Df   Draft
DfS   Draft signed
ADf   Autograph draft
ADfS Autograph draft signed

L   Letter
LS   Letter signed
AL   Autograph letter
ALS   Autograph letter signed.

Form of letters

For consistency a letter takes the following form, irrespective of the form used in the manuscript:

- the location and date appear in the top right corner;

- if stated in the letter, the addressee and his address are placed on the left immediately below the location and date;

- paragraphing is never altered;

- any interlineations by the writer are incorporated silently into the text;

- deleted passages are disregarded unless of unusual significance, in which case they are set out in footnotes;

- enciphered words are italicised and underlined;

- words emphasised by underlining etc are italicised, as are words or short phrases in foreign languages and the names of ships;

- significant additions appearing on the back, foot or top of a letter are placed at the end, preceded by the word '[*Endorsed*:]', '[*Subscribed*:]', or '[*Superscribed*:]'.

Interpolations

Apart from lost words or lost parts of words inserted into the text, all interpolations are printed in italics and enclosed in square brackets.

Blank spaces are represented by the word '[*blank*]'.

One or more words irretrievably lost by mutilation, defacement or illegibility are replaced by the word '[*torn*]', '[*blotted*]' or '[*illeg*]'.

If a lost word or the lost part of a word can be inferred with reasonable certainty from the context, it is printed in square brackets but not italicised. A mere conjecture, as distinct from a reasonably certain inference, is treated in the same way, except that it is followed by a question mark. Doubtful or alternative readings are placed in footnotes.

Spelling

Spelling is the same as in the manuscripts. If a misspelt word is not readily recognisable, it is the subject of a footnote.

Abbreviations, contractions, and symbols

Abbreviations and contractions are spelt in full, except when used in the proper names of persons.

The ampersand is replaced by 'and', except that 'etc' is substituted for '&c' and '&ca'.

The letter 'y', representing the thorn, is expanded to 'th'.

Punctuation and capitalisation

By the time of the revolutionary war punctuation and capitalisation had in many cases degenerated so that there was often no logicality or consistency in the ways in which they were employed. It would be tiresome for the general reader (for whom this work is partly intended), if not for the academic historian, to be faced with text in such a form. Accordingly punctuation and capitalisation have been altered to conform to the rules of consistency generally operative at present. As applied to this work, they are outlined in G V Carey's *Mind the Stop: A Brief Guide to Punctuation* (Revised edition, Cambridge University Press, 1958; reprint, Penguin Books, 1976). The effects are as follows:

- where the meaning of the text is certain, Carey's rules of punctuation are followed;

- where the meaning is uncertain, the original punctuation is retained;

- in compliance with Carey, colons, commas, periods, question marks, and semicolons replace dashes used in manuscripts in these senses. Dashes used in other senses, for example as a resemblance to brackets or as an introduction to an afterthought or interjection tacked on to the end of a sentence, are retained;

- each sentence terminates in an exclamation mark, period, or question mark;

- Carey's rules of capitalisation are followed.

Misdated or undated papers

The correct date of a misdated paper is provided in a footnote. The paper is placed in the correct sequence.

An undated paper is placed in what appears from the context to be the correct sequence. As a general rule no specific date is provided.

Omitted papers

Though belonging to the period covered by this volume, the following papers in the series PRO 30/11/- are omitted on the ground that they do not relate to the southern campaigns or are too inconsequential: 1(7) and (38); 2(19), (46), (60), (66), (77), (104), (335), (407), and (408); 102(16); and 106(1) and (17).

As a general rule it is not a purpose of this or later volumes to incorporate papers which are adverted to in the series PRO 30/11/- but are missing from it. Such a paper is in each case the subject of a footnote, where a reference to the paper being no longer extant is a reference to its being no longer extant in the Cornwallis Papers but not necessarily elsewhere.

Footnotes

It goes almost without saying that footnotes are there partly to provide biographical information and partly to elucidate otherwise the text. Biographical footnotes usually appear at the first mention of persons, but in all cases references to such footnotes are highlighted in the index. Without exception a cross-reference to another paper or footnote contains its page number and, in the case of a footnote, the note number.

Titles of works cited in abbreviated form in footnotes

Alden, *The South in the Rev*
  John Richard Alden, *The South in the Revolution 1763-1789* (Louisiana State University Press, 1976)

Appletons'
  Appletons' Cyclopædia of American Biography (New York, 1888-)

Army Lists
  A list of the general and field officers... (London, 1754-77), together with *A list of all the officers of the army...* (London, 1778-)

Bailey and Cooper, *SC House of Representatives*
   Walter and N Louise Bailey, Elizabeth Ivey Cooper, et al, *Biographical Directory of the South Carolina House of Representatives* (University of South Carolina Press, 1977-81)

Bass, *Gamecock*
   Robert D Bass, *Gamecock: The Life and Campaigns of General Thomas Sumter* (Holt, Rinehart and Winston, 1961)

Bass, *The Green Dragoon*
   Robert D Bass, *The Green Dragoon: The Lives of Banastre Tarleton and Mary Robinson* (Sandlapper Press Inc, 1973)

Boatner, *Encyclopedia*
   Mark Mayo Boatner III, *Encyclopedia of the American Revolution* (D McKay Co, 1966)

Cashin, *The King's Ranger*
   Edward J Cashin, *The King's Ranger: Thomas Brown and the American Revolution on the Southern Frontier* (Fordham University Press, 1999)

Cashin Jr and Robertson, *Augusta*
   Edward J Cashin Jr and Heard Robertson, *Augusta and the American Revolution: Events in the Georgia Back Country 1773-1783* (Richmond County Historical Society, 1975)

Charnock, *Biographia Navalis*
   John Charnock, *Biographia Navalis: or Impartial Memoirs of the Lives and Characters of Officers of the Navy of Great Britain from the Year 1660 to the Present Time* (London, 1794-98)

Clark, *Loyalists in the Southern Campaign*
   Murtie June Clark, *Loyalists in the Southern Campaign of the Revolutionary War*, volume I (Genealogical Publishing Co, 2003)

Coldham, *Loyalist Claims*
   Peter Wilson Coldham, *American Loyalist Claims* (National Genealogical Society, 1980)

DAB
   Dictionary of American Biography (New York, 1928-1958)

Davie, *Revolutionary War Sketches*
   William R Davie, *The Revolutionary War Sketches of William R Davie,* edited by Blackwell P Robinson (NC Department of Cultural Resources, Division of Archives and History, 1976)

Davies ed, *Docs of the Am Rev*
   K G Davies ed, *Documents of the American Revolution 1770-1783,* volume XVIII (Irish Academic Press, 1978)

DeMond, *Loyalists in NC*
   Robert O DeMond, *The Loyalists in North Carolina during the Revolution* (Duke University Press, 1940)

DGB
   Dictionary of Georgia Biography, edited by Kenneth Coleman and Charles Stephen Gurr (University of Georgia Press, 1983)

DNB
   Dictionary of National Biography (London, 1885-1901)

Draper, *King's Mountain*
   Lyman C Draper, *King's Mountain and its Heroes* (Cincinnati, 1881)

Drayton, *Memoirs*
   John Drayton, *Memoirs of the American Revolution from its Commencement to the Year 1776 inclusive* (Charleston, 1821)

Ewald, *Diary*
   Johann Ewald, *Diary of the American War: A Hessian Journal,* translated and edited by Joseph P Tustin (Yale University Press, 1979)

Fortescue, *British Army*
   Sir John Fortescue, *A History of the British Army,* volume III (Macmillan & Co Ltd, 1902)

Garden, *Anecdotes* (1st Series)
   Alexander Garden, *Anecdotes of the Revolutionary War* (Charleston, 1822)

Garden, *Anecdotes* (2nd series)
   Alexander Garden, *Anecdotes of the American Revolution, Second Series* (Charleston, 1828)

'Joseph Graham's Narrative', *The Murphey Papers*
   Joseph Graham, 'Narrative', in William Henry Hoyt ed, *The Papers of Archibald D Murphey* (Publications of the NC Historical Commission, 1914)

The Greene Papers
   The Papers of General Nathanael Greene, volumes VI-IX, edited by Richard K Showman, Dennis M Conrad, Roger N Parks, et al (University of North Carolina Press, 1991-7)

Gregg, *The Old Cheraws*
   Alexander Gregg, *History of the Old Cheraws* (The Reprint Company, 1975)

Gregorie, *Sumter*
   Anne King Gregorie, *Thomas Sumter* (R L Bryan Co, 1931)

Hanger, *An Address to the Army*
    George Hanger, *An Address to the Army in reply to Strictures of Roderick M'Kenzie (late Lieutenant in the 71st Regiment) on Tarleton's History of the Campaigns of 1780 and 1781* (London, 1789)

Hay ed, *Soldiers from NC*
    Gertrude Sloan Hay ed, *Roster of Soldiers from North Carolina in the American Revolution* (Reprint, Genealogical Publishing Co Inc, 1988)

Heitman, *Historical Register*
    Francis B Heitman, *Historical Register of the Officers of the Continental Army during the War of the Revolution* (Reprint, Clearfield Publishing Co Inc, 2000)

James, *Marion*
    William Dobein James, *A Sketch of the Life of Brig Gen Francis Marion* (Reprint, Continental Book Co, Marietta GA, 1948)

Johnson, *Greene*
    William Johnson, *Sketches of the Life and Correspondence of Nathanael Greene* (Charleston, 1822)

Johnson, *Traditions*
    Joseph Johnson, *Traditions and Reminiscences chiefly of the American Revolution in the South* (Charleston, 1851)

Johnston, *Commissioned Officers in the Medical Service*
    William Johnston, *Roll of Commissioned Officers in the Medical Service of the British Army: 20 June 1727 to 23 June 1898* (Reprint, The Wellcome Historical Medical Library, 1968)

Lambert, *SC Loyalists*
    Robert Stansbury Lambert, *South Carolina Loyalists in the American Revolution* (University of South Carolina Press, 1987)

Lee, *Memoirs*
    Henry Lee, *Memoirs of the War in the Southern Department of the United States* (Revised edition, New York, 1869)

Lossing, *Pictorial Field-Book*
    Benson J Lossing, *The Pictorial Field-Book of the Revolution* (New York, 1855)

MacKenzie, *Strictures*
    Roderick MacKenzie, *Strictures on Lt Col Tarleton's History of the Campaigns of 1780 and 1781 in the Southern Provinces of North America* (London, 1787)

Marshall, *Royal Naval Biography*
    John Marshall, *Royal Naval Biography* (London, 1823-35)

McCowen Jr, *Charleston, 1780-82*
    George Smith McCowen Jr, *The British Occupation of Charleston, 1780-82* (University of South Carolina Press, 1972)

McCrady, *SC in the Rev 1775-1780*
    Edward McCrady, *The History of South Carolina in the Revolution 1775-1780* (The Macmillan Co, New York, 1901)

McCrady, *SC in the Rev 1780-1783*
    Edward McCrady, *The History of South Carolina in the Revolution 1780-1783* (The Macmillan Co, New York, 1902)

McRee, *Iredell*
    Griffith J McRee, *Life and Correspondence of James Iredell* (New York, 1857)

Moss, *SC Patriots*
    Bobby Gilmer Moss, *Roster of South Carolina Patriots in the American Revolution* (Genealogical Publishing Co Inc, 1983)

Moultrie, *Memoirs*
    William Moultrie, *Memoirs of the American Revolution* (New York, 1802)

Raymond, 'British American Corps'
    W O Raymond, 'Roll of Officers of the British American or Loyalist Corps', *Collections of the New Brunswick Historical Society*, ii, 1899

Robinson, *Davie*
    Blackwell P Robinson, *William R Davie* (University of North Carolina Press, 1957)

Robinson, *NC Guide*
    Blackwell P Robinson ed, *The North Carolina Guide* (University of North Carolina Press, 1955)

Rogers Jr, *Georgetown County*
    George C Rogers Jr, *The History of Georgetown County, South Carolina* (University of South Carolina Press, 1970)

Ross ed, *Cornwallis Correspondence*
    Charles Ross ed, *Correspondence of Charles, First Marquis Cornwallis*, volume I (London, 1859)

Royal Regiment of Artillery
    List of Officers of the Royal Regiment of Artillery from the Year 1716 to the Year 1899 (London, 1900)

Sabine, *Biographical Sketches*
    Lorenzo Sabine, *Biographical Sketches of Loyalists of the American Revolution* (Boston, 1864)

Salley Jr, *Orangeburg County*
A S Salley Jr, *The History of Orangeburg County, South Carolina, from its first Settlement to the close of the Revolutionary War* (Orangeburg, 1898)

SCHGM
The South Carolina Historical and Genealogical Magazine (Charleston, 1900-)

Stevens, *Clinton-Cornwallis Controversy*
Benjamin Franklin Stevens, *The Campaign in Virginia 1781: the Clinton Cornwallis Controversy* (London, 1887-8)

Syrett and DiNardo ed, *The Commissioned Sea Officers*
David Syrett and R L DiNardo ed, *The Commissioned Sea Officers of the Royal Navy 1660-1815* (Navy Records Society, 1994)

Tarleton, *Campaigns*
Banastre Tarleton, *A History of the Campaigns of 1780 and 1781 in the Southern Provinces of North America* (London, 1787)

Valentine, *The British Establishment*
Alan Valentine, *The British Establishment, 1760-1784: An Eighteenth-Century Biographical Dictionary* (University of Oklahoma Press, 1970)

Wallace, *South Carolina*
David Duncan Wallace, *South Carolina: A Short History, 1520-1948* (University of South Carolina Press, 1961)

Ward, *The War of the Rev*
Christopher Ward, *The War of the Revolution* (The Macmillan Co, New York, 1952)

Wheeler, *Historical Sketches*
John Hill Wheeler, *Historical Sketches of North Carolina from 1584 to 1851* (Reprint, Clearfield Company Inc, 2000)

Wheeler, *Reminiscences*
John Hill Wheeler, *Reminiscences and Memoirs of North Carolina and Eminent North Carolinians* (Reprint, Genealogical Publishing Co, 1966)

Wickwire, *Cornwallis*
Franklin and Mary Wickwire, *Cornwallis: The American Adventure* (Houghton Mifflin Co, 1970)

The Cornwallis Papers

PART ONE

The Siege of Charlestown

1st April to 12th May 1780

CHAPTER 1

Introduction to the rest of Part One

The Cornwallis Papers deal with Britain's last throw of the dice in the American Revolutionary War.

By the close of 1779 British possessions in the revolted colonies were confined in the north to New York City, Long Island, and Penobscot. An army had been lost at Saratoga. In the south a tenuous hold on lower Georgia had been gained, East and West Florida had remained loyal, but West Florida was threatened by Spain. Elsewhere in the revolted colonies the revolutionaries were firmly in control.

Britain was losing the war.

To turn the tide a bold strategy was evolved. By a series of campaigns beginning in the south at Charlestown the British would move north through the Carolinas into Virginia and form the numerous loyalists of the Carolinas into militia as they progressed. Material reliance would be placed on the militia to maintain control of the territory that had been conquered, freeing regular and British American troops for the onward advance. If all went well, the south would be recovered and civil government eventually reinstated there under the Crown.

A most important factor in the equation was the paucity of available troops. Sir Henry Clinton, the British Commander-in-Chief, had at his disposal an entire force which at most amounted to only 27,000 rank and file fit for duty, including the troops in Georgia and the Floridas. Of these 12,000 to 15,000 men were required to maintain the posts at New York and Long Island, so that only a dangerously small balance remained for service in other quarters.

If the strategy were to succeed, a new base — Charlestown — had first to be taken and held. As the troops advanced into the interior, posts had to be established to support the militia in maintaining control of conquered territory, and lines of communication sufficiently guarded. In short, two complete armies were really required: one in the south; and another at New York to hold the forces of New England in check and to deter an offensive against Canada. It would be Clinton's task to make one army do the work of two by relying on the sea for communication between the different parts of his force. If command of the sea were kept, the troops detached to the south could if necessary be supported and might succeed; if command of the sea were lost, they or part of them ran the risk of defeat in detail.

Embarking on the first step in the strategy – the Charlestown campaign, Clinton set sail from New York on 26th December 1779 during the coldest winter in living memory. Accompanied by Cornwallis and 8,700 troops, he arrived off Tybee, Georgia, at the end of January, having been escorted by ships of war under the command of Marriot Arbuthnot, the naval Commander-in-Chief. Despite a harrowing passage almost all the troops arrived safely, but few horses survived and much of the artillery was lost together with many valuable supplies.

On 10th February Clinton sailed for Simmons (now Seabrook) Island, South Carolina, and began landing troops there the following day. Advancing cautiously on Charlestown, he eventually established himself on Charlestown Neck on 29th March and three days later broke ground within 800 yards of the town's defences. In the meantime he had been reinforced with 1,500 troops from Georgia under Brigadier General James Paterson, a corps which had at first been intended for a diversionary move on Augusta.

Charlestown lay at the tip of a peninsular ('the Neck') bounded on the west by the Ashley River, on the east by the Cooper, and on the south and south-east by the harbour. Occupying it was a combined force of Continental troops and militia commanded by Major General Benjamin Lincoln. At the capitulation it would have been augmented to almost 5,500 men.

Not the sharpest tool in the box, Lincoln had been seduced by Clinton's leisurely advance into concluding that he might strengthen Charlestown's defences in time to withstand a siege. It would prove a fatal mistake. Not only would he lose the garrison and town but by concentrating his available force there he would open the whole of South Carolina to control by the British.

Having completed the first parallel of his approaches and erected batteries there, Clinton joined with Arbuthnot on 10th April in issuing a summons to surrender. It was rejected. Lincoln was now invested on three sides: by Clinton's forces to the north and west of Charlestown and by Arbuthnot's frigates in the harbour. The only way open lay to the east across the Cooper River, where a number of revolutionary vessels were sunk or anchored behind a log-and-chain boom to obstruct passage by the Royal Navy.

To close the noose around the town Clinton detached Lt Colonel James Webster to the east of the Cooper on 12th April, placing under his command a corps of 1,400 men comprising the 33rd and 64th Regiments, Tarleton's British Legion, and Ferguson's American Volunteers. Only two days had elapsed when Tarleton and Ferguson, of whom we shall speak later, routed the only revolutionary force operational in the field west of the Santee, a body of Continental cavalry and militia posted at Monck's Corner.

In the meantime Clinton's approaches were progressing steadily under the supervision of the commanding engineer, Major James Moncrief, and by 19th April they were within 250 yards of the lines of Charlestown. Convinced at last of the hopelessness of his situation, Lincoln proposed two days later a capitulation allowing the unmolested withdrawal of his garrison to whatever destination he chose, together with that of the shipping. The proposal was rejected.

On 18th April Rawdon had arrived from New York with a reinforcement of 2,566 rank and file effectives, of whom 1,863 were fit for duty. It enabled Clinton to strengthen the corps east of the Cooper, which on the 23rd was placed under the command of Cornwallis. It is at this point that chapter 2 begins.

Charles, Earl Cornwallis was now in his forty-second year. Educated partly at Eton, he was disfigured there for life when he was accidentally struck in the eye during a game of hockey. Instead of going on to Oxford or Cambridge, he attended the military academy at Turin for several months before taking part in the European theatre of the Seven Years' War, first as an aide-de-camp to Lt General the Marquess of Granby, and second as Lt Colonel of the 12th Regiment. In the years after the war he became, *inter alia*, an aide-de-camp to the King (1765), Colonel of the 33rd Regiment (1766), Vice-Treasurer of Ireland (1769), Privy Councillor (1770), and Constable of the Tower of London (1771). Politically, he had the foresight to vote against the Stamp and Declaratory Acts and generally sympathised with the grievances of the American colonists. Nevertheless, his sympathy did not extend to support for breaking the constitutional ties with the Crown. After the revolutionary war broke out, he was promoted to major general (29th September 1775) and shortly after to lt general in North America (1st January 1776). He went on to take part in the New York, New Jersey, and Philadelphia campaigns and in the Battle of Monmouth. A dynamic officer best suited to offensive operations, he was beloved by the troops, who would have gone — and did go — through hell and high water for him. Possessing many admirable qualities, not least affability, high courage, decisiveness, endurance, honesty, humanity and self-assurance, he was tactically astute, but as these Papers later reveal, he was temperamentally unsuited to defensive warfare and would display a crucial lack of strategic awareness at a critical juncture. Third in the chain of command behind Clinton and Knyphausen, he held a dormant commission to succeed Clinton should the latter die or become incapacitated.

By now relations between Clinton and Cornwallis were strained. At first the two men were friends, but in 1777 Clinton had taken exception to Cornwallis advising Howe of a derogatory comment that Clinton had made privately about the then Commander-in-Chief. On the surface the two patched up their relationship, but Clinton had a long memory.

Another fly in the ointment was Clinton's perception of Cornwallis's recent behaviour. In the summer of 1779 Clinton had written to Germain, submitting his resignation. It was widely expected that Cornwallis would be named to succeed him, but neither man had any way of knowing when or if the succession would occur. While awaiting Germain's reply, Clinton had felt it prudent to consult Cornwallis on every step in the Charlestown campaign, but it was not the involvement of Cornwallis that caused Clinton's irritation. Rather it was his conviction that Cornwallis was tattling behind his back and persuading many officers to act as if Cornwallis had succeeded to the command. For this and other reasons Clinton considered Cornwallis guilty of unfriendly and unmilitary conduct.

On 19th March Clinton had received Germain's long awaited reply. It advised him that the King, for all his confidence in Cornwallis, was too well satisfied with Clinton's conduct to wish to see the command in any other hands. Instead of lancing Clinton's irritation with Cornwallis, it only served to exacerbate it, for Cornwallis, no doubt deeply disappointed, reacted by asking not to be consulted any longer on plans. Quite legitimately Clinton took the view that he was entitled to a subordinate's advice whenever he wished it. Of course he might have compelled Cornwallis to give his views formally in a council of the general and field officers, but he feared that they would carry too much weight there. What he really wanted was to be able to continue consulting Cornwallis privately. By closing the door on this alternative, Cornwallis irritated Clinton more.

Clinton for his part was not the easiest of men to serve under. The son of an admiral who had served as Governor of New York, he was a first cousin of the Duke of Newcastle and had entered the army in 1745. After serving for four years as an aide-de-camp to Lord Ligonier, the Commander-in-Chief in Britain, he went off in 1760 to the European theatre of the Seven Years' War as a captain and lt colonel in the 1st Regiment of Foot Guards (the Grenadier Guards), but instead of serving with the regiment, he acted as aide-de-camp to the Duke of Brunswick, an officer of superior ability. In late 1762 he returned to London as a colonel and two years later was appointed a groom of the bedchamber to the Duke of Gloucester, the King's favourite brother. It was a post he would occupy for many years, even while he was in North America. In May 1772 he was promoted to major general and two months later was elected to the Commons as the Member for Boroughbridge, becoming the Member for Newark in 1774. A supporter of the North administration, he dreaded the direction that its American policy was taking and hoped against hope that the quarrel with the colonies would not come to war. Nevertheless, as a serving officer, he considered it his duty to go out with Howe to Boston in 1775, and when Howe succeeded to the overall command in September, Clinton became his second. Less than three years later he replaced Howe as Commander-in-Chief, having by then become a full general and a Knight of the Bath.

Shy and diffident, Clinton did not mingle easily. Possessing fragile self-confidence, with an underlying sense of inadequacy, he reacted in typical ways when dealing with fellow officers. As a subordinate, he was overassertive, overcritical, and overly resentful when his advice was rejected. As Commander-in-Chief, he was prickly, belittling of his colleagues, and quick to assume they were incompetent. Perceived grievances he stored up aplenty. Yet, for all his faults, he was proving to be a humane and — for the time being — able Commander-in-Chief, who would soon capture Charlestown with the minimum of losses, always an important factor when highly trained regulars were too few to waste. On 16th April he had just celebrated his fiftieth birthday.

So on 23rd April, having requested a separate command, Cornwallis was detached to take charge of Webster's strengthened corps east of the Cooper. It was a step which Clinton promptly regretted, uneasy as he was at having his second out of sight. 'He will play me false,' he feared, a premonition which would come true, not in the Charlestown campaign, but later.

Of the principal events which now unfolded in Cornwallis's sphere of operations, only the action of 6th May at Lenud's[1] Ferry on the Santee, in which Tarleton routed a force of enemy cavalry, was removed from the immediate vicinity of Charlestown. The rest were the taking possession of Haddrell's Point on 25th April, the enemy's evacuation of the fort at Lemprière's on the 28th, Ferguson's capture of the redoubt at Mount Pleasant on 2nd May, and the surrender of Fort Moultrie to the navy five days later.

Meanwhile on the Neck Clinton had been cautiously advancing. By early May his troops were so close to Charlestown that they had drained almost dry a canal protecting the defensive works. As far as he was concerned, the only blot on the landscape, aside from his suspicions of Cornwallis, was Arbuthnot's refusal, despite assurances to the contrary, to consolidate the town's investment by sending frigates into the Cooper. A risky venture it would have been, but Arbuthnot's volte-face did not endear him to Clinton.

Marriot Arbuthnot was now approaching his seventieth year and looked much older. After an undistinguished naval career he was promoted to vice admiral of the blue on 19th March 1779 and came out to the North American station as the naval Commander-in-Chief in the summer of that year. A flawed officer past his prime, he was the worst possible choice for the job. There are those in authority — we all have met them — who take pleasure from displaying their power in a negative way by frustrating the will of others. Arbuthnot was just such a man. That there was in his make-up a flaw of this kind is revealed later in these Papers by the almost grovelling way in which he is addressed by other officers. Negative, inconsistent and unreliable, he would, in short, have tried the patience of a saint — and Clinton was no saint.

On 8th May Clinton and Arbuthnot issued a further summons to surrender. It was rejected, but a terrifying bombardment of the town and the threat of an imminent assault broke the will of the inhabitants, who petitioned Lincoln to capitulate. He now accepted the terms which had previously been offered. The Continental troops and sailors were to be prisoners of war, whereas the civil officers, armed citizens of Charlestown, and the militia then in garrison were to become prisoners on parole and to be secured in their persons and property. The militia would be permitted to go home. All other persons in the town were to be prisoners on parole.

On 12th May the defenders marched out and delivered up the town together with a mass of ordnance, shot, powder, firearms and ammunition. It was the greatest victory so far gained by the British in the war.

The Union Jack was raised on the ramparts and again flew over Charlestown.

§ - §

---

[1] *Lenud's*: pronounced Lenew's.

Principal works consulted in the writing of this chapter

Anthony Allaire, 'Diary', Appendix to Lyman C Draper, *King's Mountain and its Heroes* (Cincinnati, 1881)

Mark Mayo Boatner III, *Encyclopedia of the American Revolution* (D McKay Co, 1966)

Sir Henry Clinton, *The American Rebellion*, edited by William B Willcox (Yale University Press, 1954)

Sir John Fortescue, *A History of the British Army*, vol III (Macmillan & Co Ltd, 1902)

Edward McCrady, *The History of South Carolina in the Revolution 1775-1780* (The Macmillan Co, NY, 1901)

Charles Stedman, *History of the Origin, Progress, and Termination of the American War* (London, 1792)

Banastre Tarleton, *A History of the Campaigns of 1780 and 1781 in the Southern Provinces of North America* (London, 1787)

Bernhard A Uhlendorf ed, *The Siege of Charleston* (University of Michigan Press, 1938)

Christopher Ward, *The War of the Revolution* (The Macmillan Co, NY, 1952)

Franklin and Mary Wickwire, *Cornwallis: The American Adventure* (Houghton Mifflin Co, 1970)

William B Willcox, *Portrait of a General: Sir Henry Clinton in the War of Independence* (Alfred A Knopf, 1964)

§ - §

CHAPTER 2

Correspondence between Cornwallis and Clinton

Clinton to Cornwallis, 23rd April 1780   *2(5): LS*

Head Quarters
23rd April 1780

Rt Hon Earl Cornwallis etc etc etc

My Lord

The inclosed instructions were intended for Colonel Webster[1], who, being at a distance, required something explicit as to my wishes.

As I have thought it proper to increase the corps, I request your Lordship to take the command of it.

In detaching this body of men, my object was to seize the rebel communications, which Colonel Webster has effected to the utmost of my expectations. Your Lordship will have to prosecute this measure and to give the Admiral all the assistance you shall judge adviseable in his projected passage into the Cooper River.

---

[1] The son of Dr Alexander Webster, an eminent clergyman of Edinburgh, James Webster (*c.* 1743-1781) had for the past six years been Lt Colonel of the 33rd Regiment, a Yorkshire regiment of which Cornwallis was Colonel. Having been involved in the New Jersey and Philadelphia campaigns and in the occupation of Verplanck's Point, he was now to take a distinguished part in southern operations, notably commanding the British right wing in the Battle of Camden and the British left wing in the Battle of Guilford, an action in which he was mortally wounded. Esteemed on both sides of the political divide for his high character and talents, he was described by an adversary as uniting to consummate skill and intrepidity 'a generous forbearance and humanity towards such of his enemies as fell within the influence of his power, as secured their gratitude and most exalted admiration'. (Stevens, *Clinton-Cornwallis Controversy*, ii, 463; Fortescue, *British Army*, iii, 213; Garden, *Anecdotes* (1st Series), 280-2; *The Cornwallis Papers*)

I have the honor to be
Your Lordship's most obedient and most humble servant

H CLINTON

Enclosure
Clinton to Webster, 23rd April 1780   *2(7): C*

Head Quarters
Charles Town Neck
23rd April 1780

Lt Colonel Webster

Dear Sir

I received your note of yesterday. As this goes to you by a tolerable safe conveyance, I will venture to be a little explicit.

The ships have not passed and the Admiral now tells me they cannot 'till the enemy is dislodged from Mount Pleasant, where he has taken post.

I shall now give you a few hints respecting my ideas of your situation, that of the navy, and the besieged; such of them as you chuse to act under, you may consider as orders, if you think it necessary. The siege is so forward that things cannot hold out much longer without extremity. They may, however, pass in force to Lampries and try to escape, but as I have already desired the Admiral to send a naval force to Spencer's and Chewee, those doors will be shut. Your operations on Oandaw Creek must shut one — at least your post on Christ Church Neck would give the enemy a great jealousy for it[2], if you have not already done it. As you have withdrawn the post at Monk's Corner, Simcoe[3] will occupy it when I can spare him for that purpose. The Volunteers of Ireland, New York Volunteers and Carolinians join you. With this additional force you may probably detach towards Mount Pleasant. Reconnoitre it and let me know whether you will wish it to be attacked or can take a position near Sullivan's Island, masking at the same time Lampries, in which case the marines and sailors, as proposed by the Admiral, may land and take possession of it. Let me have your opinion respecting these matters. The move to Mount Pleasant is only to enable the ships to

---

[2] *a great jealousy for it*: a great apprehension of it.

[3] John Graves Simcoe (1752-1806) was Lt Colonel of the Queen's Rangers, a British American corps formed in 1777 and used for light and active service. Educated at Eton and Merton College, Oxford, he had entered the army in 1771 and, while serving as a captain in the 40th Foot, was severely wounded at the Battle of Brandywine. Part of a reinforcement, he and his corps had arrived in South Carolina on 18th April 1780 and were soon to return with Clinton to New York. In December they accompanied Arnold to Virginia, where they remained until they capitulated with the rest of the British forces there at Yorktown. Having published in 1787 an account of the Queen's Rangers, he was to become an MP, Lt Governor of Upper Canada, and a lt general. (*DNB*; Boatner, *Encyclopedia*, 1009; *Appletons'*)

pass into the Cooper. If you think the business is done without them, they will be of course employed in other material services; but you must first consider how long you can subsist in your present post without being fed by us, for, tho' upon a pinch we may throw something to you these dark nights, we are not sure of doing it 'till we are masters of the Cooper. Consider all this and let me know. I do not, as I said before, send you any instructions, but I repeat that any hints I give you may be considered as orders if you wish to have it so.

The news from Sir George Rodney[4] is mostly confirmed. Vaughan[5] and he are in the West Indies. The French have 24 of the line, Rodney 23, but, being heavy ships, he is judged to have the superiority.

Faithfully yours

HC

Clinton to Cornwallis, 23rd April 1780   2(9): LS

Head Quarters
23rd April 1780
11 o'clock at night

Rt Hon Earl Cornwallis etc etc etc

My Lord

I have just now received a letter from the Admiral in which is the following paragraph, which makes it necessary for me to say a few words to your Lordship upon the subject of it. I will first give it you in his own words. Speaking of the necessity of securing the post of Lampries: 'I then thought, as I now do, that should the rebels have batteries on that side, no ships could lay in Cooper River with any security. Every letter I have written since that time intimates the same idea.'

It is plain from this that he will not only object to the entering Cooper before we are in possession of the supposed fort at Mount Pleasant, but likewise that at Lampries. Your Lordship in your exertions to facilitate the Admiral's passing a naval force into Cooper will be the best judge how far it will be possible to effect either or both of these objects.

---

[4] Admiral Sir George Brydges Rodney (1719-1792) had in January relieved Gibraltar before reaching St Lucia on 27th March to assume command of the fleet on the Leeward Islands station. Besides frigates, he had twenty ships of the line, whereas the Comte de Guichen, the French admiral, had twenty-five. (Charnock, *Biographia Navalis*, v, 211-4)

[5] Major General the Hon John Vaughan (*c.* 1731-1795), a younger son of the 3rd Viscount Lisburne, had seen distinguished service in North America during the revolutionary war. On returning to England in 1779, he was appointed Commander-in-Chief of land forces in the Leeward Islands. Having arrived at Barbados in February 1780, he managed to reinforce St Lucia, by concentrating troops from Antigua and St Kitts, in time to abort with the navy an attempt by de Guichen to recapture the island on 23rd March. (Fortescue, *British Army*, iii, 334-6; *DNB*; Valentine, *The British Establishment*, ii, 886)

Lampries, independent of the Admiral's reason for wishing to occupy it (which, as far as I can presume to pass an opinion on naval matters, is not founded), is on other accounts of consequence to us, but not to be attempted at any considerable risk. In all this, however, I rely on your Lordship's zeal and knowledge to act in every respect in the manner most beneficial to the King's Service.

I have the honor to be
Your Lordship's most obedient and most humble servant

H CLINTON

Clinton to Cornwallis, 24th April 1780 — 2(13): LS

Head Quarters
the 24th April 1780

Rt Hon Earl Cornwallis

My Lord

I have just learnt from Colonel Balfour that he has halted at Boneau's Bridge. Your Lordship will, of course, order him to join you, which the inclosed letter[6] will fully satisfy him to be my intention.

I have the honour to be
Your Lordship's most obedient and most humble servant

H CLINTON

Clinton to Cornwallis, 25th April 1780 — 2(11): ALS

25th April

My Lord

I have received a message from the Admiral this morning that the *Richmond*, *Blonde*, *Rawley*[7] and *Sandwich* with gallies and armed sloops were to pass into Cooper River this morning at 10 o'clock if the wind would persist. As they have not passed this day, they may probably do it to morrow, but by what channel I know not. I thought it, however, right to mention this circumstance to you, and have the honor to be

---

[6] *the inclosed letter*: no extant copy.

[7] *Rawley*: Raleigh.

Your Lordship's most obedient servant

H CLINTON

Clinton to Cornwallis, 25th April 1780   2(15): ALS

April 25th 1780

My Lord

I am honored with your Lordship's letter[8] and will freely give my opinion respecting the possition which I should recommend to be taken to answer all the purposes intended.

If Owandaw Bridge is destroyed and cannot be easily repaired, if the *Fowey* lays in Sewee Bay and an armed force in Spencer's Inlet, I think the rebel communications by Christ Church is gone and your Lordship then might extend yourself towards the Cooper after fortifying certain points on the forks of the Wando. The holding the district between Cooper and upper Wando can alone in my opinion effectually stop their principal communication with Santee River, and if a post could be fortifyed on a narrow part of Cooper River, the investiture would in my opinion be compleat from Cooper to the sea. Of this, however, your Lordship on the spot is the best judge. I will order this side of Cooper to be explored, and when that is done and I have collected all the information I can get, your Lordship shall hear from me. In the meantime you may possibly shew yourself towards Mount Pleasant. I have this day ordered a supply of flour and rum to be sent to Chewee Bay, and should you in a future day take a possition with your gros[9] near Cooper, you will, of course, be supplyed that way. Nothing extraordinary since we parted. I have stopt all musket firing at night. *'Tis so dark we cannot see their ambrasures.*

I have the honor to be
Your Lordship's obedient servant

H CLINTON

---

[8] *your Lordship's letter..*: no extant copy.

[9] *gros*: a misspelling of 'gross', meaning 'main body', now archaic.

Clinton to Cornwallis, 28th April 1780 2(17): LS

> Camp before Charles Town
> 28th April 1780

Rt Hon Earl Cornwallis

My Lord

I am honored with your Lordship's letter dated 9 o'clock, 26th, at night[10]. 'Tho not for the same reasons he gives, I agree with the Admiral that the possession of Lampries is of importance; and if he will cooperate, and begin by removing the rebel naval force, and your Lordship thinks it may be attempted, I have no objection. Be so good to let me know your sentiments.

As I am writing this, I am told the enemy have retired the post of Lampries. If your Lordship hears nothing of them your way, they are probably gone to town. I shall immediately give notice to the Admiral, who will, of course, pass a force into the Cooper. I do not know enough of Lampries to say whether it will be safe to occupy it before we are masters of the navigation. You are best judge; but at all events the cavalry may visit it in the day, and that will prevent their reoccupying it. 'Tis possible they may wish to draw you in force to it and then give you the go by, land at Cain Hoy, and try to escape — I mean such as may intend doing so.

I have the honor to be
Your Lordship's most obedient and most humble servant

H CLINTON

Cornwallis to Clinton, 28th April 1780 72(1): ADfS

> Camp at Wappetaw
> April 28th 1780

His Excellency Sir Henry Clinton etc etc etc

Sir

I am just honoured with yours of this date by Captain Hanger. In answer to the first part proposing an attack on Lamprieres, I have only to say that the works, as they appeared to me, assisted by their shipping and gallys, would subject an attempt to storm them to considerable loss, and perhaps the event would be uncertain. The objection to any other mode of attack would be the leaving the west side of the Wando too long unguarded. The report you mention, in the second part, of the evacuation of Lamprieres gives me the greatest pleasure,

---

[10] *your Lordship's letter..*: no extant copy.

as it opens the door to the only compleat investiture of Charlestown on this side the Cooper, which in my opinion is having a superior naval force in the Cooper and Wando. I see no objection to the occupying it as soon as the navy comes up. Before that happens, it will be destitute of canon and not easily supply'd with provisions without my detaching more than I can well spare, but if the Admiral earnestly wishes it, I think it may be risk'd, and provisions may be run over in the night from Scott's Landing.

I have order'd Ferguson to push his patroles to it and shall receive his report early in the morning, which shall be immediately transmitted to you.

I have this day reconnoitred the whole of Owendaw Creek and found all the accounts of it totally erroneous. There is a tract of six or seven miles of country between that creek and the Wando which is perfectly good and practicable, and several bye roads that communicate with the roads to the Santee. I will send you a sketch of that country tomorrow. There is no man of war yet in Bulls Bay. Run by Scot's Ferry.

If the report of the evacuation of Lamprieres proves true, I shall immediately move to the west of Miller's Bridge.

I am, Sir,
Your most obedient and most humble servant

CORNWALLIS

Clinton to Cornwallis, 1st May 1780

2(20): LS

Camp before Charles Town
1st May 1780

Lt General Earl Cornwallis

My Lord

As you are informed that the navy took possession of Lampries, it is needless for me to say any thing to the first part of your letter. And as the Admiral *now* gives us little hopes of his intention to pass a naval force into Cooper and Wando, I submit to you the propriety of keeping Lampries. I have written to the Admiral for something more positive respecting his intentions of sending a naval force into Cooper and Wando. 'Till he determines, if you have no objection, we may keep it, and it can be supplied by night from hence.

I always thought that possession of the Cooper was material. As to the Wando, I thought such a position could be taken on or near its forks as would effectually shut all the avenues leading from Christ Church Parish to the Santee when Owendaw Bridge was destroyed, for, tho' there may be many communications across the Wando Swamp leading to that river, a corps near Miller's Bridge is upon them in an instant and the Santee is not passable without great difficulty any where lower than Murray's and Nelson's Ferries.

I inclose you part of the Admiral's last letter, by which you will observe there is little chance of his sending a force into Cooper.

Our affairs on this side advance, our third parallel finished, and we shall, I hope, have twenty guns mounted in a day or two. I hope likewise to be able to bleed the canal about the same time, but we are in want of some assistance to enable us to go on with the duty. I am therefore to request that you will order the 64th to join us as soon as possible; they may be passed by Scot's Ferry. If the 64th does not lay immediately for that purpose, you will be so good to send the 23rd.

I wrote to your Lordship, by Mr Bradshaw[11] of your regiment, my opinions respecting your situation on the other side. I hope you received the letter.

I have the honor to be
Your Lordship's most faithfull humble servant

H CLINTON

Enclosure
Extract, Arbuthnot to Clinton, 29th April 1780   2(22): C

I will endeavor to push a force into Cooper, but in my opinion equal good consequences would ensure were the vessels you have taken above it to be armed, in which Captain Elphinstone[12] will assist.

---

[11] Commissioned a cornet in the 17th Light Dragoons on 1st June 1777, J Smith Bradshaw had been promoted to a lieutenancy in the 33rd Regiment two years later. He would become a captain in the 17th from 7th August 1780. (*Army Lists*)

[12] The Hon George Keith Elphinstone (1746-1823) was born near Stirling, the fifth son of the tenth Lord Elphinstone. Captain of the frigate *Perseus*, he had stationed galleys to cover the British Army in its passage over Ashley River to Charlestown Neck. He was now commanding a detachment of seamen on shore. At the capitulation he would convey to England dispatches with news of the event. In 1781, as Captain of the man of war *Warwick*, he was to command a convoy of troop reinforcements from Cork to Charlestown, arriving off the bar at the beginning of June. He remained on the North American station till the close of the war. In later life he would become an MP, have a distinguished naval career, advance to the rank of admiral, and be elevated to the peerage. Steady, persevering and cautious, he was invariably equal to the necessities of the moment without ever towering above them. (*DNB*; Tarleton, *Campaigns*, 9, 10, 44, 47, 49; *The Cornwallis Papers*)

Cornwallis to Clinton, 1st May 1780   72(3): C

Camp at Cape's
May 1st 1780
8 o'clock pm

His Excellency Sir H Clinton etc etc

Sir

I am just honoured with your letter of this date and have in consequence ordered the 64th Regiment to march to Scott's Landing to morrow morning. If you can send, in the boats that are to transport them, some rum and salt, it will be very acceptable to us.

When I was at Lampries yesterday, I saw the *Sandwich* and other armed vessels in the Hog Island Channel and was assured by the officers of the navy that they would come up the first fair wind. If they should come up, the post at Lampries is absolutely necessary; if not, I cannot help thinking it very material, as it will deter the enemy from attempting to escape by the Wando Neck. Depending on the post at Lampries for that purpose, I have ordered the corps to move to morrow morning to Dr Smith's, which appears to be the most convenient position to guard the Cooper and have a great probability of intercepting any thing that attempts to go off by the West Wando. I propose to leave Lt Colonel Innes[13] with the South Carolinians and New York Volunteers near the forks of the Wando. The Wando Swamp extends but a few miles above Wappetaw Bridge, and there is a space of several miles, between it and the Owendaw Creek, of firm ground, with several roads in constant use. All this you will see distinctly by a sketch of the country which I send you inclosed[14]. You will see by the state of this corps, which I have the honour to inclose to you[15], that, including the garrison of Lampries, I have about 1,900 men fit for duty. It will therefore be necessary for me to keep the greatest part of them together to be able to act with any efficacy. Yesterday and this day I have had repeated accounts of some Virginians and North Carolinians being assembled at Lenew's Ferry, and that they intend passing the Santee River. I do not, however, apprehend any thing very formidable from that quarter.

---

[13] Alexander Innes (1743-?) was a Scot who had been Secretary to Lord William Campbell, the last royal Governor of South Carolina. On 26th May 1778 he was commissioned Lt Colonel of the South Carolina Royalist Regiment, a British American corps composed of Back Country loyalists who had come overland from South Carolina to East Florida in the same year. On 5th March 1780 he marched with his corps from Savannah, forming part of a reinforcement of some 1,500 men for Clinton. His involvement in forthcoming events is fully set out in these Papers. Besides holding the lt colonelcy of his corps, Innes was at this time, and until the close of the war, Inspector General of Provincial Forces, a post responsible for the Provincial Stores and for the mustering and inspection of British American regiments. In this capacity he returned to New York at the beginning of 1781, with effective command of the South Carolina Royalist Regiment devolving on Major Thomas Fraser. Promoted later to colonelcy of this corps, Innes was placed on the Provincial half-pay list on its disbandment. (Drayton, *Memoirs*, ii, 38; Treasury 64/23(15), W0 65/164(6) and (40), WO 65/165(10) and (15) (National Archives, Kew); Draper, *King's Mountain*, 108, 484; Clark, *Loyalists in the Southern Campaign*, i, *passim*; The Cornwallis Papers)

[14] *sketch..*: no extant copy.

[15] *the state of this corps..*: no extant copy.

I am etc

[CORNWALLIS]

Clinton to Cornwallis, 2nd May 1780   2(24): ALS

May the 2nd 1780
11 o'clock

My Lord

I am honored with yours of yesterday 8 o'clock. A week's rum and some salt will be sent to Scott's Landing immediately.

Captain Elphingstone does not seem to think that the Admiral has any idea of sending a force into Cooper. On the contrary, he is desired to collect all the vessels that can be found in Cooper and Wando and arm them. I am therefore to request that they may be deliver'd over to such officer as Captain Elphingstone sends.

Faithfully
Your Lordship's most obedient servant

H CLINTON

Cornwallis to Clinton, 5th May 1780   72(5): C

Camp at Smith's House
5th May 1780

Sir

Upon examining this country thoroughly, I have determined to move to morrow to Manigolt's near Quinby Bridge, three miles on this side of Huger's Bridge and about seven miles from hence. My reasons for it are these: I shall only be ten miles from the head of Owendaw Creek; I shall certainly be able to get, before the garrison of Charlestown, to the ferrys of the Santee if they land to the east of the Cooper, and shall have a very good chance of getting up with them if they land to the west of it; and if the enemy should attempt to pass a small corps from the north of the Santee to awe the inhabitants who are daily coming in to us to give paroles, I shall probably be near enough to strike a blow at them. I shall keep a small corps of the Legion infantry at Foggarty's Ferry and three companies of the New York Volunteers at St Thomas's Church to communicate by small posts and patroles to Foggarty's to catch any officers or people of consequence that may attempt to escape. The remainder of the New York Volunteers, the South Carolinians and mounted light infantry will be at the Widow Wigfall's near the head of Owendaw. I shall break Wappetaw and Miller's Bridges. I shall leave a small post of the Legion with a guard boat at Aikins's and a very small post to take care of the ferry boat at Bonneau's. I shall likewise have a guard at Huger's. Colonel Malmedy[16] has certainly been there three days in the woods near us, but we have not yet been able to catch him, altho' he must be in great distress. Governour Rutledge has taken up and imprisoned a man whose parole we had taken. I have wrote to him and threatned severe reprisals if he is not released, and I propose being as good as my word.

I am, Sir, etc

[CORNWALLIS]

Clinton to Cornwallis, 6th May 1780   2(28): LS

Camp before Charles Town
6th May 1780

Rt Hon Earl Cornwallis

My Lord

I am honored with your Lordship's letters of the 3rd instant[17], but the weather has been so boisterous for these three days past that I could not acknowledge the receipt of them sooner.

I visited the post of Fuller's yesterday a second time. If the battery could be compleated at Scott's and secured by a close work, the two channels of the Cooper would be effectually stopt and a short and safe communication established with your Lordship.

As there are now no hopes of any naval force being sent into Cooper, we must do the best we can with such as we have.

Our third parallel is quite compleat, and the cannal, notwithstanding the rain of yesterday, nearly drained. I begin to think these people will be blockheads enough to wait the assault. *Je m'en lave les mains*[18].

---

[16] François Lellorquis, Marquis de Malmedy, had landed in North America in late 1775 and risen to be a colonel in the Continental line. In the action at Stono Ferry on 20th June 1779 he commanded a flank battalion of light infantry. During the present siege he had been placed in command at Lemprière's Point, but evacuated the post on 28th April in great confusion, thereby allowing the British to complete their investment of Charlestown. He accordingly became unpopular in the garrison, was assigned no further command, and was advised to quit the town. In early 1781 he would be appointed to the command of a corps of North Carolina horse and on 8th September would lead, with great gallantry and good conduct, two North Carolina militia battalions at the Battle of Eutaw Springs. (McCrady, *SC in the Rev 1775-1780*, passim; *The Greene Papers*, vi-ix, passim; Boatner, *Encyclopedia*, 670-1; Heitman, *Historical Register*, 377)

[17] *your Lordship's letters..*: no extant copies.

[18] *Je m'en lave les mains*: I wash my hands of them, a favourite expression of Clinton's.

The capture of Rutledge[19] etc proves that their communication is totally stopt.

I have the honor to be
Your Lordship's most obedient and most humble servant

H CLINTON

[*Subscribed in Clinton's hand:*]

I shall have the honor of answering your Lordship's letter of yesterday when I know how you like your present station.

Cornwallis to Clinton, 7th May 1780[20]   72(6): C

Camp at Manigolt's
May 7th 1780
9 o'clock pm

Sir

I received very early this morning the favour of your letter of yesterday's date. I went this morning over the country between this place and Widow Wigfall's, where Lt Colonel Innes is posted. I found it about 14 miles from hence. However, upon the whole, I think this at present the best position. The garrison of Charlestown, if they should try to escape, must land within me so that, if my posts are tolerably alert, and attentive to sending me intelligence, I should be able to meet them instead of marching after them; and my neighbourhood to the Santee renders it impossible for the enemy to be in force on this side of that river without my knowing it and being able instantly to attack them. I have ordered Colonel Innes to keep a good look-out and, if any force appeared from the Santee, to fall back on the Cooper to the westward of me; if the garrison of Charlestown retired his way, to fall back on my post. In regard to what you mention of the communication being entirely stopped — as the posts are now fixed, we have a very good chance of picking up stragglers by our small detachments

---

[19] Edward Rutledge (1749-1800) was the youngest brother of John Rutledge, the revolutionary Governor of South Carolina, and like him had been admitted to the Middle Temple in London and called to the English bar. Returning to South Carolina in 1773, he became a delegate to the Continental Congress between 1774 and 1776, signed the Declaration of Independence, and was at the same time elected to the Provincial Congresses of 1775 and 1776. When a new revolutionary constitution for South Carolina was adopted in 1778, he was returned to the lower house of the legislature while serving as a captain in the Charlestown battalion of artillery. As such, he took part under William Moultrie in the action on Port Royal Island in February 1779. At the beginning of May 1780 he was captured soon after leaving Charlestown with intelligence for his brother, the Governor. Accused by the British of subversive activity incompatible with his parole, he would in September be transported to St Augustine before being exchanged in 1781 and elected to the revolutionary assembly at Jacksonborough. In the years following the war he would remain in public life, have a successful law practice, and invest in plantations in partnership with his brother-in-law, Charles Cotesworth Pinckney. (*DAB*; McCrady, *SC in the Rev 1775-1780* and *1780-1783*, passim)

[20] Extracts from the latter part of this letter appear in Ross ed, *Cornwallis Correspondence*, i, 43-4.

and patroles, but should any considerable body land, our taking them must be uncertain, as the country is very extensive, woody, and every where practicable to infantry unincumber'd with cannon and baggage. If they should attempt it, you may depend on our utmost vigilance and diligence, but I think now there is little chance of their quitting the town. I have ordered a serjeant and eight men of the New York Volunteers and a serjeant and two dragoons to remain at Scott's Ferry so that, if you would please to order a small row boat to remain always at that ferry, our communication would be always certain. I am glad to hear that every thing looks so well on your side. I thought it proper to send Major Manson[21] and the *other person* to you, as it was probable you might get some material intelligence from them. If you find that the enemy are obstinately bent on trying the fate of a storm, I shall take it as a favour if you will let me be of the party. I can be with you in eight hours from your sending to me. I should be happy to attend my old friends the grenadiers and light infantry, and perhaps you may think that on an occasion of that sort you cannot have too many officers. I can only say that, unless you see any inconvenience to the service, it is my hearty wish to attend you on that occasion. As it may not be proper to commit to writing, if you should approve of it, your saying your Lordship will *take a ride* at such an hour will be sufficient. I forgot to mention last night[22] that Tarleton's loss[23] was only one man killed, one lost in the swamp, and two horses wounded.

I am etc

[CORNWALLIS]

---

[21] A Scot, Daniel Manson (1739-1816) had migrated to South Carolina in the 1760s and set himself up in business as a shipbuilder in Charlestown. Refusing to take the test oath, he had had to sell up in 1778 and sail into exile with several other refugees in the *Providence*, a vessel with cargo which he had acquired for the voyage. After three days at sea it was stopped by HMS *Rose* and taken into New York, where three months were to pass before the Vice Admiralty Court determined that it was not good prize. While the other refugees then proceeded to England, Manson went on to be commissioned major in the Royal North Carolina Regiment, a British American corps formed of loyalists who had fled North Carolina rather than take the test oath. He was now being sent by Cornwallis to Clinton in case his familiarity with Charlestown and its people might be of use in the siege. In 1781 he would acquit himself well while serving under James Craig at Wilmington. On the disbandment of his regiment at the close of the war, he retired to England and was placed on the Provincial half-pay list. He died in Berwick. (Treasury 64/23(17) and WO 65/165(11) (National Archives, Kew); Lambert, *SC Loyalists*, 27, 63; Sabine, *Biographical Sketches*, ii, 47; *The Cornwallis Papers*)

[22] *I forgot to mention last night*: No copy of the letter is extant.

[23] *Tarleton's loss*: in the action of 6th May at Lenud's Ferry, in which he had routed a corps of revolutionary horse under Colonel Anthony White.

Clinton to Cornwallis, 8th May 1780

2(30): LS

Camp before Charles Town
8th May 1780
6 pm

Rt Hon Earl Cornwallis

My Lord

Lincoln seems desirous of accepting the terms the Admiral and I offered. We are now in treaty, but it may break off, and it is not impossible but that the Continentals may try to escape. Your Lordship's vigilance will, I am persuaded, render that impracticable.

Faithfully
Your obedient servant

H CLINTON

Clinton to Cornwallis, 10th May 1780

2(42): ALS

May 10th

My Lord

I am honored with your Lordship's letters and inclosures of the 8th of May[24]. You will have been informed by the cannonade of last night how matters go. Your Lordship's knowledge of their situation and ours will tell you how they are likely to go. Your dispatches by the *Bonetta* are arrived. Broderick[25] has got them. They will be sent by the first safe opportunity, and by that I will write more at large.

Faithfully
Your Lordship's humble servant

H CLINTON

---

[24] *your Lordship's letters and inclosures..*: no extant copies.

[25] A younger son of George Brodrick, the 3rd Viscount Midleton, the Hon Henry Brodrick (1758-1785) was a second cousin of Cornwallis. His mother, Albania (née Townshend), was a first cousin of the 3rd Viscount Townshend's daughter Elizabeth, who had married Cornwallis's father. Commissioned as an ensign into the 33rd Regiment on 23rd March 1775, Henry had been promoted to lieutenant on 8th August 1776 and to captain in the 55th on 12th June 1777. He was now serving in Cornwallis's suite. He would soon sail for England for the recovery of his health, but in mid January 1781 would rejoin Cornwallis in time to take part in the winter campaign as one of his aides-de-camp. Afterwards he would be sent home with Cornwallis's dispatches, setting sail from Charlestown on 3rd May in HM Sloop *Delight* and arriving in England by mid June. On Cornwallis's solicitation he would be promoted to major and in due course become a lt colonel in the Coldstream Guards. Although not of age, he was MP for Midleton from 1776 to 1783. As in the *Army Lists*, his name is frequently misspelt. (Valentine, *The British Establishment*; Wickwire, *Cornwallis*, 15; *The Cornwallis Papers*; Stevens, *Clinton-Cornwallis Controversy*, ii, 408; *Army Lists*)

CHAPTER 3

Miscellaneous papers

1 - Tonyn to Cornwallis

Tonyn to Cornwallis, 3rd April 1780 *2(3): CS*

St Augustine
3rd April 1780

The Rt Hon Earl Cornwallis

My Lord

I cannot resist this opportunity of paying my respects to your Lordship and acknowledging the very great satisfaction I have in your safe arrival in the southern provinces, where your Lordship's great influence and abilities will have due weight and effect in the reduction of His Majesty's enemies and restoring the Constitution. It is with great pleasure I recollect that I have had the honour of being known to you for many years past and ever had a sensible share in whatever concerned your Lordship.

When you was in the northern provinces, I took the liberty of making several attempts to send to your Lordship and others of my friends some barrels of sweet oranges, the produce of this province, but was disappointed by the vessels not reaching their destined port.

The Ordnance's stores for the army have been waiting eight days for the convoy. I determined to send the brig in charge of an armed ship of twenty guns on whom I can depend. That arrived yesterday from a cruize, and it will make me happy to hear they are in good time to answer the service Sir Henry Clinton intends for them.

Although our condition is such that the stores can be very ill spared, a thought shall not intrude of any bad apprehensions during their absence, trusting to our good fortune and Sir Henry Clinton engaging to return fresh supplies. I shall be happy upon all occasions to give the strongest assurances of my great respect and esteem for your Lordship, and that

I have the honour to be
Your Lordship's most obedient and most humble servant

PAT TONYN[1]

2 - Cornwallis to Tarleton

Cornwallis to Tarleton, 25th April 1780[2]   *77(1): C*

Camp near St Thomas's Church
25th April 1780

Lt Colonel Tarleton

Sir

The Commander in Chief having directed me to use every effort to prevent supplies and reinforcements being thrown into Charles Town, but particularly to guard against the garrison's escaping out of it and its dependent fortresses, I find it necessary at present to place the corps under my command on the east side of Miller's Bridge, keeping a redoubt on the west side to secure a communication. I must therefore commit the care of the country between the Cooper and Wandoo to your charge with the cavalry and infantry of the Legion. The principal objects of your care will be the landing places on the west side of the Wando and in Daniel's Island, and I trust in your vigilance that I shall receive the earliest information of any material movement of the enemy in that quarter. I must likewise recommend it to you to take every opportunity of procuring intelligence either from the town or the Santee River and the Back Country. I leave it to your discretion to take such positions as you shall find most convenient. You will please to report to me whenever you move that I may know where to find you. As you will be so constantly moving, you will not of course be able to embarrass yourself with the care of such stores as may fall into your hands. If you apprehend that any such may be in danger of being retaken by the enemy and that they will be usefull

---

[1] Almost certainly an Irish Protestant, Patrick Tonyn (1725-1804) had first seen service in the military line. Entering the 6th (Inniskilling) Dragoons as a cornet on 16th March 1744, he was promoted to captain on 10th May 1751 and served with the regiment in Germany in 1758. On 12th August 1761 he assumed the lt colonelcy of the 104th Foot, a regiment which was disbanded two years later. Transferring to the civil line, he became Governor of East Florida in 1774 and was to hold office for ten years until the province came under Spanish dominion at the peace. He died in London. (Boatner, *Encyclopedia*, 1109; Lambert, *SC Loyalists*, 262)

[2] The original of this letter appears in Tarleton, *Campaigns*, 37-8. There are no differences.

to them, you will please to destroy them. I must recommend it to you in the strongest manner to use your utmost endeavours to prevent the troops under your command [fro]m committing irregularities, and I am convinced that my recommend[atio]n will have weight when I assure you that such conduct will [be hi]ghly agreeable to the Commander in Chief.

I am etc

[CORNWALLIS]

3 - Return of captured property

Return of captured property, 2nd May 1780   **90(40): DS**

Return of effects belonging to the rebels, captured by the 23rd Regiment of Foot (or Royal Welch Fuzileers), delivered to Doctor Frazer[3], 2nd May 1780

Articles in small trunk n° 1:	*Articles in small trunk n° 2:*
A pair of silver plated candle sticks	1 necklace and silver pin
2 silver tankards	1 box with 13 small tea spoons and a pair of sugar tongs
4 ditto salt sellars	1 pair of stone buckles
1 ditto bread baskett	1 opera glass
1 ditto salver	1 case containing a necklace and 2 small hair pins and drops
1 ditto sugar box	1 silver salver
1 ditto cream jugg	11 tea spoons, 1 pair tea tongs
2 ditto punch laidles	13 tea spoons, 1 pair tea tongs
2 ditto coffee potts	2 pair steel nut crackers
1 pair of silver scissers	1 silver punch laidle
18 silver spoons	4 salt spoons
3 soop laidles	1 silver tea pott

---

[3] Dr James Fraser was a Scot who had migrated to South Carolina in the 1760s and established a lucrative medical practice in Beaufort. A loyalist, he claimed that the test oath was never administered to him by the revolutionaries, probably because he was the only 'medical man' in his community. His position as a general factotum for the British was soon to be regularised, when by 1st September he was formerly appointed by Balfour to be an assistant to the Commandant of Charlestown. (Lambert, *SC Loyalists*, 27, 66; *The Cornwallis Papers*)

1 pair of tea tongs	2 silver butter boats
1 pencil case	1 pair of stone buckles
1 wine strainer	1 pair of gold buckles
3 silver wine labels	3 sugar casters
[torn] pair of silver candle sticks	10 large table spoons
1 ditto gorget	1 small silver tankard
2 ditto goblets	1 silver sugar bowl
6 small ditto salvers	1 box with 2 pair earrings
3 silver cups	1 box with hair pins
18 large table spoons	1 cream jugg
4 silver bottle stands	4 caster tops
4 salt sellars and spoons	1 pen knife
1 purse containing several pocket pieces, 1 pair of gold sleeve buttons	1 piece of striped cotton
A box containing rings and several other small articles	1 ivorey tablet
A box containing 2 shirt buckles, a ring, a pail	Several account books
4 silver spoons	*Articles in large trunk nº 3:*
13 tea spoons	Containing women's wearing apparel etc
1 pair of sugar tongs	*Articles in large trunk nº 4:*
1 pair of knee buckles	Containing men's wearing apparel etc
2 silver pap boats	
1 snuffer stand	
1 set of castors	
1 salt spoon	
1 small box with 2 earings and 2 rings	
1 etwee case furnished	
2 cruett tops	
1 hydrostatic [sic] ballance	
1 pocket book	N BALFOUR Lt Colonel, Royal Welch Fuzileers

[*Endorsed:*]

MEMORANDUM

Supposed to be the property of Colonel Motte[4], being taken on the march to Monk's Corner in a waggon belonging to him by information from his own servants.

---

[4] Of Huguenot descent, Isaac Motte (1738-1795) had received a military education and served in Canada in 1756. A nascent revolutionary, he was commissioned lt colonel of the second regiment raised by the Provincial Congress in June 1775 and as such served as second in command to his colonel, William Moultrie, in the action at Fort Sullivan on 28th June 1776. In September of that year, when Moultrie became a brigadier general, he was promoted to the colonelcy of his regiment and was transferred with it to the Continental establishment. Quitting the military line by the beginning of 1779, he was elected at that time to the Privy Council of South Carolina under the new revolutionary constitution. He would now be taken prisoner in the capitulation of Charlestown before being exchanged in 1781 and elected as a senator to the revolutionary assembly at Jacksonborough. In later life he would be a member of the South Carolina convention which ratified the United States constitution. His brother was Jacob Motte. (*Appletons'*; McCrady, *SC in the Rev 1775-1780* and *1780-1783, passim*; Garden, *Anecdotes* (1st series), 17; Heitman, *Historical Register*, 405)

PART TWO

Consolidation of British authority in South Carolina

13th May to 25th June 1780

CHAPTER 4

Introduction to the rest of Part Two

Chapter 5 begins on 18th May as Cornwallis is about to march from Manigault's Plantation with some 2,500 men for Camden.

By now appointed to command in the southern provinces, he describes the circumstances of his appointment in a letter of 12th November: 'When I came to town after the surrender, Sir Henry mention'd my going with him to the northward. I said that I was ready to serve wherever he thought fit to employ me, and had no objection to remain in Carolina if he thought my services cou'd be usefull in that province. He said something civil about the climate. On my assuring him that it was no objection, he then wished me to take this command. However painfull and distressing my situation has been, and however dark the prospect then was, it cannot be supposed that as a military man I shou'd not rather chuse to command to the southward than be third at New York... I did not interfere in any degree with Sir Henry's arrangement [*the appointment of Paterson as Commandant of Charlestown*], nor did I say more or express myself stronger on the subject of my own staying than I have described...'

Crossing the Santee at Lenud's Ferry with part of his corps, Cornwallis marched up the eastern side of the river while Rawdon with the rest proceeded by way of Monck's Corner and Nelson's Ferry. Camden was reached on 1st June.

At first named Pine Tree Hill, the village lay to the east of the Wateree River about 35 miles north of its confluence with the Congaree. Settled about 1750 and laid out in plots and streets around a square, it was now inhabited mostly by Scotch-Irish Presbyterians, whose meeting house and that of the Quakers were features of the place. Besides Joseph Kershaw's country store, it was home to saw- and grist-mills, one or more taverns, breweries, distilleries, a pottery, and various other artisan shops. Nine years earlier a courthouse had been built. All in all, trade was brisk and by now the village had become a principal entrepôt for the back settlements.

Politically, occupation of Camden was of course inevitable, but militarily its location left much to be desired. As Rawdon remarked many years later, 'Camden had always been reprobated by me as a station, not merely from the extraordinary disadvantages which attended it as an individual position, but from its being on the wrong side of the river and covering nothing, while it was constantly liable to have its communication with the interior district cut off.'

Headquarters at Camden was established in Joseph Kershaw's mansion. He was a leading incendiary.

As Cornwallis approached Camden, Lt Colonel Nisbet Balfour began his march for Ninety Six, a village which lay to the south of the Saluda River some sixty miles west of its confluence with the Broad. In the Back Country it was second in importance to Camden. Leaving Charlestown on 26th May, Balfour commanded a mixed corps of some 600 men comprising three companies of the 7th Regiment (the Royal Fusiliers), a detachment of light infantry, the Prince of Wales's American Regiment, and Ferguson's American Volunteers. His advance along what was once an Indian trading path is minutely recorded in Allaire's Diary, with which Chapters 6 and 7 should be compared. Ninety Six was reached by Balfour and Ferguson's men on 22nd June.

The Back Country is an amorphous expression describing the vast swathe of territory now entered by the British. Though other interpretations are wider or more restrictive, it is used here to refer to the then Districts of Camden and Ninety Six. In the east the outer boundary began at the confluence of the Congaree and Wateree, extended northwards to the North Carolina line, continued westwards along that line to the Cherokee nation, and followed the Georgia line to a point just below Augusta. From there it proceeded in the south to a point on the Saluda midway between the village of Ninety Six and the Broad River before following the Saluda and Congaree eastwards.

If the momentous events soon to be seen unfolding in the Back Country are to be placed in their proper context, it is necessary to supplement the Cornwallis Papers by drawing a brief sketch of the region, its inhabitants, and those developments which had led many to remain loyal to the Crown.

Today the Back Country presents a very different aspect from that encountered by the first white settlers in the middle of the 18th century. It was then a region interspersed with extensive plains widely covered by cane; with open forests of ash, birch, cedar, chestnut, elm, hickory, oak, pine, poplar and walnut, between which lay a rich carpet of peavine; and with numerous ponds, rivers and streams, along which stretched vast canebrakes. It was partly flat, partly undulating, and partly hilly terrain, which rose to the Great Smoky Mountains in the distance. It abounded in many species of game ranging from bison, deer and elk to turkeys and other wildfowl. Common were the beaver, muskrat, opossum, raccoon, and squirrel. Among beasts of prey, the bear, polecat, puma, wildcat, and wolf were numerous, while the rattlesnake was widely to be found. Edible fish such as the shad were prolific.

By 1780 the Back Country had become dotted with small farms and settlements, but much of the landscape remained as it was thirty years earlier. The bison and elk had been hunted to extinction there, but the other wild animals were still to be found, though in diminished numbers.

The Back Country had yet to evolve into a uniform society. Of the national groups the Scotch-Irish were the most numerous. Disliked by others, they were aggressive, courageous, emotional, fiercely intolerant, hard-drinking, and in many cases inclined to indolence. Of the other groups the Germans from the Palatinate, who had settled mostly in the Dutch Fork, predominated. Better farmers, they were pacific, law-abiding, temperate, and devoted to the ideal of a well-ordered society. The rest were composed of other immigrants from the Old World or their descendants, a number of whom – less than 10 per cent of the back inhabitants – were slaves. Clannishness, through which many clung tenaciously to their cultural heritage, was the order of the day, while mutual dislike or suspicion more often than not triumphed over brotherhood and charity. Not a melting pot, the Back Country was more akin to the Tower of Babel.

By 1776 the proportion of South Carolina's population living above the fall line had soared to some 83,000, 50 per cent of its entire population and 79 per cent of its white inhabitants. By the opening of the seventies the small farm had become the means by which 95 per cent of the Back Country settlers made a living. Nevertheless, clearing land and developing a farm involved too much backbreaking toil for some, who contented themselves with a small corn patch and hunting. Overall, the Back Country had begun to produce an amazing amount of grain and meat, and towards the end of the colonial era as many as 3,000 waggons per year were being sent down from there to Charlestown.

Living in log cabins or primitive shelters on the edge of western civilisation, very many Back Country settlers no longer conformed to accepted standards of behaviour. Criminality, immorality, and irreligion were rife, accentuated by the severe shortage of ministers of religion and the lack of education. Admittedly, odd meeting houses were to be found, for example at Bush River, Camden, the Dutch Fork, Fair Forest, Fishing Creek, Turkey Creek, and the Waxhaws; itinerant preachers came and went; but in general the vast majority of the population caught neither sight nor sound of a minister. 'In the back parts of Carolina,' recalled Major George Hanger many years later, 'you may search after an angel with as much chance of finding one as a parson; there is no such thing – I mean when I was there. What they are now, I know not. It is not impossible, but they may have become more religious, moral, and virtuous since the great affection they have imbibed for the French. In my time you might travel sixty or seventy miles and not see a church or even a schism shop[1]. I have often called at a dog-house in the woods, inhabited by eight or ten persons, merely from curiosity. I have asked the master of the house: "Pray, my friend, of what religion are you?" "Of what religion, sir?" "Yes, my friend, of what religion are you – or to what sect do you belong?" "Oh! now I understand you; why, for the matter of that, *religion does not trouble us much in these parts*."' As to honesty, Cornwallis would soon observe, 'I will not be godfather to any man's honesty in this province.'

The ignorance and illiteracy of most Back Country settlers went hand in hand with a lack of intellectual curiosity. According to the Reverend Charles Woodmason, 'Few or no books are to be found in all this vast country,' besides a few religious works. 'Nor do they delight

---

[1] meeting house.

in historical books or in having them read to them.., for these people despise knowledge, and instead of honouring a learned person or any one of wit or knowledge, be it in the arts, sciences or languages, they despise and ill treat them.'

Quite a few of the settlers would once have been the orphaned or neglected children who swarmed over the Back Country on the eve of the revolution. Described as then living 'expos'd in a state of nature', they had been 'oblig'd almost to associate with villains and vagabonds for subsistence'.

Of the few meeting houses most were attended by Scotch-Irish Presbyterians, who surpassed all other sects in bigotry and fierce denominationalism, going to lengths which are almost unbelievable. Men of God, their ministers brought politics into the pulpit, exhorted rebellion, and in some cases — for example the Reverend John Simpson of Fishing Creek - took up arms themselves.

Scattered among the Back Country population was a body of hardy, illiterate and lawless backwoodsmen whom the British came to fear more than most. They tended to have no settled habitation and lived partly by hunting and partly by preying on their neighbours. 'This distinguished race of men,' declared George Hanger, 'are more savage than the Indians and possess *every* one of their vices but *not one* of their virtues. I have known one of these fellows travel two hundred miles through the woods, never keeping any road or path, guided by the sun by day and the stars by night, to kill a particular person belonging to the opposite party. He would shoot him before his own door and ride away to boast of what he had done on his return... I speak... of that *heathen race* known by the name of *crackers*.'

Despite the vaunted levelling spirit of the Back Country, a gentry of sorts had arisen composed of the wealthy who had acquired extensive land holdings, merchants, surveyors, lawyers, and men of status in other fields. Few though they were, their influence was profound, but sadly for the British almost all were of the revolutionary persuasion.

An endemic vice in all ranks was the excessive consumption of alcoholic liquor. Rough cider and peach or apple brandy were common beverages, rum was consumed in large quantities, but rye whiskey, favoured in particular by the Scotch-Irish, was the grand elixir. Except the temperate Germans, who preferred their beer, almost everyone drank to excess: the morning bevvy, the dinner dram, the evening nightcap, and the more or less frequent tipple in between times. Taverns, still houses, and drinking cabins did a roaring trade, whereas stores commonly held among their stock a pretty liberal quantity of something to keep the spirits up.

Amid the hardships of Back Country life a high old time was had with recreational pursuits. From the simple pleasures of hunting and fishing they extended to horse racing and shooting matches, but more often than not they centred around the tavern, where drunkenness, gaming, cheating, quarrelling, and brawling were commonplace, particularly on days when court or other public business was transacted. Completing the picture were communal harvest days, dances, and occasions such as musters and vendues, all of which gave ample rein to the wild frolicking common on the frontier.

Of the factors that had led many Back Country settlers to remain loyal to the Crown, a combination of three predominated. Partly it was a sense of belonging to a wider British community, besides being Americans; partly it was a feeling of gratitude to the Crown for the grant of land; and partly it was antagonism to the Low Country élite, whose gross neglect of the Back Country only a few years earlier had turned many settlers against them and the revolutionary cause which they came to espouse. Admittedly, a framework of local government had recently been established, representation in the legislature was lately secured, but memories of past grievances were long.

Now divided politically, as well as in other ways, the Back Country was a place where emotions often ran free, unrestrained by concepts of civilised behaviour. A powder keg waiting to explode, it would be ignited by the coming of the British.

When writing to Clinton on 30th May, Cornwallis refers to an event thought by many to have instigated the merciless barbarity with which the war was waged by the revolutionary irregulars and state troops of the Carolinas in the coming months. It was Tarleton's defeat of Buford at the Waxhaws. Henry Bowyer, Buford's adjutant, rode forward with a flag of truce — after the action commenced — to advise Tarleton that Buford was now prepared to surrender. According to Bowyer, 'When close to the British commander, he delivered Beaufort's [sic] message, but a ball at the moment striking the forehead of Tarleton's horse, he plunged and both fell to the ground, the horse being uppermost.' Exasperated at the dishonouring of the flag, and fearing that Tarleton was dead, his cavalry reacted, in Tarleton's own words, with 'a vindictive severity not easily restrained'. Upwards of one hundred of Buford's corps were killed, many mangled, whereas Tarleton's casualties came to only nineteen. Whilst running amok cannot be remotely condoned, no matter what the justification for it, it remains debatable whether the effect on the revolutionary mind was as marked as we have long been led to believe. If the action had not occurred, the revolutionaries of the Carolinas, embittered against their neighbours and unfettered by civilised restraints, would most likely have continued to behave as badly as they did. 'Tarleton's quarter', meaning no quarter, seems to have served simply as an excuse.

When we left Nisbet Balfour earlier in this chapter, he had gone forward with Ferguson's men to occupy the village of Ninety Six. A son of the Laird of Dunbog in the County of Fife, he was born in 1743 and commissioned an ensign in the 4th or King's Own Regiment in 1761. As the revolutionary war began, he was serving as a captain in Boston, where he would be wounded at the Battle of Bunker Hill. His bravery there brought him to the notice of Howe, who appointed him one of his aides-de-camp. At the close of the New York campaign he was sent home with Howe's dispatches and promoted by brevet to major. Returning to America, he was involved in the Battle of Germantown before being promoted on 1st January 1778 to the lt colonelcy of the 23rd Regiment or Royal Welch Fusiliers, now posted at Camden.

Balfour would not remain long in the Back Country. Cornwallis would soon appoint him Commandant of Charlestown in place of Paterson, who on 18th July was conveniently shipped off to New York for the recovery of his health. It was an exemplary appointment. Arriving in Charlestown at the beginning of August, Balfour at once applied himself efficiently and indefatigably to the job, which involved not only managing the very complex civil affairs of the town and country but also supporting militarily the troops in the field. An imposing figure, he is accurately described as being 'altogether a very fine specimen of physical manhood, with an erect person fully six feet in height, broad-chested and athletic, with cheeks unwrinkled, a skin clear and florid, eyes large, blue and tolerably expressive, and features generally well-chiselled'. In the uniform of his regiment he was, in the words of a lady who knew him well, 'as splendid as scarlet, gold lace and feathers could make a man'.

Occupying as headquarters a mansion at N° 11 Lower King Street belonging to the estate of Miles Brewton, Balfour soon began to ruffle the feathers of revolutionary Charlestonians. According to David Ramsay, a leading firebrand who was transported to St Augustine for breaking his parole, he displayed in the exercise of his office 'the frivolous self-importance and insolence which are natural to little minds when puffed up by sudden elevation and employed in functions to which their abilities are not equal'. In particular Ramsay objected to Balfour and his assistants exercising legislative, judicial and executive powers over citizens in the same manner as over the soldiery under their command. For his part William Moultrie accused Balfour of 'violent and arbitrary administration', asserting that 'Balfour, a proud, haughty Scot, carried his authority with a very high hand. His tyrannical, insolent disposition treated the people as the most abject slaves.'

Fortunately for Balfour the passage of time has led to a less emotive and more balanced assessment of his conduct. Like Cornwallis, he was faced with the realities of power. In the situation in which he found himself he had inevitably no option but to adopt measures which were designed forcibly and inescapably to put down rebellion. This being so, it was only natural for the revolutionary party to consider those measures oppressive. Indeed, they cannot have been otherwise if the aim was eventually to reinstate civil government under the Crown. As the saying goes, you cannot make an omelette without breaking eggs.

Extraordinarily preoccupied with the heavy duties of his office, Balfour personally had little time for those incorrigible revolutionaries who persevered at times in trying to score points. Rather short with them he may have been, but his arduous responsibilities did not allow him the freedom to be otherwise. Politically, they were beyond redemption.

As revealed in these Papers, Balfour's immense contribution to the war effort in the Carolinas speaks for itself. Always an entertaining writer, he comes across as an officer who never shirked responsibility but rather took it upon himself, an officer never loath to take the tough decision. Right, for example, in promoting the transportation of incendiaries to St Augustine, undoubtedly right, as we shall see later, in confirming the sentence of death on Isaac Hayne, he may, for example, be criticised for closely confining Continental and militia captives on prison ships, a decision which led many to die of small pox or putrid fevers. Yet taken together, his decisions were invariably sound in furthering the interests of the Crown.

If Balfour was more commonly fallible, it was in his assessment of subordinate officers. While right to a degree about Ferguson, he was, for example, quite wrong in criticising Cruger, whose sterling qualities were amply displayed in the siege of Ninety Six. Devoted to Cornwallis, he only once came close to regretting his judgement, namely to march from Wilmington into Virginia.

After the war Balfour was rewarded by promotion to colonel and by appointment as an aide-de-camp to the King. He went on to become an MP and see service as a major general in Flanders. Unmarried, he died a full general at Dunbog in 1823.

Patrick Ferguson, whose men we left entering the village of Ninety Six, was destined to play a prominent but ultimately tragic part in the events of the coming months. Born in 1744, he was the second son of James Ferguson of Pitfour, Aberdeenshire, a Lord Commissioner of Justiciary for Scotland. His mother, the Hon Anne Murray, was a daughter of the 4th Lord Elibank. At the age of fifteen he became a cornet in the Royal North British Dragoons – the Scots Greys — and for the next two years studied fortification, gunnery etc in the Royal Military Academy at Woolwich. He then served with his regiment in Germany during the latter part of the Seven Years' War. In September 1768 a captaincy was purchased for him in the 70th Regiment and three months later he set sail with his company for the West Indies. Back in London by 1773, he soon began to devise plans for breechloading and other improvements, which he patented in December 1776. In the same year he demonstrated his famous breechloading rifle before a number of distinguished officers at Woolwich and also before the King at Windsor. He set sail for New York in March 1777, seconded to the command of a corps of one hundred men armed with his rifles. Six months later the corps, supported by the Queen's Rangers, did good service at the Battle of Brandywine, but Ferguson was severely wounded in the right elbow and never fully regained the use of his arm. His corps was disbanded. In May 1778 he returned to active duty and five months later commanded a detachment of three hundred men which sailed to Little Egg Harbour in New Jersey to root out a nest of privateers. In a night attack nearby, he demolished much of Pulaski's Legion. On embarking with Clinton for the south in late December 1779, he was appointed a lt colonel on the Provincial establishment and given the command of the American Volunteers, a small corps of some 120 men drawn from British American regiments. On 18th April he was promoted to a majority in the 71st (Highland) Regiment, backdated to 26th October, and therefore had to relinquish his Provincial commission. Many continued to address him all the same as colonel.

During the siege of Charlestown Ferguson and his corps were involved in support operations, notably in the rout of a revolutionary force at Monck's Corner on 14th April. At the conclusion of the siege Clinton appointed him Inspector of Militia and charged him and his corps with the task of forming the loyalists, predominantly those of the Back Country, into companies or battalions of royal militia. The younger men unencumbered with large families were to be liable for offensive operations, whereas the rest were to undertake domestic duties.

Of almost all British officers Ferguson best understood the important contribution of the royal militia to the strategy outlined in chapter 1. Tragically for him, and sadly for the Crown, he consistently held an exaggerated view of the extent to which the militia was dependable. Less committed than the revolutionaries, and perhaps more pacific, many loyalists were disinclined to go out on a limb in support of the Crown, preferring to leave the prosecution of the war to the regular forces. Accordingly, when they came to be embodied in the royal militia, their fighting qualities were suspect. Indeed, Ferguson himself would soon admit, 'Their loyalty having made them avoid service, they are, it is true, less warlike than the rebels...' He nevertheless believed that, if once fairly pitted, they would gain confidence.

Besides overrating the royal militia, Ferguson may have had one or two other weaknesses which contributed to the debacle at King's Mountain. We shall address them later.

Otherwise, Ferguson emerges from these Papers as a humane, benevolent officer who, despite trying circumstances, applied his best endeavours to discipline the militia and suppress their irregularities. He was nonetheless vilified in revolutionary propaganda, which has percolated down to the present day.

Accompanying Ferguson as far as the Congarees was his deputy, the Hon George Hanger, the youngest son of Lord Coleraine. Born in 1751, he was educated partly at Eton, from where he went on to study for one year at the University of Göttingen, applying himself to mathematics, fortification, and the German language. The next two years he spent in Hanover and Hesse-Cassel, where, *inter alia*, he received practical instruction in the discipline of light cavalry. In the meantime (on 31st January 1771) he was commissioned an ensign in the 1st Regiment of Foot Guards (the Grenadier Guards) and was eventually summoned home to join it. Promoted to lieutenant on 20th February 1776, he resigned his commission one month later in disgust at a junior officer being promoted over his head. Still intent on a military career, he was drawn by the events in North America to obtaining a commission as a staff captain in the Hessian Jäger Corps. Although he variously states that he 'served the whole war', his commission was dated 18th January 1778 and it was not until 26th May that he arrived at New York aboard Gambier's fleet. Three days later he embarked for Philadelphia to join his corps. He then took part in the withdrawal across New Jersey before commanding for the rest of the year a company of chasseurs drawn from the Hessian regiments. With it he was involved in small-scale operations to the north of New York City. During 1779, being fairly fluent in German, he served as an aide-de-camp to Clinton, almost certainly to facilitate liaison with Knyphausen and his staff. For the expedition to South Carolina he was given the command of a detachment of Hessian chasseurs, but their transport, the *Anna*, was dismasted and driven across the ocean to England. Hanger for his part arrived safely in Georgia, having taken passage in the *John* to see that three of Clinton's favourite horses were properly attended to. With no men to command he acted during the siege of Charlestown as one of Clinton's aides.

Appointed Ferguson's deputy at the conclusion of the siege, Hanger enjoyed the militia rank of major, but unlike Ferguson he soon became disenchanted at the prospect of forming the militia. On 7th June, while at Thomson's plantation, he took leave of Ferguson's corps and rode over to Camden, where, supported by his good friend Tarleton, he persuaded Cornwallis to appoint him major in the British Legion in succession to the Hon Charles Cochrane, who was returning home on personal business. He would go on to play a significant part in the Battle of Camden before falling ill of yellow fever at Charlotte. He never saw active service again.

On 21st June Hanger set out with Cornwallis and Tarleton for Charlestown, where he remained until the end of July. Despite such a brief sojourn there, he left a lasting impression on Charlestonians. A womaniser who even at an early age 'had a most decided preference for female society', he, perhaps of all British officers, played fast and loose, ever mindful that for many of his calling life was short.

At the close of the war he was placed on the British half-pay list and in 1793 was promoted to lt colonel. One of the convivial companions of the Prince of Wales, to whom he became equerry, he was disposed to participate in all the dissipations of higher society, 'but as the Prince advanced in life, the eccentric manners of the Colonel became somewhat too free and coarse for the royal taste.' In June 1798 he was jailed in the King's Bench Prison for debt, but succeeded in paying off his creditors ten months later and set himself up as a coal merchant.

Despite all his frailties, Hanger was a committed Christian who was blessed with an innate goodness of heart. Fundamentally a kind and honourable man, he married his housekeeper, Mary Anne Katherine Greenwood, by whom he had had an illegitimate son John. When he succeeded to the Barony of Coleraine in 1814, he would have liked nothing better than to enter more fully into public life, but not wishing to embarrass his wife, who was of lowly estate, he declined to assume the title and was always somewhat peevish when he was addressed by it. Percipient and farsighted politically, he gave vent to his enlightened views in *The Life, Adventures, and Opinions of Col. George Hanger*, published in 1801. A roller coaster of a ride, in which Hanger plays to the gallery, it in many respects has stood the test of time, often dealing with subjects tacitly avoided by later writers. Containing common-sense views on social subjects — views far in advance of the general opinions of his day, it also provides excellent descriptions of debtors' prisons and the rogueries of attorneys at the end of the 18th century, besides frankly avowing a hatred of hypocrisy. However, it is perhaps best remembered for Hanger's famous prophecy of the American Civil War, a prophecy made, he says, before a distinguished gathering at Philadelphia in 1783. A witty man who was a source of wit in others, he was at times likened to Falstaff and became 'one of the prominent features of his time'.

Hanger died of a convulsive fit at his house near Regent's Park on 31st March 1824 and was buried in the family church at Driffield, Gloucestershire. His epitaph reads:

> *NEAR this place lieth*
> *the Body of GENERAL GEORGE HANGER,*
> *LORD COLERAINE.*
> *He lived and died a firm Believer*
> *in one God and in one God only.*
> *He was also a Practical Christian*
> *as far as his frail nature*
> *did allow him so to be.*

Over the years his detractors have had a field day in malevolently denigrating his character, and even the *ODNB* accuses him of 'promoting himself' to general. The fact is that he was promoted to the Hessian rank of major general *à la suite der Armée* in 1818, having been invested with the Hessian Order *pour la vertu militaire* three years earlier. A striking portrait of him in the uniform of the British Legion, painted by Thomas Beach *c.* 1785, is in the Royal Collection.

Throughout the period covered by Part Two a false calm prevailed in South Carolina, broken only by the actions at Mobley's Meeting House, Alexander's and Beckham's Old Fields, and Hill's Iron Works. Revolutionaries in great numbers allowed that the game was up and came in to submit. All in all, the outlook could not have seemed brighter for consolidating and furthering British success in the south.

Of particular interest in Part Two are the arrangements being made to form the royal militia. It was to be formed only of loyalists, but in reality persons of doubtful character crept in. No problem was foreseen in appointing captains and subalterns, but the selection of field officers was not so easy, for, as we shall see, virtually all the principal men were of the revolutionary persuasion.

If anything, Part Two gives the lie to the oft repeated assertion that Clinton's proclamation of 3rd June in itself led many dormant revolutionaries to take up arms against the British. Yes, it cancelled the paroles of those not in the military line, but as interpreted by Cornwallis, it did not cancel the paroles of those who had served in the revolutionary forces during the British operations in South Carolina. Of the disaffected to whom the proclamation applied, we shall see that none were to be permitted to enter the royal militia, so that none were to be required to take up arms against their fellow revolutionaries. Instead, having been disarmed, they were to be allowed to remain at home, being required only to contribute a measure of supplies in lieu of their personal attendance in the militia. *Ipso facto*, the notion that the proclamation in itself precipitated the disaffected into choosing between fighting for the British or fighting for the enemy is patently false.

The damage was in fact done, not by the proclamation and the eminently reasonable way in which it was applied by Cornwallis, but rather by the gloss placed on it by militant revolutionaries, who, though relatively few, propagated a most deceitful and persuasive interpretation of its effect, an interpretation which has gained uncritical acceptance down the years. As Turnbull soon observes, when citing another instance of revolutionary propaganda, 'It is inconceivable the damage such reports has done.'

Besides misrepresentation of British policy, another reason for becoming actively disaffected may have been plundering by 'men cloathed in *green*' — presumably British Legion cavalrymen, who were notorious for it — and by loyalists or settlers professing to be loyalists. However, many of those soon to take up arms would require no such reasons and, if subject to paroles or protections, would be unconcerned about the niceties of observing them. Once the shock of the occupation had passed, some, committed as they were to the revolution, and others, influenced or intimidated by the committed into supporting it, would quite simply take up arms in its defence.

Having left the command at Camden to Rawdon, Cornwallis arrived back in Charlestown on 25th June.

§ - §

Principal works consulted in the writing of this chapter

Anthony Allaire, 'Diary', Appendix to Lyman C Draper, *King's Mountain and its Heroes* (Cincinnati, 1881)

Annual Register, xix (1776), 1148

Carl Bridenbaugh, *Myths & Realities: Societies of the Colonial South* (Atheneum NY, 1976)

John A Chapman and John Belton O'Neall, *The Annals of Newberry* (Newberry SC, 1892)

Dictionary of National Biography (London, 1885-1901)

William Henry Foote, *Sketches of North Carolina, Historical and Biographical, illustrative of the Principles of a Portion of Her Early Settlers* (New York, 1846)

Alexander Garden, *Anecdotes of the American Revolution, Second Series* (Charleston, 1828)

Gentleman's Magazine, May 1824, 457-8

Marianne McLeod Gilchrist, *Patrick Ferguson, 'A Man of Some Genius'* (NMS Publishing, 2003)

Geoffrey Grigson, 'Some Tablets on the Wall', *Country Life*, 17th November 1955

George Hanger, *The Life, Adventures, and Opinions of Col. George Hanger* (London, 1801)

George Hanger's entry in *A List of General and Staff Officers on the Establishment in North America*, 16th October 1781 (Clinton Papers, William L Clements Library)

Hangher, Sir George, später Lord Coleraine, Die Worringer'sche Offizierskartei (Hessisches Staatsarchiv, Marburg)

George Howe, *History of the Presbyterian Church in South Carolina* (Columbia SC, 1870)

Johann Karl Philip von Krafft, 'Journal', *Collections of the New-York Historical Society for the year 1882*

J B O Landrum, *Colonial and Revolutionary History of Upper South Carolina* (Greenville SC, 1897)

Henry Lee, *Memoirs of the War in the Southern Department of the United States* (Revised edition, New York, 1869)

John H Logan, *A History of the Upper Country of South Carolina* (Columbia SC, 1859)

Lewis Melville, *The Beaux of the Regency* (London, 1908), ch II

William Moultrie, *Memoirs of the American Revolution* (New York, 1802)

The New-York Gazette, 1st June 1778

Oxford Dictionary of National Biography (Oxford University Press, 2004)

David Ramsay, *The History of the Revolution of South-Carolina from a British Province to an Independent State* (Trenton, 1785), ii, 263-4

Charles Stedman, *History of the Origin, Progress, and Termination of the American War* (London, 1792)

Banastre Tarleton, *A History of the Campaigns of 1780 and 1781 in the Southern Provinces of North America* (London, 1787)

Mark Urban, *Fusiliers: Eight Years with the Redcoats in America* (Faber and Faber Limited, 2007)

David Duncan Wallace, *South Carolina: A Short History, 1520-1948* (University of South Carolina Press, 1961)

Henry Alexander White, *Southern Presbyterian Leaders* (New York, 1911)

Franklin and Mary Wickwire, *Cornwallis: The American Adventure* (Houghton Mifflin Co, 1970)

Charles Woodmason, *The Carolina Backcountry on the Eve of the Revolution*, edited by Richard J Hooker (University of North Carolina Press, 1953)

§ - §

CHAPTER 5

Correspondence between Cornwallis and Clinton or Arbuthnot

Cornwallis to Clinton, 18th May 1780[1]   *72(8): C*

Camp at Manigold's Plantation
18th May 1780

Sir

Lt Colonel Webster arrived this morning and informed me of the message which you sent by him relative to reinforcing the corps under my command. The service on which I am going is undoubtedly of the most important nature, and in my opinion, without some success in the Back Country, our success at Charlestown would but little promote the real interests of Great Brittain; but at the same time it is as necessary that your situation to the northward should be respectable. It would be with great regret that I should see you leave behind any part of that corps destined for your first embarkation. The garrison then of Charlestown and Sullivan's Island will consist of three British regiments, two of them very weak, and two Hessian and the one weak Provincial[2], the latter of which perhaps will be sent to Fort Moultrie. This garrison will have the charge of 2,500 prisoners. The corps at present under my command is in my opinion fully equal to the purposes intended by it, unless some considerable reinforcement of Continentals should come from the northward. I have not yet heard that fact ascertained by any intelligence that has come to my knowledge. If troops are on their march and not very near, your embarkation given out publickly for the Chesapeak will probably stop them. I think therefore, sir, if you please, with proper deference and

---

[1] Published with no material differences in Stevens, *Clinton-Cornwallis Controversy*, i, 210.

[2] Provincial regiments were those raised on the British North American establishment. The rank and file consisted of loyalists, with the officers being either American or partly American and partly British.

submission to your opinion, that the business may be settled in the following manner: if no certain intelligence arrives, before you are ready to sail, of a considerable corps of the Continental troops being far advanced, that the disposition should then remain the same as you mentioned when I had the honour of seeing you; if such intelligence should arrive before that time, I should then wish to be joined by five or six hundred men, British or Hessian, and submit it to your judgement, on the spot, from whence they could be best supplied. I think, at all events, Lt Colonel Balfour's expedition should go on immediately, as the season of the year makes it necessary that he should lose no time. The more pains that can be taken to establish the belief of your going to Virginia, the greater will be the probability of stopping their reinforcements.

I am etc

[CORNWALLIS]

Clinton to Cornwallis, 18th May 1780[3]   *2(36): L*

Charles Town
May 18th 1780

Lt General Earl Cornwallis

My Lord

Colonel Webster informs me that your Lordship has received confirmation of what I had heard from an intercepted letter to General Lincoln dated George Town, 5th May, and that you suppose the number of the enemy may by the 23rd amount to 4 or 5,000.

Respecting their number, I cannot conceive that so great a one can be collected in both provinces or that of those collected any great part are Continentals. By information I have received, I have every reason to believe that the Maryland and Pennsylvania line, and Lee's Legion[4], passed the Delaware on the 20th of April. They may be about 1,000, possibly more. I should suppose it will take them two months at least in any season to get here. I cannot conceive it is their intention to come so far, but by the intercepted letter from George Town and your information they seem greatly advanced. This reinforcement, however, can only have had for object the relief of Charles Town. The instant they are informed of its fate they naturally will fall back apprehensive of what may happen elsewhere, except the North and

---

[3] An extract from the third paragraph, but dated 17th May, is published in Stevens, op cit, i, 209.

[4] Lee's Legion was a mixed corps of three troops of cavalry and three companies of infantry under the command of Major Henry 'Light-horse Harry' Lee, an officer who would play for the most part a distinguished, but at times controversial, role in the events of 1781 in the Carolinas.

South Carolina militia, Scot's Brigade (what can this brigade be, as one is taken in town?)[5], Armand's corps[6] and Lee's Legion. It is possible, however, that the whole may advance to obstruct your move into the Back Country.

Your Lordship has already with you 2,542 rank and file, but if you have the least reason to suppose the enemy likely to be in great number, you shall be reinforced with the 42nd, the light infantry and any other corps you chuse. As your move is important, it must not be stinted. I will give you all you wish of every sort; let me but know what it is as soon as possible. In the mean time I shall order the 42nd and light infantry to prepare, depending upon it that, as soon as you can spare them, you will return them to me, for all operations to the northward must be cramped without them. If you chuse to keep the 17th Dragoons, you are heartily welcome to them during this move. Respecting the first part of it, I wish the Admiral had consented to have passed his gallies into the Pedee with the Legion, threatening a landing. This would have tempted the rebels to stay in George Town, and their retreat was no longer possible after your Lordship has passed the Santee. As it is, I am apprehensive they will escape the moment you pass. Respecting the last part of the move, it is important for you to know that Rutledge[7] is probably at a bluff on the other side Santee about 70 miles

---

[5] A brigadier general in the Continental line, Charles Scott of Virginia (*c.* 1739-1813) had seen action at Trenton, Brandywine, Germantown, and Monmouth. Arriving in Charlestown on 31st March 1780, he had been expected to bring a reinforcement of Virginia State troops but had brought none. Now a prisoner, he would not be exchanged until the close of the war but by June 1781 was on parole in Virginia. In 1785 he removed to Kentucky, of which he became Governor in 1808. (Boatner, *Encyclopedia*, 993; McCrady, *SC in the Rev 1775-1780*, 455; *The Cornwallis Papers*)

[6] Armand's corps comprised the remains of Pulaski's Legion (see p 133, note 23). It now amounted to sixty horse and sixty infantry and would soon join Kalb in North Carolina before performing poorly in the Battle of Camden. Armand, as its commanding officer was called, was the surname adopted during the war by a French nobleman, Armand-Charles Tuffin, Marquis de la Rouërie (1750-1793). Arriving in America in 1777, he had been commissioned a colonel of horse in Pulaski's Legion, seeing extensive action in the north. Going south with Pulaski, he had assumed command of the Legion, which was renamed after him, when Pulaski was mortally wounded on 9th October 1779 in the failed assault on Savannah. In February 1781 he would sail for France on six months' leave to obtain clothing and equipment for his corps, returning in time for the closing operations in Virginia. In 1783 he would be promoted to brigadier general in command of the Continental cavalry. (Boatner, *Encyclopedia*, 1127-9)

[7] John Rutledge (1739-1800) was at this time the revolutionary Governor of South Carolina. The eldest son of a doctor of medicine, and a brother of Edward Rutledge, he had studied law at the Middle Temple in London before being called to the English bar in 1760. Returning soon afterwards to South Carolina, he promptly embarked upon a glittering political, and then judicial, career, becoming a Member of the Commons House of Assembly in 1761 and a delegate to the Stamp Act Congress in 1765 and to the Continental Congress in 1774 and 1775. A member of the committee which framed a temporary revolutionary constitution for South Carolina, he was elected President of South Carolina by the legislature in March 1776, although he continued to hope for an accommodation with Britain short of independence. Two years later, as one who profoundly distrusted democracy, he resigned rather than sign into law a new revolutionary constitution which replaced the Legislative Council, elected by the General Assembly, with a Senate directly elected by the people. In January 1779 he nevertheless allowed the legislature to elect him Governor (as the President was restyled) in view of a possibly imminent invasion from Georgia, and in the ensuing events of that year he was to play a prominent if not altogether uncontroversial role. Having been invested with absolute powers by the legislature in early 1780, he made his way through the lines at Charlestown on 13th April with three members of the Privy Council so that a nucleus of revolutionary government might remain in South Carolina in the event of the town falling. Soon two of those members, Daniel Huger and Charles Pinckney, would abandon the revolutionary cause, swearing allegiance to the Crown, whilst the third, John Lewis Gervais, would repair to Virginia and remain inactive. The rest of the civil leadership having been captured at Charlestown, Rutledge alone would remain responsible for maintaining the legitimacy of the revolutionary state.

from hence, collecting cattle, and Washington[8] in the forks of Black River near Kingstree Bridge. I send you an intelligent person of the district from whom I have this information.

I have the honor to be
Your Lordship's most obedient and most humble servant

[H CLINTON]

It was a responsibility he did not shirk. In the coming months he would commission and tirelessly support officers in the field, visit the north and seek aid, and skilfully apply himself to the restoration of civil government towards the close of 1781. Relinquishing office in January 1782, he entered upon a judicial career in 1784. He nevertheless attended the Federal Convention of 1787, where he argued against restrictions on the slave trade, and sat from 1784 to 1790 in the South Carolina House of Representatives, where he voted conservatively but not illiberally. In 1791 he became Chief Justice of South Carolina, but infirmity of mind caused him to retire from public life four years later. A plantation and slave owner, Rutledge owed his political success, first to the support of the politically dominant planters, with whom he identified, and second to personal qualities which well suited him for public life, not least a facility for public speaking, political adeptness, the capacity to inspire, impressive administrative ability, and the courage of his convictions. (*DAB*; McCrady, *SC in the Rev 1775-1780* and *1780-1783, passim*; *Appletons'*; *The Cornwallis Papers*)

[8] Born in Virginia and educated for the church, William Washington (1752-1810) was a distant relation of George Washington, possibly a second cousin once removed. At an early date in the war he forsook thoughts of the ministry and entered the 3rd Virginia Continental Regiment as a captain in time to take a gallant part in the New York and New Jersey campaigns, being twice wounded. Having by 1780 become Lt Colonel of the 3rd Continental Dragoons, he moved south with a mixed force of cavalry and skirmished in March with Paterson's reinforcement on its march from Savannah to Charlestown. Afterwards, in actions of 14th April and 6th May at Monk's Corner and Lenud's Ferry, he was fortunate to escape with his life when the revolutionary forces there were routed by Tarleton. He would now retire to eastern North Carolina to recruit and re-equip his corps before playing a prominent and courageous part in the events of 1781, notably in the Battle of Cowpens (where he gained his revenge on Tarleton), in the retreat to the Dan, and in the Battles of Guilford, Hobkirk's Hill and Eutaw Springs. Wounded and captured in the last affair, he played no further part in the war. On his physique, character and accomplishments Henry Lee, who knew him well, commented: 'He possessed a stout frame, being six feet in height, broad, strong, and corpulent. His occupations and his amusements applied to the body rather than to the mind, to the cultivation of which he did not bestow much time or application, nor was his education of the sort to excite such habits, being only calculated to fit a man for the common business of life. In temper he was good-humored; in disposition amiable; in heart upright, generous, and friendly; in manners lively, innocent, and agreeable. His military exploits announce his grade and character in arms. Bold, collected, and persevering, he preferred the heat of action to the collection and sifting of intelligence, to the calculations and combinations of means and measures, and was better fitted for the field of battle than for the drudgery of camp and the watchfulness of preparation. Kind to his soldiers, his system of discipline was rather lax and sometimes subjected him to injurious consequences when close to a sagacious and vigilant adversary.' Towards the close of the war he established himself at Sandy Hill, South Carolina, the ancestral seat of his wife, and although he would serve in the legislature, he would refuse to run for Governor 'because he could not make a speech'. In 1798 he was commissioned a brigadier general and would serve for two years. (*Appletons'*; Boatner, *Encyclopedia*, 1169; Draper, *King's Mountain*, 487-8; Tarleton, *Campaigns*, 8, 16, 20; Lee, *Memoirs*, 587-9)

Cornwallis to Clinton, 19th May 1780[9]

72(10): C

Camp at Manigold's Plantation
19th May 1780

Sir

I received very early this morning the favour of your letter by Lt Colonel Innes, to which the letter which I had the honour of sending to you yesterday by Major Dansey[10] will serve as an answer. I can only add that I have received no intelligence whatever of reinforcements coming to the enemy from the northward or of their being in force in this province. The day before I left the army, after having taken my leave of you, I received a letter from Webster mentioning such a report to which he gave no credit. I met him the next morning at the ferry and told him that I had not thought it worth while to trouble you with it and that, if he pleased, he might mention it in conversation to you. I have received accounts that the enemy have quitted the ferrys of Santee. The cavalry and infantry of the Legion marched early this morning and I have reason to think that they will be able to get some boats. The greatest part of my corps will march this night to Lenew's Ferry.

It will be a convenience for some days at least if you will be kind enough to order two boats to attend at Scott's Ferry and a non-commissioned officer's guard of a Provincial corps to be stationed on this side. I write to the Admiral my wish about the gallies, boats etc.

I have in consequence of your permission appointed Captain Manly[11] of the 33rd Regiment to act as Major of Brigade, and perhaps you will think it necessary to put him in general orders.

I am etc

[CORNWALLIS]

---

[9] The first two sentences of the first paragraph are published with no differences in Stevens, op cit, i, 211.

[10] Commissioned a lieutenant in the army on 17th January 1763, William Collins Dansey had entered the 33rd Regiment as such on 31st October 1766. Remaining there, he was promoted to captain on 27th January 1774 and to major on 14th October 1778. (*Army Lists*)

[11] John Manley had spent his entire service in the 33rd Regiment. Commissioned an ensign on 26th December 1770, he was promoted to lieutenant on 28th August 1775 and to captain on 14th October 1778. He would be mentioned in dispatches after the Battle of Camden. (*Army Lists*; *The Cornwallis Papers*)

Clinton to Cornwallis, 20th May 1780[12]

2(38): LS

Charles Town
South Carolina
May the 20th 1780

Rt Hon Lt General Earl Cornwallis

My Lord

I deferred answering your Lordship's letter until I could tell you the co-operating corps under Lt Colonel Balfour had received my final instructions.

Of the three routes by Savannah River, Orangeburgh and along the Santee which lead to the districts supposed most friendly to us, the latter only can with convenience be adopted, as it affords a prospect of subsistence, which the want of carriages and the barrenness of the country would render too precarious by the others.

Lt Colonel Balfour will therefore move next Monday with the 3rd, light infantry, Brown's corps, and Ferguson's detachment by this road. Your Lordship may give such orders as you judge proper for giving Colonel Balfour's march a relation to your own, as, until he quits the Santee and crosses the country towards 96, he will not be distant from the route I understand your Lordship proposes to take.

The light infantry and 42nd Regiment march this evening to Goose Creek, and thence to Monk's Corner, where they will remain at your Lordship's call in readiness either to join you or to return and embark, as shall have become expedient.

As to the Negroes, I will leave such orders as I hope will prevent the confusion that would arise from a further desertion of them to us, and I will consider of some scheme for placing those we have on abandoned plantations on which they may subsist. In the mean time your Lordship can make such arrangements as will discourage their joining us.

I shall immediately issue a proclamation, the substance of which I enclose you. Colonel Balfour will have several copies with him.

I have allowed Major Ferguson to take the charge of the militia under the title of Inspector of Militia Corps and to propose regulations for them. This, however, is of course subject to your Lordship's controul, or to being reversed and otherwise settled if you think fit.

I have sent out an emissary or two, who I hope will bring you some intelligence. They will, as proof of being employed by me, give your Lordship the words 'Fellinghausen' and 'Lord Broome'. Any persons you address to me may bring the words 'Bukkeburg',

---

[12] The fourth, penultimate and final paragraphs are published with no material differences in Stevens, op cit, i, 211, 212.

'Diesenburg', 'Hohen Wippel' etc.[13]

Such instructions as I shall find it necessary to leave, your Lordship will find with General Paterson[14], who is to be Commandant of Charles Town.

Matters relative to money, provisions, stores etc will be settled as well as our time and circumstances will permit.

Every jealousy has been and will be given on *my* part as a blind to our real intentions.

And now, my Lord, having entered into everything that occurs to me as necessary to be thought on at present, I heartily wish success to your important move. I cannot doubt your having it, for, as much as I agree with you that success at Charles Town — unless followed in the Back Country — will be of little avail, so much I am persuaded that the taking that place, in the advantageous manner we have done it, ensures the reduction of this and the next province, if the temper of our friends in those districts is such as has always been represented to us.

I have the honor to be, my Lord,
Your most obedient servant

H CLINTON

Enclosure
Draft proclamation[15]   *2(34): Df*

South Carolina

By his Excellency Sir Henry Clinton, Knight of the Most Honorable Order of the Bath, General and Commander in Chief of all His Majesty's forces within the colonies lying on the Atlantic Ocean from Nova Scotia to West Florida etc etc etc

---

[13] Clinton is using, besides the name of Cornwallis's son, misspelt place names that featured in the German theatre of the Seven Years' War.

[14] James Paterson, as he signed his surname, had been appointed Lt Colonel of the 63rd Regiment on 15th June 1763. By now a brigadier general, he went south with Clinton in 1780 and was put in command of a force that was to make a diversion from Savannah towards Augusta, but these orders were countermanded. Instead, he was in March summoned to South Carolina to reinforce Clinton with some 1,500 men. After the capitulation of Charlestown he was appointed by Clinton to be Commandant of the town, but overwhelmed by the confusion, perplexity and civil nature of the business, he was not up to the job, finding himself 'embarked on a situation out of the line of my profession'. Fortunately for Cornwallis, Paterson fell ill and on 18th July was conveniently shipped to New York for the recovery of his health. Notwithstanding the ostensible reason for his departure, Josiah Martin, who was privy to Cornwallis's views, gives the game away in the postscript to his letter of 24th July (pp 368-9). Promoted to major general on 20th November 1782, Paterson was to command British land forces in Nova Scotia after the war. At times his name is misspelt by historians. (*The Cornwallis Papers*; Stevens, op cit, ii, 449; WO 65/164(1) (National Archives, Kew))

[15] The actual proclamation, as signed by Clinton on 22nd May, is in the same terms. A copy is in Tarleton, *Campaigns*, 71-2.

PROCLAMATION

WHEREAS, notwithstanding the gracious offers which have been made to receive to His Majesty's peace and protection, with pardon and oblivion for their past offences, all those His deluded and infatuated subjects who should return to their duty and a due obedience to the laws, yet there are some wicked and desperate men who, regardless of the ruin and misery in which the country will be involved, are still endeavouring to support the flame of rebellion and, under pretence of authority derived from the late usurped legislatures, are attempting by enormous fines, grievous imprisonments and sanguinary punishments to compel His Majesty's faithful and unwilling subjects to take up arms against His authority and Government, and it is therefore become necessary, as well for the protection of the loyal subjects as to procure the establishment of peace and good government in the country, to prevent by the terror of example such enormous offences being committed in future, I have therefore thought fit to issue this my proclamation to declare that, if any person shall hereafter appear in arms in order to prevent the establishment of His Majesty's government in this country or shall, under any pretence or authority whatsoever, attempt to compel any other person or persons to do so, or who shall hinder or intimidate, or attempt to hinder or intimidate, the King's faithful and loyal subjects from joining His forces or otherwise performing those duties their allegiance requires, such person or persons so offending shall be treated with that severity so hardened and criminal an obstinacy will deserve, and his or their estates will be immediately seized to be confiscated. And for the encouragement of the King's faithful and peaceable subjects I do again assure them that they shall meet with effectual countenance, protection and support, and whenever the situation of the country will permit of the restoration of civil government and peace, they will by the Commissioners appointed by His Majesty for that purpose be restored to the full possession of that liberty in their persons and property which they had before experienced under the British Government. And that so desirable an event may be the more speedily accomplished, I do hereby, in His Majesty's name, require and command all persons whatever to be aiding and assisting to His forces, whenever they shall be required, in order to extirpate the rebellion and thereby restore peace and prosperity to this at present desolated and distracted country.

Given under my hand at Head Quarters in Charles Town
the [*blank*] day of May 1780

By his Excellency's command

Cornwallis to Clinton, 21st May 1780[16] 72(12): C

Camp at Lenew's, east side of Santee
21st May 1780

Sir

I have just received your letter by Major Dansey of yesterday's date. I yesterday passed the Santee with the cavalry and infantry of the Legion and the 23rd Regiment and sent

---

[16] The last sentence of the first paragraph is published with no differences in Stevens, op cit, i, 212.

Tarleton very early this morning to Georgetown. The remainder of the corps now with me and provision waggons will get over in the course of this day. I shall march on the 23rd for Cambden, at which place I am convinced that it is necessary I should arrive as soon as possible. I have directed Lord Rawdon to march by Monk's Corner to Nelson's Ferry, which will save time, and as every account agrees that whatever force the enemy had in this country is gone to Camden, there can be no danger in our marching so far on different sides of the river. The march of the light infantry and 42nd to Monk's Corner will be of use to those corps and will help to spread alarm thro' the country, but from what I hear I do not believe that there can be any necessity for detaining any part of the first embarkation a moment after the ships are ready for them.

You may depend on my utmost attention and exertions to draw the most usefull consequences from the great and important success of His Majesty's arms in this province. I most sincerely hope that all your other undertakings and operations in the different parts of this continent may be equally fortunate.

I have the honour to be etc

[CORNWALLIS]

Cornwallis to Clinton, 26th May 1780   72(14): C

Camp at Sumpter's
May 26th 1780

His Excellency Sir H Clinton etc etc etc

Sir

I beg leave to recommend Mr Elias Ball[17] and Mr Theodore Gaillard[18] to your favour

---

[17] Elias Ball Sr of Wambaw, the brother-in-law of Theodore Gaillard, was of a prominent local family owning large rice plantations and numerous slaves in St James Santee Parish. He was soon to accept the colonelcy of a royal militia regiment in the lower division on the west side of Santee, and both his and Wigfall's regiments were mainly charged with securing the ferries from Murray's downwards on that river. In return for his loyalty his estates were confiscated in 1782 by act of the revolutionary assembly, and after retiring with 200 slaves to East Florida, he sailed for England when the province was ceded to Spain. His son, Elias Ball Jr of Comingtee, was lt colonel of his regiment, and although his estates were likewise confiscated, he later obtained relief. (Lambert, *SC Loyalists*, *passim*; Clark, *Loyalists in the Southern Campaign*, i, 183-4; *The Cornwallis Papers*)

[18] A descendent of Huguenots who migrated to South Carolina about 1685, Theodore Gaillard owned an estate near Murray's Ferry on the Santee. On the one hand he is described as a planter and on the other as a Charlestown merchant. For a few years immediately before the revolution he sat in the Commons House of Assembly before being elected to the first Provincial Congress. A man of influence, he was assiduously courted by Cornwallis and soon persuaded to accept a lt colonelcy in the royal militia, though no record exists of any regiment to which he was assigned. Lying low, he was to take little or no part in the operations in South Carolina. As the tide of events turned, he fled his estate and sought refuge in Charlestown, where he received pay as a refugee militia officer. In 1782 his property was confiscated by act of the revolutionary assembly, but in 1784 it was restored subject to an amercement of 12 per cent. His brother John, who served as a captain in Elias Ball Sr's regiment, also saw his

and protection. They have both given every assistance in their [power?] to His Majesty's forces and shewn the most evident proofs of their loyalty. It was owing to the zeal and activity of Mr Ball that we procured the intelligence which gave Lt Colonel Tarleton the opportunity of striking the decisive blow at Lenew's Ferry.

All accounts say that the enemy are retiring with precipitation and that they are moving from Camden to Charlotte Town and Salisbury. I shall continue my march with all possible expedition.

I am, sir, etc

[CORNWALLIS]

Cornwallis to Clinton, 30th May 1780 72(15): C

Camp at Beach Creek 20 miles from Camden
30th May 1780

Sir

When I arrived at Nelson's Ferry, I was assured that the enemy had no intention of making a stand at Camden and that they had sent off four out of six of their field pieces. As they had 60 miles start of me, I had no hopes of coming up with them with my infantry. The Virginia troops by the best accounts amounted to about 300, the North Carolina militia to about 4 or 500. I thought it would have the best consequences in this province to strike a blow at this corps. I therefore mounted the infantry of the Legion and sent the whole of that corps under Tarleton to harrass their retreat and to attack them if he could with any prospect of success. The enemy separated on their leaving Camden. The North Carolina militia took the route of Cross Creek, the Virginians under Colonel Buford[19] that of Salisbury. Tarleton wisely followed these last. I had the most sanguine hopes from the zeal, spirit and abilities of that

---

property confiscated, but it too was restored on the same basis. (Rogers Jr, *Georgetown County, passim*; Lambert, *SC Loyalists*, 113-5, 291-2; Clark, *Loyalists in the Southern Campaign*, i, 183-4, 491; *The Cornwallis Papers*)

[19] Abraham Buford (1749-1833) was a Virginian who had served in the military line throughout the war, first raising a company of minutemen, and shortly afterwards transferring to the Continental establishment. Now Colonel of the 11th Virginia Continental Regiment, he had come south in 1780 with 300 to 400 men but arrived on the Santee too late to affect operations at Charlestown. Withdrawing towards North Carolina, he was overtaken by Tarleton at the Waxhaws on 29th May and routed in controversial circumstances. In mid September he would join Gates with the remnants of his troops augmented by 200 recruits. After these were assigned to Morgan's light infantry, he himself was eventually placed in command of the post at Salisbury, North Carolina, the site of the Continental hospital. Falling ill in February 1781, he would return on leave to Virginia and play no further part in the events of that year. In later life he would migrate to Kentucky, become a deputy surveyor, and settle on a fine estate near Georgetown, Scott County, where he died. (*DAB*; McCrady, *SC in the Rev 1780-1783*, 11; *The Greene Papers*, vi-viii, *passim*)

excellent officer; by the inclosed letter[20] which I just received from him, you will see they were well founded. The action happened 40 miles beyond Camden. Tarleton had marched 100 miles in little more than two days. I shall write more particularly when I arrive at Camden. I fear we shall be very soon distressed for rum and salt. I should be very much obliged to you if you would please to order 20 or 30 puncheons of rum and three or four waggons loaded with salt to be sent as expeditiously as possible to Nelson's Ferry. I will send waggons to meet them there. You will please to let me know by express the time of their leaving Charlestown. I send this letter by a young man who accompanied Tarleton, whose family have been remarkably loyal, and who deserves any gratification you may think proper to bestow on him.

I am etc

[CORNWALLIS]

Clinton to Cornwallis, 28th May 1780

2(50): LS

Head Quarters
Charles Town
28th May 1780

Lt General Earl Cornwallis

My Lord

As your Lordship will of course see Major Ferguson, he will tell you that I have appointed him Inspector of Militia and major commandant of the first battalion that shall be raised.

I shall leave blank commissions for 4 majors, 20 captains, 20 lieutenants and 20 ensigns, which will be delivered to your Lordship to be disposed of as you may judge most proper for the interest of His Majesty's Service; to be paid and victualled when employed at the same rate with the King's troops.

Your Lordship is at full liberty to give other commissions, and of higher rank, for any new levies you may make to promote the general service, with a certain assurance that you will meet with every confirmation in my power to give.

I have the honor to be
Your Lordship's most obedient and most humble servant

H CLINTON

---

[20] *the inclosed letter*: briefly describing the action of 29th May at the Waxhaws and written in great haste on the field of the encounter, it appears in Bass, *The Green Dragoon*, 81-2. Tarleton's formal account, which Cornwallis forwarded to Clinton on 2nd June, is published with supporting documents, in Tarleton, *Campaigns*, 77-9 and 82-4.

Clinton to Cornwallis, 29th May 1780 *2(54): A(in part)LS*

Head Quarters
29th May 1780
11 at night

Lt General Earl Cornwallis

My Lord

I have the honor to inclose the copy of a letter I sent your Lordship yesterday under cover to Major Ferguson.

From every information I receive, and numbers of the most violent rebels hourly coming in to offer their services, I have the strongest reason to believe the general disposition of the people to be not only friendly to Government but forward to take up arms in its support.

I have not as yet thought proper to call upon the services of the inhabitants of the town and neighbourhood, who appear to be equally zealous; but I shall leave directions with the Commandant to issue such orders to them as he shall, upon consulting with the Superintendent of the Police, judge requisite for the preservation of order and good government. In the mean time they will hold themselves ready to obey your Lordship's summons whenever you shall have occasion to call upon them.

People are this moment come in from Savanna. The whole country between this and that river are coming in and offer to join with their arms. The rebels that plundered Georgia are all gone to the northward and of course will be met either by your Lordship, Colonel Balfour or our friends of the Back Country.

Faithfully
Your Lordship's most obedient servant

H CLINTON

Cornwallis to Clinton, 2nd June 1780[21] *72(16): C*

Camden
June 2nd 1780

His Excellency Sir Henry Clinton KB etc etc etc

Sir

I am honour'd with your letters of the 28th and 29th and have seen Lt Colonel

---
[21] Short extracts from this letter appear in Ross ed, *Cornwallis Correspondence*, i, 45.

Hamilton[22]. Appearances in this province are certainly very favourable, and the important success of Lt Colonel Tarlton at this critical juncture will be of the greatest service. I shall most earnestly endeavour to regulate the government of South Carolina, to act towards the inhabitants, and to establish such kind of force as I think most likely to conduce to the essential good of His Majesty's Service. As soon as I have been able to form a compleat plan, I will have the honour of transmitting it to you. I have no doubt of your agreeing with me that, in a business of such infinite importance, regulations must not be too hastily made nor professions too easily accepted. I have no doubt of being able to subsist a body of troops here this summer without bringing any thing from Charlestown but rum and salt. I have taken every occasion to inform myself of the state of North Carolina and am sorry to find that the back part of that province is in a want of provisions nearly approaching to famine, so that it will be impossible to establish any post there 'till after the harvest. I have sent emissaries to our friends in that country to state my situation to them and to submit to them whether it would not be prudent for them to remain quiet untill I can give them effectual support, which could only be done by a force remaining in the country. At the same time I assured them that if they thought themselves a match for their enemies without any regular force and were determined to rise at all events, I would give them every assistance in my power by incursions of light troops, furnishing ammunition etc.

I will only add my assurances to you that I will use the utmost exertions to perform the important services which you have intrusted to my care and that, altho' in this sanguine moment I may appear slow and cautious to some who overflow with zeal, I must trust you will find my conduct in this business both active and vigorous.

I beg you will accept my most sincere good wishes for your success, and have the honour to be

---

[22] John Hamilton (1747-1817) was a Scot who had migrated to North Carolina and become a prosperous and important merchant in Halifax. When he refused to take the test oath in 1777, the revolutionary authorities expelled him and confiscated his property two years later. By January 1778 he had arrived in New York and was in due course to be commissioned a lt colonel in the Royal North Carolina Regiment, a newly formed British American corps composed of loyalist refugees from North Carolina. During 1779 he and his men were involved in British operations in the south, notably in the action at Stono Ferry and in the defence of Savannah during the siege. In 1780 they reinforced Clinton. Assigned now to Cornwallis's command, they were to be with him at the Battle of Camden, where part of the regiment was on the British left wing, and to play a supporting role in the winter campaign. Having left the rest of the regiment at Wilmington, Cornwallis took Hamilton and his light company with him to Virginia, where they formed part of the troops that capitulated at Yorktown. Placed on the Provincial half-pay list at the close of the war, and compensated by the Crown in 1794 for his losses, Hamilton, who died in England, was to become British consul for many years at Norfolk, Virginia, from where he often visited Halifax and mingled freely with friends of pre-war days. Described by a contemporary as a short, red-faced man, full of gaiety and fond of high living, he was beloved by his troops and respected by his opponents, to whom he was generous and humane. Extremely popular in North Carolina, he was marked by 'the openess of his temper and extreme affability of his manners, so indispensably necessary in conciliating the affections of the people, especially in this country where all ranks are so much upon the level'. According to Stedman, the British nation owed more perhaps to Hamilton than to any other individual loyalist in the British service. Cornwallis, on the other hand, perhaps in a moment of irritation, accused him on one occasion of imprudence and of being 'one of the most obstinate blockheads I ever met with'. O'Hara, for his part, when in Virginia, thought poorly of Hamilton and his light company, describing them as being among 'all our rubbish'. (DeMond, *Loyalists in NC*, 52-3, 181-2; Wheeler, *Reminiscences*, 214; Sabine, *Biographical Sketches*, i, 511-2; Lossing, *Pictorial Field-Book*, ii, 530; McCrady, *SC in the Rev 1775-1780*, 388; *The Cornwallis Papers*; WO 65/165(11) (National Archives, Kew); Stevens, op cit, ii, 436)

Your most obedient and most humble servant

[CORNWALLIS]

Clinton to Cornwallis, undated[23]   4(13): D

Memorandum from Sir Henry Clinton to Lord Cornwallis

That the principle inhabitants were dayly coming in, declare they will never carry arms against His Majesty, nor do they wish to fight against the Americans; but shou'd any part of the southern colonies be invaded by the French or Spaniards, they will to a man be in readiness to join the British forces.

Sir Henry did not intend to embody any militia below for the present.

Lord Cornwallis to act as he thinks proper with the militia in the Back Country and to make such movements with the army as his Lordship may think most conducive for His Majesty's Service.

Sir Henry was to go to town on Wednesday last to inquire into the conduct of Rutledge and others and intended to make an example of some.

Yagers and Hessian grenadeers embarked Tuesday last. The British light infantry and grenadeers with the Queen's Rangers were to embark on Thursday or Friday.

Sir Henry Clinton to go on board Friday evening and wou'd write Lord Cornwallis fully before he sail'd.

To send a flagg to North Carolina offering a general pardon and protection to the inhabitants, provided they wou'd lay down their arms, or such other terms as his Lordship may think proper to offer.

Clinton to Cornwallis, 1st June 1780[24]   61(3): LS

Head Quarters
Charles Town
1st June 1780

Lt General Earl Cornwallis

My Lord

Upon my departure from hence you will be pleased to take the command of the troops

---

[23] Internal evidence suggests that this document was written on or around 1st June.

[24] Published without the enclosure in Stevens, op cit, i, 215. There are no other material differences.

mentioned in the inclosed return[25], and of all other troops now here or that may arrive after I am gone. Your Lordship will make such change in the position of them as you may judge most conducive to His Majesty's Service for the defence of this important post and its dependencies. At the same time it is by no means my intention to prevent your acting offensively in case an opportunity should offer consistent with the security of this place, which is always to be regarded as a primary object.

All provision and military stores of every denomination now here or which may hereafter arrive are submitted to your Lordship's orders together with every power you may find necessary to enforce in my absence for the promotion of the King's Service. To this end the principals in departments and the Inspector General of Provincial Forces[26], who has the charge of the stores designed for their use, are directed to give in returns to your Lordship of the states of their several departments so far as respects their stores in possession, and of every other particular relative to their trusts which can tend to your fullest information, communicating to you at the same time their general instructions from me.

I am persuaded I need not recommend the utmost œconomy in the issue of ordnance and other stores, and particularly of the arms, of which there are two thousand stored in boxes, and about eight hundred serviceable, and as many more repairable, which were saved out of the magazine that was blown up.[27]

Your situation in respect to the two Floridas and Georgia will naturally engage you in a correspondence with the officers commanding His Majesty's troops in each of those posts. Wherefore it is my desire that all letters directed for me from thence should be opened by your Lordship and that you may give such orders thereupon as the exigencies of the service may require, forwarding to me the letters so received and report of your orders in consequence, to which those officers will of course pay due obedience.

Mr Newton[28], Assistant Deputy Paymaster General, has orders to receive your Lordship's warrants for pay or subsistence in all cases as final, and to furnish money upon your warrants on the requisition of the public departments or on account of contingencies — the vouchers for the disbursements of the first of which, after being submitted to your Lordship's inspection, will of course remain with the principals, as they are amenable to Government. And your Lordship will be pleased to transmit to me at the close of every quarter a list of the warrants you have issued for extraordinaries within that period.

---

[25] *the inclosed return*: not extant.

[26] *the Inspector General of Provincial Forces*: this post was occupied by Lt Colonel Alexander Innes.

[27] On 15th May the Charlestown magazine had blown up. It was being used by the British to store arms taken at the capitulation. How the accident happened was uncertain, but it was supposed that by throwing loaded muskets into the magazine one had gone off and ignited the powder. The explosion killed three officers and about thirty privates. (Draper, *King's Mountain*, 495; McCrady, *SC in the Rev 1775-1780*, 505-6)

[28] His first name was William. (Stevens, op cit, ii, 447)

A number of blank warrants for presidents and deputations for judge advocates will be delivered to you for holding general courts martial. And I do hereby authorise and appoint you to approve of the sentences of such courts in all cases not capital if in your judgement the necessity of the case should require it, excepting only the reduction of commissioned officers unless under very singular circumstances.

Major Moncrief[29] of the Corps of Engineers will communicate to you the orders he has received for the services required for that department, which are, however, submitted to your Lordship's future instructions.

It is my intention that the troopers belonging to the detachment of the 17th Light Dragoons now here shall follow me as soon as the service will admit of it and proper vessels and a convoy provided for transporting them. I am therefore to desire that they may be held in readiness to embark accordingly.

Having judged it to be for the good of His Majesty's Service that some fit and qualified persons should be appointed to superintend the militia in the southern provinces, I have made choice of Major Ferguson of the 71st Regiment and Captain Hanger of the Corps of Jagers for that service; and I have accordingly given them commissions appointing Major Ferguson Inspector of Militia and major commandant of the first battalion of militia to be raised, and Captain Hanger Deputy Inspector with the brevet rank of major of militia, with orders to Major Ferguson to lay his instructions before your Lordship and pay all due obedience to such regulations and commands in every thing respecting his department as you may think proper to give him.

Whenever any packet or advice boat may arrive here from Europe, your Lordship will be pleased to apply to the commanding officer afloat for a convoy and order them to proceed to the army, having first taken from the mails all letters for the troops under your command. These packets will return with my dispatches without touching at any port after the receipt of them, but care will always be taken to give your Lordship the earliest account of the time intended for their sailing that your dispatches and all letters from hence may arrive in time to go by them.

---

[29] Born in Fifeshire in 1744, James Moncrief, as he signed his surname, had entered the Royal Military College, Woolwich, in 1759, being commissioned an ensign in the Corps of Engineers three years later. Having been severely wounded during the siege of Havana in 1762, he was to serve for many years in the West Indies and North America. On the opening of the revolutionary war he was present as a captain lieutenant at the capture of Long Island before taking an active part in the Battle of Brandywine and other operations of 1777 and 1778. It was, however, in the south where he gained his fame as an extraordinary military engineer, notably in 1779 in the defence of Savannah, in 1780 in the siege of Charlestown, and subsequently in the formidable fortification of that place. For his services in Georgia he was promoted by brevet to major, and for those at the siege of Charlestown, to lt colonel. It is perhaps no surprise that, assiduous as he was in his duties, and occupying the house of John Rutledge, the revolutionary Governor, he came to incur the displeasure of the revolutionary party in South Carolina, being accused of malignity, oppression and implacable resentment. And when Charlestown was evacuated in 1782, he is said to have carried off 800 slaves employed in his and the Ordnance departments and to have sold them in Jamaica for his personal profit. In 1793 he was mortally wounded at the siege of Dunkirk and was buried in Ostend. His name is frequently misspelt by historians. (*DNB*; Boatner, *Encyclopedia*, 712-3; *Appletons'*; Garden, *Anecdotes* (1st series), 234, 268-9; Johnson, *Greene*, ii, 369)

In order that I may be furnished with every information necessary to be communicated to the Secretary of State[30] for His Majesty's information, or to the other departments of office, I am to request you will from time to time communicate to me such intelligence as you may think interesting to His Majesty's Service, that you will report the arrival of all troops and stores from Europe, and more particularly I beg to be informed of every thing relative to your own immediate situation, with a full assurance of a like communication on my part.

I understand that Captain Henry[31] is to remain here in the command of the naval force. His zeal for the service will of course lead him to cooperate with your Lordship in every measure that can promote it. Your applications to him for the conveyance of your dispatches at any time will, I am persuaded, be readily complied with.

I have the honor to be, my Lord,
Your obedient servant

H CLINTON

Enclosure
Blank warrant for deputy judge advocate 99(3): DS

By his Excellency Sir HENRY CLINTON, Knight of the Most Honourable Order of the Bath, General and Commander in Chief of all His Majesty's forces within the colonies laying on the Atlantic Ocean from Nova-Scotia to West-Florida inclusive etc etc etc

To [blank]

of HIS MAJESTY'S [blank] Regiment of [blank]

Greeting,

BY virtue of the power and authority to me given and granted by HIS MAJESTY, I DO hereby constitute and appoint you to be deputy judge-advocate at a general court-martial to be held to-morrow morning at [blank] o'clock, being [blank] of this instant month of [blank]

---

[30] Lord George Germain.

[31] Born at Holyhead, Anglesea, John Henry (1731-1829) had entered the Royal Navy about 1744 and served as 1st lieutenant of the 64-gun *Hampton Court* at the reduction of Havana in 1762. Promoted to post-captain in November 1777 for his conduct at the capture of Mud Island, he in the following May commanded in the Delaware a flotilla which cooperated with light infantry in destroying the frigates *Washington* and *Effingham*, six smaller armed vessels, nine large merchantmen, twenty-three brigs, and a number of schooners and sloops. It was, however, during the siege of Savannah in 1779 that he greatly distinguished himself, when he commanded the 20-gun *Fowey* and the rest of the naval force stationed there. On 15th May 1780 he was appointed to the *Providence*, a revolutionary frigate of 32 guns taken at Charlestown, and was to remain in town as naval officer commanding until he sailed for England on 3rd September to convey Alexander Ross and Cornwallis's dispatches after the Battle of Camden. His active service ended in 1793 when, as Captain of the 74-gun *Irresistible*, he assisted in the reduction of French islands in the West Indies. In 1804 he was promoted to admiral. (Marshall, *Royal Naval Biography*; *The Cornwallis Papers*)

at [*blank*] in the Province of [*blank*], whereof [*blank*] of HIS MAJESTY'S [*blank*] Regiment of [*blank*] is President; you are therefore carefully and dilligently to do and perform all and all manner of duties and things belonging to the said office of judge-advocate as becometh you. For the doing of which, this shall be to you a sufficient warrant and authority.

GIVEN under my HAND and SEAL at Head-Quarters
the [*blank*] day of [*blank*] 17

By his EXCELLENCY'S COMMAND

JOHN SMITH[32]

H CLINTON ◯

Clinton to Cornwallis, 1st June 1780[33]   *2(68): LS*

Head Quarters
June 1st 1780

My Lord

By the accounts which I have received from an officer this moment returned from escorting Lincoln's aid de camp to Pedee, I am told that Caswell[34] had passed that river soon after the capitulation of Charlestown, disbanded his militia, destroyed his boats and a galley, and himself retired to Wilmington. He further tells me that the report of the country is that our friends in North Carolina are in arms. From information I likewise receive from him and indeed from all quarters, your Lordship was probably at or near Campden last Sunday. Colonel Balfour's march was delayed longer than I expected by the difficulty of getting boats to pass part of the troops which composed his corps from Sullivan's Island. While in hourly expectation of hearing from your Lordship, I have to inform you that all the country in

---

[32] Captain John Smith was secretary to Clinton. He had remained at New York.

[33] Extracts from this letter are published with material differences in Stevens, op cit, i, 213.

[34] Gifted and versatile, Richard Caswell (1729-1789) had migrated in 1746 from Maryland to North Carolina, where he not only became a surveyor, lawyer and Member of the House of Commons but also commanded Governor Tryon's right wing at the Battle of Alamance in 1771. Siding with the revolutionaries, he became a delegate to the Continental Congress in 1774 and 1775 before being involved as a colonel of rangers in the defeat of Scots Highlanders at the Battle of Moore's Creek Bridge on 27th February 1776, an event which effectively suppressed loyalism in North Carolina from then till mid 1780. In November 1776 he presided over the Provincial Congress which adopted a revolutionary constitution for North Carolina. Now, having only recently left office as the revolutionary Governor of North Carolina, he was serving as a major general in command of the militia there and would soon lead his men to defeat in the Battle of Camden. Superseded for a while by William Smallwood, he would quickly recover his reputation and play a prominent part in the political life of North Carolina until his sudden death from a stroke. He was respected by Cornwallis for his private character, but not of course for his politics. (Lossing, *Pictorial Field-Book*, ii, 379; *Appletons'*; *DAB*; *The Cornwallis Papers*)

general, from Pedee to Savannah and within your march, have either come themselves or sent to accept the offers of the proclamation. Many honestly confess that they have always served against us. They seem to have some scruple about carrying arms against the Congress, and perhaps I may have some of trusting them with them 'till they have given me more convincing proofs of their loyalty than can have appeared in so short a time. I shall permit them, however, to form companies of militia for their protection against robbers, but commanded by *loyal officers.* One and all will join most heartily against French and Spaniards. We shall probably leave this in a day or two. I dare not be so sanguine as to suppose that your business will be compleated in time for us to meet before I sail, and as our communication will become precarious, I think it necessary to give your Lordship the outlines of my intentions where your Lordship is likely to bear a part. Your Lordship knows it was part of my plan to have gone into Chesapeak Bay, but I am apprehensive the information which the Admiral and I received may make it necessary for him to assemble his fleet at New York, in which case I shall go there likewise. When your Lordship has finished your campaign, you will be better able to judge what is necessary to be done to secure the south and recover North Carolina. Perhaps it may be necessary to send the gallies and some troops into Cape Fear to awe the lower counties, by far the most hostile of that province, and to prevent any succours being conveyed by inland navigation, the only communication that will probably remain with the northern parts of North Carolina and Virginia. Should your Lordship so far succeed in both provinces as to be satisfied they are safe from any attack during the approaching season — after leaving a sufficient force in garrison at Charlestown and such other post as you think necessary, and such troops by way of a moving corps as you shall think sufficient, added to such Provincial and militia corps as you shall judge proper to raise - I should wish you to assist in operations which will certainly be carried on in Chesapeak as soon as we are relieved from our apprehensions of a superior fleet and the season will admit of them in that climate. This may happen perhaps about September or, if not, early in October. I am clear this should not be attempted without a great naval force. I am not so clear there should be a great land force. I therefore propose that your Lordship with whatever you can spare at the time from your important post, which is always to be considered as the principal object, may meet the Admiral, who will bring with him such additional force as I can send, in the Chesapeak. I should recommend in the first place that one or two armed ships (Vigilants) should be prepared and that as many gallies as can go to sea may likewise accompany you from hence. Our first object will probably be the taking post at Norfolk or Suffolk or near Hampton Road and then proceeding up the Chesapeak to Baltimore. The force will depend in great measure upon the situation of the country at the time it is undertaken. 3,000, I should think, would be quite sufficient to bring with you and probably more than can be spared. To these I will add what *I* can spare and what from my knowledge of things at the time I may think necessary. I recommend Baltimore as an object of importance because 'tis there our friends invite us to. 'Tis, however, impossible to say at present what is best to be done. The only thing in which we all agree is that our next operation must be in Chesapeak, and when it is settled your Lordship shall have my opinions about it. The army under my immediate command will of course make such movements as I shall judge necessary. Should these operations in Chesapeak be delayed, I should wish to have with me, whenever you can well spare them, such troops as you please in the following order: 63rd, 64th, 7th, 71st, York Volunteers, Ferguson's, Volunteers of Ireland, Ditford.

Untill operation goes on in Chesapeak, I will not trouble your Lordship, but when it does, I must request that you will direct it. Should it be necessary to move the whole army there,

I shall of course accompany it, but whilst any corps can be usefull acting to the northward I shall remain with it. I shall not presume to say any thing by way of instruction to your Lordship except in the articles where you wish it, and if you will do me the honour to inform me of your wishes by the first safe opportunity, I shall pay every attention to them upon this subject or any other.

The Admiral assures me that there will be ships enough left for convoy ready by the 24th June. Your Lordship will be the best judge what use can be made of them.

Correspondence may, and I hope will, be kept up by the cruizers which the Admiral or the officer stationed here will employ, but if you find it necessary, you will be so good to press or hire armed vessels. Your dispatches for England and those of the corps under you may be sent to New York, from whence they will be forwarded as opportunities occur.

The hurry we are in obliges me to request your Lordship will accept of this hasty copy, which there is not time to transcribe.

Your Lordship will observe that on the above arrangement I have not named the 33rd. You will of course dispose of them as you please, but wherever you are, I shall naturally expect to find them.

I have the honour to be
Your Lordship's most obedient and most humble servant

H CLINTON

Clinton to Cornwallis, 1st June 1780

2(74): LS

Head Quarters
the 1st June 1780

My Lord

Your Lordship may well conceive that the success of your detached corps gave me the greatest satisfaction. I expected no less from troops under your Lordship's orders.

The rum and salt will leave Charlestown under escort tomorrow.

I have the honour to be
Your Lordship's most obedient and most humble servant

H CLINTON

[*Subscribed in Clinton's hand:*]

The troops are embarked.

Clinton to Cornwallis, 3rd June 1780   61(7): DS

Answers to several queries and memorandums relative to the command in Carolina

Questions	Answers
Whether East Florida is included?	East and West Florida are included.
A sum of money to be left with one of the agents for the contractors and a Paymaster General.	One of the agents for the contractors will remain here for the purpose of raising money. Mr Newton will remain as Paymaster.
A stock of provisions for the troops, prisoners etc.	A fair proportion will be left but rice must be purchased and stored for the use of the Negroes; and indeed the troops will wish to have it.
Some transports in case of a necessity for any movement by water.	Some transports will be left under Captain Knowles[35].
Blank warrants for holding general courts martial.	Blank warrants for holding courts martial, judge advocates etc will be left.
Blank commissions or powers for embodying militia.	Blank commissions and power for embodying militia are given.
Regulations about Negroes.	All I can do about Negroes is already directed to be done, but care must be taken that they are not ill treated — something is now in contemplation.
A proportion of the Corps of Artillery to be left.	A good proportion of artillery is left.
Public departments, Commissary General, and of Captures.	All the public departments are filled. A commissary of captures your Lordship has with you in the field, at which season only the appointment is to subsist.

Memorandums in addition

Your Lordship will be pleased to grant assistance to suffering loyalists thro an inspector of refugees, as is practised at New York.

---

[35] John Knowles (?-1801) had been commissioned a naval lieutenant on 19th January 1759. Promoted to commander on 29th September 1778, he would attain the rank of post-captain on 1st July 1780. He died a rear admiral. (Syrett and DiNardo ed, *Commissioned Sea Officers*)

I have given my permission to Major Moncrief to go to Europe in the autumn, so it meets your Lordship's approbation.

I beg your Lordship will settle with Colonel Tarleton his account of horses taken or purchased to mount the cavalry.

General Prevost[36] having, as I am informed, appointed Mr Rory McIntosh[37] Governor of Sunbury, I have thought proper to change his appointment to that of Captain of Guides with an allowance of ten shillings sterling per day.

I could wish no exchange of officers prisoners to take place nor any to go on parole until we have some tokens that the rebels have adopted a more liberal system in these transactions. Your Lordship will, however, act according as you think best.

---

[36] Augustine Prevost (1723-1786) was born in Geneva, Switzerland, and followed his father into the British Army. As a major in the 60th (or Royal American) Regiment, he was dangerously wounded while serving under Wolfe at Quebec. At the start of the revolutionary war he was a lt colonel commanding land forces in East Florida and was soon to be promoted to colonel. On 9th January 1779 he took Sunbury, Georgia, when on his march with some 2,000 men to cooperate with the expeditionary force from New York which had taken Savannah. Assuming overall command, and promoted to major general in February, he saw most distinguished service throughout the year, notably in the victory at Briar Creek, the raid to Charlestown, and the defence of Savannah. At the end of May 1780, having obtained Clinton's leave to go to Europe on his private affairs, he relinquished the command in Georgia to Lt Colonel Alured Clarke. He arrived at Falmouth, England, in mid July, having served twenty-two years in North America and the West Indies. (Boatner, *Encyclopedia*, 889; *Appletons'*; *The Cornwallis Papers*)

[37] Roderick (or Rory, as he was commonly called) McIntosh was a Highland Scot of the Jacobite persuasion who had emigrated to Georgia many years before the revolutionary war. Rather eccentric and a speaker of both English and Gaelic, he resided comfortably at Mallow Plantation in what is now McIntosh County, where he possessed a large stock of cattle and a few slaves. Hunting was a business and amusement, which in those days supplied a bountiful table. With the overthrow of the royal government he supported the Crown, fleeing to St Augustine, and came to be appointed Governor of Sunbury as a result of a singular and foolhardy act of bravery there. According to John Couper, who knew him well, Rory accompanied Prevost's forces in their advance into Georgia and attached himself particularly to the light company of the 4th Battalion, 60th Regiment, commanded by Captain Murray. Besieging a small fort at Sunbury commanded by Captain (later General) John McIntosh, 'the British opened lines, in which Captain Murray's company was placed. Early one morning when Rory had made rather free with the "mountain dew", he insisted on sallying out to summon the fort to surrender. His friends could not restrain him, so out he strutted, claymore in hand, followed by his faithful slave Jim, and approached the fort, roaring out, "Surrender, you miscreants! How dare you presume to resist His Majesty's arms?" Captain McIntosh knew him and, seeing his situation, forbad any one firing, threw open the gate, and said, "Walk in, Mr McIntosh, and take possession." "No," said Rory, "I will not trust myself among such vermin; but I order you to surrender." A rifle was fired, the ball from which passed through his face, sideways, under his eyes. He stumbled and fell backwards, but immediately recovered and retreated backwards, flourishing his sword. Several dropping shots followed. Jim called out, "Run, massa – de kill you." "Run! poor slave," says Rory, "Thou mayest run, but I am of a race that never runs." In rising from the ground, Jim stated to me, his master, first putting his hand to one cheek, looked at his bloody hand, and then, raising it to the other, perceived it also covered with blood. He backed safely into the lines.' Of Rory's age and appearance Couper remarked, 'In 1777 he must have been about sixty-five years of age, about six feet in height, strongly built, white, frizzled, bushy hair, and large whiskers (then uncommon) frizzled fiercely out, a ruddy, McIntosh complexion, handsome, large and muscular limbs. In walking, or rather striding, his step must have been four feet. I have seen him walking along and a small man trotting by him...' By the close of the war Rory's health was impaired. Returning to England in the brigatine *Ranger*, he died on board at Gravesend. (George White, *Historical Collections of Georgia* (New York, 1854), 470-4; T W Lipscomb to the editor, 24th September 2004)

The hospital staff I have left will require another apothecary and some mates. These I will send as soon as possible. Mates, if to be had here, your Lordship will appoint. Dr Hayes[38] I leave Inspector of the Rebel Prisoner Hospital.

H CLINTON

Clinton to Cornwallis, 3rd June 1780

2(79): L

Head Quarters
the 3rd June 1780

Rt Hon Earl Cornwallis

My Lord

As during the operations previous to the taking of Charlestown a number of receipts have been given for cattle where the titles for payment may, from the owners being in rebellion or from the want of authority in the persons who gave the said receipts, not be in every case valid, I have ordered the receipts to be called in by advertisement that they may be examined by such persons as your Lordship will be pleased to appoint and those be confirmed which the Commissary General is to pay.

Your Lordship will then be pleased to order payment of such as are thus certified.

I have the honour to be
Your Lordship's most obedient and most humble servant

[H CLINTON]

---

[38] John McNamara Hayes (c. 1750-1809) was born in Limerick, Ireland, and on 1st January 1776 was appointed a surgeon on the staff of the General Hospital in North America, the body responsible for hospitals other than small ones run by regimental surgeons. Promoted to physician on 26th November 1779, he would, besides occupying the post mentioned by Clinton, be placed in charge of HM Hospital at Charlestown. According to Cornwallis, its management could not have been 'in abler or better hands'. At the close of the war he was placed on the half-pay list and in March 1784 obtained a doctorate in medicine at Rheims. Having been appointed Physician Extraordinary to the Prince of Wales in 1791, he was created a baronet six years later. In 1806 he became Inspector General of the Ordnance Medical Department. He is buried at St James's, Piccadilly. (*DNB*; Johnston, *Commissioned Officers in the Medical Service*)

Clinton to Cornwallis, 4th June 1780 *2(88): LS*

John transport
June 4th 1780

Lt General Earl Cornwallis

My Lord

Mr McLeane[39], who will have the honor of delivering your Lordship this letter, is a gentleman well acquainted with North Carolina and, having formerly been an officer in the service, is desirous of raising a battalion in that province

As Mr McLeane has been recommended to me by Governor Martin[40], I am willing to comply with his request and shall have no objection to your Lordship's permitting him to raise a Provincial battalion with the rank of major if you approve of it.

I have the honor to be
Your Lordship's most obedient and most humble servant

H CLINTON

Arbuthnot to Cornwallis, 7th June 1780 *2(99): ALS*

Europe
Charles Town Road
June the 7th 1780

My Lord

A very respectable number of the citizens of Charles Town have presented an address expressing their wishes to be restored to the bosom of peace and enjoyment of those civil

---

[39] The variants and misspelling of Scottish surnames, together with the many McLeans who settled in North Carolina, do not enable a positive identification to be made. He may, for example, have been the McLeane who received a commission from Governor Martin and was involved in the defeat of the Scots Highlanders at Moore's Creek Bridge, North Carolina, on 27th February 1776. If so, he fled with other leaders of the uprising and with great difficulty found his way to Martin on the *Scorpion* sloop of war off Brunswick, an acquaintance which may have led Martin to recommend him to Clinton. (Extract, Martin to Germain, 2nd March 1776, quoted in Wheeler, *Reminiscences*, 104)

[40] Born in Antigua, Josiah Martin (1737-1786) had at first seen service in the military line, being promoted to Lt Colonel of the 22nd Foot on 24th December 1762. Having resigned his commission, he was appointed the royal Governor of North Carolina in 1771 but was forced to flee in 1775. Described as amiable, able, energetic and honest, though somewhat stubborn and insistent on prerogative, he had attempted to conciliate the colony without violating his conception of his duties, but had ultimately failed to reconcile the differences between the nascent revolutionaries and Great Britain. He was now to serve as a volunteer in the Battle of Camden and to accompany Cornwallis during the autumn and winter campaigns, but due to broken health he would depart on 3rd May 1781 from Charlestown for England in HM Sloop *Delight*. (*Army Lists*; *DAB*; *The Cornwallis Papers*)

priviledges they have so long been estranged from. I think every encouragement ought to be given to promote in them this disposition and I had formed as an earnest thereof an answer to that address, but it met not with Sir Henry Clinton's aprobation and *I have submited.* Your Lordship's wishes, I know, coincide with mine to put a speedy end to this destructive broile, and when aplication is made to you for leave to export their just property, being the produce of Carolina, to Britain, your Lordship can have no objection to grant such permission because we have been fighting to produce that end.

I know the proper objects of indulgence are in your hands, and your Lordship will not only consider your self as comanding in chief but as counselor in those and every other situation.

I know that you will conduct your self as Earl Cornwallis. More than that cannot be added as far as is the opinion of, my Lord,

Your Lordship's most faithfull, most obedient and most humble servant

M.r ARBUTHNOT

Clinton to Cornwallis, 8th June 1780[41]   *2(106): LS*

Romulus
the 8th June 1780

Rt Hon Earl Cornwallis

My Lord

I have the honour to transmit to your Lordship the names of several inhabitants of the town of Charlestown who have signed an address[42], the copy of which Brigadier General Paterson will send. Inclosed is a copy of the answer the Admiral proposed sending[43] until I represented to him that the subscribers were unknown to us as to their several characters, that the Intendant was not with us to be consulted, that the permitting exportation amounted to opening the port, which we were not empowered to do, and that I reluctantly would at the hour of my departure change the conditions of so many persons within your Lordship's command without knowing their merits. I also considered that property in the late troubles might have been unwarrantably acquired and that exportation realised it to the present possessors.

---

[41] An extract omitting the last three paragraphs is published without the enclosures in Stevens, op cit, i, 220. There are no other material differences.

[42] *an address*: dated 5th June, it is published in Davies ed, *Docs of the Am Rev,* xviii, 102-4.

[43] *a copy of the answer...*: not extant.

In consequence the enclosed answer was substituted bettering their present condition and opening the prospect of trade and of the restoration of civil government.

To this, my Lord, I have to add in the Admiral's and my own name that you are empowered still further to indulge men who exhibit sincere prooffs of a return to their duty by admitting them to any greater degree of liberty, to the fullest enjoyment of their property, and to the permission in particular cases of shipping it, when the officer commanding the King's ships shall furnish convoy — which advantages I will ratify either as Commissioner or Commander in Chief.

With respect to the Province of North Carolina, concerning which I have your Lordship's opinions, I beg leave to recommend the mode by gallies and a few troops up the Cape Fear River as the most eligible at this season to succour our friends there. Governor Martin will, however, I hope, be of great assistance to your Lordship in these considerations and I trust, from your Lordship's observations and the information the Governor will give you, the best measures will be adopted.

I am very sensible of our good fortune in the last coup by Tarleton and no less so of the judgement with which it was concerted or of the spirit and courage with which executed. I sincerely hope this very deserving officer will be distinguished by His Majesty.

We are under sail.

I have the honour to be
Your Lordship's most obedient and most humble servant

H CLINTON

Enclosure
Subscribers to the address   2(110): D

Subscribers to the address				
John Wragg		Hopkin Price		Alex^r Harvey
William Glen		George Denholm		John Passford
John Hopson		Roger Browne		Thos Philpot
John Rose		James Strickland		Samuel Knight
William Greenwood	5	William McKinney	75	Archibald Carron	145
Jacob Valk		Michael Hubert		Thos Elliot
James Cook		David Bruce		Thos Clar
Christ^r FitzSimons		Hendrick Blowdecker		Thos Hopper
John Davis		John Gregg		Charles Snether

Benjⁿ Baker Senr	10	Thos Dawson	80	Robert Lindsay	150
John Fisher		Thos Winstanley		J Richardson	
Charles Atkins		Charles Ramage		James Rack	
Gideon Dupont Junr		William Bower		Peter Dument	
Jeremiah Savage		Alex^r Walker		S Saunders	
Andrew Reid	15	John Lyon	85	Edward Legge Junr	155
Zephaniah Kingsley		Robert Philp		Henry Hairnsdorff	
Alexander Oliphant		Robert Johnson		Aaron Loocock	
Paul Hamilton		David Taylor		Archibald Browne	
Robert Wilson		John Lahiff		William Russell	
Leonard Askew	20	John Gillmour	90	Thos Coran	160
Andrew McKenzie		John Pearson		James Hartley	
Robert Lithgow		James Donevar Junr		Andrew Thompson	
William Wayne		Nicholas Boden		William Layton	
James Gⁿ Williams		James McKenzie		Nicholas Smith	
James Ross	25	Henry Walsh	95	Andrew Stewart	165
John Moncrieff		Isaac Clark		William Hardy	
John Wells Junr		John Durst		Thomas Stewart	
Allard Belin		W Cameron		Hugh Irvin	
John Wagner		John Russell		Lewis Coffare	
John Ward Taylor	30	John Bell	100	Hugh Kirkham	170
Joel Holmes		John Hayes		William Farrows	
James Megcour		James Mackie		William Ancram	
William Davie		Giner Gaillerdean		Thos Deighton	
James Dunning		Charles Boucheroneau		R Pattison	
John Spird	35	John Burg	105	John Parkinson	175
William Nicholls		Daniel Bayne		John Love	
John Daniel		Peter Lambert		Alex^r Inglis	
John Callun		Hendⁿ Bookless		Willm Mills	
John Smith		William Edwards Sadler		James Duncan	
Lewis Dutarque	40	Thos Buckle Junr	110	James Blackburn	180

James McKeown		H Ephraim Schultz		John Johnson	
William Burt		John Hart		Samuel Perry	
John Watson		James Carmichael		G Robert Williams	
Anthony Montelle		Samuel Adams		Mathias Thurskine	
James Lynch	45	Christ[r] Sheets	115	Edward Petrie	185
George Grant		Alex[r] Smith		W[m] Nesbitt	
Abraham Pearce		John McCall		Geo: Cooke	
John Miot		John Abercromby		Peter Ponnereau	
Frederick Augustin		Joseph Jones		Gilbert Chalmers	
John Webb	50	Henry Braton	120	Arthur Downes	190
Robert Williams		John Callaghan		Alex[r] Johnson	
Alex[r] Macbeth		John Ralph		James Fagan	
John Robertson		Samuel Bower		James Bryan	
John Liber		Geo: Younge		James Courtonne	
Hugh Rose	55	Joseph Milligan	125	Joseph Wyatt	195
Patrick Bower		Anthony Gabeau		John Cuple	
Thomas Tod		William Smith		Ja[s] McLanachan	
Bryan Forky		James Robertson		William Jennings	
James Wright		Michael Luimme		Pat[k] McKane	
Tho[s] Eustace	60	John Gourlay	130	Robert Beard	200
Emanuel Marshall		Walter Rosewell		Stephen Townshend	
Andrew Mitchell		Richard Demich		James Snead	
Farq[d] McCollm		John Walter Gibbs		Charles Burnham	
William Valentine		Benj[n] Tucker		Robert McIntosh	
Christ[r] Williman	65	John Bostels	135	John Smyth	205
D Pendergrass		John Sorrell		Charles H Simmonds	
Will[m] Bell		William Miller		George Thomson	
Edward Hare		John Burgess		Isaac Lesesne	
Tho[s] Timms		Thomas Hutchinson		Isaac Mazzich	209
Tho[s] Buckle Sen[r]	70	Thomas Elfe	140		

Enclosure
Clinton and Arbuthnot to Paterson, 7th June 1780
Response to the address

June 7th 1780

Brigadier General Paterson

The Commissioners having received an address signed by a number of inhabitants of Charlestown, prisoners on parole, requesting to be admitted to the condition of British subjects, it may be signified, if you please, in return to them that the Commissioners will transmit their address to England to be laid before the King.

In the mean time the Commander in Chief puts them upon their parole at large in the province and their Excellencys the Commissioners inform them that, by an Act expected daily, the port will be opened and trade restored, that civil government will speedily be reestablish'd and that they doubt not by this early tender of their allegiance [they] will meet a return of clemency from their Sovereign.

H CLINTON
M ARBUTHNOT

CHAPTER 6

Correspondence between Cornwallis and Balfour

Balfour to Cornwallis, 20th May 1780 *2(40): ALS*

Saturday, 20th

My Lord

You will find by Major Dancy's dispatches that every part of the plan you did me the honor to communicate and entrust me with is altred, owing, I conceive, to the interposition of Ferguson. What the present one is *I do not know but in a very general point of view*. The corps, as I *understand*, which he means to give me is Graeme's, Brown's Provincials and Ferguson's, amounting to 580 men of the stuff your Lordship knows well.

Ferguson's being with me I could not parry more than guess how he came to send him, as it appeared to me that he had no idea of it a few hours before he was ordred.

Your Lordship must, I doubt not, know when and where I am to make my first marches to, and I hope after the first days to have your instructions how to proceed in every respect. I will keep clear of particular ones as much as possible before I move, and as I find it would be perfectly impossible for your side of the water to direct any plan that would be forwarded and followed here, I apprehend the only means left to do the service you wish is to leave this as little hampred as possible and to hope for your instructions the moment you can get at me.

Of all the corps that ever marched I can scarce conceive one worse calculated to second your intentions respecting regularity than this. However, you may depend upon my part of the business being as steadily attended to as possible.

I beg my compliments to Ross[1], and have the honor to be truly

Your much obliged and obedient humble servant

N BALFOUR

[*Subscribed:*]

This moment only I learnt of Major Dancy's going and must beg excuse for the shortness and confusion of this.

Balfour to Cornwallis, 30th May 1780   3(10): ALS

Tuesday
Eighteen miles from Nielson's Ferry

My Lord

At last I have got away and am thus far advanced in my road to hear of you, with a corps composed as the state inclosed[2] will shew.

I have only verbal instructions of any kind, but am strangely hampred by the gentleman I mentioned, who is appointed Inspector of Militia etc etc.

The idea of getting a militia to take arms and *join* you imediately is to me a very extraordinary one. As far as I am able to judge, the disarming the present militia in the first place and new modelling their officers are the first necessary steps; a centrical place must be fixed upon to do both; and if then it appears likely to succeed, they might be assembled and regulated with orders to meet at all times of danger, when called upon, at stated periods etc.

Ferguson, beside being Inspector, has a commission of major commandant of the 1st battalion of militia to be raised, with two other majors he has here ready to take post.

The line I have taken with him is to be on very good terms, but *have* and *shall* wave every particular idea of proceeding untill I hear from your Lordship.

---

[1] Alexander Ross (1742-1827) was born in Scotland and entered the army in 1760, seeing service in Germany. Promoted to captain in May 1775, he came to America and served with distinction. Now principal aide-de-camp to Cornwallis, with whom he shared a close life-long friendship, he was to sail for England in September with Cornwallis's dispatches following the Battle of Camden. Promoted by brevet to major, he rejoined Cornwallis at the commencement of the winter campaign and was to be still with him at Yorktown, where he acted as a commissioner with Dundas to arrange the details of the capitulation. Arriving with Cornwallis in England in January 1782, he was to become Deputy Adjutant General in Scotland before serving in India under Cornwallis in a similar capacity. In 1812 he attained the rank of general. (*Appletons'*; *DNB*; *The Cornwallis Papers*; Stevens, *Clinton-Cornwallis Controversy*, ii, 454-5)

[2] *the state inclosed*: not extant. For the composition of Balfour's detachment, see p 32. It is taken from Allaire, 'Diary', 26th May 1780, Appendix to Draper, *King's Mountain*, 496.

Sir Henry Clinton informed me severall times, and at parting repeated his wishes, that what part of the plan you thought proper to alter was to be done etc etc; but it was impossible to impress him with the idea of the impropriety of an apointment of this nature while you, who was on the spott and actually trying the people, was not consulted, or that it was not left soly to your management who was to command in the country.

I shall be at Nielson's Ferry on Thursday and shall wait there untill the return of this party and your answer how far or where to proceed. I have about eighteen days' rum and flour from tomorow, and Ferguson has a train of his *own*, for his intended militia, of rum, spare arms, ammunition etc etc.

The getting to the Congries as fast as possible was my idea, and there either to be called in to you if necessary, or establishing a post, setting about the militia, seizing violent people, and so on; but your situation will direct every thing and I shall hope to receive your full directions how to move and act in every respect; and to fulfill your intentions, be assured, will be my principal object. As to Ferguson, his ideas are so wild and sanguine that I doubt[3] it would be dangerous to entrust him with the conduct of any plan, and it is not necessary to hurry on any establishment untill a through knowledge is gained of the people who are your friends — and foes.

I beg my best compliments to Ross, and am with sincere regard

Your Lordship's much obliged and very humble servant

N BALFOUR

Balfour to Cornwallis, 6th June 1780 2(96): *ALS*

Camp at Thompson's House
6th June

My Lord

I had the honor of receiving your letter of the 2nd[4], but having received informations of flower being about this place, and other stores, belonging to the Americans, not yet removed, I thought it best to march this way and did not wait the return of Captain Dunlopp[5] at

---

[3]   *doubt*: used in the now archaic sense of 'fear'.

[4]   *your letter...*: no extant copy.

[5]   On 27th November 1776 James Dunlap had been commissioned a captain in the Queen's Rangers, a British American corps formed mainly of loyalists from Connecticut and the vicinity of New York, and later augmented by the incorporation of the Queen's Own Loyal Virginia Regiment. Now seconded to Ferguson's corps, he was to play a controversial role in the operations in the Back Country and the adjoining border region of North Carolina. While seeking to promote Ferguson's plan of campaign, he was involved in the actions at Earle's Ford on 15th July, Cedar Spring on 8th August, and Cane Creek on 12th September, where he was severely wounded

Neilson's but mett him on my way here, where I arrived this day and found some indian flour with nearly a puncheon of rum, some cattle, and other trifling articles. I sent forward a small party of mounted infantry to Sailor's Mills and towards the Congrees, who have procured plenty of flour and meal but no rum or salt. I shall halt here untill the return of the bearers, as, from your wishing me to remain till the 6th at Neilson's, I conclude my moving sooner is not necessary; also as this is a centrical and a disafected district. What I have hitherto mett with is very submissive and an appearance of readiness to take up arms in defence of their property. I have only as yet given paroles, and those in considerable numbers, but have been obliged upon good information to break in upon one of yours granted to one Teurtle[6], late Governor of Georgia. Passing by his plantation, I was mett with a party of about thirty inhabitants who had made him prisoner and intended taking him to town. He shewed me your parole granted him, but owned he did not inform you the capacity he had acted in, upon which I sent him with the same party to Charles Town with a letter to Sir Henry Clinton telling him of my reasons for sending him, which were chiefly the violent part he had acted, especialy in bringing over his countrymen the Dutch[7], and the necessity of removing him from this part of the country to quiet those whom he had injured etc; but indeed he is so poor a creature that it matters little what side he takes. I hope you'l excuse my taking this liberty, as he came exactly under the description mentioned in your letter. Also I was obliged to change a parole granted by Lord Rawdon to one King[8], a representative, and a very violent one: from his plantation to go to James's Island on the 4th of July and remain there till called for etc. Several others I have been obliged to confine to certain boundarys and have made

---

in the leg. As he recuperated at Gilbertown, a failed attempt was made to murder him in which he was shot in the body. Recovering by early November, he had been promoted to major of an irregular corps of horse to be raised in the District of Ninety Six. While foraging with seventy-six of his men on 24th March 1781, he was attacked at Beattie's Mill on Little River and surrendered after stiff resistance. On his way to Virginia as a prisoner he had got as far as Gilbertown when he was shot and killed in cold blood by a set of men who forced the guard. Accepted by all as an active, spirited officer, Dunlap has had his drive and determination vilified by revolutionaries as severity, an accusation to be treated with caution, for it is scarcely supported by concrete examples and would have been so contrary to the humane, conciliatory policy followed by his commanding officer, Ferguson. It is a peculiar fact of civil wars that adherents of one party tend to blackguard those of the other more bitterly than is common in other forms of warfare, and so it has been with Dunlap. Accused by revolutionaries of raiding Pickens' plantation and causing him to break his parole in late December, he was in fact in Charlestown in November and early December before being engaged at Ninety Six in forming his corps of horse. He had still not done so by mid January. Entrusted with this task, he had neither men nor opportunity to trouble Pickens, a course so at odds with British policy to conciliate this man of influence. (Draper, *King's Mountain*, passim; Lambert, *SC Loyalists*, passim; *The Greene Papers*, viii, 70-2; *The Cornwallis Papers*; Alice N Waring, *The Fighting Elder: Andrew Pickens, 1739-1817* (University of South Carolina Press, 1962), 41-2)

[6] John Adam Treutlen (c. 1730-1782) was born in south-west Germany. In the mid 1740s his widowed mother brought him and his brother to Georgia, where the family were indentured to a Swiss inhabitant of Vernonburg. Faring well at school in Ebenezer, he opened a small store there, prospered, and eventually became a substantial planter, owning slaves. Having mastered English, he for a number of years served as a Justice of the Peace and represented his parish in the Provincial Assembly. Siding with the revolutionaries while championing the interests of yeoman farmers and small planters, he was elected the revolutionary Governor of Georgia in May 1777, an office he held until January 1778. When Savannah and Ebenezer fell to the British later that year, he moved to a family plantation near Orangeburg, where he was assassinated in the spring of 1782 by James Swinney, a loyalist outlier who had taken to the swamps and woods. (*DGB*; Lambert, *SC Loyalists*, 226)

[7] *Dutch*: used here and elsewhere to mean 'Germans' or 'German'.

[8] Under the new revolutionary constitution of 1778 Charles King had been returned to the legislature as Senator for the Lower District between Broad and Saluda Rivers. (Salley Jr, *Orangeburg County*, 276)

the distinction you wished for on every occasion. Old Mr Midleton[9] and Mr Motte[10] of this place mean to be with you soon. The first, I believe, has long since given up all management of publick affairs, and the other is a man of property to whom a confinement to his plantation *here* might be of use; but I would beg leave to warn the officers giving paroles to examine nearly into those at so great a distance as those here, who have presented their paroles to me got from the other side the river although some very violent ones are amongst them, residing near this.

I have employ'd a faithful person near Orangeburgh who assures me of the loyalty of that district, and propose empowering him to raise an association to take up arms and keep the peace untill the militia is formed, which I think there is no doubt of effecting. This will secure all that part of the country and prevent robberys etc. Tomorow I expect to see the heads of the association and mean also to establish one, if I can, betwixt this and the Congrees — but the difficulty in this, as well as for a militia, will be to get men of property and consequence to take the lead.

I am very glad to hear that I am to be joined by Colonel Innes and shall not fail to give his corps every asistance in my power.

It appears to me that a post at the Congrees or near the forks of Saluda and Broad River would be highly necessary, as there great plenty of corn might be procured, ground, and put in magazines with rum and salt; and it would be a communication betwixt Camden and Ninety Six[11] with stores placed with a small detachment which would command all this

---

[9] Of a wealthy, politically influential Charlestown family, Henry Middleton (1717-1784) had been educated in England before he became one of the greatest landowners in South Carolina, owning nearly twenty plantations with a total of 50,000 acres and some 800 slaves. Having been a Member and Speaker of the Commons House of Assembly, he progressed to membership of His Majesty's Council, but he resigned his seat on it in September 1770 to become a leader of opposition to British policy. Elected to the Continental Congress in July 1774, he briefly served as its second President, but as a moderate who looked for an accommodation with Britain short of independence, he resigned from that body in February 1776 when the radicals began to obtain control. He was succeeded by his radical son Arthur, who was to be a signer of the Declaration of Independence. Returning to South Carolina and to his membership of the Provincial Congress, he assumed his seat on the Council of Safety and was appointed to a committee charged with drafting a temporary revolutionary constitution. On its adoption in March 1776, he was elected by and from the General Assembly (as the Provincial Congress had reconstituted itself) to the Legislative Council, which was to be the upper house of the legislature. In 1778, when a new revolutionary constitution was adopted, he was returned to the Senate. Now, in 1780, he would abandon the revolutionary cause and take protection, swearing allegiance to the Crown. Surprisingly, when the revolutionary assembly met at Jacksonborough in 1782, he was subjected to neither confiscation nor amercement for his action. (*DAB*; McCrady, *SC in the Rev 1775-1780* and *1780-1783*, *passim*; *Appletons'*)

[10] A prominent planter of Huguenot descent, Jacob Motte had taken an active part in the earlier revolutionary movement. Dead by May 1781, presumably of natural causes, he was to have his mansion fortified by the British and named Fort Motte. It lay on the southern side of the Congaree, a little above its confluence with the Santee. He was the father-in-law of Thomas Pinckney. (McCrady, *SC in the Rev 1780-1783*, 233; Lossing, *Pictorial Field-Book*, ii, 477, 479; *Appletons'*; *The Cornwallis Papers*)

[11] Ninety Six was so named because it lay within ninety-six miles of Fort Prince George on the Keowee River, a fort constructed in 1753 above and opposite to the Cherokee town of Keowee. At this time, before its fortification by the British, Ninety Six was a village containing about twelve dwelling houses, a courthouse and a jail. It was situated on an eminence six miles below the Saluda River, some sixty miles westward of the confluence of the Saluda and Broad. Around it the land had been cleared for a mile. (Lossing, *Pictorial Field-Book*, ii, 483;

country, Orangeburgh and that great district towards Ninety Six.

A proper person to gather in flower etc could be easily procured, but from this detachment there is neither a proper corps or officer to leave, should you approve the idea.

A march to Ninety Six *now* will be as much as we can manage fully. I hear that Williamson[12] is there and in arms with a small force, who are all threatning to leave him, but I have no certain intelligence.

I propose getting some waggons hereabouts and, by bribing them with a little salt, send them for some rum and salt to Charles town, which can be brought to the Congrees easily, and so on if necessary, but for all this I shall wait your directions.

As to the militia arming to defend the country, I have not the smallest doubt of it whenever you think it necessary, and I own I think the sooner it was done the better.

Major Ferguson remains perfectly quiet since he received your letter[13], but seems very desirous to raise a militia upon his plan of six months' service etc.

I shall not fail to take the names of those fitt for militia officers as I go along.

Wallace, *South Carolina*, 171; Draper, *King's Mountain*, 498-9)

[12] A Scot, Andrew Williamson (*c.* 1725-1786) had migrated by the 1750s to the Back Country of South Carolina, where he worked in his early days as a cattle and hog driver. Illiterate but very energetic and possessing a good natural understanding, he moved on and settled at White Hall, a plantation some six miles west of Ninety Six on Hard Labour Creek. Raising cattle and grain, he became a man of influence and by 1775 a major in the royal militia. Of the revolutionary persuasion, he was to oppose the non-associators in 1775, crush the Cherokee uprising in 1776, participate in the ill-fated expedition against East Florida in 1778, and be involved in the failed siege of Savannah in 1779. In the meantime he had been promoted to colonel (in 1776) and to brigadier general (in 1778) of the revolutionary militia. Inactive in 1780, he would submit, and instead of being sent on parole to the off-shore islands, as Cornwallis originally intended, he would be permitted to remain on parole at home, being assiduously courted by the British in a vain attempt openly to turn him. Contrary to assertions by various writers, who have at times confused paroles with protection, there is no concrete evidence, either in these Papers or elsewhere, that Williamson ever took protection, an act which involved swearing allegiance to the Crown. Instead, he adopted a more duplicitous approach, remaining outwardly true to his revolutionary convictions while more covertly acting in the British interest, whether by offering confidential advice, for example on the use of the Cherokees against Georgia insurgents, or by persuading his fellow countrymen not to go off to the enemy. Although his motives are not entirely clear, it seems that he wished to stay peaceably at home, doing whatever little was necessary to achieve this end, rather than to refuse to submit, openly opposing the British in the field, or, having submitted, to refuse to cooperate and face banishment to the off-shore islands. Losing heart in the revolutionary struggle, he had, in short, opted for the quiet life. As matters turned out, increasing disorder in the Back Country would lead him to abandon White Hall by summer 1781 for his plantation in St Paul's Parish, some seven miles from Charlestown. Here, on 5th July, he was captured by revolutionary militia but was promptly rescued, precipitating the Hayne affair. Later, true to his duplicitous nature, and contrary to his parole, he would communicate to Greene useful information about the Charlestown garrison. In January 1782 his extensive properties were confiscated by act of the revolutionary assembly, but none was advertised or sold by the confiscation commissioners. Instead, in 1784, he was quietly amerced and disqualified. When he died, apparently on his plantation near Charlestown, he left an estate valued at nearly £2,500. (Johnson, *Traditions*, 144-5; McCrady, *SC in the Rev 1775-1780*, *passim*; *The Cornwallis Papers*; Lambert, *SC Loyalists*, 4, 300; Johnson, *Greene*, ii, 386; Alden, *The South in the Rev*, 328n)

[13] *your letter*: of 2nd June, p 101.

I have the honor to be with sincere esteem
Your most obedient and most humble servant

N BALFOUR

[*Subscribed:*]

I hope Ross can send me either paper or printed paroles as I have neither at present.

Balfour to Cornwallis, 7th June 1780　　　　　　　　　　2(101): ALS

Camp
7th June 1780

My Lord

I did myself the honor of writing you yesterday, and having the opportunity of Captain Hanger's going to Camden, I wish to mention that I have used the liberty of sending to Nielson's Ferry for three or four puncheons of rum ordred by you there, as we now draw short and I fear by all acounts have not the least chance of any supply further up the country. From this place or Camden there can be but little difficulty in getting any quantity up, and I propose, with your approbation, falling upon some plan to get rum and salt up, even as far as I shall go, in time.

I have used my best endeavours to find out proper people for militia officers in this and the other districts, but I cannot find a single man of any property or consequence that has not been in the rebel service; and from the Congrees to Nielson's Ferry is a very disafected and populous district.

Colonel Thompson[14] is the leading man here, and I am informed, although active on the other side, yet he has not been harsh or oppressive, and from a good many reasons I believe he may be made useful in taking the other side, especialy as he is fond of money. What they have with him in town I cannot conceive, as there are no acounts here about him since he was carried there, but I am clear, if he cannot be brought to act for us, he ought to be sent away

---

[14] William Thomson (1729-1796) was born in Pennsylvania and as a child moved with his Scotch-Irish parents to the west side of Congaree River. A frontiersman and expert rifleman, he was a trader to the Cherokees before becoming an indigo planter. Active in local affairs, he served in the colonial era in several public offices ranging from Member of the Commons House of Assembly to Colonel of the Orangeburg militia. Elected to the first Provincial Congress in 1775, he was appointed to its Executive Committee and to the lt colonelcy of the 3rd regiment (of rangers) which it raised. After serving in the Snow Campaign later that year, he was to take a signal part in the Battle of Fort Moultrie in June 1776, blocking with 700 rangers the British attempt to land on the eastern end of Sullivan's Island. When in the following month his regiment was transferred to the Continental establishment, he was promoted to colonel, resigning his commission in 1778, a year in which he was returned to the Senate under the new revolutionary constitution. Captured now by the British, he was to be confined for several months in the Provost before being exchanged in June 1781. Described as amiable, energetic and without brilliance, he is said to have contributed to the revolutionary party the stabilising influence of his solid dependability and common sense. (Johnson, *Traditions*, 90-105; Salley Jr, *Orangeburg County*, *passim*; *DAB*)

from this part of the country immediately, for nothing will or can effect the purpose of getting the country so essentialy as the removing all violent and principal people, who pay no sort of obedience to paroles or any thing of that nature. Already it has had strong effects, and I shall not fail to second your intentions whenever I meet with men under this description. Associations here and for Orangeburgh district will be formed tomorow, to remain in force till discharged, for the purposes of watching over the peace of the country untill a militia is formed, preventing commotions of every kind, and watching over the disafected.

But when you think it a proper time to call out and form the militia, I believe you will find it necessary to put officers at the head of regiments from the reasons I already mentioned; and I think there will be no fear of the soldiers rising, and even as far as captains could be procured. I think the associations will keep every thing quiet in all this part of the country, but *only* for a short time.

By the best acounts I can get, Williamson is still in arms, as I mentioned, with a Colonel Pickens[15], but believe they mean not to continue in a body but in small partys in the Back Country. From this, and to have the means of quickly securing those you want to seize, I would beg, if you can spare me, a troop of the Legion or a detachment equal to one. The mounted infantry of Ferguson's can do no more than get cattle, press provisions, and other triffling dutys, but having a small body of cavalry ready to act, I am convinced, would overawe the country and keep the peace infinitely more than any body of infantry.

The chance of getting the rum from Nielson's and the settling the Orangeburgh business will keep me here till Friday night. On Munday I shall be at the Congrees at Friday's Ferry, where I hope to meet with the cavalry if you think them necessary for the service.

I have the honor to be
Your Lordship's most obedient humble servant

N BALFOUR

---

[15] Andrew Pickens (1739-1817) was born in Pennsylvania of Scotch-Irish immigrants who drifted south to Waxhaw Creek, South Carolina. Having volunteered in James Grant's expedition against the Cherokees in 1761, he moved two years later to Long Cane Creek, where he farmed and became a Justice of the Peace. In November 1775, as a captain of militia, he took part with his company in the defence of Ninety Six against the non-associators, and then, promoted to Colonel of the Long Cane militia, he commanded in the defeat of North Carolina loyalists at Kettle Creek, Georgia, in February 1779. Now, in 1780, he would be granted a parole by the British and be assiduously conciliated. Nevertheless, he would break his parole in controversial circumstances (see p 74, note 5) and go off to the enemy in late December with a number of his men. Whatever we may think of him for breaking his word, he was to play a courageous and prominent part in operations the following year, notably in the Battle of Cowpens (as a result of which he was promoted to brigadier general), the siege of Augusta, and the Battle of Eutaw Springs. Afterwards he was mainly occupied in warfare with the Cherokees. Elected to the legislature in 1781, he would continue to sit there until returned to Congress in 1793. Until the close of the century he would be repeatedly appointed to handle relations with native Americans. A Presbyterian who was reputedly so strict that he would have suffered martyrdom before singing one of Watt's hymns, Pickens was of medium height, lean and healthy, with strongly marked features. He seldom smiled and never laughed, conversing so guardedly that 'he would first take the words out of his mouth, between his fingers, and examine them before he uttered them'. Buried at the Old Stone Church, Oconee County, South Carolina, he has been the subject of more than one biography, the most recent being Alice N Waring's *The Fighting Elder: Andrew Pickens, 1739-1817* (University of South Carolina Press, 1962). (*DAB*; McCrady, *SC in the Rev 1775-1780* and *1780-1783, passim*; Lambert, *SC Loyalists, passim*; Waring, op cit, 41-2; *The Cornwallis Papers*)

Balfour to Cornwallis, 9th June 1780
2(81): ALS

Camp, Friday

My Lord

I received your letter, instructions etc[16] this morning and shall not fail to put them in forwardness imediately, but it will not be possible to get names for militia officers in so short a time as my passing quickly through the country will allow.

The steps I have taken are by the means of a Mr Fisher of Orangeburgh[17], a confidential and trusty man, who has formed an association nearly upon the plan you intend for the militia, and from which the best militia can be formed. By his means I mean to get the names of those fitt for officers, but no higher rank than captains I should think ought to be granted untill we can get a more through knowledge of the people, and the fact is that all the leading men of property have been on the rebel side so that a proper person to head them will be difficult to get.

The district of one battalion was from Neilson's Ferry to Beaver Creek, including Orangeburgh. This battalion was commanded by a Colonel Heatley[18], and he has signed at *Charles Town* his allegiance and is come home, as has most of the violent people in the country, which I confess I think ought imediately to be stoped, for this will be otherwise a constant dissatisfaction and these gentry will throw every impediment in the way of settling the country.

The militia for Orangeburgh I have no doubt will be well conducted; and in order to forward the settling of that for this part of the country, which is by much the most *disafected*

---

[16] *your letter, instructions etc*: no extant copies.

[17] John Fisher had come to South Carolina from Scotland in 1760. He later acquired over 3,000 acres in Orangeburg Distict, together with lots in the town, and was chosen as one of the commissioners to build the courthouse and jail. In 1773 he became the first sheriff of the district. Cornwallis was soon to appoint him to the colonelcy of the royal militia regiment raised there. (Lambert, *SC Loyalists*, 104-5; *The Cornwallis Papers*)

[18] William Heatly was born about 1720, not long after his parents, Richard and Mary, who were planters, moved from Cooper River and became among the first to settle the area between the lower Congaree and upper Santee Rivers. His father died a few years later and his mother married Captain Charles Russell JP, Commandant of the Congaree garrison, who died in 1737. Although of influential parentage, William himself does not appear to have played a prominent role in public life outside the militia. In October 1776, as a member of the Grand Jury of Orangeburg District, he was party to an address extolling the virtues of the new revolutionary constitution, whereas in 1778 he was appointed an inquirer and collector under the newly enacted Tax Act. Now, in 1780, he was to be sent away from his neighbourhood by Cornwallis, presumably to the islands, and would play no further part in the war. In 1755 his half-sister, Eugenia Russell, married Colonel William Thomson, and in 1775 his son Charles (1749-?) became a lieutenant and soon after a captain in Thomson's regiment of rangers, a corps raised by the Provincial Congress and transferred in 1776 to the Continental line. (Salley Jr, *Orangeburg County, passim*)

and *consequential*, I have thought it necessary to leave Major Graham[19] of the light infantry with a detachment of the two flank companies of Brown's corps and the convalescents of the corps, amounting in all to 100 men. I have left him in an excellent post where he will get indian meal and plenty of cattle, and with seven days' rum and flour.

He is a steady, trusty officer and well enough calculated for the situation. I have put the best people I can find here in his hands, and from them I expect a list of proper people and associations to be imediately formed. And he will deliver them to any people appointed to receive them, but I conceived a post here highly necessary to asist and forward the business, and if, when I come to the Congarees, I can get no better informations than here, I must leave some small one there for this purpose, for it will be impracticable for me to do much in passing. And Ferguson's plan being now greatly changed, I imagine we can expect but little asistance from him further than bare inspection, although as yet he seems contented.

If the service of six months every year for the second class was mitigated, I conceive it would be more readily assented to. If for four months, or three months, the second year, and so on diminishing, it would be more readily entrd into, as every man *now*, except the elders, are liable to be sent out of the country — soldiers — for six months every year.

This objection was made to me today by those I showed the plan to of our friends in the country.

As to those officers who have served in the rebell militia, would you choose to allow *any* of them to serve in the present?

I must again mention Colonel Thompson of this place, who has the greatest influence here. I certainly *think* that he ought by no means to be allowed to remain in this part of the country unless he takes a very strong and active part for us. If he does, by all acounts he may be trusted, but if he declines, he ought to be sent on parole imediately somewhere else. If you choose to admit any of those officers into the militia who have served against us before, be so good as let me know, that the best and most moderate may be admitted — and I own I think some might be of service, but not too many.

Ammunition will be wanted. Shall I have any? They all deny having allmost a single round.

On Munday I shall be at the Congres, where I hope to find Innes and where I hope to have the honor of hearing from you, and I shall proceed on Wednesday towards Ninety Six with all the expedition possible, and exerting myself to the uttmost of my power to put your intentions in train, and should be glad to know, as soon as you think it necessary, how I am

---

[19] Now commanding a detachment of light infantry partly from the 16th Foot, Colin Graham had entered the regiment as a captain on 17th April 1769, having risen to the rank eight and a half years earlier. On 29th August 1777 he was promoted to major. During the defence of Savannah some two years later he played a conspicuous part, commanding a successful sortie on the morning of 24th September. He would now be mainly involved in arranging the Orangeburg militia, but would return to Charlestown in mid July due to ill health. His detachment would be broken up. (*Army Lists*; J P MacLean, *An Historical Account of Scotch Highlanders in America prior to the Peace of 1783...* (Heritage Books Inc, 2001), ch 13; *The Cornwallis Papers*)

to dispose of the corps should I find the Back Country at peace, as some arrangement will be necessary if a post is to be left there.

I mean to try if some rum and salt cannot be brought to the Congrees, as both these articles will be very soon scarce with us.

I hope your Lordship will excuse the liberty with which I mention my opinions as I can safely assure you it proceeds from the best intentions in, my Lord,

Your most grateful servant

N BALFOUR

NB

Some stopp ought to be put, *if possible*, to the depredations of the cavalry, who in small partys and as expresses committ every enormity.

Major Graham will write to your Lordship of his success in the militia business etc etc.

Cornwallis to Balfour, 11th June 1780[20]   *87(3): C*

Camden
June 11th 1780

Lt Colonel Balfour

Dear Balfour

I last night received yours of the 9th. In a letter which I wrote to Innes[21] to be communicated to you, I gave you a latitude of appointing only captains of militia where proper field officers could not be found. I likewise left the present disposal of your corps totally to your discretion. I cannot approve of admitting any officers of the rebel militia into ours for the present. The associating companies is a good thing 'till the militia is formed. They will perhaps be better men than the militia in the field but they will not answer so well the purpose of internal government. I should apprehend that arms and ammunition would be found by disarming the disaffected – sufficient for the present use of the militia. However, if that should not be the case, I will order supplies from town. By my regulation the second class of militia is liable to be called upon for six months of the twelve, but you may desire them to place confidence in me and to believe that I will not call on the whole of the second class at the same time or keep them out six months unless the imminent danger of this province should make it absolutely necessary. I would, however, have it understood that I

---

[20] An extract from the second paragraph appears in Ross ed, *Cornwallis Correspondence,* i, 46-7.

[21] *a letter..*: no extant copy.

shall very soon embody a part of the 2nd class.

I yesterday met by accident with a proclamation issued by the Commissioners of the 1st of June[22]. I was at first startled at it and at the effect it had on the people of the country. However, on considering it attentively, it appears vague and nugatory and does not materially affect any part of my plan. I likewise find that the aid-de-camps at Head Quarters have been distributing protections, declaring some of the most violent and persecuting rebels good and loyal subjects. I must, however, notwithstanding these little obstacles, persevere steadily in my plan. All those possessing these protections who come under the discription of being sent to the islands must have their protections taken away and proper paroles substituted in their stead, and all others who are not thought by the commanding officers of each district to be sufficiently loyal to be admitted into the militia must have their protections changed for common paroles. I agree with you perfectly about the danger of suffering such men as Heatly and Thomson to remain in the country and would have them sent away without loss of time.

There is a considerable quantity of salt at Colonel Simmonds's, which does not belong to him. You may send for part of it when you please, ordering strictly that civility should be shewn to Colonel Simmonds and his family. You will write a line to Colonel Simmonds on the occasion.[23]

I beg you will continue to mention your opinions freely to me. Without the assistance of my friends I could never get through this arduous task, particularly as every measure taken at Charlestown has counteracted me as much as possible. Poor Hanger, who is deputy to Ferguson with the rank of major, does not think he can give me much assistance in regulating the militia.

I am most faithfully yours

[CORNWALLIS]

[*Subscribed:*]

If powder alone will be of use to you, I can spare you some barrels if you will send a waggon or two with a small escort for them.

---

[22] *a proclamation..*: printed in Tarleton, *Campaigns*, 74-6, it offered a full and free pardon to those guilty of treasonable offences who would return to their allegiance, excepting those 'polluted with the blood' of loyalists 'shed under the mock forms of justice'. It assured the well affected of protection and support, called for their assistance, and promised the inhabitants (as soon as the situation of South Carolina would allow) a reinstatement of their rights and immunities formerly enjoyed under the British Government, together with an exemption from taxation except by their own legislature.

[23] Cornwallis may be referring to Maurice Simons (1744-1785), who had been Colonel of the Charlestown militia during the siege. If so, his delicacy is understandable, for Simons was to abandon the revolutionary cause and swear allegiance to the Crown. For his sins he was amerced by act of the revolutionary assembly in 1782 and killed in a duel with William Clay Snipes almost four years later. (McCrady, *SC in the Rev 1775-1780*, 427, 472-3, *SC in the Rev 1780-1783*, 587; McCowen Jr, *Charleston, 1780-82*, 52-3; Lambert, *SC Loyalists*, 294; Moss, *SC Patriots*, 865)

Innes sent me a letter from Williamson[24] asking his terms. If he should surrender, you will give him a parole for the islands, with directions to call on me in his way thither. Perhaps I shall be gone to Charlestown before he can set out. You will able to inform him of that.

Balfour to Cornwallis, 12th June 1780 2(137): ALS

Camp, Hampton's House
Munday, 12th June 1780

My Lord

Upon my arrival here this morning I received your letter of yesterday. From every appearance I am allmost certain of no resistance from the Back Country and apprehend it will be absolutely necessary to have a post here, but am distressed to a degree who to leave. In fact, I have not a man. Pattison[25] commands Brown's regiment, a very *poor* captain is with the Fusiliers, the light infantry have only two captains that cannot possibly be spared, and Ferguson's must go with us. My idea is that Trumbull[26] should come here from Camden and Pattison's corps come over in their room, and that Trumbull should remain in this post to array the militia after they are in train, disarm etc and keep up the communication. As to Pattison, he is so dead a weight that he cannot be trusted *any where* to himself, and his only use will be under some one at the principal post — and his regiment is stronger than Trumbull's. If you approve of this idea, the York Volunteers could march on Wednesday, and as I shall not be able to leave this before Thursday, Pattison would be here only one day. If you do not approve of this, I do not know what other plan to take, as a post must be here, unless *Hanger* can come over to keep Pattison right, which I think would be impossible. I shall therefore wait your determination, which I hope to have on Wednesday.

Innes has sent on Captain Murphy[27] of his regiment to Frieves's Ferry on Broad River and he moved this morning with the remainder of his battalion to Weaver's Ferry. I have

---

[24] *a letter from Williamson*: of 5th June. See p 115.

[25] Of Thomas Pattinson (1738-c. 1781) little is known except that he was an Englishman who was promoted from the 17th Light Dragoons to the lt colonelcy of the Prince of Wales's American Regiment (otherwise known as Browne's corps). Balfour's assessment of him in this letter is echoed later by Rawdon and Cornwallis. Ordered to Camden with six companies of his corps, Pattinson would leave Balfour on 16th June. Due to exigencies, Rawdon had soon no option but to entrust him with the command of the post at Hanging Rock, but, finding him drunk there late in the evening of 29th July, placed him under close arrest. Rather than face court martial, Pattinson would resign his commission and be placed on the Provincial half-pay list. He died in Charlestown before its evacuation by the British. (*The Cornwallis Papers*; Treasury 64/23(35) and WO 65/165(16) (National Archives, Kew); Sabine, *Biographical Sketches*, ii, 153)

[26] *Trumbull*: Balfour means Lt Colonel George Turnbull commanding the New York Volunteers.

[27] John Murphy had been a settler on Cuffeetown Creek in the Dutch Fork. In response to overtures from Thomas Brown in East Florida, he and Benjamin Gregory assembled some 400 loyalists in 1778 and took them there. On arrival they were enlisted into the newly formed South Carolina Royalist Regiment, of which Alexander Innes became Lt Colonel. Murphy resigned his captaincy in early 1781 and was not placed on the Provincial half-pay list when the regiment was disbanded at the close of the war. (Lambert, *SC Loyalists*, 70, 72; Treasury 64/23(15), WO 65/164(40) and WO 65/165(10) (National Archives, Kew))

agreed with him in opinion that he should march up the side of Broad River while my road is up the banks of Saluda. The ridge road being impracticable, I mean to march to the eastward of the Saluda upon a road which I am informed is good and where there is water and pasture. Innes will halt near the Ennoree River and wait my arrival at Ninety Six, when he will cross over and join me, leaving recruiting partys etc etc. Innes thinks he will send in Williamson. If so, good and well, but if he does not, I think the light infantry, Fusiliers and Ferguson's are sufficient to meet him, and Brown's can be spared for Camden. I find I must take with me flour and salt, as I have only to expect the first after the harvest.

Graham and Ferguson are gone to meet this day at Orangeburgh the associated companies and to inform them that they will be formed into a militia, according to your plan, imediately.

As to associations, I can't help thinking it the luckiest plan that could have been thought of, as it is their *own* act entirely and the best foundation for a militia. They choose their own officers and will not admitt but loyal people amongst them; and they also associate upon your plan, so that — when the whole have given in their lists and chosen their officers — as soon as you get the names, you have it in your power to call them together imediately and regiment them into a militia, by which means you are sure of arms being only in the hands of your friends, for, upon a day fixed, I would certainly order every man not in the militia to bring in his arms and ammunition and then give him a fresh parole properly worded, for at present there are all sorts of paroles, protections, and allegiances, all which, when I disarmed them, might be called in and proper paroles granted. The proper places for disarming, I think in my walk, will be: McCord's Ferry by Major Graham; and Orangeburgh, also under his eye, where Mr Fisher, protected by him, can receive the arms; the Congarees under Colonel Trumbull; and Ninety Six under any one you please. As to ammunition, it surely will be wanted, for the rebels will hide theirs and they took care that the loyalists should not have much. The ammunition can be sent by water to McCord's, from thence to Orangeburgh, and *that* for this quarter proceed up here. The country at present is in that state that they will do any thing, but sooner the dissafected are disarmed the better, and if you please, I will do it immediately at Ninety Six. The fixing magistrates as soon as possible will also much strengthen you, and if I can get a proper person at Ninety Six or near it, I shall get him to act as a justice of the peace imediately. As soon as Ferguson comes back on Wednesday, I shall take him up with me, and having done our business there, he can come to you. We are on good terms, but as I do not communicate or follow his ideas *entirely*, of course, I do not expect his exertions, although I beg leave to assure you that he has been ready on all occasions when he was desired, and has done what he could to keep his people in order, in which he and the rest of the corps have succeeded wonderfuly.

As to protections granted, where I have been certain of their impropriety I have taken them away and given paroles, a proper copy of one of which I should wish you to send me tomorow to give to those who are disarmed.

I should wish to know, if matters can be settled, what part of the corps you would wish to stay at *96*, or if the whole. Innes's appears to me by much the properest for one, but he says *he* is under your orders to return to Charles Town as soon as he can, and I cannot see who I have to asist them, unless the corps from Augusta and Ferguson's, which, if things are as I expect, will be enough for both posts. The light infantry and Fusiliers I suppose you mean should return, but their march back will be a very arduous one, I suspect, at that season.

I beg leave to mention these things that I may know and second your wishes, as you are at so great a distance. When at Charles Town much time will be lost if I have not a general idea of your plan, which I hope you think will be perfectly safe with me.

As to provisions, I shall take from hence enough to last me fourteen or fifteen days, in flour trusting to providence and the harvest for a supply. Salt and rum I shall try to get up this length at least as soon as possible.

Innes has got two very good men, Messrs Laud[28] and Ancrum[29], who have undertaken the care of all the publick stores here. I shall put them in the proper way before I go, and leave orders for their being asisted etc, but they desire me to say that if you can only get boats and send them here, they will load them instantly and send them off. As to waggons, they fear they can't be got here. In the mean time every care will be taken to preserve the present and find out more.

I found thirty six barrells of good flour here and shall be as sparing as possible of it, but must take some to carry with me – but in future I wish to know if I am to give receipts for the cattle and provisions voluntarily brought to us by friends of Government.

I certainly should send every horse that was fitt for the cavalry to you, but I assure you that we have come over a country so drove and pillaged before us that there are not six good horses in the corps. I am sorry to say that I have received many and *wonderful* complaints of men cloathed in *green* plundering singly every house they cross or can get at when in search of horses or expresses.

This is a very tiresome letter but it is not to be helped, and I only beg you will make what use of me you think best. Although I am not the best bearer of heat in the world, yet I have not found any inconvenience from it, and good will allways gets on.

I have the honor to be
Most sincerly yours

N BALFOUR

---

[28] Of Andrew Lord little is known. A wealthy trader at the Congarees, he was, according to Cornwallis, 'certainly a rebel', but was judged by him too harshly. By May 1781 Lord had sought refuge in Charlestown, at which time his estate was plundered by Sumter. (*The Cornwallis Papers*; Gregorie, *Sumter*, 161)

[29] Owning an estate near Friday's Ferry, George Ancrum, whose brother William was residing in Charlestown, had been involved with him in mercantile business for a number of years. Politically, he had become a turncoat, having been a Justice of the Peace in 1776 and a major of revolutionary militia in the action at Stono Ferry in 1779. Suspecting him of duplicitous behaviour in keeping with his past conduct, Cornwallis was soon to observe, 'Mr Ancrum is a smooth tongued gentleman, but I very much suspect his loyalty. His overseers were constantly going backward and forward to Sumpter, and every one he recommends is inclined to rebellion.' His estate, like Lord's, was plundered by Sumter in May 1781. (*The Greene Papers,* ix, 326; Bass, *Gamecock*, 162; McCowan Jr, *Charleston, 1780-82*, 83; McRee, *Iredell,* i, 21; Lambert, *SC Loyalists,* 298; Salley Jr, *Orangeburg County*, 265; Moss, *SC Patriots*, 17; *The Cornwallis Papers*; Gregorie, *Sumter*, 161)

NB

Major Graham will inform you of any thing extraordinary his way. He understands the plan of the militia and will be ready to disarm etc when you order.

Cornwallis to Balfour, 13th June 1780   77(7): C

Camden
June 13th 1780

Dear Balfour

I have just received your letter. Turnbull is detached to Rocky Creek in the neighbourhood of two very troublesome districts, and indeed very near the frontier of the province, so that it is impossible to move him. I should therefore propose your leaving the best captain you can find of Brown's corps with about 40 men at the Congarees, with orders to act under the direction of Major Graham, who might come over to him on any particular occasion; and I think Innes on his return may pass a few days there to compleat the arrangement of the militia. The remainder of Brown's corps you may either take on with you or send to Camden, as you think best for the service. The detachment of the Fuziliers should undoubtedly be sent back directly to Charles Town, as it must otherways render that very serviceable regiment useless. At present I cannot form any plan for the disposition of the troops as I don't know what further demands Sir Henry means to make on me. I fear they will be considerable. I cannot either decide upon the post at Cheraws, which is very important and distant and close to North Carolina, untill I get an account of it from McArthur[30]. As soon as the militia is established in any kind of order, very few posts will be necessary. Something will probably be necessary for the greatest part of the summer at Ninety Six, which is a kind of head quarter of the Back Country, and it will probably be right that Lt Colonel Balfour should remain there some time. He may depend on my releasing him as soon as the service will admit of it. As I have not been of late much in the secret, I know nothing of a corps *at* or going to Augusta. You will oblige me by telling me what you know on that subject. I approve very much of the associations you mention. They will undoubtedly be the best foundation for a militia, into which form I wish you would put them without delay. As soon as you get the list of names, I should wish you, or whoever you appoint, to

---

[30] An accomplished, judicious officer of great experience and many years' standing, Archibald McArthur had served with the Dutch Scots Brigade before entering the British Army and becoming a captain in the 54th Regiment. Promoted in 1777 to major in the 71st Highlanders, a corps raised two years earlier by Simon Fraser, sometime Master of Lovat, he accompanied his regiment to Georgia in 1778 and participated in its distinguished service there and in South Carolina during the next year. After the return to England of Archibald Campbell, Lt Colonel of the 2nd Battalion, and with the forthcoming departure for New York of Alexander MacDonald, Lt Colonel of the 1st Battalion, command of the regiment would devolve upon McArthur. It was to be his misfortune to serve under Tarleton at the Battle of Cowpens on 17th January 1781, where, commanding the 1st Battalion, he was captured with the remains of his men. Paroled and exchanged, he would in April be promoted to Lt Colonel of the 3rd Battalion of the 60th (Royal American) Regiment and continue to serve in South Carolina. Esteemed on both sides of the political divide, he was said by an adversary to have had 'no act of inhumanity or of oppression' ever attached to his name. (MacKenzie, *Strictures*, 108-9, 111; Hanger, *An Address to the Army*, 99, 107; Boatner, *Encyclopedia*; *DNB*; Garden, *Anecdotes* (1st Series), 264, *Anecdotes* (2nd Series), 103; *The Cornwallis Papers*)

approve of it and name a field officer to command them (perhaps Mr Fisher or somebody he would recommend). You will give him a commission according to the copy I inclose to you, by which you will find that the commanding officer of a regiment of militia is invested with the power of a magistrate. You will explain to our friends that this is only a temporary expedient to obtain immediately some form of government, and that commissions in a more regular form will be issued as soon as I can get proper advice at Charlestown, where I hope now to be in a few days. The steps taken at the Congarees relative to provisions are perfectly right. Some boats are now going round. You will order receipts for cattle and provisions to be given to our friends. I inclose to you the proclamation I mentioned in my last and one I received yesterday of the Commander in Chief's[31]. They are not just what I should have dictated but do not materially affect my plan. The exception made in that of Sir Henry's to the cancelling the paroles of those in a military line undoubtedly comprehends all those who have been actually arrayed as militia since we attacked this province. The exception in that of the Commissioners of pardon to those who have been concerned in shedding innocent blood by mock trials undoubtedly puts it into my power to confine in any manner I may think proper all legislators and magistrates 'till their conduct can be enquired into. The only difference is whether common paroles given to those who have not acted in a military line, that is, have not been arrayed as militia during our attack of the province, shall be cancelled by the proclamation or by the means I proposed. Of course it is now done by the former. Every thing else will go on as before directed.

At so great a distance and in so complicated a business I should have been under the necessity of giving the most discretionary powers to any officer acting in your situation, but I have so thorough a confidence in your ability and attention that I give them to you with the greatest satisfaction, and you may depend on it that every step you take shall meet my hearty approbation and confirmation. As I may have frequent occasions to write to you, I wish you could fix half a dozen horsemen of the country, in whom you can place dependence, at the Congarees to bring my letters to you and to return with yours. It will save both the dragoons and the country. Allow them what you think proper.

I am very sincerely yours

[CORNWALLIS]

---

[31] *one... of the Commander in Chief's*: dated 3rd June, the proclamation is printed in Tarleton, *Campaigns*, 73-4. It declared that all inhabitants of South Carolina who were prisoners on parole and had not been in the military line (excepting, principally, those in Charlestown at the time of its capitulation) would, from and after 20th June, be freed from their paroles and restored to all the rights belonging to inhabitants. If thereafter any such persons neglected to return to their allegiance, they would be considered as enemies and treated accordingly.

Enclosure
Commission for colonel of militia 101(36): D

By Charles Earl Cornwallis, Lt General of His Majesty's forces etc etc etc

To [*blank*] Esq

By virtue of the powers in me vested, and reposing special trust and confidence in your courage, loyalty and good conduct, I do hereby constitute and appoint you the said [*blank*] Esq to be Colonel of the Militia and Conservator of the Peace of the District [*blank*]. And you are hereby empowered to grant commissions to persons properly qualified for field officers, captains and subalterns of the said militia, and you are to take them under your charge and command, and array and form them, in such manner and numbers as you shall see expedient for His Majesty's Service and the defence of this province. And you are likewise authorized to act in the character, and to discharge the duties, of Justice of the Peace according to the laws of England and the usages of this province, and to grant similar powers to the field officers and such captains acting under your command as you shall think proper untill civil government can be re-established. And you are to observe and obey such orders as you shall from time to time receive from me, the commanding officer of His Majesty's forces within this province for the time being, or any other your superior officer according to the Rules and Discipline of War. And for the discharge of the several duties required of you this shall be your sufficient warrant.

Given etc

[CORNWALLIS]

Balfour to Cornwallis, 14th June 1780 2(153): ALS

Camp at Congrees
14th June

My Lord

I received your letter and inclosures, and have the pleasure to send you inclosed the capitulation of Fort Ruttlidge[32], sent me by Innes, with Paris's letters etc. By these fortunate strokes following one another I have no doubt of this country being totally yours and have every day strong marks of it, but Mr Paris[33], a fellow of infamous character, has a sett with

---

[32] Fort Rutledge had been erected by Andrew Williamson in June 1776 during his expedition against the Cherokees. It was meant to serve as a protection against them and was located at Esseneca town on the Keowee River. (McCrady, *SC in the Rev 1775-1780*, 192-9)

[33] Richard Pearis, a veteran of Indian trading and diplomacy in Virginia and Maryland, had an indifferent reputation for straight dealing. Moving to the Back Country of South Carolina before the revolution, he received from the Cherokees a land cession twelve miles square in the valley of the upper Saluda. When the cession was nullified by John Stuart, the British Superintendent of Indian Affairs in the Southern Department, he sided with the nascent

him that must imediately be sent home; otherwise there will be much distress amongst the inhabitants. I have therefore desired Innes to proceed to General Williamson's, take the command, and send the militia home untill I come to embody them; also to take care of Fort Rutlidge, and to send Colonel Paris to me, and afterwards to meet me at Ninety Six, leaving recruiting partys etc; but allways leaving him every latitude to act as circumstances occurr; and indeed this is the idea I think he has himself. When he comes to me, I shall keep him but a very short time and send him here in his way to Charles Town, a place he has no kind of objection to visit – I *alledge*. His asistance will always be of use, as he is very active and clear in every thing.

Finding by every acount that I have no chance of any flour, I must take with me enough for a small corps till harvest comes on. I have therefore divided this corps in the following manner, conceiving that force is no longer necessary and subsistance very difficult.

Lt Colonel Pattison with six companies march this evening to Camden, the Fuzileers with forty men or two companies of Brown's remain here under Captain Peacock[34] of the 7th with Major Graham to visit them and give necessary directions. The light infantry and Ferguson's go forward. I hope you will approve of this distribution, as, upon recollection, so long a march to the Fuzileers to return immediately would distress them to no purpose; and when you think proper to order them to town, you will be able to send up the flank companies of Brown's from McCord's Ferry to relieve them, and *they* have two very tolerable captains, but I think I would not send for the Fusiliers till the militia was throughly regulated.

Ferguson is come today from Orangeburgh, where he has associated, exactly upon the plan you fixed, about three hundred men, and as soon as we can get the other companies here of that battalion, they shall instantly be regimented into a militia and if possible a good field officer found. The districts I shall try to regulate will be Orangeburgh, Colonel Heatley's battalion which reaches up to Weaver's Ferry from Nielson's, the battalion of the Dutch Forks betwixt Saluda and Broad River commanded by a Colonel Beard[35], the battalion on the north

---

revolutionaries in 1775, hoping that their Provincial Congress would confirm his claim and appoint him as an agent to the Cherokees. Suspecting the Congress of double-dealing, he changed sides in the same year and immediately became a leader of the failed loyalist uprising in the Back Country. In summer 1777 he was again active there, enlisting men in the service of the Crown. Evading capture, he made his way to Pensacola, where he was commissioned as a captain in the West Florida Loyalists, a British American corps raised for temporary service, and took part in operations which led to the recovery of Manchac on the Mississippi in 1778. After serving on command in East Florida the following year, he next appeared in South Carolina on the mission to the Back Country set out in *The Cornwallis Papers*. Following service in 1781 as an ensign in the King's Rangers at Augusta, he settled at the close of the war on Great Abaco in the Bahamas, where he received a handsome award of £5,624 for property losses, together with half pay of £70 per year for his service in the Rangers. He died some time after 1800. (Lambert, *SC Loyalists,passim*; Clark, *Loyalists in the Southern Campaign*, i, *passim*; Treasury 64/23(16) and (37) (National Archives, Kew))

[34] Commissioned a lieutenant on 2nd March 1763, George Peacocke entered the 7th Foot (Royal Fusiliers) on 7th January 1767 and was promoted to captain in the regiment ten years later. He would die in October 1780 during the withdrawal from Charlotte to Winnsborough, possibly of yellow fever, which had broken out among the troops. (*Army Lists*; *The Cornwallis Papers*)

[35] Jonas Beard had played a prominent part in revolutionary affairs in South Carolina. Elected to the first Provincial Congress held in January 1775, he was appointed to its Executive Committee subversive of the royal government. In April 1776, following the adoption of a temporary revolutionary constitution, he was commissioned a Justice

side of Congrees commanded by Goodwyn[36], and the one of Ninety Six — and I have no doubt of any but Goodwyn's, who are very disafected. How soon all this can be well done I cannot well say, but Ferguson seems determined to go through it with good humour, and it shall be done. I have left some spare arms and powder, which was brought by Ferguson, with the detachment here for the militia. If the arms are wanted at Camden, they can be sent for. Some osnabirgs sent for here, finding you had received bad information of, and supposing they were wanted, have sent some of Ferguson's. He goes up with me to Ninety Six and returns to complete the regulation of the battalions here, and so down to Head Quarters.

I send the list of paroles taken from people confined to particular places, that the Commissary of Prisoners may know of them, and have also sent a most oppressive dog, a Justice of Peace, one Patrick[37], who is a most excellent example to make for every kind of violence and oppression. I hope he may be confined at least some time, and care taken he does not return here. One Ships[38] is also sent prisoner for being convicted of ordering a man of good character, a loyalist, to be tyed up and scoorily[39] flogged — another good example. All other people, within the description, I have taken notice of (that I could hear of) but of course many are passed over which we could not get intelligence of.

---

of the Peace for Orangeburg District. When a more permanent constitution was adopted in 1778, he was returned to the General Assembly as a Representative for Saxe-Gotha Township. By that time he had assumed a colonelcy of revolutionary militia in the Dutch Fork. Considered a firebrand by the British, he was to be consigned to the Provost in Charlestown before being exchanged in 1781. Later that year he would be elected to the revolutionary assembly which was to meet at Jacksonborough. (Salley Jr, *Orangeburg County, passim*; McCrady, *SC in the Rev 1780-1783*, 368)

[36] Born in Surrey County, Virginia, Robert Goodwin (1739-?), as he signed his surname (2(85)), moved on to South Carolina and in 1764 served as an inquirer and collector under the Tax Act. On 18th June 1775 he was commissioned a captain in William Thomson's regiment of rangers, one of three regiments raised by the Provincial Congress which were transferred to the Continental line in 1776. He resigned his commission on 30th May 1778 and in the same year assumed the colonelcy of revolutionary militia between the Congaree and Wateree Rivers. Now, in 1780, he would, unlike many of his men, become a turncoat, at first discovering corn and flour for the use of the British, and then, in November, acting for them as an agent and spy. Afterwards he took no further part in the war. In the meantime Cornwallis had appointed James Cary to the command of the militia in his area. (Salley Jr, *Orangeburg County, passim*; *The Cornwallis Papers*; Heitman, *Historical Register*, 253; information from Charles Ferdinand Carson Jr, 9th October 2005)

[37] In 1775 Henry Patrick had been commissioned a Justice of the Quorum for Orangeburg District under the royal constitution. He nevertheless sided with the nascent revolutionaries and was in August of that year elected to the new Provincial Congress which convened in November. When in March 1776 the Congress went on to adopt a temporary revolutionary constitution for South Carolina, Patrick was in the following month commissioned a Justice of the Peace for Orangeburg District, holding office until 1780. An artful character, he was, despite Balfour's description of him, soon to inveigle himself into John Fisher's regiment of royal militia as a lieutenant before changing sides again and going over to the enemy. (Salley Jr, *Orangeburg County*, 249, 260, 265; Clark, *Loyalists in the Southern Campaign*, i, 197, 208)

[38] Notwithstanding Balfour's comments, David Ships, like Henry Patrick, may have been treated leniently. In the spring of 1781 he was able to abscond to the enemy and served in the revolutionary militia until the end of August, latterly as a lieutenant. (Moss, *SC Patriots*, 860)

[39] *scoorily*: a misspelling of "scourily" (now obsolete), meaning "scouringly".

As to Augusta, I have good information that Colonel Brown with two other small corps, Delancey's and Wright's[40], will be at Augusta by the 18th or 19th, and I have sent to them this day to inform me of the state of the country there but not to move till they hear further from me; and I should beg to know what you would wish done with them. If Crugar could be sent there, he would be a good man to be at Ninety Six, and Brown sent to the Indians.

Although *by no means* in the secret, Sir Henry told me of this corps moving, and I never doubted but you knew of it and expected allways your directions concerning them, which I again beg before you leave Camden. I march tomorrow morning, but, having Rall's Ferry[41] to cross, can be easily overtaken.

As to my movements, believe me I most sincerely wish them to cooperate with your intentions in every respect, and I should be much dissapointed if you brought me from the present business before it was finished to your satisfaction.

I conceive that the Provincials had better remain at Augusta and cover that province there, and send for Crugar to command hereafter at Ninety Six — or any one else you choose.

Six country people are hired to carry your Lordship's dispatches and will be allways here with the detachment.

I have the honor to be most sincerly
Your Lordship's most obliged humble servant

N BALFOUR

Enclosure (1)
Pearis to Innes, 12th June 1780　　　　　　　　　　　　　　　　　*2(134): ALS*

Camp
12th June 1780

Colonel Ennes

Sir

I received yours of the [*blank*] instant and express. Inclosed is a copy of instructions from his Excellency the Commander in Chief and also a copy of capitulation with the persons therein mention'd on behalf of the people on the south side of Saludee. By the former you

---

[40] *Wright's*: the Georgia Loyalists, a British American corps commanded by Major James Wright Jr, the son of Sir James Wright, the Governor of Georgia. It would be amalgamated with Thomas Brown's King's Rangers in 1782. (Treasury 64/23(35) (National Archives, Kew))

[41] The ferry, which lay near the confluence of the Saluda and Broad Rivers, had been owned by John Rall, who had died intestate a few years earlier. (T W Lipscomb to the editor, 11th January 2007)

will perceive that my conduct and opperations have been conformable thereto. I am now on my march to White Hall (the habitation of General Williamson) to receive the arms etc deposited there; from thence I shall proceed to Fort Rutledge on the same business.

I am, sir,
Your most obedient servant

RICH^D PEARIS, Captain
West Florida Loyalists

[*Annotated in Innes's hand:*]

Letter from Captain Pearis with sundry inclosures.

NB

I had wrote to him to know by what authority he acted.

Enclosure (2)
Simpson to Pearis, 2nd May 1780[42]

2(131): C

Head Quarters
Charles Town
May 2nd 1780

Sir

His Majesty having thought proper to direct a force to be sent to Carolina to reestablish His Government and to extinguish the most wicked and daring rebelion, which still subsists notwithstanding the gracious terms repedatly offered in order to reclaim his rebelious subjects in the collonees, there Excelanceys the Commanders in Chief of the army and navy have come hither in person with a very powerfull fleet and army for those purposes and to resave[43] the King's faithfull subjects from the misery and opposition and oppression they are now suffering from those men whose ambitious politicks have overwhelmed North America with misery and ruin.

Although the force already in the province may be sufficently competent for every purpose of conquest, yet the exertions of the King's loyal subjects will much accelerate and facalatate the establishment of the peass and quite of the contry and it is not to be doubted but that they will use there utmost endavours to accomplish as soon as possable a measure so conducive to there own saifty and interest and happyness; and his Excelancey Sir Henry Clinton hath

---

[42] Undoubtedly a copy of a genuine document, possibly misspelt from being dictated to a semi-literate copyist, who was not Pearis.

[43] *resave*: here and in a later paragraph an archaic spelling of 'receive'.

judged it proper to send fit persons amongst the inhabitants of the interiour parts of the province, in whose loyalty from there past exertions and later possesions[44] there is much reason to confide in, and to inform them of these there intentions that they may be the better enabled to be assisting in reasteblishing His Majesty's Government together with peass and happyness in this almost ruined and distracted country; and as you have agreead to go upon this service it is his Excelancey's pleasure that in endeavouring to execute it you will have regard to the following rules for your conduct:

1st, you will proceed with all convenient expedition to such places in the country as are inhabited by the loyal subjects and be diligent to inform them of the force which is arived, and you are authorised to give them the strongest assurance of effectual countenance, protection and suport.

2ndly, you will inform that it is the General's intentions, as soon as Charlestown is reduced, to march a force into the Back Country and that it is therefore his pleasure that they should hold themselves in readiness to assemble on the first notice of the King's troops being in motion; and in the mean time advise them to colect as much amunition and provisions as they can procure that they may not be distressed for want of these articles untill they join the royal army.

3rdly, as soon as they are assembled in suffient numbers they will endavour to seize and secure such of the people as have been most subservent to the purposess of the rebelious leaders in enforcing there tyranical laws and thereby prevent the mischief they will attemp and the distresses they will cause to the defensless familys left behind, but it must always be remembered that no time is to be lost and that there junction with the King's troops as soon as possable is of the first consquence and every other consideration must be posponed it.

4th, as it will be of great consquence to procure as many horsess as possable, they will be carefull to bring with them all they cann colect and also any provisions that belongs to the rebels; or, if it cannot be brought away with conveyanance, let it be destroyed but not so as to leave the wimen or childerin absolutely destitute, but they must not destroy the corn in the grownd as the distress it would occasion would probely chiefly fall upon themselves.

5thly, if in there march down the country they should be opposed by the rebbels, they must resoluetly endavour to cutt there way through them, but it will be proudent not to attemp any doubtfull opperations that can be avoided untill they meet the King's troops and they themselves are form'd under proper officers to guide and conduct them.

6thly, whenever they join the King's troops they will be furnished with amunition and arms where they are wanted. It is the intention of his Excelancey the Commander in Chief to embody them as militia, to appoint such fit persons as will be agreable to themselves to be there officers, to employ them only for the purpass of extirpating the rebelion in this and the two adjoining provinces, and, as soon as that is effected, to dismiss them to there own

---

[44] *possesions*: probably 'professions' in the original document, which the copyist misheard.

habitations after establishing nevertheless such police[45] as will be effectual speedly to assemble them upon any emergancey or to repel any hostile attemps of the rebels; and when ever they are in actual service they will resave the same pay and draw the same rations as the King's troops.

7th, when they march down the country, they will of course destroy all stores belonging to the rebels if they cannot bring them away, and they will also destroy all posts or places of strength erected by the rebels if any shall fall in there way.

Although the Commander in Chief is persuaded that the loyal disposition of most of the inhabitants in the Back Country will be sufficent to induce them to exert themselves on the present ocation, yet, in order more speadly to procure peass and good government to the country, the powers vested in the Crown by the laws and Constitution will be resaved to[46] and the pains and penaltys prescribed in case of disobedience or neglect will most assuredly be inflicted on all delinquents.

8th, it will be proper not to make the purposses of your errand generly known amongst the common people untill you have disclosed it to such persons whose consequence and influences amongst them will probely induce there example to be followed; and it will also be right to digest with some men of sence and direction a proper plan for conducting them untill that care shall devolve upon persons properly commisioned for that purpass; and lastly you must not omit frequently to send fit and inteligent persons to head quarters to give information of your proceedings and success.

It cannot fail to occur to you that much will depend on the secrecy with which you conduct yourself untill the time shall arrive when the people are to assemble, and that vigor and dispatch after they are assembled will be nessasary to crush any attempts of the rebels to withstand them. The exigency of the moment must govern your conduct but you must never forget the junction with the King's army is the object to which every other consideration must give way.

I am, sir,
Your very humble servant

JA^S SIMPSON[47], Secretary to the Commissioners

---

[45] *police*: a misspelling of 'policy'.

[46] *resaved to*: possibly a misspelling of 'resorted to'.

[47] At the date of this letter James Simpson was acting as Secretary to the King's Commissioners, namely Clinton and Arbuthnot. Highly esteemed as a percipient adviser on political, constitutional and legal affairs, he had by 1775 become Clerk of HM Council in South Carolina, a body which acted in two capacities, first as a privy council advising the royal governor in the exercise of his functions, and second as a legislative council forming the upper house of the legislature. In 1777, two years after the royal government was overthrown, he was banished from South Carolina for retaining his allegiance to the Crown. Two years later he went on commission to Savannah and from there reported to Clinton on the extent of loyalist sympathy in South Carolina, particularly in the Back Country. On 23rd June 1780 he was to be appointed Intendant General of Police for South Carolina, but his role would extend wider. He would continue to act as a valued political and legal adviser to Cornwallis and Balfour

Enclosure (3)
Articles of capitulation, Fort Rutledge   *2(133): C*
and south side of Saluda[48]

In order to the immediate restoration of that harmony, peace and happiness which we once experienced under the Government of His Britanick Majesty, and by virtue of His authority to us by his Excellency Sir Henry Clinton, Commander in Chief in North America, we do receive His Majesty's most gracious pardon and protection agreeable to the terms of the proclamation issued by his Excellency the 22nd May 1780[49] — all the inhabitants on the south side of Salludy River — on the following terms:

First, you are to deliver up to any officer we shall appoint the arms, amunition and military stores at General Williamson's and Fort Ruttlidge and all other places of strength occupied by you, together with all publick warlike stores, arms, ammunition, artillery and provisions.

The independent companies, excepting those in garrison at Fort Rutledge, shall be immediately discharged and received on the same conditions as the other inhabitants. The garrison of Fort Rutledge will continue to occupy that post untill they are relieved by us, when they shall march out without their arms, be also discharged and receiv'd on the same conditions as the other inhabitants, each officer having charge of such publick stores to render on the delivery thereof an account of the same on oath if required.

Secondly, the arms belonging to private persons to remain in care of the person appointed to receive the same untill the pleasure of his Excellency shall be known, for which purpose we assent that a memorial be sent down.

Thirdly, we will remove the publick arms and stores to Ninety Six, you furnishing waggons and horses sufficient for that purpose, which waggons and horses shall be immediately discharged on the delivery.

---

and be involved in adjusting much of the very complex business of Charlestown and the country. He may have been a Scot, for, aside from his official duties, he was soon to be elected President of the St Andrew's Society, a Charlestown club established in 1729 of which most of the Scottish community were members. Respected on both sides of the political divide, he would in February 1781 return to New York at the urgent behest of Clinton to resume his duties as Secretary to the King's Commissioners. On his service in South Carolina an adversary was to comment many years later, 'It should forever redound to the honour of Mr Simpson... that the only use which he ever made of his power and influence was to mitigate the sufferings of the unfortunate and by generous attention to free them from every taint of political animosity...' In December 1781 he would accompany Cornwallis on his passage to England. (Drayton, *Memoirs*, i, 160, ii, 4; McCowen Jr, *Charleston, 1780-82*, 16, 17, 44, 124; *The Cornwallis Papers*; Lambert, *SC Loyalists*, 27; Garden, *Anecdotes* (2nd series), 104)

[48] A confusing document. In the first paragraph the first person subject refers to the inhabitants and the first person indirect object to Pearis and Rees. In later paragraphs the first person refers to the latter and the second person to the former.

[49] *The proclamation..*: see p 49.

We will relieve the garrison at Fort Rutledge with our troops as soon as may be, to defend the inhabitants from the incursions of the Indians.

Fourthly, we will advertize and publish in all quarters of your district his Excellency's proclamation, that no person may be ignorantly kept from the benefit thereof, and we will be ready on Monday the 12th instant to grant protection at [*blank*].

Done at the camp at James Williams's[50] this 10th June 1780

RICH[D] PEARIS, Captain
West Florida Loyalist

DAVID REES[51], Captain

We assent to the above on behalf of the people:

JOHN BOWIE[52]   R A RAPLEY[53]
JAMES MOORE[54]   GEO WHITEFIELD[55]

---

[50] The plantation of Colonel James Williams, the noted revolutionary, lay some 16 miles from Ninety Six between Little River and Mudlick Creek on the old Island Ford road. It would be long occupied as a fortified post by the royal militia. (Draper, *King's Mountain*, 69, 500)

[51] A settler in the Back Country, David Rees had in 1775 been a leader there of loyalist opposition to measures of the Provincial Congress subversive of the royal government. Classified by nascent revolutionaries as a 'powder man', that is to say, an inveterate opponent, he had been involved in the seizure of gunpowder being sent to the Cherokees by the Congress's Council of Safety. Now a captain on half pay in the South Carolina Royalist Regiment, he had been sent into the Back Country when the British forces lay before Charlestown. (McCrady, *SC in the Rev 1775-1780*, 88; Lambert, *SC Loyalists*, 44-5, 48, 106; Clark, *Loyalists in the Southern Campaign*, i, 47)

[52] In November 1775 John Bowie had served as a captain of militia in the defence of the stockade at Ninety Six against Patrick Cuningham and the non-associators. On 1st March 1777 he was commissioned a captain in the 5th South Carolina Continental Regiment and on 9th October 1779 was wounded in the assault on Savannah. He was not among the Continentals captured at Charlestown, presumably because he had lost out when his regiment was reduced and consolidated with others in the South Carolina Continental line. Now a major in Andrew Pickens' regiment of militia, he would in December go off with him to the enemy and serve as his aide-de-camp. (Salley Jr, *Orangeburg County*, 309-11, 315; Heitman, *Historical Register*, 112; McCrady, *SC in the Rev 1775-1780*, 507; Moss, *SC Patriots*, 88; *The Greene Papers*, vi, 558; *The Cornwallis Papers*)

[53] A leading backcountryman in the civil line, Richard Rapley was associated with Andrew Pickens and may have lived in the Long Cane settlement. (*The Cornwallis Papers*; *The Greene Papers*, vi, 558)

[54] Another leading backcountryman in the civil line, James Moore had been appointed an inquirer and collector under the Tax Act 1777 for the district between the Savannah and the north fork of the Edisto. In the following year he was appointed one of the election commissioners for the same district. (Salley Jr, *Orangeburg County*, 271, 274) An associate of Andrew Pickens, Moore would continue to reside after the war in what became Edgefield County.

[55] As captain of an independent company, George Whitefield had in 1775 been in command of Fort Charlotte on the Savannah River. (McCrady, *SC in the Rev 1775-1780*, 11, 13) He surrendered the fort to the nascent revolutionaries, being of a like persuasion.

Cornwallis to Balfour, 20th June 1780   77(16): C

Camden
20th June 1780

Lt Colonel Balfour

Dear Balfour

I propose setting out for Charlestown tomorrow and shall leave the command of this post to Lord Rawdon. I find the utmost difficulty in getting up the supplies and stores requisite for the troops in this part of the country owing to the total want of waggons and horses in Charlestown. The Commander in Chief, it seems, has taken them with him. The waggons you have carried on will empty fast and then be of no further use to you. I wish therefore, as soon as ten or twelve are empty, you would send them by the Congarees to Monk's Corner. The detachment of the Fuzileers may go with them or *in them* thither, and then proceed to join their regiment at Charlestown, which I am very desirous of their doing. I shall see Major Graham on my journey and shall order the parties which you left with him and at the Congarees to come to this place, except the Fuzileer detachment and perhaps a small guard at the store. I should likewise wish the remainder of Graham's corps to be sent hither as soon as you can spare them, and if you should think any thing necessary to be left at Ninety Six besides Innes's corps and Ferguson's, you will take it from the corps at Augusta. I desire you will please to continue sending your waggons as fast as you can spare them to Monk's Corner.

I am your most obedient and faithfull servant

[CORNWALLIS]

CHAPTER 7

Correspondence between Cornwallis and Ferguson

Ferguson to Cornwallis, 30th May 1780   *2(58): ALS*

Camp, 39 miles from Charles Town
May 30th 1780

Lord Cornwallis

My Lord

The employment of Inspector of Militia to which Sir Henry Clinton has done me the honor of naming me, altho it is attended with no rank or emolument, I feel myself much obliged to him for, as affording me an opportunity of receiving your Lordship's commands in a line which I cannot but hope will be attended with very important and probably decisive advantages with regard to the southern provinces at a small expence.

The instructions I have received were, I believe, sent to your Lordship by a better opportunity. I shall, however, seize the first certain means of transmitting a second in order to receive what further instructions your Lordship may honor me with and to pay obedience to what alterations in the present ones you may think proper to direct.

Least any dispatches to your Lordship may have miscarried, inclosed are a printed proclamation, a hand bill, a certificate meant for the militia men, and another lately substituted in place of paroles to those who come in to submit[1], all of which accord thoroughly with the instructions.

---

[1] The proclamation, which would have been Clinton's of 22nd May, and the certificates are missing.

I am this day inform'd by Major André[2] that by late accounts from the Back Country the Commander in Chief has no reason to doubt that the inhabitants are very well disposed to take an active part.

Being ignorant of the thorough safety of this conveyance, I shall only add that under your Lordship's patronage of the militia I have much confidence that great benefit will be derived from that body to the King's Service as well as to the internal peace and prosperity of these provinces, and that the army will so far forget professional prejudice as to encourage an establishment which, independant of the immediate beneficial consequences, may render it unnecessary to emasculate a great number of regular troops in garrison in an unhealthy climate.

Begging your Lordship's indulgence to this lefthanded scrawl wrote on the ground, I have the honor to be with the greatest respect, my Lord,

Your Lordship's most obedient humble servant

PAT FERGUSON

Enclosure
Hand bill   *1(46): C*

When the royal army arrived in South Carolina, the Commander in Chief avoided as much as possible every measure which might excite the loyal inhabitants to rise in favor of Government and thus bring danger and trouble upon themselves at a time when the King's army, being employed in the reduction of Charlestown, could not assist or second their struggles.

The blood of the loyalists that had been unhappily shed, and the severities which had been inflicted on them by the rebels, in consequence of the former spirited but ill timed insurrections of the King's numerous friends on the back of both Carolinas[3] had already occasioned too much grief and regret to His Majesty and their fellow subjects in Europe for him wantonly to bring again into hazard the lives and happiness of men who deserve so well of their country.

But Charlestown with its harbour and Fort Moultrie being now reduced, and their garrisons to the amount of 6,000 men with all their arms, stores, artillery and ships of war being in

---

[2] John André (1751-1780) was the son of a Genovese merchant settled in London. Commissioned in 1771, he came to America three years later as a lieutenant in the 7th Regiment. Now Adjutant General with the rank of major, he was to be involved in the Benedict Arnold affair, being captured outside the lines of New York, convicted of espionage, and hanged on 2nd October. (*DNB*; Boatner, *Encyclopedia*, 21-2)

[3] Ferguson is referring to two risings. The first was in the Back Country of South Carolina in 1775 under Patrick Cuningham. It was put down in December during the Snow Campaign. (McCrady, *SC in the Rev 1775-1780*, ch 5) The second was of Scottish Highlanders in North Carolina in 1776, who were defeated in the action at Moore's Creek Bridge on 27th February. Thereafter most loyalists remained quietly at home until the British captured Charlestown in 1780. (Alden, *The South in the Rev*, 197-8, 201)

possession of His Majesty's forces, the time is come when it is equally the interest and duty of every good man to be in readiness to join the King's troops and assist them in establishing justice and liberty and in restoring and securing their own property when they shall march to support them against the small rebel parties that still linger at a distance in the province.

After so much disorder, violence and oppression the helping hand of every man is wanted to reestablish peace and good government; and as the Commander in Chief wished not to draw the King's friends into danger when any doubt could remain of their success, so, now that that is certain, he trusts that one and all will heartily join and by a general concurrence give effect to such necessary measures for that purpose as from time to time may be pointed out to them; and they may rest assured that every means will be used to avoid giving them any trouble that may not be necessary to secure to them peace, liberty and prosperity.

In order to attain these happy ends it is the duty of all men who wish well to themselves and their country to be ready at a moment with their arms to regain their just rights and support the free Constitution of their forefathers under which we all encreased and prospered.

Those who have families will form a militia to remain at home, and occasionally to assemble in their own district when required, under officers of their own choosing for the maintenance of peace and good order. Those who have no families and can conveniently be spared for a time it is hoped will chearfully assist His Majesty's troops in driving their rebel oppressors and all the miseries of war far from the province.

For this purpose it is necessary that the young men be ready to assemble when required, and serve with the King's troops for any six months of the ensuing twelve that may be found requisite, under proper regulations. They may choose lieutenants to each company to command them and will be allowed, when on service, pay, ammunition and provisions in the same manner as the troops. When they join the army, each man will be furnished with a certificate that he is only engaged to serve as a militia man for the time specified, that he is not to be marched beyond North Carolina and Georgia, and that, when the time is out, he is freed from all claims of military service except the common and usual militia duty where he lives.

He will then have paid his debt to his country and be entitled to enjoy undisturbed that peace, liberty and prosperity at home which he had contributed to secure.

Cornwallis to Ferguson, 2nd June 1780   77(2): C

Camden
June 2nd 1780

Major Ferguson

Sir

I received yesterday your letter by Captain Dunlap and have not the least doubt of your zealous exertions in any service in which you may be employed. I have no account from Sir

Henry Clinton of any instructions he has given to you. He notified your appointment by the following paragraph: 'I have allowed Major Ferguson to take charge of the militia under the title of Inspector of Militia Corps and to propose regulations for them. This, however, is of course subject to your Lordship's controul, or to being reversed and otherwise settled if you think fit.'

I agree, sir, perfectly with you that it is absolutely necessary to regulate the militia of this province and am now busied in forming a plan for that purpose. As soon as I have been able to compleat it, I will transmit it to you. In the mean time I must desire that you will take no steps in this business without receiving directions from me.

I am, sir,
Your most obedient and most humble servant

[CORNWALLIS]

Ferguson to Cornwallis, 6th June 1780 *2(92): ALS*

June 6th 1780

Lord Cornwallis

My Lord

I had the honor of your letter dated June the second enjoining me to take no steps whatsoever in the militia business untill I should receive directions from your Lordship, to which it is unnecessary to say I shall pay the most implicit obedience.

At the time when Sir Henry Clinton first did me the honor of conversing to me about the establishment of a militia in Carolina, I was ignorant of the force meant to be left in this country and of your Lordship's being to penetrate into the back settlements. It appear'd to me that a rising of the loyal inhabitants, if critically excited and supported by a battalion or two, might re-establish the King's authority in the back of the Carolinas and secure the possession of the southern provinces; and I could not but be proud of being employ'd in a service of such importance and of little expence, and was glad to have the sanction of Sir Henry Clinton's authority to the measures he was pleas'd to point out to me relative to the militia, as well as to some details which he allow'd me to enter into. The instructions which I did myself the honor of mentioning to your Lordship, and which are inclosed, he accordingly furnish'd me with, in which those articles relating to the speedy forming of a militia, the limiting their service to a precise term and removing all distrust of being forced into the regular service, the restraining them from acts of violence and inhumanity, the establishment of a defensive as well as of an active militia, and the being entirely under your Lordship's direction, were particularly from his Excellency. The other articles, containing details which of some sort or other were necessary, met with his approbation.

I will beg leave further to observe to your Lordship that, at the time these instructions were drawn out, I expected to go by a route from which there was little chance of communicating with North Carolina untill the exertion was over, and that his Excellency has since repeatedly and strongly enjoin'd me to pay the utmost obedience to your Lordship in every respect, a command which, I beg permission with the less scruple to say, I shall with pleasure obey, as my future views are such as to give me no expectations from your Lordship further than the honor of your approbation.

I am with the greatest respect, my Lord,
Your most obedient and most humble servant

PAT FERGUSON

PS

Sir Henry Clinton was so good as to appoint me at my request major commandant of the first battalion of militia in my commission as Inspector, which he undoubtedly meant with your Lordship's approbation, and if this appointment should in any respect interfere with your Lordship's arrangements, of course it becomes my duty to lay it aside.

Enclosure
Clinton's instructions to Ferguson[4]   *2(44): C*

Instructions to Major Ferguson, Inspector of Militia

By virtue of the commission of Inspector of Militia with which you are vested you will use your best endeavours without loss of time to form into corps all the young or unmarried men of the provinces of Georgia and the two Carolinas, as opportunity shall offer, to serve under the orders of Lt General Earl Cornwallis or other general officer commanding in these provinces.

This militia you will form into companies consisting of from 50 to 100 men each and will, when the local and other circumstances will admit of it, form battalions consisting of from 6 to 12 companies each, allowing such as cannot conveniently be assembled in battalions to remain as independent companies.

Each company to be under a lieutenant chosen by the men, to whom you may add, if you find it necessary, an ensign from the non-commissioned officers and others who have served in the army to assist in establishing a certain degree of order, regularity and discipline, which, however, must be done with great caution so as not to disgust the men or mortify unnecessarily their love of freedom.

---

[4] Published in Howard H Peckham ed, *Sources of American Independence* (University of Chicago Press, 1978), ii, 358-360. There are no material differences.

Major Timpany[5] of the 3rd Battalion, Jersey Volunteers, will act under you as major and Captain Lieutenant Frederick De Peyster[6] as captain in the 1st battalion, to which you will appoint an adjutant and quarter master, each to do the duty of the other when necessary, also a surgeon.

The officers during actual service to have army pay, and those already in the regular service only one pay.

Each company may be allowed two serjeants, two corporals and one horn[7].

The other battalions to have a similar establishment.

In order to procure the general and hearty concurrence of the loyal inhabitants it is of the first importance to limit their service to a precise term and to remove all distrust that they may entertain of being drawn into the regular service without their consent, for which purpose you will furnish each of them, when they engage, with a written certificate in the following words:

> 'By order of Sir Henry Clinton KB, Commander in Chief etc, I hereby certify that AB has joined the British Army as a militia man, and not as a regular soldier, and has only engaged to serve any six months of the ensuing twelve that may be required.
>
> 'I further certify that he is entitled to six pence sterling per day and provisions during the time of his actual service and is not to be obliged under any pretence to march beyond North Carolina or Georgia; and he is hereby absolutely freed from all

---

[5] At the outset of the revolutionary war Robert Timpany was a schoolmaster at Hackensack, New Jersey. On 18th November 1776 he was commissioned a major in the 4th Battalion, New Jersey Volunteers, but when the battalion was reduced from ten to five companies in April 1778, he retired on half pay. Returning to active service for the Charlestown campaign, he was seconded to Ferguson's corps and would be wounded several times while in the south. At the close of the war he was placed on the Provincial half-pay list and settled in Nova Scotia, where he died when more than one hundred years of age. (Nan Cole and Todd Braisted, '4th Battalion, New Jersey Volunteers - Major Robert Timpany's Company', 'New Jersey Volunteers - List of Officers, 1776-1783', and 'A History of the 4th Battalion, New Jersey Volunteers' (*The On-Line Institute for Advanced Loyalist Studies*, 7th March 2006); Treasury 64/23(30) (National Archives, Kew))

[6] Commissioned into the New York Volunteers in 1778, Frederick De Peyster (1759-?) was of a prosperous New York family whose ancestors had occupied important public offices in the province or city. A Dutchman, his great-great-grandfather had emigrated to New Amsterdam before 1649. Seconded now to Ferguson's corps, Frederick was to be with it until the last days of August, when he was directed by Cornwallis to try and model the militia regiments of Samuel Tynes and William Henry Mills. After inspecting part of the first regiment, he accompanied Wemyss to Cheraw Hill to see what could be done with the second, but the task was hopeless. On his way there he attended Moncrief at Georgetown, where he inspected part of James Cassells's, John Wigfall's and Elias Ball Sr's militia regiments. Returning with Wemyss to Camden, he arrived on 4th October and was fortunate not to be with Ferguson at the Battle of King's Mountain three days later. Promoted to captain in the New York Volunteers on 18th October 1781, he was placed on the Provincial half-pay list two years later when the regiment was disbanded. At the close of the war he settled in St John, New Brunswick, and in 1792 served as a magistrate in the County of York. He afterwards moved to the United States. His brother, Abraham, was Ferguson's deputy, and another brother, James, also served in the south. (Treasury 64/23(1), WO 65/164(31) and WO 65/165(2) (National Archives, Kew); *Appletons'*; *The Cornwallis Papers*; *DAB*)

[7] *horn*: a cornet, otherwise known as a bugle-horn.

further claims of serving with the army after the [*blank*] day of [*blank*], being the expiration of his term.'

Such as freely engage to enlist in the regular forces after 3 days' consideration are not to be refused, but the militia men are to be protected from those snares and frauds frequently employed to entrap men against their consent to the prejudice and dishonor of the profession.[8]

You will furnish each man with ammunition and oznabergs for a rifle shirt and, when practicable, supply those with arms who have none. Those who are averse to serve on foot may be allowed to serve on horse back at their own expence, and, in a word, you are to endeavour to derive as much advantage as possible from their services at as little expence as may be.

All disbursements of pay above mentioned and unavoidable contingencies you will receive from the Pay Master of the Army or of the Provincial Forces by warrant from the Commander in Chief or general officer commanding in Carolina.

On every occasion you will pay particular attention to restrain the militia from offering violence to innocent and inoffensive people and by all means in your power protect the aged, the infirm, the women and children of every denomination from insult or outrage, endeavouring as much as possible to subsist your men and supply their wants at the expence of the known and obstinate enemys of the King and Constitution alone.

Beside this body of militia to act offensively with the army, you will promote the establishment of a domestick militia for the maintenance of peace and good order throughout the country, composed of the men who have families under their own officers ready to assemble occasionally in their several districts.

These instructions and every thing relating to the militia to be subject to such alterations and restrictions as may be ordered by Lt General Earl Cornwallis or other general officer commanding His Majesty's forces in the Carolinas and Georgia for the time being.

Given under my hand at Head Quarters in Charlestown
May the 22nd 1780

H CLINTON

---

[8] Drink generally played a key role in the process of entrapment. If all honest means failed, the last recourse was to get the potential recruit drunk, slip a shilling into his pocket, swear he enlisted, and bring the rest of the recruiting party to prove it. (Richard Holmes, *Redcoat: The British Soldier in the Age of Horse and Musket* (HarperCollins, 2001), 144-5)

Ferguson to Cornwallis, 14th June 1780 *2(145): ALS*

Camp at Congarees
June 14th 1780

Lord Cornwallis

My Lord

Some days ago I was honor'd with a letter from your Lordship of the eighth instant[9]. It shall be my endeavour to obey your Lordship's orders and instructions to the best of my power and not to disappoint the favorable opinion you are pleased to express of me.

An association having been form'd at Orangeburgh by the very loyal and oppress'd inhabitants of that neighbourhood in favor of the King's Government and transmitted to Colonel Balfour, he thought proper to direct a 2nd meeting on the 12th, on which day I went to Orangeburgh in order to mention to the inhabitants your Lordship's militia arrangements as a foundation for a more regular association, which has been subscribed by 294 men, the majority of whom have long refused to acknowledge the rebel authority and all of whom have a confidence in each other. A few others offer'd themselves but, being objected to by individuals and their objections approved of by their companys, were not admitted. They chose to each company two officers, and I repeatedly on the parade call'd upon any man to object to each of them, but they were unanimous. Two of the officers chosen have been in the Assembly, into which they were voted by their constituents without their knowledge or consent on purpose to protect them. Their names are Sally[10] and Rowe[11], and they are universally allow'd by the inhabitants to be steady friends of Government, and indeed, from the best information I have been able to get, it has been a scheme of policy among the people

---

[9] *a letter..*: no extant copy.

[10] John Sally Sr (1740-1794) was born in Orangeburg District to Swiss immigrants and lived near the river swamp about half a mile from Orangeburg village. In 1775 he was elected to the second Provincial Congress, and when it reconstituted itself as the General Assembly in 1776, he ipso facto became a member of that body. In 1777 he served as a commissioner for clearing the Edisto River and making it navigable. Now, in 1780, he was to be commissioned a captain of a company in John Fisher's Orangeburg Regiment of the royal militia. A considerable landowner, he was granted more than 6,500 acres between 1767 and 1793, the majority of which lay in the vicinity of the North and South Edisto Rivers. According to the Federal census of 1790, he owned thirty-three slaves. (Bailey and Cooper, *SC House of Representatives*, iii, 631; Salley Jr, *Orangeburg County*, 489; Clark, *Loyalists in the Southern Campaign*, i, 197, 209)

[11] A Scot, Samuel Rowe had settled in Orangeburg Township about 1740. Before the Revolution he held at various times several offices under the Crown ranging from Justice of the Peace and commissioner for building a chapel to captain in the militia and inquirer and collector under the Tax Act. When the revolutionaries in South Carolina adopted a temporary constitution in 1776, he was again commissioned a Justice of the Peace, and when they adopted a new constitution in 1778, he was one of three representatives elected from Orange Parish to the lower house of the legislature. A covert loyalist, he sided with the British in 1780 and was commissioned a captain in Fisher's regiment of the royal militia. In May 1781 he was part of the garrison in Orangeburg village which surrendered to Sumter. Unlike fourteen of the prisoners who were summarily shot, he was spared, temporarily joined the revolutionaries, and deserted to the British when Rawdon was on his march to relieve Ninety Six. (Salley Jr, *Orangeburg County, passim*; Clark, *Loyalists in the Southern Campaign*, i, 202; Lambert, *SC Loyalists*, 105, 201)

of that quarter as their last resource to vote in members and procure magistrates favorable to them in order in some degree to protect them in the Assembly, and slurr over the exceptionable parts of the State oaths, which latterly every man of them have been compeled to hear administer'd to them.

I have taken the liberty of giving the commanding officers the inclosed directions untill further orders, which I believe are conformable to your Lordship's instructions and approved by Colonel Balfour, and have furnished them with certificates of their being members of the militia entitled to protection. I have also applyed to General Paterson for one hundred weight of powder and as much ball, of which they are much in want; and their known fidelity, the importance of their situation upon the mid road to the Back Country (at the only practicable passage of the forks of Eddisto for carriages) commanding also in a great degree all the approaches to Charles Town from Augusta, Ninety Six, Congaree and Cambden between Savannah and Santee, will, I am persuaded, induce your Lordship to approve of this and every other reasonable indulgence and mark of confidence to these first associations on this side.

There is at Orangeburgh a very well executed field fort, with four bastions, upon an eminence. It is only 60 yards square. Within it is a court house 40 feet by 60 which would be an excellent barracks. The situation is healthy and there is a very large brick jail in tolerable repair, which from its centrical situation may perhaps be of use. The inhabitants could furnish the commissary with flour and cattle for 50 or 100 men and the post would be render'd sufficiently strong by a good abattis. A copy of the association is inclosed.

As I have only had half an hour's warning after a ride of 40 miles, I hope your Lordship will pardon this scrawl.

I have the honor to be with the greatest respect, my Lord,
Your most obedient humble servant

PAT FERGUSON

PS

By the few opportunitys of mixing with the inhabitants which I have had on this side it appears to me that the loyalists and others who from distress and experience are disgusted with the rebel government will be very sufficient with two or three small detachments to secure this country, and that the militia will be infinitely more to be trusted to, more willing and indeed more strong if they are allow'd to reject men of doubtfull characters and if your Lordship's instructions about imprisoning very obnoxious criminals is steadily followed. There are very few men upon whom the people wish to do justice; and unless they are favor'd and the militia forced to give up their voice and receive men they dislike, there will be a militia in this province soon form'd upon the foundation of a free association, much more numerous and ten times more to be trusted than any the rebels ever turn'd out.

Enclosure
Instructions to the commanding officers of the Orangeburgh association

2(143): C

Orangeburgh
June 13th 1780

Untill particular instructions and orders shall arrive from Lord Cornwallis, the captains chosen by the militia at Orangeburgh will if necessary exert themselves to preserve the publick peace. They will get a return, from every inhabitant within the bounds of their company, of all arms and ammunition in their possession as well as of all property belonging to the rebel States or plundered from loyalists and prevent them from being removed or embezzled. They will get attested accounts in writing from such of their men as have suffered injurys particularly grievous from any individual during the rebel government and, if the crimes are of a very black name and that[12] there is any danger of escape, secure their persons and report them to Major Graham. In a few days they will assemble again their companies and admit into the association any good subjects that their men shall think worthy of being trusted with arms; and they will prepare returns of their companys, specifying the unmarried men under forty and the married with the number of their children, and also a return of those inhabitants within their bounds that ought not to be received into the militia or be intrusted with arms.

Enclosure
Articles of association

2(129): C

Orangeburgh
June 12th 1780

We the subscribers belonging to the companies of malitia in the district of Orangeburgh, South Carolina, happy in an opportunity once again of assembling in freedom to express our sentiments without force or constraint, do hereby one and all testify our earnest desire and intent to enter into an association for the purpose of extirpating rebellion, restoring real liberty, and maintaining peace and good order, and hereby express our firm resolution to contribute to the outmost of our power to the reestablishment of the British Government in this once happy but now distracted country.

And as it is our opinion equally the duty and interest of men united in society under the blessings of a free and mild Government, such as we formerly enjoyed under our gracious Soverign, George the Third, to be ready at all times to stand forth like men in suport and defence of that Constitution by which they are protected from oppression and secured in their liberty and property, we the subscribers do therefore unanimously resolve and agree, conformable to some arangements for the millitia which we understand are adopted by Lord Cornwallis, that all such men of this association as are under fourty years of age and are not

---

[12] *that*: the meaning is 'if'. As in modern French, a subordinate conjunction, if repeated in 18th-century English, was often replaced by 'that'.

burthened with more than three children do, when required, embody themselves and co-operate with the troops within the limits of the two Carolinas and Georgia against His Majesty's enemys natural and foreign according to the orders they may receive from the Commander in Chief or officer acting by his authority, whenever the publick service shall require it, providing that the associators on serving shall receive pay and provisions whilst embodyed and that the term of such service do not exceed six months out of the twelve. And we do further resolve that every member of this association shall whilst at home be ready at all times to assemble when required and perform millitia duty within the limits of his own district according to the regulations that may be established for that purpose.

Moreover, in consideration of the foul terror and intrigues employed by the abetors of the late rebellion in this province, by which means many well meaning men were either compelled or seduced to act with those then in power contrary to their duty and best interest, we the subscribers do unanimously agree to do our outmost to protect from molestation and injury those unhappy men in the hope that they must now see the ruinous consequence of the designs of their leaders and that they will shew themselves by their future conduct worthy of being again received with confidence into this free, happy and loyal community.

Cornwallis to Ferguson, 16th June 1780   77(14): C

Camden
June 16th 1780

Major Ferguson etc

Sir

I have just received the favour of your letter of the 14th by Lt Colonel Pattison. I approve very much of every thing that has been done at Orangeburgh and am much obliged to you for your care and attention to it. Your ideas relating to the forming the militia of loyal subjects only are exactly conformable to mine, and you will find those express words in the plan for regulation which I sent to you. My intention was that all others should have remained prisoners on parole and have been obliged to contribute to the publick service in provisions, horses, waggons etc in lieu of their personal service. The Commander in Chief has released all persons from their paroles on the 20th of this month except those who were in a military line etc, but the other part of my plan obliging those, whom the loyal part of the district do not chuse to receive into the militia, to furnish contributions in lieu of service shall be put in force as soon as the militia is sufficiently regulated to enable us to enforce any orders by their means. You may depend on my steadily pursuing my plan of imprisoning those who have rendered themselves obnoxious by their cruelty and persecution of our friends, and I shall release them only by the consent and forgiveness of the injured party. You have engaged in a most troublesome business, but in my opinion a most important one; I have no doubt of your perseverance in carrying it through. You shall [have] every assistance and support I can give you.

I am etc

[CORNWALLIS]

CHAPTER 8

Correspondence between Cornwallis and Innes

Innes to Cornwallis, 8th June 1780 2(114): ALS

Friday's Ferry, Congaree River
Thursday, 8th June 1780

My Lord

After two days' long march through a country almost a perfect desert, I arrived on the banks of the Congaree Tuesday forenoon. Notwithstanding my expedition, a flying party from Colonel Balfour had been as high as this place on the other side the river, conducted by a Lieutenant Dawkins[1] of my battalion and one Taylor[2] of Ferguson's, a noted ranger from

---

[1] George Dawkins (1754-?) was an inhabitant of the Dutch Fork who had made his way to East Florida with other Back Country loyalists in 1778. There they were formed into the South Carolina Royalist Regiment, in which Dawkins was a commissioned a lieutenant. While Dawkins' service in South Carolina would have been inseparable from that of his regiment, two specific facts are known: first, he was promoted to the captaincy of a company on 24th October 1780; and second, he was badly wounded in August 1782 during an attack on an enemy force near Charlestown that had forewarning. After accompanying his regiment to East Florida, he commanded 64 officers and men of the regiment who moved in 1783 to Nova Scotia and settled on land grants beside Country Harbour. He still resided there in 1791. Placed on the Provisional half-pay list, he also received an award of £984 for losses directly attributable to his loyalty. (Lambert, *SC Loyalists, passim*; Clark, *Loyalists in the Southern Campaign*, i, *passim*; Treasury 64/23(15), WO 65/164(40) and WO 65/165(10) (National Archives, Kew))

[2] Lieutenant John Taylor (1742-1822) was born near Amboy, New Jersey, and had been commissioned into the 1st Battalion, New Jersey Volunteers, in 1776. Seconded now to Ferguson's corps, he was to command its troop of twenty horse. After being taken prisoner at the Battle of King's Mountain, he was led to Bethabara, North Carolina, from where, accompanied by two other officers and a militiaman, he fled in November 1780 to Ninety Six, claiming that he had been ill treated by his captors and that he had entered into no parole. In the meantime, on 25th October, he had been promoted to captain in his battalion but was to take no further part in southern operations. At the close of the war, having been placed on the Provincial half-pay list, he retired to Weymouth, Nova Scotia. (Draper, *King's Mountain, passim*; Treasury 64/23(6), WO 65/164(35) and WO 65/165(6) (National

Monmouth County in the Jerseys. As they had traversed the finest part of the Congarees, I have not been able to send Colonel Tarlton such horses (or in such numbers) as I expected, but I doubt not that Balfour will supply the deficiency. I can assure your Lordship the best I could procure are now sent, but this part of the country had been much drained and many sent off to Virginia. The *cursed* capitulation of Charles Town has been presented once or twice in demur of delivery of some good horses.

The quantity of corn and corn flour we have found is very great — there is also some wheat flour, and a large quantity of tobacco, all belonging to the publick. At least thirty thousand bushels of indian corn was at first collected. Some of it has been ground and sent off, much of it embezzled no doubt, but still a very great quantity remains. I am now endeavoring to get as exact a return made as possible of every thing, but as the corn and meal is at nine or ten different plantations, it will take a little time. Mr Godwin pretends he was empowered by your Lordship to collect those returns, but as I have the best grounds to entertain the worst opinion of that man, I shall not trust entirely to his report. I have already found out where the different depots are, and my quarter master with a trusty guide will, I hope, be able to see the whole to day and give a strict charge as to their preservation.

The misery of the wretched inhabitants above this fork on both rivers is already very great and I fear will be still more so. Indeed, without your Lordship's assistance, I fear many will starve. The greatest part of the industrious hands were either drove off or dragooned to be absent from their families on military duty when they should have been providing for their subsistance, and the rich country on this river was drained to supply magazines for Charles Town. I have already met with poor loyalists from Turkey Creek, above a hundred and twenty miles above this place, coming down to purchase a little corn for their subsistance, and every account I have from Orangeburgh, Ninety Six, Saluda and Broad River Districts are full of the distress of the back inhabitants throughout the province. Thank God the rebels here have good stocks, and with proper care much may be drawn for the supply of Charles Town, the army and the poor country people if care is only taken.

As to the general disposition of the country, I have found it as favourable as your Lordship can wish. Several of our friends from the different districts have been with me and are returned to assure the loyal of every protection. They are assembling in many places, and the most violent rebels are candid enough to allow the game is up and are coming in to make their submission in great numbers. A sensible clever scoundrel came in as deputy from a large body on Broad River; the names of some of the chief of them I have the honor to inclose[3]. They desired to know on what terms they might be admitted to surrender. I showed him the parole, at the same time explained your Lordship's intentions not to grant indiscriminately the same indulgence to all but to have regard to characters in settling the places of confinement. He allowed the justice as well as good policy of that measure. Indeed, every one I have spoke to (and I have told all who came for paroles the same) seemed much pleased at the intention (a few obnoxious people excepted), and some gentlemen near this of good fortune who I knew in Charles Town has candidly hinted that, while a knot of

---

Archives, Kew); *The Cornwallis Papers*)

[3] *the names..*: not extant.

violent rascals from Virginia remain here, they never can be in peace or security. At the head of this gang are Colonels Thompson, Godwin, Beard and others. It was with some difficulty I prevented Godwin from being put to death on Tuesday night by my people. He was recognised by the wife of an old German who has been three years a soldier in the Carolina Regiment and accused of having tied up her son who is also a soldier in the corps, then quite a boy, and flogging him most unmercifully to make him discover where his father was concealed. Godwin denied the fact and accused his brother, who must not come to this place. One Reeves[4] and a Strother[5], violent rascals, I have been obliged to stop and a fellow who tied Captain Murphy to a black and ordered him to be fired at because he would not march in that situation. It was necessary to secure those men to save their lives from the just resentment of the people they have persecuted.

I wrote to Colonel Balfour and inclosed your Lordship's letter[6]. He received it last night and I expect to hear from him every moment. He was at Thompson's last night, about thirty five miles from this post. I intend to meet him this night or early tomorrow morning, represent the present state of this part of the country that he may regulate his future operations accordingly. I can assure your Lordship there will not be a shadow of opposition in this province attempted, and I speak from the best authority. Williamson's people are in general gone home. There are not now fifty men in Augusta and I am told Williamson means to remain peaceably at home. In this situation your Lordship must judge of the necessity of sending so large a body of troops through a country so wretchedly circumstanced as to provisions; they can hope for nothing but cattle and those chiefly a breeding stock. I will pledge my life that three hundred men shall march to the Indian line[7] and from thence to Augusta without firing a shot, and I am also clear that the very followers that attend our troops would so effectually ruin the Back Country it must be left a desart.

It was necessary for me (that no time should be lost) to acquaint some leading people in the different districts of Saluda, Broad River, Ninety Six and Orangeburgh of the heads of your Lordship's plan with regard to the militia. It was received with the most universal satisfaction and I could not resist their importunities to give them in writing the description of the different classes that they might proceed immediately to throw their neighbours into one or other of the lists. Captains and subalterns will easily be found. Men of consequence enough to command districts cannot now so easily be had. I therefore recommended them

---

[4] Possibly Daniel or Green Reeves, both of whom at one time or another served in revolutionary corps from Orangeburg District. (Moss, *SC Patriots*, 807)

[5] Of the various Strothers in Orangeburg District, George or William would have been the one to whom Innes was adverting. George had been commissioned a Justice of the Peace under the royal government in 1770 before acting from April 1776 in the same capacity under the temporary revolutionary constitution. William had served as Sheriff of Orangeburg District since 1779. In September or October 1780 one of them was to die in captivity at Camden. (Salley Jr, *Orangeburg County*, 248, 265; Moss, *SC Patriots*, 904; *The Cornwallis Papers*)

[6] *your Lordship's letter*: no extant copy.

[7] The old Indian line was the boundary between the Cherokees and South Carolina settlers. It was established at the conclusion of the Cherokee War in 1761 and ran forty miles east of the Keowee River. (Fred Anderson, *Crucible of War: the Seven Years' War and the Fate of the Empire in British North America, 1754-1766* (Faber and Faber Ltd, 2000), 457-471)

to begin with companies till things were more settled. I hope in this business I have only anticipated the Inspector General of Militia — not offended by seeming to encroach on his department, which really is not my intention. Your Lordship has been the ablest assistant he could have had, for the people so warmly approve your plan that I doubt if I shall have one offer to raise a Provincial corps in this quarter, and indeed I hardly expect to keep up my present numbers but rather think the whole regiment will disperse. If that is the case I have no concern but for the officers and I must rely on your Lordship's goodness to recommend them for some provision.

I mean to propose to Colonel Balfour to proceed *alone* through the fork of Saluda, or with a very small addition to my numbers. If he agrees to this, I will beg your Lordship's permission to move to the very upper part of it, but if that is not thought eligible and the whole moves on, I will in that case take the benefit of your Lordship's indulgence and return to head quarters immediately.

Colonel Godwin has just called with a memorandum of the corn and flour he has found, which I beg to inclose[8]. He allows much more may be discovered. The meal must be immediately used or it will very soon be spoilt.

I have the honor to be with equal sincerity and respect, my Lord,
Your Lordship's most obedient and most humble servant

ALEX INNES
Lt Colonel

NB

I shall move the bulk of my people over the river this day for the readier communication with the fork of Saluda, leaving a company to protect this side and to secure the ferry.

NB

Not a drop of rum but what has been seized by Balfour, nor a bushel of salt.

Innes to Cornwallis, 10th June 1780   *2(118): ALS*

Friday's Ferry
10th June

My Lord

Since I had the honor of writing you last, I received the inclosed letter from Captain Reisinger, which made it necessary for me to establish a post at Weaver's Ferry yesterday, and I mean to move the battalion there tomorrow as it is of the last consequence our people

---

[8] *a memorandum..*: not extant.

on the fork should be supported. On the road to the ferry I received a letter from General Williamson, which I also have the honor to inclose, and have acquainted him I am empowered by your Lordship to receive as prisoners such persons as are in arms against their Sovereign, that paroles will be granted to those whose characters deserve them, and that great lenity has been hitherto showed on every occasion. Captain Kinloch[9] will inform your Lordship of the absolute impossibility of my know[ing] what I write, such crouds are every moment coming in. I must therefore refer your Lordship to him for some other particulars, and have the honor to be most respectfully, my Lord,

Your Lordship's most obedient and most humble servant

ALEX INNES
Lt Colonel

Enclosure (1)
Reisinger to Innes, 8th June 1780   2(112): ALS

Head Quarters
Shieries Ferry, Broad River
June 8th 1780

Colonel Alexander Ennis Esq
Commander of the South Carolina Royalists

Honoured Sir

I just now received an express from Captain Reece on the frontiers of the province, which informs me he is likely to be attacked by a party of rebels and wants me to reinforce him, which is out of my power. I therefore have advised him to retreat from his station in order to join the Royal Army, as is my intention to do immediately, and I hope you will proceed with the Royal Army up to the Widow Weaver's Ferry on Saludy in order to reinforce His Majesty's subjects in the back inhabitants. I make not the least doubt but we shall be able to suppress all the attempts of the rebels in a short time.

---

[9] A lieutenant in the 1st Battalion, 71st (Highland) Regiment, David Kinloch had transferred to the British Legion as a captain of horse when that British American corps was formed in 1778. He had recently been involved in the action at the Waxhaws, commanding part of the Legion cavalry in the charge against the centre of Buford's force. During the Charlottesville raid in June 1781 he would capture his cousin, Francis, who was a delegate from South Carolina to the Continental Congress. Five years later he would be residing in Moffat, Scotland. (*Army Lists*; Bass, *The Green Dragoon*, 47, 179; Tarleton, *Campaigns*, 29; Peter Wilson Coldham, *American Migrations: 1765-1799* (Genealogicial Publishing Co, 2000), 270)

I am, sir, with respects
Your honourable servant

FECH REISINGER[10]
Captain, 1st Batalion, Royal Americans

Enclosure (2)
Williamson to the officer commanding, north of Saluda 2(90): *LS*

June 5th 1780

To the officer commanding the British troops
　on the north side of Saluday River

Sir

Understanding from several persons who have been stoped on the north side of Saluday River that parties of men are embodyed and pretend to have authority from the Commander in Chief of the British Army to treat with the inhabitants or, on their refusal, to reduce them by force of arms, being desirous on my part to prevent the effusion of blood and the ruin of the country, I send the bearers, Major John Bowie, Richard A Rapley and James Moore Esquires, and request you will inform them of the tenor of the powers you are invested with.

I am, sir,
Your most humble servant

A WMSON
Brigadier General, South Carolina militia

---

[10] A settler in the Dutch Fork, Fecht Reisinger had been part of some 400 loyalists who had made their way from the Back Country to East Florida in 1778. There he was commissioned a captain in the newly formed South Carolina Royalist Regiment. With the reduction of South Carolina he would shortly resign his commission, but would later see service as a captain and express rider in Daniel Clary's Dutch Fork Regiment of the royal militia. By December 1781 he had fled to Charlestown, where he was paid as a refugee until its evacuation. Why he should sign himself as a captain in the 1st Battalion of the 60th (Royal American) Regiment is puzzling, as there is no record in the *Army Lists* of his ever holding a commission in that corps. Formed in the 1750s of German officers and recruited mainly from Pennsylvania Germans, it may nevertheless provide a clue to his origin. (Clark, *Loyalists in the Southern Campaign*, i, 7, 8, 234, 493-500; Boatner, *Encyclopedia*, 947-8)

Innes to Cornwallis, 14th June 1780 *2(149): ALS*

Sheires's Ferry above Cannon Creek
June 14th 1780

Lt General Earl Cornwallis etc etc etc

My Lord

The bearer of this, Mr Mills of North Carolina[11], who collected some men and joined the loyalists of this province assembled on the Fair Forest two or three days ago, wishes to wait on your Lordship to request assistance I am not empowered to give him. He requests I will give him a few lines to your Lordship and I must beg leave to refer to Governor Martin for his character and to himself for other particulars. I have wrote so fully to Lt Colonel Balfour of the state of this part of the country, to be transmitted to your Lordship, that I shall only add that I arrived here this morning, am busy in putting things into some little order, and shall, I hope, be able to move from this place towards 96 tomorrow evening. In the course of next day's march I shall have the honor of addressing your Lordship and sending my letter across the country, should any thing happen worthy your attention.

I have the honor to be with great respect, my Lord,
Your Lordship's most obedient and most humble servant

ALEX INNES
Lt Colonel

Enclosure
Proclamation issued by Innes *2(157): ACS*

By Lt Colonel Innes, Inspector General Provincial Forces, commanding a detachment of His Majesty's forces at Sheires's Ferry, Broad River

Whereas I have received information that a number of dissorderly people are now ranging through the back settlements of this part of the province, pretending to be friends to His Majesty's Goverment, and under that pretext are pilaging and oppressing the people, seizing their horses and cattle and robbing their houses:

---

[11] Ambrose Mills (c 1722-1780) was born in England and was taken while young to Maryland. On marrying he settled on James River, Virginia, before moving to the frontier of South Carolina, where his wife was killed by native Americans, probably in 1760 during the Cherokee War. Marrying the sister of the wife of Colonel Thomas Fletchall, who was to become a leading figure in Back Country loyalism, he settled about 1765 on Green River in North Carolina. After taking part in the 1776 campaign against the Cherokees, he and David Fanning raised a corps of 500 men to join the British at St Augustine. He was discovered and jailed for a time at Salisbury. As colonel commanding a North Carolina battalion of loyalist militia, he was put under the command of Major Patrick Ferguson and joined with him in attempting to pacify the Back Country and frontier region. Present with some 300 of his men at the Battle of King's Mountain, he was taken prisoner, subjected with others to a mock trial, and summarily hanged at Bickerstaff's Old Fields in the evening of 14th October 1780. (Draper, *King's Mountain*, *passim*)

As this outrageous and dissorderly conduct is contrary to all order and prevents many of His Majesty's deluded subjects from taking the benefit of His gracious clemency signified by the Commissioners' proclamation of the 22nd of May[12], I do hereby strictly forbid all such illegal proceedings under pain of the most severe punishment, which I will inflict on the spot, and I also direct that no person in the district within my command do presume to seize or carry away any horses, cattle, corn or goods of any kind from any person whatever unless it is for the publick service and they have my order in writing for it. Such as have committed outrages on the persons or properties of His Majesty's loyal subjects will hereafter be amenable to the laws of their country if they do not make satisfaction to those they have injured, but under the just and mild government of His Majesty they shall not be liable to the caprice, cruelty or malice of every individual who chuses to take the law into his own hands. I do also hereby promise all persons inclined to return to their duty and allegiance every protection His Majesty's troops can possibly afford them.

Given under my hand at Sheires's Ferry, Broad River, South Carolina this 14th of June 1780

ALEX INNES, Lt Colonel
Inspector General Provincial Forces

Innes to Cornwallis, 15th June 1780   2(160): ALS

Sheire's Ferry above Cannon Creek

15th June 1780

Lt General Earl Cornwallis

My Lord

Every thing being perfectly quiet here, the militia sent home, and some little order established, I intended to have march'd this evening to Ninety Six with the regiment, but about an hour ago Captain Robert Cunningham[13] arrived here from that place and I find it

---

[12] The Commissioners' proclamation was dated 1st June 1780. See p 83, note 22. The one of 22nd May 1780, a draft of which appears on p 49, was issued by Clinton alone and did not deal with clemency.

[13] Robert Cunningham (1739-1813) had settled with three brothers in the Back Country in 1769, having migrated from Pennsylvania by way of Virginia. Almost immediately he was looked on in his neighbourhood as a man of consequence, becoming a captain of militia, a deputy surveyor, and a Justice of the Peace. A prominent Regulator, he was dismissed from his offices by Lord Charles Montagu, the royal Governor, but seems to have retained the respect of leaders in the Back Country. Opposed to British taxation of the colonies without their concurrence, he did not go so far as to favour severing the constitutional ties between Britain and America, believing that it would lead to arbitrary, oppressive rule by the revolutionary party. Accordingly in 1775, with his brother Patrick and others, he led loyalist opposition in the Back Country to the subversive measures of the Provincial Congress. As a result he was confined in Charlestown jail from November to the following summer. Typically of the times, Andrew Pickens was to malign his motives, ascribing them to thwarted ambition with respect to revolutionary appointments in the militia line. When in 1778 an election was held under the new revolutionary constitution, he was returned as Senator for the Middle District of the Dutch Fork, but he did not take his seat, being unwilling to swear the oath of allegiance. On 22nd November 1780 he was to be commissioned a brigadier general of the

absolutely necessary some officer should be there as soon as possible. I shall therefore take the few mounted men I have with me and push on as fast as possible to White Hall[14], leaving the regiment to follow under the command of Captain Murphy. I did hope for Colonel Balfour's permission to have joined your Lordship at Camden by way of 25 Mile Creek after clearing the country on the other side Broad River, but as there is not the least appearance of an enemy on this side the North Carolina line, and Colonel Balfour wishing that in that case I should go to Ninety Six, I cannot hope to see your Lordship before your arrival in Charles Town, for which place I shall immediately set out after Colonel Balfour's arrival with us.

I wrote your Lordship a few lines yesterday by a Mr Mills, a poor old man from North Carolina, and inclosed a copy of a placart[15] I was under a necessity of publishing, and I find from Captain Cunningham something of the same kind is very necessary in that part of the country.

Captain O'Neale[16], who commands a number of militia 40 miles from this place, was with me yesterday. He went back this morning to dismiss all the militia excepting about 50 under his own immediate command and whose regularity he can depend on. Those he conceives quite sufficient to keep peace in the country, which at present is suffering from so many useful hands being unemployed or rather doing mischief. I have ordered him to enforce my orders with regard to marauding, which I am sorry to find was too necessary. The good management of Captain Cunningham has contributed greatly to finish things so well to the southward. I would not have entrusted Pearis with a corporal's guard, and, added to that, he is a man of very indifferent character. With this your Lordship will receive a letter for Sir Henry Clinton inclosing the capitulation which I had the honor of sending your Lordship by

---

royal militia in the District of Ninety Six, but by that time it was a spent force following Ferguson's defeat on 7th October. By mid 1782, with his property confiscated by act of the revolutionary assembly, he was receiving pay as a militia refugee in Charlestown. At the close of the war he was placed on the Provincial half-pay list and eventually settled in New Providence in the Bahamas, having been refused permission to return to South Carolina. He was awarded £1,080 by the Crown for his losses. Cunningham signed himself with a double 'n' in his surname, whereas his brother Patrick signed himself with one. (Lambert, *SC Loyalists, passim*; George Atkinson Ward ed, *Journal and Letters of the late Samuel Curwen...* (London, 1842), *passim*; Sabine, *Biographical Sketches*, i, 346-7; McCrady, *SC in the Rev 1775-1780, passim*; *The Cornwallis Papers*; Clark, *Loyalists in the Southern Campaign*, i, 495, 497, 500; Treasury 64/23(36) (National Archives, Kew))

[14] *White Hall*: the home of Andrew Williamson.

[15] *placart*: an obsolete form of 'placard', having the outdated meaning of 'proclamation'.

[16] A settler on Little River in the Dutch Fork, Henry O'Neaill (as he signed his surname) had been in 1775 a leader of the non-associators in the Back Country, that is to say, of those who refused to sign the association of the Provincial Congress subversive of the royal government. When elections were held in late 1778 to the General Assembly under the new revolutionary constitution, his district returned him and two other loyalists, Robert Cunningham and Jacob Bowman, but, unlike them, he took his seat. With the coming of the British in 1780, he was appointed a captain in the Little River Regiment of the royal militia. In November 1780 he signed an address to Cornwallis from militia officers in the Ninety Six District recommending Moses Kirkland to superintend all the royal militia regiments there, but Robert Cunningham was appointed. Otherwise, apart from acting as an infrequent emissary between Cruger or Kirkland and headquarters, he has left no record of his service. In late 1782 he moved to East Florida, where he settled about three miles from the mouth of St Mary's River and became the local magistrate. With the transfer of sovereignty to Spain he indicated his intention to remain. (Lambert, *SC Loyalists, passim*; Clark, *Loyalists in the Southern Campaign*, i, 309; *The Cornwallis Papers*)

Colonel Balfour[17].

I have the honor to be with great respect, my Lord,
Your Lordship's most obedient and most humble servant

ALEX INNES
Lt Colonel

NB

Lieutenant Gregory[18] of my regiment has been so good as to take charge of this as Captain Cunningham wishes to return with me and will be very useful.

I am now reduced to my last sheet of paper.

Cornwallis to Innes, 16th June 1780[19]   77(13): C

Camden
June 16th 1780

Lt Colonel Innes

Dear Sir

I received both your letters this morning. Governour Martin knew by some papers delivered to him by Major André that Mills was most perfectly to be depended upon. He has been premature in his rising, but as he lives in a remote corner of the country quite out of our way and insists on defending the settlements of himself and his followers, we must let him act. I have used every expedient in my power to induce our friends in North Carolina to remain at home and get in their harvest, and by no means to think of rising 'till I send to them, and I have reason to think now that they have all acquiesced, tho' very unwillingly. I must beg you will let Mills have a little ammunition, and you must absolutely send some tolerably intelligent officer with him to insist positively on his acting only on the defensive and to put him in the way of doing so. Should he act offensively, he might endanger the bringing on a premature rising in the province and ruin all our plan for the reduction of North Carolina. I trust the management of every thing about Ninety Six to your discretion in the

---

[17] Of the letter to Clinton there is no extant copy. For the capitulation, see p 96.

[18] Benjamin Gregory had been a settler on Crim's Creek in the Dutch Fork. In response to overtures from Thomas Brown in East Florida, he and John Murphy assembled some 400 loyalists in 1778 and took them there. On arrival they were enlisted into the newly formed South Carolina Royalist Regiment, of which Alexander Innes became Lt Colonel. Gregory was to resign his lieutenancy some time before 24th February 1781 and transfer to the royal militia, becoming a lt colonel. A refugee in Charlestown, he died on 31st July 1782. (Lambert, *SC Loyalists*, 70; Clark, *Loyalists in the Southern Campaign*, i, 33-5, 48, 498)

[19] An extract from this letter appears in Ross ed, *Cornwallis Correspondence,* i, 47.

first instance, and then to Balfour's. You are both thoroughly in possession of my plan and ideas relative to the regulation of this province. You judged very rightly in sending home the useless militia to attend their harvest. I have sent you a quire of paper by Lieutenant Gregory, and am etc

[CORNWALLIS]

CHAPTER 9

Other correspondence etc

1 - Between Cornwallis and Paterson

Paterson to Cornwallis, 6th June 1780 *2(94): ALS*

Charles Town
June 6th 1780

His Excellency Earl Cornwallis etc etc etc

My Lord

I have been extremely uneasy at the delay and disappointment of your convoy. The inclosed state of the Quarter Master's Department[1] will explain and account for the causes of it.

I have found every thing here in so confused and perplexed a state as to be almost out of the reach of recovery. My whole time is devoted to it, and I have not half enough; and I find my self, for want of magistrates and a civil judicature, embarked on a situation out of the line of my profession, in which I can not expect either to give or receive satisfaction. No exertion on my part, however, shall be wanting to bring matters into order and establish some kind of arrangement in the complicated scene before me, in which, if I am fortunate enough to succeed, I shall look up to your Lordship's approbation as the great and only reward of it.

---

[1] *The inclosed state..*: not extant.

I have the honor to be with all possible respect and esteem, my Lord,
Your most obedient humble servant

J PATERSON
Brigadier General

Cornwallis to Paterson, 10th June 1780[2] 77(3): C

Camden
June 10th 1780

Brigadier General Patterson
Commandant
Charlestown

Dear Sir

I inclose to you as much as I have been able to form of a plan for settling this province, regulating the militia etc. It is with great concern that I find the Commander in Chief adopted the idea of granting indiscriminate protections, by which means some of the most violent rebels and persecutors of the whole province are declared faithfull subjects and are promised to be protected in their persons and properties. You will see by the inclosed regulation[3] that all persons in whom we can place any confidence will be militia men. The remainder therefore must be considered as disaffected. All persons who have got these protections, and who cannot in the opinion of the commanding officers of each district be safely received into the militia, must be obliged to give up their protections, and their paroles must be taken as prisoners of war. You will see by the plan that there is a distinction of paroles. If, therefore, any in the neighbourhood of town, not in the capitulation of Charlestown, have got common paroles[4] who come under the discription of those who are to be sent to the islands on the coast, you will be kind enough to call them in and give them paroles to find themselves in one of the islands by the 15th of next month. I should wish it to be publickly known that no more protections will be granted and that those already given will be recalled unless the conduct and characters of the possessors entitle them to be trusted to bear arms in the militia or Provincial corps. I hope to be in town by the end of the month, perhaps sooner. In the mean time I shall be obliged to you if you will look out for proper persons to command the militia of the districts near Charlestown. To save time and trouble we have adopted the division made by the rebels so that we have only to appoint *A* to command the district late of *B*.

---

[2] Extracts from this letter, not accompanied by the enclosure, appear in Ross ed, *Cornwallis Correspondence,* i, 46.

[3] *the inclosed regulation*: a reference to the enclosed plan.

[4] *common paroles*: the inference from the following enclosure and letter is that such paroles were to permit the holders to remain at home.

I am, dear sir,
Your most obedient and faithfull servant

[CORNWALLIS]

[*Subscribed:*]

I should wish you to disarm the districts near you as we cannot shew too soon that we are in earnest.

Enclosure
Draft plan for dealing with the disaffected and the militia   *2(86): Df*

*Part of a General Plan for regulating the Province
and forming a Militia*

Camden
4th June 1780

Those who have been in publick stations such as Governour, Lt Governour, Members of the Council, Senate or Assembly, acting magistrates, field officers of militia, and some individuals who are particularly obnoxious to friends of Government, are to be sent prisoners on parole to James, John's, Edisto, St Helena or Port Royal Islands. Those that have been violent persecutors will be sent to prison and the remainder of the disaffected will be disarmed and permitted to remain[5] at their own homes. The loyal subjects will be formed into militia by districts according to the present division of the province. This militia is to be divided into two classes. The first to consist of men:

—   above 40 years of age

—   having four children or upwards

—   having one hundred Negroes or upwards

—   who have served three years or upwards in any regular or Provincial corps

—   who have any bodily infirmity that renders them unfit to bear fatigue.

This class will remain at home to preserve order and will not be called out of their respective districts except in case of an insurrection or invasion of the province.

The second class to consist of the remainder of the men above eighteen years of age, and is to be liable to be called upon to serve six of each twelve months — during that period with pay and provisions as Provincial troops — in the provinces of Georgia, South and North Carolina when the exigencies of the publick service make it necessary.

---

[5]   *to remain*: the following words, 'prisoners on parole', are deleted.

The prisoners, whether on parole or in confinement, and the disaffected who are not admitted into the militia are to furnish contributions from their properties for the publick service in provisions, horses, waggons etc in lieu of their personal services, and their proportions will be regulated by the militia officers of the district to which they belong.[6]

It is believed that there is a sufficient quantity of arms and ammunition in the country for the present purposes of the militia that will be formed, but if they should prove deficient in any district, a supply will be sent as soon as possible from Charlestown.

Cornwallis to Paterson, 10th June 1780   77(5): ADf

Camden
June 10th 1780, pm

Brigadier General Paterson
Commandant at Charlestown

Dear Sir

Since I wrote to you this morning, I have by accident met with a proclamation of the Commissioners dated the 1st of this month. I do not, however, see occasion in consequence of it to alter any thing of what I said to you in my letter of this day's date. The sending the persons described in my regulation on parole to the islands untill we can inquire how far they have been concern'd in taking the lives of the innocent and well affected, and putting others on parole 'till we can judge of the sincerity of their repentance, is perfectly conformable to the words and spirit of the proclamation, and I am sure that without it there will be no possibility of regulating the militia or introducing order and government into the country. Those who were taken in Charlestown can have nothing to do with the proclamation, having no power to surrender themselves untill they are regularly exchanged, unless hereafter good reasons should appear for releasing them from their parole.

I am, dear sir,
Your most obedient and faithfull servant

[CORNWALLIS]

---

[6] The following paragraph is deleted: 'Paroles are cancelled by any of those at present under parole entering into a Provincial corps or being received into the militia.'.

Paterson to Cornwallis, 12th June 1780

2(135): ALS

Charles Town
June 12th 1780

His Excellency Lt General Earl Cornwallis

My Lord

I have the honor to transmit to your Lordship several letters and dispatches from the Commander in Chief, one from General Robertson, which I thought my duty, from the wording of the inscription, to open. It contains confirmation of Dalrymple's packet, and as the fleet sailed the 9th with a fair wind, it was impossible to overtake them so as to communicate it to the General or Admiral. A copy shall follow. By order of the General I inclose also the proceedings of a general court martial[7].

Several applications will certainly be made to your Lordship for several indulgences which I am, in obedience to my instructions, under a necessity to refuse; and the absolute stile in which the solicitations are couched makes my situation not exactly a bed of roses.

Captain Henry (of the navy) is preparing transports for bringing the Hessian Regiment of Trombach from Savanna. As soon as they arrive we shall be strong enough to take post, with your Lordship's permission, at Monk's Corner, where, it appears to me, we want something to cover the convoys and communication with Camden, which must be incessant.

I am endeavoring (but with difficulty) to establish a kind of police for the good order and cleanlyness of the town, without which some infectious disorder will infallibly take place.

I have a great many matters to lay before your Lordship, but as I hear with great satisfaction I am soon to hope for the honor of seeing you, I shall only at present beg leave to assure your Lordship how much I have the honor to be most respectfully, my Lord,

Your most obedient and most faithful humble servant

J PATERSON
Brigadier General

PS

The address alluded to in the General's letter is not sent to me. Every assistance Colonel Tarlton can wish for he may depend upon from me, but our means are very unequal to our wishes.

---

[7] *the proceedings..*: not extant.

Enclosure (1)
Robertson to Cornwallis, 30th May 1780　　　　　　　　　　　　　　　　　　*2(56): LS*

New York
30th May 1780

Earl Cornwallis

My Lord

Four rebel privateers attacked the pacquet near Sandy Hook. The captain, finding resistance could not save his ship, run her aground and at great risque brought the mail here in his boat. General Knyphausen[8] being extremely desirous to send Sir Henry Clinton's dispatches, and no man of war being to be spared, I have at his desire engaged a vessel remarkable for fast sailing to carry them. To prevent their falling into the enemy's hands an officer takes care of them, but to prevent any ill consequences from their being lost Captain Smyth keeps the originals and only sends copys. As this precaution cannot be taken with your Lordship's, I reserve them for a safer occasion and only send one package which appears to be news papers. There are two packages from the Secretary of State's Office, one from the War Office, and five private letters.

The *Iris* has put in to replenish the water which the great number of prisoners she has taken on the passage had consumed.

The surrender of Charlestown, without loss on our part, is all he can relate, and this is enough to make me conclude that America will return to its duty, to justify me in troubling you with congratulations, and begging leave to be considered among, my Lord, your Lordship's most obedient and most humble servants.

JAMES ROBERTSON[9]

---

[8] Freiherr Wilhelm von Knyphausen (1716-1800) was a lt general commanding the German troops in North America. During the Charlestown campaign he had remained at New York in overall command there. In the event of Clinton's death or incapacity Knyphausen would have succeeded him had not Cornwalliis held a dormant commission to do so. (Boatner, *Encyclopedia*, 588; Ewald, *Diary*, 460)

[9] Born in Fifeshire, James Robertson (*c.* 1710-1788) had risen from the ranks to be at this time a major general and civil Governor of New York. Having served as a field officer in the Seven Years' War, he was for many years barrack master at New York. Promoted to colonel in 1772, he led a brigade in the Battle of Long Island four years later. What is known of his character rests entirely on the testimony of Thomas Jones, the Chief Justice of New York, a malevolent and disappointed man, who in his history of the place accuses Robertson of peculation, extortion and other uncomplimentary traits. It is an assessment to be treated with caution, being so at variance with his principled stand on plundering taken later in these Papers. By then a lt general, he was to return to England on 15th April 1783. (*Appletons'*; *DNB*; *The Cornwallis Papers*)

Enclosure (2)
McKinnon to Paterson, 12th June 1780 6(218): ALS

Charlestown
12th June 1780

To General Paterson

Sir

In consequence of the difficulty of supplying the troops at Cambden with provisions from the length of the land carriage and the contract'd scale of the department I went yesterday in obedience to your commands to Monk's Corner to see if there was any means of obviating this difficulty.

I find there is a road from Wadboo's Landing on the Cooper River to Cook's on the Santee, the distance only 15 miles. The navigation of the Santee from Ca[m]bden to this place, tho' in some places difficult, is in none impractible. By availing ourselves therefore of the navigation of the two rivers I will undertake, if agreable to you, to have above 20 puncheons of rum, with all the salt and necessaries for the regiments that may be wanted, at Cook's Landing every week. The first convoy shall be there in three days from my receving your orders. I am also informed there is on the banks of the Santee a great many corn blades and some lumber, both articles very much wanted here, which might be brought down in the empty waggons and boats.

I am, sir,
Your most obedient humble servant

JN McKINNON[10]
Deputy Quarter Master General

§ - §

---

[10] John McKinnon was a captain in the 63rd Regiment who had been assigned to duty in the Quartermaster General's Department. Commissioned a lieutenant in the 47th Regiment on 15th June 1764, he had been promoted to captain in the 63rd on 27th July 1776. (*Army Lists*)

2 - Rawdon to Cornwallis

2(123): ALS

Lesslie's House
Waxhaw
June 11th 1780

Earl Cornwallis etc etc etc

My Lord

I have the honor to report to your Lordship that I arrived at this settlement yesterday and have fixed my camp in a spot the most centrical within the district. Being met by a number of the people, I required that they should appoint among themselves a certain number of the principal inhabitants with whom I might transact all business. This committee has been with me today. As they professed the warmest desire to live under the British Government, I strongly recommended to them to take up arms for their own defence, but this they declined, wishing rather to be considered as prisoners. I believe in this instance the sound of the word *parole* decided their judgement, for, with a very envious and nice distinction, they expressed their desire that their arms might be left with them and that they might be empowered to use them against the rebel militia of Mecklenburg County in case the latter should make inroads into the district. To this request they did not find me inflexible. I am very sure that if they were convinced any other district in the province had arrayed a militia, they would immediately follow the example, but they fear to take a step which they imagine others have refused. I think it would be very expedient that Mr Rugeley[11] (if he can be spared) should come hither before I quit the place. The idea of an administration of justice by a conservator of the peace is very pleasing to them, and I think Mr Rugeley may induce them to stand forth in support of that regularity. They are apprehensive here that they shall be troubled by the North Carolina militia and by the Catawba Indians[12]. Many people have quitted

---

[11] Although nothing in his background suggested a marked partiality for loyalism before the fall of Charlestown, Henry Rugeley was by early August appointed colonel of a royal militia regiment in the Camden District. Beginning with a store in Charlestown dealing in general merchandise and country produce, he had gone on to acquire property in the interior. On one such tract just north of Camden he constructed Rugeley's Mills, where he employed twenty slaves. It consisted of a sawmill, gristmill, two bolting mills, a waterwheel, tanyard, store and several log houses. Nearby he built 'Clermont', a dwelling described by one contemporary as 'elegant'. Rugeley is chiefly remembered, not for his minimal contribution to the war effort, but for the manner of his abject surrender to the enemy. Surrounded in his fortified post at the Mills, and faced with a fake cannon made of a pine log, he and 103 rank and file submitted on 1st December without firing a shot. Exchanged in 1781, he sailed the following year for Jamaica after his property was confiscated by act of the revolutionary Assembly. He was later removed from the act, amerced, and permitted to return to South Carolina, where most of his lands were put into trust for the benefit of his many creditors. (Lambert, *SC Loyalists, passim*; Ward, *The War of the Rev*, ii, 745)

[12] The Catawbas were a small tribe occupying a tract fifteen miles square mostly south and east of the point where the Catawba River enters South Carolina. They had been confirmed in possession of this land by the Treaty of Augusta in 1763. Small pox and whiskey had done much to reduce their numbers. In 1700 they were said to have 1,500 warriors, in 1750 only 400, and in 1787 only 150. During the present conflict they sided with the revolutionaries. In 1780 a small party was with Sumter during the action at Hanging Rock, another reportedly

Charlotteburg and retired in arms to the pass in the mountains near Salisbury; to induce them to behave peaceably I have sent them an address, a copy of which is enclosed. I have taken the liberty of mentioning your Lordship's name in it, but it was on a point which I knew to be accordant with your sentiments. I took this step principally on account of a number of people who came in to me from North Carolina and who, on account of their families, cannot well remain with the army till it should penetrate thither. I have recommended to them to remain quietly at home for the present, and they think my paper may secure them from molestation. The Catawba Indians have retired into North Carolina with their families and every thing which they could carry away. Lest they should be troublesome by coming down to plunder for support, I have empowered the committee here to assure them that, if they return to their settlement and behave quietly, they shall receive protection but that, if they commit any act of hostility, their settlement shall be utterly destroyed. As they have good crops on the ground and fled from an apprehension that a body of Cherokees were advancing with some detachment of our troops, I dare say they will return. I do not see that by prolonging my stay here any advantage can accrue, nor do I at present observe any point to be gained by advancing further. Therefore, if nothing particular happens or if I do not receive your Lordship's orders to the contrary, I shall in three or four days set out for Camden. The country, tho' thickly settled, is poor in itself and much drained. I am regularly supplied with cattle, tho' even in that article they plead poverty, but the neighborhood is totally destitute of grain or any kind of dry forage. I send five waggons tomorrow for a reinforcement of provisions, upon which head I have written to Captain Ross. I have this day written to Lt Colonel Turnbull. The inhabitants here insist that the party which attacked Leonard and his companions were not disaffected to the King and only defended their property against the unwarranted depredations of a set of men who have long lived in a loose manner; they wish much that evidence should be heard upon it.[13]

I have the honor to be, my Lord, with sincere respect and affection
Your very faithful servant

RAWDON
Colonel, Volunteers of Ireland

Enclosure
Address to the inhabitants of Charlotte, 11th June 1780 2(127): ACS

To the Inhabitants of Charlotteburg, North Carolina

Being informed that many of the inhabitants of Charlotteburg and its neighborhood have deserted their plantations thro' apprehension of suffering for their late association, I think it necessary to give them the following intimation.

---

    joined Davie, and in 1781 some thirty or more were with Greene. The rest of the tribe sought refuge in Virginia when Cornwallis advanced to their settlement in September 1780. (Wallace, *South Carolina*, 6; Douglas Summers Brown, *The Catawba Indians: The People of the River* (University of South Carolina Press, 1966), 251, 269, 270)

[13] According to colonial land records, a David, John and Thomas Leonard were landowners in the vicinity of Broad River and Fishing Creek. The incident to which Rawdon refers may have been that at Mobley's Meeting House or, less likely, that at Alexander's Old Fields. (T W Lipscomb to the editor, 18th and 22nd August 2006)

It is the generous wish of Lt General Earl Cornwallis to reclaim rather than to subdue the country, to incline the inhabitants to peace by giving them time and encouragement to consider their own interest rather than to make them sigh for it from suffering the scourges of war.

In obedience to the instructions which I have received from his Lordship, I do earnestly recommend to the inhabitants of the district above mentioned to return immediately to their farms, where they shall gather their crops without fear or interruption, provided always that they do demean themselves peaceably and do not attempt to distress either in person or property any friend to Government either in their own or in the neighboring settlements.

After this warning, should any person be unadvised enough to foment further disturbance in the country or to instigate his neighbors to a ruinous and unavailing shew of opposition, to him alone must be charged the severities which such misconduct may draw upon the district.

Given at Waxhaw this eleventh of June 1780
RAWDON

§ - §

3 - Between Cornwallis and McArthur

Cornwallis to McArthur, 14th June 1780 *77(10): C*

Camden
14th June 1780

Major McArthur
71st Regiment

Sir

I inclose to you two proclamations, one issued by the Commissioners, the other by the Commander in Chief. They do not affect the plan which I gave you for regulating the province, except in the article of paroles — all those given by persons not in a military line, that is, not serving in the army or militia, being cancelled on the 20th of this month. It must, however, make no difference as to legislators and magistrates, or those who have taken away the lives of the innocent and well affected, for, altho' many of the Assembly men, magistrates etc may not prove guilty of this charge, yet it is very necessary that they should remain prisoners on parole or otherwise 'till their conduct can be enquired into. The paroles of all other persons who have not acted in a military line are cancelled, of course, by the General's proclamation.

I have certain information that one *Mason*[14] at Long Bluff[15] about sixteen miles from your post down the Pedee is in possession of some property of Governour Rutledge's, which, by letter a few days ago from the Governour, he was directed if possible to dispose of for hard money. My authority for this fact is undoubted. You will therefore take what steps you think proper with Mr Mason. I have delayed sending any thing to you, being in hourly expectation of hearing from you. However, I shall send some rum and salt in a day or two if I hear nothing.

I am, sir,
Your most obedient and faithfull servant

[CORNWALLIS]

[*Subscribed:*]

Whatever Mr Mason may say, I am sure of the fact I have mentioned. You must therefore be very peremptory in insisting on his giving up the Governor's property.

McArthur to Cornwallis, 13th June 1780   *2(141): ALS*

Camp at Cheraw Hill[16]
June 13th 1780

My Lord

I have just time to inform your Lordship by Captain Treville[17] that I arrived here the 9th.

---

[14] A prominent inhabitant of St David's Parish, Charles Mason had contributed £15 at the beginning of 1771 to the committee set up to consider ways and means of encouraging domestic manufactures and the non-importation of tea and other luxury goods. He had since served for a time in the 5th South Carolina Continental Regiment. Now lying low, he would continue to do so until 1782, when, the fate of the war decided, he would act as a commissary for Marion. (Gregg, *The Old Cheraws*, 159, 410; Moss, *SC Patriots*, 663)

[15] Long Bluff was so named from its being one of the longest bluffs on the Pee Dee, extending without break for some three miles. (Gregg, op cit, 118)

[16] Cheraw Hill had been built about 1766 on land granted to Ely Kershaw. Being at the head of navigation on the Pee Dee, with an extensive and fertile country to be developed, and mainly dependent on it for supplies, it was in a particularly advantageous location from the standpoint of trade. As late as 1792 it is said to have contained no more than a dozen dwelling houses. (Gregg, op cit, 118, 119)

[17] A Frenchman in the revolutionary service, Jean François de Treville (?-1790) had served as a captain in the 4th South Carolina Continental (Artillery) Regiment since at least June 1777. On 3rd February 1779 he took part under Moultrie in repulsing the British in the action on Port Royal Island, where he gallantly commanded one of the artillery pieces and did great execution. Nine months later he was wounded in the assault on Savannah. Now, having been captured at the capitulation of Charlestown, he was acting very much as a soldier of fortune, being on his way back to Cornwallis with intelligence from the north. In the ensuing months he would continue to act as a paid spy for the British before being exchanged in June 1781 under the cartel with Greene. On 30th

A flagg was sent, which met me a few miles from this place, but the dragoons and Harrison's people, whom I detached the night before, were already in possession of this Hill. The flagg was totally inadmissible. I therefore gave only a verbal message and went next morning with all that was mounted to the court house at Long Bluff sixteen miles down the Pedee, where I met General McIntosh[18] and several of the principal inhabitants, who immediately submitted and gave their paroles. Most of the rebel officers of the militia regiment of this district have come in and given their paroles. The Colonel (Hicks[19]) is not yet come in; his wife was with me this day and promised to use her endeavours for that purpose. I am busy in taking paroles and forming a militia. The country people in general seem desirous to return to their allegiance and form a militia as the only means to prevent plunder from a banditti that are robbing indiscriminately. I have sent an officer's party to the court house to be at hand to support Dr Mills[20], whom I have prevailed with to take the command of the militia. He was formerly in the 46th Regiment and is a man of good character. He has been more than once elected to their Assembly but always declined acting. We are plentifully supplied with

---

September 1783 he would be promoted by brevet to major in the Continental line. Although perhaps suspected, his duplicity was not to come to light until many years after his death. (Heitman, *Historical Register*, 195; Garden, *Anecdotes* (2nd series), 178-9; Johnson, *Traditions*, 211-2; Boatner, *Encyclopedia*, 65; *The Cornwallis Papers*)

[18] Alexander McIntosh was a Scots Presbyterian who had settled in the late 1750s on the eastern side of the Pee Dee a few miles below Long Bluff in the Welch Neck. Said to have been the first of the early planters who brought slavery to the region, he amassed a large fortune. A handsome, decisive man of commanding presence, better educated than was common in his day, he was appointed a Justice of the Peace in 1761 and commissioned a captain of militia four years later. On 17th June 1775 he was appointed to the majority of the 2nd regiment raised by the Provincial Congress before being promoted in 1776 to the lt colonelcy of the 5th regiment, which was transferred to the Continental line. Politically active too, he was a Member of the General Assembly, which in 1777 elected him to the Legislative Council. On the passing of the Militia Act in 1778, he was appointed a brigadier general in command of the eastern brigade. The following year, as Lt Colonel of the 5th Continental Regiment, he took a minor part in operations against the British. He would die in the Welch Neck on 18th November 1780, apparently of natural causes. (Gregg, *The Old Cheraws, passim*)

[19] Accompanied by nine relatives and eleven slaves, George Hicks (c. 1720-1793) moved from Virginia to the Welch Neck in 1747, where he had received a land grant of 4,450 acres. Amassing a large fortune, he was appointed a Justice of the Peace in 1756 and commissioned a captain of militia in 1762. A nascent revolutionary, he was in August 1775 Chairman of the Committee of Observation for St David's Parish and by December had become a major in the revolutionary militia of the Cheraws District. When a temporary revolutionary consitution was adopted for South Carolina in March 1776, he was commissioned a Justice of the Peace for his district before being returned to the General Assembly in a by-election five months later. By December 1777 he had become colonel of his militia regiment. A fair-weather friend to the revolutionary cause, he would by August 1780 remove with his family to Virginia and take no further part in the war. (Gregg, op cit, *passim*)

[20] Coming to North America in 1754 as surgeon to the 46th Regiment, William Henry Mills retired ten years later to South Carolina, where he became a substantial planter, owning 2,000 acres and a number of slaves on or near the Pee Dee. A popular figure, he was appointed Sheriff of the newly formed Cheraw District in 1773, stood in a by-election to the Provincial Congress in January 1776, and, when a new revolutionary constitution was adopted for South Carolina in 1778, served as Foreman of the Grand Jury of Cheraw District and was returned to the legislature as a Representative for St David's Parish. Accepting now the colonelcy of the Cheraw royal militia, he was soon to resign his commission after his regiment mutinied and no reliable men could later be embodied, events set out in these Papers, together with his subsequent path of pillage and the reasons for it. In January 1782 his property, which had been burnt to the ground, was confiscated by act of the revolutionary assembly. Shortly afterwards he is said to have migrated to New Providence in the Bahama Islands to resume planting, though other accounts say that he moved to Jamaica and became involved in the production of sugar. He was later compensated by the Crown for his losses. (Lambert, *SC Loyalists*, 116, 267; Gregg, op cit, 254, 288-9, 380-1; *The Cornwallis Papers*; Draper, *King's Mountain*, 373; Sabine, *Biographical Sketches*, ii, 84)

beef, indian meal and rum. I have encamp'd the battalion in an airy situation and covered their hatts with plank[21]. The day I got here we marched 27 miles without leaving a man behind — the reason was information received that a firing had been heard in this neighbourhood, from which I concluded our dragoons, who marched in the night, had met with opposition, but it was only a false alarm, though some attempts had been made to collect the militia for that purpose without effect. If this opportunity had not offered, I did not purpose to trouble your Lordship till I had setled the militia so as to enable them to preserve order, which is much wanted. The only obstacle is the want of people proper for officers from the rebellion's having been so universal, for the lower class are all desirous of being inrolled. I shall administer the oath of allegiance to all that are admitted into it. I suppose it will be governed by the militia laws in force during His Majesties Government before the rebellion broke out. These people have a great avidity for news. Some of the Charlestown papers sent here would produce a good effect. I thought to write a few lines only, but have insensibly proceeded far owing to Treville's horses being so long in getting ready.

I have the honor to be, my Lord,
Your Lordship's much obliged and most obedient humble servant

ARCH[D] McARTHUR
Major, 71st Regiment

McArthur to Cornwallis, 14th June 1780   2(155): ALS

Camp at Cheraw Hill
June 14th 1780

The Rt Hon Lt General Earl Cornwallis
Camden

My Lord

As I did myself the honor to write to you yesterday by Captain Treville, nothing material having happened since, I would not again so soon trouble your Lordship, only Major Harrison going to Camden on the recruiting duty was desirous I should write by him. Fellinghausen[22] wrote me a letter from North Carolina and was much surprised to find it had not come to hand; I this day received it safe. I am sorry to inform you that three of the dragoons deserted in the night of the 9th with their horses — two of them came from Polasky's at Savannah[23], the 3rd was of Delancey's — and the day after we got here a soldier of the 71st (an officer's

---

[21] *plank*: felt cloth for protection against the sun.

[22] *Fellinghausen*: the code name for a spy. See Clinton to Cornwallis, 20th May, p 48.

[23] Pulaski's Legion, a Continental cavalry corps commanded by Count Casimir Pulaski, a Polish nobleman, had taken part in the failed assault on Savannah by the French and revolutionaries on 9th October 1779. After Pulaski, a brigadier general, was mortally wounded in the assault, he was succeeded in command by Armand, a French nobleman and colonel in the corps. (Boatner, *Encyclopedia*, 900-1, 1128)

servant) was carried off by three lurking villains as he was looking for forage within a mile of the camp. The men are very healthy, and I am hopefull some of our convalescents from Charlestown are by this time got to Camden as well as the necessarys for the men, which are much wanted, for, though we fare well enough in point of provisions, no wearables can be procured.

I have the honor to be, my Lord,
Your Lordship's most obedient humble servant

ARCH[D] McARTHUR

Cornwallis to McArthur, 18th June 1780

77(15): C

Camden
18th June 1780

Major McArthur
71st Regiment

Dear Sir

I received the favour of your two letters by Mr T[revill]e and Major Harrison and am very glad to hear so good an account of your post. It was very fortunate that you found so proper a person to command the militia of the Cheraw District as Dr Mills. As soon as you can find a good man to be major, you may appoint Dr Mills to be lt colonel. I shall be much obliged to you if you will endeavour to find out proper field officers for the districts down the Pedee and on the coast and either appoint them yourself or, if you have any doubt, send me the best account you can get of them to Charles Town, whither I am going in two or three days and where I shall probably get some accurate account of George Town and its environs. I was much pleased to hear that you had captured a considerable quantity of rum and salt as those articles are not very plentifull at this place, our convoy having been long coming up and having met with considerable losses on the road. If you should seize any other articles of rebel property that cannot be immediately applied to the use of the troops under your command, you will take the opportunity of any returning waggons to send them to the Commissary of Captures at this place. Lord Rawdon will command here in my absence. You will please to communicate any material intelligence to him and let him know whether you wish that your post should be reinforced and how many men you can subsist untill the harvest.

I inclose all the news papers I have received and will give orders for your being constantly supplied with them. I know no more particulars of the action of the 17th April than you see.[24] A Mr Johnson[25] about 10 miles on this side of Cheraw Hill can direct you where

---

[24] Cornwallis is referring to an inconclusive engagement between the fleets of Rodney and de Guichen in the West Indies.

to find four hundred bushells of salt supposed to be rebel property. I fancy you must put on the appearance of forcing him to discover it.

I am etc

[CORNWALLIS]

McArthur to Cornwallis, 18th June 1780 *2(169): ALS*

Camp at Cheraw Hill
June 18th 1780

The Rt Hon Lt General Earl Cornwallis
Camden

My Lord

I did myself the honor to write to your Lordship on the 13th and 14th instant, and on the 16th I was honored with your Lordship's letter and the proclamations by Mr McBean[26]. The inhabitants appear much pleased with the terms offered by the Commissioners. I was at the court house at Long Bluff on the 15th and administered the oath of allegiance to about one hundred and fifty people. I told your Lordship I had appointed Dr Mills colonel of the regiment of militia in this district. I have since appointed Mr Gray[27], a Scotch gentleman, lt colonel and Mr Palmer[28], a moderate Tory from near Pon Pon, major. He has resided some time in this neighbourhood. These gentlemen are well respected and I have good hopes will render the militia usefull — at least with regard to preserving order and securing of property, which is much wanted. I must depend chiefly on their recommendations for proper

---

[25] Johnson shared such a common surname in South Carolina that he cannot be positively identified. He may have been James or John Johnson, both of whom lived in the Cheraw District and briefly served in the revolutionary militia in 1782. (Moss, *SC Patriots*, 502)

[26] Alexander McBean acted as an emissary between Cornwallis and McArthur. He had been commissioned on 15th March 1771 as a 2nd lieutenant in the Royal Artillery, from which he resigned on 21st October 1776 on being commissioned a lieutenant in the 2nd Battalion, 71st (Highland) Regiment. (*Royal Regiment of Artillery*, 13; *Army Lists*)

[27] Robert Gray acquired land on the Pee Dee in 1774. Apart from references in *The Cornwallis Papers*, little else is known about him other than that he wrote a thought-provoking commentary on the war in the Carolinas which appeared in the North Carolina University Magazine, I (1858) and the SCHGM, XI (1910). When in September 1780 William Henry Mills gave up all hope of raising a royal militia in the Cheraw District, Gray was appointed colonel in his place. He fared no better. Nevertheless, according to Cornwallis, he appeared 'a very sensible, spirited man', a view echoed by Balfour, to whom he seemed 'by much the best militia man I have seen'. In 1781 and 1782 he acted as Paymaster to the Royal Militia, at which time his estates were confiscated by act of the revolutionary assembly. (*The Cornwallis Papers*; Lambert, *SC Loyalists*, 116; Clark, *Loyalists in the Southern Campaign*, i, *passim*; Gregg, *The Old Cheraws*, 380)

[28] Of Palmer and lesser officers in Mills' regiment little is known. They with Mills and Gray were seized by their men and carried captive into North Carolina when McArthur quit Cheraw Hill on 24th July. (Lambert, *SC Loyalists*, 117; *The Cornwallis Papers*)

officers and have given Colonel Mills several warrants signed for him to fill up. Before I received your Lordship's letter, Mr Mason, understanding I had heard something about the Governor's effects, made an open confession. There is between thirty and forty pieces of blue Negroe cloth, a hogshead of rum, a litle coffee and some sugar, which is secured. I gave a litle memorandum on a loose paper to Major Harrison, signed with my initials, of a quantity of salt and rum that was likewise seized below the bluff and hid in a swamp; these goods are now coming up by water and shall be taken care of. They belonged to one Wade, son of the notorious Wade[29] of Anson Court House. He and his father are both fled, as are the principal leaders in that county. Colonel Love[30], who commanded a regiment of militia, is the only person of consequence in it who has come in. He gave his parole two days ago.

Yesterday Alex[r] McCraw from McClendon's Creek in Cumberland County came in and informed me that Duncan McCraw, who was lately sent by Governor Martin into North Carolina, was taken on his return in Chatham County by two men of the name of O'Neale and carried to Chatham Court House, and, as the express sent by Mr Conner Dowd of Deep River to McClendon's Creek inform'd, he was tried, condemned and said to be ordered for execution.[31] The man who brought this account was told that Duncan McCraw had a letter found upon him. This day one Watson, who lived near Smith's Ferry on Cape Fear River, came in from that neighbourhood, which he left on Friday, and says General Kaswell a few days ago arrived at his son's (Colonel Kaswell's[32]) camp the other side of Cape Fear River at the ferry of Cross Creek with 200 light horse and from 1000 to 2000 foot with some pieces

---

[29] A delegate from Anson County to the North Carolina Provincial Congress in 1775, Thomas Wade (1720-1786) was appointed by it colonel of the minute men (later revolutionary militia) in the Salisbury District. The following year he was returned to the new Provincial Congress which in December adopted a revolutionary constitution for North Carolina. Appointed by Governor Rutledge of South Carolina, he was from December 1780 to act as a contractor for the supply of provisions to Greene's army and would be assisted by his son as a purchasing commissary. At the same time he would be active in trying to suppress loyalists, particularly those on Drowning Creek and the Little Pee Dee towards Cape Fear River, but was not always successful, being routed in the actions at Cole's Bridge in March and at Bettis's Bridge in September. His grave lies in Mount Pleasant, some 50 yards west of the site of old Anson Courthouse. The town of Wadesboro, the present seat of Anson County, is named after him. (Hay ed, *Soldiers from NC*, 498, 500, 502; Wheeler, *Historical Sketches*, i, 72, 85; *The Greene Papers*, vi-ix, *passim*; Robinson, *NC Guide*, 410, 503)

[30] Like Thomas Wade, David Love was a delegate from Anson County to the North Carolina Provincial Congress in 1775, being appointed by it major of a company of minute men in his county. When the Congress reconvened in April 1776, he was promoted to the lt colonelcy of the militia there. Later that year he would be re-elected to the new Provincial Congress. (Wheeler, *Historical Sketches*, i, 77, 81, 85; Hay ed, *Soldiers from NC*, 498, 502)

[31] Duncan McCraw may have escaped the noose. Although variants and misspelling of Scots surnames do not enable him to be positively identified, a Duncan McCra (on one occasion spelt McCraw) was in August to be nominated for an ensigncy in the North Carolina Highland Regiment, and in September for a lieutenancy, but the regiment was never embodied. An Alexander McCra would be nominated for a captaincy in the same corps. Both were placed on the Provincial half-pay list at the close of the war. (Clark, *Loyalists in the Southern Campaign*, 409, 425-6, 469); Treasury 64/23(32) and WO 65/165(17) (National Archives, Kew))

[32] William, the son of Richard Caswell, had not reached his majority when in September 1775 he was commissioned an ensign in the 2nd North Carolina Continental Regiment, being promoted in April 1776 to captain in the 5th and serving there for two and a half years. Now a colonel in the North Carolina revolutionary militia, he was by March 1781 to be promoted to brigadier general of militia and command in the vicinity of Wilmington. In 1783 he would be awarded 1,280 acres of land for his service in the Continental line. (Lossing, *Pictorial Field-Book*, ii, 379, 380; Heitman, *Historical Register*, 148; *The Greene Papers*, vii, viii and ix, *passim*; Hay ed, *Soldiers from NC*, 78, 236)

of cannon, and that he was throwing up works t'other side that river. The guns, he says, were taken out of the *Walker* privateer. Watson had this account from other people; he was too well known to venture into their camp. From reports current I understood Lord Rawdon was gone to Charlotte Town, but I am pretty well informed he was not there three days ago. If not an improper request, I would be glad to know his post.

We are much obliged to your Lordship for your intention of sending us rum and salt, but you see we want neither and we have got some barrels of flour for the use of the officers. The soldier of the 71st who was carried off is returned. They took him no further than 20 miles and then allowed him to return, but not the horse. I did not explain to your Lordship my reason for sending the dragoons and Harrison's people so far before me to occupy this post. It was in consequence of advice received that some publick stores here were removing and nobody in arms. The information respecting the stores was groundless, there being none except some indian corn belonging to Mr Kershaw[33], which we now live upon. A Mr Miller[34] (absconded) has also left us a quantity of the same so that we apprehend no want till the new crop comes in.

I have the honor to be, my Lord,
Your Lordship's most obedient humble servant

ARCH^D McARTHUR

[*Subscribed:*]

I hope Captain Ross will send me some paper. Without it business will be at a stand.

§ - §

---

[33] As both Joseph and Ely Kershaw had had interests in Cheraw Hill, it is unknown to which of them McArthur is referring. They were Yorkshiremen from Sowerby who had migrated together to South Carolina in about 1755, bringing with them considerable wealth. Some three years later Joseph moved to Pine Tree Hill on the eastern side of the Wateree at the head of navigation. It was later renamed Camden. Here he built a large country store, developed a very extensive country trade, and purchased a good deal of adjoining land, becoming one of the most influential proprietors. A nascent revolutionary, he was returned to both the first and second Provincial Congresses, being in November 1775 appointed to a committee to report on the state of the colony and its defences. When a temporary revolutionary constitution for South Carolina was adopted in March 1776, he was elected by the General Assembly (as the Provincial Congress had reconstituted itself) to the Legislative Council, which was the upper house of the legislature. Between 1776 and 1780 he was also colonel of revolutionary militia in and about Camden but took no active part in military operations. Like Joseph, Ely had extensive property interests and was in 1766 granted the lands on which Cheraw Hill was built, setting up there a large trading establishment with his brother which was sold in 1774. With the coming of the revolution, Ely was in June 1775 commissioned a captain in the regiment of rangers raised by the Provincial Congress and was transferred with it to the Continental line in 1776. He resigned his commission in October 1777. Both Joseph and Ely are mistakenly said to have participated in the defence of Charlestown in 1780 and to have been captured there. In fact, both gave their paroles in the country and were required to remove to one of the off-shore islands. Presumably for activities incompatible with their paroles, they were transported off to Bermuda in August 1780, but Ely died of typhus on the passage. Joseph would be exchanged in 1781 and was elected to the revolutionary assembly at Jacksonborough. (Johnson, *Traditions*, 463-9; McCrady, *SC in the Rev 1775-1780* and *1780-1783, passim*; Drayton, *Memoirs*, ii, 239-241; Gregg, *The Old Cheraws*, 104, 118-9; Heitman, *Historical Register*, 330; *The Cornwallis Papers*)

[34] Miller has not been identified. The name was common in the Carolinas.

4 - Between Cornwallis and Turnbull

Turnbull to Cornwallis, 14th June 1780   2(147): ALS

Rocky Mount
June 14th 1780

The Rt Hon Lord Cornwallis

My Lord

In answer to your Lordship's proposal of joining three Carolina independent companies to the New York Volunteers, I hope you will be well assured that my zeal and attachment for His Majesty's Service will never be awanting to forward His interest.

If your Lordship will do me the honor to put any number of companies under my command, I will do my utmost to discipline them and give them every assisstance in my power, but I do imagine it wou'd not answer to enroll such people in a corps with ours, who are high disciplin'd and not indulged with the same conditions.

I do flatter myself, when this province is quieted, that your Lordship will espouse our cause by taking our case into consideration and if the service permitts to send us to our own province, where we not only wou'd have an opportunity of compleating the corps but our services in a place where we are known must exceed that of strangers.

When I speak of that matter, how it affects me personally, I really have scarce words to express it. There is surely a duty which a man owes his family, and if I see no relief after settling the peace and quiet of this province, I shall be drove to the dissagreable necessity to quit the service intirely.

Forgive me the expression. It may be improper language for an officer on duty, but I have already declared that I will see this service out and the peace of the province established. I dare venture to say your Lordship will have compassion for one in my situation.

I am with the greatest respect
Your Lordship's most obedient and most humble servant

GEO TURNBULL[35]

---

[35] George Turnbull (1734-1810) was a Scot who had seen twenty years' service in the British line, being a lieutenant and then a captain in the 60th (or Royal American) Regiment. From 1776 he began to serve on the Provincial establishment and was commissioned a captain in the Loyal American Regiment. For his intrepidity, particularly in the capture of Fort Montgomery on 6th October 1777, he was promoted to the lt colonelcy of the New York Volunteers with effect from the following day. Going south with his regiment late in 1778, he took part in the capture of Savannah and then distinguished himself during the siege of the town in 1779. Commanding now the post of Rocky Mount, he would ably withstand an assault on it by Sumter on 30th July. His later involvement in

Turnbull to Cornwallis, 15th June 1780   *2(158): ALS*

Rocky Mount
June 15th 1780

The Rt Hon Lord Cornwallis

My Lord

Captain Hook[36] and his party returned yesterday, having made a circular tour of about forty miles to the westward. The rebells who were embody'd fled so fast to the mountains that he could not come up with them. From information that some of them had taken post at Simson's Meeting, he surounded the house and, finding them gone, recoinoitring the roads which led to it, two men with rebell uniforms were discover'd running through a field of wheat. The militia fired upon them, killed one and wounded the other.

Colonel Patten[37], Bratten[38], Wynne[39] and a number of violent people have abandon'd their habitations. It is believed they are gone amongst the Cataba Indians, and some say that the Indians likewise have retired further back.

The rebells have propagated a story that we seize all their young men and send them to the Prince of Hesse. It is inconceivable the damage such reports has done.

---

    southern operations is set out in these Papers. When his regiment was disbanded at the close of the war, he was placed on the Provincial half-pay list. He was married to a daughter of Cornelius Clopper of New York and died at Bloomingdale, New Jersey. (*Army Lists*; Treasury 64/23(2), WO 65/164(31), and WO 65/165(2) (National Archives, Kew); Sabine, *Biographical Sketches*, ii, 367; Stevens, *Clinton-Cornwaliis Controversy*, ii, 460)

[36] Christian Huck had been a lawyer in Philadelphia. Joining the British at New York, he was commissioned a captain in Emmerich's Chasseurs (a corps which was disbanded in 1779) before transferring to the British Legion as a captain of horse. Criticized by revolutionaries for severity and profanity, he was to be killed in an action near Bratton's plantation on 12th July. (Sabine, *Biographical Sketches*, i, 552-3; Treasury 64/23(33) (National Archives, Kew); McCrady, *SC in the Rev 1775-1780*, 591-9; *The Cornwallis Papers*)

[37] Of Robert Patton little is known and little else is heard. In October he would be directed by Governor Rutledge to pay over to Sumter, who had just been commissioned a brigadier general of revolutionary militia, whatever public money might be in his hands. (Gregorie, *Sumter*, 110)

[38] A colonel of a revolutionary militia regiment in the New Acquisition, William Bratton (1743-1815) was already active, having dispersed a body of loyalists who had gathered at Mobley's Meeting House on 26th May. He would soon take part in the defeat of Huck before joining Sumter and being involved in the actions at Fish Dam Ford and Blackstocks. (McCrady, *SC in the Rev 1775-1780*, *passim*; Moss, *SC Patriots*)

[39] Richard Winn (1750-1818) had by 1771 moved from Virginia to the Back Country of South Carolina, purchasing lands near the future town of Winnsborough, which was named after him. A nascent revolutionary, he was in 1775 commissioned a 1st lieutenant in the regiment of rangers raised by the Provincial Congress, taking part in the action at Sullivan's Island on 28th June 1776. A few months later, when commanding Fort McIntosh, Georgia, he was captured with the fort, having put up a stout defence. By 1780 he had become colonel of a regiment of revolutionary militia in the Back Country and, going off with a number of his men, was soon to join Sumter and take part in the actions at Hanging Rock, Fish Dam Ford, and Blackstocks. In 1781 he would be elected to the revolutionary assembly at Jacksonborough and for many years afterwards would play a prominent role in political life. (*DAB*; Johnson, *Traditions*, 334-5; McCrady, *SC in the Rev 1775-1780* and *1780-1783*, *passim*)

Corn begins to be scarce. I have now about ten days' meal, but when that is out, I don't know which rout to take.

There is an Irish settlement at Turkey and Bullock Creek which abounds with provision but it is thirty miles westward. I do believe those fellows would be much the better for some troops to keep them in order for a little; they have been very violent.

It is difficult to support dragoons without corn. I am in hopes, if our mounted men arrive and the militia continue their good countenance when they meet here against[40] Saturday, that in such case we might spare the Legion altogether if your Lordship had any service for them.

I forgot to mention an iron works about fifty miles to the westward. It has been a refuge for runaways, a forge for casting ball and making rifle guns etc. I wou'd propose, with your Lordship's permission, to destroy this place. I think a small party might be found against Saturday at the muster that wou'd compleat this affair, sending some of our own officers and men with them.

I have given no receipts for any provisions as yet, but I fancy it will be necessary on some occasions to give receipts.

While I am writing, I have received a letter from Lord Rawdon dated yesterday. He mentions that he is about returning to Camden and that there is a body of rebell militia still in arms between Charlotteburgh and Salisbury, but, as he has no dragoons or mounted men, he says he has no chance of giving them a blow. I flatter myself your Lordship will see the necessity of dispersing those men, for, while such a body of rebells keeps in arms so near us, our militia affairs will not go well.

I have appointed one captain of militia at Cedar Creek untill your Lordship's pleasure is further known. Indeed he was the choice of the people and I thought him deserving.

I shall endeavour to make some arrangement on Saturday forenoon when I expect them all at Rocky Mount, but am much afraid I will not be able to get any body fit to make a field officer.

I have the honor to be with the greatest esteem and respect
Your Lordship's most obedient and most humble servant

GEO TURNBULL

---

[40] *against*: an obsolete temporal preposition meaning 'towards'.

Cornwallis to Turnbull, 16th June 1780 77(11): C

Camden
16th June 1780

Sir

I have just received your letter and am sorry to find that meal grows scarce already. I shall send you some salt and rum, and your cavalry and infantry as soon as they arrive. I should then advise your going to the Irish settlement you mention and staying there as long as you find it convenient and bringing back some meal to your present post. If the horses of the Legion suffer for want of corn, I wish you would send back immediately some of the best of them, and the remainder as soon as your people join you. I likewise approve of your destroying the iron works and beg you will take upon yourself to act in all those matters as it shall appear to you to be best for the King's Service. You will give permission to the militia to do what they please with the plantations abandoned by the rebels. If they can get in the crops and turn them to their own use, it will be the best plan, but if it is more convenient now and then to destroy one, I have no objection, only I strictly forbid and will severely punish any act of cruelty to their wives and children. You are to give receipts for provisions to all friends, and I would have you take the utmost pains to settle a militia and if possible to appoint a major commandant to each district where the enemy had a field officer. A very plain man with a good character and tolerable understanding will do. He is to act more in a civil than a military character, and as we are not at present troubled with law, all that is required of him is to have sense enough to know right from wrong, and honesty enough to prefer the former to the latter. I send you a form of a commission[41] which you may sign and deliver to the field officer 'till I can have an opportunity of sending one. I do not apprehend any great danger from the enemy's militia which you mention said to be posted between Charlottetown and Salisbury. They are above an hundred miles from us and would certainly retire on our approach; and the country between us and them is a perfect desart. I think whilst we keep, which I promise to do, a strong post at this place with a large body of cavalry, the militia on this frontier of South Carolina need not fear being properly supported. I wish you would endeavour to explain this to them and to instill as much confidence as possible into them.

I am, sir,
Your most obedient and most humble servant

[CORNWALLIS]

[*Subscribed:*]

I inclose you two late proclamations. They do not materially affect my plan. Only those who have not served in the army or militia, or acted as magistrates, will be released from their paroles on the 20th of this month according to Sir Henry's proclamation of the 3rd of June.

---

[41] *a form of commission..*: no extant copy.

Turnbull to Cornwallis, 16th June 1780 2(162): ALS

Rocky Mount
June 16th 1780

The Rt Hon Earl of Cornwallis

My Lord

Yesterday afternoon I was favour'd with a visit from a Mr Floyd[42] who lives about sixty miles to the westward. He appears to be a sensible man and a staunch friend to Government – has been persecuted and lain some time in Charlestown jail. He brought about thirty men with him, all volunteers, to serve the King.

I appointed his son captain of the company, as he was their choice, and I thought I cou'd not get so good a man to command that upper district as Mr Floyd, so that I appointed him colonel.

Our joy was very soon interrupted by a couple of expresses, who assured us that a party of rebels had sally'd forth from the iron works and had gone into the settlement of Mr Floyd and his company and were tearing every thing to pieces.

I immediately order'd Captain Hook of the Legion to get ready, that with Captain Floyd's company and the other militia which we cou'd assemble it was necessary to give these fellows a check. The weather prevented their setting off last night, but they took the morning early. I have taken the liberty to give Captain Hook orders to destroy the iron works. They are the property of a Mr Hill[43], a great rebell. I hope the marching of this party will do something towards quieting our frontier. Those rebels embody'd between Charlotburgh and Salisbury overawes great part of the country and keeps the candle of rebellion still burning. Lord Rawden's retreat, I dare say, confirms them in the belief that we are only here for a few days.

---

[42] Matthew Floyd (?-1826) was an Irishman who had migrated from Pennsylvania to the Back Country many years before. A settler on a branch of upper Broad River, he had been a Justice of the Peace and militia captain before the revolution. In 1775 he was dispatched by the loyalists to seek advice from Lord William Campbell, the royal Governor, after a treaty was concluded ending hostilities between them and nascent revolutionaries at Ninety Six. After conversing with Campbell on the *Tamar* in Charlestown harbour, he was seized on landing and jailed by order of the Council of Safety. On being appointed a colonel of the royal militia in 1780, he took command of the regiment between and about the Tyger and Enoree Rivers, but apart from some sixty men, all went over to the enemy. He and the rest of his men were fortunate not to be with Patrick Ferguson at the Battle of King's Mountain. (Lambert, *SC Loyalists*, 119; McCrady, *SC in the Rev 1775-1780*, 93, 94, 590; *The Cornwallis Papers*; Stevens, *Clinton-Cornwallis Controversy*, ii, 430)

[43] William Hill (1741-1816) was born in the north of Ireland and migrated to Pennsylvania before soon moving on to the Back Country of South Carolina in 1762. Part owner of the iron works on Allison's Creek, he was now to have it destroyed by Huck with the loss of his home, mills and ninety slaves. Joining Sumter as a lt colonel of militia, he would take part in the actions at Rocky Mount, Hanging Rock, where he was wounded in the arm, Fish Dam Ford, and Blackstocks. A vigorous personality, very influential in his community, he was elected in 1781 to the revolutionary assembly at Jacksonborough and after the war continued to serve many terms in the South Carolina legislature, where he spoke often. He is buried in an unmarked grave at Bethal Presbyterian Church, York. (*DAB*; McCrady, *SC in the Rev 1775-1780* and *1780-1783*, passim; Draper, *King's Mountain*, passim)

I confess, my Lord, I have no particular attachment to any part in South Carolina but I wou'd not wish to leave the worst spot in it untill the neck of rebellion was broke.

In my former letter I mentioned to your Lordship that we had meal for about ten or twelve days. When that is done we shall be much at a loss.

The inhabitants are constantly teezing me for proclamations. I wish your Lordship cou'd send me some.

I meant tomorrow to have had a general muster of the militia to arrange them in the best manner I could. This alarm will discompose it a good deal.

I am with great esteem
Your Lordship's most obedient and most humble servant

GEO TURNBULL

Turnbull to Cornwallis, 19th June 1780   2(171): ALS

Rocky Mount
June 19th 1780

The Rt Hon the Earl of Cornwallis

My Lord

I have the pleasure to acquaint your Lordship that, by a letter from Captain Huck of the British Legion dated yesterday some miles this side of the iron works, that the rebells were assembled at that place about one hundred and fifty strong; that he with his detachment of the Legion and about sixty militia attacked them; the rebells had time to pull down a bridge very near the iron works, which impeded them for some time; that, repairing the bridge, they were lucky enough to overtake their rear, killed seven, and took four prisoners; the rest fled to the mountains.

I am likewise to inform your Lordship that Captain Huck has compleatly destroy'd the iron works, which has been the head quarters of the rebells in arms for some time past.

I am taking every step to arrange the militia, although my progress is but slow as most of their former officers are run off. I can't get people to warn them and bring them together, yet I expect in the course of this week to do a good deal.

I beg leave to put your Lordship in mind that, when our detachment passes, we may not be forgot in the articles of rum and salt.

Some more arms, cartridges, flints and a barrell of powder are likewise wanted.

A Captain Henderson[44] was taken some days ago. He was a great persecutor and expected to be hanged. Some of his friends told him that he shou'd do something in favor of Government to intitle him to be restored to favor. He proposed to seize Governor Rutledge and bring him a prisoner. I told him, if he succeeded, he shou'd be handsomely rewarded, and have sent him of to try his luck. He assured me that Rutledge and Twigg[45] from Georgia were at a widdow woman's house near Salisbury about ten days ago and that his guard had left him.

Some times great villains will do services. At all events I thought it best to put it to the tryal.

I have the honor to be with the greatest respect and esteem
Your Lordship's most obedient and most humble servant

GEO TURNBULL

§ - §

5 - Paroles

Parole of Daniel Huger, 2nd June 1780[46] 2(78): DS

I, Daniel Huger of the Province of South Carolina, acknowledge myself to be prisoner to His Majesty's troops and hereby promise upon my parole of honour that I will repair to James Island, John's Island, Edisto Island or Edings's Island in the said province on or before the fifteenth day of July next (notifying the place of my residence to the commissary of prisoners

---

[44] Probably John Henderson (1756-?), who was born in Rowan County, North Carolina, and captured at this time. Artfully escaping the clutches of Turnbull, he went off to become a captain under Sumter, being present in the actions at Rocky Mount, Fishing Creek, Fish Dam Ford, and Blackstocks. He is said to have also taken part in the Battles of King's Mountain and Cowpens. In later life he would move to Georgia, Tennessee and Alabama. (Moss, *SC Patriots*, 435)

[45] John Twiggs (1750-1816) was born in Maryland and brought to Briar Creek, Georgia, between 1755 and 1757. A carpenter or millwright by trade, he commanded a company of Burke County militia in the Cherokee War of 1776 and became colonel of his regiment in June 1778. After being involved in the action at Fishdam Ford on 9th November 1780, he was to take part in the action at Blackstocks eleven days later, asssuming overall command of the revolutionary forces when Thomas Sumter was wounded. On 4th December he and Elijah Clark entered the Long Cane settlement but failed to persuade Williamson, Pickens and most of the disaffected there to join them. One week later they and their men were routed by Isaac Allen commanding 150 of the Ninety Six garrison and some 270 royal militia. Promoted to brigadier general of militia in August 1781, Twiggs was to become a wealthy man after the war, accumulating property with the initial purchase of nearly 1,500 acres of confiscated land just below Augusta. (*DGB*; Gregorie, *Sumter*, 116, 123; Bass, *Gamecock*, 108-9; *The Cornwallis Papers*)

[46] The paroles of the following persons, which are couched in the same or similar terms, are also extant from this period: James Beames (2(174)), Charles Cantey (2(49)), Robert Ellison (unsigned) (2(151)), Robert Goodwin (2(85)), Robert Heriot (2(233)), Ely Kershaw (2(121)), Joseph Kershaw (2(120)), Richard Richardson Jr (2(152)), James Sinkler (2(49)), John Winn (2(103)), and John Wyly (2(122)).

at Charlestown within two days after my arrival) and there remain untill regularly exchanged or permitted or ordered to remove, and that while prisoner I will not write, speak or act directly or indirectly against His Majesty's interest, and that I will surrender myself at any time and at any place when ordered by the Commander in Chief or any other of His Majesty's officers.

D^L HUGER[47]

Earl Cornwallis's Quarters
2nd June 1780

Witness:

GEO TURNBULL
Lt Colonel

BANASTRE TARLETON
Lt Colonel, British Legion

§ - §

---

[47] Of Huguenot descent, Daniel Huger (1741-1799) was born on Cooper River to an influential planting family whose forebears had been settled there for generations. One of four brothers, all of whom were to take an active part in the revolutionary movement, he was educated in Europe. When a new revolutionary constitution was adopted for South Carolina in 1778 he was elected to the General Assembly and by 1780 had become a member of the Privy Council. On 13th April 1780, as the noose tightened round Charlestown, he made his way through the lines with Governor Rutledge and two other Privy Councillors so that, should the town fall, there might remain a nucleus of revolutionary government in South Carolina. Events thereafter might have led him to play a pivotal role in maintaining revolutionary legitimacy, for the constitution provided that in the case of the Governor or Lt Governor (Gadsden, who remained in Charlestown) being sick or absent from the seat of government the Governor might empower any one Privy Councillor to act in his place. Huger would, however, be guilty of a gross dereliction of duty. Having progressed as far as Rugeley's Mills and evaded capture there by Tarleton, he suddenly abandoned the revolutionary cause, turning himself in at Camden and entering into a parole. Some three and a half months later he would go so far as to take protection, swearing allegiance to the Crown, and would subscribe to a notice in the *Royal South-Carolina Gazette* which congratulated Cornwallis on his victory at Camden, execrated the revolution, and extolled the virtues of British government. The revolutionaries would exact no price for his actions, subjecting him to neither confiscation nor amercement. Indeed, he would in later life be returned to serve two terms in Congress. Described as 'not a very lovely person in his private life', he is summarised, unsurprisingly, as not 'a very effective person' politically. (*Appletons'*; Rogers Jr, *Georgetown County*, 175-9; McCrady, *SC in the Rev 1775-1780* and *1780-1783, passim*; Wallace, *South Carolina*, 306)

PART THREE

Incipient Unrest

Revolutionary Forces from the North

26th June to 15th August 1780

CHAPTER 10

Introduction to the rest of Part Three

In this Part we see how British ascendancy in South Carolina began so soon to unravel in the face of internal uprisings and an external threat.

By mid July Major General Johann Kalb had advanced from the northward to Coxe's Mill on Deep River, North Carolina. Under his command were 1,400 Delaware and Maryland Continentals, three companies of artillery, and Armand's corps of 60 horse and 60 infantry. Also in the field were some 1,450 poorly armed Virginia militia besides a body of 1,200 North Carolina militia under Major General Richard Caswell.

Fearing that his post at Cheraw Hill might be taken out in detail, Rawdon promptly ordered McArthur to withdraw with the 71st to Black Creek and eventually to the vicinity of Camden. It was an inevitable but fateful decision. Apart from Georgetown, the High Hills of Santee, Kingstree and the high road south and north of Camden, the British would never again command the expanse of territory to the east of the Santee and Wateree. Forays into it would be made, for example by Harrison, Tarleton, Watson, and Wemyss, but for all practical purposes British authority there had ended.

Elsewhere in South Carolina there appeared on the scene a revolutionary leader whom the British considered one of their greatest plagues. Born in Virginia, Thomas Sumter (1734-1832) had served in the ranks during the Seven Years' War. In 1763 he was imprisoned for debt in Staunton but escaped and fled Virginia to South Carolina. Opening a country store midway between Eutaw Springs and Nelson's Ferry, he prospered and three years later purchased a 200-acre plantation to the south of the Santee in Berkeley County. Shortly after, he married a fairly wealthy widow and moved across the river to a plantation on the Great Savannah in St Mark's Parish. A slave owner, he went on to become an extensive land speculator and man of property. As the crisis with Britain deepened, he was elected to the Provincial Congresses, served as Richardson's aide-de-camp during the Snow Campaign, and in February 1776 was commissioned lt colonel commandant of a rifle regiment. While commanding it in the Cherokee expedition later that year, he was transferred with it to the

Continental line. By then a member of the General Assembly, as the Provincial Congress had reconstituted itself, he would be re-elected to it when a more permanent revolutionary constitution was adopted in 1778. In the same year he resigned his Continental commission and returned to his neglected private affairs. Two years later he took no part in opposing Clinton, but when a house of his was set alight by Tarleton during the pursuit of Buford, it reputedly 'roused the spirit of the lion'. Repairing to Tuckaseegee Ford on the northern border between the Carolinas, he was elected leader of a band of irregulars and began to style himself as a general. After sending parties in mid July across Broad River, he led 500 men to attack Turnbull's post at Rocky Mount on the 30th. Repulsed, he attacked with Davie the post at Hanging Rock one week later. Again repulsed, he nevertheless did great execution, demolishing the Prince of Wales's American Regiment, which ceased from then to be an effective fighting force. Later, on 15th August, he marched down the Catawba with 700 men and 100 Continentals, capturing Cary's redoubt, about thirty prisoners, a number of horses, and thirty-eight waggons filled with supplies. During the same day he went on to capture about seventy regulars going from Ninety Six to Camden.

Wishing to act independently, Sumter was disinclined to cooperate wholeheartedly with Gates and Greene, the Continental commanders-in-chief, for example by uniting his force with those under their immediate command. Proud and supercilious, though affectionate, open-handed and loyal to his friends, he possessed a sarcastic tongue, but one tempered with a sense of humour. Yet it is a dark side of his nature which comes to the fore in coming months, for, as we shall see, he consistently displayed a marked streak of ruthlessness which did not scruple to employ measures such as cold-blooded murder on a grand scale in furtherance of his ends. We shall return to him later.

As other bands of revolutionary irregulars, notably ones under Clark, McDowell and Shelby, took to the field north of the Congaree and Saluda, the British hold on the Back Country also began to weaken, Amid the rising unrest there, four events in particular exemplified the worsening situation: on 12th July Captain Huck of the British Legion, while commanding a party near Bratton's plantation, was defeated and killed; on 15th July Prince's Fort on a branch of the North Fork of Tyger River had to be abandoned by Captain Dunlap of Ferguson's corps after he found himself greatly outnumbered in an action at Earle's Ford on North Pacolet; on 30th July the royal militia surrendered Thicketty Fort near Goucher Creek without firing a shot; and on 8th August Dunlap, and later Ferguson, took part in an action near Cedar Spring, eventually forcing a large body of revolutionary irregulars to flee over Pacolet River.

Events began to take a turn for the worse in the Low Country[1] too. On 8th July Major Wemyss occupied Georgetown with no more than half of the 63rd Regiment, but when the country to the north was overrun by revolutionary irregulars after the withdrawal of McArthur from Cheraw Hill, he found it out of his power to attain his principal objective, the formation of a battalion of royal militia in the Georgetown District. Therefore ordered by Cornwallis to join the rest of the 63rd on the High Hills of Santee, he and his men quit Georgetown on 9th August. By then bands of 30 or 40 revolutionary irregulars had threatened even the Low

---

[1] For a vivid description of the Low Country and its people, see Carl Bridenbaugh, *Myths & Realities: Societies of the Colonial South* (Atheneum NY, 1976), ch II.

Country west of the Santee, the area most securely controlled by the British.

Throughout large parts of South Carolina we begin to see the revolutionary irregulars adopting what would become a consistent practice of 'breaking up', as they termed it, the habitations of loyalists, whom they detained, drove off, or, as the months progressed, maltreated, mutilated or murdered in cold blood. 'Breaking up', or plundering as the British called it, inevitably attracted many in pursuit of gain to the revolutionary cause, but the underlying aim was of course to cleanse the areas in which the revolutionaries operated, or over which they exerted control, of members of the opposing party, who might act against them.

In their own way the British were rigorous too. In September the homes of many who had taken up arms would be burnt by Wemyss and Moncrief during their punitive expeditions to the east of the Wateree and Santee. Elsewhere the estates of others who, *inter alia*, had gone off to the enemy or had continued openly to avow rebellious principles would soon become liable to sequestration, and in the meantime supplies were appropriated wholesale from those estates. A measure of supplies was also appropriated from the estates of the disaffected who remained quiescently at home, or who were on parole or in confinement, in lieu of their service in the royal militia. In addition, unauthorised plundering was practised by loyalists, regulars and British American troops.

Increasingly apparent in Part Three is the fragility of the royal militia. Ill armed and at times slow to turn out, it displayed a patchwork of confidence, timidity, fidelity, and disloyalty in the face of the revolutionary forces taking to the field. Precipitated by McArthur's withdrawal from Cheraw Hill, Mills' entire Pee Dee Regiment promptly defected, whilst in the Back Country most of Turner's Rocky Mount and Floyd's Enoree-Tyger Regiments did likewise. Perhaps Fisher's Orangeburg Regiment was the most zealous, but other regiments in the Back Country were for the most part hesitant and in need of support, particularly those toward the North Carolina line. Overall, the fighting qualities of the royal militia were inevitably diminished, first by admitting disaffected persons, and second by incorporating Quiet men, as Ferguson termed them, to the extent of no more than one for every three loyalists.

Amid the mounting unrest the command at Camden could not have been in safer hands. The eldest son of the Earl of Moira in the Irish peerage, Francis Lord Rawdon was only in his twenty-sixth year. Educated at Harrow and University College, Oxford, he entered the army as an ensign on 7th August 1771, distinguished himself as a lieutenant at the Battle of Bunker Hill, and took part as a captain in the New York campaign. While at Philadelphia he raised at his own expense a British American regiment called the Volunteers of Ireland, of which he became Colonel. Promoted to the regular rank of lt colonel on 15th June 1778, he began to serve as Clinton's Adjutant General, but in autumn 1779 the two quarrelled and Rawdon quit the post.

Charged by some with being a martinet, Rawdon emerges from these Papers as a discriminating officer of outstanding military ability. Combining high courage with keen strategic and tactical awareness, he dealt unerringly with every situation, whether it called for exceptional enterprise, due caution or retrenchment, or simply the routine and efficient conduct of his command.

Like Balfour, Rawdon was rewarded for his service in South Carolina by promotion to the regular rank of colonel and by appointment as an aide-de-camp to the King. In addition he was created an English peer by the style of Lord Rawdon of Rawdon in the County of York. He soon became a lifelong friend and confidant of the Prince of Wales. In June 1793 he succeeded to the Earldom of Moira on the death of his father, and one year later distinguished himself when as a major general he commanded an expeditionary force of 7,000 men in the Low Countries. Promoted to full general in September 1803, he went on to serve briefly as a very popular Commander-in-Chief in Scotland. Opposed to Pitt, he did not achieve political office until February 1806 when as a member of the Ministry of All the Talents he began to serve for one year as Master of the Ordnance. It was, however, in India that he most notably added to his reputation, not only as a consummate military strategist, but also as a skilful politician and able administrator. Appointed Governor General and Commander-in-Chief in India on 18th November 1812, he landed at Calcutta eleven months later and served for nine years. During this period he established the supremacy of British power through most of the Indian sub-continent and was rewarded in February 1817 by elevation to the Marquisate of Hastings. While Governor and Commander-in-Chief at Malta, he died aboard HMS *Revenge* in Baia Bay off Naples on 28th November 1826.

An imposing figure with a stately manner, Rawdon was tall, dark, and in his younger years athletic. A full-length portrait of him by Sir Joshua Reynolds, painted in 1789-90, is in the Royal Collection.

Another exceedingly able British American officer soon succeeded to the command at Ninety Six in place of Balfour. As evinced by these Papers, John Harris Cruger, Lt Colonel of De Lancey's 1st Battalion, would gain a well deserved reputation for courage, activity, decisiveness, resolution, resourcefulness, vigilance, and exceptional leadership in the face of adversity. His measure was rightly taken by Alured Clarke, the officer commanding in Georgia and East Florida, when he observed to Cornwallis, 'If I may be allowed to judge from a very short acquaintance, I am convinced your Lordship will not be disappointed in your expectations from this gentleman, who will be greatly assisted by the zeal and good sense of Lt Colonel Allen and the harmony that subsists between them.' Isaac Allen, Lt Colonel of the 3rd Battalion, New Jersey Volunteers, would ably serve as Cruger's second throughout the coming months.

Writing to Cruger on 5th August, Cornwallis remarked, 'The keeping possession of the Back Country is of the utmost importance. Indeed, the success of the war in the Southern District depends totally upon it.' They are words which would come to haunt Cornwallis in 1781, when, as we shall see, he inexplicably forsook South Carolina and marched from Wilmington into Virginia.

A false calm continued to prevail in Georgia, where, according to the Governor, Sir James Wright, 'the flame of rebellion is pretty well extinguished at present, yet it may revive and break out again if we are not very circumspect.' A worrying problem were the settlers on the Ceded Lands. Hardy, numerous and ill disposed, they were ready to give trouble as soon as an opportunity offered. As we shall see, it would not be long before they rose.

Besides the small garrison of Savannah, the only military post in Georgia was at Augusta, the seat of the Indian trade for forty years. Between the coast and Augusta the Savannah

River was navigable by boats of sixty tons, but not for three or four months from mid September, and the journey was tedious, lasting on average more than three weeks. Occupying the village were 250 men of the King's Rangers, a British American regiment under the command of Lt Colonel Thomas Brown, who was also Superintendent of Indian Affairs in the Southern Department.

An inspirational leader, Brown had migrated only six years earlier from Yorkshire to Georgia, where, as he himself relates, he was savagely treated in the Up Country for his loyalism. A controversial figure, he in turn has been accused of severity.

Despite the approach of the British, the loyalists in North Carolina began to suffer worse than ever. Comprising a half to two-thirds of the population there, they had sat idly by, relying on the Crown to act, while nascent revolutionaries had organised themselves and put in place a framework of control which eventually usurped the royal government. Too late, the Scots Highlanders rose, but were defeated at the Battle of Moore's Creek Bridge in February 1776. Repression had by then become the order of the day and was so successful that loyalists were cowed into submission for the next four and a half years. Unwilling to forego their allegiance to the Crown, many were imprisoned, brought to the whipping post, banished, subjected to confiscation, and executed for treason, particularly under an Act of 1777. However, it was not so much the revolutionary authorities whom the loyalists came to fear as mobs of revolutionary irregulars who, unrestrained by concepts of civilised behaviour, took advantage of the disordered times and practised all sorts of enormities ranging from plundering and destruction of property to severe chastisement, murder, and rape. Lawlessness was rife, and nothing could be done by the revolutionary authorities to suppress it. Indeed, matters were so bad that many loyalists took to lying out in the swamps for safety.

Correspondents of the day were led by delicacy to cloud over the fact that rape and other sexual villainy were widely committed by the revolutionary irregulars of the Carolinas, and later writers tacitly followed suit. We owe it to Caruthers for peeling away the layers of obscuration, acquainted as he was with those who had lived through the war. Yet even he, though unmistakable in his meaning, could only bring himself to generalise when, for example, he described the treatment of Scots Highlanders in and near Cross Creek: '... individuals and irresponsible companies, who acted without any special authority, seemed to think that, because the Highlanders had risen in arms against the country and had been vanquished, they were at liberty to insult them, plunder them and trample upon them as they pleased. In this way a great many cruelties and outrages on decency were practised which were too disgusting to appear on the pages of history, and we pass them over with the names of the actors, leaving them to the imagination of the reader, but assuring him that when he has given his imagination full play he will hardly go beyond the reality.'

Though it is difficult to conceive, repression of North Carolina loyalists became even more severe in the summer of 1780, initiated when they rose prematurely in Tryon County and were defeated at Ramsour's Mill. Faced with joining the revolutionary militia or going to prison, Samuel Bryan and near 800 loyalists were forced to flee the forks of the Yadkin and joined McArthur at Cheraw Hill on 30th June.

In South Carolina the communication between Charlestown and Camden soon became a matter of concern. As Cornwallis observed to Rawdon, 'The great difficulty of our communication is that we can have no fixt posts on any of the rivers, or indeed in any part of the lower country. No way occurs to me but sending some of those loose corps to make incursions and intimidate.' Partly for this purpose, though ultimately bound for Camden, Tarleton and Hanger marched from Charlestown on 31st July with thirty of the British Legion cavalry. Battered by violent winds and heavy rains which had been raging for the past eight days, the Low Country was so completely flooded that the detachment did not cross the Santee at Lenud's Ferry until 6th August. It then moved on to Black River to punish those in that quarter who had revolted. While there, an incident occurred which exemplified the skill of American riflemen. It was described by Hanger many years later: 'Colonel, now General Tarleton and myself were standing a few yards out of a wood, observing the situation of a part of the enemy which we intended to attack. There was a rivulet in the enemy's front, and a mill on it, to which we stood directly with our horses' heads fronting, observing their motions. It was an absolute plain field between us and the mill, not so much as a single bush on it. Our orderly-bugle stood behind us, about three yards, but with his horse's side to our horses' tails. A rifleman passed over the mill-dam, evidently observing two officers, and laid himself down on his belly, for in such positions they always lie to take a good shot at a long distance. He took a deliberate and cool shot at my friend, at me, and the bugle-horn man.[2] Now observe how well this fellow shot. It was in the month of August and not a breath of wind was stirring. Colonel Tarleton's horse and mine, I am certain, were not anything like two feet apart, for we were in close consultation how we should attack with our troops, which laid 300 yards in the wood and could not be perceived by the enemy. A rifle ball passed between him and me. Looking directly to the mill, I evidently observed the flash of the powder. I directly said to my friend, "I think we had better move or we shall have two or three of these gentlemen shortly amusing themselves at our expence." The words were hardly out of my mouth when the bugle-horn man behind us, and directly central, jumped off his horse and said, "Sir, my horse is shot." The horse staggered, fell down, and died.' Tarleton and his detachment moved on to Camden, which they reached by the 10th.

A most controversial figure in the southern campaigns, Banastre Tarleton was born in Liverpool in 1754, the second son of a prosperous merchant. At the age of seventeen he entered University College, Oxford, where he became a good friend of Rawdon, but rather than concentrate on the study of law he preferred to spend most of his time on athletic and sporting pursuits, gambling, and other social amusements. He went on to study at the Middle Temple but soon exhausted his finances, having squandered an inheritance of £5,000 from his recently deceased father. He therefore turned his thoughts to the military line and was purchased a cornetcy in the 1st Regiment of Dragoon Guards. In February 1776 he set sail for North America as part of the reinforcement commanded by Cornwallis. Ten months later he played a prominent part in the capture of Major General Charles Lee of the Continental Army. Tarleton, like Hanger, was an inveterate womaniser, playing fast and loose, but he also proved himself to be an exceedingly able, active cavalry officer. Appointed a captain in the Liverpool Volunteers in January 1778, he was promoted to the same rank in the 1st Regiment of Dragoon Guards five months later. While serving as brigade major to Sir William Erskine, he was rewarded for his exemplary service by promotion in August 1778 to the lt colonelcy of the British Legion, a newly raised British American regiment consisting

---

[2] I have passed several times over this ground and ever observed it with the greatest attention, and I can positively assert that the distance he fired from at us was full four hundred yards.

of cavalry and infantry. With it he accompanied Clinton to the south and had recently routed revolutionary forces at Monck's Corner, Lenud's Ferry, and, controversially after a forced march of 105 miles in only 54 hours, the Waxhaws.

A charismatic leader of men, Tarleton was now gaining a deserved reputation for severity and indeed, when we read his letter of 5th August[3], he may be thought to have damned himself with his own pen. Yet underlying his words is a defensible approach to the war which has received scant attention, particularly from American writers, who have superficially and uncritically followed revolutionary propaganda in demonising the man.

Of the factors which formed the backdrop to Tarleton's conduct, two predominated. First, inevitably, was the paucity of British, Hessian, and British American troops. As he himself states, South Carolina contained only about 5,400 effectives, and Georgia only about 1,100. Second, there was the nature of the war itself, where the constitution and, for those living in North America, one's very sense of national identity were at stake. In such a contest it was unrealistic to assume that committed members of the revolutionary – and indeed the loyalist – party could ever be persuaded to change their views. Dissemble in public they might well be prepared to do, but in their heart of hearts they were as unlikely to forsake their allegiance as to sell it for a mess of pottage.

If we are to draw the correct inferences from Tarleton's *Campaigns*, it was considerations such as these which led him to conclude that the war in the south could not be won by lenity and conciliation. In Tarleton's eyes such a policy, as practised by Cornwallis, would not succeed in winning over the committed. Instead, by minimising the consequences if they were captured, it served only to induce many to take up arms. Such lenity and its pernicious effect were graphically described by Colonel Robert Gray when he reflected on the war in March 1782: '... when the rebel militia were made prisoners, they were immediately delivered up to the regular officers, who, being entirely ignorant of the dispositions and manners of the people, treated them with the utmost lenity and sent them home to their plantations upon parole; and in short, they were treated in every respect as foreign enemies. The general consequences of this was that they no sooner got out of our hands than they broke their paroles, took up arms, and made it a point to murder every militia man of ours who had any concern in making them prisoners.' Gray contrasted British policy with that of the revolutionaries, who, having a better understanding of what was in part a civil war, treated their royal militia captives with severity: '... when ever a militia man of ours was made a prisoner, he was delivered, not to the Continentals, but to the rebel militia, who looked upon him as a State prisoner, as a man who deserved a halter, and therefore treated him with the greatest cruelty.'

Like the revolutionaries, Tarleton understood that it was quite useless to try and reconcile political differences in a conflict in which they were so acute. As he might well have said, 'A leopard cannot change his spots.' In such a polarised situation he, like them, had an intuitive conviction that a winning policy had no option but to rely primarily on deterrence. Indeed, as he saw it, the greater the deterrence, the sooner the restoration of peace and good government under the Crown. Accordingly, in his treatment of 'malefactors' who disturbed

---

[3] Inexplicably this important letter does not form part of Robert D Bass's *The Green Dragon*.

the peace, as in his encounters generally with the enemy, he came down hard, so that, in the words of Clinton's proclamation of 22nd May, he might deter 'by the terror of example'. With so few troops in South Carolina and Georgia it seemed to him the only practical way to keep a lid on dissension there.[4] And as we have seen, it was a policy which had been successfully practised on a much grander and severer scale by North Carolina revolutionaries during the past five years.

As far as South Carolina's white inhabitants were concerned, we should avoid exaggerating the impact of Tarleton's approach. Although no reliable figures are available, perhaps only one third were committed revolutionaries, and of them only those who took up arms and came within Tarleton's sphere of operations were affected. What is clear, however, is that Tarleton had the stomach for the necessary but disagreeable measures involved in suppressing the rebellion. Cornwallis had not, as the Wickwires make clear: 'He [*Cornwallis*] never quite understood that to quell revolutionaries — men fired with dedication to an ideal above themselves — he had to be as ruthless as they; that he had to use terror, oppression, confiscation, and brutality on a grand scale; that to eliminate the revolution he had to eliminate revolutionaries, not just beat their armies in the field. Even if he had understood it, he could not have won, for he would have resigned his commission rather than use such methods... Although by the time of Guilford he had learned that kindness won few adherents to George III, Cornwallis never stooped to meanness. He had come to realize that terror was perhaps the most effective weapon, so he threatened the rebels with death and destruction. But against every threat worked his natural humanity. In the final analysis, because he rarely carried out his threats, they stimulated opposition rather than fear, boldness rather than retreat, disorder rather than order. And as opposition grew, loyalist support necessarily diminished. Fearless in battle, magnanimous in victory, honest and humane, a gentleman in the truest sense — Cornwallis had no place in a civil war.'

Perhaps the reason why Tarleton was so demonised in the revolutionary propaganda of his day was the realisation that his approach to the war, if it had been generally adopted by the British high command, would have afforded the surest means of pacifying the south. Akin in various respects to Henry 'Light Horse Harry' Lee (Pyle's massacre), he has ever since been subjected to double standards by American writers, who, if he had operated on the revolutionary side, would no doubt have lauded him down the generations. It is high time that the man was reappraised in a sensible way.

Having so far proved himself in small-scale actions, Tarleton was yet to perform on a larger stage. His further involvement in the war we shall comment on later.

At the close of hostilities he was placed on the British half-pay list, became a close friend of the Prince of Wales, and served as MP for Liverpool, speaking in Parliament against the abolition of slavery. In 1816 he was created a baronet and four years later was invested with the GCB. Crippled by gout and arthritis, he died a full general at Leintwardine, Herefordshire, on 16th January 1833 and was buried in the local church. A full-length portrait of him in the uniform of the British Legion, painted by Sir Joshua Reynolds in 1782,

---

[4] His motto might well have been, 'Oderint, dum metuant!' — 'Let them hate, so long as they fear!' —, a saying attributed to Accius (170-*c*. 90 BC).

is in the National Gallery, London.

Scattered among Part Three are various references to the intense heat and unhealthiness of the climate. Wherever troops were posted, they were falling down with dysentery, malaria, spotted or yellow fever, or typhoid. On 10th July a thermometer at Savannah registered 98°F in the shade.

As Part Three begins, preparations were afoot for the autumn campaign in North Carolina, the strategy being set out in Cornwallis's dispatches to Clinton. Yet by 6th August a great part of the supplies for the campaign were still not very far advanced on their way to Camden. They were being conveyed, not by land carriage, which their extent, the length of the journey, and the wear and tear on horses made impractical, but almost entirely by water: along the Cooper River and Wadboo Creek from Charlestown to Wadboo Landing, and from Cooke's Landing on the Santee to Camden, with only the fifteen miles between the two landings being covered by road. By the close of Part Three all preparations for the campaign were at risk as Gates menaced Camden.

Horatio Gates, a major general in the Continental Army, had been appointed on 13th June to supersede Johann Kalb. On 13th July he arrived at Hillsborough, North Carolina, and twelve days later joined Kalb at Coxe's Mill. Despite the wretched state of his troops, he immediately ordered a direct march across Deep and Pee Dee Rivers through barren terrain towards Camden. Joined by Richard Caswell on 7th August, he marched on, but finding four days later that Rawdon occupied a very strong position on Little Lynches Creek, he moved westwards to Rugeley's Mills. There he was joined by Edward Stevens and some 800 Virginia militia. Meanwhile Rawdon concentrated his force and fell back to Camden, towards which Gates advanced from Rugeley's in the late evening of the 15th. It lay only thirteen miles to the south.

As the British hold on South Carolina gradually weakened, Cornwallis was preoccupied in Charlestown with regulating the civil and commercial affairs of the town and country, endeavouring to form a militia in the lower districts, and forwarding the preparations for the autumn campaign. After handing over the business to Balfour, who arrived as Commandant on 3rd August, he set out for Camden one week later. In the night between the 13th and 14th he arrived there with a fixed resolution to attack Gates at all hazards.

Coincidentally, as Gates advanced south towards Camden in the late evening of the 15th, Cornwallis marched north to meet him.

§ - §

Principal papers and works consulted in the writing of this chapter

John Richard Alden, *The South in the Revolution 1763-1789* (Louisiana State University Press, 1976)

Robert D Bass, *The Green Dragon: The Lives of Banastre Tarleton and Mary Robinson* (Sandlapper Press Inc, 1973)

Holly Calmes, 'Banastre Tarleton, a Biography' (www.banastretarleton.org, 1st December 2007)

E W Caruthers, *Interesting Revolutionary Incidents and Sketches of Character, chiefly in the 'Old North State': Second Series* (Philadelphia, 1856)

The Cornwallis Papers (UK National Archives, Kew)

Robert O DeMond, *The Loyalists in North Carolina during the Revolution* (Duke University Press, 1940)

Dictionary of National Biography (London, 1885-1901)

Lyman C Draper, *King's Mountain and its Heroes* (Cincinnati, 1881)

Sir John Fortescue, *A History of the British Army*, vol III (Macmillan & Co Ltd, 1902)

Robert Gray, 'Colonel Robert Gray's Observations on the War in Carolina', *The South Carolina Historical and Genealogical Magazine*, XI (July, 1910), 139-159

Anne King Gregorie, *Thomas Sumter* (The R L Bryan Co, 1931)

George Hanger, *Colonel George Hanger to all Sportsmen, and particularly to Farmers and Gamekeepers* (London, 1814)

Paul David Nelson, *General Horatio Gates, a Biography* (Louisiana State University Press, 1976)

Charles Stedman, *History of the Origin, Progress, and Termination of the American War* (London, 1792)

Banastre Tarleton, *A History of the Campaigns of 1780 and 1781 in the Southern Provinces of North America* (London, 1787)

Franklin and Mary Wickwire, *Cornwallis: The American Adventure* (Houghton Mifflin Co, 1970)

§ - §

CHAPTER 11

Correspondence between Cornwallis and Clinton or Arbuthnot

Cornwallis to Arbuthnot, 29th June 1780[1]   *77(18): C*

Charlestown
June 29th 1780

His Excellency Vice Admiral Arbuthnot etc etc etc

Dear Sir

I received the favor of your letter of the 7th[2], but as I have been in town but a very short time and have had much business on my hands, I have not been able to form an opinion as yet relative to the matter which you have mentioned to me.

I have been very earnestly employed in the country in regulating the affairs of this province and in endeavouring to insure the most permanent advantages from our success. I hope you will not be offended when I assure you that the proclamation of the Commissioners of the 1st and that of the General of the 3rd did not at all contribute to the success of my operations. Nothing can in my opinion be so prejudicial to the affairs of Great Britain as a want of discrimination. You will certainly lose your friends by it, and as certainly not gain over your enemies. There is but one way of inducing the violent rebels to become our friends, and that is by convincing them it is their interest to be so. I hope to hear that your reinforcement has joined you and that we have nothing to apprehend from a French fleet on

---

[1] An extract from the second paragraph appears in Ross ed, *Cornwallis Correspondence*, i, 48.

[2] *your letter..*: see p 66.

this coast.

I am with the most sincere good wishes for your success
Your most obedient and faithfull servant

[CORNWALLIS]

Cornwallis to Clinton, 30th June 1780[3]   72(18): C

Charlestown
30th June 1780

His Excellency Sir Henry Clinton KB etc etc etc

Sir

In my letter from Camden of the 2nd instant[4] I had the honour to inform you that I was employed in regulating the militia and establishing some kind of government in this province; and I likewise mentioned the state and the steps that I had taken relative to our friends in North Carolina. I will first proceed with the affairs of South Carolina. As the different districts submitted, I, with all the dispatch in my power, formed them into militia and appointed field officers according to the old divisions of the province. I invested these field officers with civil as well as military power as the most effectual means of preserving order and reestablishing the King's authority in this country, and I divided the militia into two classes: the first to consist of men above 40, and of certain property, family or service, this class to be depended upon for the preservation of order in their respective districts and to do the patrole duty but never to be called out except in case of an insurrection or an actual invasion of the province; the second class composed of the younger men not only to assist in the home duties but liable to be called out for six of each twelve months to serve in either of the Carolinas or Georgia — promising, however, to call upon this class in such proportions as to occasion the least distress possible to the country. This militia, both officers and soldiers, is composed of men either of undoubted attachment to the cause of Great Britain or whose behaviour has always been moderate; and the field officers of the rebel militia, Members of their Council, Assembly men, and acting magistrates were ordered to go on their paroles to the islands on the coast between Charlestown and Beaufort, to remain there untill their conduct and characters could be enquired into, and that their presence in the country might not awe those that were inclined to return to their duty and our friends from assuming the authority necessary to give vigour to our government. The rest of those that were notoriously disaffected I ordered to be disarmed and to remain at home on their parole, but subject, in lieu of personal services, to furnish moderate contributions of provisions, waggons, horses etc towards carrying on the war; and about this time I readily agreed to a proposal

---

[3] Published with no material differences in Stevens, *Clinton-Cornwallis Controversy*, i, 221.

[4] *my letter...*: see p 54.

made by a Mr Harrison[5] to raise a Provincial corps of 500 men with the rank of major to be composed of the natives of the country between the Pedee and Wateree, and in which it is at present extremely probable that he will succeed.

I had advanced thus far when I was met on the 11th of this month by two gentlemen, one of whom had been in an high station and both principally concerned in the rebellion, who said they were come to surrender upon the proclamation of the Commissioners of the 1st June. However extraordinary it might appear to them, I was forced to acknowledge that no proclamation of that date had been communicated to me and that consequently I could not acquiesce in the terms of their professed submission; and indeed when I saw that proclamation as well as your Excellency's of the third of June, which was soon after transmitted to me, I found that those gentlemen had overstrained the meaning of the first, for, upon considering both, I thought myself at liberty to persevere in sending on parole to the islands the field officers of militia, the Members of Council, Assembly men, acting magistrates etc, the former as falling under the exception of the military line in your Excellency's proclamation, and the latter as under the description of those polluted with the blood of their fellow subjects, excepted by the proclamation of the Commissioners. This measure appeared absolutely necessary for the security of the province, especially as our hold is much loosened of a considerable number of people who, being notoriously disaffected, cannot with prudence be trusted with arms and admitted into the militia but are disengaged from their paroles by the proclamation of the third instant. The submission of General Williamson at Ninety Six, whose capitulation I inclose with Captain Paris's letter, and the dispersion of a party of rebels, who had assembled at an iron work on the north west border of the province, by a detachment of dragoons and militia from Lt Colonel Turnbull put an end to all resistance in South Carolina. After having made the following disposition of the troops, I arrived in town on the 25th: Major McArthur with the 71st Regiment, a troop of dragoons and a six pounder on the Cheraw Hill, with orders to cover the raising of Major Harrison's corps and to establish the militia in the districts on the Pedee; the remainder of Lt Colonel Webster's brigade and the Provincials that marched with me and Brown's corps remain at Camden, and Lt Colonel Turnbull with some cavalry at Rocky Mount; the whole under the command of Lord Rawdon. Lt Colonel Balfour's detachment is dispersed from the forks of Santee by the Congarees to Ninety Six, whilst he, and Lt Colonel Innes and Major Graham, are giving orders for the militia of those districts. I have directed Major Ferguson to visit every district of the province as fast as they get the militia established, to procure lists of each, and to see that my orders are carried into execution. I apprehend that his commission of major commandant of a

---

[5] A native of Virginia, John Harrison (1751-?) had migrated to Sparrow Swamp above Lynches Creek. At the beginning of 1779 he managed to reach the British at Savannah, from where he was sent back into the interior of South Carolina to recruit loyalists. Although in June 1780 Cornwallis agreed to his proposal to raise a corps of 500 men on the Provincial establishment from among those residing between the Pee Dee and Wateree, he failed, raising only a motley band of some eighty irregular horse, neither Provincials nor militia, of which he was styled major. Known by the British as Harrison's corps, they rarely numbered more than fifty or so in the field. Accompanying Wemyss on his punitive expedition to Cheraw Hill in September 1780, they were, remarked Wemyss, 'if possible worse than militia, their whole desire being to plunder and steal and, when they have got as much as their horses will carry, to run home,' an assessment later confirmed by Rawdon. They nevertheless served a useful purpose in helping at times to subdue or keep in subjection areas to the east of Camden. In 1782 the remnant was incorporated into Innes's South Carolina Royalist Regiment. In the same year Harrison moved to East Florida, where he settled on St John's River. He was placed on the Provincial half-pay list at the close of the war. (Lambert, *SC Loyalists, passim*; *The Cornwallis Papers*; Treasury 64/23(15) and WO 65/165(10) (National Archives, Kew))

regiment of militia can only take place in case a part of the 2nd class should be called out for service, the home duty being more that of a justice of the peace than of a soldier. I have given to the militia regiments temporary commissions, which perhaps your Excellency will find more convenient to confirm by a line in your next dispatch than to take the trouble of signing, as the number for the whole province will amount to some hundreds. I have had some conversations with Brigadier General Paterson and Mr Simpson and have made a little progress in the arrangement of this place.

In regard to North Carolina I have established the most satisfactory correspondence and have seen several people of credit and undoubted fidelity from that province. They all agree in assurances of the good disposition of a considerable body of the inhabitants, and of the impossibility of subsisting a body of troops in that country 'till the harvest is over. This reason, the heat of the summer and the unsettled state of South Carolina all concurred to convince me of the necessity of postponing offensive operations on that side untill the latter end of August or beginning of September, and in consequence I sent emissaries to the leading persons amongst our friends, recommending in the strongest terms that they should attend to their harvest, prepare provisions, and remain quiet untill the King's troops were ready to enter the province. Notwithstanding these precautions, I am sorry to say that a considerable number of loyal inhabitants of Tryon County, encouraged and headed by a Colonel Moore[6], whom I know nothing of, and excited by the sanguine emissaries of the very sanguine and imprudent Lt Colonel Hamilton, rose on the 18th instant without order or caution and were in a few days defeated by General Rutherford with some loss.[7] I still hope this unlucky business will not materially affect the general plan or occasion any commotions on the frontiers of this province. The force of the enemy in North Carolina consists of about 1,000 militia at Cross Creek under General Caswall, 4 or 500 militia at or near Salisbury under General Rutherford[8], and 300 Virginians in that neighbourhood under one Potterfield[9]. Monsieur

---

[6] John Moore, whose father and family resided about six miles from Ramsour's Mill, had served as Lt Colonel of the Royal Volunteers of North Carolina. Composed of two companies, one of foot and one of horse, it was formed in February 1779 out of North Carolina loyalists who had fled to Georgia. It was later expanded and renamed the Royal North Carolina Regiment, but Moore ceased to be connected with it, being replaced as commanding officer by John Hamilton. What became of Moore is uncertain. On the one hand, according to family tradition, he moved to Carlisle, England, the town from where his father, Moses, had migrated. On the other, according to a North Carolina loyalist, he was taken prisoner by Wade Hampton near the Wateree and hanged. ('Joseph Graham's Narrative', *The Murphey Papers*, ii, 218; Nan Cole and Todd Braisted, 'An Introduction to North Carolina Loyalist Units', *The On-Line Institute for Advanced Loyalist Studies*, 11th March 2006; Draper, *King's Mountain*, 298; *Political Magazine* (London, April 1783))

[7] Brigadier General Griffith Rutherford arrived too late to take part in the action of 20th June at Ramsour's Mill, but his son, Major James Rutherford, was involved in it. James would be killed at the Battle of Eutaw Springs in September 1781. ('Joseph Graham's Narrative', op cit, ii, 224-5)

[8] Born in Ireland, Griffith Rutherford (c. 1731-c. 1800) had settled in North Carolina to the west of Salisbury. Described as 'uncultivated in mind or manners but brave, ardent and patriotic', he was appointed in 1775 to the Committee of Safety for Salisbury District, and having been elected to the Provincial Congress which met in April 1776, he was commissioned by it brigadier general of militia for his district. When the Cherokees later rose that year, he marched into their lands with 2,400 men and, in co-operation with forces from South Carolina and Virginia, laid them waste, compelling the Cherokees to sue for peace. Late in 1778 he was dispatched with a force of militia to the aid of South Carolina and Georgia but did not materially affect the situation. Now, in 1780, he would command North Carolina militia at the Battle of Camden, where, disabled by a musket ball through the thigh, he was captured. Transported to St Augustine, he would be exchanged in 1781 under the cartel with Greene

Treville returned with information that he saw 2,000 Maryland and Delawarre troops at Hilsborough under Major General de Calbe[10]. Other accounts have corresponded with his, but I have since heard that the greatest part of the last have returned to Virginia.

After having thus fully stated the present situation of the two Carolinas, I shall now take the liberty of giving my opinion with respect to the practicability and the probable effect of further operations in this quarter and my own intentions, if not otherways directed by your Excellency. I think that with the force at present under my command (except there should be a considerable foreign interference) I can leave South Carolina in security and march about the beginning of September with a body of troops into the back part of North Carolina with the greatest probability of reducing that province to its duty; and if this be accomplished, I am of opinion that (besides the advantage of possessing so valuable a province) it would prove an effectual barrier for South Carolina and Georgia and could be kept with the assistance of our friends there by as few troops as would be wanted on the borders of this province if North Carolina should remain in the hands of our enemies. Consequently, if your Excellency should continue to think it expedient to employ part of the troops at present in this province in operations in the Chesapeak, there will be as many to spare as if we did not possess North Carolina. If I am not honoured with different directions from your Excellency before that time, I shall take my measures for beginning the execution of the above plan about the latter end of August or beginning of September and shall apply to the officer commanding His Majesty's ships for some co-operation by Cape Fear, which at present would be burdensome to the navy and not of much importance to the service. I have seen a letter from

---

and again take the field near Wilmington. When the town was evacuated by the British, its remaining citizens, almost all of the revolutionary persuasion, 'experienced brutality, outrage and spoliation' at the hands of his militia, the streets for days being 'the scenes of riot and debauchery'. For his part he was denounced as a 'petty scoundrel'. After the war he would serve as a senator for Rowan County before moving on to Tennessee, where he became President of the Legislative Council. Immoderate in his views, he described loyalists as 'imps of hell'. (*Appletons*'; Wheeler, *Historical Sketches*, i, 74, 78-9, ii, 383; McCrady, *SC in the Rev 1775-1780*, 198-9, 331-2, 677; McRee, *Iredell*, i, 562; Alden, *The South in the Rev*, 326)

[9] Born in Frederick County, Virginia, Charles Porterfield (1750-1780) had been involved militarily from the beginning of the war, first in the expedition against Quebec in 1775, where he was captured, and then, when exchanged, as a captain in the Continental line from 1777 to 1779. Resigning his commission for the lt colonelcy of a Virginia State regiment, he had come south with it to join the revolutionary forces in North Carolina. In the very early morning of 16th August, while his corps formed the right flank of the van as Gates marched on Camden, he would be severely wounded in the leg, which was shattered below the knee. With the defeat of Gates he would be taken captive to Camden, where the leg had to be amputated. Although treated with great kindness and attention, and granted permission to go on parole to Virginia, he would not be in a fit state to do so, dying at Camden of his wound about the beginning of December. (*Appletons*'; Heitman, *Historical Register*, 448; Otho Holland Williams, 'A Narrative of the Campaign of 1780', Johnson, *Greene*, i, 492, 495; *The Cornwallis Papers*)

[10] Johann Kalb (1721-1780) was a German who for many years had been in the service of the King of France: as a subaltern in the War of the Austrian Succession, as a field officer in the Seven Years' War, and as a secret emissary to North America in 1768 to report on the affairs of the British colonies. Promoted to brigadier in November 1776, he returned to North America with the spurious title of Baron and was appointed one year later a major general in the Continental Army. Having served without conspicuous distinction, he was placed in command of a reinforcement for the south on 3rd April 1780, but on 13th July he would be superseded by Horatio Gates while at Coxe's Mill on Deep River, North Carolina. He would die on 19th August at Camden of wounds received while bravely commanding Gates' right wing in the battle there. On his body was found an encrypted document (PRO 30/11/3), which, despite seeking advice from eminent cryptanalysts, the editor has been unable to decipher — a pity, for, liaising as he was known to do with the French mission, it might well indicate where Kalb's ultimate loyalty lay. (*DAB*)

St Augustine which mentions that two officers had arrived there from Pensacola, who reported Don Galvez was at Mobile when they came away and short of provisions, and that the *Mentor* had taken three Spanish victuallers on their passage from the Havannah to Mobile and brought them into Pensacola.

I shall immediately, in compliance with the directions contained in your letter of the 8th of June[11], order proper people to examine the receipts granted for cattle previous to the taking of Charlestown and to certify such as they think ought to be paid. A great number of claims are likewise made for provisions delivered to the troops through the Commissary of Captures and for which no receipts were given. These claims shall undergo the same examination as the receipts and shall depend upon similar certificates. You will be pleased to direct from what fund the whole sum when ascertained is to be paid.

I opened the inclosed letter from Governour Tonyn, but as the point appears to be out of the common line of Indian business and the service suffers no inconvenience from a little delay, I herewith send Mr Moore's letter to General Paterson on the subject and have likewise directed Mr Moore to transmit his other papers to New York for your Excellency's determination.[12]

Mr Graham[13], Lt Governour of Georgia, has presented an account of money advanced for refugees, to which is added a charge of twenty shillings per diem to the 24th of June as Inspector of Refugees in Georgia, but as he informs me that his commission for that office is not signed, I beg to know your pleasure whether this account is to be allowed. I must likewise beg to know whether the pay is to be continued to the Commissaries of Captures and, if it is, to what fund it is to be charged, or, if your intention is that it should cease while the

---

[11] *your letter..*: dated 3rd June. See p 65.

[12] Philip Moore was a captain under Thomas Brown in the Indian Department of the Southern District. He was serving as Brown's deputy in East Florida. At the close of the war he would be placed on the Provincial half-pay list. If Cornwallis kept copies of Moore's and Tonyn's letters, they are not extant. (Clark, *Loyalists in the Southern Campaign*, i, 470; Treasury 64/23(38) (National Archives, Kew); *The Cornwallis Papers*)

[13] John Graham (c. 1718-1795) was a Scot who had migrated to Georgia in 1753. Engaging in trade at Savannah, he was appointed to HM Council ten years later, and soon after became receiver of monies from sales in the vast lands ceded by the Cherokees and Creeks. His income from this source averaged £2,000 a year. Quitting business for agriculture, he had by 1776 developed three large plantations and acquired over 260 slaves, with the gross produce from his property amounting to £2,700 annually. On 19th January 1776 he was arrested by the nascent revolutionaries, together with Governor Sir James Wright and the rest of HM Council, but was paroled the next day. Fearing rearrest, he fled to the man of war *Scarborough* in the Savannah River and on 13th May sailed for England, having been appointed Lt Governor two months earlier. After the reduction of Georgia he returned there in July 1779 with Sir James Wright and other royal officials. One year later, having been requested to do so by Balfour, he would come to Augusta to form the royal militia, and after Clarke's attack on the town in September he would be involved in forming a militia regiment on the Ceded Lands and otherwise arranging matters there. In July 1782, having been appointed Superintendent of Indian Affairs in the Mississippi Region, he would quit Savannah at the time of its evacuation and repair with more than 200 slaves to East Florida, where he received five grants of land of 500 acres for himself and each of his four sons. In the following November he removed to England for the sake of his health, and having had his property in Georgia confiscated by the revolutionaries, he was compensated by the Crown with an annuity of £400 and a lump sum of more than £1,000. Becoming joint agent of the Georgia loyalists, he set himself up as a merchant in London to supplement his income. He died at Naples. (*DAB*; *The Cornwallis Papers*; Sabine, *Biographical Sketches*, i, 486)

troops are inactive, whether you wish that, when the troops take the field, the office should be revived in the persons of the present commissaries.

Judge Pendleton[14], who in his judicial character committed a number of barbarous murders on the persons of His Majesty's loyal subjects, has escaped from his parole, and I find by returns which I called for that not less than 500 Continental prisoners have made their escape since the town was taken. I have now taken measures which I hope will enable us to keep those that remain untill an exchange can take place.

Brigadier General Paterson shewed me a letter which he received from Major André relative to the general court martial left with him, in which he expressed your desire that I should give my opinion of the proper objects of mercy or severity. I must lament the fate of those unhappy people who have been and must remain so long confined, but as all those under sentence of death are convicted of desertion and carrying arms against their country, I cannot bring myself to say that they are proper objects of mercy.

The morning that I left Camden I had the honour to receive your Excellency's dispatches and instructions that had been left in charge of General Paterson. Your Excellency may depend on my utmost attention to them and on my zeal in fulfilling your wishes in every respect. The detachment of the 17th Dragoons will sail for New York with the 1st convoy, which Commodore Henry informs me will go in a week or ten days, and I now think, having compleatly tired both your Excellency and myself, I shall only add that I have the honour to be

Your most obedient and most humble servant

[CORNWALLIS]

---

[14] Born in Culpeper County, Virginia, Henry Pendleton (1750-1789) had sat on the bench since April 1776 when a temporary revolutionary constitution for South Carolina was adopted. A man of unusual activity and progressive ideas, he sought to stir interest in the framing of a more permanent constitution through his charges to the grand juries, an agency then frequently employed in the absence of local agencies of public opinion. When a new constitution was adopted in 1778, he was elected to the lower house of the legislature as the Representative for St David's Parish and, while remaining a judge, would continue to serve after the war. Like Jefferson in Virginia, he would display a zeal for reforming the criminal code and be appointed in 1785 to a committee of the House charged with preparing a new draft. Its recommendations would, however, fall on stony ground. Only one substantive reform advocated by Pendleton, namely a County Court Act establishing courts of inferior jurisdiction, was passed, leaving the rest of the existing code, with its severities, cruelties and injustices, intact. Pendleton County, South Carolina, was named after him. (Gregg, *The Old Cheraws*, 297-8, 432; Wallace, *South Carolina*, 279; Alden, *The South in the Rev*, 339; *Appletons'*)

Cornwallis to Arbuthnot, 14th July 1780 78(14): C

Charlestown
14th July 1780

His Excellency Vice Admiral Arbuthnot etc etc etc

Dear Sir

As I found from the appearance of things in North Carolina that it would be impossible long to constrain our friends there from acting or even to keep the frontiers of this province quiet without moving soon in considerable force into North Carolina, I saw that there would be an absolute necessity of asking assistance from Captain Henry in order to get our supplies either up Cape Fear or some of the principal rivers in that country. I therefore desired him to detain the *Sandwich* here unless he thought that it was absolutely necessary for the service that she should go to New York. At the same time I will freely own that I gave my opinion that you could do very well there without her. Captain Henry has agreed to keep her, and we both hope for your forgiveness and approbation. When the fleet is gone, we shall have nothing left here but the *Providence* and the *Sandwich*. If therefore a ship of some force is wanted to co-operate and protect the galleys in North Carolina, we shall still have one left in this port, which I am sure you will think necessary. Mr Gordon[15] tells me that you was so good as to recommend it to them at home to send some money directly here, for which I think myself very much obliged to you. Affairs on the borders do not look so peaceable as they did. I am much afraid that I shall be obliged to move very soon notwithstanding the heat of the season, as an offensive war in the present circumstances of this country is far preferable to a defensive one. I had the pleasure of hearing last night of your safe arrival at New York, but no news either of the French fleet or Admiral Graves. I will neither forget nor neglect the commercial business you mentioned to me.

I am, dear Admiral, with great regard
Your most obedient and faithfull servant

[CORNWALLIS]

---

[15] Gordon was the Assistant Paymaster General in charge of the office at Charlestown. He would be recalled to New York by early November. (*The Cornwallis Papers*)

Cornwallis to Clinton, 14th July 1780[16]

72(26): C

Charlestown
July 14th 1780

His Excellency Sir Henry Clinton KB etc etc etc

Sir

About the time that the *Beaumont* sailed with my last letters, Lieutenant Gordon of the 16th Regiment[17] arrived with dispatches from General Campbell[18] at Pensacola, which he will have the honor of delivering to your Excellency. I was extremely sorry to learn that the state of the place, and that of their enemies in the neighbourhood of it, was very different from what I had heard a few days before through the channel of a private letter from St Augustine; and I am the more concerned, as the relative situation of this place, the state of the naval affairs here, and the present condition of the province render it utterly impossible for me to give assistance, for, to attempt it with any degree of prudence and to do it effectually, a convoy would be wanted of more considerable force than could be given from hence, and a greater detachment of troops than could be spared, consistent with the security of this important province. And indeed I think it right to take this opportunity of remarking to your Excellency that, if even Pensacola should escape the present danger, the navigation of a fleet of transports from North America must always be tedious and difficult and much exposed to the cruisers from St Domingo. I should therefore be of opinion that it would be fortunate if His Majesty's Ministers would think proper to annex it to the Jamaica command, to which it is contiguous and from which it might be speedily supported.

In case of a misfortune at Pensacola St Augustine becomes a frontier in this quarter, and I think I shall direct Lt Colonel Clarke to take the command there with the Regiment of Wissenbach and some Provincials and remove the detachments of the 60th (upon which, from

---

[16] Published with no material differences in Stevens, op cit, i, 231.

[17] Hugh Mackay Gordon had served as a volunteer under Sir William Howe in 1775-6 before being commissioned an ensign in the 71st (Highland) Regiment on 11th March 1777. Promoted to lieutenant in the 16th Regiment on 27th April 1778, he accompanied John Campbell (see below) to Pensacola. Now charged with Campbell's dispatches, he would return to Pensacola in January 1781 and be captured with the garrison the following May while acting as Campbell's aide-de-camp. In later life he would see service in India, rise to the rank of major general, and in 1816 become Lt Governor of Jersey. (Stevens, *Clinton-CornwallisControversy*, ii, 433; *Army Lists*)

[18] Born in Strachur, Scotland, John Campbell (c.1725-1806) had entered the army as a lieutenant in Loudoun's Highlanders in 1745 and helped put down the Jacobite Rebellion. Having served in Flanders in 1747, he took part in the Seven Years' War, being wounded at Ticonderoga in 1758 as a captain in the 42nd Highlanders, and being involved in the expeditions against Martinico and Havana four years later, when, as a lt colonel, he commanded the 17th Foot. Appointed lt colonel of the 57th Foot in 1773, he came with it to America in 1776 and for the next two years was stationed at New York, where, with the local rank of brigadier general, he apparently commanded at Staten Island. Late in 1778, having been promoted the previous year to the regular rank of colonel, he was detached by Clinton to take command in West Florida, and on 19th February 1779 was further promoted to the regular rank of major general. Left out on a limb at Pensacola, he would, on 10th May 1781, capitulate to the Spanish in the face of overwhelming odds, having put up a stout defence of the town. (*Army Lists*; *Appletons'*; Boatner, *Encyclopedia*, 171-2)

their composition, there can be no great dependence) to Savannah to assist in the interior business of the province, for, with East Florida in our possession on one side and South Carolina on the other, it is not probable that Georgia can be an object to a foreign enemy.

Since my arrival at this place I have been employed in the internal regulations of the province and settling the militia of the lower districts, both of which are in forwardness, and I have kept up a constant correspondence with the frontiers and the interior parts of North Carolina, where the aspect of affairs is not so peaceable as when I wrote last. Major General de Kalbe is certainly at Hilsborough with 2,000 Continental troops, including some cavalry, and said to be preparing to advance to Salisbury. Porterfield is in the neighbourhood of Salisbury with 300 Virginians, and Rutherford with some militia with him. Caswall with 1,500 militia is marched from Cross Creek to the Deep River between Hilsborough and Salisbury, and Sumpter with about the same number of militia is advanced as far as the Catawba settlement. Lord Rawdon reports to me that many of the disaffected South Carolinians from the Waxhaw and other settlements on the frontier, whom he had put on parole, have availed themselves of the general release of the 20th of June[19] and have joined General Sumpter.

Accounts from Virginia through different channels say that two thousand five hundred of their militia had followed de Kalbe, that the Assembly had voted five thousand men to be immediately drafted to serve as a corps of observation and had vested their Governor with absolute power during their recess. The Government of North Carolina is likewise making great exertions to raise troops, and persecuting our friends in the most cruel manner, in consequence of which Colonel Bryan[20], altho' he had promis'd to wait for my orders, lost all patience and rose with about 800 men on the Yadkin and by a difficult and dangerous march join'd Major McArthur on the borders of Anson County. About two thirds only of his people were armed, and those, I believe, but indifferently.

The effects of the exertions which the enemy are making in those two provinces will, I make no doubt, be exaggerated to us, but upon the whole there is every reason to believe that their plan is not only to defend North Carolina but to commence offensive operations

---

[19] See page 88, note 31.

[20] Samuel Bryan (1721-1800) was a committed loyalist who in January 1776 had been authorised by Governor Martin to raise men in Rowan County in what proved to be a failed attempt to support the Crown. Remaining loyal, he had seen his property confiscated three years later by act of the revolutionary legislature. Now, in 1780, having been drafted to serve in the North Carolina revolutionary militia, he and near 800 of his followers had refused to be so. Professing to have had no option but to join Cornwallis or go to jail, they would be posted to Hanging Rock, and although performing poorly there in the action of 6th August, they would suffer no considerable loss. Ten days later a number of them would support the extremity of the British left wing in the Battle of Camden. In September they were intended to accompany Wemyss on his punitive expedition to Cheraw Hill, but only fifty did so and the rest formed part of Cornwallis's force which in the same month marched to Charlotte. After the capitulation of Yorktown Bryan returned to the forks of the Yadkin in the northern end of Rowan County but was soon arrested for high treason. Convicted in March 1782, he was pardoned by the Governor, exchanged, and by the summer was receiving pay in Charlestown as a colonel of militia. At the close of the war, by then forgiven for his loyalism, he again returned to the forks of the Yadkin, where he spent his remaining years, becoming a valued member of the community. (Sabine, *Biographical Sketches*, i, 272; *The Cornwallis Papers*; Tarleton, *Campaigns*, 95, 105, 138; Robinson, *Davie*, 157-8; Clark, *Loyalists in the Southern Campaign*, i, 361-2; John Robertson, 'Southern Campaign — Rev War' (Internet, 11th November 2005))

immediately, which reduces me to the necessity, if I wanted the inclination, of following the plan which I had the honour of transmitting to your Excellency in my letter of the 30th June as the most effectual means of keeping up the spirits of our friends and securing this province. To enable me to begin first I am using every possible dispatch in transmitting to Camden rum, salt, regimental stores, arms and ammunition, which on account of the distance and excessive heat of the season is a work of infinite labour and requires a considerable time. In the mean while, the measures that I have directed Lord Rawdon to take will, I trust, put it out of the power of the enemy to strike a blow at any of our detachments or to make any considerable inroads into this province. I have the satisfaction to assure your Excellency that the numbers and disposition of our militia equal my most sanguine expectations, but still I must confess that their want of subordination and confidence in themselves will make a considerable regular force always necessary for the defence of the province untill North Carolina is perfectly reduced. It will be needless to attempt to take any considerable number of the South Carolina militia with us when we advance. They can only be looked upon as light troops and we shall find friends enough in the next province of the same quality; and we must not undertake to supply too many useless mouths.

When the troops march into North Carolina it will be absolutely necessary to get supplies up some of the principal rivers of that province. I therefore thought it proper to apply to Captain Henry to detain the *Sandwich*, which will be more usefull to us than any frigate in the service and could not in my opinion be much wanted at New York, where the Admiral will have it in his power to fit up so many vessels of the same kind. Captain Henry has consented and I hope to procure with her assistance and the galleys a tolerable water communication pretty high up the country. The bringing the troops down towards the coast before the month of November would be leading them to certain destruction.

I have agreed to the proposal of Mr Cunningham in the Ninety Six District to raise a corps on the footing of Major Harrison's, which I believe will be the last Provincial corps that I shall attempt. I have rejected all plans for raising cavalry, except the augmentation of the Legion to seventy men a troop.

I inclose a duplicate of a letter from Governor Tonyn[21], with some accounts. The former ones were, I believe, forwarded to you by Brigadier General Paterson.

It gave me great pleasure to hear last night, by a vessel from New York, of your Excellency's safe arrival.

I have the honour to be
Your most obedient and most humble servant

[CORNWALLIS]

---

[21] *a letter..*: no copy.

Cornwallis to Clinton, 15th July 1780 72(30): C

Charlestown
July 15th 1780

His Excellency Sir Henry Clinton KB etc etc etc

Sir

I have just received intelligence from Lord Rawdon that de Kalbe has certainly joined Caswall at Cox's Plantation on the Deep River. His Lordship in consequence has withdrawn Major McArthur's detachment over the Black Creek, where he means to join him with two battalions and post Lt Colonel Webster at Hanging Rock Creek. This will make his situation pretty compact, but I fear the enemy will make incursions into the country and shake the confidence, and consequently the fidelity, of our friends. I propose going down in a few days, altho' you will easily imagine that *arrangements* here are much wanted and that I can be but ill spared. The other business is, however, the most pressing.

Lord Rawdon likewise inclosed to me a letter from Lt Colonel Turnbull at Rocky Mount on the west bank of the Wateree thirty miles from Camden, who reports that, having heard that some of the violent rebels about thirty miles in his front had returned to their plantations and were encouraging the people to join them, he sent Captain Huck of the Legion with a detachment of about 30 or 40 of that corps, 20 mounted men of the New York Volunteers and sixty militia to seize or drive them away. Captain Huck, encouraged by meeting with no opposition, encamped in an unguarded manner, was totally surprised and routed. The Captain was killed, and only twelve of the Legion and as many of the militia escaped. This little blow will, I fear, much encourage the enemy and greatly increase the difficulty of protecting our borders. I see no safety for this province but in moving forward as soon as possible.

I have the honour to be, sir,
Your most obedient and most humble servant

[CORNWALLIS]

Cornwallis to Clinton, 16th July 1780 72(32): ADf

Charlestown
July 16th 1780

His Excellency Sir Henry Clinton KB etc etc etc

Sir

Upon examining the state of the hospital I am much concern'd to find that there is a most alarming deficiency of medicine and a want of medical assistance and of stores. I have directed Dr Hayes to make his requisition to Dr Nooth[22] and to write to André relative to their being sent to us in the most expeditious manner. May I suggest that your Excellency will be pleased to give orders that no time may be lost in this important business, as the sickly season is advancing and the troops will be exposed to much fatigue.

I have the honour to be
Your most obedient and most humble servant

[CORNWALLIS]

Cornwallis to Clinton, 16th July 1780   72(34): AdfS

Charlestown
July 16th 1780

His Excellency Sir Henry Clinton etc etc etc

Sir

When I arrived in this town I found Brigadier General Paterson in a very indifferent state of health, and indeed he then seemed to apprehend that he could not survive the heat of a Carolina summer. At my request, however, he determined to persevere for some time. He has ever since been gradually growing worse and, some very alarming symptoms having appeared lately, Dr Hayes has given it as his opinion that to preserve his life it is absolutely necessary that he should immediately remove to some more temperate climate. I have therefore, altho' very unwillingly, insisted that he should take the opportunity of this convoy to go to New York on his way, with your Excellency's permission, to Europe, where he will have the only chance of reestablishing his health.

I have sent for Lt Colonel Balfour and intend to appoint him Commandant of Charlestown. His zeal and abilitys and his experience in the business of this province give me the strongest assurances that the management of this town will go on very well under his direction.

In justice to Brigadier General Paterson I think it my duty to represent to your Excellency that he has shewn on all occasions the greatest attention to the business of his station and the most earnest zeal to promote the good of His Majesty's Service, and indeed his great exertions in this very laborious command have contributed as well as the climate to the present declining state of his health.

---

[22] An MD from Edinburgh University, John Mervin Nooth (c. 1745-1828) had been Superintendent General of Hospitals for the British Forces in North America since April 1779, a post which he would occupy until the close of the war. He died at Bath. (Johnston, *Commissioned Officers in the Medical Service*, 47)

I have the honour to be
Your most obedient and most humble servant

CORNWALLIS

Clinton to Cornwallis, 14th July 1780[23]

2(296): LS

Head Quarters
Philipsburg
July 14th 1780

Rt Hon The Earl Cornwallis

My Lord

The Admiral having spared a frigate to convoy the cloathing, camp equipage etc belonging to the regiments in South Carolina, I embrace the opportunity to inform your Lordship that I arrived here, with the corps I brought from Charlestown, on the 17th ultimo.

On my arrival I found General Knyphausen with a considerable force in Jersey, but as his Excellency was disappointed in the object of his move, I thought proper to withdraw the army from thence and take a position on the North River (extending my line towards East Chester) in order to give some rest to the troops after their long campaign.

We have had no late arrivals from Europe except the *Speedwell* packet on the 26th ultimo in six weeks from Falmouth. My letters by her are of the 3rd of May. Captain England[24], who goes to join the southern army as major of brigade, is charged with those for your Lordship. Your Lordship's appointment of Captain Manley will, however, of course stand, as you will want majors of brigade with you, and I am to request that if any come with the troops you destine for us, it may be Captain Benson[25], if you please.

---

[23] A very short, mistranscribed extract from this letter appears in Ross ed, *Cornwallis Correspondence*, i, 52.

[24] Richard England had been serving as a captain in the 47th Regiment since 1770. Now being sent south to act as a major of brigade, he would arrive at Charlestown in late July, but not having a brigade for him, Cornwallis would employ him in a public department as Deputy Quartermaster General at Camden until the close of 1780. In between times he would act as Deputy Adjutant General at the Battle of Camden, for which he was mentioned by Cornwallis in dispatches, and be promoted to major with effect from 17th November. An active, assiduous officer who had great merit, he would be variously praised by Cornwallis and Rawdon for his attention and exertions in aid of the service. Accompanying Cornwallis on the winter and Virginia campaigns, he would continue to act as Deputy Quartermaster General, being with the troops who capitulated at Yorktown. (*Army Lists*; *The Cornwallis Papers*)

[25] Having been commissioned an ensign in the 9th Regiment on 6th February 1770, George Benson had been promoted to lieutenant and then to captain in the 44th Regiment with effect from 5th June 1771 and 4th October 1776 respectively. With his regiment seeing service in Canada, he himself came in 1780 to Charlestown, where he was to act as Major of Brigade. A prudent officer, he would become a highly esteemed aide to the Commandant and be always employed in the most confidential situations. When he proposed relinquishing his office in June 1781, Balfour commented to Cornwallis, 'Although I am certain that the service of this province will suffer

Agreable to the intimation I had the honor of giving your Lordship in my letter of the 1st June[26], I have to request that you will send me as soon as possible what troops can be spared from the army under your command and that your Lordship will be pleased to take them in the order I mentioned, applying to Captain Henry or officer commanding the navy at Charlestown for a convoy, who, if he has not already got them, will receive orders from the Admiral by this opportunity for that purpose.

Thinking it possible that your Lordship may spare as far as *2,500 men*, I have not sent the baggage etc of the regiments that will compose that number, but should your Lordship think it necessary to detain them, I shall of course forward it by the first opportunity.

I have no reason to doubt the intention of the enemy, when the French fleet arrives, to send two very powerfull expeditions against Canada. Washington has not as yet been able to recruit his army to any great amount, but if the French shew a force here, I cannot doubt of its influencing the whole continent and that he will in that case be able to do it very considerably. And, should they succeed in Canada, I am naturally to expect a great effort on this side. I cannot say, however, that I am under any apprehensions while we remain superior at sea, which is likely to be the case from what the Admiral tells me. I have the honor to inclose a list of the force come out with Admiral Graves[27]. That of the French is said to be no more than seven ships of the line (six of which of 64 guns) and only 6,000 troops of the first embarkation, but a second is talked of to Chesapeak, which may possibly frustrate our views in that quarter. Indeed, without I am reinforced considerably, I dare not go there in force, and, without I do, nothing can be expected.

I have the honor to be
Your Lordship's most obedient and most humble servant

H CLINTON

---

exceedingly by Benson's leaving the situation, yet I cannot think of objecting to it, as his friends in Ireland under the administration of Lord Carlisle have very considerable interest and influence and his presence there might be the means of his obtaining a very desirable situation. I own likewise that the prospect of my own movement soon from Charles Town makes me the more readily join in the request, as I assure you I could not go on as we have done without his asistance.' Benson sailed for England in the following August and carried a letter from Balfour to Germain in which Balfour hinted that some mark of approbation be bestowed on this 'most deserving officer'. (*Army Lists*; *The Cornwallis Papers*)

[26] *my letter..*: see p 60.

[27] *a list..*: not extant.

Clinton to Cornwallis, 15th July 1780 2(301): LS

Head Quarters
New York
15th July 1780

Lt General Earl Cornwallis

My Lord

I have the honor to transmit herewith a proclamation of the Commissioners dated the 15th instant[28] permitting prizes taken from the enemy to be carried into the ports of New York and Charles Town, which your Lordship will be pleased to cause being published in South Carolina.

I have the honor to be
Your Lordship's most obedient and most humble servant

H CLINTON

Clinton to Cornwallis, 15th July 1780 2(303): ALS

July 15th 1780

My Lord

I received last night the letter your Lordship did me the honor to write to me[29] and learn with great satisfaction the compleat state of submission to which the Province of South Carolina is reduced. The regulations your Lordship has made respecting the militia and the government of the country I intirely approve of and hereby ratify such military commissions as you have thought fit to grant. In summoning the inhabitants under particular circumstances to substitute a declaration of allegiance and promise of military service to the parole by which they were bound, I conceived their connection with the rebel cause would be broken and their delinquency by word or deed rendered still more inimical. I am sorry the notice of the proclamation did not reach your Lordship earlier. When I mentioned to your Lordship my hope that affairs in North Carolina would be in such forwardness as to admit of your sending me the regiments I named, it was without knowledge of the state of the country, which had been represented to me in a very different light with respect to provisions. The operations I had proposed carrying on in Chesapeak Bay will *now* be confined to sending 1,000 men into Elizabeth River (when the Admiral can spare a naval force for the purpose), which will secure an important post and favor your Lordship's measures; it may also become a place of rendezvous when the service in North Carolina shall have been compleated and token troops

---

[28] *a proclamation..*: missing.

[29] *the letter..*: of 30th June, p 160.

can be spared from your Lordship's command. With respect to the payment of cattle I will consult the Commissary General and transmit to your Lordship my further direction. The Commissaries of Captures are to be paid to the time of our entering Charlestown and from the stoppages in the hands of Lieutenant Gratton of the 64th Regiment[30] unless your Lordship should find that this fund would be too much reduced by such a charge, in which case it will be paid as the cattle. When the troops may move again on hostile ground your Lordship will of course appoint either the same gentlemen or such other persons as you think fit to act in the above capacity. Brigade Major England will have the honor of delivering this letter to your Lordship. You will doubtless, notwithstanding his presence, require for the many detached posts several majors of brigade. The officers you think proper to appoint will therefore remain as such. Should your Lordship at any time find it convenient with any troops you may send to me to attach one of the majors of brigade, I beg it may be Brigade Major Benson. The Admiral's impatience to send off the convoy obliges me to finish my dispatches rather hastily and before I can say all I wish in answer to yours. I heartily wish you success and have the honor to be, my Lord,

Your Lordship's most faithfull obedient servant

H CLINTON

Cornwallis to Clinton, 6th August 1780[31]　　　　　　　　　　　*72(36): Adf*

Charlestown
August 6th 1780

Sir

I received by Major England your letters of the 14th and 15th of July and am very glad to find by the latter that you do not place much dependance on receiving troops from hence. My letter of the 14th by the *Halifax* will have convinced you of the impossibility of weakening the force in this province, and every thing which has happened since that time tends more strongly to confirm it. The general state of things in the two provinces of North and South Carolina is not materially alter'd since my letters of the 14th and 15th of last month were written. Frequent skirmishes with various success have happen'd in the country between the Catawba River and Broad River. The militia of the district about Tiger and

---

[30] Having been appointed quartermaster to the 64th Regiment on 10th April 1769, William Gratton had been promoted seven years later to lieutenant in the regiment, which was then commanded by Alexander Leslie. A prudent officer, he would be dispatched by Balfour to convey and back up Rawdon's letter of 24th October to Leslie (vol II, p 55), by then a major general commanding in Virginia, to whom Gratton was much attached. As Balfour was to remark, 'Knowing the good opinion the General has of him and that he was well informed of matters here, I thought his being the bearer would be a great satisfaction to the General and a good *channel of communication* to and from that army.' Gratton's usefulness, prudence and good management on this occasion were later commended by Balfour, who on his return would send him to steady McLeroth to the east of Santee. (*Army Lists*; *The Cornwallis Papers*)

[31] Published with no material differences in Stevens, op cit, i, 235.

Ennoree Rivers was formed by us under a Colonel Floyd. Colonel Neale[32], the rebel colonel, had fled, but Lt Colonel Lisle[33], who had been paroled to the islands, exchanged on his arrival in Charlestown his parole for a certificate of his being a good subject, returned to the country, and carried off the whole battalion to join General Sumpter at Catawba. We have not, however, on the whole lost ground in that part of the country. Turnbull was attack'd at Rocky Mount by Sumpter with about 1,200 men, militia and refugees from this province, whom he repulsed with great loss. We had on our part an officer kill'd and one wounded and about ten or twelve men kill'd and wounded. Colonel Turnbull's conduct was very meritorious. The affair of Captain Huck turn'd out of less consequence than it appear'd at first. The captain and three men of the Legion were kill'd and 7 men of the New York Volunteers taken.

On the eastern part of the province we have been more unfortunate. Major McArthur, seeing the importance of the post at Cheraw Hill and finding himself perfectly secure from any attack of the enemy, desired to continue there longer than it was intended he should when I had the honour of writing to you on the 15th. At last, however, the 71st Regiment grew so exceedingly sickly that he found it absolutely necessary to move and march'd on the 24th to the east branch of Linches Creek. Gates[34], who has taken the command of de Kalb's corps, was still on Deep River, and Rutherford no farther advanced than Rocky River, Pedee. Knowing of no enemy within many miles, he ventured to send about one hundred sick in

---

[32] Of Andrew Neel few personal details are known. The son of Colonel Thomas Neel (1730-1779), who had been killed in the action at Stono Ferry, he had come to command the regiment of revolutionary militia to which Cornwallis refers. Most of the regiment (see below) was carried off to Sumter by its lt colonel, John Lisle, but in the meantime Neel, fleeing on account of 'his violent persecution of the loyalists', had been elected colonel of a party of revolutionary irregulars at the time of Rawdon's stay in the Waxhaws between 10th and 14th June. He was then involved in Christian Huck's defeat on 12th July before being killed in Sumter's attack on Rocky Mount some three weeks later. (Moss, *SC Patriots*, 719; McCrady, *SC in the Rev 1775-1780*, 590, 597, 624; Bass, *Gamecock*, 65)

[33] Before the overthrow of the royal government John Lisle had been lt colonel in Thomas Fletchall's Upper Saluda regiment of the royal militia. By 1780 he was serving as lt colonel in Andrew Neel's regiment, and on being paroled to the islands by the British, he obtained a certificate of his being a good subject. Reinstated in the lt colonelcy of the regiment, now commanded by Matthew Floyd, he carried most of it off to Sumter. In mitigation of his breaking his word it has been claimed that he was influenced by Clinton's proclamation of 3rd June which cancelled the paroles of certain persons not in the military line, willy-nilly restoring them to the rights and duties of loyal subjects, but as Lisle was in the military line, the proclamation did not apply to him. Little else is known of him except that from now on he would play no conspicuous part in the war. (McCrady, *SC in the Rev 1775-1780*, 12, 620; Tarleton, *Campaigns*, 93)

[34] Horatio Gates (1728-1806) was born in Maldon, Essex, and had served for many years in North America as an officer in the British Army, rising to the rank of major. After leaving the army, he came out from England to Virginia in 1772 and purchased a 659-acre plantation in Berkeley County. Of decidedly Whiggish views, he sided with the revolutionaries and in June 1775 was appointed Adjutant General of the Continental Army with the rank of brigadier. As a competent organiser and administrator he was ideally suited for the job. Promoted to major general eleven months later, he went on to command at Saratoga, but whether he himself deserved the victor's laurels has been hotly debated ever since. Possessing no great military talent in the field, he was socially a mild-mannered, amiable and convivial person, but one who was contentious and quarrelsome with his superiors and subordinates in the army and Congress. Whether true or not, he gained a reputation for scheming against Washington, whom he would dearly have liked to supersede. Now commanding in the south, he would make the strategic mistake of marching on Camden, where, as we shall see in Part Four, he was disastrously defeated. He died in New York City and was buried in Trinity Churchyard. (Paul David Nelson, *General Horatio Gates, a Biography* (Louisiana State University Press, 1976)

boats down the Pedee to Georgetown. By this time the reports industriously propagated in this province of a large army coming from the northward had very much intimidated our friends, encouraged our enemies, and determined the wavering against us, to which our not advancing and acting offensively likewise contributed. Colonel Mills, who commanded the militia of the Cheraw District, 'tho' a very good man, had not complied with my instructions in forming his corps, but had placed more faith in oaths and professions and attended less to the former conduct of those whom he admitted. The instant that this militia found that McArthur had left his post and were assured that Gates would come there the next day, they seized their own officers and the hundred sick and carried them all prisoners into North Carolina. Colonel Mills with difficulty made his escape to Georgetown, where I was much alarmed for Wemys, whose party was much weakened by sickness. The whole country between Pedee and Santee has ever since been in an absolute state of rebellion. Every friend of Government has been carried off and his plantation destroy'd, and detachments of the enemy have appeared on the Santee and threaten'd our stores and convoys on that river. I have not heard that they have as yet made any attempt on them and I hope by this time that the steps I have taken will secure them. This unfortunate business, if it should have no worse consequences, will shake the confidence of our friends in this province and make our situation very uneasy untill we can advance. The wheat harvest in North Carolina is now over, but the weather is still excessively hot, and notwithstanding our utmost exertions a great part of the rum, salt, clothing and necessaries for the soldiers, and the arms for the Provincials and amunition for the troops, are not very far advanced on their way to Camden. However, if no material interruption happens, this business will be nearly accomplish'd in a fortnight or three weeks. It may be doubted by some whether the invasion of North Carolina may be a prudent measure, but I am convinced it is a necessary one and that, if we do not attack that province, we must give up both South Carolina and Georgia and retire within the walls of Charlestown. Our assurances of attachment from our poor distress'd friends in North Carolina are as strong as ever, and the patience and fortitude with which those unhappy people bear the most oppressive and cruel tyranny that ever was exercised over any country deserves our greatest admiration. The Highlanders have offer'd to form a regiment as soon as we enter the country and have desired that Governor Martin may be their chief. I have consented with the rank of lt colonel commandant. The men, they assure us, are already engaged.

An early diversion in my favour in Chesapeak Bay will be of the greatest and most important advantage to my operations. I most earnestly hope that the Admiral will be able to spare a convoy for that purpose.

As Major Graham's corps grew very weak and was very unequally composed, some of the men of the 16th being totally unfit for light infantry, and as the major himself is not in a good state of health, I thought it best to break up that corps. The 71st I shall send to their regiment, except as many as will compleat those already with Tarleton to a troop of 70. The Provincials will likewise join their respective corps, and the detachment of the 16th consisting of about 60 men will be attach'd to the field artillery, except 17 or 18 who are represented to me to be active young men and whom I intend at present to lend to Tarleton. I propose taking the following corps with me into North Carolina: 23rd, 33rd, 63rd, 71st, Volunteers of Ireland, Hamilton's, Harrison's new raised, Legion cavalry and infantry, North Carolina refugees. I intend to leave on the frontiers from Pedee to Wateree (to awe the disaffected, who I am sorry to say are still very numerous in that country, and to prevent any insurrections in our rear) the New York Volunteers and Brown's corps, and some of the militia of the

Camden District who are commanded by Colonel Rugeley, a very active and spirited man. I shall place Ferguson's corps and some militia of the 96 District, which Colonel Balfour assures me are got into very tolerable order owing to the great assiduity of Ferguson, on the borders of Tryon County with directions for him to advance with a part of them into the mountains and secure the left of our march. Lt Colonel Cruger, who commands at Ninety Six, will have his own corps, Innes's and the remainder of the militia of that district to preserve that frontier, which requires great attention and where there are many disaffected and many constantly in arms. Allen's corps, and for a time the Florida Rangers, are stationed at Augusta under the command of Lt Colonel Allen, he being by all accounts a much properer man than Colonel Brown to trust with command. Besides, the latter will have sufficient business in the Indian Department. Poor Hanger is always willing to do his best but he did not think that he should be very usefull in collecting the lists, fixing the officers and establishing the militia in the different districts, and as he found that the attempt would take him up many months and would be entirely a civil employment, he beg'd that he might act as a volunteer major of Tarleton's cavalry. As Tarleton seemed to wish it very much, I have given my consent untill your pleasure shall be known.

Major Stuart[35] is rather inconveniently placed with the 63rd Regiment, and as he and Major Wemys are not on very good terms, and the regiment being joined with other troops would occasion a constant change of command from one to the other, which would be prejudicial to the regiment and the service, I have given him leave to go to New York, where he tells me he was appointed to remain as Major of Brigade before the sailing of the expedition. Major Graham has no farther duty to detain him here, his corps being dissolved; I beg leave to assure your Excellency that he has served with zeal and attention. I forgot to apologise to you for letting Lt Colonel Macdonald[36] go to New York to solicit leave to go home. His business in Europe seemed pressing and I did not see any inconvenience in the command's devolving upon Major McArthur, who is an excellent officer.

Lt Colonel Balfour is arrived and I have great reason to think that he will render very essential service at this place. It will be a great convenience to us if your Excellency will please to authorise the Paymaster General to grant money from the warrant of the Commandant at Charlestown for the subsistance of the garrison etc, as I may probably be at a very considerable distance. A deputy paymaster will for the same reason be much wanted for the troops in the field.

As I have the strongest assurances that your Excellency intended that Lt Colonels Webster and Clarke should receive pay and forage money as brigadier generals, I shall take it upon me to give it to them. It is absolutely necessary that Balfour should have it, or he would be ruined by being Commandant of Charlestown. I likewise think it highly proper that, as Lord

---

[35] Charles Stewart had entered the 63rd Regiment as a captain on 15th August 1775, having been commissioned a captain in the army on 20th October 1761. He was promoted to major in the army on 29th August 1777. (*Army Lists*)

[36] Alexander MacDonald had been appointed Lt Colonel of the 1st Battalion, 71st (Highland) Regiment, on 25th October 1779 immediately following the death of his distinguished predecessor, John Maitland. In practice, he had commanded both battalions of the regiment, as Archibald Campbell, Lt Colonel of the 2nd Battalion, had departed for England earlier that year. (*Army Lists*)

Rawdon is acting with, and commanding, all these officers, he should be offer'd the same allowance. I have appointed Lt Colonel Clarke to command in East Florida as well as Georgia and he is gone with Moncrief to inspect the condition of St Augustine.

I have already explained the measures I had taken for establishing a government and securing this country by means of a militia. I have likewise paid as much attention as possible to the civil and commercial matters. The principal objects of my attention will appear in the five proclamations which I have issued[37] and which I have the honour of inclosing to your Excellency.[38]

[I have the honour to be, sir,
Your most obedient and most humble servant

CORNWALLIS]

Cornwallis to Clinton, 10th August 1780[39]   72(40): C

Charlestown
10th August 1780

His Excellency Sir Henry Clinton KB etc etc etc

Sir

I yesterday received an express from Camden informing me that Gates with Caswall and Rutherford were advancing and making every appearance of attacking Lord Rawdon. He had assembled, at the west branch of Linches Creek at Robertson's, the 23rd, 33rd, 71st and

---

[37] *five proclamations..*: 'five' is substituted for 'six'. The sixth proclamation was to be the one dealing with sequestration and the appointment of John Cruden as Commissioner for Sequestered Estates, but it was not to be finalised until 16th September when Cornwallis issued it in the Waxhaws. As far as the rest of the proclamations were concerned, they, among other things, prohibited the impressment of cattle except by field officers of militia acting under authority, permitted loyal subjects to discharge their debts to merchants and manufacturers in Great Britain by exporting there such rice or other produce as was not needed by the army, navy or inhabitants, prohibited persons from migrating who had not settled with their lawful creditors, and prohibited, subject to exceptions, persons who were not loyal subjects from engaging in trade or commerce. They were published in the *South Carolina Gazette* and three appear in Tarleton, *Campaigns*, 121-6.

[38] Because Cornwallis had yet to finalise the sixth proclamation (see above), he deleted the following passage: 'If the delay of the last would not have been attended with many inconveniences and given opportunities for the concealment and fraudulent conveyance of a considerable part of the rebel property, I should have been glad to have waited for the sanction of the Commissioners, but from a consideration of the above mentioned reasons and a conviction of the rectitude of the measure, from an assurance how highly agreeable and satisfactory it would be to our friends and how much it would tend to intimidate our enemies, I determined to take it upon myself. My reasons for appointing Mr Cruden were his universal good character, his being a person with whom I have not the least connexion, and his being strongly recommended by Governor Martin, who is the most likely person in my opinion to have the management of this province as soon as any civil officers are appointed.'

[39] An extract from this letter appears in Ross ed, *Cornwallis Correspondence*, i, 54-5.

Volunteers of Ireland. Our troops are in general sickly, the 71st so much so that the two battalions have not more than 274 men under arms. Sumpter attacked his post at Hanging Rock, where the infantry of the Legion and Governor Browne's corps were posted. He was repulsed but not without difficulty. Our loss was considerable: five officers killed and four wounded. These accounts, added to the infidelity which we have experienced of our militia, are not pleasing. I am just going to set out to join the army and hope to get there before any thing of consequence happens. As I thought it material that you should be acquainted as early as possible with the state of affairs in this province, and that[40] Captain Henry's ship could not be ready in less than a month at soonest, I desired Captain Lutwidge[41], who in the mean time was unemployed in a copper frigate, to carry my letters to New York. If we succeed at present and are able to penetrate into North Carolina, without which it is impossible to hold this province, your Excellency will see the absolute necessity of a diversion in the Chesapeake, and that it must be made early.

I have the honour to be
Your most obedient and most humble servant

[CORNWALLIS]

Cornwallis to Arbuthnot, 10th August 1780   79(21): C

Charles Town
August 10th 1780

His Excellency Vice Admiral Arbuthnot etc etc etc

Dear Sir

As the situation of affairs is in some degree changed in this province, I thought it very material that Sir Henry Clinton should be acquainted with it as early as possible. As the *Providence* cannot possibly be ready to go to sea in so short a time as a month, I desired Captain Lutwidge to run to New York, from whence he may easily return before Henry can get away. I think it possible, when you hear the state of the *Providence*, that you may leave her here this winter. She is of a very convenient draft of water and Henry is vastly attentive and anxious to promote the good of the service. The rebel privateers are constantly off the bar and taking vessels in our sight, and the eight and twenty gun frigates cannot get except at spring tides. All this, however, is submitted to your better knowledge and judgement. I am setting out this evening to the frontiers to meet Gates, who is, I am told, in full march to attack Lord Rawdon. I hope to get up before any thing of consequence happens. I have

---

[40] *that*: the meaning is 'as'. See p 108, note 12.

[41] Skeffington Lutwidge (?-1814) had been commissioned a lieutenant in the Royal Navy on 15th August 1759. Promoted to post-captain on 15th October 1773, he was now commanding the frigate *Triton*. After the war he would rise steadily in the service, commanding the *Terrible* at the occupation of Toulon in 1793 and becoming an Admiral of the Red in 1810. (Syrett and DiNardo ed, *The Commissioned Sea Officers*; Stevens, *Clinton-Cornwallis Controversy*, ii, 443)

inclosed to you my proclamations[42], which I hope you will approve of. I am writing in the greatest haste and must refer you to Captain Lutwidge for the particulars of our situation.

I am etc

[CORNWALLIS]

---

[42] *my proclamations*: see p 179, notes 37 and 38.

CHAPTER 12

Correspondence between Cornwallis and Rawdon

Rawdon to Cornwallis, 22nd June 1780　　　　　　　　　　　　　*2(179): ALS*

Camden
June 22nd 1780

Earl Cornwallis etc etc etc

My Lord

    It grieves me that the first intelligence which I have occasion to transmit to you should be of unpleasing tenor. Mr Moore, in spite of your Lordship's earnest advice and in contradiction to your express direction, has called forth the loyalists in Tryon County. The consequence was that early on the 20th instant, the second day after their assembling, they were attacked near the south fork of the Catawba River by General Rutherford and entirely dispersed. I received the intelligence this morning thro' Lt Colonel Turnbull, who forwarded to me a person that had been in the engagement. This man says the number of the loyalists was about eight hundred and that of the rebels was estimated about six hundred. He complains much of ill management on our side, and indeed by his account it seems to have been a strange business. He imagines the loss to have been exceedingly trifling on both sides, but says the loyalists were completely scattered. Lt Colonel Turnbull informs me that in consequence of this disaster he was just going to march for Major Brown's, where Captain Huck with the dragoons lay, and he requests a reinforcement of cavalry. The reason given for this step (which, as far as I can judge, I do not think adviseable) is that this advantage on the part of the rebels may shake the fidelity of our new-formed militia on the borders unless the troops are present to awe them to their duty. Brown's is five and thirty miles advanced from Rocky Mount. I should conceive Lt Colonel Turnbull would not have made the movement had he not been thoroughly convinced there was no risque in it; and as I am unacquainted with the circumstances of that district, I repose myself on his prudence. I have, however, very fully signified my doubts to him, and, lest this accident should encourage any turbulence, instead of sending twenty dragoons as Lt Colonel Turnbull requested, I have detached Captain Kinloch with sixty of the cavalry to visit that district and to return immediately if he sees no cause of apprehension. If he thinks the post hazarded, he is to prevail on Turnbull to fall back. As I had some rum and ammunition to send to Rocky Mount, I have detached an escort of an hundred men under Major Carden[1] with it. They are to meet Lt Colonel Turnbull's directions at that place and, according to them, are either to join him should he find it necessary or to return immediately. I thought that if no more material purpose was to be effected by this movement, a report of the march of troops might probably fix any wavering spirits. The proclamation strikes home at us now, for these frontier districts, who were before secured under the bond of paroles, are now at liberty to take any steps which a turn of fortune might advise. However, from the present disaster I foresee no consequences unless that it may possibly tempt some of the rebel militia within Kinloch's reach. The detachment of the 71st Regiment which was at Rocky Mount arrived here this day, the party belonging to the New York Volunteers having rejoined their corps. The 2nd Battalion of the 71st marches in the course of this night to reinforce Major McArthur. As the inhabitants of Waxhaw still endeavor to temporize, I have bidden Major Rugeley summon them to take up arms immediately under His Majesty's standard. If they hesitate, he is directed to require that they shall surrender all their arms and ammunition, denouncing military execution against any person who shall presume to secrete either.

I have just secured a quantity of bacon and flour, with some rum, belonging to Colonel Kershaw at a house about ten miles off. We narrowly missed a box containing a very large quantity of gold. Kershaw unfortunately saw the man who gave me the intelligence, and, inspecting the matter, sent for his box, which was brought hither safely to him before the Commissary of Captures arrived at the hoard. I shall not fail to give your Lordship the earliest information respecting the event of that affair in Tryon County. In the mean time I have the honor to profess myself, my Lord,

Your most obedient and affectionate humble servant

RAWDON

---

[1] John Carden had been commissioned a major in the Prince of Wales's American Regiment in the summer of 1777. When its commanding officer, Lt Colonel Thomas Pattinson, was placed under close arrest on 29th July, being found drunk when in charge of the post at Hanging Rock, Carden assumed command of the troops there, comprising a detachment of his own corps, the British Legion infantry, and Bryan's North Carolina refugees. Eight days later the post was vigorously attacked by Sumter and Davie, who so roughly handled Carden's own regiment that it afterwards ceased to be a materially effective force. According to some accounts Carden lost his nerve during the action and relinquished command to Captain John Rousselet of the British Legion. He died in Charlestown on 31st October 1782. Historians frequently confuse Browne's corps (as the Prince of Wales's American Regiment was commonly called) with Thomas Brown's King's Rangers, who played no part in the above action. (Raymond, 'British American Corps'; *The Cornwallis Papers*; Tarleton, *Campaigns*, 92; Gregorie, *Sumter*, 93; Bass, *Gamecock*, 70; Sabine, *Biographical Sketches*, i, 294; *Royal Gazette* (New York), 4th December 1782)

Rawdon to Cornwallis, 24th June 1780   *2(189): ALS*

Camden
June 24th 1780

Earl Cornwallis etc etc etc

My Lord

I have just received the fullest account of the misfortune in Tryon County concerning which I had the honor of writing to you yesterday, for Colonel Moore, who commanded the party, has arrived here. He says that he had collected about eight hundred men. The rebels had nearly a thousand, two hundred of which were Continentals. The loyalists were badly armed and had little ammunition, so that they retired after a very slight action. Colonel Moore thinks that between twenty and thirty were killed or wounded and he believes that an hundred and fifty may have been made prisoners. The rest separated and fled. They were not pursued, so that Moore thinks most of them will join Lt Colonel Turnbull. Colonel Floyd was at Brown's and told Moore that our militia were turning out with great spirit. The affair, I fancy, must necessarily stop here, for neither party could trust to the country for provisions on a march. Colonel Moore says that he embodied those unfortunate people at the express instance of Major Walsh[2] and rather in contradiction to his own opinion. By this account Major Walsh appears to have acted diametrically opposite to his instructions. He has escaped and is hourly expected here. It should be observed that they assembled on the 18th, altho' their plan, had your Lordship approved it, was not to have risen till the 24th, so that they did not wait to learn your final sentiments.

I have the honor to be, my Lord, with great respect and affection
Your very faithful servant

RAWDON

---

[2] Nicholas Welch, like John Moore (see p 162, note 6), had lived in the vicinity of Ramsour's Mill before going off to join the British in Georgia at the beginning of 1779. A major now in the Royal North Carolina Regiment, he would cease to serve by 1783 and was therefore not placed on the Provincial half-pay list at the close of the war. ('Joseph Graham's Narrative', *The Murphey Papers*, ii, 219; Clark, *Loyalists in the Southern Campaign*, i, 376-8; Treasury 64/23(17) and WO 65/165(11) (National Archives, Kew))

Cornwallis to Rawdon, 29th June 1780[3] *77(20): C*

Charlestown
29th June 1780

Rt Hon Lord Rawdon

My dear Lord

The affair of Tryon County has given me great concern, altho' I had my apprehensions that the flame would break out somewhere. The folly and imprudence of our friends is unpardonable. I desire you will inform Lt Colonel Hamilton that I wish him to come to town immediately, and would have him acquaint his officers before he leaves the regiment that, if I hear of any more instances of irregularity about recruiting or disobedience of orders, that I will put the regiment into garrison on Sullivan's Island. I likewise desire that you will examine Major Walsh very strictly as to what pass'd between him and Colonel Moore. You will likewise please to inform yourself whether Captain McNeal[4] of that corps went without leave into North Carolina, and if he did, you will send him up to me to answer for his conduct. You will please to order Major Doyle[5] to examine all recruits that are brought to any of the Provincial corps, and if it appears that any of them are rebel prisoners, they must be sent to town escorted by an officer and party of the corps which has inlisted them; and you will report to me the name of the officer by whom they were inlisted. I approve perfectly of every thing you have done relative to Lt Colonel Turnbull's march and the detachment you have made. I think I mentioned to you that it will be proper to give higher rank to the majors of militia as soon as proper persons can be found to succeed them as majors. Perhaps you

---

[3] Extracts from this letter appear in Ross ed, *Cornwallis Correspondence,* i, 49-50.

[4] Daniel McNeil (1755-?) was an American who had been commissioned into the Royal North Carolina Regiment when it was formed in Georgia in 1779. He and his company would take part in the winter campaign but would be left at Wilmington with the rest of the regiment when Cornwallis took Hamilton and the light company with him to Virginia. They would remain at Wilmington until its evacuation and then be posted in 1782 at the Quarter House near Charlestown. When the regiment was disbanded at the close of the war, McNeil was placed on the Provincial half-pay list and settled with eighty-one of the men at Country Harbour, Nova Scotia. (Clark, *Loyalists in the Southern Campaign*, i, 356, 395-7, 423, 468; Treasury 64/23(17) and WO 65/165(11) (National Archives, Kew))

[5] Born in Dublin, John Doyle (*c*. 1750-1834) was commissioned an ensign in the 48th Regiment in March 1771 and promoted to lieutenant two years later. Transferring to the 40th Regiment, of which he soon became adjutant, he was involved in many of the earlier engagements in the northern theatre of the revolutionary war. When Rawdon raised the Volunteers of Ireland on the Provincial establishment in 1778, Doyle transferred there as a captain, coming south with the regiment in 1780. He was now acting as Major of Brigade at Camden, where he would soon be assisted by Richard England. After the Battle of Camden he would be mentioned in dispatches by Cornwallis, and, after the Battle of Hobkirk's Hill, by Rawdon. When his regiment was disbanded at the close of the war, he was placed on the British half-pay list. He was then involved politically, first as a Member of the Irish House of Commons and Irish Secretary of War, and later as Lt Governor of Guernsey, but also continued in the military line, first raising the 87th Regiment and accompanying his lifelong friend Rawdon, now Earl of Moira, to the Netherlands in 1794, and later seeing distinguished service in Egypt. After briefly acting as private secretary to the Prince of Wales, he was created a baronet in 1805 and made a Knight of the Bath in 1812. Unmarried, he died a full general. His younger brother was Wellbore Ellis Doyle. (*DNB*; *Appletons'*; *Army Lists*; *The Cornwallis Papers*)

need not wait even for that, as the being called colonel will help to give them authority. You will please to give orders to all the districts with which you have any communication to continue to send on parole to the islands all those who come under the description of my order. There is nothing new. They talk of several actions in the West Indies, but none decisive. I have received from my brother a very pleasing and satisfactory account of his engagement with La Motte Picquet.[6]

I am, my dear Lord,
Most sincerely yours

[CORNWALLIS]

Rawdon to Cornwallis, 25th June 1780   2(197): ALS

Camden
June 25th 1780

Earl Cornwallis etc etc etc

My Lord

Mews[7], who was sent into North Carolina by Lt Colonel Hamilton, has returned, having found it too dangerous to attempt penetrating as far as he proposed. The enemy secure every person against whom the smallest suspicion lies. Mews says that two of our emissaries, besides McCrea, have been take up, but he could not learn their names. One Eli Branson[8] is likewise apprehended, who I believe was sent out by the Commander in Chief. The disposition of the rebel force by Mews's account is: 1,000 militia at Cross Creek under Caswell; 500 Virginians at Guildford, of whom 100 are mounted; and 150 at Hillsborough. He adds that he heard it reported that, 3,000 men from the northward having entered the

---

[6] The Hon William Cornwallis (1744-1819) was at this time captain of the 64-gun *Lion* in the West Indies. Between 20th and 22nd March, while in command of a small squadron comprising his ship and two others, he had had an inconclusive engagement off Monte Christi with four French 74-gun ships of the line under La Motte Piquet. (Charnock, *Biographia Navalis*, vi, 534-5; *DNB*)

[7] James Mews had been captain of a light horse company under Donald McDonald at the time of the loyalist uprising in North Carolina in early 1776. Captured, presumably at the Battle of Moore's Creek Bridge, he was imprisoned at Halifax before being sent on to Philadelphia. He either escaped from there or was exchanged. (Clark, *Loyalists in the Southern Campaign*, i, 345; DeMond, *Loyalists in NC*, 231)

[8] Eli Branson (1743-?) had been commissioned a captain in the Provincial line by Governor Josiah Martin on 5th February 1776. On the defeat of the loyalists in North Carolina some three weeks later he made his way to New York, from where he had now come south. By early 1781 he would be released from captivity and was placed in command of the North Carolina Independent Company of 35 men raised during the winter campaign. With it he accompanied Cornwallis on the Virginia campaign and was among the troops who capitulated at Yorktown. At the close of the war he repaired to Nova Scotia, but finding the climate uncongenial and clearance of the ground impossible, he indicated his inclination to settle in the Bahamas. Placed on the Provincial half-pay list, he was also awarded £450 for his losses. (DeMond, *Loyalists in NC*, 232-3, 251; Clark, *Loyalists in the Southern Campaign*, i, 347, 414-6, 538; Treasury 64/23(20) and WO 65/165(14) (National Archives, Kew); *The Cornwallis Papers*)

province, they were recalled after making three days' march. The rebels are driving as many of the cattle as they can across Cape Fear River. Those which are not worth driving they kill in the woods, and they attempt to destroy the wheat by turning their horses into it. Mews reports that much of the wheat there is entirely fit to reap; I doubt this testimony, for I observe all these people wish to precipitate the affair and make representations suitable to their own desires.

I have the honor to be, my Lord, with great respect
Your very faithful and affectionate servant

RAWDON

Rawdon to Cornwallis, 29th June 1780   2(216): ALS

Camden
June 29th 1780

Earl Cornwallis etc etc etc

My Lord

A person from North Carolina whose intelligence may be depended upon has just been forwarded to me by Major McArthur. He reports that on the 21st the last of de Kalbe's army reached Hillsborough. Not daring to be seen there himself, the informant sent an intelligent friend, who brought back word to him that the numbers of the rebels were estimated at two thousand two hundred and that they had seven pieces of cannon with them. A person who had left Kaswell's camp on the Cape Fear River but a few days before informs McArthur that there are not above three hundred men there and he saw no cannon, tho' he was told there were some. The man reports that Kaswell, having deluded a poor country fellow to own that his principles were in our favor, ordered him without any further charge or trial to be executed immediately. The militia, to a man, refused to perpetrate the murder, but the unfortunate wretch being tied to a tree, four of Colonel Washington's dragoons shot him. Sumpter is appointed a general and is near Charlotteburg. About three hundred militia who assembled forty miles in front of McArthur's post have marched, as is supposed, to join this new general. I have no account of Kinloch but imagine that he must have come up with Rutherford. It is a circumstance which I scarcely wish, for a victory which is not immediately in the line of our great object is of no consequence to us but a repulse might be of infinite detriment. Were it not for my reliance personally upon Kinloch, I should be uneasy, as this is a step beyond my intentions. The five hundred Virginians who were at Guilford are certainly gone back, plundering the country cruelly the whole way. Our friends are very uneasy and pressing. I take every means of keeping up their patience. They represent their wheat harvest as having already begun and say it is uncommonly plentiful. They are apprehensive that the rebels will destroy a great deal of it. What they can save is to be ground immediately. I have had a great deal of business about the Waxhaw people. They declare their readiness to take arms for the King, but having taken that step, unless they have troops (which they cannot yet support) to protect them, they say all their crops will be destroyed by the North Carolinians. There is some truth in that representation. I have therefore bidden them remain quiet till called upon, only requiring that they should enroll themselves with the usual oaths. This they have done in general and have recommended three very good men for captains. Some indeed have retired into North Carolina. I have ordered their crops to be secured for the public service. We stand much in need of some spare arms here, which perhaps your Lordship might be able to send from Charlestown.

I have the honor to be, my Lord, with great respect and affection
Your very faithful servant

RAWDON

Rawdon to Cornwallis, 30th June 1780   2(218): ALS

Camden
June 30th 1780

Earl Cornwallis etc etc etc

My Lord

Captain Kinloch with his detachment have just returned hither. He had proceeded across the country about fifteen miles beyond Brown's house, but finding that the enemy (who were all mounted) fell back upon his first movement, he judged that any attempt to get up to them would be ineffectual. The enemy were in detached parties amounting possibly in all to seven hundred. The party which attacked our friends scarcely exceeded 300. The loyalists were completely surprized and made very little defence, as your Lordship will suppose when I mention that the rebels fought on horseback during the whole action. Colonel Moore with all the officers were holding a council of war to determine who should command the corps, when the attack began. I fear likewise there was too much whisky in the neighborhood.

Many persons who were engaged on the rebel side that day have since joined Colonel Turnbull; Colonel Patten is treating for terms; he and Lacey[9] offer to bring in their whole

---

[9] Born in Shippensburg township, Pennsylvania, Edward Lacey Jr (1742-1813) had run away from home in 1755 and, while serving in the packhorse department of the Pennsylvania troops, had been involved in Braddock's defeat. Found by his father two years later, he ran away again when sixteen to the Back Country of South Carolina, accompanying William Adair, to whom he bound himself to learn bricklaying and from whom he received a good English education. In 1775, having settled nine years earlier on the headwaters of Sandy River, he was elected captain of a volunteer company and in 1776 participated in Andrew Williamson's Cherokee expedition. A colonel by July 1780, he would with Bratton lead the party which defeated Christian Huck and go on to serve under Sumter in the actions at Rocky Mount and Hanging Rock. Routed with Sumter at Fishing Creek, he would join William Hill in taking interim charge of the corps while Sumter's dispute with James Williams over the command was being settled. Leading 270 of Sumter's men, he would take part in the Battle of King's Mountain before again serving under Sumter in the actions at Fish Dam Ford and Blackstocks, the expedition in early 1781 down the Saluda and Santee, and the actions at Quinby Bridge and Thomas Shubrick's plantation in the following July. A member of the revolutionary assembly at Jacksonborough, he would continue to serve in the legislature after the war and be appointed a brigadier general of militia and a county court judge. In 1797 he migrated to West Tennessee, moving on two years later to Livingston County, Kentucky, where he became a county judge. As prophesied by a gypsy

party, provided they may remain on their plantations and not be sent to Charlestown, with which offer I believe Turnbull has closed. Kinloch thinks some advances of the same nature have been made from Sumpter, but Turnbull has not mentioned it. I think that a better capitulation may be allowed to those officers who, without being driven to extremity, surrender their troops as well as their own persons than to those who, being in no command, have no sacrifice to purchase remission with; but upon this point I should wish to know your Lordship's sentiments lest I should furnish any precedent that may inconvenience you in the prosecution of your general plan. Turnbull can assemble 800 militia upon very short warning. He keeps two hundred with him. He has received a messenger from Ferguson with a plan for the junction of their two armies on the Saluda. Turnbull replied that he neither wanted to make a junction nor to go to near the Saluda. One McWilliams[10] has been sent to me by Turnbull. I was much tempted to hang him that I might have spared your Lordship the trouble of deciding about him, but as I did not know what considerations might occur, I shall keep him safe till I hear from you. The charges against him (which appear clear beyond possibility of doubt) are that he was with Moore's party in Tryon County; that the night before the attack he went to the rebels and gave them information; that on the morning of the action he was in Moore's camp and, having seen the officers go to council, took that opportunity of going off and guiding the rebels to the post. He then went to Turnbull and offered himself as a spy but, being sent with Kinloch, was taxed with treachery by some of the country people and in consequence secured. I have gotten seven prisoners who escaped from the barracks in Charlestown. They say that six more got out at the same time with them. The centries that night were Hessians.

I have the satisfaction to say that every thing here goes on as regularly as your Lordship could wish, and I hope that upon your return you will find every thing in the state you desire.

I have the honor to be, my Lord, with sincere respect and affection
Your very faithful servant

RAWDON

[*Subscribed*:]

It was only young Rutherford who was in Tryon County.

---

woman in his youth, he was never wounded in battle but drowned, an event which occurred from a cataleptic fit while crossing the swollen waters of Deer Creek. His father Edward was a staunch loyalist. (Draper, *King's Mountain*, 168, 214n, 463-4; McCrady, *SC in the Rev 1775-1780*, 593-4, and *1780-1783*, 322, 331, 337, 559)

[10] McWilliams has not been identified.

Rawdon to Cornwallis, 2nd July 1780   *2(235): ALS*

Camden
July 2nd 1780

Earl Cornwallis etc etc etc

My Lord

I have just heard from Major McArthur that Colonel Bryan has been obliged by the oppressions of the rebels to take up arms. On the 30th of June he was within twenty-seven miles of McArthur, who advanced with his cavalry and two companies of infantry to meet him. The number of Bryan's men is said to be above fifteen hundred. McArthur talks of placing them near Anson Court House but I think they will be too numerous. I have some idea of moving about five hundred of them to Waxhaw, where, with a few troops to support them, they may defend the frontier and certainly will not oppress a single friend. The inhabitants of that district are playing such a double game that I find it necessary to send troops among them, altho' it is too early to do it with convenience. However, I see clearly that if I do not take that step, all the wheat of that country will be carried off to the enemy. I therefore propose that Major Mecan[11] shall march for Waxhaw tomorrow morning with the 23rd Regiment and the infantry of the Legion, mounted as well as dismounted. He shall likewise have powers to embody any part of Rugeley's militia which he may think necessary. I am told that the wheat left by persons who have gone over to the enemy will be a real object for the public service. I shall put refugees from Tryon County upon the plantations which have been thus quitted and will allow them a sufficient share of the crops for the subsistence of their families. The wheat shall immediately be ground and the stills shall be set to work for a supply of whisky. Desertion still continues from my regiment, but the others do not seem to be vitiated by the example. I have not been fortunate enough to retake any of the fugitives and I have reprehended the militia for never impeding their escape. The measures I have taken will, I hope, at length stop it. I have gotten some distant light that temptations were used to make them desert and am in hopes that I may trace it further.

I have the honor to be, my Lord, with great respect
Your affectionate humble servant

RAWDON

---

[11] Thomas Mecan (*c.* 1738-1780) was a long-serving officer in the 23rd Regiment (Royal Welch Fusiliers). Having entered the regiment as a 1st lieutenant on 12th October 1760, he was promoted to captain on 25th May 1772 and to major on 24th April 1779. He was now in charge of the regiment after the secondment of Nisbet Balfour, his lt colonel, to the command of a motley corps destined for Ninety Six. Mecan would briefly command at Hanging Rock later in July before retiring ill to Camden, where he died on 9th August. Clinton appointed Frederick Mackenzie in his room. (*Army Lists*; *The Cornwallis Papers*)

Cornwallis to Rawdon, 6th July 1780   78(7): C

Charlestown
6th July 1780

Rt Hon Lord Rawdon

My dear Lord

Your letter of the 2nd took off very much from the satisfaction which I received from that of the 30th and makes me apprehend the most disagreeable and dangerous consequences from the spirit of precipitation which seems to have seized all our friends in North Carolina. I can hardly flatter myself it will stop with Colonel Bryan. I must, however, for a time at least keep firm and defer moving as long as possible. Perhaps they may oblige me to march much sooner than I intended or than I think right, but for some time at least it is impossible.

In regard to settling these unhappy people in some place where they may get provisions 'till we can take the field, I think, as they are pretty numerous, they may be able to maintain their ground at Waxhaw on the borders of Charlotte county, where they may keep up a scrambling kind of war with the militia and fall back towards Camden if any thing more serious from de Calbe should move that way; but I cannot be of opinion that the Welsh Fuzileers and the mounted and dismounted infantry of the Legion should remain in that country. I think your force at Camden ought to be very respectable, and I have seen in the course of this war so many bad consequences from a distant separation that I would not risk it without an absolute necessity. The refugees, and any militia that may be embodied towards Rugeley's to support them, may come back in a hurry without any bad consequence, but if any part of the regular force remains at Waxhaw, on any report of an enemy's advancing you must march to support them, as a retreat of those troops would dishearten the whole country. I wish therefore, after disarming the inhabitants of Waxhaw if you think that a proper measure, or taking any step that may tend to intimidate those people from acting against us, that the troops may rejoin you at Camden. It will be very right to keep some part of Rugeley's militia embodyed, but not in such number as to be any inconvenience to the managing the harvest. If you should find any material objection to the stationing the North Carolina refugees at Waxhaw, I don't think their sending off their wheat to the enemy of much consequence, as we must at all events carry some days' bread and flour with us and it is on the further side of North Carolina that I shall be most anxious to find supplies.

I do not think that we should allow better terms to those men who have persisted in rebellion to the last than to those who were the first to submit. As to what they say of bringing in their followers, I conclude they were only a set of banditti that could be kept together whilst there were hopes of plunder, but if they have any real influence over these people, it only makes them the more dangerous to us. I must therefore insist that their field officers and magistrates may be put on the same paroles as the rest. If Colonel Patton or any of those gentlemen object to it as a breach of treaty, they are welcome to return from whence they came, leaving their property in the state it was before they submitted.

As to McWilliams, if you are thoroughly convinced of his guilt, you have my order to execute him. I wish you could authenticate the murder said to be committed by Caswall, and if it really is as it has been represented, I should be very anxious for your seizing a proper object, if possible from North Carolina, for retaliation. It will always be a prudent measure to have some objects of this sort ready and will certainly save the lives of some of our friends. The story of Caswall, however, surprizes me, for altho' he is a violent rebel, he has a good private character.

I wish you would order the roads in all your neighbouring districts to be repaired. If the old commissioners whose duty it is by the law of the province are absent or unable to do it, the commanding officers of the militia will appoint new ones and see that they execute their office. There is no occasion for their being very trusty friends. The number of rebel prisoners who have escaped from hence could hardly be credited. I hope I have taken such measures as will in a great degree prevent that evil for the future. I have been obliged to send every recruiting party out of town; near two hundred have been already inlisted; I suspect several to be in Hamilton's corps. I shall write to you again by Governor Martin, who sets out for Camden on Saturday next. No news here from any part of the world except from Pensacola, the account not very pleasing from thence.

I am, my dear Lord,
Very sincerely yours

[CORNWALLIS]

Rawdon to Cornwallis, 4th July 1780   *2(242): ALS*

Camden
July 4th 1780

Earl Cornwallis etc etc etc

My Lord

Colonel Bryan has been with me, his party being all safe at Anson Court House. There are near eight hundred of them in all, of whom about six hundred are armed. They come from the forks of the Yadkin and that neighborhood. They say that they had been drafted to serve in the militia and, refusing to march, had no alternative but joining us or going to prison. Their march has been difficult and, I believe, was well conducted. Bryan seems a shrewd man and, I am told by McArthur, has great influence. I have directed Bryan to put himself under the direction of Major McArthur and to consult him about modelling his men into companies etc. I am in hopes they will embody upon the same terms as Harrison's people. Bryan says that another body of loyalists meant to follow his example; I have sent to entreat (if it be not too late) that they will remain quiet. Lest these risings should force your Lordship to move earlier than you intended, I shall immediately order magazines of flour to be laid up on the frontier, equally at every post, that the route you purpose to take may not be pointed out by them.

I have had the honor of receiving your Lordship's letter of the 29th of June. Lt Colonel Hamilton shall set out directly for Charlestown and probably will carry this letter. He had reported to me that three of the recruits which he had received owned themselves to have been prisoners and he was much concerned at the circumstance. The men say that the recruiting officer did not know them to be prisoners. They shall be sent to town directly. The others shall be examined and an account of them transmitted that the Commissary of Prisoners may detect them by the name and circumstances if they belong to his flock. If any other regiment has received recruits, they shall be examined strictly.

Both Lt Colonel Moore and Major Walsh are at present with Colonel Turnbull, but I will cause them to be confronted in presence of the refugees from Tryon County and will report the result of the enquiry. Colonel Hamilton declares upon his honor that Captain McNeal was not in North Carolina at the time suspected, and I can find no evidence to criminate him.

Allow me to take a share in the pleasing account which you have received from your brother, and believe me, my Lord, with the greatest affection and respect

Your very faithful servant

RAWDON

[*Subscribed*:]

I have just received a letter from Lt Colonel Turnbull mentioning that he has been joined by a body of two hundred men from Tryon County and that he meant to march from Rockey Mount this morning. He says that bodies of the rebel militia are collecting on the frontier.

Rawdon to Cornwallis, 7th July 1780   *2(252): ALS*

Camden
July 7th 1780

Earl Cornwallis etc etc etc

My Lord

That unfortunate proclamation of the 3rd of June has had very unfavorable consequences. The majority of the inhabitants in the frontier districts, tho' ill disposed to us, from circumstances were not actually in arms against us. They were therefore freed from the paroles imposed by Lt Colonel Turnbull and myself, and nine out of ten of them are now embodied on the part of the rebels. I must own that several likewise who were excepted from the indulgence have, notwithstanding their paroles, taken the same active part against us. Yet here again the proclamation wounds us, for should any person in this predicament fall into our hands, his guilt, which before could not have been controverted, becomes matter of nice disquisition and the punishment due to his crime may by misrepresentation furnish a pretext to the rebels for exercising inhumanity upon some friend of ours in their hands. Perhaps I ought not to question the expediency of that proclamation, but I so immediately feel the effects of it that I may fairly be excused. The greater part of the Waxhaw people have joined the rebels; the rest live under the enemy's protection. The Irish settlement on the west of the Catawba River has taken the same part. General Sumpter is encamped near the old ford in the Catawba lands with from a thousand to fifteen hundred militia. Upon his assembling that force, and upon general symptoms of disaffection among the people around him, Turnbull fell back to Rockey Mount, much to my satisfaction. By advancing in force, I could remove Sumpter immediately, but that alone is not a real object, and the bare credit of making him retire cannot be put in competition with what I think I might risque by the move. He is sixty miles from me, so that I could not hope to make the march undiscovered. He would retire to Salisbury, and when I fell back to Camden (as I should be obliged to do), he would return to his post. The reason for my not being able to leave any considerable force in that country is that I have not lately had any exact account of de Kalb. My last intelligence was that stores were preparing for him in Salisbury. If he comes thither whilst a principal part of my force is at Waxhaw, he has a good move to make: he may advance to Charlotteburg as if intending to oppose my detachment, which would not be equal to seek him there; then he might strike suddenly into a cross road which leads by the heads of Brown's Creek into the Cheraws road, aiming at McArthur; having thus two days' march of me, he might rout that corps before they could be sustained. This struck me some time ago, and in consequence I sent directions to McArthur that as soon as he should hear of the arrival of de Kalb's army at Salisbury, he should immediately fall back with his infantry behind Black Creek, leaving only light troops on the Pedee. Exclusive of the cross road from Charlotteburg there is only one cut from the Waxhaw road, which makes a small angle to Linches Creek, but it is a rough and difficult track. Should the enemy think of taking an offensive part, I imagine they would advance to Camden by two routes, the Waxhaw and the Brown's Creek roads, and there is no intermediate position by which you can cover both. The letters which I have the honor to transmit make de Kalb's force, when his parties are united, near six thousand men, without including the Meclenburgh and Rowan militia. I should not think his numbers so great at present, but they will probably be completed to that amount when the Virginians are delivered from their fears of invasion. I am tampering with his commissaries and think I shall succeed. Lacey[12] is the only one of Captain Ross's emissaries who has returned to me or given me any information. I fear the rest have been taken up. I have been making liberal offers of the secret service money, but should your Lordship have to pay any of my drafts in that line, I hope you will find that the object has been adequate to the expence. Mecan is stationed at Hanging Rock, and Kinloch with the cavalry is to try if any thing can be done. I have bidden him try to *purchase* a detachment of the enemy from the Waxhaw people. Gold will, I think, outweigh the spirit of rebellion, tho' it is very strong in my old friends. As I claim a particular interest in those gentlemen, I wish your Lordship would let me forward as many of them as I can pick up to the commanding officer of the navy in Charlestown. I think two hundred of my countrymen would be admirably placed aboard your brother's squadron, and it would be the only chance that any one of them would ever have of doing a meritorious action. I am not without hope of drawing Sumpter forward a day's march, in which case I shall try to get at him. Upon that scale I should be confident enough, but I should be very

---

[12] Perhaps George Lacey, a private in the Royal North Carolina Regiment, or possibly Edward Lacey Sr, a staunch loyalist and father of Colonel Edward Lacey, the noted revolutionary. (Clark, *Loyalists in the Southern Campaign*, i, 378; McCrady, *SC in the Rev 1775-1780*, 595-6)

much concerned were the parrying of more decisive movements to rest upon my little experience. The post with which your Lordship has honored me is not an idle one at present, but the advance of an enemy in force would make this a critical command, for there is no position to maintain and the station (tho' a most useful one) is awkwardly circumstanced. The want of communication between the roads leading from the town is a sad difficulty. The militia in a line with us, and those in our rear, seem not only well disposed but very zealous. Many of them, however, want arms. Rugeley's militia are embodied and advanced with Kinloch, but Turner's[13] have for the most part joined the rebels. I am apprehensive that your Lordship will find it necessary to move earlier than you proposed. To advance upon the enemy would be the surest stile of defence for this territory, as you did me the honor to observe to me, but it will be attended with more difficulty should the enemy make a similar move first. I know your goodness will excuse my stating my sentiments with such freedom, and I think it right to mention what opinion I form from the course which I see affairs take in this quarter. I have sent Balfour notice that some rebels in Georgia are pressing Sumpter to advance to Ninety Six, promising to join him with a number of men. There is one Levi Allen[14] gone to Charlestown upon a parole and pass from me. Since his departure I have learned that he is brother to Ethan Allen. Perhaps your Lordship would chuse to see him.

I beg pardon for so long and so scrambling a letter and have the honor to be most truly

Your Lordship's very affectionate servant

RAWDON

---

[13] William Vernon Turner had been commissioned Colonel of the Rocky Mount Regiment of the royal militia on the recommendation of Lt Colonel George Turnbull. It was a recommendation that Turnbull was later to regret, at least for a time. Writing to Cornwallis from Camden on 1st October, he remarked, 'I have superceeded Colonel Turner for absenting himself from his duty. It seems he had been at Charlestown selling tobacco, and never made his appearance till last night. It makes me blush to think I recommended such a man.' Although Cornwallis acquiesced, it appears that Turnbull relented, for in the latter half of 1782 Turner was still being paid as colonel of his regiment. He was not subjected to confiscation or amercement by the revolutionary assembly at Jacksonborough. (*The Cornwallis Papers*; Clark, *Loyalists in the Southern Campaign*, i, 152; McCrady, *SC in the Rev 1780-1783*, 586, 785)

[14] Born in Connecticut, Levi Allen (*c*. 1750-1801) had by 1772 become actively interested in the affairs of the New Hampshire Grants, as Vermont was then known. Unable to secure Congress's recognition of Vermont as an independent state, Levi and his brothers Ethan and Ira were now about to become deeply implicated in an attempt to negotiate a treaty with Britain which would have made Vermont a province under the Crown. Whether they actually wanted this or were merely trying to force Congress to recognition of Vermont has never been determined, but it is against this background that Levi's visit to Charlestown, affording the possibility of discussions with Cornwallis, needs to be considered. Despite the cessation of hostilities in April 1783, the Allens, particularly Levi, who had in 1779 been publicly condemned by Ethan as a loyalist, continued to foster the idea of making Vermont a British province, mainly for commercial reasons. To this end Levi was unofficially in London for two years from 1789, but the matter was settled when Vermont was admitted to the Union as a state in 1791. Returning then to Vermont, Levi would die in jail, having been consigned there for debt. (*DAB*)

Enclosure (1)
McArthur to Rawdon, 5th July 1780   *2(246): ALS*

Camp at Cheraw Hill
July 5th 1780

The Rt Hon Lord Rawdon
Camden

My Lord

Since I did myself the honor to write your Lordship yesterday, I received the inclosed letter from Dr Mills, colonel of militia in this district and a true friend to our cause, and as the part of it relative to Caswell's march and numbers is confirmed by a person I sent eight days ago into his camp and who is just now returned, 'tis probable the other part is equally just. The man I sent was detained four days as a spy but had address enough to get released. He marched three days with Caswell's army upwards on the north side of Cape Fear, their numbers about 1,500 with six field pieces (2 brass and four iron), 28 waggons and near thirty carts. He left them on Sunday at ten o'clock as they were coming over Cape Fear at Sprowle's Ferry, and they intended for Cox's settlement about thirty miles this side Hillsbro'. To him they appeared to be all militia. They gave out the reason of their march was only to get into a more plentifull country.

I have the honor to be, my Lord,
Your Lordship's most obedient humble servant

ARCH[D] McARTHUR

Enclosure (2)
Mills to McArthur, 3rd July 1780   *2(239): ALS*

3rd July 1780

Major McArthur
Commandant of His Majesties Forces at Cheraw Hill

Dear Sir

I am very sorry to hear of your indispossition, which I apprehend to proceed from the great fatigue you lately took in your incurssion up into Anson County. By Mr John J Pringle[15] of Charles Town, who is just returned from England via Holland and St Ustatia to

---

[15] The son of a Scot who had migrated to South Carolina about 1730 and become a merchant, John Julius Pringle (1753-1843) was born in Charlestown and educated at the College of Philadelphia, graduating in 1771. He went on to read law in England, where he published articles in defence of colonial rights, and then moved to France at the outset of the revolution. In 1778 he became secretary to Ralph Izard, a revolutionary diplomat, who had been

Virginia, where he has resided attending his studys this seven years past, and brings a flagg from General Caswel at his camp near Cross Creek, I have the following inteligence, viz:

That he left Petersburgh in Virginia ten days ago; that Baron de Calb had marched through there about three weeks ago with eighteen hundred Continental infantry and two hundred horse of the Maryland line with Captain Harison's artilery[16]; that two thousand five hundred of the Virginia militia had followed them a few days after and that they were going to Hillsborough; that the Assembly of Virginia had voted five thousand troops to be imediately draughted as an army of observation and had vested their Governor with absolute power during their recess; that General Caswell had about fifteen hundred men at Cross Creek, with whom he began his march for Coxes settlement (about thirty miles on this side Hillsborough) last Thursday in order to make a junction with the other two near Hillsborough.

He, Mr Pringle, assures me he saw those three different parties and believes their numbers to be as above stated; and as I believe him a gentleman of varasity and appears asured[17] to the British Constitution and Govournment and purposing to reside under it, induces me to give it credit. He says there was no accounts there of General Clinton when he left it, but in passing through North Carolina, he herd of a fleet's ariving in Chesapeak said to be French, which I believe to be the General.

I have the honour to be, dear Major,
Your most obedient humble servant

W^M H^Y MILLS

PS

I had almost forgot to thank you for your very frendly and oblidging letter.

---

appointed by Congress as Commissioner to Tuscany but who remained in France, attempting to frustrate the activities of Benjamin Franklin. Recalled in June 1779, Izard would arrive at Philadelphia in early August 1780, circumstances which no doubt had some bearing on Pringle's decision to return to South Carolina. Be the reasons as they may, his return was self-evidently marked by duplicitous conduct, first by his concealing his revolutionary activities from William Henry Mills, and second by his imparting intelligence which might have been injurious to the revolutionary cause. He was soon to be admitted to the bar, going on to become a prominent advocate, Speaker of the House of Representatives between 1787 and 1789, and Attorney General of South Carolina from 1792 to 1808. He would also occupy minor public offices such as the presidency of the Charleston Library Society in 1812. For a time his country seat was Arundel Plantation on the Waccamaw River. (*Appletons*'; Boatner, *Encyclopedia*, 546-7; *The Cornwallis Papers*)

[16] Mills is referring to Charles Harrison, Colonel of the 1st Continental Artillery. (Heitman, *Historical Register*; *The Greene Papers*, vi, 480n)

[17] *asured*: a misspelling of 'assured', with the obsolete meaning of 'engaged', 'covenanted' or 'pledged'.

Cornwallis to Rawdon, 13th July 1780

78(12): C

Charlestown
July 13th 1780

Rt Hon Lord Rawdon

My dear Lord

I have received yours of the 7th and Ross has that of the 9th[18]. I am sorry that your post turns out more troublesome than we apprehended when I left you. I can only in general terms recommend the greatest care of your detachments and that you would keep every thing as compact as possible. I shall come to you much sooner than I intended and in the mean time shall do every thing in my power to hasten the stores to Camden and to procure waggons. I have wrote to Balfour to send on the 1st of next month fifty waggons with four good horses in each to the Cheraws, but to call at Camden to take up stores to carry thither. You understand that I mention the Cheraws only as a blind, and I would wish to use every means to make it believed that we intend to penetrate by Cross Creek. If our water carriage succeeds from Cooke's, I hope every thing necessary for our moving will get to Camden in good time. Any demands you may have on me for secret service shall be duely answered. That is not in my opinion a proper article for economy.

I am, my dear Lord, with the most sincere good wishes
Ever faithfully yours

[CORNWALLIS]

Rawdon to Cornwallis, 10th July 1780

2(262): ALS

Camden
July 10th 1780

Earl Cornwallis etc etc etc

The enclosed[19], my Lord, arrived here this day, directed to your Lordship. As the bearer told me that it came from Augusta, I thought it might possibly contain matter respecting the frontiers and therefore judged it necessary to open it. Finding that it treats of subjects upon which I cannot decide, I forward it to your Lordship and have the honor to remain with great truth, my Lord,

Your most faithful and obedient servant

RAWDON

---

[18] *that of the 9th*: not extant.

[19] *The enclosed*: Brown to Cornwallis, 28th June, p 272.

Rawdon to Cornwallis, 11th July 1780 2(264): *ALS*

Camden
July 11th 1780

Earl Cornwallis etc etc etc

My Lord

I have the honor to acknowledge the receipt of your letter of the 6th. Since I wrote by Lieutenant Peterson[20], nothing particular has occurred. Mecan continues at Hanging Rock, in which situation I think him well placed on every account. He communicates pretty readily with Rockey Mount, he covers the country from petty alarms, and should I have occasion to support McArthur, his infantry would lose little time by passing along the old path to Linches Creek which I mentioned in my last letter. It was not my design that Mecan's detachment should have been posted for any length of time at Waxhaw. His business was to disarm such of the inhabitants as did not enroll in the militia and to collect grain, which I proposed to store at Rugeley's Mills. By the time this service was performed, I designed that Bryan's followers with the refugees from Tryon County should have been collected at Waxhaw and left there, with only a small detachment in their rear to have received them in case they should be pressed. Sumpter's collecting his force on the Catawba lands prevented my scheme from taking place, for I did not think it of consequence enough to carry it through at the expence of any considerable movement. My last letter will shew your Lordship that I feel all the necessity of being in force at Camden, and if I hazard a step from it, it is not without measuring carefully what the enemy could do in consequence. I think it both right and necessary to inform your Lordship of every minute change of appearance which circumstances wear, altho' I sometimes fear to perplex you at a time when I am too conscious of the complicated difficulties under which you labor. I cherish hopes that I may prevail on our friends to remain quiet till they are called upon. If that prospect deceives me, I must endeavor to facilitate their escape, and I will take care to feed them till your Lordship's arrival.

Of this at least, my Lord, be convinced, that doubting my own judgement, I shall not easily be induced to risque any thing which can have extensive consequences, but should I by circumstances find myself necessitated to act, I hope it will be in such a manner as will prove to you that I have well weighed what may happen and have beforehand considered what steps would be expedient under any possible event. If I can flatter myself that by zealous attention I may relieve your Lordship in any trifling degree under the variety of cares which must arise from your present disjointed command, and if I can prove to you that I am anxious to fulfil exactly your wishes, it will be a most real satisfaction to, my Lord,

---

[20] Robert Peterson had been commissioned a lieutenant in the 1st Battalion, New Jersey Volunteers, on 4th April 1777 and was taken prisoner four months later. He then went on to half pay, perhaps while on parole awaiting his exchange, or perhaps as a result of his battalion being amalgamated with the 5th in April 1778. He returned to active service on 25th December 1779, entering the New York Volunteers as a lieutenant. In 1783 he would absent himself without leave, being succeeded by Ensign Isaac Du Bois, so that he was not placed on the Provincial half-pay list when the regiment was disbanded. (Raymond, 'British American Corps'; Treasury 64/23(1), WO 65/164(31), and WO 65/165(2) (National Archives, Kew))

Your very faithful and affectionate servant

RAWDON

[*Subscribed*:]

Mr Daniel Huger, who was under parole to be on the islands by the 15th of this month, having represented that three of his children are now ill of the small pox, I have taken the liberty of extending his term till the first of August.

Rawdon to Cornwallis, 12th July 1780   2(281): ALS

Camden
July 12th 1780

Earl Cornwallis etc etc etc

My Lord

I have this day received notice from Captain Dickson[21] (to whom Governor Martin desired me to pay attention) dated July 8th, signifying that de Kalb with his army was advanced to Deep River, forming a junction with Caswell. I can see no other object in this but a move against McArthur, whom I have therefore ordered to fall back to this side of Black Creek. Should the enemy approach him, I mean to join him with two battalions, the cavalry and two pieces of cannon. Webster shall be posted with the remainder of my force at Hanging Rock to check the militia under Sumpter and Rutherford. I am uneasy lest this plan of defence should not meet your Lordship's approbation, but I do aver that it proceeds not in any degree from a wish of coming to action or from a hope of distinguishing myself. It is the result of repeated reflection, and I state it to myself as the safest game I can play. Here, I have no position, and if I am beaten, I am gone. If I am routed at one creek, there is hope of rallying for a stand at another, and ultimately to fight for the town. I am sure you would not have me retire before any force without trying it. In Germany it would have no bad effect, but here, where as much is to be done by opinion as by arms, it would be ruinous. I am fearful of alarming you falsely, but I cannot reconcile it to myself not to give your Lordship immediate notice of every circumstance, stating it in the exact light which I view it in. Having said this, let me add that, having made my dispositions, I feel every confidence that an officer ought to feel, and if I err, it shall be a decided error of judgement. I cannot at present say all I wish, as a violent headache has made me find infinite difficulty in writing the above. I will ease your Lordship upon these points as early as possible. In the mean time, with anxious desire to merit your good opinion as an officer, I have the honor to remain

Your Lordship's most faithful and most affectionate servant

RAWDON

---

[21] Dickson has not been identified. His surname was common in North Carolina.

[*Subscribed:*]

I am grieved to enclose a letter of bad news from Turnbull.

Enclosure
Turnbull to Rawdon, 12th July 1780   *2(285): ALS*

Rocky Mount
July 12th 1780
One o'clock past noon

The Rt Hon Lord Rawdon commanding at Camden

My Lord

I have just now received yours of yesterday.

By intelligence from the other side that Kinloch had pursued the rebels partly up the Waxhaws on Sunday last, and hearing that a noted partizan McLure[22] was come home and reaping his grain about twenty two miles above and that Colonel Bratton, who lived about twelve miles farther, was publishing proclamations and pardons to who shou'd return to their duty, I proposed to Captain Huck that I wou'd mount twenty of our men and give him some militia to the amount of sixty to beat up those two quarters.

The party marched from this Monday evening and found only one of the McLures[23] and no person at Bratton's. My orders to him was not to go farther than prudence shou'd direct him. He very unfortunately encamped about a quarter of a mile beyond this and was attack'd this morning about sunrise by a large body of rebels and has been totally defeated. Captain Huck, they inform me, is killed. Cornet Hunt[24] is wounded and supposed to be prisoner.

---

[22] John McClure (?-1780) was one of four brothers who, like their mother and sister, were firmly of the revolutionary persuasion. Mary, his mother, was born in North Carolina while his father was long dead. The family lived up the Catawba near its west bank. A captain in the revolutionary militia, John had already taken a leading role with William Bratton in dispersing loyalists who had gathered at Mobley's Meeting House on 26th May. With Bratton and Lacey Jr he had now been involved in the defeat of Christian Huck. Joining Sumter, he would next participate in the action at Rocky Mount before being mortally wounded in the action at Hanging Rock while courageously leading his men. He died at Charlotte on 18th August. (Johnson, *Traditions*, 339-346; McCrady, *SC in the Rev 1775-1780*, 588, 594)

[23] Turnbull is referring to James McClure, a brother of John (see above), who had been caught by Huck in the act of melting down pewter dishes and turning them into bullets. It is said that Huck, had he not been defeated at sunrise, would have hanged him later in the day. (Johnson, *Traditions*, 341-3)

[24] Cosby Hunt (1758-?) had enlisted as a private in the Prince of Wales's American Regiment on 24th June 1777. Now a cornet in the New York Volunteers, he would assume the adjutancy on 24th October and be promoted to lieutenant. When the regiment was disbanded at the close of the war, he was placed on the Provincial half-pay list. (Treasury 64/23(1), WO 65/164(31), and WO 65/165(2) (National Archives, Kew))

Lieutenant Adamson[25] and Lieutenant McGregor[26] of the New York Volunteers and all our twenty are missing. Ensign Cameron[27] of the New York Volunteers, Lieutenant Lewis[28] of the militia, and twelve dragoons and twelve militia are returned.

This is a very unfortunate affair, my Lord. If Major Ferguson does not advance from Fair Forest or some large body of troops make head against them, I am afraid they will give us trouble. Their successes will no doubt encourage them to pay us a visit[29] and they may distress us in provisions.

I hope your Lordship will be assured that what ever I plann'd I thought cou'd have been executed without much danger. Mr Cameron says the ground they were on was not very favourable, and they advanced so rapidly that the dragoons had not time to mount.

Lt Colonel Moore nor Major Walsh is neither of them here, nor do I know where they are.

I am with great respect
Your Lordship's most obedient and most humble servant

GEO TURNBULL

---

[25] William H Adamson had been commissioned a lieutenant in the New York Volunteers on 1st March 1778. Now a prisoner, he was to be paroled by 22nd July. A very zealous and active officer who had ingratiated himself exceedingly with the people of the country, he would be proposed for immediate exchange by Rawdon, who had in mind Adamson's raising an independent company. Little else is known about him except that he would have ceased to be an officer in the Provincial line by the close of the war. (Ibid; Raymond, 'British American Corps'; *The Cornwallis Papers*)

[26] A Scot, John McGregor (1759-?) had been commissioned an ensign in the New York Volunteers on 25th August 1777 and was promoted to lieutenant on 15th January 1779. He would serve in the regiment until its disbandment at the close of the war, when he was placed on the Provincial half-pay list. (Raymond, 'British American Corps'; Treasury 64/23(1), WO 65/164(31), and WO 65/165(2) (National Archives, Kew))

[27] Allan Cameron had been commissioned an ensign in the New York Volunteers in 1779. He would soon be promoted to lieutenant in the cavalry of the British Legion with effect from 25th April 1781. Having been taken prisoner at Yorktown, he would be placed on the British half-pay list at the close of the war and settle in Canada, having received a grant of one hundred acres in Port Hebert, East District of Queen's Ferry, Nova Scotia. (Raymond, 'British American Corps'; WO 65/164(38) (National Archives, Kew); Michael C Scoggins, 'Loyalist Trails', UELAC Newsletter, 14th April 2005 (Internet))

[28] Lewis has not been identified. His surname was common in South Carolina.

[29] *pay us a visit*: a prescient warning. See Rawdon to Cornwallis, 31st July, p 222.

Doyle to Ross, 12th July 1780 *2(283): LS*

Camden
July 12th 1780
11 at night

Captain Ross
Aid de camp etc etc etc

My dear Sir

Lord Rawdon, being forced to bed by a very feverish attack and head ach against which he has fought all day, desires me to take up the pen for him and to say something more of the state of our affairs here than he has been able to do to Lord Cornwallis.

I have the honor to enclose to you a duplicate of his Lordship's letter of this date to Major McArthur (which will give you an idea of matters in that quarter), in pursuance of which he has ordered the 33rd Regiment and Volunteers of Ireland to march at 10 this night to *Robertson's* on the road to Cheraw Hill, where they are to halt untill they hear from Major McArthur, to whose assistance (if required) they are to march with two six pounders which are attached to them. The distance from hence to Robertson's is called sixteen miles, and to Black Creek I think thirty five, so that it is nearly half way. Shou'd Major McArthur not want them, they are to remain there untill further orders.

Major Rugely is just returned from Hanging Rock, where he left every thing quiet. He was with Kinloch's people and some mounted militia up at the Waxsaws. Upon their approach Mr Sumpter left his strong holds in the Catawba lands and fled in great disorder. I am sorry to say a different fate has attended our friends on the other side of the river, as you will see by Colonel Turnbull's letter enclosed to Lord Cornwallis.

The friends of Goverment in North Carolina suffer much more severity since the rising of Bryan, though it is agreed on all hands *it* was unavoidable. Lord Rawdon has endeavoured to keep them quiet a little longer, and they have promised they will if possible.

Shou'd the enemy move towards Camden, his Lordship has consented to a general rising of our friends in their rear. It is to be done in one day and they have orders to disarm all disaffected or suspicious persons.

I have the honor to be, dear sir, with great regard
Your most faithful humble servant

J DOYLE
Acting Major of Brigade

[*Subscribed:*]

July 13th, 7 in the morning

I have the pleasure to tell you that Lord Rawdon is much better this morning, but Doctor Hill[30] has given him so much employment he has not time to write.

Enclosure
Rawdon to McArthur, 12th July 1780 2(275): C

Camden
July 12th 1780
¼ past two afternoon

Major McArthur commanding at Cheraw Hill

Sir

I have just received intelligence from North Carolina, dated on the 8th, that de Kalb has marched from Hilsborough to Deep River. My information comes from a person of the surest fidelity. He says it was supposed that de Kalb meant to join Caswel at Rockfish, but as we know the latter has moved, the junction wou'd probably be formed at Coxe's settlement.

That movement marks decidedly in my opinion the enemy's intention of advancing upon us immediately, as I cannot see any other object towards which that march can point. You had better (without you have strong reasons to the contrary) fall back to Black Creek, for at Coxe's settlement they are so near you that if they can steal one day's march upon you, your situation wou'd be critical. I wou'd have Bryan's corps at all events withdrawn into a post of safety. After you retire, I shou'd think Harrisson's corps and the mounted militia might hover about the Pedee without much risque as they might retreat down the river if any thing stronger than themselves shou'd advance upon them; but of this you must be the best judge. I am ready to march in support of you in half an hour after I shall hear that the enemy are moving towards you, but I have many reasons for not advancing untill that fact shall be ascertained. The express who has brought me the intelligence has been obliged to walk all the way through the swamps, which has occasioned my receiving it so late. Shou'd the enemy get near you, you must endeavor to gain time, with the fullest confidence that we shall not lose a moment in sustaining you. Rum will be sent for you this evening. If you fall back to Black Creek, you shall be supplied with meal and cattle.

---

[30] West Hill (1742-1834) was a surgeon on the staff of the General Hospital in North America, the department responsible for hospitals other than small regimental ones. Appointed there on 5th November 1778, he had previously served as surgeon to the 33rd Regiment. Now in charge of the general hospital at Camden, he would remain so until joining Cornwallis at Winnsborough to accompany him on the winter campaign. After the Battle of Guilford he would be left at New Garden Meeting House to care for the badly wounded under the sanction of a flag. An MD from St Andrews University, he would see service after the war as a staff surgeon in St Vincent, retiring on half pay in 1802. He died at Chippenham, Wiltshire. (Johnston, *Commissioned Officers in the Medical Service*, 46; *The Cornwallis Papers*)

Let me hear from you directly.

I have the honor to be, sir, with great regard
Your most obedient servant

RAWDON

[*Endorsed*:]

Sent by Captain Leggit[31], North Carolina Regiment.

Cornwallis to Rawdon, 15th July 1780   78(18): C

Charles Town
July 15th 1780

Rt Hon Lord Rawdon

My dear Lord

I received early this morning your letter of the 12th. I approve very much of your moving Major McArthur to your side of the Black Creek, and should Mr de Kalbe advance, I would by all means wish you to join him. In regard to the forward position you mention, it is difficult for me, having no knowledge of that country but by a bad map, to give a positive opinion about it. I therefore shall content myself with only saying that, if the enemy come within any possibility of reaching you, *be compact* and prefer that to any other considerations. Every [thing] else I shall leave to your Lordship's judgement, and I am well convinced that I do not misplace my confidence. I foresee that it will be absolutely necessary to act offensively very soon to save our friends in North Carolina and to preserve the confidence, in which is included the friendship, of the South Carolinians. I am hastening our preparations but we must do it, ready or not ready, rather than submit to any serious insult. I will come to you as soon as possible, and I think it will be very soon, for altho' every thing here is in the most confused state, yet I see no hopes that any possible stay of mine could put them into a good method. There is but one thing[32] could do it. You will easily guess what I mean. If not, Governor Martin will help you.

Lt Colonel Turnbull's letter gave me very serious concern, and is indeed a very serious misfortune. Cavalry acts chiefly upon the nerves, and if once it loses its terror, it loses its greatest force. Tarleton will join in a few days. In the mean time let me conjure you to take

---

[31] John Legget (1753-?) was an American who by now had seen some four years' service in the Provincial line. A captain in the Royal North Carolina Regiment, he would be placed on the Provincial half-pay list when the regiment was disbanded at the close of the war. (Treasury 64/23(17) and WO 65/165(11) (National Archives, Kew); Clark, *Loyalists in the Southern Campaign*, i, *passim*)

[32] *one thing*: the replacement of Paterson by Balfour as Commandant of Charlestown.

care of the cavalry and to give the most positive orders against small detachments; they are always dangerous, especially under ignorant and careless officers. I am sorry to find that you are indisposed but hope it is now over. Doyle mentions to Ross what you have done about our friends in North Carolina. I think you perfectly right and would draw this line for them: that if de Kalbe comes one day's march on our side of Charlotte town, that the rising should be general and every possible attack made on the stores and convoys in his rear, and then at all events we must go on.

I am etc

[CORNWALLIS]

[*Subscribed*:]

If, in consequence of that unlucky affair of the Legion, the rebels should be troublesome between the Wateree and Broad River, your Lordship will please to send to Balfour for any militia assistance he can give you. I have ordered up Innes in a few days to assemble his corps. Perhaps Major Graham might move a few miles higher than Friday's Ferry. I shall talk to Innes and write to Balfour about these matters, but if you find any pressing inconveniencies, you will, to save time, correspond with Balfour yourself and make what requisitions you think necessary.

Rawdon to Cornwallis, 14th July 1780   2(294): ALS

Camden
July 14th 1780

Earl Cornwallis etc etc etc

My Lord

As our express sets out this morning for McChord's Ferry, I take that opportunity of informing your Lordship that nothing particular has occurred since I last had the honor of writing to you, excepting that I have had notice of the junction being formed between de Kalb and Caswell at Coxe's settlement. From the measures which I have taken I think every thing in a safe condition, and Doctor Hill has fitted me for any service by dispelling a little fever which had attacked me. The enclosed letter from Turnbull will shew your Lordship that the misfortune of Huck's party has not been so bad as it first appeared. In the course of this day I hope to learn with certainty something respecting the enemy's movements, an account of which I should certainly dispatch.

I have in the mean time the honor to remain with equal respect and affection
Your Lordship's most faithful and obedient servant

RAWDON

Enclosure
Turnbull to Rawdon, 12th July 1780 2(277): ALS

Rocky Mount
July 12th 1780
Nine o'clock in the evening

The Rt Hon Lord Rawdon commanding at Camden

My Lord

I was unfortunate enough to be oblidged to tell you a very dissagreable story some hours ago.

Nine of our missing men have come in, and one dragoon.

A Negroe boy who was taken has made his escape and says that Lieutenant Adamson fell of his horse (being much bruised, is taken prisoner), that seven of ours and a serjeant, and two of the dragoons, are likewise wounded and taken prisoners.

Lieutenant McGregor and Cornet Hunt, we suppose, have made their escape, but have not yet arrived. Captain Huck is the only person who was killed dead on the spot.

My militia are so allarmed it will be some days before they recover their spirits.

There are some wounded militia I send down by the bearer in a waggon to the care of Doctor Hill.

The Negroe boy is very intelligent. He says the rebells will send down Lieutenant Adamson and our wounded men tomorrow.

By what I can learn, the only bait which led Huck to encamp at this cursed unlucky spot was an oat field that was near, but by every acount the position was very unfavourable.

My paper and sealing wax is almost expended. In a few days I don't believe I shall have any materials to keep up a correspondence.

Our doctor resign'd last week and we have no body of the faculty but a mate who is not very regularly bred.

I have wrote to Stapleton of the Legion[33] and Mr Gibbs, the surgeon's mate of the

---

[33] Wynne Stapleton (1744?-1780) was a doctor of medicine who was serving as surgeon to the British Legion. He may have been a Yorkshireman, perhaps the Dr Stapleton who sailed from Scarborough for Nova Scotia in April 1774. He would die of a violent fever in September while at the Waxhaws. What little we know of his service in the south is dependent on a single revolutionary source which is unflattering. He is said to have refused at first to treat one of Buford's severely wounded officers after the affair at the Waxhaws, and then, when ordered to do so, to have treated him only perfunctorily. (Raymond, 'British American Corps'; Gerald Fothergill, *Emigrants from*

33rd[34]. I believe the latter will accept of it if Lord Cornwallis will permitt him. He writes me he is now going to Charlestown and expects to join us on his return. In the mean time, if Doctor Hill cou'd spare one of his mates with some medicine, it wou'd oblige us much.

I can learn nothing of those deserters mention'd by Major Carden. The house which the[y] frequented is on the Waxhaw side.

I am with much esteem
Your Lordship's most faithfull humble servant

GEO TURNBULL

PS

I have just discovered that our salt is out. Some musket cartridges and ammunition for the militia is wanted. I beg your Lordship wou'd be pleased to send a small guard with the waggon.

GT

Rawdon to Cornwallis, 17th July 1780   *2(329): ALS*

Camden
July 17th 1780

Earl Cornwallis etc etc etc

My Lord

I have the satisfaction to acquaint you that I have now secured a source of information which will enable me in future to form the best judgement of the enemy's intentions. Rutherford is ordered to join de Kalb near Deep River. I am persuaded this step is taken because they find I will not give into the snare by following him to Waxhaw. When this junction shall have been formed, the enemy propose to advance to the Pedee. I understand that de Kalb has been down as low as Drowning Creek to recconnoitre. The rebels, I am informed, had an idea of entrenching themselves at the Sand Hills, and de Kalb has certainly been at great pains to collect all the spades and shovels in his neighborhood. I am to acknowledge the honor of your Lordship's letter of the 13th. You express your wishes that

---

England 1773-1776 (Boston, 1913), 67; Michael Tepper ed, *Passengers to America* (Genealogical Publishing Co, 1980), 288; 'Yorkshire, England, to Nova Scotia, 1774', *Genealogical Reference Builders Newsletter*, i, N° 9 (October-November 1967), 4; Kenneth Scott, *Rivington's New York Newspaper Excerpts from a Loyalist Press, 1773-1783* (University of Virginia Press, 1973), 244; James, *Marion*, appendix, 6)

[34] Thomas Gibbs was to be appointed surgeon to the New York Volunteers with effect from 6th September. He resigned his commission before the close of the war and was not placed on the Provincial half-pay list. (Treasury 64/23(1), WO 65/164(31), and WO 65/165(2) (National Archives, Kew))

the corps should be kept as compact as possible, and as I conceive your Lordship means by that expression that one part should be in the most advantageous situation for supporting another, I think I may say the detachments are so stationed at present. The support of McArthur's corps (which I do not think it politic, nor indeed do I esteem myself authorised, to withdraw without strong reasons) must influence all my measures. The corps at Hanging Rock have a route, which I have lately discovered, to Black Creek at least ten miles shorter than the road from Camden. At the same time, by a communication of twelve miles, they support Rockey Mount. The troops which I thought it necessary to send to Robertson's that they might be within a march of Black Creek are in a most healthy and agreable situation. They have a road (the same which I formerly described as making a small angle from Hanging Rock to Linches Creek) by which they are at least eight miles nearer to Hanging Rock than they were at Camden. As I remain centrical here and within a gallop of all the posts but Cheraws, I can, upon the first intelligence that makes it necessary, unite all my force at any point from Black Creek to Rockey Mount. I may add that I believe the present positions of the troops to be much more healthy than Camden. I have had a severe attack of the ague, but I have taken such a quantity of bark that I hope it will not return.

I have the honor to be with great respect and affection, my Lord,
Your most faithful and obedient servant

RAWDON

Cornwallis to Rawdon, 20th July 1780   78(34): C

Charlestown
July 20th 1780

Rt Hon Lord Rawdon

My dear Lord

I have received your letters of the 16th[35] and 17th and they are indeed very satisfactory. Your Lordship understood my meaning perfectly by the word compact (that no part of your corps should be so detached but that it might be withdrawn without hurry or disgrace or sufficiently supported before it was possible for a superior force of the enemy to come upon it). Your present position appears perfectly proper and judicious as long as it is certain that McArthur is safe at Cheraw Hill. It is very desirable that he should stay there. Whenever you think him at all exposed, you will without scruple bring him back to any place of security that you may think proper. The accounts you have given me of all your movements are so clear, and your reasons so good and your ability and attention so evident, that I feel the most perfect confidence in you and think myself most fortunate in having the advantage of your Lordship's assistance. The only thing that makes me uneasy is the state of your health, of which I shall be very anxious to receive better accounts. You have heard that our Commandant of Charlestown is gone and that I have ordered Balfour to replace him. Innes

---

[35] *16th*: perhaps a slip of the pen, as Cornwallis appears to refer to Rawdon's letter of the 14th.

is gone to assemble his regiment and to relieve Balfour untill the arrival of Colonel Cruger, who is to take the command of the posts of Augusta and Ninety Six. I have ordered fifty good waggons to be sent from Ninety Six to Camden early next month. I have likewise directed Innes to order some waggons to be collected at Congarees, either to be sent directly to Camden or, if our water carriage should not be sufficient, to go first either to Cook's Landing or to Manigault's Ferry and to bring on any thing that may be left at either of those places. McKinnon is just returned from Cook's Landing and gives a good account of things there. The baggage and stores of the regiments were gone up and there were seven boats in readiness to receive rum and artillery stores, and he hopes soon to have more. I shall pay the greatest attention to expediting those matters. Lieutenant McCleod of the Artillery[36] is going to Camden. He takes up two of the light infantry three pounders, and I should wish to have two of the six pounders sent back, being well convinced that two much artillery is a great embarrassment in this country. McCleod is a very good officer. Unless de Kalbe should advance so as to make things critical or that[37] some other event in that part of the country should hasten me, I should wish to stay here untill Balfour arrives and is a few days settled in his command. I have, however, every thing ready and can move away at a moment's warning.

I beg my respects to the Governor and am, my dear Lord, with great truth
Most sincerely yours

[CORNWALLIS]

---

[36] Having entered the Royal Regiment of Artillery as a cadet in 1767, John Macleod (c. 1752-1833) was commissioned a 2nd lieutenant four years later and promoted to 1st lieutenant on 15th March 1779. Highly esteemed by Cornwallis, whose personal friendship he gained, he would command Cornwallis's field train of artillery throughout the southern campaigns. 'He is,' observed Cornwallis to Balfour, 'an excellent officer and a pleasant man to serve with in every respect.' Mentioned by Cornwallis in dispatches after the Battles of Camden and Guilford, he would be part of the troops who capitulated at Yorktown. On returning to England, he was placed on the staff of the Master General of Artillery and was engaged till his death in the organisation of the regiment and in its arrangement and equipment for all expeditions, of which there were no fewer than eleven. Fulfilling the potential which Cornwallis had seen in him, he held successively the offices of Chief of the Ordnance Staff, Deputy Adjutant General, and Director General of Artillery, being promoted to major general in 1809 and to lt general four years later. In 1809 he also commanded the artillery during the expedition to Walcheren. As a mark of his long and distinguished service, he was made a knight in 1820, being invested with the Grand Cross of the Royal Guelphic Order. He died at Woolwich. (*Royal Regiment of Artillery*, 13, 167-8, 199, 232; *Army Lists*)

[37] *that*: the meaning is 'unless'. See p 108, note 12.

Rawdon to Cornwallis, 19th July 1780   *2(327): ALS*

Camden
July 19th 1780

Earl Cornwallis etc

My Lord

I am happy to find from your Lordship's answer to me by Ensign Garret[38] that you do not disapprove of the measures which I intended to pursue had de Kalb continued to advance. Two days ago an ensign of the 5th Maryland Regiment (by name Clarke[39]) came in to McArthur with fourteen men of the same corps who had been sent out under his command to search for some Tories. He says that they meant to have advanced upon us by the Pedee, but, learning that we were too well prepared for them in that quarter, a council of war has been held and it has been judged best to march to Salisbury. This information he says he received from one of de Kalb's aide de camps on the 14th, who further told him that he supposed the march to Salisbury would immediately take place. Clarke asserts that de Kalb has sent back to Hillsborough all his field pieces excepting six. He had (Caswell's included) thirteen, and two mortars or howitzers. The rebels commit great devastation and cruelty in the country, yet I hope that by the assistance of Governor Martin's influence I may prevail on our friends to remain quiet.

Lt Colonel Balfour writes me word that a party of the enemy consisting of 400 had attempted to surprize his advanced post in the fork of Tyger River. Captain Dunlop, who commanded there, patroling with a dozen regulars and about sixty militia, all mounted, unexpectedly fell in with this body. He attacked them and killed or wounded near thirty of them and, having made them give back a little, took that opportunity of securing his retreat, which the flight of most of his militia made rather difficult. Balfour has upon this advanced to Fair Forest and asks me to cooperate with him, which I can never do to any purpose, nor do I think the enemy will collect there in any great force. Bryan has been with me to apologize for the impatience of his people, and they promise strict obedience in future.

---

[38] Patrick Garrett had entered the Prince of Wales's American Regiment as an ensign in 1777 and was now serving on secondment to Ferguson's corps. For most of 1781 he would be seconded to the 23rd Regiment (Royal Welch Fusiliers), but how he came to be serving there is unknown. He was taken prisoner with the Fusiliers at Yorktown. In the same month as the capitulation he was promoted to lieutenant in his own regiment, but deciding that the regulars were for him in preference to the prospect of half pay, he obtained a commission in the 30th Regiment with effect from 17th April 1783. (Raymond, 'British American Corps'; Nan Cole and Todd Braisted, 'A History of the Prince of Wales' American Regiment' (*The On-Line Institute for Advanced Loyalist Studies*, 10th March 2006))

[39] Clark(e) was a very common name in the Maryland line. See Bernard Christian Steiner ed, *Archives of Maryland: Muster Rolls and Other Records of Service of Maryland Troops in the American Revolution*, xviii (Baltimore, 1899).

Stedman[40] being dismissed from his office as Commissary of Captures, Knecht[41] wished to have him in his bureau. I promised to mention it to your Lordship and must say that I have had every reason to be satisfied with Stedman.

I have the honor to be with great respect
Your Lordship's very affectionate servant

RAWDON

Cornwallis to Rawdon, 24th July 1780　　　　　　　　　　　　78(44): C

Charles Town
July 24th 1780

Rt Hon Lord Rawdon

My dear Lord

I received last night by Mr Stedman your letter of the 19th and am perfectly satisfied with every thing in your quarter. I am in great hopes we shall get boats enough to Cooke's to carry up every thing. However, least we should be disappointed, it will be well to hurry down those that arrive at Camden as fast as they are unloaded. I do not see how [you] can co-operate with the division under Balfour more than you do. Innes will assemble his corps immediately. I have this moment received Balfour's account of Dunlap's business. He thinks that by Turnbull's being watchful he might make their parties afraid of passing the Catawba River. I am sure you will do all you can with safety, but I cannot hope for any tranquillity on the borders untill we move forward. I shall enquire about Mr Stedman's situation and settle it in the best way for him. I was very glad to get from him a good account of your health, which you did not mention.

I am etc

[CORNWALLIS]

---

[40] Charles Stedman (1753-1812) was the son of a Jacobite lawyer who had fled to America and become a judge of the High Court in Philadelphia. Educated for the law at William and Mary College in Virginia, he, like his father, remained loyal to the Crown on the outbreak of the war. While his father withdrew to England, Charles was appointed a commissary under Howe and had recently acted as a commissary of captures under Clinton during the Charlestown campaign. He would soon be reemployed by Cornwallis in the same capacity, and after becoming responsible for securing provisions between the Congaree and Wateree, he would accompany Cornwallis on the winter campaign. At the close of the war he retired on half pay to England, where in 1794 he published his history of the American war. A standard work for many years, it is still valuable, particularly for its portrayal of his personal experiences as set against the broad canvas of the events in which he himself was involved. In 1797, through the influence of Cornwallis, he was appointed to the office of Deputy Controller of the Revenue of Stamps. He died in London and was buried at Paddington. (*DNB*; *The Cornwallis Papers*)

[41] Anthony Knecht was an acting assistant commissary general. (*The Cornwallis Papers*)

Rawdon to Cornwallis, 22nd July 1780

2(341): ALS

Camden
July 22nd 1780

Earl Cornwallis etc etc etc

My Lord

I have the honor to inform you that every thing here is at present quiet. The rebels remain in the same positions as when I last wrote, but Sumpter's people begin to tire and I understand his force has mouldered considerably. I have received assurances from our friends in North Carolina that they will bear their distresses patiently till we are able to advance to their relief, and I have taken all possible pains to keep their minds easy and secure that the hour of their deliverance is at hand. Lieutenant Adamson of the New York Voluntiers, who was taken by the enemy in Huck's affair, is now here on parole. I wish much to have him exchanged as he has ingratiated himself exceedingly with the people of the country. I am confidant that he can immediately raise an independant company should your Lordship have no objection, and from my knowledge of the man I can recommend him as a very zealous and active officer. Should your Lordship think it expedient to release a lieutenant for him, I would, immediately upon receiving a certificate of it, instruct Lieutenant Adamson to collect his men. Turnbull tells me that no force of any consequence has marched towards Balfour's quarter. I am happy to hear from Captain Ross that there is now a prospect of getting the business of the town into a train which will in some measure lighten your Lordship's burthen. Let me assert that a similar consideration makes the business of this district a satisfaction to

Your Lordship's very faithful and affectionate servant

RAWDON

Cornwallis to Rawdon, 26th July 1780

78(48): C

Charlestown
July 26th 1780

Rt Hon Lord Rawdon

My dear Lord

I received this morning with great pleasure your Lordship's letter of the 22nd. The preserving so extensive a frontier and surmounting so many difficulties both in and out of the province can only be attributed to the prudence and firmness of your conduct.

I do not care to propose to the enemy an exchange of any of the prisoners here, as the General in his instructions to me seems very averse to it, but Tarleton by my consent, before I had received those instructions, wrote to the commanding officer in North Carolina to propose an exchange of some of the officers taken at Waxhaw for some of the Legion taken at sea. He received no answer. De Kalbe was not then come into North Carolina and I doubt whether any Continental officer was there. Tarleton will be with you in a few days and will give you a further account of this business, when I can see no impropriety in your writing to de Kalbe to renew the proposition and to add Lieutenant Adamson. If he should by this means get released before I come down, I beg your Lordship will give what orders you think proper about his company. If, however, any lieutenant of the rebels should be actually or should hereafter fall into your hands (those taken by the Legion excepted, who certainly should not be exchanged without the release of the officers of the Legion, who by all accounts have been most cruelly treated), you have my leave to negotiate Lieutenant Adamson's immediate exchange.

Poor Osborne[42] is dead, which is at present a great distress. I have directed the Town Major to give notice that all letters for officers in the Camden District should be sent to my quarters, and I will continue to send often, as I know the satisfaction it gives at a distance to receive letters.

We have heard nothing from any part of the world.

I am, my dear Lord,
Most sincerely yours

[CORNWALLIS]

[*Subscribed*:]

My best respects to the Governor.

Cornwallis to Rawdon, 29th July 1780   78(55): C

Charlestown
July 29th 1780

Rt Hon Lord Rawdon

My dear Lord

By your letter to Ross[43] I find that McArthur has moved from Cheraw Hill and that the militia under Rutherford had advanced to Rocky River, Pedee. The approach of the enemy and the sickness of his troops made it very necessary for him to move. I have no doubt but

---

[42] Osborn(e), who apparently served as a courier, has not been otherwise identified. He may have been a non-commissioned officer, there being no record of him in the *Army Lists* or in the Roll of officers on the Provincial establishment.

[43] *letter to Ross*: dated the 24th, it is not extant.

your Lordship will receive the best intelligence of de Kalbe's motions and make the best dispositions possible. I assure you I feel much for the uneasiness and anxiety of your situation but hope it will not affect your health. I expect Balfour about the middle of next week and should wish to stay here about a week after his arrival, but if things look at all serious, I can come at the shortest notice. I was very uneasy, before I heard from New York, for fear of a positive order to send troops thither. The dispatches I have received by the *Pearl* make me easy on that subject. I therefore should wish to undertake our march in as great force as possible and with as good troops. We must expect of course that our battalions will be much weakened by sickness, for which reason I intend to take an English regiment from hence, the 7th I believe. In order to effect this it will be necessary to put a Provincial corps into Sullivan's Island, and Brown's appears to me in every respect the properest for that purpose. I would, to have obliged Turnbull, have been glad to have ordered down the New York Volunteers, but as some corps must for a time be left at Camden, and then perhaps moved on to secure the communication with this province and to awe any disaffected districts near the boundary, I cannot think Paterson proper to be trusted with such a command; and the York Volunteers, when joined by their light company and the flank corps of Brown's, would be very sufficient for this service; and tho' Turnbull is not a great genius, he is a plain righteaded man. I am sensible that he will be mortifyed at not getting away to his family in New York, but the service here is too important to sacrifice publick to private motives, and as we are likely to meet with much more opposition than was expected when I promised to let him go, he must be satisfyed with an assurance that he shall go as soon as I can possibly spare him. I am not quite sure whether you have six or eight companies of Brown's corps with you, but whichever it is, you will please to order that corps to march immediately for this place. Their baggage will come by water to Cooke's. By the time that corps can arrive, I hope to get Wemyss back from George town, and then the 7th can be spared. If any material objection occurs to you or that[44] you cannot at present part with that corps, let me know by the return of the express that I may try some other mode of doing it. I cannot be easy about this place without two English regiments in it. I wish you would employ emissaries on the Pedee to give information to Wemyss at Georgetown in case the enemy should attempt any thing against him. He has not above half his regiment with him and consequently must keep a good look out. England is come to act as a major of brigade with us. I have not just now a brigade for him, but will take him with me when we march, and shall find some employment for him. In the meantime, as he is idle here and as Doyle is sick, I thought you might want some assistance. I have therefore sent him to you 'till I come up. Don't apprehend that he will interfere with Doyle's appointment; I have received sufficient authority from Sir Henry to insure him. I think you should do every thing in your power to persuade both friends and enemies that we mean to penetrate by Cross Creek — in short, every thing that can tend to save the country about Salisbury. Altho' I fear it will be all in vain, it is worth trying. I wish you could get Harrison's corps to Camden as early in the month as possible, whether perfectly compleat or not, and tell them that cloathing, arms and money will be sent thither for them.

---

[44] *that*: the meaning is 'if'. See p 108, note 12.

List of the ships arrived at New York under Admiral Graves:

	Guns
London	90
Resolution	74
Royal Oak	74
Bedford	74
America	64
Prudent	64.

I am, my dear Lord,
Most sincerely yours

[CORNWALLIS]

Cornwallis to Rawdon, 30th July 1780   78(60): C

Charles Town
30th July 1780

Rt Hon Lord Rawdon

My dear Lord

I inclose to you a letter I this morning received from Major Wemyss with my answer[45]. It is a very unpleasant business, but we must expect many mortifications in our trade. I cannot help lamenting that McArthur was not better informed. This blow certainly might have been avoided. I have, you see, determined that the 63rd should join the army, and as we shall by that means keep two compleat British regiments here, I will not, for the present at least, bring up Brown's corps. You will either send that corps, or any other detachment that you may think more convenient or proper, to the High Hills of Santee. In short, the communication by that river must not be lost. The grenadier company, and I believe two battalion companys, of Brown's corps are at Friday's Ferry. I do not see any use they are of there; your Lordship therefore had better send to the commanding officer to collect as many waggons as he conveniently can from that district, without seriously distressing the friendly inhabitants, and join you with them at Camden. The friends may be assured that the waggons shall be returned to them as soon as possible and that they shall be paid for the hire of them. I must leave every thing else to your discretion and shall join you as soon as possible.

I am etc

[CORNWALLIS]

---

[45] For enclosures, see pp 319 to 322.

[*Subscribed*:]

July 31st

Tarleton sets out this evening with about 40 of the Legion. I have directed him to pass at Lenew's Ferry and proceed from thence to Camden. He will make a favourable diversion for Wemyss and endeavour on his way to encourage our friends and intimidate the enemy.

Rawdon to Cornwallis, 27th July 1780   2(369): ALS

Camden
July 27th 1780

Earl Cornwallis etc etc etc

My Lord

The letter which accompanies this, dated on the 24th, would have been dispatched on that day had I not expected that Osborn would have furnished me a better conveyance than the Congaree express. Being disappointed in that hope, I proposed sending it by Colonel Rugeley, who intended to have set out yesterday for Charlestown, but that expectation also failed me. The delay has given me the opportunity of acknowledging your Lordship's letter of the 24th. Turnbull has had directions to take every step which will not expose himself to risque in order to prevent the enemy from passing in force towards the Ninety Six District; and to render his efforts effectual, I gave him the absolute disposal of all the militia between the Wateree and Broad River; but by the accounts which Turnbull transmits to me respecting the royal militia west of Broad River, they by no means stand in need of our assistance. Every thing continues more quiet than could possibly have been expected. Rutherford with a considerable body of militia is upon Rockey River, Pedee. A few of our militia have had what they call a skirmish with some of his people; that is, as far as I can make out, both parties came unexpectedly to the banks of the river, fired, and retired. I am surprized at not being able to inform your Lordship exactly where de Kalb is. I have many people out, but I fear some accident has befallen them. I believe de Kalb to be now at Salisbury. The rebel officer, who came with the flag of truce, in his way back stopped at Rugeley's. Having enquired for Rugeley, who was not at home, he very privately slipped a note into the hand of Doctor Harper's wife[46]. She retired into another room and attempted to read the note,

---

[46] A niece of John Witherspoon, President of Princeton College, Sarah Dickey Harper had married Daniel Harper MD on the death of her first husband, Dr Jean Cantzon (Canson), a Frenchman who had practised medicine in and around the Waxhaws and who was the father of her four children. Daniel (1745-1791) had migrated to South Carolina from Ireland in 1767, and after setting up in practice with Dr James Knox in what was later Chester County, he now resided in the Waxhaws. In late September 1780 Cornwallis would remark that 'he has been a great sufferer and very active and zealous in our service'. It is presumably for this reason that later in the war he felt it necessary to flee with his family to Ireland. He was reputedly warned not to return to South Carolina, did so, and is said to have been murdered. He lies buried in the cemetery of the Old Waxhaw Presbyterian Church. (Viola Caston Floyd, 'Descendants of William Harper, Irish Immigrant to Lancaster County, South Carolina' (np, 1965), 4-5; *The Cornwallis Papers*; Lark Emerson Adams ed, *Journals of the House of Representatives,1785-1786 (The State Records of South Carolina)* (South Carolina Department of Archives and History, 1979), 428; T W

but, as it was written in a cramp hand, she had not time to make it out before the officer followed her and asked with emotion whether she was Mrs Rugeley. Upon her replying, 'No!' he snatched the paper with much confusion, put it into his pocket and left the house immediately. He likewise put some very improper questions to some of our militia officers. As he was out of my reach before I was made acquainted with these circumstances, I wrote to de Kalb, complaining of this prostitution of a public pledge of faith and prescribing that, should he in future have occasion to send any letter to this army, the messenger should stop as soon as he came within sight of our advanced post, should there deliver his letter, and immediately retire. Mrs Harper says that, as far as she could make out, the note was an application from Rutledge to Rugeley. A Negro having given me information that Captain Chesnut[47] and his overseer used daily to dress a quantity of victuals and carry them out into the woods, never employing a Negro in that office, I sent a party of dragoons to surround the plantation and to endeavor by threats to extort from the overseer where the party was concealed which he and his master fed so cautiously. After much difficulty, the overseer guided the dragoons to a swamp, in the heart of which they took Chesnut's nephew (Alexander Irwin[48]) and four other rebels. Their business appears to have been to collect Negroes and horses belonging to the army and to carry them up the country to sell. I am astonished at Chesnut's conduct, as every possible attention had constantly been paid to him. He is now in gaol and in irons. Having secured these people, I soon traced a further connection and, before they were alarmed, seized some others of the set. I cannot find any proof of their having held communication with the enemy's army and rather think that, Chesnut having resolved to fly, he was willing first to carry off as much as possible both of his own and of his neighbor's property. Colonel Bryan, not being able to find forage for his horses on the Cheraws road, is now stationed at Hanging Rock. My letter of the 24th to Captain Ross will have informed your Lordship that McArthur was drawn back to the eastern branch of Linches Creek. His men fell sick so fast at Cheraws Hill that, not being able to bring off all his invalids, he sent no less than ninety of them by water to Georgetown. This is all ague, for very fortunately we have had no appearance yet of any kind of bad fever among the men. I have picked up a few of the Continentals who escaped from Charlestown. Would your Lordship have them exchanged for the men of the New York Volunteers and Legion who were taken in Huck's affair? Two of the six pounders shall be sent down immediately. I think the best method (if I find it can be done with perfect safety) will be to send them in boats returning to Cook's Landing. I do not reccollect whether your Lordship before your departure gave any directions about the two cohorns. If they are to remain here, shells for them must be sent from Charlestown. Lieutenant Adamson, whom I mentioned in

---

Lipscomb to the editor, 23rd and 25th February 2005)

[47] Born in Virginia, John Chesnut (1743-1818) had served as a captain and paymaster in the 3rd regiment of rangers, which, having been raised by the Provincial Congress in June 1775, was transferred to the Continental establishment in 1776. Resigning his commission, he later entered the South Carolina revolutionary militia as a captain and was among the troops who capitulated at Charlestown. Under article 4 of the capitulation he had been permitted to return home, but now found in breach of the parole to which he had been required to subscribe, he had been consigned to the jail at Camden, loaded with irons, and chained to the floor. For his sins he would also lose $5,000 worth of indigo. (Moss, *SC Patriots*, 167; McCrady, *SC in the Rev 1775-1780*, 619)

[48] Of Alexander Irvin little is known except that he served under John Chesnut (see above) in the South Carolina revolutionary militia and was consigned with him to the jail at Camden, loaded with irons. (Moss, op cit, 485; McCrady, op cit, 619)

a former letter to your Lordship, will have the honor of delivering this packet. He is upon parole.

I have the honor to be, my Lord, with great respect and affection
Your very faithful and obedient servant

RAWDON

[*Subscribed*:]

I have just had notice that on the 23rd de Kalb was still on Deep River but had moved from Coxe's settlement towards Guildford Court House. The militia, who are spread all over the country, delayed and nearly took my messenger.

Enclosure (1)
Rawdon to Cornwallis, 24th July 1780   2(352): ALS

Camden
July 24th 1780

Earl Cornwallis etc etc etc

My Lord

I was last night honored with your letter of the 20th and feel the highest satisfaction in finding that I have answered your wishes. There is such appearance of quiet at present that I flatter myself your Lordship will not be obliged to leave Charlestown till you shall have arranged every thing to your satisfaction. I am much indebted to Governor Martin for the assistance he has afforded me in quieting the minds of some of our friends who began to grow impatient. At present I do not dread any further rising till we shall call them forth. I am in hopes that Bryan will immediately be able to form a corps on the Provincial Establishment with the rank of major for himself. I have had Harrison with me. He says he has collected four hundred men, who are to be mustered before me on the 5th of August. The Highlanders in the neighborhood of Cross Creek have proposed to me to raise a regiment. Their plan is that the men shall not come in here, but that the officers shall be appointed immediately, so that the privates, being secretly enrolled at present, may be collected without delay in their respective companies whensoever we penetrate into the country. The enemy having left that district open, there is no difficulty in making that arrangement. They entreat that Governor Martin may be their colonel. Mr Cruden[49] is proposed by them for lt colonel,

---

[49] A son of the Reverend William Cruden of London, John Cruden had been a merchant in Wilmington, North Carolina. In March 1775 he had at first refused to sign the association subversive of the royal government but had later been pressured into doing so. Declining to take the test oath two years later, he was banished and saw his property confiscated. Repairing to the Bahamas by way of East Florida, he for a time resided at Nassau. On 16th September 1780 Cornwallis would appoint him Commissioner for Sequestered Estates in South Carolina, an office whose nature, and his occupancy of it, is fully set out later in these Papers. On the evacuation of Charlestown in December 1782 he would sail for East Florida before moving on to Rawdon Harbour in the Bahamas by May 1785.

and Captain Stewart[50] (who commanded the Negro pioniers) is recommended as major. The rest of the officers are mostly from the Provincial half pay list. Not thinking myself authorised to decide upon the ranks of colonel and lt colonel, I have waved the scheme of forming the regiment till I shall receive your Lordship's orders, but, that the opportunity of securing a serviceable body of men may not be lost, I have agreed to issue warrants for raising as many independant companies on the principle above mentioned as, when united, would form the battalion. A rebel captain with a flag of truce arrived here last night, having been mistakenly suffered to pass the post at Hanging Rock. He wished to proceed to Charlestown with a letter to your Lordship from de Kalb[51], and upon my absolutely refusing him that liberty, he requested that I would give an answer to the letter, as he was directed to bring one back. I therefore opened it, but finding that the business was beyond my sphere, I promised to forward it to your Lordship and to transmit the answer as soon as it should arrive. He got here after dark and I dispatched him two hours before day — not much to his satisfaction, for he seemed desirous to look about him.

I have the honor to be most faithfully
Your Lordship's very affectionate humble servant

RAWDON

Enclosure (2)
Warrant for independent companies destined to form   *101(2): ACS*
   the North Carolina Highland Regiment

By etc

    To [*blank*] Esq

Reposing especial confidence in your loyalty to His Majesty and in your courage and discretion, I do hereby empower you to raise an independent company on the Provincial

---

Three years later, with his father dead and his mother, sister and her children dependent on him, he would present a claim to the royal commission in respect of his losses. (PRO 30/11/7(52), (53) and (57); DeMond, *Loyalists in NC*, 54, 66, 184; Lambert, *SC Loyalists*, 236, 264; Coldham, *Loyalist Claims*, 111)

[50] A veteran of the Seven Years' War, Allan Stewart (1725-?) was a Scot who had settled in North Carolina about 1775. At the time of the loyalist uprising there in early 1776, he was commissioned a captain in the Provincial line by Governor Josiah Martin, but when the uprising was put down, he fled to New York and on 13th July 1777 took command of the Black Pioneers, a unit initially consisting of forty to fifty escaped slaves from the Carolinas who were employed on labouring duties. With them he saw service at New York and Philadelphia before coming south and commanding them during the siege of Charlestown. They had returned with Clinton to New York, but he did not, as promotion was in prospect. Cornwallis was soon to appoint him a lt colonel in the North Carolina Highland Regiment (of which Martin was to be appointed Lt Colonel Commandant), but the regiment was never embodied. Stewart would nevertheless be placed on the Provincial half-pay list in that capacity at the close of the war. (Nan Cole and Todd Braisted, 'A History of the Black Pioneers' (*The On-Line Institute for Advanced Loyalist Studies*, 11th March 2006); Raymond, 'British American Corps'; Clark, *Loyalists in the Southern Campaign*, i, *passim*; Treasury 64/23(21) and (32) and WO 65/165(15) (National Archives, Kew))

[51] *a letter..*: of 16th July. See p 375.

establishment from among the Highlanders settled in North Carolina, to consist of a captain, lieutenant, ensign, three serjeants, one drummer or piper, and fifty six rank and file, exclusive of three contingent men.

You may promise your men that they shall not be obliged to serve beyond the two Carolinas and Virginia unless with their own consent; neither shall they, without their own approbation, be liable to be incorporated into any battalion, excepting into the North Carolina Highland Regiment to be commanded by his Excellency Governor Martin; and the term of enlistment is to be only during the present rebellion.

I hereby command the said company to obey you as their captain, and you are diligently to observe and fulfill all such orders and instructions as you may from time to time receive from me or any other your superior officer.

For all which this (from the powers vested in me by Lt General Earl Cornwallis etc etc etc) shall be your sufficient warrant.

Given under my hand and seal at Head Quarters
in Camden, South Carolina,
this first day of July 1780

RAWDON

Cornwallis to Rawdon, 1st August 1780　　　　　　　　79(2): C

Charlestown
August 1st 1780

Rt Hon Lord Rawdon

My dear Lord

I yesterday received your letters of the 24th and 27th, by which I find you had not then heard of the disaster of McArthur's sick or the confusion and terror of Colonel Mills's district. I am still afraid of some party getting over to the Santee and disturbing our convoys, especially as I find that Major Manson, whom I supposed to be attending on the artillery boats with a detachment of convalescents, had yesterday got no farther than Monk's Corner and that the convalescents were left in parties without orders and in the utmost confusion. McKinnon has been twice at Cooke's, but I do not see that he has done any good there. I have ordered an officer of this garrison to go express to Cooke's to pick up all the convalescents he can find, which may I suppose amount to about 24 men, and march on the road to Camden by short stages, keeping as nearly as possible opposite to the artillery convoy. I should hope that your Lordship will send something either that way or down Linches Creek for a few days untill we see what turn things will take in that quarter. Our officers in general want exertion and had rather see things go on ill than give themselves the smallest trouble or undertake at least[52] responsibility. To compleat all, during the storm on Sunday night they allowed near fifty of the rebel prisoners to escape.

I am much pleased with the offer of the Highlanders and with the testimony they bear of their esteem for their Governor. I approve of what you have done in regard to the companies. I will certainly desire the Governor to take the command of them, but as so much has been said about Provincial rank, and the Commander in Chief has been in such different humours about it, I do not care to meddle with the rank of colonel. The Governor is so good as to say that it is immaterial to him by what military title he is called. I shall therefore appoint him lt colonel commandant with a lt colonel under him, as I hope to see him soon lead the province instead of that corps. Mr Cruden would have been very agreeable to me as lt colonel, but as I have determined to employ him in the very important business of the sequestrations, they or the Governor must fix on some other person.

I totally forgot the coehorns. Your Lordship will please to send them hither. I trust the navigation of Santee is safe. If we lose our convoy of arms and artillery stores, we are undone.

I am, my dear Lord,
Most sincerely yours

[CORNWALLIS]

[*Subscribed*:]

I will answer de Kalbe's letter by the next express.

Rawdon to Cornwallis, 31st July 1780   *2(399): ALS*

Camden
July 31st 1780

Earl Cornwallis etc etc etc

My Lord

Finding my health pretty firm, and no immediate business pressing upon me, I made an excursion on the evening of the 29th to examine the state of our post at Hanging Rock. Upon my arrival there about eleven at night, I found Lt Colonel Pattinson drunk. I therefore ordered him hither into close arrest till I shall receive your Lordship's orders respecting him. If your Lordship has not the power to confirm the sentences of general courts martial in such cases, I don't know whether it would not be better to accept his resignation, which I doubt not he would be very glad to give in, for the resignation so immediately following the crime may perhaps furnish a better example than his dismissal from the service three months hence

---

[52]   *at least*: perhaps a copying mistake. The sense suggests 'the least'.

when the army may be separated and the circumstances almost forgotten. It may require explanation why I should entrust the command of a considerable post to an officer of such doubtful character. In my defence I plead necessity, for Mecan, McArthur and Carden are all sick in this town, and the Fuziliers were so miserably circumstanced as to cloathing that I was absolutely forced to recall them on the arrival of their baggage lest they should have been unfit to march when called upon for business of greater consequence. Webster is at the eastern branch of Linches Creek, whither I have advanced the 33rd Regiment in support of the 71st, the Voluntiers of Ireland still remaining at Robertson's with the cannon to sustain either the post above mentioned or Hanging Rock, as may prove requisite. Under these circumstances I was obliged to make use of Pattinson, trusting that by keeping a constant eye upon him he could not do much mischief.

I have very unluckily missed an opportunity of making a stroke against the enemy of so advantageous a nature that a similar occasion is scarcely to be expected. Having given such directions as I thought necessary for the security of Hanging Rock and of the communication from that post hither, I mounted my horse about ten yesterday morning to return to Camden, for I think it wrong, without important motives, to be long absent from this place, where information and business from every quarter naturally center to me, much of which is of such a nature that the delay of its seeking me at a distant post might be very prejudicial. Before I set out, a countryman mentioned that there had been firing in the morning near Rockey Mount. I examined the man, and from his account it appeared to me that there was no room to suppose that it had been more than that some patrole of Turnbull's had fallen in with a plundering party of the enemy, several of which Turnbull had mentioned to have come very near his post. I thought it sufficient to order an officer with a party of dragoons to patrole to the river, and I set out for Camden. When I got within four miles of the town, I met an express who informed me that two dragoons were arrived who had escaped from Rockey Mount, which post had been surrounded and assaulted at day break by a great body of rebels. I took every step which this tardy intelligence admitted, but my precautions were happily superfluous. I have just received a detail of the affair from Turnbull and, thro' the modesty of his recital, I can observe that the circumstances were much to the honor of his vigilance and firmness. As his account was very hastily written, I think it best only to send an abstract of it. His dragoons, having been saddled all night, were soon after day-break ordered out to grass, but they had scarcely passed an abbatis, which surrounds the post, when they fell in with three large columns of the rebels, by whom they were fired upon and dispersed. The New York Voluntiers, who were as usual at that hour standing to their arms, were immediately thrown into some log houses constructed for the purpose of defence; and some militia, abandoning a redoubt which they were appointed to garrison, likewise ran into the houses. The rebels advanced to the assault but were speedily driven back to a more respectful distance. They kept possession, however, of the redoubt, from which and the cover of rocks, trees etc they continued to fire for a long time. At length Sumpter (for it was his corps of militia that made the attack) summoned Turnbull to surrender, giving him ten minutes only to consider of it. The proposal was rejected and the attack was repeated with as little success as at first. Sumpter continued before the post till three in the afternoon, I suppose to cover the carrying off his killed and wounded, for, either during the truce or by means of a valley which from the loss of the redoubt was not flanked, they carried off all who fell, excepting three dead and one wounded who lay too near the post. Turnbull therefore cannot ascertain the enemy's loss, but imagines it to have been pretty severe. A Colonel Neal is one of the dead, and the wounded man says that a Colonel Bratten was likewise killed. At five Turnbull sent out two dragoons to recconnoitre, who brought back intelligence that they saw a large body of the enemy on an island at half a mile's distance. I suspect this to have been a party of our militia, for I think the corps at Hanging Rock must have been alarmed long before that time and have attempted, according to their instructions, to sustain Colonel Turnbull. I do not despair yet of hearing that the enemy have suffered in their retreat. I enclose to your Lordship a copy of Turnbull's loss in the action[53]. Many of those returned missing have come in here. Had a single man of them fled to Hanging Rock (which, being only a third part of the distance, was much more natural for them), I might in little more than an hour after receiving the intelligence have crossed the Catawba above the rebels with sixty of the Legion cavalry and Bryan's refugees, who are all well mounted. Advancing in that manner upon an enemy dispirited by repulse and ignorant of my numbers, I should have gone to sure victory, which circumstances would have made both creditable and useful, altho' there might have been but little of real merit in the success. I shall not, however, repine at want of fortune so long as I am conscious that I have acted from cool deliberation and that I have not omitted any of the arrangements which my situation required. I should have held myself highly blameable had I gone to Rockey Mount upon vague intelligence, thereby absenting myself another day from Camden whilst the enemy might have broken in upon my right. I will make no other excuse for exceeding my two sheets of paper than that I think it better to risque tireing your Lordship a little than to leave any thing unsaid which can tend to give your mind satisfaction respecting this part of your command. Colonel Rugeley will have informed your Lordship that a party of the enemy had pillaged our waggons between this and Hanging Rock. That party was intercepted by a Captain Cole of our militia, who, with half their numbers, routed them, killing and wounding several.[54] The same night a party of Colonel Bryan's routed two different scouting parties close to the rebel camp, killing some and bringing off a few prisoners. These little successes have put them in spirits. Kinloch commands at Hanging Rock for the present, but I purpose bringing Turnbull with his regiment thither and sending Carden (who is recovering) with the Prince of Wales's to Rockey Mount. Rutherford is at Waxhaw. Loose parties of militia under the direction of a Colonel Wade are on Rockey River and Pedee. De Kalb and Caswell were near the Quaker Meeting House on Deep River on the 24th, upon which day Gates arrived and took the command of the army. The strict defensive, which circumstances require me to maintain, gives great advantage to an enemy, who, having no precise point to cover, may throw himself at will upon any part of my extensive district; and as I should feel myself highly culpable were I to risque our great object by any attempt upon the enemy which did not carry with it almost a certitude of success, my apparent inactivity not only gives presumption to the rebels but also shakes the fidelity of many who had joined us. An advantage that could not be followed would be of little use to us, excepting where it is to shew that our posts are not to be attempted with impunity. It would be irksome enough, however, to submit, with every consciousness of superiority, to the appearance of being curbed and intimidated by the enemy were it not for the consideration that patience and temper should be as much the soldier's virtues as intrepidity. I could not any where so properly acknowledge the receipt of your Lordship's

---

[53] *a copy..*: not extant.

[54] The waggons had been captured by revolutionary militia led by William R Davie. On the way back to their camp on the north side of Waxhaw Creek they were ambushed in the early hours of 22nd July and routed. (Davie, *Revolutionary War Sketches*, 9-10; Revolutionary pension application of Richard Clinton of Davidson County, Tennessee, 10th December 1834) Apart from commanding the ambush, Cole has not been identified.

letter of the 26th as after what I have just been saying, as the commendation with which you have honored my conduct gives me new strength in those sentiments. Be assured, my Lord, that your praise has all the effect upon me that you wish. It convinces me that you at least think I strive to merit your esteem and, by encouraging me in that view, supports under every difficulty the zeal of

Your Lordship's most faithful and affectionate humble servant

RAWDON

Rawdon to Cornwallis, 1st August 1780 63(3): ALS

Camden
August 1st 1780

Earl Cornwallis etc etc etc

My Lord

I had the honor of writing to you yesterday by Lieutenant Chapman of the 23rd Regiment[55], giving your Lordship an account of a repulse which the rebels received in an attack on Rockey Mount. By very singular ill-fortune no intelligence of that affair reached Hanging Rock before the express which I mentioned to have met me close to this place upon my return. Him I sent forward to Captain Kinloch, but before he could arrive, it was too late. The enemy have thus escaped without paying the full penalty for their presumption – yet not entirely unpunished. It is impossible as yet to form even a guess at their loss, but the people of the country say that the number of dead and wounded which they carried off was very great. I am grieved to inform your Lordship that the 71st are miserably sickly, and I am in great pain about the ninety sick which they sent down the Pedee for Georgetown, being assured that a person who had taken the oath of allegiance collected a party expressly to pursue them.

I have the honor to be with great respect
Your Lordship's very faithful and affectionate servant

RAWDON

---

[55] Thomas Chapman was commissioned a 2nd lieutenant in the 23rd Regiment (Royal Welch Fusiliers) on 20th May 1776, being promoted to 1st lieutenant on 30th May 1778. (*Army Lists*)

Cornwallis to Rawdon, 4th August 1780   79(8): C

Charlestown
August 4th 1780

Rt Hon Lord Rawdon

My dear Lord

I yesterday received your letter of the 31st and am very glad to find that all the attempts of the enemy to disturb us in that part of the country have proved ineffectual. I beg you will give my thanks to Lt Colonel Turnbull and the troops under his command. I am still frightened about the situation of the country between the lower part of Pedee and Santee. A party of the enemy were on the 1st at the house of Gaillard at Murray's Ferry, which is not very distant from Cooke's Landing. Our great convoy of artillery, stores and arms has not yet reached the Wateree. Tarleton's march has been greatly impeded by the floods, and he will not be able to cross at Lenew's Ferry before tomorrow at soonest. Wemyss is still detained at Georgetown, partly by the country's being under water and partly by waiting for a sloop to bring away his sick. Every two or three hours I receive an express from some person near the Santee representing their terrors and great distress. I am told that Colonel Mills attributes all these misfortunes to his having received no notice of McArthur's quitting Cheraw Hill. It is absolutely necessary to inflict some exemplary punishment on the militia and inhabitants of that part of the country. On the moment we advance, we shall find an enemy in our rear. I thought perhaps that Bryan's and Harrison's corps with a small regular force to support them might be equal to this service and, with the word discrimination strongly impressed on their mind, might be trusted to punish the guilty by securing those whom they could catch and by burning and destroying the plantations of those who have fled. You, who know the situation of these corps, will best judge how adequate they are to this service, but some force must be sent to reduce and intimidate that country or the communication between the upper army and Charlestown will be impracticable; and unless we can get at our stores, I don't see how we can advance.

Balfour arrived last night and gives a good account of the situation of things at Ninety Six. The letter I sent to him ordering the waggons from Ninety Six was committed to Captain Ryarson[56], who fell sick on the road and forgot to send on the letter. The waggons, however, Balfour says, were to set out about this time under the convoy of the light infantry and were to pass by Fishdam Ford. If you wanted flour, perhaps by sending off an officer immediately, you might get a considerable supply as I am told there is great quantity in that country. I have no power to confirm general courts martial and consequently should be extremely glad that you got Lt Colonel Pattison's resignation, and beg you will make any use

---

[56] Of Dutch descent, Samuel Ryerson (1751-?) was a native of New Jersey and had been commissioned a captain in the 4th Battalion, New Jersey Volunteers, on 25th March 1777. He was now serving on secondment to Ferguson's corps and would be wounded and captured in the Battle of King's Mountain on 7th October. Paroled to Charlestown four months later, he would find on his arrival that he had been exchanged. At the close of the war he was placed on the Provincial half-pay list and retired to New Brunswick, where he lived to a ripe old age. (Draper, *King's Mountain*, 360, 479, 480; Treasury 64/23(8), WO 65/164(36), and WO 65/165(7) (National Archives, Kew))

you please of my name to accomplish it, as that wretch renders the corps totally useless. I have just received your Lordship's letter of the 1st, by which I find that you are still uncertain about the fate of the sick of the 71st and uninformed of the uproar and confusion down the Pedee. The arrival of Balfour will soon set me at liberty and I will most certainly advance as soon as possible, but we must first have the stores that are absolutely necessary, and I look on the severe chastisement of the traitors at Cheraws to be absolutely necessary. If you think it unsafe to send a corps too near the frontier, we may punish the interior part of the country now and reserve the borderers untill we move on, when it can be done with safety. I am much concerned to hear that the 71st are so sickly. I fear the 63rd will be in the same state. The great difficulty of our communication is that we can have no fixt posts on any of the rivers, or indeed in any part of the lower country. No way occurs to me but sending some of those loose corps to make incursions and intimidate. I intend to let the light company of the New York Volunteers join their corps, the light companies of the 71st their regiment except so many as will compleat those that are now with the Legion to a troop of 70 men. Of the detachment of the 16th Regiment I mean to take about 18 or 20, if so many are fit, for the cavalry and the remainder will be attach'd to the guns. I believe Captain Campbell of the 71st[57] will be the properest man to command the troop of that regiment. Without good cavalry we can do nothing in this country. I would have it of as good a species as possible, and not too numerous for very obvious reasons. I feel very much for your anxiety, but I can assure you I have had and still have my full share. If you send letters for New York, I believe I shall in about ten days have an opportunity of a safe conveyance. You had better direct your letters for the future to me or Colonel Balfour, as I shall try hard to get away in the course of next week.

I am, my dear Lord,
Most sincerely yours

[CORNWALLIS]

[*Subscribed:*]

My best respects to the Governor. I have at last finished my proc[essing] of the composite order.

---

[57] Having been commissioned a lieutenant in the 1st Battalion, 71st (Highland) Regiment, in November 1775, Charles Campbell (*c.* 1755-1780) had been promoted to captain in the same battalion three years later. By some accounts he is mistakenly said to have been involved in the burning of one of Thomas Sumter's houses on 28th May 1780 when Tarleton's force passed there in pursuit of Buford, but according to Tarleton, who was better placed than anyone to know, no element of the 71st Regiment accompanied him on that occasion. Now commanding the 71st's light companies at Ninety Six, Campbell would depart with them for Camden on 9th August, arriving there on the 13th. After the defeat of Gates three days later, he would command a detachment of the 71st's light troops forming part of Tarleton's force in pursuit of Sumter. Near the end of the ensuing action on 18th August he would be killed. 'His death,' remarked Tarleton, 'cannot be mentioned without regret. He was a young officer, whose conduct and abilities afforded the most flattering prospect that he would be an honour to his country.' It was a view shared by Cornwallis, who described him as 'a very promising officer'. (*Army Lists*; Tarleton, *Campaigns*, 27, 102, 111-115; Bass, *Gamecock*, 52; Gregorie, *Sumter*, 74; *The Cornwallis Papers*)

Rawdon to Cornwallis, 2nd August 1780　　　　　　　　　　　　　　　　*63(5): ALS*

Camden
August 2nd 1780

Earl Cornwallis etc etc etc

My Lord

I have this afternoon been honored with your letter of the 29th of July. The information which your Lordship will have received from me since you wrote that letter will prove to your Lordship that my situation requires constant vigilance and full as much force as I can at present bring into the field. The posts of Rockey Mount and Hanging Rock are both of infinite consequence to me and Linches Creek must never be exposed. The supporting this chain and other immediate considerations make me feel myself bound to use the latitude which your Lordship has allowed me by delaying the march of Brown's regiment till the light infantry shall arrive. I dispatch this letter by the Congaree express, as your Lordship desired, to give you information of the delay, altho' I think it probable that I shall have to send another messenger in the course of the night. The enemy are moving about me but, as far as I can yet see, not with any combined plan, and I think it possible they may suffer for it. I hope I shall not be forced to make any movement but what is to be included in a defensive plan, so that your Lordship may not be hurried from Charlestown before every thing is fully arranged; but as I conceive your sentiments entirely, I bid fair to satisfy them. I am grieved to tell your Lordship that the ninety sick of the 71st were taken by the scoundrel who pursued them. The enemy have not been able to move them from the Pedee and probably will not before we move. I could push a party to where they are, but do not see a possibility of bringing them off. Our artillery stores are not arrived, which is very unfortunate as they may cause delay.

I have the honor to be with great respect
Your Lordship's very affectionate servant

RAWDON

Rawdon to Cornwallis, 3rd August 1780　　　　　　　　　　　　　　　　*63(9): ALS*

Camden
August 3rd 1780

Earl Cornwallis etc etc etc

My Lord

In my letter of yesterday afternoon I mentioned that it was probable I should have to dispatch another messenger in the course of the night. That expectation was occasioned by the state of affairs at Rockey Mount. On the 1st instant I received notice from Hanging Rock that Turnbull had sent information thither of the enemy's being again in march towards him in considerable force, in consequence of which Captain Kinloch, according to his instructions, immediately marched to the relief of Rockey Mount with the Prince of Wales's American Regiment, part of the Legion, two hundred of Colonel Bryan's volunteers and a three-pounder. The Royal North Carolina Regiment and four hundred of Bryan's were left at Hanging Rock under the command of Captain McCulloch[58] of the Legion, a very careful officer; but suspecting that the demonstration against Rockey Mount might be a feint to draw troops from Hanging Rock and facilitate an attack there, I ordered the flank companies of the Volunteers of Ireland to march by the cross road from Robertson's to Hanging Rock and further reinforced that post with about an hundred militia. Lt Colonel Turnbull's force had likewise received an addition of ten dragoons, and a captain and fifty men from the 23rd Regiment, which detachment I had sent with a supply of provisions and ammunition to him. Besides this, I had ordered Carey's regiment of militia to join him with all dispatch, for I thought it probable that the enemy might make a second attempt with cannon against Rockey Mount. I have this day had two expresses from Hanging Rock forwarding the news received from Rockey Mount. The first mentioned that Sumpter, having notice that the post was reinforced, had halted behind Fishing Creek ten miles distant from Rockey, in which position he was on the night of the 1st instant when Turnbull marched in hopes of surprizing him. The second letter tells me that Turnbull, hearing the ford of Fishing Creek was impassable on account of the late heavy rains, had made a detour of six miles to head the creek. If he succeeded in that step before the rebels were alarmed, they could not possibly escape as the Catawba is very much swelled. I meant not to have written till I had learned the event lest I should raise hopes which may fail us, but I thought your Lordship would be anxious to hear from me at present and I thought it but just to your Lordship to detail our fair prospects as well as those which are unfavorable. I have judged it necessary to remain here that I may be in readiness to meet Gates if he crosses the Pedee. However, I hear nothing of him, tho' I have many emissaries abroad.

I have just received your Lordship's letter of the 30th with the postscript of the 31st and the two enclosures. It is too true that the sick of the 71st have been taken, but the rest of Colonel Mills's account appears a good deal tinged by his own apprehensions. I have heard of plundering parties distressing the country which McArthur's retreat uncovered, but of no uproar that betokened revolt. On the contrary, a number of the Pedee militia have (with their wives and families) fallen back to our posts. I sent orders some days ago to Colonel Moore[59] to assemble his regiment of militia, and I will immediately send something to the High Hills, but I protest I cannot yet say what it will be. I expect that the intelligence which I shall receive this night will either set me exceedingly at my ease or require my best

---

[58] Commissioned a captain in the Roman Catholic Volunteers on 14th October 1777, Kenneth McCulloch had transferred to the British Legion infantry on 30th September 1778. He would be mortally wounded on 6th August when commanding them with bravery and distinction in the action at Hanging Rock. (Raymond, 'British American Corps'; Bass, *The Green Dragoon*, 47; Tarleton, *Campaigns*, 95; *The Cornwallis Papers*)

[59] Of Moore little is known apart from his briefly commanding the royal militia on the High Hills of Santee. By the close of August he would be superseded by Samuel Tynes. As these Papers later make clear, he was not Isham Moore, who also lived in the vicinity, but he may have been the James Moore whose loyalism would eventually lead him and his four sons to be killed in cold blood by the revolutionaries. (*The Cornwallis Papers*; Lambert, *SC Loyalists*, 211)

exertions. With regard to force, I must say I think I have quite enough, but, tho' the enemy do not give me any apprehension, from the nature of the country they are enabled to give me full employment for all my troops on my defensive plan. I learn that the Continental regiments in Gates's army are much reduced by desertion; many indeed have come in to us and I am told that Generals de Kalb and Guest[60] are gone back to Maryland. I am not in any fear for Wemyss; the people about Black River are disaffected but they are not collected in any part; nor do I believe that any party of the enemy has come down from the northward towards that district. I will make some trusty persons take a sweep and go to Wemyss with their intelligence. I must hope that your Lordship's goodness will attribute the haste in which this is written to my desire of forwarding without delay an express which your Lordship may be impatient to receive.

I have the honor to be, my Lord, with great respect and affection
Your most faithful and obedient servant

RAWDON

Cornwallis to Rawdon, 6th August 1780   79(19): C

Charlestown
6th August 1780

Rt Hon Lord Rawdon

My dear Lord

I this day received your letters of the 2nd and 3rd and expect another very soon. I am not, however, too sanguine, having had so much experience of military events. I am most perfectly convinced that every thing has been done to ensure success as far as your arrangements are concerned. Tarleton passed Lenew's Ferry this day. He was much delayed by the floods. I shall be very happy to hear of the arrival of the artillery stores. I write now by way of sending back one of the expresses as we have three here.

I am, my dear Lord,
Yours very sincerely

[CORNWALLIS]

---

[60] Mordecai Gist (1743-1792) had seen service as a field officer in the Maryland line during operations in the northern theatre of the war before being promoted on 9th January 1779 to brigadier general commanding the 2nd Maryland Brigade. Sent south with Kalb, he and his brigade were to fight bravely in the Battle of Camden. When all was lost, he would escape with some one hundred men by wading through a swamp on the western side of the battlefield. (Boatner, *Encyclopedia*; McCrady, *SC in the Rev 1775-1780*, 678)

Rawdon to Cornwallis, 4th August 1780
63(15): ALS

Camden
August 4th 1780

Earl Cornwallis etc etc etc

My Lord

I am sorry to tell you that Turnbull's march has proved fruitless. His disappointment at the ford gave time for the enemy to receive the alarm, and as they were all mounted, they escaped with only a fright. Four or five of their worst mounted were picked up by our dragoons. Had he succeeded in giving them a stroke, it would have had very beneficial consequences upon the sentiments of the country people. No opportunity shall be lost of giving the enemy a blow where it can be done securely, but the most brilliant prospect of distinguishing myself would not tempt me if its event could put this station to hazard. I shall feel sufficient satisfaction if I can surrender this command to your Lordship in the condition in which you have a right to expect to find it. Many difficulties have surrounded me but they have merely arisen from the necessity of my acting on the defensive and they will disperse the moment we press upon the enemy. A party of the Legion cavalry march this afternoon to join Colonel Moore's militia at the High Hills, and the mounted infantry of the Legion will follow tomorrow. They are the troops which just at present I can best spare.

I have the honor to be with sincere affection and respect
Your Lordship's very faithful and obedient servant

RAWDON

Rawdon to Cornwallis, 11th August 1780
63(34): ALS

Camden
August 11th
11 at night

My Lord

Tho' I take it for granted that this letter will travel but a short distance before it meets you, yet it may be acceptable, as it may save your Lordship from some hours of anxiety concerning us. This consideration would have made me write frequently to your Lordship during these last two or three days had not constant hurry and the want of every convenience prevented me. I have endeavored to delay Gates as much as possible in his progress without risquing any thing, and I have in some degree succeeded. No opportunity offered of attacking him consistent with the safety of our magazines, tho' I thought my force fully equal to the attempt. Gates's army is called five thousand, but I do not believe they exceed three thousand five hundred. Whensoever he threatened to pass round my flank and get between me and Camden, I was always obliged to fall back. At last I have collected every thing but

Turnbull's regiment at this place. Gates may attack me tomorrow morning. If he does, I think he will find us in better spirits than he expects. If he does not, it will become every day more difficult and he will be seriously distressed by want of provisions. No exertion shall be wanting on the part of

Your Lordship's very faithful and affectionate servant

RAWDON

[*Subscribed*:]

    I understand that Gates is two miles on this side of Rugeley's Mills but am not positive. Part of his troops are there. I can procure but miserable intelligence.

Return of the troops etc at Camden, 13th August 1780[61]

State of the Troops and Public Departments at Camden under the command of the Rt Hon Lord Rawdon, August 13th 1780

	Present fit for Duty			Sick Present			Total			Men without Arms		
	S:[62]	D:[63]	R & file	S:	D:	R & file	S:	D:	R & file	S:	D:	R & file
23rd Regiment	17	9	328	-	1	32	17	10	360	-	-	-
33rd ditto	13	1	261	3	-	44	16	1	305	-	-	-
71st Regiment:												
1st Battalion	14	6	138	13	5	147	27	11	285	-	-	-
2nd Battalion	5	3	90	20	14	226	25	17	316	-	-	-
Prince of Wales's American Regiment	9	5	37	10	1	71	19	6	108	-	-	-
Volunteers of Ireland	23	12	269	-	2	25	23	14	294	-	-	-
British Legion:												
Cavalry	12	8	189	2	-	30	14	8	219	-	-	-
Infantry	10	7	143	3	3	59	13	10	202	-	-	-

61   This document would have been delivered to Cornwallis when he arrived at Camden during the night of the 13th to 14th August.

62   S: serjeants.

63   D: drummers

North Carolina Regiment	15	6	206	4	122	19	8	328	-
Major Harrison's millitia	8	-	64	-	-	8	-	84	20
Colonel Rugely's regiment ditto	12	-	116	-	-	12	-	169	53
Colonel Bryant's ditto	30	-	172	-	-	30	-	326	154
Stragling militia supposed	3	-	30	-	-	3	-	30	-
Total	171	57	2043	55	756	226	85	3026	227

State of the Detachment of Royal Artillery under the command of Lieutenant Macleod

	Guns				
	S:	D:	R & file		
Present fit for Duty	2	-	20		
Sick Present	-	-	6		
Total	2	-	26		

	Six pound	Three pounder	Cohorns	Unserviceable
Guns	4	3	2	1

NB: One of the three pounders belongs to the Legion

The unserviceable gun is a six pounder but it would answer for slow firing

State of the Waggons, Horses etc in the Quarter Master General's Department

Distribution	Waggons	Carts	Ox teams	Oxen	Horses
Fit for Duty in the Yard	22	1	2	22	124
Repairing in the Yard	10	-	-	-	-
With the different corps	13	-	-	6	48
Total	45	1	2	28	172

14 men of the Pioneer Corps

NB: in the Present fit for Duty are included bat men and officers' servants

RAWDON
Colonel, Volunteers of Ireland

234

CHAPTER 13

Correspondence with Ninety Six and Augusta

1 - Between Cornwallis and Balfour or Cruger

Balfour to Cornwallis, 22nd June 1780   *2(185): ALS*

Ninety Six
Thursday 22nd

My Lord

I arrived this day here and received your Lordship's letter of the 20th[1] just after my coming to the ground.

Colonel Innes, to whom I am extremly indebted for his activity and asistance, having informed me of your desire that he should return to Charles Town (and give leaves of absence to his men and officers), will best inform you of the state of things here. Having not had an hour to look about me, I cannot speak to any thing from my own knowledge but shall give you a full acount the moment I am master of the business in this very extensive district.

---

[1] *letter of the 20th*: see p 98.

The dilemma I find myself in, respecting the capitulations of Williamson and Hammond[2], Innes will explain, and I must beg your instructions upon that head. At present my own idea is clearly to remove all the leading men of the rebell party at least for a time from the country that I may have ful *scope* to establish the militia.

As to sending the light infantry immediately to Camden, I realy think it would be imprudent at present, as Ferguson's corps has not above seventy infantry and Innes's corps is to a *man* gone on furlough for two months. Any attempt to regulation under so *slender* a protection in this distant country, by no means yet well at peace, would be a good deal retarded, if not insulted. I will therefore hope you will allow that corps to remain here untill the business is throughly done, which, be assured, shall be followed up every moment. The want of field officers keeps me back extremly, and at present Colonel Kirkland[3] seems to me the proper hands to put the chief command in here in the militia line. However, I am by no means well enough informed to speak upon the subject as yet.

---

[2] Samuel Hammond (1757-1842) would soon renege on his capitulation, made to Thomas Brown, and go off to the enemy. Born in Richmond County, Virginia, he had participated in Dunmore's War in 1774 and in the action at the Great Bridge in December 1775. Going south in 1779 to join Lincoln, he was involved in the action at Stono Ferry and in the siege of Savannah. By mid 1780 a colonel in the South Carolina revolutionary militia, he would no doubt have taken with him much of his regiment, which was largely disaffected, when he broke the capitulation. In the coming months he would take part in the actions at Musgrove's Mill and Blackstocks, the Battle of King's Mountain, the siege of Augusta, and the Battle of Eutaw Springs, where he was wounded. Described as polished in manner, a brilliant conversationalist, and having an exceptionally attractive personality, he would play after the war a prominent role in the public affairs of Georgia, Louisiana, Missouri and South Carolina, besides serving a term in Congress. (Draper, *King's Mountain, passim*; *The Cornwallis Papers*; *The Greene Papers*, viii, *passim*; *DAB*)

[3] Born and raised in America, Moses Kirkland (*c.* 1715-1787) was a semi-literate, ambitious, naturally acquisitive and hard-driving man, having begun by the 1750s to take up lands in the interior of South Carolina well beyond the established townships of Amelia, Orangeburg and Saxe-Gotha. Not above selling rum to native Americans or dealing in fraudulent land claims, he soon accumulated numerous tracts, built a sawmill, and ran a ferry on the lower Saluda before amassing a sufficiency of slaves to develop a large tract on a tributary of Stevens Creek, a branch of the Savannah. In a career characterised by opportunism and skirting close to the fringes of the law, he nevertheless succeeded in being commissioned a Justice of the Peace and an officer in the militia. Later he would take a leading role in organising the Regulators. As the revolution rapidly approached in 1775, he accepted a captain's commission in the Provincial Congress's regiment of rangers, but soon resigned, perhaps from pique at not obtaining higher command or from a conviction that he had chosen the wrong side. He immediately became a leading figure among Back Country loyalists and undertook a mission to Lord William Campbell, the royal Governor, in the hope of receiving aid and advice. Campbell at once dispatched him to convince Thomas Gage, the British Commander-in-Chief at Boston, that troops should be dispatched to support loyalism in the Back Country, but Kirkland's ship was captured. Taken to Philadelphia, he was imprisoned by the Continental Congress, who forwarded incriminating documents found on him to Charlestown for publication. Escaping, Kirkland made his way to Pensacola, from where he began to act as John Stuart's deputy to the Seminoles and Creeks. At the same time he continued his efforts to convince the British that loyalism in the southern Back Country made the Carolinas and Georgia ripe for recovery. Calling at St Augustine in 1778, he was sent by Prevost to New York, where his ideas led in part to Clinton invading Georgia later that year. Reaching Savannah after its recovery, Kirkland served during the siege in 1779 before returning to South Carolina when Charlestown fell. He would now be commissioned lt colonel of a regiment of royal militia, and although its pay rolls have not survived, preventing till now its catchment area from being determined, these Papers indicate that it lay towards the Savannah River with four companies adjoining the Long Cane settlement. These Papers also set out Kirkland's later involvement in southern operations. Resigning his commission on 25th November 1780, he retired to Ebenezer, where he owned land, and when Savannah was evacuated in 1782, he took his family to Jamaica. In the meantime his property in South Carolina was confiscated by the revolutionaries. He would be lost at sea while on passage to England to press his claim for compensation from the Crown. (Lambert, *SC Loyalists*, 4, 36-7, 40-1, 80-1, 111, 154-5, 291; McCrady, *SC in the Rev 1775-1780*, 37-8; *The Cornwallis Papers*)

A party not under fifty men I think should be at the Congrees, and shall order Brown's to remain there if you have not sent them to Camden. The Fuzileers will come with the waggons, which I shall dispatch the moment they can travell according to your order, and hope they may sett off on Saturday.

I must again referr your Lordship to Innes for further information as things appeared to him, and have only to add that the prospect of a powerful militia is undoubted.

I have the honor to be with sincere regard and respect
Your most obedient and humble servant

N BALFOUR

Balfour to Cornwallis, 24th June 1780   2(191): ALS

Ninety Six
24th June

My Lord

I did myself the honor of writing you by Colonel Innes, but since he left us we have been put into a violent hurry by a scramble betwixt a General Rutherford and a Colonel Moore upon the Catabaw on the borders of North Carolina, our friend Moore having been obliged to get away as fast as he could spread the allarm, and they conceived Rutherford already advanced into the heart of the country.

To quiet their fears I sent them some arms and ammunition, desired that the neighbouring districts of loyal subjects would embody, and above all sent them Ferguson with his mounted people with the view of getting the militia plan forwarded by being on the spott. They chose a post far enough from the enemy at a place called Sugar Creek upon the Tyger River, where they will remain to face Mr Rutherford if he comes near them, and to go home if he does not, which I have no sort of doubt will be the case; but for fear of any check that might happen, which would by no means agree with us at present, I wrote to Lord Rawdon to inform him of the matter, that, in case of their advancing towards our militia on the Tyger, he might move to intercept them, but I cannot conceive there is the least probability of their coming nearer than they are to this province. However, I fear it may have some bad effects in regard to the North Carolinians and hasten their rising too early.

As to my boasted good humour with Ferguson, I fear it cannot last. In this last business he has been ridiculous and I fear will carry matters to a length which will make us but bad companions. He is so extremly capricious and violent in his whims that I doubt[4] it will be impossible to keep him to any steady plan, but I will keep him up to the business as long as I can and must prepare you for his breaking out violently — at least I fear it may happen. Colonel Brown has been here and I find by his acount that his capitulation with Hammond

---

[4] *doubt*: used in the now archaic sense of 'fear' or 'suspect'.

is in substance the same as Paris's: to go on parole, deliver up their arms etc. He has brought up to Augusta two hundred and fifty men made up from his own battalion and detachments of all the other Provincials at Savanah, Major Wright[5] being his second.

I desired he might relieve Fort Rutledge with fifty men and, as he is Superintendant, that he would send proper people to manage the Indians; also that he would imediately inform the savages of our being in posession of South Carolina etc. He says he has already done it and likewise ordred the principal men to meet him at Augusta from the Creeks and Cherokees, where he has ordred presents for them. He begs me to be informed from your Lordship whether he may not order the Indians to drive away a sett of banditti who have settled by force upon the lands of the Creeks and Cherokees that lye on the back parts of North Carolina and Virginia. He says they are all rebells and carry on a trade with the Spaniards by the Ohio down to the Misisipi, receiving arms etc; that it had been allways complained of by the Indians as a grievous incroachment and was intended to have been remedy'd by us whenever it was in our power. The mode he proposes is to warn these people to leave these lands in a certain time and in case of non compliance to take the consequences. He represents this as a matter of consequence to which the Indians look for redress, and, if not attended to, they will think the change at present of no advantage to them.

Fort Ruttlidge, he says, they also think a grievance, but if you wish to keep it a short time longer to open the communication with the Indians, he would reconcile them to it in their next talk. And of all these matters he wishes instruction as soon as possible. My own idea is that, as soon as all the militia are formed, that it ought to be destroyed, as it is not strong enough to resist any force of consequence in case of disafection amongst the rebells and may easily be turned against us. Also I conceive that the nearer the Indians are brought to these gentry the better.

As to the post at Augusta, upon enquiry both sides of the river are much disafected. It has been, and will be, the depot for the Indian business and, besides covering Georgia, is a support to this post, where I am clear a force ought to be kept. Provisions of all kinds can be brought up by water during the year, and this post supply'd from it. I conceive a small work will be necessary, as it is so straggling a village and as there are guns and necessarys upon the spot, but particularly as there can only be Provincials in garrison, under whose care stores can be ill trusted or surprises guarded against. I should think a work for two hundred men perfectly sufficient with barracks, and they have six four pounders on the spott. An additional engineer is come up with Brown from Savanah with carpenters etc, and I am told that the loyal inhabitants are all willing to give their Negroes, which, with those of the rebels, can very soon finish the business.

---

[5] James Wright Jr (1748-1816) was the eldest son of Sir James Wright Bt, the royal Governor of Georgia. On 1st May 1779 he had been commissioned major in command of the Georgia Loyalists, a a British American corps who were then forming, and with them took part in defending Savannah during the siege. Now, in 1780, recruiting irregularities would soon lead to the recall of his corps from Augusta to Savannah, where it would play no material part in southern operations, being incorporated into Thomas Brown's King's Rangers in 1782. At the close of the war he was placed on the Provincial half-pay list and in 1785 succeeded to the baronetcy. On his death without issue, the title passed to his brother, Alexander. (*DNB*; Clark, *Loyalists in the Southern Campaign*, i, *passim*; *Appletons'*; *The Cornwallis Papers*; Treasury 64/23(16), WO 65/164(42), and WO 65/165(11) (National Archives, Kew)

As to this post, it is so situated that three small redoubts well abattis'd, I think, can easily defend it. The court house is an excellent barrack in the centre of the village sufficient for two hundred men, and a guard in each of the redoubts will, I am certain, keep every thing quiet, prevent surprises etc. The Negroes belonging to rebells, especialy Ruttlidge's, can sett about these redoubts, if agreeable to you, immediately. We have carpenters enough and ammunition, and the small cannon at Fort Rutlidge could be put into them. If not, the field pieces here could be spared, I dare say, but without these small works I think the post, with the Carolinians in garrison, a little ticklish. Lieutenant Frazer of the 42nd[6], who is the additional engineer, could do both the business at Augusta and here with ease — without *Ferguson's asistance.*

The principal object of the militia is a good deal interrupted by this business of Moore's but is going on. I find it absolutely necessary to fix on field officers immediately, as I must look to *them* more than the Inspector General. The companies are going on forming and I shall not lose a moment in regimenting them, but it will absolutely require time, longer than I fear you expect.

Things are by no means in any sort of settled state, nor our friends so numerous as I expected from Saluda to Savanah River. Allmost the whole district from the former up to the Indian lands are dissafected and, althow at present overawed by the presence of the troops, yet are ready to rise on the smallest change. As to their disarming, it is a joke; they have given in only old useless arms and keep their own good ones.

It appears to me there are two lines of conduct for this back country: the first, to march into the dissafected districts and by punishments etc dissarm every suspicious person, break the agreements of Paris and Brown and send off imediately every leading man of the rebell party, and arm the well affected only; the second, to keep the capitulations, let the dissarming stand as it is, get the leading men to be answerable for the conduct of the people and trust them in a certain degree, allow such of the dissafected as have not been violent to be incorporated with the militia, who will choose them, and give them a part in the defence of the country.

I have had several private conversations with Williamson, who has every appearance of candour and sincerly wishing to remain under the British Government. He has a strong sound understanding and, if I am not much deceived indeed, will be infinitely useful here if properly treated. The amount of our conversations is that from decency as well as inclination any active military part would be impossible for him at present, should we choose to trust him; that he knows his influence in asisting the civil as well as military arrangements will conduce more to bring the country to quiet and submission than if he took a more publick part; that he is ready to give us every pledge in his power for his remaining steady to the part he now takes; that he has lived so long in the country that he has a through knowledge of the people here, who are of all mankind the least to be depended upon, and is therefore of opinion that, in order to keep them entirely under, a stronger force would be necessary than we would wish

---

[6] There were three lieutenants named Fraser in the 42nd Regiment: Hugh, commissioned on 19th October 1778; Henry David, commissioned on 23rd November 1778; and William, commissioned on 25th August 1779. (*Army Lists*)

to spare; and the only mode, he thinks, to get government established is by degrees to get the leading men to exert themselves and to insist upon their being answerable for the people, not to trust them too far till we are convinced they are steady, and to take part of them into the militia.

That he will immediately interest himself in gaining every man in his power to join heartily in settling the country and will let me know those we can depend upon and what degrees of trust can be put into them. The leading men are Pickens and Hammond, Bowie and Rappillie[7], and could the two first be gained, he seems to be certain their influence is so great that, with his own, the whole country could be brought to act for us as heartily as ever they acted against us.

To bring about this he is now employed, and if you will trust him to me, I hope he will not deceive you. At the same time permit me to say that, if you think it in the least dangerous, that I beg to receive your directions.

Provincial corps cannot I fear at present be brought to any thing. The militia affects them in some degree, but the fact is the people are averse to engage untill they see how things turn. If possible, I will get two Provincial troops of light dragoons that I think will be of service. The only want will be officers.

Many Negroes captured from people who have left the country, and all Ruttlidge's, are brought in here. I have, in order not to feed them, distributed them amongst the inhabitants, taking receipts for them, making them responsible when called for, and mean to make use of some of them on the publick works should you approve of their being begun.

Provisions for any corps necessary here may be allways supply'd by the country in beef and flour, rum and salt by Augusta. The latter I mean to send for now to Savannah.

Innes's corps for this place, when things are throughly settled and government settled, but not before, I should think the best garrison, and, as Brown is Superintendant General to command at Augusta, the whole under an intelligent officer I apprehend the best arrangement.

My friend Innes would not like it, but if he did, I fear he has not temper for it. I beg to send enclosed a return of stores I found here, the arms being allmost all unserviceable, but the main point — the ammunition will do for the militia.

Many smaller articles of information, I believe, may be excused from the length of this letter — only to add that I shall send some villains of the first magnitude from this jail[8] by the militia in a few days with their crimes to Charles Town. I hope as soon as possible to have any directions you may think proper in answer to this, and have the honor to be

---

[7] *Rappillie*: Richard A Rapley.

[8] According to Lt Allaire's Diary for the 22nd and 24th June (Draper, *King's Mountain*, 499), about forty revolutionaries were confined in the jail, having been brought in by loyalists. They included magistrates and an executioner. At one court 75 loyalists had been condemned, five executed in April 1779, and the rest reprieved.

Your Lordship's most obedient servant

N BALFOUR

PS

I have wrote to Sir James Wright to beg that Lt Governor Graeme may come to Augusta and form the militia, and that I have sent your Lordship's plan for those of this province to Colonel Brown.

[*Annotated:*]

Eighteen waggons left this yesterday in their way to Charles Town — 25th June.

Enclosure
Return of arms etc taken from the enemy   *2(173): DS*

An Account of Arms, Ammunition and Stores taken from the Rebels and now in the possession of the Commisary at Ninety Six
19th June 1780

1 two pounder	1 pair bullet moles
20 blunderbusses	578 bayonetts
21 swivells	11 shovels
638 stand of arms fit and unfit for service	2 spades
15 barrels of powder	2 cross cutt saws
4 boxes of cartridges	2 whip ditto
1 barrel of ditto	1 keg of small hinges
1 box of ditto	25 pair of door hinges
1 keg of ditto and part of 1 keg ditto	Small quantity of nails
1 barrel of spikes	3 drums
2 boxes of bullets	1 gouge
3 kegs of ditto not full	6 pickaxes
14 large bars of lead, each bar computed to weigh 180 lbs	8 pair hand cuffs
12 small bars of ditto	5 iron potts

2 small kegs of shott	
⅓ barrel of ditto	JOHN CUNNINGHAM[9]
8 bags of ditto	Commissary Public Stores
2½ kegs of cannisters	
½ barrel of flints	
— quantity of gun locks	
215 cartridge boxes	
63 shot bags	

Balfour to Cornwallis, 27th June 1780   2(200): ALS

27th June

My Lord

I did myself the honor of writing you a few days ago and now *realy* inclose a return of stores etc[10].

Ferguson and the militia at Sugar Creek have great matters in view and I find it impossible to trust him out of sight. He seems to me to want to carry the war into North Carolina himself at once. He has got with Mr Mills about 800 militia, who distress the country to a degree, and as it appears to me there is not the smallest danger of an enemy coming near them, I have therefore desired that, unless the enemy are crossed into this province, that he will dismiss the militia since nothing appears sufficient to keep them embodyed, leaving a few young men volunteers and his mounted people as an advanced guard to give intelligence in case of a movement to Camden and this post — also have desired him to come to me here in order to carry on the militia business, which is infinitely retarded by this scramble. How he will receive these mandates I know not, but they must be obey'd. The militia will go on to a wish, I am certain, in a little time, but it cannot be effected so very quickly as one would wish. There are no less than seven battalions in this district, six of whom I think are in a fair way, as is the Orangeburgh. I have got lists of mostly all the companys in four battalions, the officers as far as captains chose. The getting field officers to them all is not yet effected, but am in hopes will be soon, when returns will be made, I should think, of five thousand men ready to assemble upon a short notice — I mean from the 96 District, the Orangeburgh and Goodwyn's battalions included.

---

[9] John Cunningham may have been the brother of that name who accompanied Robert, Patrick and David to the Back Country in the late 1760s (see p 117, note 13). If so, he would have been acting unofficially as commissary at Ninety Six.

[10] *a return..*: not extant.

There is not a doubt that the troops employed in establishing this business cannot be better made use of. As I look upon it, it is the gaining of the province, nor did I ever see people more desirous of getting government amongst them. A rising in the Long Cane settlement was suspected and I sent to Williamson, who immediately brought the people to me and shewed clearly it was a falsity. In short, if temper and management can be made use of here for some time, I think your Lordship will find this part of the country soon settled, but great attention will be necessary to the Georgians, and a post at Augusta with one here are indispensably necessary. Nor do I think Innes's corps sufficient untill the militia are firmly fixed and some works finished.

I send the bearer, Lieutenant Frazer[11] of Trumbull's corps, who, from his activity and abilitys, I think will be a proper person to raise a small corps of Provincial light horse, a kind of troops I think absolutely necessary to be kept in this part of the Back Country. One troop consisting of 1 captain, 2 lieutenants, 1 cornet, 1 quarter master and 100 private rank and file, I mean with corporals, would be sufficient for this duty, and part might be kept here and part at Augusta.

I have not a doubt that he could allmost immediately raise the men, especialy if they are taken immediately while the spirit of loyalty is so high etc. If deferred, it may not be so easy. Horses can also be got; arms and cloathing will only be wanted; and should you approve of the plan, I think you may depend upon its being no jobb and that it will be well and quickly done. I would recommend a separate corps and not attached to Innes's or any other. The want of all sort of discipline in the South Carolinians will not admitt of any interference, nor will that corps *do* here unless they be seriously attended to as soon as they assemble, which I think ought to be on the 1st of August at furthest.

Frazer has acted as Quarter Master to this detachment, and very short time is sufficient to shew any one that he is extremly intelligent and active. His name, I own, is against him. He will report the particulars of the plan to whoever your Lordship chooses.

Our detachment at Augusta, I fear, is made up of very sad stuff. Mr Wright and Brown are vying to complete their corps, and by what I learn, the former would be fully as well with his father. All sorts of irregularitys are going on and must be stoppt immediately. Your answer respecting the works there and here I hope to have soon.

---

[11] Thomas Fraser (1755-?) was a Scot who had settled before the war in New Jersey. Commissioned a lieutenant in the New York Volunteers in August 1777, he had served lately as its adjutant and then as quartermaster. He was now acting on secondment as quartermaster to Balfour's detachment. A spirited and able officer, he would, as recommended now by Balfour, receive a warrant from Cornwallis to raise a company of which he was appointed captain. He proceeded to take part on 19th August in the action at Musgrove's Mill, where he was wounded. Shortly afterwards Cornwallis appointed him to the majority in the South Carolina Royalist Regiment, backdated to 10th August. With the recall soon afterwards of his commanding officer, Alexander Innes, first to Charlestown and then to New York, Fraser would take command of the corps in the field and play with it an active part in operations in South Carolina, a part which is mostly outlined in these Papers. When the regiment was disbanded at the close of the war, he was placed on the Provincial half-pay list and retired to South Carolina. Marrying there, he engaged at first in the lumber business, establishing saw mills on the Edisto River, but did not appear to prosper. He then became a factor or commission merchant in Charleston. Until his death he continued to receive half pay, and his widow was granted a pension by the Crown. (Raymond, 'British American Corps'; Lambert, *SC Loyalists*, 151; Treasury 64/23(1), (15), WO 65/164(40), and WO 65/165(10) (National Archives, Kew); Clark, *Loyalists in the Southern Campaign*, i, 47; *The Cornwallis Papers*; Johnson, *Traditions*, 362-3)

I have desired the Fuzileers to return to Charles Town immediately but wish the detachment of Brown's to remain under Major Graham a little longer, if agreeable to you, at the Congrees.

By what I can perceive, there is not any danger of flour and beeff here for any detachment that will be left, but rum and salt will be necessary and can be got from Savanah.

Brown's corps at Augusta, I am informed, meant to have raised two troops to be added to his battalion. From every acount it will be so much money thrown away, if he is permitted. Wright's corps and his, I am told, understand and practise all the arts of Provincial plunder and imposition.

If these corps are to be permitted to recruit here, I beg to know. They have apply'd, as also has Colonel Trumbull, from whom there is an excellent light company here, but I have only allowed Innes's yet till I receive your directions. Not less than one hundred men are sick of the Augusta detachment, and if the rebells had the most distant idea of rising, every hour would give them an opportunity.

I hope also soon to have an answer to my last upon different points.

I have the honor to be, my Lord, with sincere gratitude
Your most obedient and faithful servant

N BALFOUR

Cornwallis to Balfour, 3rd July 1780   78(3): C

Charles Town

3rd July 1780

Lt Colonel Balfour

Dear Balfour

I am to acknowledge the receipts of your letters of the 22nd, 24th and 27th. I approve of keeping the capitulations, for altho' it was very unwarrantable in the gentlemen who granted them, yet there is no object that makes it worth while to break them. Those, however, who are too dissaffected to be trusted with arms and have imposed upon us by bringing in old useless arms and keeping good ones must be properly disarmed when the militia is established. I give you *charte blanche* as to Williamson and shall approve of every step you may take to fix him and bring over usefull people to our interest; I have the most implicit faith in your discretion and experience. I have ordered Cruger to go up immediately to Ninety Six, where you will explain every thing minutely to him and then invest him with the command. His battalion is to follow him, and you will please to order Major Wright and his corps to return immediately to Savannah and on no account to inlist a man in South Carolina. You will likewise let him know that I am much surprized that, contrary to the General's orders, he has sent a party to Charles Town, from whence I suspect he has carried off several rebel prisoners, and that I am determined to bring that affair to a court martial. Colonel Brown's corps will likewise return to Savannah as soon as Colonel Cruger's arrives at Augusta; I insist on his being put under the same restrictions as to recruiting as Major Wright; the Colonel himself may stay to manage the Indian business but not to keep any military command. I have directed Clarke to send up Allen's corps as soon as Brown's returns to Savannah. In regard to Indian affairs, I would demolish Fort Rutledge, but on no account enter into that boundary business. They may be encouraged to expect that, when affairs are a little more settled, that business will be attended to. I beg you will explain to Colonel Brown in the most positive manner that I wish to keep the Indians in good humour, but on no account whatever to bring them forward or employ them. In regard to the works you mention at Augusta and Ninety Six, as you seem to approve of them I have no objection to their being executed, provided they can be made on the footing of field works, but I shall certainly admit of no engineer's account whatever. Pray have that matter fully understood. The business of Colonel Moore is very provoking and has been greatly owing to the folly and indiscretion of Colonel Hamilton, who is one of the most obstinate blockheads I ever met with. I hope no ill consequences will follow. I must beg you will inform Major Ferguson that I would have him lose no time in procuring the states of the militia in the neighbourhood of Ninety Six. I would then wish him to do the same at Orangeburgh and proceed to Charles Town, where he will receive further directions from me. *Entre nous*, I am affraid of his getting to the frontier of North Carolina and playing us some cussed trick. I cannot consent to the plan of Provincial troops of dragoons. It will open a door to endless applications and jobs, and cost a great deal of money and hurt the recruiting of the infantry. The commanding officer may, if he thinks proper, either mount some of his own men or embody some mounted militia if any particular service should require it. I have told Clarke that the supplies for Augusta and Ninety Six must come from Savannah. We have no news nor any account of the French fleet.

I am etc

[CORNWALLIS]

NB

I have no objection to Mr Frazer's raising a company to be added to the New York Volunteers, but they must be inlisted on the same terms as that corps.

You will please to give orders in all the districts round your post that the roads should be repaired by the old commissioners. The commanding officers of militia will see that the duty is done and, where there is a difficiency of old commissioners, will appoint new ones. I forgot to tell you that I had long since appointed Colonel Carey[12] to command Colonel

---

[12] James Cary (?-1794) was a Virginian of some education and legal training who had been a man of local prominence in Northampton County, North Carolina, before migrating to the South Carolina Low Country in 1764. Six years later he moved to the west side of the Wateree near Camden Ferry to manage a plantation which he later purchased together with other property. By mid 1780 he was raising indigo and tobacco and owned a sawmill, an orchard, and a dozen or more slaves. A one-time Regulator, he had been commissioned a Justice of the Peace for Camden District in 1776 under the temporary revolutionary constitution adopted in that year. Now colonel of the

Goodwyn's district.

Balfour to Cornwallis, 4th July 1780   2(244): ALS

Ninety Six
4th July 1780

Earl Cornwallis etc etc etc

My Lord

I trouble you with this to inform you that I have received an application to raise a Provincial corps from Mr Robert Cunningham, who with his brothers are people of very considerable influence here, and I rather think it probable they will succeed if they embark in it. I beg to know if you still continue in the idea of raising more Provincial corps here and what number of men you would wish this to consist of.

The number of men in this part of the country ensures success to any popular person who may attempt to raise a corps, although in some degree it will hurt the militia, from whom I own I conceive only the hopes of their defending the country when well supported, for, although numerous, they are a sad banditti.

I have got Ferguson back after having satisfy'd himself with manœuvring the militia to his whistle and shall not allow him to shirk untill the militia is formed. All the field officers are to be here on Saturday and I hope in a few weeks to get every thing very forward.

A post of Ferguson's mounted men are left on Pacolet River to watch the militia of the

---

    royal militia between the Wateree and Congaree, he with thirty of his men was to be captured by Sumter while guarding Camden Ferry on 15th August. He subsequently escaped and his men were released by Tarleton in the action at Fishing Creek three days later. Accused soon after by Balfour of mismanagement, credulousness and inactivity, he was stoutly defended by Cornwallis, who commented, 'I will answer with my life for Carey, but he has had infinite difficulties to struggle with and is a modest, diffident man. Five out of six of his whole district are rebels and he has been constantly called out with part of his regiment on actual service during the whole summer. He opposed Sumpter in arms until he was deserted by his people, and afterwards contrived to make his escape before Tarleton's action. So far from being desirous of command, it was with the utmost difficulty I could prevail on him to take it, and I am very sure that nothing but his determined zeal for the cause could make him continue in it.' When in November Balfour hinted at Cary's misappropriating private property, Cornwallis replied, 'In regard to Carey, you know I am more partial [*than to William Henry Mills*], altho' I will not be godfather to any man's honesty in this province.' In the following month Cornwallis observed to Rawdon, when declining Cary's proposal to raise a kind of district troop of light horse, 'I have no opinion of Carey's raising any good cavalry. However loyal he may be, he certainly is not much of a soldier.' On the abandonment of Camden in May 1781 Clary fled to Charlestown, where he was paid as a refugee militia officer until its evacuation in December 1782. Sailing with a number of slaves to Jamaica, he attempted to produce sugar but fell into debt, finally turning over his land and slaves there to creditors in 1790. In the meantime, having had his property in South Carolina confiscated, he moved first to Nova Scotia, and then to England, in order to pursue his claim for compensation before the royal commission. Settling in Bristol, he received a pension backdated to 1783 and an award from the commission, both of which enabled him and his wife to live in modest comfort. (Lambert, *SC Loyalists*, 118-9, 269, 273, 278-9, 281, 291; *The Cornwallis Papers*; Gregorie, *Sumter*, 99, 102; Clark, *Loyalists in the Southern Campaign*, i, 491 et seq)

enemy, and as they are commanded by a good captain, I have no fears about them. I mean to bring them off soon if there are no appearances of any embodying on the frontiers.

I have sent the worst of the prisoners I found in jail here. Their characters are so bad and they have acted such parts that while they staid, things were in hott water by the different partys.

I have the honor to be
Your Lordship's most humble servant

N BALFOUR

Cornwallis to Balfour, 13th July 1780   78(10): C

Charlestown
13th July 1780

Lt Colonel Balfour

Dear Balfour

I inclose to you a warrant for Major Cunningham's corps, which, if you still think him likely to succeed, I desire you will give to him immediately. I should likewise wish Innes's corps to be ordered to assemble at the Congarees in the first week of next month. You will please to make a requisition from the District of Ninety Six of fifty good waggons with four good horses in each to march on the 1st of next month to the Cheraws. They will, however, be to call at Camden for stores. I understand from Williamson's account that the district could on an emergency furnish a much greater number without suffering any material inconvenience. They shall be returned to them again as soon as they have performed the service, and if any belong to friends, they shall be paid for the hire of them. I would, however, take as many as possible from the enemy. The first object must be the horses being good and capable. If Colonel Cruger should be then arrived, you may at that time, if you please, leave Ninety Six and go to Camden, where you will hear from me. I should be glad to know what troops you think it necessary to leave at Ninety Six. Perhaps, if Cruger's battalion was come up, that might be sufficient. Whilst we are in force at Camden, I cannot see much danger in that quarter. However, if you come away, I desire you will take it upon you to give any orders you think proper about it for the present. I do not answer Ferguson's letter[13], as I think it probable he may have left you to come towards this place before this letter reaches you. If he has not, you will hasten him about making up his lists and then send him this way, where his inspection is much wanted. Nothing is yet arrived from New York, nor have we any foreign news whatever.

---

[13] *Ferguson's letter*: of 22nd June, p 285.

I am, dear sir,
Most faithfully yours

[CORNWALLIS]

Balfour to Cornwallis, 12th July 1780 *1(15): ALS*

Ninety Six
Wednesday, 12th July

My Lord

I had the honor of receiving yours and am truly sensible of your kind approbation, which, permit me to assure you, is the greatest satisfaction I can possibly receive.

The business here I think in a very fair way, but, from the scarcity of field officers, magistrates were absolutely necessary exclusive of them. I therefore have appointed the old Justices of Peace, who acted before the rebellion, to renew their offices, and very luckily there are some very good ones who have retained their attachment to Government. They have begun their magistracy to the great satisfaction of the country, who conceive their old government renewed and fixed and obey them implicitly. They are not to decide in cases of consequence, where property is concerned, and the decision of the law is necessary, but in all smaller disputes they will act by arbitration and other prudent methods, but chiefly they will establish civil authority and strictly watch the dissafected, and I have no doubt you will find that, asisted by the militia, they will keep the country in peace and good order except on the frontiers, where I fear the consequences of Mr Moore's affair will be felt untill the war is carried into North Carolina.

A General Sumpter has embody'd about a thousand militia on the Catabaw with a few Continentals and has made inroads into this province with large plundering partys, chasing the loyalists from their plantations over Broad River. Their complaints and the earnest petitions of the principal inhabitants about Tiger and Ennoree Rivers determined me to send them a force to cover the country to the westward of Broad River etc.

A refusal might have been of bad consequences, as the two battalions of militia were not yet throughly formed. I therefore detached all Ferguson's infantry to join the mounted (that were left there since their last allarm) and ordred up Brown's light company from the Congrees to join at a very strong post near Fair Forest, which from its situation effectualy covers the country. A volunteer corps of militia under an active man, joined to the North Carolina refugees, will amount the corps to about four hundred and fifty men, who can be reinforced at pleasure by the two battalions of that district consisting of seven hundred or near it. They will assemble at the proposed post this night.

Captain De Peister[14] of Ferguson's corps will command this advanced guard, a very steady officer and who will obey his orders exactly.

I have desired that he will take the position described and, in case of a movement in force against him, that he will fall back toward Saluda so as to give time for my support; that he will embody the militia in case of necessity *only* and give every kind of countenance and support to the inhabitants, but on no acount to run any risk or make any movement across Broad River.

I hope the establishing this post will have good consequences and I think cannot have bad ones in the hands of an officer of any prudence.

I have kept Ferguson from it, and trust me he shall not have it in his power to do the mischief you suspect. He is gone to inspect some militia companys, which office I mean he should continue untill he gets to Charles Town. I have been able to get one field officer for each regiment and, by taking time, they are better than I once hoped for. Upon the whole, I think you will be satisfied with the state of the militia business when it gets to you. Major Graham will be the bearer of this. He wished much to come to Charles Town on acount of health and business. He has been very desirous of forwarding every thing entrusted to him and has got the Orangeburgh battalion arranged very properly. We have, I believe, ammunition enough here for the militia, but shall want arms I believe, although I cannot exactly ascertain the number now. I have transmitted your orders to Brown, as you directed, in explicit and positive terms. I own I am sorry that Fraser's troop did not take place, as I am convinced it could have been raised quickly and would have been of service.

As to the offer of the Cunynghams to raise a corps, I believe still they may raise the men, but officers will be wanted much if you approve of the offer — shall send them down to Charles Town with their proposals. The fact is that there are a great many men in this country that could be brought to inlist by the men of influence in the district. I think Innes's corps must be compleated soon.

When Cruigar arrives, I shall be ready for him and put him in full posession of the business, which I think will be nearly finished by that time, and if he answers the character I have heard of him, this back country will be kept steady and made very useful. The light infantry being now the only troops here, I beg to receive your directions about them and when you would wish them to move, but I by no means think this post can be left without troops. Innes's corps can be called in, or *they* can remain here (having good barracks) until Cruigar's arrive. As to Ferguson's, I believe it will be best to keep them where they are as yet some time to give the confidence that is very necessary there at present. Some magistrates and field officers sent by me to the islands have been returned and has given much dissatisfaction in

---

[14] Commissioned a captain in the King's American Regiment on 12th December 1776, Abraham De Peyster (1753-*c.* 1799) was now serving on secondment to Ferguson's corps and acting as Ferguson's deputy. A reliable and assiduous officer, he would on 7th October be left to capitulate at the Battle of King's Mountain when on Ferguson's death the situation became hopeless. He himself had been paid off on the morning of the engagement, and when he was struck by a bullet, its course was stopped by a doubloon among the coins in his vest pocket. At the close of the war he retired on half pay to St Johns, New Brunswick, and became Treasurer of the province. His brothers Frederick and James also served in the south. (*Appletons'*; WO 65/164(34) (National Archives, Kew))

the country, especialy one Lightner and Sommers[15]. It will counteract all the plan if this is continued, and I hope you will give positive directions to prevent it in future. I believe I can establish a good channel for intelligence from this quarter, and at little or no expence, except that of assuring a man of considerable consequence that he will have merit with you in getting it. The number of Continentals in North Carolina, the magazines, and intentions of Congress in the defence of that province are all points to be learned from Governor Ruttledge and their General Sumpter by this man's means, who now assures me that the Virginians backed by Washington insist to keep the war in North Carolina by a strong force in the inland part of the country, and that a very considerable magazine is now forming at a place called Shallow Ford. As to my movements, when Cruigar arrives and is perfectly master of the business, I wish to come to Charles Town for a short time if you have no object.

I have the honor to be
Your Lordship's most obedient servant

N BALFOUR

Cornwallis to Balfour, 17th July 1780   78(20): C

Charles Town
July 17th 1780

Lt Colonel Balfour

Dear Balfour

Brigadier General Paterson is so ill that he is obliged to go to the northward and takes the opportunity of the fleet that sails to morrow. I must therefore appoint you Commandant of Charles Town. I know you will say that you would rather go with your regiment, but men of merit must go where they are most wanted, and it is absolutely necessary for the good of the service that you should take the management of the town, which will in fact be the management of the province. I must insist in having no excuses, and I will give you such appointments that you shall not be ruined. Innes will come to Ninety Six and take the command untill the arrival of Colonel Cruger. I wish you would be ready to set out as soon as Innes gets to Ninety Six, as I should wish to see you here and my stay in the present situation of things is very precarious. The unlucky affair that happened to the detachment under Captain Huck of the Legion has given me great uneasiness. It will certainly make the rebel parties much more troublesome. Innes has orders to assemble his corps immediately. If in the mean time any assistance can be given by the militia about it I trust to your giving

---

[15] Both Michael Lightner and Adams Sommers (Summers) had settled in the Dutch Fork, becoming respectively a captain and a major in the revolutionary militia. Echoing Balfour, Moses Kirkland was later to describe them as 'two of the worst rebels that were in the fork'. It seems that, despite Balfour's comments, they were allowed to remain at home, for on 3rd November James Liles would write to Lightner, and Thomas Sumter to Sommers, inviting them to embody their men, or rather those of the revolutionary persuasion, and repair to Sumter at Shirer's Ferry. The letters were intercepted, Lightner was taken, and Sommers fled. Some two years later Lightner would act briefly as a commissary in the revolutionary service. (*The Cornwallis Papers*; Moss, *SC Patriots*, 568, 907)

proper orders. I wish you to form if possible a close connexion with Williamson before you part. I will promise to perform any engagements you may enter into. You must bring Ferguson this way. He is much wanted to form the militia and collect the lists in the lower districts. I inclose a letter[16] which you will please to forward to Colonel Brown.

I am etc

[CORNWALLIS]

Balfour to Cornwallis, 17th July 1780　　　　　　　　　　2(317): ALS

Ninety Six
17th July 1780

Earl Cornwallis etc etc etc
Charles Town

My Lord

I did myself the honor of writing you a few days ago by Major Graeme and at present am obliged to send for a supply of medicines, which are much wanted, as I am sorry to say we are turning sickly fast and our surgeon very ill. The express will be able to bring us a sufficient supply for our stay.

I must also mention an unlucky accident to a captain and twenty of our militia who were sent with an order to seize some robbers and plunderers on the back settlements and very unfortunately fell in with a party coming round from Georgia to join the rebels in North Carolina, who surprised our people, killed one, and took the rest prisoners. This rebell party, amounting to about one hundred men, has gone off from a mismanagement in the disarming the people in Georgia by the officer commanding at Augusta. However, not one man is gone from this province, but if speedy means are not taken to form the militia in Georgia and dissarm the dissafected, they will greatly impede the establishment of government here. The rebell general on Catabaw still holds his post and sends large partys across into this province. I shall do all I can to cover every thing on this side of Broad River and do not doubt to succeed, although the militia are extremly allarmed at their approach.

Ammunition, and all the arms I have, is given out, and I think in a few days there will be but few dissafected people with arms in this back country, but there are not near arms enough for the whole. I have therefore desired three battalions, those nearest to Charles Town, to send *there* for a supply and have given them directions and passes in writing for their waggons. They will apply to the Commandant upon their arrival and I hope good arms, if such can be spared, will be given them.

---

[16] *a letter*: of 17th July, p 274.

Ferguson goes to day to inspect the battalion lying towards Savanah, Kirkland's, and when he returns I propose he should sett out towards Charles Town, inspecting as he goes along, and think you will see him in about a fortnight with all his returns, which indeed are hard to bring to any degree of precission. However, the numbers are fully more than I expected, and I apprehend that at least fifteen hundred young and active men could be got from these eight battalions here to operate with the army, leaving a very sufficient and large force to defend the country. I have been surprised for some days past to find the violent and active magistrates in this district appear, having returned from Charles Town with protections from Major Benson by order of the Commandant. I had, according to your Lordship's instructions, sent those oppressive and violent gentry to the different islands, but it seems one of them found his way to Charles Town and succeeded in his applications, which encouraged others, and I suppose allmost every one are now at their homes that were ordred down. I fear this mistake will counteract the plan intended and do mischief if not remedy'd directly. Major McLaurin[17] of Innes's corps, a useful and sensible man, proposes to raise a second battalion if permitted. I think this country will easily afford one corps if Cunyngham's is not adopted. I hope the express with the medicines may be sent as soon as possible. I am now convinced that this place can afford to maintain one thousand men, if necessary, in provisions of all kinds.

I am your Lordship's most obedient servant

N BALFOUR

[*Endorsed*:]

Received 17th July and immediatly forwarded by express.

ANDREW MAXWELL[18], Captain commanding at Congaree

---

[17] Born in Argyle, Euan McLaurin had migrated to the Dutch Fork as a young man in the late 1760s, operating a country store there in partnership with a fellow Scot, Joseph Currie. A man of sense and some influence in the Back Country, and connected with many principal people there, he was commissioned a Justice of the Peace and in 1775 was a leader of the non-associators in their failed opposition to measures of the Provincial Congress. Evading capture by Richardson and making his way overland to St Augustine, he arrived there in August 1776 and was soon commissioned as major in Thomas Brown's Rangers. Having transferred in 1778 to Alexander Innes's South Carolina Royalist Regiment, he would by mid August 1780 have resigned his commission but would later obtain a warrant from Cornwallis to raise a Back Country battalion on the Provincial establishment. He would fail, as Cornwallis suspected, and play no further part in southern operations. While paid as a refugee, he died in Charlestown in June 1782. According to Balfour, he had but one fault, which was that he drank sometimes rather hard. (Lambert, *SC Loyalists, passim*; Clark, *Loyalists in the Southern Campaign, passim*; *The Cornwallis Papers*)

[18] Andrew Maxwell (1750-?) was a Scot who had migrated to the eastern shore of Maryland before the war. Making his way to the British lines, he had been commissioned a captain in the Prince of Wales's American Regiment on 5th April 1777. He was now in command of Fort Granby, a square redoubt enclosing two or three storehouses, which was situated on an eminence near the Charlestown road, about three-quarters of a mile from Friday's Ferry on the Congaree. According to Lee, Maxwell was an inexperienced officer, not fit to meet an impending crisis, and more zealous of spoil than of military reputation. Balfour, on the other hand, variously describes him as intelligent, prudent and dispassionate, adding that 'I have a good opinion [*of him*] as a man of sense, temper and, as far as he has seen service, a good officer'. Cornwallis evidently concurred, for to give Maxwell some credit with the people of the country, he promoted him by brevet to major in January 1781, even though, as he rightly assumed, he was not empowered to do so. Maxwell would maintain his post when invested by Sumter in February

Balfour to Cornwallis, 20th July 1780 2(320): ALS

Camp betwixt Ennoree and Tyger Rivers
Thursday night

My Lord

Soon after I had the honor of writing you last, I found that the business of Moore and Huck had given such spirits to the rebels that they had began to make risings in small partys on the frontiers, encouraged by the leaders of the party who had fled from their propertys.

The dissafected from Georgia, having also found means to get to them, in their way fell in with a captain of our militia with twenty men, surprised and took them, and soon after, being joined by some militia from Catabaw, came with an intention to attack Captain Delapp of Ferguson's, who, with good intentions, yet had delayed to obey my order for his retiring and joining the principal body at Sugar Creek. The consequences of his being *obliged* to retreat soon appeared, and I found by numberless *expresses*, and terrors masked in them, that, unless some step was immediately taken, that the militia would make a shameful business of it and, retiring, leave the country to be laid waste. To prevent this and support the shaking faith of the newly adopted loyalists, I marched immediately towards them and arrived here to day within a few miles of their encampment with the light infantry and three pounders. The better part of the four battalions of militia are embody'd that lye near to this district, and two are already mett. The others I expect tomorow.

I find the enemy exerting themselves wonderfuly and successfully in stirring up the people. Many that had protections have already joined them and a very great number are ready at the smallest reverse of our fortune. Their posts at present, as I am informed, are: at Catabaw, from whence they feed very strong plundering partys across Broad River just to the heart of this settlement; another post at North Pacolett, consisting of nearly five hundred; and a third, smaller, betwixt the forks of Tiger and Ennoree. These are all, or principaly, militia and Catabaw Indians, but I fear they have from long superiority so terrify'd our friends that they have not yet got the better of that idea, and, without giving them a little confidence, they are shy of meeting them.

I propose trying to get at the post upon Pacolett if possible, but fear they will retire, when I shall then clear all this side of Broad River and leave the militia with Ferguson's corps and Brown's light company to guard every thing on this side and return to Ninety Six with the light infantry, who feel the severity of the heat and are not able to go much further for want of shoes.

1781 and be praised for his good conduct by Rawdon and Balfour. He would, however, tamely capitulate to Lee the following May, lending some credence to Lee's assessment of him. Among the private property which the garrison were permitted to take with them on parole to Charlestown were two covered waggons, which Lee took to be filled with plunder. When Maxwell's regiment was disbanded at the close of the war, he was placed on the Provincial half-pay list and settled at Fredericton, New Brunswick. (Treasury 64/23(11), WO 65/164(34), and WO 65/165(8) (National Archives, Kew); Lee, *Memoirs*, 350-2; Lossing, *Pictorial Field-Book*, ii, 482; *The Cornwallis Papers*)

I hope you will excuse my quitting Ninety Six (where I left Major McLaurin with some of Innes's corps, our invalids, and some militia), as it appeared to me that the whole country east of Saluda would get into the enemy's hands, for a time at least, unless I moved to support these very ticklish friends here abouts. McLaurin is to call in Innes's corps immediately, and as things appear, they will be wanted, as the enemy can so easily disturb us. One lucky stroke at a post would have an exceeding good effect at present and I shall do my uttmost to effect it, but should that not happen, I hope the militia will be able to keep this part of the country perfectly clear, and if Turnbull is active, I should think he might make their incursions too dangerous to be often attempted over Catabaw.

We are much in want of medicines and feel considerably this very hott weather. In all probability I shall be at Ninety Six when I receive your Lordship's answer to this, and shall find Colonel Crugar there.

When I marched, I wrote to Augusta to stop the return of Brown's corps untill further orders, thinking it necessary to be watchful over that post in the neighborhood of so many dissafected settlements until I returned — and if they are not wanted at Savanah, should imagine they will not be useless at present where they are.

Inclosed is Captain Dunlapp's letter upon his retreat.

I have the honor to be
Your Lordship's most humble servant

N BALFOUR

Enclosure
Dunlap to Balfour, 15th July 1780   2(315): ALS

McAlwain Plantation
15th July 80

Lt Colonel Balfour

Sir

Having received such information yesterday as made me suspect there was some *stroke* against me in meditation, I thought it necessary to be very watchful, for which purpose I made a strong patrole in the evening consisting of a sergeant and 14 of the mounted infantry and 60 mounted militia. I had also in view a party of 25 from Georgia who had been plundering that day within a few miles of my post and who I expected would lie that night in the settlement.

To my great astonishment I fell in with a body of near 400 men on their march to surprise my post. Taking them for the Georgia plunderers, I dismounted the militia and attack'd them. They gave way on the first fire. I then charged with the mounted with good success, killing and wounding about 30 of the rebels and making them retreat some distance. A prisoner then informing me of their numbers and destination, I took the opportunity of their retreating to remount the militia (who had got into confusion) and made the best of my way to my post at Prince's Fort[19]. The rebels, getting the better of their consternation and finding the smallness of my force, pursued me with a party of horse. The moment they appeared in my rear, the militia ran off to the woods and left me with (then) only ten mounted infantry to make good my retreat. However, as I was near home, I got in without any other loss than a wounded man who is (I am afraid) made prisoner and some prisoners I had taken, which they retook. Upon my return to the fort I found that some of the militia had got in before me, had alarm'd the rest and they had all taken to their heels together, except about twelve who remained with the 20 infantry under Lieutenant Stephenson[20]. Thus situated and expecting every moment to be attack'd, nothing offer'd but to retreat with speed, which I have done without molestation to McAlwain Plantation within ten miles of the post at Sugar Creek occupied by the detachment of infantry and militia under the command of Captain Abraham Depeyster, who detach'd 100 men to cover my retreat. My loss is one of the mounted infantry and one militia man killed, one private of the militia, one sergeant and two privates of the mounted not dangerously wounded, one of which last I mentioned as believing to have been taken. I met the rebels about 10 miles from Prince's Fort near Baylis Earls's towards the border line. It had been a long concerted scheme, though they were but nine hours about embodying that force. They give out that they now intend desolating the country in bulk as they have hitherto done in small parties whenever it was in their power. I shall move to Sugar Creek tomorrow.

I am, sir,
Your obedient humble servant

J DUNLAP
Captain, Queen's Rangers

---

[19] Prince's Fort stood on a commanding height near the head of one of the branches of the North Fork of the Tyger River, seven miles north-west of the present town of Spartanburg. Some twenty years previously, early settlers had used it as a place of resort in time of danger from native Americans. (Draper, *King's Mountain*, 80)

[20] William Stevenson (1758-c. 1818) was a native of Monmouth County, New Jersey, and had been commissioned a lieutenant in the 2nd Battalion, New Jersey Volunteers, on 22nd December 1776. He had now been seconded to Ferguson's corps and would soon be taken prisoner at the Battle of King's Mountain. In November 1780 he would flee from his captors with two other officers and a militiaman, the reason and the circumstances the same as set out at p 110, note 2. Safely reaching Ninety Six, he would take no further part in southern operations. At the close of the war he was placed on the Provincial half-pay list and retired to Nova Scotia, where he died without issue at the home of his old comrade in arms, John Taylor. (Draper, op cit, 480; Treasury 64/23(8), WO 65/164(36), and WO 65/165(7) (National Archives, Kew); *The Cornwallis Papers*)

Cornwallis to Cruger, 5th August 1780[21]

79(12): C

Charlestown
August 5th 1780

Lt Colonel Cruger

Sir

Lt Colonel Balfour delivered your letter to me[22] and has given me a very full account of the state of your post. The keeping possession of the Back Country is of the utmost importance. Indeed, the success of the war in the Southern District depends totally upon it. I have at present determined to leave your corps and Lt Colonel Innes's at Ninety Six. I have given a warrant to Major Cunningham to raise a corps of 500 men of which he is to be lt colonel commandant. I desired him, as soon as he got his companies in any forwardness, to send them to Ninety Six, where I was sure that you would give him all possible assistance towards forming them and teaching both officers and men the common rules and discipline of the army. I sent about a fortnight ago an order to Savannah for the immediate march of Lt Colonel Allen's battalion to Augusta. Lt Colonel Balfour tells me that it will be necessary that this battalion should proceed to disarm some disaffected persons who live up the Savannah River beyond Augusta, and that Colonel Brown's corps will be wanted at Augusta 'till they return. I therefore leave it to your discretion to keep Colonel Brown's corps at Augusta as long as the safety of that country requires it, desiring that, when their stay at Augusta shall appear to you to be no longer necessary, you will order them to return to Savannah.

I am in general averse to allowing the corps which were raised in the northern provinces to recruit in this country, but as I hear a particular good character of your regiment, and as it must be a great satisfaction to you to have that corps, in which you can place dependence, on a respectable footing, I consent to your endeavouring to get some men, trusting that you will pay the strictest attention that the recruits are not imposed upon and that the terms of their inlisting, which must be the same as that of your corps, are fully explained to them. I have likewise sent up three hundred pounds, two hundred of which you will please to advance to General Williamson and keep the other for any contingencies that may occur. I propose leaving this place in a few days, so that you will direct all letters of business to Charlestown to Lt Colonel Balfour, and as my arrival at Camden may be uncertain, you will please to direct to Lord Rawdon at Camden untill you hear that I have joined the army.

I am, sir,
Your most obedient and most humble servant

[CORNWALLIS]

---

[21] Cruger did not receive this letter until 22nd August. See Cruger to Cornwallis, 23rd August, vol II, p 170.

[22] *your letter to me*: not extant.

Cruger to the officer commanding at Camden[23]　　　　　　　　　*63(13): ALS*

Ninety Six
August 4th 1780

Officer commanding at Camden

Sir

I make no doubt but Colonel Ferguson has sent to Camden the intelligence I have received from him of the rebels being in considerable force from 12 to 1500 advancing towards him at his post near the Tyger, that 'no man with him doubts but that there are two very considerable rebel partys within ten miles of Broad River amounting by all conjecture to thrice his numbers, that some of our militia had surrender'd to the rebels a stockade fort on Thicketty'. This is the substance of his intelligence of yesterday, which (with accounts of a similar nature that I have for some days received from him) very possibly on their way to Camden may have been intercepted. I am therefore induced by express to repeat the situation of the country on this side Broad River. I can make no remarks of my own, knowing nothing beyond Saluda but what I get from Colonel Ferguson. On this side the Saluda, about the Savannah, in the neighbourhood of the Ceded Lands in Georgia[24], a Colonel Clark[25] (rebel) is very busey stirring the people up. I am told he has 300 men with him. His rout is from Georgia by the line of this province to North Carolina without molestation. I beleive his corps is daily increasing. For Ferguson's support I have order'd Clary's regiment of militia to be immediately assembled and to receive his orders. The rest of the militia I have desired Colonel Ferguson to call out as the service may require, of which he on the spot must be the best judge.

---

[23] This letter was presumably passed to Cornwallis when he arrived at Camden during the night of the 13th to 14th August.

[24] 'The Ceded Lands' was an expression commonly used to refer to part of the territory ceded to Georgia by the Cherokees and Creeks in 1773. It was located in the Up Country above Augusta, extending from the headwaters of the Oconee downwards and between that river and the Savannah. (Charles Hudson, *The Southeastern Indians* (The University of Tennessee Press, 1978), 443; James H O'Donnell III, *Southern Indians in the American Revolution* (The University of Tennessee Press, 1973), 14 (map 2) and 142 (map 3); *The Cornwallis Papers*)

[25] Elijah Clark (?-1799), as he signed his surname, was born in North Carolina, from where he removed to the Back Country of South Carolina in the mid 1760s before going on to settle in the Ceded Lands of Georgia by September 1773. Some time in 1778 he was appointed lt colonel in John Dooly's Wilkes County Regiment of the Georgia revolutionary militia and played a major role in the defeat of loyalists at Kettle Creek in February of the following year. Now, in 1780, Dooly had entered into a parole, but Clark had refused to do so and gone off with a party of his men. In the coming months he would serve at both sieges of Augusta besides taking part in the actions near Cedar Spring and at Musgrove's Mill, Blackstocks, and Beattie's Mill, where he would defeat and capture James Dunlap. Described as an illiterate cracker, he would play a prominent if controversial role in public life after the war, despite being, with his old comrades, increasingly tried and fined for the drunken brawling and the violent personal vendettas which they once practised unhindered. (*DGB*; *DAB*)

I have the honor to be with due respect, sir,
Your obedient humble servant

J H CRUGER[26]
Lt Colonel commanding 96

Cruger to Cornwallis, 7th August 1780 — 63(22): LS

August 7th 1780

Rt Hon Earl Cornwallis etc etc etc

My Lord

Taking it for granted that Colonel Ferguson has punctually advised your Lordship with the different bodies of rebels in his front as well as on his right and left, I will not trouble you, sir, with a repetition, but observe that from every intelligence it was found requisite to detain Captain Charles Campbell with the light infantry at this post for the present. It is Colonel Innis's opinion and I hope will meet with your Lordship's approbation, especially when you understand that the detachment I brought here is only 125 rank and file, and not one hundred of Colonel Innis's regiment arm'd fit for duty, the militia amazing slow in turning out and ill arm'd. Colonel Ferguson has retired on this side the Tyger. I have this instant an account from him that by a person he had imployed towards Pacolet he hears that 1,200 militia and 400 Continentals had advanced on Fair Forrest within 16 miles of him. If Ferguson should be hard push'd, we must support him, but I shall decline quitting this post untill real necessity can justify the measure. Colonel Clark from the Ceded Lands in Georgia is return'd there and has imbodied 300 rebels and has a prospect of getting more (this I depend on as fact). I cannot as yet discover their intentions but have laid out for it. I have sent an express to

---

[26] Born in 1738, John Harris Cruger belonged to an extended family which had been prominent in the public affairs of New York before the revolution. He himself had been a member of HM Council for the Province, the Chamberlain of NY City, and, being well established in business, a member of the NY Chamber of Commerce. A son-in-law of Oliver De Lancey the elder, he was commissioned Lt Colonel of the 1st Battalion of De Lancey's Brigade on 6th September 1776 and for the next two years was posted to Long Island. In November 1778 he came south with his men as part of the expedition which seized Savannah, and in autumn 1779 commanded one of the principal redoubts during the unsuccessful siege of the town by the French and revolutionaries. In 1780 he had remained there as part of the garrison, but on 12th July, having been ordered to succeed Balfour in the Back Country, he marched with his battalion for the village of Ninety Six, where he arrived by the beginning of August. The Cornwallis Papers go some way to revealing the sterling qualities of the man, but it was in the siege of Ninety Six and at the Battle of Eutaw Springs that they were most amply displayed. At the close of the war his men settled in what became the Parish of Woodstock, New Brunswick, whereas he himself removed to London. Placed on the Provincial half-pay list, he sought compensation from the royal commission for his losses, having been subjected to confiscation by the revolutionary authorities. He died in London on 3rd June 1807. (Sabine, *Biographical Sketches*, i, 343-6; *Appletons'*; John Austin Stevens, *Colonial Records of the New York Chamber of Commerce, 1768-1784* (NY, 1867), 370; 'The Memorial of John Harris Cruger of New York', together with 'A History of the 1st Battalion, DeLancey's Brigade', *The On-Line Institute for Advanced Loyalist Studies*, 22nd November 2007; W O Raymond, 'Provincial Regiments: De Lancey's Brigade', *A Raymond Scrapbook* (Fort Havoc Archives CD, i); Treasury 64/23(9), WO 65/164(33), and WO 65/165(7) (National Archives, Kew))

hasten Allen[27] up to Augusta. I could wish the corps with 150 militia just now on their march into the Ceded Lands, that those fellows might be disarm'd *positively*. I received your Lordship's letter to Colonel Balfour for waggons. I made the requisition immediately to different parts of the country, have been obliged since to give press warrants, and have now every reason to beleive that the 50 waggons will be at Camden this week.

I have the honor to be with the highest respect, my Lord,
Your Lordship's most obedient and very humble servant

J H CRUGER
Lt Colonel commanding 96

Cruger to Cornwallis, 11th August 1780   *63(30): LS*

August 11th 1780

Earl Cornwallis, Lt General etc etc etc

My Lord

I did myself the honor to write your Lordship the 7th instant and accounted (I hope to your Lordship's satisfaction) for the light infantry's being detain'd a day or two. They march'd the day before yesterday. The preceding night the prisoners here broke gaol and ten made their escape, none of consequence except a Colonel Thomas[28] and his son[29]. They

---

[27] A son of an Associate Justice of the New Jersey Supreme Court, Isaac Allen was born in 1742, graduated from Princeton in 1762, and was admitted to the New Jersey Bar three years later. He practised in Trenton and was a warden of St Michael's Church when the revolutionary war broke out. On 3rd December 1776 he was commissioned Lt Colonel of the 6th Battalion, New Jersey Volunteers, and when it was incorporated into the 3rd, he was appointed Lt Colonel of the expanded battalion on 25th April 1778. Like the 6th, the 3rd was posted to Staten Island, but in November 1778 it formed part of the expedition to Georgia. When the Franco-revolutionary assault on Savannah was repulsed eleven months later, the battalion occupied a position on the front left of the British line. In March 1780 the light company marched with Paterson to reinforce Clinton, while Allen and the rest of his men remained in garrison at Savannah. At the end of July he was ordered to march with them to reinforce Cruger, who had gone ahead to the Back Country. Like Cruger, Allen was an excellent officer commanding a well disciplined unit and would serve as an able second in the coming months, notably in the siege of Ninety Six. At the close of the war he was placed on the Provincial half-pay list and settled with his men in what became the Parish of Kingsclear, New Brunswick, where he resumed the practice of law. Besides holding other offices, he went on to become a Judge of the Supreme Court, of which his grandson, Sir John Allen, later served as Chief Justice. He received partial compensation of £925 from the Crown for his property confiscated by the revolutionaries, which comprised a two-storey dwelling house in Trenton, a farm outside the town, and property in Philadelphia. He died at Kingsclear on 12th October 1806. (Hamilton Schuyler, chapter II of *A History of Trenton 1679-1929* (Princeton University Press, 1929); Nan Cole and Todd Braisted, 'A History of the 3rd Battalion, New Jersey Volunteers', *The On-Line Institute for Advanced Loyalist Studies*, 23rd November 2007; W O Raymond, 'Provincial Regiments: The New Jersey Volunteers', op cit; Lossing, *Pictorial Field-Book*, ii, 530; Treasury 64/23(7), WO 65/164(35), and WO 65/165(6) (National Archives, Kew))

[28] Born in Wales, John Thomas Sr (*c.* 1718-1811) was brought up in Chester County, Pennsylvania. Having been involved in Braddock's defeat in 1755, he moved on to the Back Country of South Carolina, from where he is supposed to have participated in the Cherokee War of 1760 and 1761. As the revolution approached, he was residing on Fair Forest Creek, and besides being a founder of the Presbyterian church there, he had become a

had procured tools to open the doors and did it so quietly as to knock down the sentry at the foot of the stairs before he was apprised of their bussiness.

I take the liberty to enclose the present state of this garrison, and thinking it my duty to observe to your Lordship that the South Carolina Royalist[s] in point of discipline are quite militia and not an hundred of them arm'd. My convalescents and sick from Savannah in number 50 I expect here next week. Colonel Allen's battalion, about 200 strong, I have ordered on immediately to Mill Creek or Horn Creek on the Augusta road hither, there to halt untill about 150 of Kirkland's militia join them. I chose one of those creeks (especially as it is not out of the way) for the place of rendezvous to avoid giving any jealousy to the traitors on the Ceded Lands, with whom I mean Colonel Allen to be by recrossing the Savannah before they have an opportunity to get off or become dangerous, not only to suppress their turbulent spirits with a resolute and determin'd countenance more to frighten than to hurt, but to disarm every suspicious man. This necessary bussiness, proposed by Colonel Balfour, will, I think, be carried into execution properly by Colonel Allen. I take the liberty to trouble your Lordship with a petition from the inhabitants on the western frontiers of the province[30].

The stores from Fort Seneca[31], demolish'd, I have receiv'd agreeable to the enclos'd return.

In my last I told your Lordship that I expected to have in Camden this week 50 waggons. The great distance to the westward they have to come, and the repairs many of them required, has caus'd a delay I did not expect. Eight more I have come in this day, a dozen, I am assured, will be here tomorrow and next day, which, with the 15 sent by William Meek[32] from Saluda the begining of the week and 9 by the light infantry, will come pretty near to your Lordship's order to Colonel Balfour. Clary's total disappointment will effect us a good deal[33].

---

militia captain and a Justice of the Peace under the Crown. Siding with the nascent revolutionaries, he took part in the Snow Campaign in late 1775, succeeding to the colonelcy of the Fair Forest Regiment of militia formerly commanded by the loyalist Thomas Fletchall. Considered an incendiary by the British, he had in 1780 been refused parole and consigned to the jail at Ninety Six. Escaping now from there, he would be recaptured within a week and remain in confinement for fourteen months, afterwards taking no material part in the war. Part of his regiment had been turned by the British and placed under the command of Major Zacharias Gibbs, but some sixty disaffected men had gone off under his son, Colonel John Thomas Jr. (McCrady, *SC in the Rev 1775-1780*, 95, 608; T W Lipscomb to the editor, 23rd August 1977; *The Cornwallis Papers*; Draper, *King's Mountain*, 74)

[29] John Thomas Sr had four sons, two of whom were killed in the war. (McCrady, op cit, 608)

[30] *a petition..*: not extant.

[31] *Fort Seneca*: more commonly known as Fort Rutledge. See p 89, note 32.

[32] William Meek was a private in Patrick Cuningham's Little River Regiment of the royal militia. He acted as a waggonmaster for the British. With the loss of the Back Country in 1781 he and his wife would flee to Charlestown before going on to settle in Canada. In 1791 he was acting as a tax assessor in the township of Rawdon. (Clark, *Loyalists in the Southern Campaign*, i, 258; Lambert, *SC Loyalists*, 234, 275)

[33] This sentence is added in Cruger's hand and refers to enclosure (3), p 264.

I have the honor to be with the highest respect very much, my Lord,
Your Lordship's most obedient and very humble servant

J H CRUGER
Lt Colonel commanding 96

Enclosure (1)
State of the garrison of Ninety Six

103(2): DS

Present State of the Garrison of Ninety Six commanded by Lt Colonel Cruger, August 12th 1780

Corps	\multicolumn{6}{c}{Officers Present}							Present and Fit for Duty			Sick			Total		
	\multicolumn{5}{c}{Commissioned}					\multicolumn{4}{c}{Staff}												
	Lt Col	Maj	Capt	Lt	Ens	Chap-lain	Adj	Qr Mstr	Sur-geon	Mate	S^{34}	D^{35}	R & F[36]	S	D	R & F	S	D	R & F
Detachment, 1st Batt, Genl De Lancey's	1	-	3	2	4	-	1	1	-	-	10	2	81	2	-	10	12	2	91
Ditto, 3rd Batt, Skinner's	-	-	1	1	1	-	-	-	-	-	2	1	34	1	-	3	3	1	37
South Carolina Royalist	-	1	1	1	3	1	1	1	1	1	17	5	164	-	-	26	17	5	190
Total	1	1	5	4	8	1	2	2	1	1	29	8	279	3	-	39	32	8	318

J H CRUGER
Lt Colonel commanding 96

---

[34] Serjeants

[35] Drummers

[36] Rank and file

Enclosure (2)
List of military stores from Fort Seneca 103(1): C

List of Military Stores sent from Fort Seneca to Ninety Six under the care of Wm Weatherford[37]	
1 cask gun powder	6 cross cut and whip saws
43 French musketts	A few large augers
17 old ditto - many useless	2 gouges
16 cartridge boxes	2 frows
13 bayonets	1 adze
12 pigg's lead	1 hand saw
20 lbs muskett ball	1 pair large bullett moulds
22 swivell cartridges	1 drum
A few flints and round shott	3 pieces cannon 2 or 3 pounders without carriages
½ barrell muskett cartridges	9 swivels
3 old spades	4 carriges for swivels
2 casks 4^d nails	

Fort Seneca
1st August 1780

JO^S SMITH[38]
Captain, King's Rangers

---

[37] About Weatherford's identity there is some confusion. Citing this document, Cashin identifies him as Martin Weatherford, a veteran Indian trader of Augusta who was a close friend of Thomas Brown (Cashin, *The King's Ranger*, 14, 110, 314), but the document unmistakably abbreviates the first name to 'W^m' (William). Perhaps the writer of the document was not well acquainted with Weatherford and made an error or someone else was involved, for example William Wetherford (c. 1746-?), who was born in Virginia and had served during 1775 in Ely Kershaw's company of the 3rd regiment of rangers raised by the Provincial Congress. (Moss, *SC Patriots*, 981)

[38] Joseph Smith (1754-?) was an American who by now had served some three years in the Provincial line, being promoted to captain in the King's Rangers on 10th January 1779. Serving with the regiment throughout the rest of the war, he would be placed at its close on the Provincial half-pay list and settle, like Thomas Brown, on the island of Abaco in the Bahamas, where he claimed land at a place called Spencer's Bight. (Treasury 64/23(16), WO 65/164(42), and WO 65/165(11) (National Archives, Kew); Clark, *Loyalists in the Southern Campaign*, i, *passim*; Cashin, op cit, 175)

Enclosure (3)
Cruger to Clary, 9th August 1780   63(25): *ALS*

August 9th 1780

Major Clary[39] at the mouth of Little River

By Tim McKenny[40]

Sir

As we have not called quite so soon for the waggons and horses for the King's Service as I meant we should, I presume you have procured the dozon, but whatever there are, you'll be pleased to order them on immediately in my name to the commanding officer of Camden. Some light infantry march this morning for Camden. If you could procure from Captain Campbell an escort, which you will by applying to him, provided your waggons do not lay too much out of his way, it would be best. Captain Campbell means to be at Davenport's[41] this evening.

I am , sir, your humble servant

J H CRUGER
Lt Colonel commanding 96

[*Endorsed*:]

Sir

Both Magor Clary and I has taken fathfull pans to ancer your request but can not porv^e,

---

[39] A committed and influential loyalist who had been involved in the Back Country uprising in 1775, Daniel Clary had now been commissioned major in command of the Dutch Fork Regiment of the royal militia. Barely mustering one hundred men, it was to provide a detachment led by him in the action at Musgrove's Mill on 19th August. Later in the year he would be persuaded by Cruger, who considered him a very clever, spirited man, to raise two badly needed troops of horse for the Ninety Six District, but was superseded by James Dunlap at Cornwallis's behest. Promoted at a later date to colonel, Clary would, with the loss of the Back Country in 1781, flee to Charlestown, where he was paid as a refugee officer till its evacuation. Being well liked despite his politics, Clary was not banished by the revolutionaries and he was removed from the Banishment and Confiscation Act in 1784. Amerced instead, but disqualified from public office, he settled once more in what became Newberry County. (Lambert, *SC Loyalists*, 111, 300-1; Draper, *King's Mountain*, 106, 109; *The Cornwallis Papers*; Clark, *Loyalists in the Southern Campaign*, i, *passim*; McCrady, *SC in the Rev 1780-1783*, 585)

[40] Timothy McKenny (McKinny) was a private in Major Patrick Cuningham's Little River Regiment of the royal militia, serving in Captain William Hendricks' company. Fleeing to Charlestown with the loss of the Back Country in 1781, he would from 20th November of that year become a quartermaster to the Ninety Six refugees there. (Clark, *Loyalists in the Southern Campaign*, i, 257, 259, 507)

[41] Davenport's lay some sixteen miles east of Ninety Six on the north side of the Saluda. According to Allaire, 'He was formerly captain of militia under Government. He has the name of a Tory from his neighbors; but many of his actions were doubtful.' (Draper, *King's Mountain*, 498)

for harses is not to be had in our rigment. The prasent action calls for what we can rase. Magor Clary marcht this marning with his man for Corn Forginsons camp.

From your humbl s[t]

PETER BLACK[42]

§ - §

2 - Between Cornwallis and Innes[43]

Innes to Cornwallis, 24th July 1780 *2(354): ALS*

Friday's Ferry, Congarees
Monday, 24th July
4 o'clock afternoon

My Lord

The wretched state of my horses and the scarcity of forage prevented my getting to this place sooner. I found Balfour had marched towards Fair Forest and left McLaurin at Ninety Six. The inclosed I found here from McLaurin has relieved me much with regard to that post, but the moment my horses are refresh'd, I push on there by the fork road as that route will give me an opportunity of hearing from Colonel Balfour, to whom I have this moment dispatched an express. Captain Maxwell, who commands here, tells me that Strumm's militia company[44] from this neighbourhood marched without orders to join Balfour and another was on the move if he had not prevented them.

Give me leave to hope that the alertness of the South Carolinians in forming at so short a notice will meet with your Lordship's approbation.

---

[42] Of Black nothing is known. He may soon have been killed, perhaps in the action at Musgrove's Mill, for there is no record of him in the extant rolls of Clary's regiment. (Clark, *Loyalists in the Southern Campaign*, i)

[43] On Balfour's arrival at Ninety Six Innes left for Charlestown. He was ordered back to assume command until Cruger's arrival. (Balfour to Cornwallis, 22nd and 24th June, pp 235 and 237, and Cornwallis to Balfour, 17th July, p 250).

[44] Captain Strum has not been identified. He may have been related to Henry or Jacob Strum, both of whom served as privates in John Cotton's Stevenson's Creek Regiment of the royal militia. (Clark, *Loyalists in the Southern Campaign*, i, 239, 243; Coldham, *Loyalist Claims*, 470)

I have the honor to be with the greatest respect
Your Lordship's most devoted servant

ALEX INNES
Lt Colonel commanding South Carolina Royalists

NB

I have desired Captain Maxwell to parole a few notorious scoundrels to the islands who ought not now to be at home, whoever gave them permission; and there were a knot of vilains I saw yesterday with rebel caps in Thomson's piazza that would incline me to cleanse that nest if I had time.

Enclosure
McLaurin to Innes, 20th July 1780   *2(331): ALS*

Ninety Six
20th July 1780

Colonel Alexander Innes
Inspector General of His Majesty's Provincial Forces
Charlestown

Sir

Colonel Balfour on account of some commotion is marched to Pacolet with his whole force and left me in a situation I did not much like, tho' I now plainly see his prudent conduct is to me better security than more men. I think it will be found that this alarm is only from a plundering party, yet the disaffected hereabout began to prick up their ears.

By Colonel Balfour's order I have sent to call in the whole battalion and so many are now arrived that I think myself in no danger of bringing disgrace on the South Carolina Royalists. I have information of a considerable body of rebels on the Indian line and am using all my endeavors to support this post as it will no doubt be their object if they once begin to act seriously. The leading men hereabout are no way inclined to risque their all by another effort and I think nothing will be attempted against me before I am prepared.

I am truly happy to learn that you will soon be here. Your presence is at this time necessary.

This express has been delayed all day in hopes of my hearing from Colonel Balfour. As I am disappointed, I send him on Mr Donworth's[45] arrival.

---

[45] Peter Dunworth had been commissioned a lieutenant in the South Carolina Royalist Regiment on 13th November 1779. He would cease to serve in the Provincial line by the close of the war and would not be placed on the Provincial half-pay list. (Clark, *Loyalists in the Southern Campaign*, i, 39; Treasury 64/23(15), WO 65/164(40),

His cart is not yet arrived and I send a party to meet it, plundering becoming rather common, nor can footmen prevent it.

The best account of the recruits I can get, you have herewith. My strength here is almost all the regiment and a considerable body of the best militia.

I have the honor to be, sir,
Your most humble servant

EUAN McLAURIN
Major, Carolina Royalists

[*Subscribed*:]

Number of recruits 176, but I think there are more.

Cornwallis to Innes, 30th July 1780   78(59): C

Charles Town
30th July 1780

Lt Colonel Innes

Dear Innes

I find by a letter from Balfour[46] that he is on his road hither, which I am glad of, being anxious to get away. When McArthur left the Cheraw Hill he sent his sick down the Pedee, sixty of whom with a lieutenant and surgeon are taken by the North Carolina militia. I have only to desire that you will lose no time in assembling the *gentlemen* in the *blue surtouts* and putting them into as good order as possible, and that you will send as many waggons as you can with four good horses in each to Camden with a proper escort. Make my compliments to Colonel Cruger. You and Balfour will have described accurately to him the situation of the post and temper of the people who are to be entrusted to his care. I have no doubt but he will feel the good effects of the zeal and attention of his predecessors.

I am etc

[CORNWALLIS]

---

and WO 65/165(10) (National Archives, Kew))

[46] *a letter..*: not extant.

Innes to Cornwallis, 28th July 1780   *2(373): ALS*

Ninety Six
28th July 1780

My Lord

    The South Carolina Regiment in its present state is really not fit for any active service, and however improper this time may appear for a general reform, I plainly see there is an absolute necessity for it. I was in hopes the old standers would have been induced to persevere a little longer but the age and infirmities of many, and the distresses to which their familys have been exposed during their long absence, makes it absolutely impossible to prevail on them to serve from home with any chearfulness. Most of those men never would receive any bounty. Their losses have been very great. They therefore always thought themselves entitled to a discharge as soon as they conceived they could live peaceably with their familys. There is no convincing them that this period is not yet arrived. They are persuaded it is, and as that is the case, I do think they will be of more service to the common cause by staying at home than in any active line they could take with the army. I would therefore humbly beg leave to request your Lordship's permission to discharge all aged and infirm men, also those who have familys depending on them for support and who have never received bounty. Many of the useless officers, of which I have not a few, will retire with them, but enough will remain, *natives of the country*, to compleat the regiment in a few weeks with young active unmarried men. I have near two hundred such recruits already, of my old stock I may be able to keep one hundred, and by the end of September I have no doubt of being compleat. Colonel Balfour is so perfectly master of this, as well as every other subject that has the least concern with the back part of this province, that I need not trouble your Lordship any further on this head, and he will also acquaint you with my intended motions, provided they meet with your Lordship's approbation.

I have the honor to be with great respect
Your Lordship's most devoted servant

ALEX INNES
Lt Colonel

NB

    It will not be necessary for me to stay a moment longer here than just to put this business in a train which I can do in a few days after receiving your Lordship's commands.

Cornwallis to Innes, 5th August 1780   79(16): C

Charles Town
5th August 1780

Lt Colonel Innes

Dear Innes

I am very sorry to hear so bad an account of the *blue coat gentry*. I am very sure that I told you at Camden to discharge any men you thought proper and in short to do every thing relating to them in your own way. As it is, I propose leaving them with Cruger at Ninety Six. Balfour being arrived, I shall get away from hence in six or seven days and shall be glad to see you at Camden, where I think I can depend on being before the 20th.

Yours etc

[CORNWALLIS]

Innes to Cornwallis, 12th August 1780   63(38): ALS

Ninety Six
12th August 1780

My Lord

My Lord Rawdon having thought it necessary to order Major Fergusson with all the force he can collect to pass the Broad River and join Lt Colonel Turnbull at Rocky Mount, which leaves the whole fork of Saluda open to the enemies incursions, this move and the departure of the light infantry makes a very material difference in Lt Colonel Cruger's situation here. Dawkins of my battalion has collected a few militia between the Tyger and Eneree, but I cannot flatter myself he will be able to remain there long as the rebel plunderers who have been hanging about that country will certainly join and must easily drive him back, now the principal strength of the country is moved to such a distance. Colonel Cruger wrote your Lordship[47] of his having very good intelligence that the rebels were busy in Georgia in the Ceded Lands and his intentions of ordering 200 militia to assemble at Turkey Creek to join Allen there, who he intended should march into this rebellious part of Georgia before any number of men could be got together, and dissarm them; but now it is really a hard matter to say which side requires his attention most, and some accounts he expects from Georgia tomorrow must determine him as to that movement. Lt Colonel Balfour would inform your Lordship that, as I found Colonel Cruger here, I requested he might take the command immediately to save trouble, but as he has expressed a wish I should remain here a little longer till things wear a more settled appearance, I shall take the liberty of complying with his request and of putting off for a few days longer my journey to Camden. As Colonel

---

[47] *Colonel Cruger wrote..*: on 11th August, p 259.

Cruger writes himself, I shall not trouble your Lordship with any particulars relative to this post.

I have the honor to be most respectfully
Your Lordship's devoted humble servant

ALEX INNES
Lt Colonel

§ - §

3 - Between Cornwallis and Brown or Wright Jr

Brown to [Innes?], 18th June 1780[48]   *2(166): ALS*

Augusta
June 18th 1780

Sir

I have the honor to acknowledge the receipt of your letter and am happy to congratulate you on the favorable state of public affairs.

Colonel Hammond waited upon me at Galphin's and told me he and the officers were willing to surrender themselves prisoners of war. I in consequence sent Major Wright of the Georgia Loyalists to the regimental muster field to accept of their submission on the terms offered by his Excellency the Commander in Chief.

The militia in South Carolina and Georgia offered their services on my march, but having no occasion for their assistance, I declined accepting their offers from the same motive which induced you to send them home.

The people on Savannah River on the Georgia and Carolina side have been distressed in their persons and property to the essential prejudice of the service. About ten [days] ago I gave notice to the inhabitants that I should hang without favor or distinction any person who presumed to plunder or otherwise disturb the peaceable inoffensive planters, and for the apprehending of any of the persons above described I offered a reward of fifty guineas.

About 10 days ago I received a flag from Colonel Dooley[49] and officers offering to

---

[48] This letter was no doubt written to Innes, who preceded Balfour to the Back Country. When Innes arrived in Charlestown in late June, he may have delivered it to Cornwallis.

[49] Born in North Carolina, John Dooly (c. 1740-1780) was the son of a poor Scotch-Irish family. Migrating to the Ninety Six District of South Carolina, he eventually acquired at least 2,500 acres, becoming a successful planter, trader, land speculator and surveyor. He then moved on to the back part of Georgia, where he became a deputy surveyor and acquired new lands on which he established a mill, a fort, a ferry and a plantation. At first loyal to

surrender themselves prisoners of war. I in consequence sent a person with sufficient powers to accept of their submission agreable to the terms prescribed by the proclamation of the Commander in Chief.

I purposed to have sent a company to have relieved the garrison of Fort Rutledge this afternoon. The men were paraded when I received your letter.

As this fort is in the Indian territories, I hope it will be destroyed as soon as the stores are removed. The Indians will never be satisfied whilst a fort remains in the country. They were promised that the people who have taken forcible possession of their lands should be removed.

I have sent off runners to the Creeks and Cherokees to suspend all hostilities against South Carolina and Georgia and shall give directions to the Indian commissaries to order the planters on the Indian lands to retire with their families and effects in 14 days after notice has been given.

A quantity of skins now at the fort, the property of merchants in England either bought or taken from the traders, I beg may be reserved for the just owners until I can send information to the commissaries to receive them into their charge.

I purpose to assemble the head men of the Creeks and Cherokees at Augusta to prevent their young warriors from seeking satisfaction for any losses they may have sustained. You will please, sir, to enquire of Colonel Balfour whether he wishes that I should order the Indians to drive the Virginia and North Carolina banditti who have forcible possession of their lands at Wattoga, Caen Tuck etc — I mean Henderson's settlement as it is generally called. It was chiefly from this quarter that the rebels took shipping and passed down the Ohio and Mississippi to join the Spaniards and plunder the plantations in West Florida. I shall be obliged to you for your answer.

With sincere wishes for your honor and success, I have the honor to be with just esteem, sir, Your most obedient humble servant

THO^S BROWN[50]

---

the Crown, he changed sides in late 1775 and soon became a captain in the 1st Georgia Continental Regiment, a commission which he was forced to resign in autumn 1777 after having seized a Creek peace delegation in retaliation for the death of his brother. In the same year he was elected to the Georgia revolutionary assembly and in 1778 he became the first Sheriff of the newly formed Wilkes County. Shortly afterwards he succeeded to the colonelcy of the Wilkes County militia, and of the operations in which he was involved the most notable was the defeat of North and South Carolina loyalists at Kettle Creek on 14th February 1779. Now, in 1780, he would soon be admitted to parole and allowed to return to his plantation some forty-five miles above Augusta. In August he would be murdered there by a party of loyalists. (*DGB*; Heitman, *Historical Register*, 200)

[50] Thomas Brown was born in 1750 in the North Riding of Yorkshire at Whitby, where his father was a prosperous ship owner. After receiving a liberal education, which he improved by travel as a young man to North America, he decided to become a gentleman planter on the Ceded Lands in Georgia. Setting sail from Whitby in August 1774, he arrived at Savannah in November, accompanied by 300 servants, and proceeded to establish an extensive plantation between the forks of Kiokee Creek in the Up Country besides taking up lands in South Carolina. A leading loyalist there, he summarises his involvement in the war and the events leading to it in his letter of 16th July to Cornwallis. He would play a distinguished part in repulsing Clark's attack on Savannah before

[*Subscribed*:]

I have just received intelligence that the Indians I sent to the aid of General Campbell harrassed the Spaniards so much on their debarking about 15 miles to the westward of Pensacola that they have retired.

TB

Brown to Cornwallis, 28th June 1780   2(208): ALS

Augusta
June 28th 1780

My Lord

Since my arrival in this quarter of the country with the detachment under my command I have received the submission of Hammond's (South Carolina), Garden's[51], Middleton's[52] and Dooley's Georgia regiments on the terms prescribed by the Commander in Chief.

I have given directions to have their arms collected together and conveyed to Augusta.

As the interior parts of this province have been considered for some years past a secure retreat for all the villains and murderers who have fled from justice from the southern provinces, the principal difficulty I have hitherto experienced has been the suppression of plunderers and horsethieves who under the specious pretext of loyalty have from [time] to time daringly assembled in defiance of all law and authority and indiscriminately ravaged the plantations of peaceable inoffensive inhabitants who have received protections or prisoners on parole.

It may not be unnecessary to inform your Lordship that the town of Augusta (our present quarters) has for near forty years been the seat of the Indian trade, the depot of Indian merchandize, and considered, from its vicinity to the Creeks, Cherokees and other Indian tribes, as the key to the southern provinces.

---

courageously but unsuccessfully defending the post against Lee and Pickens. As Lt Colonel of the King's Rangers and Superintendent of Indian Affairs in the Southern Department he was placed on the Provincial half pay list at the close of the war and settled in the Bahamas, first on Abaco, and then on Grand Caicos, where he again became a gentleman planter, owning 8,000 acres and over 600 slaves. He later removed with his slaves to a plantation in St Vincent, where he died on 3rd August 1825. Charged with cruelty and severity in revolutionary propaganda, which has percolated down to the present day, he has in recent years been the subject of a seminal work by Cashin which questions whether such charges are true. (Cashin, *The King's Ranger*; Treasury 64/23(16) (National Archives, Kew))

[51] Benjamin Garden's regiment came in fact from South Carolina. He was a colonel in the Granville County revolutionary militia. (Moss, *SC Patriots*, 342)

[52] Colonel Robert Middleton commanded the 1st or Lower Battalion of the Richmond County revolutionary militia. (Gordon Burns Smith, *History of the Georgia Militia, 1783-1861* (Boyd Publishing Co Inc, 2000), i, 54, iv, 151)

The River Savannah opens a navigable communication to the town for boats of 60 tons.

Provisions, rum and military stores may be with facility be brought up the river and be from hence conveyed to Ninety Six.

I have communicated my ideas on this subject to Colonel Balfour and pointed out the necessity of a work being thrown up at this place for the security of the province, our Indian connections and the vast quantitys of merchandize which will of course be lodged here for the purposes before mentioned.

Colonel Balfour informed me he would write to your Lordship on this subject.

A considerable number of the Indians from the Creek and Cherokee nations have sent to inform me that they purpose to pay me a visit at Augusta to tender their services. I have in consequence sent to Savannah for presents for them and shall be glad to know your Lordship's pleasure relative to their future operations. I sent them early notice of the inhabitants of South Carolina and Georgia having submitted to the authority of Government and orders to suspend all hostilities against these two provinces.

The Cherokees, I have every reason to believe, will renew their application of being reinstated in (possession of) their hunting grounds on Watoga, Louisa, Henderson's settlement and Cane-tuck, of which the rebels from North Carolina and Virginia have taken forcible possession to the essential prejudice of the nation.

From these settlements (the asylum of plunderers and robbers) the rebels occasionally embark upon the Ohio and proceed down the Mississippi, plunder the plantations of British subjects and join the Spaniards at New Orleans.

I have been informed from good authority that at least 500 rebels are now employed in the army of Don Galvez (the Spanish Governor).

As at this juncture it perhaps will be more politic to secure the affections of our Indian allies than to employ them on such services where there is a difficulty of discriminating between friends and foes, I can, if it is your Lordship's pleasure, order them to confine their operations within their own territories (i.e beyond the legal boundary lines of the provinces of Virginia and North Carolina).

The Cherokees, from the early active part they took in favor of Government, were exposed to the incursions of the rebels from the southern provinces, their lower and middle towns were laid in ashes, their plantations destroyed, and their wives and children driven into the woods.

From the distressed miserable condition of near 700 families I have reason to expect they will make application to me to relieve their wants. Such presents as are sent by the Lords of the Treasury I can apply to that purpose; but as I am unprovided with any funds to relieve their respective wants, particularly for the purchase of rum, provisions, tobacco etc on their arrival here with other contingent expences, and being directed to apply to the commanding officer of the Southern District for such sums as are necessary for defraying all extra expences for carrying on the service, I must take the liberty of applying to your Lordship to enable me to defray such expences as are incurred in the course of service for the purchase of provisions, salaries of the officers employed in time of war etc in such a manner as your Lordship may judge proper.

The rebel garrison at Fort Rutledge in Seneka I have at the request of Colonel Balfour sent a company of the King's Rangers to relieve. The temporary possession of this post will overawe the frontiers and I have reason to think I can reconcile the Cherokees to our retaining this post in one of their towns on representing to their chiefs that it is intended for the security of their families and property.

As the province of Georgia has been declared to be in His Majesty's peace and civil government established, I am at a loss to judge whether or how far the mode adopted for the regulation of the militia in South Carolina can be introduced in Georgia.

I have wrote to Sir James Wright (the Governor) and informed him of the plan proposed and partly executed in South Carolina.

The returns of the detachment I hope your Lordship has already received by the way of Ninety Six through Colonel Balfour.

By an express from the Indians I am informed that near 1200 hundred [sic], including the women and children, will be down in 3 or 4 weeks.

I shall endeavor to the extent of my interest and abilities to keep them in proper temper and in a disposition to act on their return to their nation whenever your Lordship may require their services.

Fourteen hundred Creeks are returned from Pensacola, having marched down at the requisition of Major General Campbell to his aid on the appearance of a Spanish fleet off the harbour of Pensacola.

I have the honor to be, my Lord,
Your Lordship's most obedient and most humble servant

THO^S BROWN

Cornwallis to Brown, 17th July 1780

78(22): C

Charlestown
July 17th 1780

Lt Colonel Brown
Superintendant of Indian Affairs

Sir

I have received from Camden your letter of the 28th of June dated at Augusta. I will in a few words tell you my ideas and wishes in regard to the Indians. I should desire that they may be kept in good humour by civil treatment and a proper destribution of such presents as are sent from England for that purpose, but I would on no account employ them in any operations of war. The business of the claims of the Cherokees is too intricate for us to enter upon it at present. They had better be told that we hope soon to be able to settle that matter to their satisfaction. I think Fort Rutledge of very little consequence, and if they are very desirous of having it destroyed, I would not refuse their request. As it is not the intention of the Commander in Chief to make any military use of the Indians, I cannot think myself justified in suffering the publick to be put to any considerable expence about them, nor can I consent to any gratuity being given to them further than the usual presents. If their houses have been destroy'd, the rebuilding an Indian hut is no very expensive affair and I dare say they will get their usual crops of corn this year. I can therefore allow nothing further on the account of provisions than for their entertainment during their stay at Augusta, and in that article, when I pass the accounts, I shall expect to find there has been no unnecessary waste. I have ordered all the Indian presents that are here to be sent to Savannah for the convenience of their being transported to Augusta.

The number of officers employed with the Indians, and their salaries, have, I conclude, been already regulated either by Sir William Howe[53] or Sir Henry Clinton. The customary charges therefore on that account will be allowed for the present and untill I see any reason for altering them.

From the report I have received from Pensacola of the behaviour of the Creeks, they have very little merit from that expedition. General Campbell says that they staid only as long as they could extort presents, that they consumed great part of his provisions, and left him just at the time that he expected an attack.

I have given my directions very fully to Lt Colonel Balfour relative to the post at Augusta.

I am, sir,
Your most obedient and most humble servant

[CORNWALLIS]

Wright Jr to Cornwallis, 15th July 1780

2(305): ALS

Augusta
15th July 1780

Rt Hon Earl Cornwallis etc etc etc

My Lord

I was yesterday honor'd with a message which your Lordship had ordered Colonel Balfour to send to Colonel Brown. It gives me infinite concern to fall in any shape under your displeasure, tho' it shou'd prove only temporary.

---

[53] William Howe (1729-1814) was Clinton's predecessor as Commander in Chief.

Sir Henry Clinton repeatedly told me, whilst he was before Charles Town, that I had his full permission to recruit there and in South Carolina, and Major André, upon my request to have the same inserted in public orders, answered that he wished me not to press the matter as it might induce other corps to trouble Sir Henry with like petitions, but that I might rest assured with a liberty of recruiting throughout the province, with which I thought it my duty to be satisfied.

Your Lordship will permit me to add a paragraph of a letter I received from Major Barrow[54] dated June 21st 1780, viz: 'Unfortunately we did not reach Charles Town Bar before the 4th of June, when Sir Henry Clinton with his suite had already embarked, generally supposed for New York. I had only an opportunity of a few minutes' conversation with Major André, who desired me to acquaint you that you certainly had the Commander in Chief's leave to recruit in South Carolina and that he wou'd give you such an authority in writing the first moment he had leisure.' This is in hopes only of regaining that opinion with your Lordship which I shall always study to deserve.

Shou'd Lieutenant Obman[55] (my recruiting officer) have been guilty of endeavouring to inlist any improper people, he will have acted contrary to my written instructions, and I have frequently repeated by letter that he was on no account to receive any prisoners.

I will take the liberty to entreat your Lordship's permission still to avail myself of Sir Henry Clinton's kind intentions towards me and to confess my great omission in not having earlier acquainted you therewith.

The different corps which have long recruited in the province of Georgia have picked up most of the young men. Shou'd there be any particular district in Carolina to which you may think proper to confine me, to that and any other orders which you may favor me with the strictest attention shall be paid.

Captain Randell[56], who will have the honor of presenting this, will wait your Lordship's determination and can explain any part of our conduct which you may condescend to inquire

---

[54] Thomas Barrow was the brother-in-law of Major James Wright Jr, whose sister, Isabella, he had married. On 20th November 1775 he had been commissioned a lieutenant in the 3rd Battalion of the 60th (or Royal American) Regiment and been promoted to captain in the battalion on 27th April 1778. He may now have been acting as a major of brigade. In December 1783, while he was serving with the regiment in the West Indies, his father-in-law, Sir James Wright, would present on his behalf a claim for compensation from the Crown. It related to the loss of a plantation at Ogechee, fifteen miles from Savannah, together with three tracts of 3,000 uncultivated acres in St John's Parish, Georgia. (Coldham, *Loyalist Claims*, 27; *Army Lists*)

[55] Jacob Daniel Obman (1749-?) was a German who had served nine years in the British line, transferring to the Provincial establishment on 27th May 1779 when he was commissioned a lieutenant in the Georgia Loyalists, a corps being newly formed under Major James Wright Jr. He would not be cashiered for his recruiting indiscretion and would transfer to Thomas Brown's King's Rangers when they and Wright's corps were amalgamated in 1782. At the close of the war he would be placed on the Provincial half-pay list. (Treasury 64/23(16) and WO 65/165(11) (National Archives, Kew); Clark, *Loyalists in the Southern Campaign*, i, *passim*)

[56] John Bond Randall (1753-?) was an Englishman who had been commissioned into the Georgia Loyalists as a captain on 29th May 1779. Like Obman, who served in his company, he would transfer to the King's Rangers in 1782 and be placed on the Provincial half-pay list at the close of the war. (Ibid)

about.

I have the honor to be
Your Lordship's most obedient and very humble servant

JAMES WRIGHT JUN[R]

PS

As Colonel Brown writes by this opportunity, I do not presume to give your Lordship any state of this part of the country.

Cornwallis to Wright Jr, 21st July 1780
78(38): C

Charles Town
21st July 1780

Major Wright

Sir

I have received your letter of the 15th.

I have understood from the most undoubted authority that your corps was originally raised out of the prison ships at Savannah. Your party that was in this town has carried off several of the Continental prisoners from the barracks. As this is in my opinion an offence of the most heinous nature, being not only a breach of a most positive order but a most cruel injustice to our poor soldiers who have been languishing four years in captivity, I must beg to be understood to be very much in earnest about it, and I must insist that you make the strictest scrutiny into your recruits, that you will return the prisoners of war if any are found, and order your officer under arrest. In regard to your recruiting in South Carolina, I cannot possibly consent to it without a positive order in writing from Sir Henry Clinton as I think it would be very prejudicial to the King's Service.

I am etc

[CORNWALLIS]

Brown to Cornwallis, 16th July 1780
2(307): ALS

Augusta
July 16th 1780

His Excellency General Cornwallis etc etc etc

My Lord

I had the honor of writing to your Lordship at Camden, which letter, I am informed by Lord Rawdon, was forwarded to Charlestown.

By a letter yesterday from Colonel Balfour commanding at Ninety Six I have received orders to send my corps (the King's Rangers) on the arrival of Lt Colonel Cruger at this place to Savannah and to remain at Augusta or such place as may be deemed proper for carrying on the Indian business, and that neither the King's Rangers or Major Wright's corps are to recruit in South Carolina.

It affords me the most sensible concern to perceive from this order I have unknowingly incurred your Lordship's displeasure.

May I be permitted to suggest to your Lordship that the King's Rangers were principally raised in South Carolina, are composed of North South Carolinians and Indian traders and -countrymen who have a perfect knowledge of the language, customs, manners and disposition of the different tribes of Creeks and Cherokees, are active expert woodsmen, capable of swimming any river in the province, have many of them served with me during the rebellion with our Indian allies, and are the best guides in the Southern District.

The officers, having acquired in the course of service a knowledge of the Indian language and being personally acquainted with the chiefs, have on various occasions enabled me to curb their natural ferocity and prevent any acts of wanton barbarity or indiscriminate outrage.

With the assistance of officers and men trained in the woods and possest of advantages (to which the other troops are strangers) from a knowledge of the Indians, inhabitants and country, I could be answerable of the peace and security of the frontiers.

My own influence and interest, I believe, are extensive, perhaps more so than any person's in the interior parts of the southern provinces; my zeal, I trust, inferior to few who have the honor to serve His Majesty. My reasons for hazarding such a declaration, I flatter myself, modesty forbids me not to mention.

Previous to the commencement of the rebellion I was engaged in the cultivation of my lands in South Carolina and Georgia with 300 servants I brought with me from Yorkshire.

Being obnoxious to the rebels on account of my principles and being represented by some artful villains as an emissary of administration and a son of Lord North sent to poison the minds of the people, I was ordered to appear before a committee then sitting in Augusta, and on my refusal to attend, a party consisting of 130 armed men headed by the committee surrounded my house in South Carolina and ordered me to surrender myself a prisoner and subscribe a traiterous association. I told them my determination to defend myself if any person presumed to molest me. On their attempting to disarm me, I shot one of the ringleaders (a Captain Borstwicke[57]). Being o'erpowered, stabbed in many places, my skull

---

[57] Chesley Bostwick, a storekeeper at Augusta, was wounded in the foot and survived. As a captain in the Georgia revolutionary militia, he was in 1776-7 to command at Fort Howe (formerly Barrington) on the Altamaha River. He may have been related to Littleberry Bostwick, a planter who was to become Lt Colonel of the 1st Battalion of the Richmond County revolutionary militia. When in 1780 Brown assumed command at Augusta, he bore Chesley no open ill will and allowed him to remain undisturbed, but after the failed assault on the town in September Chesley would be among those 'of the worst characters' sent under guard to Charlestown. He would return to Augusta by February 1783. Being active revolutionaries, both Chesley and Littleberry had been named

fractured by a blow from a rifle, I was dragged in a state of insensibility to Augusta. My hair was then chiefly torn up by the roots; what remained, stripped off by knives; my head scalped in 3 or 4 different places; my legs tarred and burnt by lighted torches, from which I lost the use of two of my toes and rendered incapable of setting my feet to the ground for 6 months. In this condition, after their laying waste a very considerable property, I was relieved by my friends and conveyed to the interior parts of South Carolina.

Having assembled the inhabitants, I prevailed upon near 2,500 to enter into a league to oppose the measures of the Congress and to support at the risque of their lives and fortunes His Majesty's crown and dignity.

I believe I can say without the imputation of vanity that to my exertions Government is indebted for the loyalty of the inhabitants of the interior parts of South Carolina. A price being set on my head and the emissaries of the Congress (a William Henry Drayton[58] and a Mr Tenant[59]), whom I opposed at every public assembly, and a number of horse thieves being employed to assassinate me, I retired secretly to Charlestown to confer with Lord William Campbell[60] (his Lordship having taken refuge aboard of an armed ship from the resentment of an unprincipled rabble) and I, being discovered, was taken into custody, banished the province by Henry Laurens[61] (chairman of a committee) as a sower of sedition

---

in the Georgia Disqualifying Act passed by the royal assembly on 1st July 1780. (Cashin, *The King's Ranger*, 27-8, 53, 62, 113; Cashin Jr and Robertson, *Augusta*, 50, 72, 77; The Georgia Disqualifying Act 1780)

[58] A nephew of Lt Governor William Bull, William Henry Drayton (1742-1779) had accompanied the Reverend William Tennent on a mission to the Back Country in August and September 1775 for the purpose of persuading the inhabitants, many of whom were loyal to the Crown, to support the subversive measures of the Provincial Congress. On the radical wing of the revolutionary party, Drayton would soon afterwards be elected President of the Provincial Congress and become Chief Justice under the temporary revolutionary constitution. He died of typhus while attending the Continental Congress as a delegate from South Carolina. (*DAB*)

[59] Born in New Jersey, William Tennent (1740-1777) was a Presbyterian clergyman who shortly before the revolution removed from a church in Connecticut to the Independent Church in Charlestown, from where he soon became the leading Presbyterian or Congregational minister in South Carolina. At the time of his mission to the Back Country he was a member of the Provincial Congress and of its Special Committee. 'Of majestic and venerable presence', he was an ardent revolutionary leader who in his public offices, the pulpit and the press industriously promoted the revolutionary cause. While a member of the lower house of the revolutionary legislature, he would in January 1777 make a powerful speech advocating religious equality and the disestablishment of the Anglican Church. It was to be his last important public act, for, while bringing his recently widowed mother from New Jersey, he would die in August at the High Hills of Santee. (Wallace, *South Carolina*, 215, 279; McCrady, *SC in the Rev 1775-1780*, 5, 206, 209)

[60] Lord William Campbell (?-1778), the fourth son of the Duke of Argyll, was the last royal Governor of South Carolina. A former naval captain, he arrived at Charlestown in June 1775 to an ominously quiet reception and found that his office had been usurped by the subversive measures of the Provincial Congress. After being discovered encouraging support for the Crown in the Back Country, he fled in September to the sloop of war *Tamar* in Charlestown harbour. In June 1776 he returned, and while a volunteer commanding the lower gun-deck of the *Bristol* during the attack on Fort Sullivan, he received a wound in the side which led to his death two years later. (McCrady, *SC in the Rev 1775-1780, passim*; *DAB*; *Appletons'*)

[61] Of Huguenot descent, Henry Laurens (1724-1792) was a very wealthy merchant and planter who for many years had been involved politically in South Carolina. Almost continually a Member of the Commons House of Assembly from 1757, he had become President of the First Provincial Congress in June 1775 besides serving concurrently as Chairman of its Council of Safety, an office in which he crossed the path of Thomas Brown. Re-

and an enemy to the liberties of America. Being every moment in danger of assassination, I made my escape to Savannah, was there thrice publicly attacked by the mob, and scarce with life got off to St Augustine.

On the arrival of Sir Henry Clinton in Carolina, I was by his order appointed lt colonel commandant of a corps by Governor Tonyn in East Florida in June 1st 1776.

The province of East Florida being laid waste, the stocks of cattle carried off, and the inhabitants and garrison comparatively starving, the corps I had the honor to command in conjunction with the Indians extended the frontiers, surprized and cut off the rebel posts, secured the inhabitants from insult and supplied the garrison and province with cattle. On the frontiers I occupied the outpost two years and a half 70 miles advanced beyond any other. On the requisition of Governor Tonyn I sent trusty guides to my friends in South Carolina, who to the number of 350 abandoned their property and connections to serve His Majesty, marched through Georgia into Florida and were formed into a battalion now commanded by Colonel Innes.

East Florida being invaded by the united force of the rebels from Virginia, North South Carolina and Georgia under the command of a General Howe consisting of 5,000 men, the corps under my command I subsisted 4 weeks on rice and palmeto cabbage, in the course of which time we dismounted the chief part of the rebel army. The rebels were in consequence obliged to retreat with considerable loss without penetrating the province.[62]

Previous to the arrival of Colonel Campbell[63] in Georgia, with 28 rangers, a reconnoitring party in the same province, from ambush I beat back the rebel army consisting of 600 men with a train of artillery, killed two of their captains and wounded and took the commanding officer, General Screven, at the head of his column prisoner.[64] I believe, my Lord, I can say with truth I have been engaged in as great a variety of service as any Provincial officer of my

---

elected to the Second Provincial Congress, he was again appointed to its Council of Safety in a like capacity, and after helping to draft a temporary revolutionary constitution for South Carolina, he became its Vice-President. By July 1780 he had moved on to the Continental Congress and had been serving there for some three and a half years, part of the time as its President. At the beginning of September 1780 he would be captured at sea while on a mission to Holland and be imprisoned in the Tower of London. Exchanged for Cornwallis in 1782, he would shortly afterwards act as a sort of unofficial envoy to the Court of St James. On his arrival in America in August 1784, he retired from public life, broken in health, to 'Mepkin', his beautiful estate on the Cooper River. (*DAB*)

[62] Brown is referring to the ill-fated invasion of East Florida in the spring of 1778 by Major General Robert Howe (1732-1786), the Continental officer then commanding in the Southern Department. It failed as a result of hunger, sickness, and insubordination. (*DAB*; *Appletons'*; Boatner, *Encyclopedia*)

[63] Archibald Campbell (1739-1791), Lt Colonel of the 2nd Battalion, 71st (Highland) Regiment, had led the expedition which captured Savannah in late December 1778. After Augustine Prevost assumed overall command on joining him with a force from East Florida, he returned on leave to England.

[64] Brown is referring to an incident of 22nd November 1778 which occurred on the high road between Midway and Sunbury. As he says, he ambushed Brigadier General James Screven of the Georgia revolutionary militia, who was advancing to oppose a British diversion against Sunbury made as part of an incursion into Georgia from East Florida. Whether Screven was mortally wounded or killed on the spot is obscured in conflicting accounts. (*DGB*; Cashin, *The King's Ranger*, 79-80; George White, *Historical Collections of Georgia* (New York, 1855), 615-6, 524-5; T W Lipscomb to the editor, 2nd March 2005)

years and standing and have had the good fortune hitherto never to receive a reprimand or rebuke from any superior officer. On the contrary, in the course of service I have had the honor to receive the thanks of General Howe, Lord Dartmouth[65], Lord George Germain, Sir Henry Clinton and Governor Tonyn, and in consequence of my services His Majesty was pleased to confer on me the office of Superintendant of Indian Affairs.

How far I have succeeded with the Indians is, I presume, well known to the people of the country. Having served with them on eight different occasions with success, I gained their confidence and attachment. On the late invasion of West Florida I prevailed, at the requisition of Major General Campbell, on 1,600 Creeks (a larger body of Indians than I believe was ever assembled for service by Sir William Johnson[66] or Colonel Stuart[67]) to march to his aid. How far I may be able to retain their future attachment by being seperated from the officers and men who can alone be useful to me, I cannot pretend to determine.

The dissafected Indians of the Creek nation have sent to inform me they purpose to pay me a visit to adjust all misunderstandings after their Busk the latter end of August. 'The Busk' is an annual festival (after a general purification) on the ripening of the corn. The Cherokees who were driven from their towns by the rebels and reduced to extreme distress inform me they purpose to accompany them in order to procure that relief to their respective wants that their distress and services justly intitle them to.

Nothing shall be wanting on my part to keep the different tribes in my department in good temper and a favorable disposition towards Government. I am apprehensive it will be a task of extreme difficulty to prevent the Cherokees harrassing the rebels who are in possession of their hunting grounds so near to their villages. It is in fact as distressing to them as the loss of their houses and corn. As they are reduced to this sad alternative, either to repossess themselves of their hunting grounds or to encroach on the territories of the Creeks or Chickesaws, the consequence of the latter is obvious.

Captain Johnson[68] of the King's Rangers is the bearer of this letter and returns on the

---

[65] William Legge (1731-1801), 2nd Earl of Dartmouth, was a stepbrother of Lord North and his friend from boyhood, though they were not always in political agreement. From 1772 to 1775 he had been Secretary of State for the Colonies before becoming Lord Privy Seal, a post he was to occupy until the resignation of the North ministry in 1782. (Valentine, *The British Establishment*, ii, 528-9)

[66] Sir William Johnson Bt (1715-1774) had been Superintendent of Indian Affairs north of the Ohio from 1756 till his death.

[67] The Hon John Stuart (c. 1700-1779) had been Thomas Brown's predecessor as Superintendent of Indian Affairs in the Southern Department.

[68] Andrew Johnston (?-1780) was a son of the Hon Lewis Johnston, a doctor of medicine at Savannah who was currently a member of HM Council in Georgia. Forced to leave Georgia in 1776 on account of his loyalism, Andrew repaired to East Florida, where in 1777 he was commissioned a captain in Thomas Brown's King's Rangers. On 12th March 1778 he distinguished himself in the storming of Fort Howe (formerly Barrington) on the Altamaha River, where he was the first man to enter the works. Shortly afterwards, during Howe's ill-fated invasion of East Florida, he was dangerously wounded when gallantly defending a breastwork with a handful of men against a great superiority of numbers. He would be killed on 14th September during Clark's assault on Augusta. (*Royal Georgia Gazette*, 28th September 1780; Cashin, *The King's Ranger*, 74, 115; Clark, *Loyalists in*

receipt of your Lordship's commands.

I have the honor to be, my Lord, with just respect
Your Lordship's most obedient and most humble servant

THO[S] BROWN

Cornwallis to Brown, 21st July 1780   78(36): ADfS

Charlestown
July 21st 1780

Lt Colonel Brown

Sir

    I have just received your letter of the 16th by Captain Johnson. As I never make any disposition of the troops under my command without maturely weighing the consequences and am guided solely by the good of His Majesty's Service without any consideration of personal favour, I do not think my self bound to give my reasons to any person but the Commander in Chief. I will, however, tell you some of those which induced me to make the present exchange: the weakness of your corps and Major Wright's; their having inlisted a number of prisoners of war; my having received accounts from the Back Country that they were practising all the tricks of recruiting to the great terror and disgust of the inhabitants; and my desire to employ Colonel Cruger and Colonel Allen and their corps. And on account of the behaviour of your recruiting officers and my having put several new corps in commission I cannot at present consent either to yours or Major Wright's corps recruiting in this province. If there should be any individuals in your corps that are Indian interpreters or for some reason particularly usefull in Indian affairs, you will keep them with you, reporting it to the commanding officer at Ninety Six. As to the disaffected Creeks who intend to pay you a friendly visit, I have undoubted authority that two hundred of their young warriors have been to pay their respects to Don Galvez. I beg leave to assure you that you have never given me the least offence and that I never entertained a doubt of your performing with the utmost zeal your duty to your King and country.

I am, sir
Your most obedient humble servant

CORNWALLIS

the Southern Campaign, i, 61)

Brown to Cruger, 6th August 1780[69]   *62(6): ALS*

Augusta
August 6th 1780

Colonel Cruger commanding His Majesty's troops at Ninety Six etc etc etc

By a dragoon

Dear Sir

The Governor of Georgia being determined to carry the Disqualifying Act[70] into full and immediate execution without distinction of persons, I beg you will be so obliging as send or communicate the contents of the inclosed letter to Lord Cornwallis, being much at a loss how to act in this business.

I am certain that a number carry on regular correspondence with the rebels, and as so large a proportion of the people on the Ceded Lands are prisoners of war, unless a considerable number of them who are most obnoxious are removed, the loyalists in the neighbouring parishes will not be able to live in peace.

It certainly will be prudent to remove all the officers — civil, military, Continental or militia — with very few exceptions, by which means the lower class of people will return to a proper sense of their duty.

Five or six hundred prisoners are certainly too many to remain (as they seem disposed) in one district.

Sir P Houstoun[71] informs me he can procure a sufficient number of waggons. He desires

---

[69] Although addressed to Cruger, this letter is included here in view of its relevance to Augusta. It was presumably forwarded to Cornwallis with the letter (not extant) mentioned in the first paragraph.

[70] The Disqualifying Act of 1780 was passed by the royal assembly of Georgia on 1st July and assented to by the Governor, Sir James Wright, on the same day. According to its long title, its main purpose was 'to disqualify and render incapable the several persons herein named from holding or exercising any office of trust, honour or profit in the Province of Georgia for a certain time'. It proceeded to name 151 persons considered active in the usurpation of the royal government before going on to disqualify all other persons who at any time or times before the passing of the Act 'have acted in the said Province of Georgia as members of any council, assembly or committee or as a commission of trade or of forfeited estates or who have held any commission or appointment under the said usurpation either in a civil or military capacity'. (Allen D Candler ed, *The Revolutionary Records of the State of Georgia*, 3 vols (Atlanta, 1908)) The other purposes of the Act are described in Brown's letter of 5th September to Cruger, vol II, p 183.

[71] Sir Patrick Houstoun Bt (1742-1785) was a planter who, like his father and a younger brother John, had taken a prominent part in the public affairs of Georgia. Succeeding to the baronetcy in 1762 (created by Charles II in 1668), he had quickly become the province's Registrar of Grants and Receiver of Quit Rents. Two years later he was elected to the Commons House of Assembly, but as the revolution approached, he lost heart for service in the House and ceased to attend. He was nevertheless nominated to HM Council in 1775. As the war began to progress, he was unable to make an early choice between the contending parties, being denounced at one time or

to be informed on what [terms] he is from time to time to engage them and in what manner they are to be supplied with provisions and forage when on service. He says, on being acquainted with these matters, he can procure as many as will be wanted.

The people in Savannah are very backward in paying the hire of boats employed in transporting provisions, rum etc to Augusta. If they should neglect being regular in discharging such accounts, there will be much difficulty in engaging the number required.

I have mentioned that if they do not send up in the course of six weeks a sufficient quantity of rum and salt for the troops for five months, the river will not be navigable for boats for 3 or 4 months after that time on account of the current from the rainy season.

You will be so obliging, dear sir, as send me the order respecting the allowance of forage for officers, as I am not acquainted what number of rations (and in what proportion) the officers have right to.

By a letter from General Campbell to me yesterday all at present is quiet, tho' the Spaniards talk of paying them a visit in the winter.

I shall be obliged to you for the Charlestown papers if you have any with you.

I am, my dear sir, with true esteem
Yours sincerely

THO^S BROWN
Lt Colonel commanding King's Rangers

§ - §

---

another by each, but towards the end of the war came down solidly on the side of the Crown. For his sins he saw part of his property confiscated by the revolutionaries and in 1784 removed to England, where he died at Bath. By contrast his brother John was firmly of the revolutionary persuasion and served as a delegate to the Continental Congress in 1775 and as revolutionary Governor of Georgia in 1778. Another brother James appears elsewhere in these Papers. (*DGB*)

CHAPTER 14

Correspondence between Cornwallis and Ferguson

Ferguson to Cornwallis, 22nd June 1780 *2(183): ALS*

Ninety Six
June 22nd 1780

Lord Cornwallis

My Lord

I had the honor of your Lordship's letter of the 16th[1] today and have only to say that, after having met with your approbation at the outset, it would make me extremely unhappy if my best endeavours should either be wanting or unsuccessfull to fullfill your Lordship's designs respecting the militia.

Inclosed are circular letters containing instructions which have been sent to the different battalions in order to promote a free militia establishment throughout, which I daresay will take place as in general they seem only to have wanted to have been put in a method of assembling and arranging themselves and heartily to approve of your Lordship's regulations.

There will be some little difficulty in avoiding to disgust those loyalists who have suffer'd in their property by the rebels and who, having refrain'd from doing themselves justice at the revolution, now expect it from the officers commanding; and there is danger of occasioning a coolness among the militia also from the necessity that some times will occur of restraining others from following the opposite extreme and taking advantage of the confusion of the times

---

[1] *letter of the 16th*: see p 109.

to plunder their rebel neighbours without having been injured by them. The importance of not damping the zeal of our friends or exasperating those rebels who are quietly disposed will render some instructions from your Lordship to those who are to act as magistrates very necessary. As to redress by the civil law, were it ever about to be immediately establish'd, many of the loyalists, being beggar'd, would have no access to that mode of redress.

By General Williamson's report the militia of the seven regiments under his command ammount to above five thousand men without reckoning the three lower regiments that lay between the Santee, Congaree and Eddisto, so that it will be some time before a perfect report can be made of them.

I have the honor to be with the greatest respect, my Lord,
Your Lordship's most obedient humble servant

PAT FERGUSON

Enclosure (1)
Ferguson to Cheney, 17th June 1780

2(164): CS

High Hill Creek
June 17th 1780

Mr Bailey Cheney[2]
Big Creek

Sir

Inclosed are some directions and arrangements for the forming of the militia, to which you will please to conform untill more particular orders shall be received from Lord Cornwallis; and you will be so good as send a copy of them and of this letter to such of the companys of your battalion as join your own, directed to any principal loyalist within the bounds of each company, and request of them to assemble the men and proceed to take the sense of the people as there directed, and also to transmit copys to the neig[h]bouring companys.

All men who have so lately and woefully experienced how much the good subjects in these very loyal districts, altho ten times as numerous as the rebels, have been govern'd and opppress'd by them (for want of being united under proper rules and arrangements so as to be unable to avail themselves of their superior strength and courage) must see the necessity

---

[2] As a young man Baily Cheney had accompanied Moses Kirkland on his mission from the Back Country non-associators to seek aid and advice from Lord William Campbell, the royal Governor. Now commanding a company in the royal militia, he would flee to Charlestown in 1781 and by mid October be promoted to a lt colonelcy of militia there. When Charlestown was evacuated in December 1782, he moved to East Florida, where he became implicated with others in pillaging settlements near the frontier with Georgia. Wishing to begin his administration peaceably, the new Spanish Governor Zespedes offered the outlaws safe conduct outside the province. Cheney accepted and obtained a pass to go to Tensaw above Mobile in West Florida. (Lambert, *SC Loyalists*, 55, 263-4; Clark, *Loyalists in the Southern Campaign*, i, *passim*)

of proper regulations and be sensible how much it is the duty and interest of every man who wishes not for a return of the rebel tyranny to lend a hand thoroughly to establish the peace and security of this province, which will not be out of danger untill the arms and authority are placed in the hands of the loyalists of both Carolinas.

It must therefore be evident to them that their own safety, as well as the oppress'd condition of their suffering fellow subjects in North Carolina, requires that they should be ready, if necessary, to assist His Majesty's troops in securing their own frontier by driving the rebels out of that province.

The proposed arrangements calculated for the above purposes are contrived so as to put the inhabitants to as little inconvenience as is consistent with their safety and happiness, and are sent to them in the confidence that they will meet with the approbation and assent of every thinking man.

It is therefore wished that no person who has any objections to them be allowed to enter into the militia, as the number of loyalists in this province is fully sufficient for its defence without the assistance of doubtful people. A militia thus composed of men whose fidelity is known and depended upon by each other, associated for their common interests under regulations establish'd with their hearty consent and approbation, and serving under officers freely chosen by themselves in support of liberty, justice and the laws of their fore fathers will give an unconquerable strength to this province, being in every respect opposite to the mock militia of the rebels, which was founded on oppression and establish'd by force against the interest and consent of the people, consequently in the end hasten'd the ruin of the rebel cause and brought its promoters under the hatred and contempt of the inhabitants.

As it is proper, in case of accidents, to have the militia arranged without loss of time, the captains, so soon as chosen, will prepare the returns of their companys and bring them to Colonel Balfour commanding at Ninety Six on the first of July; and it is hoped they will not regard a little trouble for so necessary a purpose.

I am, sir,
Your most obedient servant

PAT FERGUSON
Inspector of Militia

PS

The limits of each company are to be the same with those establish'd by the rebels.

Enclosure (2)
Directions and arrangements for forming the Royal Militia   *4(440): CS*

Hill Hill[3]

As the militia will be intrusted with arms and be employ'd to watch over the interests and safety of their fellow subjects, and as the chief officers will in a considerable degree have the authority of civil magistrates and have it in charge to preserve the peace and support the laws as well as defend the Constitution untill the thorough establishment of civil government, it is of the first consequence that such men alone are chosen for officers or admitted to carry arms in the militia as sincerely abhor the rebel tyrany and wish for a return of true Brittish liberty under the King and Old Constitution; wherefore, however much the loyalists may be inclined to forgive the former proceedings of those men who have taken an active and willing part with the rebels, it is incumbent upon them not to receive them as guardians of their rights and happiness untill time shall show the sincerity of their reformation.

After the men of each company have assembled and have chosen their captains, lieutenants and ensigns and have entered their names as militia men, and that[4] all such have been rejected as are distrusted and objected to by the others, the captains will then inform them of the following arrangements designed for the militia.

1st, that every man who is receiv'd into the militia shall be ready to assemble at all times when required and perform militia duty within the limmits of his own district according to the regulations which may be establish'd for that purpose.

2nd, that all militia men who are under 40 years of age and not incumbered with more than three children or disabled by any bodily infirmity shall, if required, embody themselves and co-oparate with the Brittish troops within the limmits of the two Carolinas and Georgia agains[t] His Majesty's enemys natural and foreign according to the orders they may receive from the Commander in Chief or officer acting by his authority whenever the publick service shall render it necessary, provided that the militia men, when embodyed, receive pay and provision and that the term of such service does not exceed six months of the twelve.

The above terms to be signed by all those who are willing to unite and act in concert for their common safety, and it is particularly recommended to the captains to take care that none but good and trusty men who are approved of by the men of their company are suffered to sign.

The several captains of militia, when duly chosen by the men of their companys, will, untill they receive further instructions, exert themselves if necessary to preserve the publick peace and suport the King's Government, taking care that nothing is done contrary to the laws that were in force before the rebellion.

---

[3] *Hill Hill*: a slip of the pen. As indicated by his letter of 17th June, Ferguson was at High Hill Creek.

[4] *that*: the meaning is 'after'. See p 108, note 12.

They will imediately get a return, from every inhabitant whatsoever within the bounds of their companys, of all arms and amunition of every sort in their possesion, as well as of all property bellonging to the rebel States or taken from loyalists, in order to keep them from being removed or embezeled.

They will without loss of time prepare returns of their companys, specifying the age of the men, whether married or batchelors, and the number of their children.

They will also procure a similar return of all those inhabitants within their bounds that ought not to be receiv'd into the militia or be intrusted with arms.

They will get attested accounts in writting from such of their men as have suffered injuries from individuals during the rebel government in order to their getting redress; and if the oppressions they have underwent have been particularly cruel and tyranical and that[5] there is danger of escape, they will immediately secure the offenders and report the circumstances to the nearest commanding officer of the troops.

They will from time to time admit into their companys any good subjects who may have been absent at their first meetings and who shall appear to their men to deserve their confidence and to be worthy of being intrusted with arms in defence of their King, country and liberties.

PAT FERGUSON
Inspector of Militia

Ferguson to Cornwallis, 11th July 1780   *2(267): ALS*

Ninety Six
July 11th 1780

Lord Cornwallis

My Lord

I am sorry to intrude upon your time so frequently but the variety of circumstances that occur leave me at a loss and some appear worthy of being laid before your Lordship.

There are claims brought in by Mr Edgehill[6], a man of character here employ'd this

---

[5] *that*: the meaning is 'if'. See p 108, note 12.

[6] Thomas Edghill had acted as commissary to some 1,500 loyalists raised by Colonel Thomas Fletchall in the Back Country in 1775 and for his sin had been imprisoned by the revolutionaries in Charlestown jail for several months.. Now, in 1780, he would soon be commissioned lt colonel of a regiment of royal militia, but impaired health, perhaps from being shot through the thigh in a skirmish, seems to have led him to relinquish the command less than two months later. With the loss of the Back Country in 1781, he would flee to Charlestown, where, as an inspector of refugees, he would be partly responsible for administering relief to those from the District of Ninety

summer as commissary by the loyalists at their first rising, for flour, cattle, bacon, a little rum and whisky, and one or two trifles (the ammount of which will, I believe, be under £200 sterling) that were conceal'd by the friends of Government for the purpose of assisting a revolution and then produced.

As this account was referr'd to me by Colonel Balfour and appears to be a generous credit given to Government upon an important and trying occasion, I think it my duty to mention the circumstances, perswaded that your Lordship will esteem it true œconomy as well as just and creditable to defray the charge without admitting the precedent.

Since that, our late alarm at Pacolet has afforded pretexts for other claims of the same kind, which if not discouraged in future will occasion a great expence and give an opening for much imposition, as these partial alarms may be frequent and no means of examining or checking the returns.

In cases where the militia run together upon any sudden alarm to defend their own district, I am not sufficiently inform'd to say how far it might be proper for them to bear their own expences as the countys and parishes in England do in many cases; but if each militia man was required on such occasions to bring three days' provision, it would certainly prevent their distressing the country and enable them, the instant they assembled, to keep in force and act with vigor, whereas at present they are obliged to employ themselves in running up and down the country, exposed to any enemy that may approach them in that scatter'd condition, in order to find subsistance.

In cases where, the alarm proving serious, any body of militia was order'd to keep together by the King's officers, an allowance of fourpence farthing sterling per day for each man appearing on the parade would more than pay for a pound of flour and beef at the medium contract prices here and also afford a farthing to the commissary for every ration; and thus the expence be small and ascertain'd.

If a strict and precise line can be drawn for these charges, and all uncertain contingencies disallow'd, except in cases of evident and serious necessity, the nation, in place of being plunder'd so as to corrupt the loyalists and become at once their prey and contempt, could, out of a tenth part of the saving, well afford liberal gratuitys to such loyalists as have suffer'd for their fidelity or shall persevere to do their duty disinterestedly.

At present it is evident here that many of the sufferers are casting about naturally enough to make up their losses by getting employ'd in one job or another either to raise Provincial corps, contract for provisions, forage or waggons, create and procure appointments etc, little thinking how much more happy and even rich they will probably become, as well as better subjects and members of society in every respect, if they are led to continue their fidelity as heretofore from a sense of common danger and general interest, and not seduced into more sordid pursuits from a facility of preying upon the public. Indeed, the priviledges they will

---

Six. When Charlestown was evacuated in December 1782, he sailed for Jamaica, where he remained for four and a half years before embarking for England. In January 1789 he presented a claim to the royal commission in London for the supply of cattle and wheat. (Coldham, *Loyalist Claims*, 141; *The Cornwallis Papers*; Clark, *Loyalists in the Southern Campaign*, i, *passim*)

derive from your Lordship's measures for putting the arms and civil authority into their hands, joined to the advantages in point of trade and barter which they must enjoy from being allow'd to range freely through the country, with the credit that they will naturally procure from the certainty that they cannot go off with their stock and moveables to the rebels (whilst the disaffected are more distrusted and confined), will be very sufficient to bind their interests with their duty.

The measure directed by your Lordship of settling differences by arbitration had in some degree been adopted by themselves with very good effects; and as those who have been injured are by this means satisfy'd and silenced and the others reliev'd from their apprehensions and have given this proof of acquiescence and a desire of peace, it is to be hoped that there will be reason to treat them by degrees with less distrust; but there are numbers who have suffer'd in person and property, who have nobody from whom to claim damages, and for whom there is no aparent means of relief unless your Lordship should see fit to apply to that use the slaves, horses and other property captured by the militia here, with some valuable crops left by the rebels who have fled.

In the articles which I did myself the honor of mentioning in my last letter[7] as necessary for the militia then serving with the army, I forgot canteens, tomahawks and camp kettles. Excellent wooden canteens are made at Orangeburgh for a trifle, and the tomahawks here if iron was sent up.

There have been some proposals here for raising volunteer troops and companys to protect the frontier, which, altho perhaps a temporary inconvenience, would, I apprehend, contribute much to debase the spirit of the militia and prevent them from ever acquiring any discipline or knowledge of service. If such covering partys are necessary, a few prime men from each company, form'd into a body under their best officers, would probably prove superior to any job-companys, be of no continued expence, and probably bring back into their battalions a degree of confidence and discipline that in place of debasing would much improve the whole in the same manner as the officers and men who accompany the army will at their return diffuse their spirit and experience through every regiment of militia and render them more fit for real service than all the theory and drilling possible.

It is not without an effort that I do myself the honor of expressing my sentiments to your Lordship without your particular commands. I am only encouraged to it from the opportunitys of partial information which my journeys through the country afford, and from the belief that, amidst the various and extensive objects of attention that occupy your Lordship, you will necessarily have to avail yourself of the observation and talents of men of very inferior experience and capacity with regard to details in order to judge of the whole; wherefore with the utmost deference I lay my ideas before you in the confidence that, however much they may in other respects be deficient, they will at least prove sincere and disinterested.

I am just inform'd by Colonel Balfour that your Lordship has determined against every thing here but field works on account of the expence. How far the work that I had the honor

---

[7] *last letter*: not extant.

to propose may come within that description I know not, but least your Lordship should conceive that my calculations were made in a hurry, I again beg leave after thorough consideration to say that I will be proud to engage (with the command of the captured Negroes, waggons etc) to erect such a work under penalty, if it is not out of reach of assault in three weeks and in a thorough state of defence in six or if it should cost £100 beyond the £500 supposed, to pay the whole expence myself. And with regard to repairs, the parapet having a broad base, little height and a natural slope, and the logs at least of 50 years' duration, a few shingles and oak rails would ten years hence renew the whole.

I set out for Pickins' regiment on the Indian line tomorrow and shall be with Hammond's regiment about Augusta on Monday, soon after which I hope to pay my respects to your Lordship with a satisfactory account of the militia of this quarter. In the mean time allow me to express the high sense I shall ever entertain of the opinion you are pleased to express of me, which it shall be my endeavour in some measure to deserve.

I have the honor to be with the greatest respect
Your Lordship's most obedient humble servant

PAT FERGUSON

Ferguson to Cornwallis, 20th July 1780   2(333): ALS

Fair Forest
July 20th 1780

Lord Cornwallis

My Lord

I am this instant apprized of an express to Charles Town, and although it is not in my power to express myself fully, being to march immediately, it appears to me necessary to mention some circumstances.

The rebels on this frontier from Georgia to Catabaw River are undoubtedly in very high spirits, enterprizing and confident of support. They talk loudly of a large force arriving under General Calve[8] and have seduced great numbers of the protected men to join them.

I am perswaded, if we do not cover the militia regiments on this frontier by a strong advanced force, that we will lose all credit and influence with our friends, and every hesitating man will rise against us.

The militia in our rear are sufficient if we cover the front, providing we had a post at 96 or else where, secured from a sudden coup, for their support and the security of our stores; but if in detail, a very small force against us may act with serious effect.

---

[8] *Calve*: Kalb.

If some hundred good cutlasses could be forwarded here, they would give our militia in their scouring courses a very great advantage against the naked rebel rifle horse-men; and if they are getting swords, as repeatedly reported, our men must have them.

There is very great difficulty in bringing the militia under any kind of regularity. I am exerting myself to effect it without disgusting them, and, on the whole, not without effect.

I find Colonel Floyd's regiment near Catabaw have all turn'd to the rebels, except about 60. The two other regiments between the Wateree and Congaree are also much against us. On our side there appears a great majority in general, except in Pickins' and Hammond's battalions; and there are two battalions in Georgia, one about Augusta, one near the Indian lands, both of which require to be form'd and the majority disarm'd speedily.

I beg your Lordship's indulgence for this scrawl and have the honor to be with the greatest respect

Your most obedient humble servant

PAT FERGUSON

Ferguson to Cornwallis, 24th July 1780   *2(360): ALS*

Mitchel's Creek
Fair Forrest
24th July 1780

Lord Cornwallis

My Lord

I did myself the honor of writing a letter to your Lordship in such a hurry some days ago that nothing but my want of time could have induced me to have sent it. It related to the bad consequence to our militia here of suffering the rebels to ruin the loyalists of our frontier regiments and to excite those who had taken protections again to rise, from the want of a body of troops near Broad River, advanced to protect the loyalists and awe the disaffected, collected in force sufficient to threaten the rebel frontier, strike powerfully at any invading detachments and detach rapidly and extensively against any plundering partys.

Colonel Balfour has been since here and the rebels are fallen back. The militia is assembled and daily gaining confidence and discipline, so that if our account of the rebel strength in reach of us is near the truth, I shall think the officer commanding very unfortunate if anything serious is done against us.

Colonel Balfour will acquaint your Lordship with the plan and arangements. I shall confine myself to what relates to the militia and principally to what appears to me the cheapest method of supplying them with provisions with the least opening for perquisite or imposition.

Beef here in the killing months, if not stall fed, and flour used formerly to sell for nine shillings sterling (two dollars) per hundred pounds, and as the tallow and hide, being a perquisite of the commissary and lost to the farmer, is valued at 1/5th of the carcass, the beef in fact costs, when served out to the troops, one penny three eight[h]s[9] per pound, and the flour one penny one twelfth. Thus a ration of a pound and a half of beef and a pound of flour will ammount nearly to 3¼d[10] and, allowing the commissary one farthing per ration, to three pence half penny, exclusive of a little salt and a little whisky or rum occasionally. This estimate is too little if south of Enoree.

It would be a check on the commissary if his receipts were counter sign'd by the commanding officer, and when detachments were sent out, the officer might be allow'd a little above the usual price to feed his men, and all confusion and fraudulent receipts prevented.

The chief commissary might be bound by oath, and give security, to have no other perquisite than the farthings, hides and tallow, nor to suffer them in others, with a promise of reward if his œconomy deserved it.

I understand that the commissary of the army at Ninety Six offers publickly a guinea for every hundred weight of flour when a third less would be reckon'd an exorbitant price. From Mr Townsend's character[11] I am perswaded he is misinform'd by some of the under commissarys, who want to begin as usual by establishing a precedent for a high price in order to turn it to their own account afterwards.

With regard to the pretence of raising the prices on account of the supposed scarcity of grain, were that really the case, yet the still greater scarcity of specie and want of all other substitute for the necessary circulation will at least enhance the value of gold and silver in an equal proportion.

With regard to waggons, horses etc for the militia, I presume that the parole men, Quakers and all others who do not assist with their personal services will, according to your Lordship's arangement, be sufficient to furnish these without hardship to them or expence to Government.

Œconomy once establish'd, the public could well afford a few liberal gratuitys to such of the militia as deserv'd them and were more ambitious of profit than honor. From the qualitys they possess, and their very great diligence at exercise, I must prove very deficient in my duty if their services do not, when they are tryed, well repay their expence. All punishments have heretofore been avoided; they have unanimously agreed to degrade, disarm and eraze from their list those who misbehave, and have come to a resolution that whatever militia man shall

---

[9] *one penny three eight[h]s*: the correct figure is almost exactly 1.3*d*.

[10] *nearly to 3¼d*: the correct figure is approximately 3*d*, which, with the farthing allowed for the commissary, makes a total of 3¼*d*, not 3½*d*.

[11] Captain Gregory Townsend was the Assistant Commissary General in charge of that department in the Southern District. He was held in high regard by Balfour. In April 1781 he would be replaced by Major John Morrison, of whom Balfour had a very low opinion, and would return to New York. (WO 65/164(3) (National Archives, Kew); *The Cornwallis Papers*)

quit the militia, when assembled on service, without leave is a traitor to his country and comrades and deserves to have his beeves and grain brought to camp for the public service.

Least any of those who are to be embody'd should plunder or return home without leave, it may be necessary that the captains who remain at home have public orders to confine in jail all such as return without a pass or who bring any plunder or property not specify'd in it, and when the service was over, a Negro or good horse from His Majesty's enemys would well reward and bind their ready obedience in an easy way.

The three regiments, late Brannan's[12], Thomas and Williams[13], are in point of discipline much more forward than the rest and indeed want only a few arms and the necessary clothing to turn out a very vigorous and numerous battalion of rangers. Williamson's, Beard's and Heatly's could well spare another that in a few days might be made to equal them. As to Pickens', Hammond's, Watson's[14], Win's and Goodwin's battalions, there is such a

---

[12] Of Scotch-Irish descent, Thomas Brandon (1741-1802) was born in Pennsylvania and migrated with his parents to the Back Country of South Carolina in 1754 or 1755. Residing at Fair Forest Shoal, he took an early part in the revolution and by the fall of Charlestown had risen to be a colonel in the revolutionary militia. Rather than enter into a parole, and with the bulk of his regiment turned and now commanded by Major Daniel Plummer, he had gone off with a small party of his men and would soon place himself under the command of James Williams, with whom he was involved in the action at Musgrove's Mill in August and the Battle of King's Mountain in October. Rough, impulsive, and with an inveterate hatred of loyalists, who received little mercy at his hands, he would, on the march from the battlefield, cold-bloodedly hack to death a prisoner who hid in a hollow sycamore tree. Although Benjamin Cleveland was the villain of the piece, there is reason to suspect that Brandon played a supporting role in the later mock trial and execution of other prisoners at Bickerstaff's Old Fields. Continuing in this manner in early November, he would, according to Cornwallis, be involved in plundering and putting to death loyalist inhabitants between the Tyger and Pacolet Rivers. He would later participate in the action at Blackstocks before serving under Morgan in the Battle of Cowpens. After the war he was frequently elected to the legislature, became a militia general, and also served as a Justice of the Court, County Ordinary. (Draper, *King's Mountain*, 129, 326, 336, 469; *The Cornwallis Papers*)

[13] Born in Hanover County, Virginia, James Williams (1740-1780) received a very limited education and on the death of his parents migrated early to North Carolina, where a brother and two cousins had settled. A Presbyterian, he removed about 1772 to Little River in the Back Country of South Carolina and shortly afterwards was elected to the Provincial Congress that convened in January 1775. Later in the year he became a member of his local committee responsible for enforcing the association subversive of the royal government. In 1776 he was appointed a lt colonel in the revolutionary militia and served in Andrew Williamson's Cherokee expedition. Two years later he stood for the office of senator but was defeated by Robert Cunningham, who declined to sit. In 1778 and 1779 he was also involved in military operations, notably in the action at Stono Ferry and the siege of Savannah. Now, in 1780, with his regiment turned by the British, he had refused to enter into a parole, going off to North Carolina. From there he returned to join Sumter and was appointed his commissary. After the action at Hanging Rock he would deviously take off with him Thomas Brandon and his men, participate in the action at Musgrove's Mill, and, leading Rutledge to believe that he had been the overall commander there, obtain from him a commission of brigadier general of militia. Sumter and his men would refuse to recognise Williams as their commander and refer the matter to Rutledge to resolve. In the meantime Williams would go off with his small band of followers, and while courageously leading them at the Battle of King's Mountain, he would be mortally wounded and die the following day, being buried in an unmarked grave some one or two miles from the battlefield. Described as rough and rash but with a remarkably good disposition, Williams was about five feet nine inches in height, corpulent, and very dark in complexion. He had black hair and eyes, a nose uncommonly large, turned up and round at the end, with nostrils which became distended by passion or excitement. (Draper, *King's Mountain*, *passim*; Johnson, *Traditions*, 483, 490-2, 494)

[14] Samuel Watson (1731-1810) had been a member of the Provincial Congress in 1775 and 1776 and had served as Lt Colonel of Colonel Thomas Neel's New Acquisition Regiment of the revolutionary militia. When Neel was killed in the action at Stono Ferry on 20th June 1779, Watson succeeded to the colonelcy. Now, in 1780, he would

proportion of disaffected that the good men may perhaps be all necessary at home.

As I imagine the blowing up of the magazine at Charles Town must have occasion'd a very great scarcity of arms, I will take the liberty of mentioning to your Lordship various little resources of supplying the militia at little or no expence, with which perhaps you may be unacquainted.

There are a hundred short German rifles in the ordnance store at Savannah that I left there, particularly suited for light horse, and in the store of the 71st Regiment there some broad swords, which, altho rather short for horse, would answer the purpose very well, and also several hundred Highland pistols that are perfectly new and which, as well as the swords, Colonel Macdonald offer'd this spring to sell for ⅔rds the original price. There are also probably both there and at Charles Town many bayonets out of repair, fitted to no firelocks, that would be of infinite use to the militia, who have many firelocks without bayonets, to which they would readily fix them in a rough way. There is moreover at Charles Town some thousand spears, which might not only with a pistol be put into the hands of the officers of militia, so as to put it out of their power to neglect doing their duty by firing themselves and throw some hundred of the best arms now idle in their hands into the ranks, but might be of use in some of the stockade forts here (some of which are very defensible against every thing but cannon and, laying upon Tyger and Thicketty advanced towards the North Carolina frontier, must be occupy'd by the militia) to supply the want of bayonets and with a pistol to arm those home militia who will otherwise be without any arms; and if there are not swords enough, a small proportion of the mounted militia would be better arm'd with a light spear and pistol than with a naked rifle. Some pistols and cutlasses, and perhaps firelocks, might be procured from the transports and ships of war. Indeed, one or two thousand common horse man's swords, bitts and spurs arriving here from England would, I apprehend, give us a more thorough and extensive command over the country inhabitants and resources of these southern colonys than any addition of fighting foot whatsoever, who, however safe themselves, can neither protect the friendly districts nor turn to their use those of the enemy, much less controul or check the horse militia, who reign uncontroul'd over every inch of the country except the foot cantonments and three miles of their environs.

Inclosed is a circular letter which it appear'd necessary to me, with Colonel Balfour's approbation, to send to the several regiments of militia, as some of the captains from timidity, and others from a desire of numbers, had already admitted improper people so as not only to disgust the loyalists but in fact arm men for the rebels, whilst other loyalists, from natural virulence of temper or interested views, have much alarm'd the quiet part of the disaffected and given them a very injust impression of the intentions of Government, which has contributed much to the late risings.

I have found myself, from the urgency of the moment, necessitated to take steps without delay for which I stood much in need of your Lordship's instructions, and I shall feel myself extremely unhappy if in any degree I have err'd or counteracted a plan which, from what I have seen and can pretend to judge of it, will establish the authority of Government and

---

command some of his disaffected men when taking part under Thomas Sumter in the action at Hanging Rock on 6th August. (Moss, *SC Patriots*, 971)

attachment of the Colonys upon the noblest and most permanent basis as well as justify the measures and adorn the success of Sir Henry Clinton, in whose glory I am bound by every tie of gratitude and respect to take a thorough interest.

The state of this frontier and the opportunity of forming and arranging so large a body of the militia occasions me to remain here. Captain Depeyster (whom Sir Henry Clinton allow'd me to take as an assistant and to whose assiduity both in expediting the returns and disciplining the militia I have been much obliged) will proceed to Ninety Six and from thence wait on your Lordship with the returns, the delay of which from the various interruptions we could not avoid; and I can assure your Lordship that, between night marches, restraining the resentment and irregularitys of the militia and arranging them, I have not slept eight hours in the last four nights.

I have the honor to be with the utmost respect
Your Lordship's most obedient humble servant

PAT FERGUSON

Enclosure
Ferguson to the officers commanding militia regiments 2(347): C

July 23rd 1780

To the Officer Commanding

Sir

As there is reason to believe that many of the captains have misunderstood the intention of the returns, so as that no very certain judgement can be form'd from some of them of the proportion of loyalists and off disaffected people in the province, I beg you will as soon as convenient get them to reexamine them.

In the Rebel column they ought to place only those men who are known to have acted heartily with the rebels from inclination and to have readily and willingly contributed to the support of the rebel government.

In the Loyal column ought only to be placed such men as have given proof of their attachment to Government privately or publickly and are known to have continued under the rebel government from necessity alone.

In the column of Quiet People they will be so good as insert all Quakers, Dunkars, Babtists and other men who are principled against fighting but wish'd for a return of the Old Constitution, also all those men who have shown no particular attachment to the rebels by their actions and who, without exerting themselves in support of the rebellion, have only comply'd with what they were ordered to do to avoid being fined or otherwise mollested. And the returns will still be more distinct if, in place of a first figure in the Quiet column, they will put the word Quaker, Babtist, Dunkar, Quiet or Doubtfull opposite to the names.

Of those men who are included in the Rebel column many have and more will no doubt see their error and, if they are men in other respects of a moral character, be by degrees received without suspicion into the militia.

In the mean time, as every proper and legal means is following to procure satisfaction to the loyalists from those who have injured them in person or property, it is the duty of every officer of militia, and indeed of every honest man, not only to avoid insulting or mollesting such of their neighbours as have been disaffected but to discourage and prevent others from injuring or irritating them.

Of those deluded men, many have acted with probity and moderation in a bad cause, and how much more is it the duty of the loyalists to show themselves worthy of being supporters of a good one by their justice, humanity and charity. Moreover, when it is consider'd by what various and artfull methods the rebel leaders seduced many honest men from their duty (not only suppressing the liberty of the press, punishing men for reporting bad news altho true, or examining freely into their conduct), keeping them in total ignorance of the truth, by misrepresenting the intention of the King and by awakening their fears with regard to a design of turning the Indians loose upon them, of employing the troops to lay waste the country, and even had the astonishing impudence to assert that Britain, the land of liberty, of toleration and of the Prodestant religion, was about to introduce popery and slavery at the time when the rebel Congress was conspiring with France and Spain in a league which threaten'd, had it prov'd successfull, to destroy liberty, peace and true religion throughout the world.

Thus mislead, there is much excuse for such rebels as have not been guilty of blood or rapine and every reason to hope that their daily experience and the knowledge they will acquire of their true interests will open the eyes of such as are not already convinced.

Of those in the Quiet column, no doubt the greatest part might now be trusted safely in the militia, was there occasion for them; but the number of known loyalists is more than sufficient, and it is impossible in so short a time either to form a just judgement of the former conduct of these people amidst the various resentments and ill founded accusations which naturally influence many well meaning loyalists and equally impossible to judge of their present disposition untill there shall be time to observe their conduct; wherefore it is recommended to the companys not to be in a hurry either to judge against any men of doubtfull character or in their favor, but to leave them for the present unmollested, and when the accusations against them shall prove false or that[15] they shall show by their conduct the sincerity of their reformation, every man whose heart and understanding is good will with pleasure receive them into the militia.

In the mean time such of the Quiet lists as are not charged with any particular acts of violence and rebellion can not be supposed to lay under any imputation of blame, and what arms are to spare, after thoroughly arming all the loyalists, may be put into their hands, but the number even of the Quiet men received at present into the militia ought not to be above one for every three loyalists, and when these prove faithfull, more can in future be admitted — where the characters are equally good, young and unmarried men ought of course to be

---

[15] *that*: the meaning is 'when'. See p 108, note 12.

admitted in preference.

At the bottom of the return should be mentioned the number of Quiet men receiv'd into the company among the known loyalists.

I am, sir,
Your most obedient humble servant

[PAT FERGUSON]

Ferguson to Ross, 26th July 1780

2(368): ALS

Fair Forest
July 26th 1780

Captain Ross
Aid de camp to Lt General Earl Cornwallis

Dear Sir

Inclosed is a memorial which I beg you will lay before his Lordship. There are numbers of emigrants here from Maryland, Pensylvania and Jersey who would probably inlist in preference in our northern corps, and our detachment is now so long on service that it could probably bear a proportion of recruits without hurting it.

I am in haste, dear sir, with true regard
Your most obedient humble servant

PAT FERGUSON

Enclosure
Memorial from officers under Ferguson seeking permission to recruit, 25th July 1780

2(362): DS

Unto his Excellency Lt General Earl Cornwallis

The Memorial of the officers commanding detachments
from different Provincial regiments
now serving under Major Ferguson

MOST RESPECTFULLY SHEWETH

That, in consequence of the orders by which the detachments have been sent to this province, the commanding officers have given them warrants to recruit men for their respective regiments.

That, on the army's landing in Carolina, it was found expedient for the publick service to prohibit all corps from recruiting except the Legion, Irish Volunteers and Carolinians, but as that prohibition we understand to be remov'd with respect to the New York Volunteers, we beg leave to solicit your Lordship's authority for recruiting our detachments, who have considerably suffered by the effects of the climate and constant services.

A DE PEYSTER, Captain
King's American Regiment

Camp
Fair Forest Ford
25th July 1780

WILLIAM STEVENSON, Lieutenant
2nd Batt, New Jersey Volunteers

FRED[K] DE PEYSTER, Captain
Nassau Blues

DUN FLETCHER[16], Lieutenant
Loyal American Regiment

WILL[M] McFARLANE[17], Ensign
3rd Batt, De Lancy's

JOHN TAYLOR, Lieutenant
1st Batt, New Jersey Volunteers

Cornwallis to Ferguson, 5th August 1780

79(14): C

Charlestown
5th August 1780

Major Ferguson

Sir

I received the favour of your letter of the 24th of last month by Lt Colonel Balfour, who has given me a full detail of the state of our affairs in the part of the country in which he has

---

[16] Duncan Fletcher (1757-?) was a Scot who had seen three years' service in the British line. In 1777 he was commissioned a lieutenant in the Loyal American Regiment on the Provincial establishment and was now serving on secondment to Ferguson's corps. On 7th October he would be taken prisoner at the Battle of King's Mountain. Promoted to captain lieutenant in his regiment on 12th March 1781, he would be placed on the Provincial half-pay list when the regiment was disbanded at the close of the war. In 1784 he was living in Wilmot, Nova Scotia. (Treasury 64/23(3), WO 65 164(37), and WO 65/165(3) (National Archives, Kew); Draper, *King's Mountain*, 480-1)

[17] William McFarlane (1756-1783) was a Scot who had served some four years in the Provincial line. An ensign in the 3rd Battalion, De Lancey's Brigade, he was now serving on secondment to Ferguson's corps and would be captured on 8th August in the action near Cedar Spring. Paroled or exchanged, he would be promoted on 26th June 1781 to lieutenant in his battalion and serve until its imminent disbandment. He was lost at sea in September 1783 while on passage to the St John River, Nova Scotia, when the *Martha* transport was wrecked on rocks near Yarmouth. (WO 65/164(33) and WO 65/165(8) (National Archives, Kew); *The Cornwallis Papers*)

commanded. He has likewise informed me of your indefatigable exertions to put the militia of that district into a respectable situation and of the success with which your labour has been attended. I beg you will accept my warmest acknowledgements for the very important services which you have rendered to your country. I have sent up by Colonel Cunningham for your disposal some arms, a little rum and salt, and three hundred pounds. You will please to give to each commanding officer of a regiment of militia one hundred dollars as a gratuity for the trouble and expence to which they have been put and to allow any other small gratuities that you think will tend to encourage the plan of militia and promote the good of the service. Whilst the militia are assembled to defend their own districts, as in the present case, they will be allowed provisions. Whenever they are called out and join in the operations of war with other troops, they will be allowed pay and provisions. You will please to appoint a commissary or quarter master to each corps at five shillings per day to supply the corps with provisions. His receipts will be countersigned by the commanding officer. I propose leaving this town in a few days and should be glad that you would come to me at Camden about the 20th of this month when I will explain to you what part I intend that the militia should take in my future operations. I will then speak to you about your corps and every other business that I have not time to take notice of in this letter. You will please to leave Captain De Peister or some carefull officer to take care of your post during the three or four days that you may be absent, as any blow just now would greatly discourage the militia. I approve very much of your attention to keep disaffected people out of the militia; our misfortune at Cheraws has been entirely owing to an inattention to my instructions on that head.

I am, sir,
Your most obedient and most humble servant

[CORNWALLIS]

Ferguson to Cornwallis, 9th August 1780   63(26): LS

Phillip Fords[18] on Fair Forest
9th August 1780

Lord Cornwallis

My Lord

I am sorry that the situation of affairs here has put it out of my power to attend to the militia returns, being otherwise employed.

By the arraingement settled with Colonel Balfour, 700 militia with my detachment were to have been upon Pacolet, and 500 under Major Robert Cunningham upon Broad River to scower the country from plundering partys, one of which consisting with about 300 men was about Gilberton, and another under Sumpter on Catabaw which was supposed to be kept in awe by our post on Rocky Mount.

---

[18] *Phillip Fords*: a slip of the pen. The letter was written at Phillip's Ford and deals with the action near Cedar Spring and the events leading up to it.

But Major Robert Cunningham having thought proper of his own accord to make an excursion towards Catabaw with 800 of our party, mostly on foot, after some runaway rebel horse men and afterwards to dismiss his militia and send them 60 or 70 miles home, against Colonel Balfour's intentions, without orders or leave, in place of 1,200 militia there were only 500 (of whom 100 without arms) at a time when the rebels about Gilberton, having finish'd there wheat harvest and being reinforced by several partys from Georgia and some hundred men from the Western Waters, were preparing to advance in force and act in concert with Sumpter, of whose offensive preparations in the rear of our right we had also an account, whilst we could not weaken ourselves to watch him by patroles in our rear on Broad River fords.

At that time I was advanced to Thicketty north of Pacolet in order to awe the plundering partys, subsist beyond our secure resources and impose upon the rebels, when I got at the same time undoubted intelligence of the approach of a body of 800 rebels calling themselves 1,200 to McNight's upon North Pacolet to turn our left, and a move of Sumpter's down from Catabaw in the rear of my right, which made it necessary to fall back a little in order to cover the country, enable our militia to assemble in our rear, and preventing the rebels from getting between us and Ninety Six. I therefore threw the Tyger in our front and employed myself to encourage the rebels, improve the discipline and confidence of our militia, and so mask'd the fords as to be able, when an opportunity offer'd, to make a march by surprise upon either flank under blind of the river.

On Sunday the 6th instant, being satisfyed that nothing could in 48 hours penetrate on the side of Broad River, and having the account that 400 of the rebels were at Ford's Mill upon Tyger River and were to be join'd that day by the main body said to consist of 1,200 (among whom they industriously reported that there were some hundreds of Continentals), I march'd all night with 700 men to surprise them, but the militia broke the line of march and we could not arrive in time, and at any rate the rebel party had, it seems, fallen back that evening 7 miles without any knowled[g]e of our advance in order to join their main body. We therefore remain'd aback all day, mask'd by the river, march'd all Monday night, and on Tuesday morning enter'd the rebel camp an hour before day, but unfortunately some intelligence had alarm'd them and for the first time their horses were tyed and their men collected; and one of our guns happening to go off a mile from their camp, they push'd off half an hour befor we came on their ground. As our men and horses were totally overcome by two successive nights' marches, and the rebels fresh and well mounted, it was in vain to follow. I therefore contented myself with detaching our mounted infantry to the amount of 15 with the least fatagued of the militia horse after some waggons said to be following their rear. The rebels had avail'd themselves of a ravin[19] to dress an ambush, and from the intemperate ardour of our mounted and of some gallant fellows of the militia, as well as from the backwardness of the rest of the militia, Captain Dunlap found himself under a necessity of attacking 300 men with 40, one half of whom are kill'd or wounded, and of the rebels as many, and half a dozen

---

[19] *ravin*: an exaggeration. According to Draper (*King's Mountain*, 95), quoting the traditions of the neighbourhood, it was a hollow which had been cleared and planted with peach trees before the war.

of prisoners on each side. Major Smith and Captain Potts of the rebels[20], and their commissary, lay dead on the field; Colonel Graham[21] is dangerously wounded. Colonel Clark, I am assured, was mortally wounded and abandon'd two miles from the field by the rebels[22]. Captain Dunlap is slightly wounded on our side, and Ensign McFarlin taken fighting in the heart of a crowd of rebels. Fatagued as the foot were, it became necessary to march upon the rebels, who upon their approach fled before them over Pacolet, and since, I understand, over Broad River, their number not exceeding 700, some having gone home with plunder.

In justice to the Provincial detachment which I have the honor to command, I think it my duty to represent to your Lordship that it has chearfully undergone much more fatague since we quitted New York than any part of the British Army, and are now in rags without shoes, shirts or cloathing, living upon half flour, and often without rum, upon constant alarts and frequent night services, and without any of the comforts usual in our army, at a time when the rest of the army are in quarters of refreshment. They wish now to be relieved as they are intirely naked, if your Lordship approves of it. As to the officers, I can with justice say I have been much obliged to their zeal, diligence and spirit and shall take the liberty, when I have the honor of seeing your Lordship, of laying before you the names of those who appear to me to have the strongest claim for promotion.

If the militia here were provided, the horse with good cutlasses and some of the foot with bayonets, I have no doubt that, when assisted with one third part of regular troops, they would do every service if a judgement can be form'd from the almost savage bravery shown by individuals in the two skirmishes and from expedition, and very respectable order and countenance, with which our line advanced on broken woody ground yesterday over three miles in presence of an enemy that had bled the horse.

I have the honour to be with the greatest respect
Your Lordship's most humble servant

PAT FERGUSON, Major, 71st Regiment

---

[20] Burwell Smith, who was major in Clark's Wilkes County Regiment of the Georgia revolutionary militia, 'had contributed greatly to the settlement of the frontier portion of Georgia, where he had been an active and successful partisan in Indian warfare'. Of Captain John Potts little is known. (ibid, 97)

[21] William Graham (1742-1835) was born in Augusta County, Virginia, and now resided in a large, partly fortified log house near the west bank of Buffalo Creek, about eight miles north of King's Mountain. In 1775 he had been elected to the North Carolina Provincial Congress which met in August, and in the following month was appointed by it to the colonelcy of the revolutionary militia in Tryon County. Almost immediately he was involved in the Snow Campaign before serving in 1776 against the Scots Highlanders and Cherokees. A member of the Halifax Convention, he was by 1779 elected to the North Carolina Senate. After his present involvement in the action near Cedar Spring, where Ferguson is mistaken that he was wounded, Graham would take no material part in the war. Called away before the Battle of King's Mountain to attend his pregnant wife, he could not resist returning on hearing the gunfire, but would arrive after the outcome had been decided. He would die near Shelby, North Carolina, a pensioner for his revolutionary services. (ibid, 145, 232, 280, 476; Hay ed, *Soldiers from NC, passim*; Wheeler, *Historical Sketches*, i, 86)

[22] Clark was only slightly wounded. He received two sabre wounds, one to the back of the neck, the other to the head, his stock-buckle saving his life (Draper, *King's Mountain*, 93).

CHAPTER 15

Correspondence between Cornwallis and Wemyss

Wemyss to Cornwallis, 11th July 1780 *2(269): ALS*

George Town
11th July 1780

My Lord

I do myself the honor of acquainting you that I arrived here on Saturday morning.

The principal inhabitants of this place have been most violent and persecuting rebells and, altho they now, to save their estates, profess a desire of becoming good subjects, ought, I think, to be treated with some marks of disscouragement.

I should therefore propose to your Lordship that the paroles of about ten or twelve of the leading people should be altered, and, in place of having liberty to reside at their own estates, should be sent to the islands. By their removal the friends of Goverment, who are much inferior to the other party both in numbers and consequence, will be pleased and will be roused to take every method of carrying on the purposes of Goverment. In doing this, the militia plan, which goes on very slowly, will be forwarded. The friends of Goverment press very much to have the country people assembled, and to tender the oaths of allegiance to them, and to have those that do not appear or decline taking the oath to be dissarmed, but as I have no directions from you on this subject, shall not interfere in it untill I receive your Lordship's opinion. As I am told this place is very unhealthy, I beg your permission, should I find it so, to carry the men to North Island, which is looked upon as very healthy and is but a few miles distant. As provision is very scarce and dear, I hope you will be good enough to order some flour, rum and a small quantity of salt provision to be sent us as soon as possible. The small pox rages so much in the town that the country people, to prevent its spreading, have stopt all intercourse with it.

I have the honor to be
Your Lordship's most obedient and most humble servant

J WEMYSS[1]

Cornwallis to Wemyss, 15th July 1780   78(16): C

Charles Town
15th July 1780

Major Wemyss

Sir

I last night received your letter of the 11th and have [ordered] a galley and sloop with provisions to proceed immediately to Georgetown. I would have you by all means seize all violent and persecuting rebels and send them directly on parole to the islands unless there are a few, very notorious for acts of cruelty, who might be sent under a guard of militia to the Provost's at Charlestown. I do not approve of indiscriminate swearing. All those who are thought by our friends worthy to be trusted with arms will of course take the oaths of allegiance on their being admitted into the militia. The remainder must be disarmed and put on parole to remain at home, with the most solemn assurance that if they break their parole by committing any act of hostility, they shall instantly be hanged without any form of trial farther than proving the identity of the person. I have no objection to your going to North Island as soon as the galley arrives, but you must look out for intelligence as hostilities have recommenced on the frontier and every thing is in motion in those parts. Lord Rawdon has withdrawn McArthur from Cheraw Hill to bring his corps more together. You will do well to establish a correspondence with Colonel Mills, who commands the militia in the Cheraw District. Any expence incurred by obtaining intelligence will be allowed. You will take care to talk with the most perfect confidence. At the same time you will give out that your stay will not be long on account of the unhealthiness of the season, and you may intimate that it is probable a battalion of militia of about 4 or 500 men will soon arrive there from

---

[1] Born in Edinburgh, James Wemyss (1748-1833) had spent some ten years serving in the 40th Regiment and the Queen's Rangers before entering the 63rd Regiment as major on 10th August 1778. An active, capable officer, he would command the regiment in South Carolina during the ensuing months, in particular a detachment of his men and others on the controversial expedition to the Pee Dee during September. Wounded in the arm and leg in the action at Fish Dam Ford on 9th November, he would be captured and paroled later the same day. Lame, and with his health much impaired, he obtained leave by January to return to New York and took no further active part in the war. In August 1783 he was promoted to lt colonel but sold his commission six years later and retired to Scotland. About 1795 to 1799 financial difficulties led him to migrate to America, where living was less expensive, and he purchased a farm in a quiet backwater of Long Island. He lived there until his death. Like the place in Scotland, his name was pronounced 'Weems', as evinced by Kirkland's letter of 31st October to Cornwallis (vol III, ch 35), where it is spelt phonetically. (*Army Lists*; *The Cornwallis Papers*; Margaret Baskin, 'James Wemyss (1748-1833)', *Banastre Tarleton and the British Legion: Friends, Comrades and Enemies* (www.banastretarleton.org, 29th June 2005))

Orangeburgh or Ninety Six. As you are so very weak and that[2] there is no possibility of reinforcing you to any purpose, should you apprehend any real danger, I would have you come away either by land or water as you think best, but endeavour to find some plausible reason for doing it. At all events I would have you return to Charlestown as soon as you have put the power and arms into the hands of our friends and see the militia in a fair [way] of being established.

I am etc

[CORNWALLIS]

[*Subscribed*:]

I have seen a memorial from some loyal inhabitants near George Town asking for ammunition. If there is any want of that sort for the militia, you will first try to squeeze all you can from the rebels and then get some powder for them from the galley, which I will replace.

Wemyss to Cornwallis, 14th July 1780

2(290): ALS

George Town
July 14th 1780

My Lord

I did myself the honor of writing to you a few days ago and now send you a kind of representation I received yesterday from the dissafected part of the inhabitants, likewise a letter from Herriot & Tucker complaining of Captain Ardesoiff's[3] having taken away their private property, and am to request your Lordship's instructions. Many who's names are at the representation are the principal people in this part of the country and have acted as chairmen of committees, sherriffs, magistrates etc.

As the forming of the militia in this district seemed to me to be your Lordship's first object, I hope you won't think me assuming in offering you such information on that subject as has immediately come under my own observation. I think that Colonel Ball is neither known or respected enough to be at the head of a militia in this part of the country. His

---

[2] *that*: the meaning is 'as'. See p 108, note 12.

[3] John Plummer Ardesoif (?-1790) had been commissioned a lieutenant in the Royal Navy on 10th October 1759. Promoted to commander on 16th November 1779, a rank which carried the courtesy title of captain, he was now commanding the *Loyalist* on the southern station. Currently busy in appropriating captured property in and near Georgetown, he has become famous in revolutionary history for a perhaps much embellished incident in which he attempted to explain the effect of Clinton's proclamation of 3rd June to Major John James (soon to be of Marion's Brigade). Promoted to post-captain on 5th May 1781, he may have been captured with the *Loyalist* when, on 30th August of that year, it struck off Cape Henry to four ships of de Grasse's fleet, its main topmast having been shot away. (Syrett and DiNardo ed, *The Commissioned Sea Officers*; *The Cornwallis Papers*; James, *Marion*, 42-3)

abilities and activity appear to be much against him, and to this I attribute the refusal of several people to be militia officers. Indeed some of them, upon my finding fault with their backwardness, have told me so plainly. The lt colonel is still more dissrespected; his principles are even called in question. Before the rebellion broke out I understand there was never more than two regiments of militia in this division, but the rebels, finding that they had many friends, formed them into three, on which plan your Lordship, I believe, means to establish the present militia.

If the militia was formed on the old plan, I think it could be settled more easily, as I am afraid the country is neither able to find officers or men for three regiments. If the middle regiment was divided betwixt the upper and lower regiments, they would be well officered and their colonels men that are looked up to, Colonel Mills for the upper, and Mr Cassills[4] for the lower, a gentleman who is, I understand, to be nominated for the middle regiment. He resides chiefly in this town and is a very sensible good man and a zealous friend to Goverment. If from your Lordship's better information you find I am mistaken in my opinion as to the militia, I hope you will allow my intentions to be good and in that view excuse the trouble I have given.

If those people who have signed the representation are not to be received as subjects, I think the leading part of them ought to be sent to the sea islands on their paroles immediately, as their remaining here on parole I think will (as they have been used to command) disscountenance the raising the militia much.

As Mr Stewart[5], the clergyman of this place, writes, I believe, many letters on the politicks of this country, I beg leave to mention that, altho he is a very good man, allowances ought to be made to all his representations as I find him exceedingly violent and disposed to

---

[4] James Cassells was a Scot who had migrated to South Carolina in 1758 and soon established himself as an indigo planter on the Waccamaw. Despite taking the test oath in 1778, he was a covert loyalist and would shortly be commissioned Colonel of the Georgetown Regiment of the royal militia. He would, however, be captured by revolutionaries while on his way from a plantation to accept the commission and be briefly imprisoned in North Carolina before making his escape by September. Balfour, who like Cornwallis had a high opinion of him, observed in November, 'Cassells's character and his whole behaviour are much more manly and worthy of credit than any other colonel of militia I have yet seen, and as far as I have had connection with him, realy seems by no means a man of chimera or capable of undertaking any plan without a rational and well founded reason.' Nevertheless, Cassells' regiment, like the rest of the royal militia, did not perform well. Upon the confinement of the British to the Charlestown area, Cassells was appointed one of the inspectors of refugees in charge of administering relief, and he himself received pay both as an inspector and as a refugee. With his property confiscated by act of the revolutionary assembly at Jacksonborough, he sailed in mid October 1782 to East Florida, accompanied by more than twenty slaves, and began planting along St John's River in partnership with Gabriel Capers, a protectionist from Christ Church Parish. On the cession of the province to Spain he indicated his intention to move to the Bahamas, but to his surprise his slaves refused to go, declaring that they would take to the woods if he did not arrange for their return to South Carolina. Making arrangements accordingly, he sold them there, not being allowed himself to remain or to obtain relief from the Banishment and Confiscation Act. (Lambert, *SC Loyalists*, passim; *The Cornwallis Papers*)

[5] James Stuart was an Anglican clergyman who, after posting bond in London in 1766, had served in Virginia and Maryland before being called to Georgetown in 1772 to serve as Minister to the Parish of St George Winyah. Marrying Ann Allston Waties, the daughter of a prominent South Carolinian and the widow of another, he remained loyal to the Crown at the onset of the revolution and was driven from his parish in 1777. (Rogers Jr, *Georgetown County*, 81-4)

persecute.

I am with much esteem
Your Lordship's most obedient humble servant

J WEMYSS

Enclosure (1)
Petition from inhabitants of Georgetown 3(1): DS

Major Wemyss commanding His Majesty's troops, Georgetown

We, inhabitants in and about George Town, Winyah, beg leave to represent to Major Wemyss that, as the original cause of the disputes between Great Britain and her Colonies was our being taxed without being represented, and as by a proclamation of the 1st June last issued by his Excellency Sir Henry Clinton, Knight of the Bath, General and Commander in Chief of His Majesty's forces in America, and Mariot Arbuthnot Esquire, Vice Admiral of the Blue and Commander in Chief of His Majesty's ships, we are assured that we shall not be taxed but by our representatives in General Assembly, we are therefore desirous of becoming British subjects, in which capacity we promise to behave ourselves with all becoming fidelity and loyalty.

CHRI^{STR} TAYLOR	GEO HERIOT	MORD^{E} MYERS
JOHN VICAR	EDW MARTIN	THO^S HENDLEN
DAN^L TUCKER	THOMAS HASELL	JOHN HAWKINS
THOMAS SMITH	PETER SANDERS	ANDREW DEHAY
WILL HERIOT	PAUL TRAPIER	SOLO^N COHEN
JOS^H BROWN	BEN YOUNG	JESSE BALLARD
RANDOLPH THEUS	THO^S MITCHELL	RICH^D BROOKS
SIMEON THEUS JUNR	FRAN MARSHALL	JOHN ALLSTON JUN^R
S WRAGG	PET^R LESESNE	EDW^D MITCHELL
JN^O WILSON	JN^O PORTER	JOHN GOFF
ABR^M COHEN	THO^S BURNHAM	GEORGE CROFT

Enclosure (2)
Messrs Heriot & Tucker to Wemyss, 12th July 1780 2(279): L

George Town
July 12th 1780

Major Wemyss
Commandant of Winyah

Sir

As commanding officer of Winyah, we beg leave to address you to inform you that Captain Ardesoif of His Majesty's Ship *Loyalist* on the 3rd instant sent two arm'd barges to the plantation of the Hon John Moultrie Esq[6] on Pedee River and carryed away from thence sundry goods, the property of the subscribers and others in Charles Town, in defiance of his own public declaration that all private property should be protected and secur'd to their owners in consequence of the people appearing under arms to testify their allegiance to His Majesty's Government. We are therefore to request you will be pleas'd to take such steps as you may judge necessary for the recovery of said property, for which you will have our most grateful acknowledgements.

We are, sir,
Your most obedient humble servants

HERIOT & TUCKER[7]

Enclosure (3)
Goods seized by Captain Ardesoif RN 102(13): D

Goods taken by Captain Ardesoif of His Majesty's Ship Loyalist

Private Property —

Heriot & Tucker

---

[6] The eldest son of a Scottish physician who had migrated to Charlestown about 1728, the Hon John Moultrie MD (1729-1798) was a loyalist who had been a member of HM Council in East Florida since 1764 and Lt Governor there since 1771. Before transferring to East Florida, he had been a physician in Georgetown but had become more involved in the cultivation of several plantations which he had acquired, including indigo lands on the Pee Dee. A younger brother was William Moultrie, a brigadier general in the Continental line who was now a prisoner in Charlestown. (*DAB*; Rogers Jr, *Georgetown County*, 93-4)

[7] Heriot & Tucker was a firm of Georgetown merchants. (Rogers Jr, op cit, 150)

13 barrels coffee
6 bags ditto

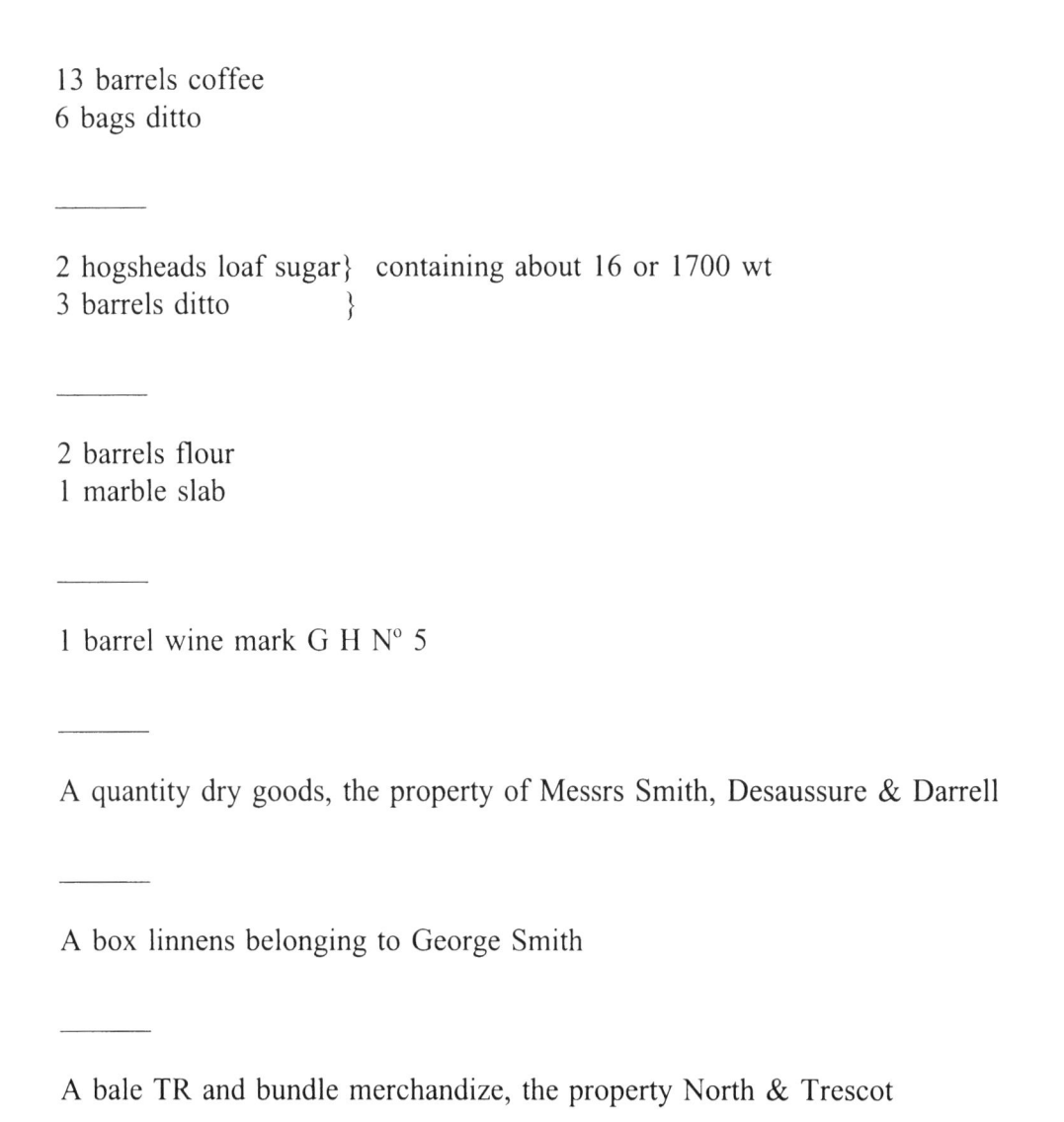

———

2 hogsheads loaf sugar} containing about 16 or 1700 wt
3 barrels ditto   }

———

2 barrels flour
1 marble slab

———

1 barrel wine mark G H N° 5

———

A quantity dry goods, the property of Messrs Smith, Desaussure & Darrell

———

A box linnens belonging to George Smith

———

A bale TR and bundle merchandize, the property North & Trescot

Wemyss to Cornwallis, 17th July 1780 — 2(325): ALS

George Town
17th July 1780

My Lord

    I had the honor of receiving your letter of the 15th last night and am very sorry to say that the longer I remain here, the more I discover the dissaffection of the people; and the motions of the rebells on the frontier will of the course add to their audacity. I shall immediatly obey your directions in altering the paroles of those people who have been exceedingly forward and zealous in rebellion, and shall, in place of permitting them to remain here, send them to one of the islands. Without this step, peace will never be restored in this country.

    As soon as I receive your Lordship's answer on the subject of the militia, shall immediately sett about to put your instructions in execution. I do not intend to go to North Island unless I find the health of the men should make it necessary. As yet they continue pretty well.

I have wrote to Colonel Mills, who, I dare say, will communicate every thing that happens on the frontiers. I shall likewise endeavour to establish a correspondence at other places along the frontier towards the sea and shall inform your Lordship of any thing that may appear to be material. Should I apprehend any real danger, I shall come off in the handsomest manner I possibly can.

I have enquired of several friends of Goverment if they knew of any application being ever made for amunition. They all say they do not. After the militia is got together, I shall be able to judge what quantity may be wanting and supply them as you have directed, but untill that is done, giving them any might have a bad effect.

I have the honor to be
Your Lordship's most obedient and most humble servant

J WEMYSS

Wemyss to Cornwallis, 17th July 1780   2(323): ALS

George Town
17th July 1780

The Rt Hon Earl Cornwallis etc etc etc
Charles Town

My Lord

I think it proper to acquaint to you that Mr Charles Pinkney[8], formerly of the Council of this State, arrived here last night and is desirous of going to Charlestown. I have taken his parole to remain here untill I receive your directions.

Mr Parker[9], the Treasurer of this province, and a Captain Lesesne[10] came here likewise

---

[8] Charles Pinckney (1731-1782) was a wealthy lawyer and planter who had been active in support of the revolutionary cause in South Carolina. Lately a Senator and Privy Councillor under the revolutionary constitution of 1778, he had accompanied Governor Rutledge and two other Privy Councillors through the lines of Charlestown on 13th April 1780 so as to maintain a nucleus of revolutionary government in South Carolina in the event that the town should fall. A fair-weather friend to the revolutionary cause, he was now to be guilty of the charge levelled at his fellow councillor, Daniel Huger (see p 145, note 47). Like Huger, he would soon take protection, swearing allegiance to the Crown, and subscribe to the notice to which the note on Huger refers. For his volte-face he was subjected to amercement by act of the revolutionary assembly which met at Jacksonborough in January 1782. (*DAB*; McCrady, *SC in the Rev 1775-1780* and *1780-1783*, *passim*; Wallace, *South Carolina*, 297, 306)

[9] A Commissioner of the Treasury under the revolutionary constitution, William Parker would be sent back to North Carolina with a flea in his ear. In December notice would be given that his property had beeen sequestered. In January 1782, when the revolutionary assembly met at Jacksonborough, he would be reappointed a Commissioner of the Treasury. By September 1785 he was dead. (McCrady, *SC in the Rev 1775-1780*, 729, and *1780-1783*, 572; Moss, *SC Patriots*, 753)

last night with a flag of truce to go to Charlestown to settle their private affairs and then to return to North Carolina. As I apprehended this would not be agreable to you, I have detained them likewise untill I hear from you. I send your Lordship a copy of the flag of truce and am with much esteem

Your most obedient and most humble servant

J WEMYSS

Enclosure
Flag of truce concerning Parker and Lesesne, 3rd July 1780   2(241): C

State of North Carolina

> The Hon Richard Caswell Esq, Major General and Commander in Chief of the militia of the said State in service

To the Commanding Officer of His Britannic Majesty's forces in South Carolina and all others whom it may concern.

These are to certify that William Parker Esq and Captain Thomas Lesesne, formerly of Charlestown in South Carolina, who were during the siege and at the time of the capitulation of Charlestown in this State, are permitted to proceed with a flag of truce to Charlestown and settle their private affairs there and return to this State. All officers civil and military in this State and others concerned are required to take notice thereof and govern themselves accordingly.

Given under my hand and seal
in camp at Sprowle's Ferry
the 3rd day of July 1780

By his Honor's command

J^NO SITGREAVES[11]   R^D CASWELL
Aid de camp

---

[10] Of Huguenot descent, Thomas Lesesne had been commissioned a 1st lieutenant in the 2nd regiment raised in South Carolina by the Provincial Congress in 1775. He was to be with the regiment, commanded by William Moultrie, in the Battle of Fort Sullivan the following year. Transferred to the Continental line with his regiment shortly afterwards, he was promoted to captain but resigned his commission in 1779. Now, in 1780, he would, like William Parker, be sent back to North Carolina with a flea in his ear, from where he would become a captain in Marion's Brigade. (Rogers Jr, *Georgetown County*, 20; McCrady, *SC in the Rev 1775-1780*, 14, 143; Heitman, *Historical Register*, 348; Moss, *SC Patriots*, 564)

[11] Born in New Berne, John Sitgreaves (c. 1740-1802) had studied and practised law there, being commissioned a lieutenant in the North Carolina revolutionary militia in 1776. Now Caswell's aide-de-camp, he would be with him at the Battle of Camden. In 1784-5 he would represent North Carolina in the Continental Congress and in 1786-9 be a member of the North Carolina legislature, an office he would relinquish on being appointed US District Judge for North Carolina. (*Appletons'*; Heitman, *Historical Register*; Gregg, *The Old Cheraws*, 320)

Cornwallis to Wemyss, 18th July 1780

78(32): C

Charlestown
18th July 1780

Major Wemyss
63rd Regiment

Sir

I have received your letters of the 14th and 16th[12]. In regard to the address of the inhabitants, I have only to answer that I cannot receive professions in contradiction to acts and believe that those who have been acting violently against us for four years are now become our friends only because they tell me so. You must therefore proceed to parole all the most obnoxious and dangerous to the islands and the remainder to their own plantations.

I am much obliged to you for the intelligence you have given me relative to the militia, and I think of forming as much of the three districts as lie on the east side of Santee into two battalions and putting the part of the lower division on this side of Santee into a third under the command of my friend Ball. By this means Mr Cassils and Mr Mills will have nearly the command you propose. I have heard an excellent character of Mr Cassils and should be glad to see him in town to talk over this business. If, however, you think his coming here will occasion too great loss of time, and that[13] your people grow sickly, you will then set about the business immediately with him and let him recommend the officers that he thinks most likely to succeed. I have sent for Mr Ball to come to me. If he happens to be at George Town he may not receive my message, in which case you will say every thing you can that is civil to him on the occasion and send him to Charlestown to settle the matter with me. You will likewise send Mr Gaillard to me if it is not very inconvenient to him to come. If it is, you will please to desire him to come to you and talk to him in a friendly manner, explain to him the critical situation of George Town and the great importance of getting our friends there to enter heartily into the militia, treat him as one engaged in the same cause with us, assure him of every mark of friendship and attention from me, and get him either to consent to be only a captain or to relinquish it altogether. I find the galley and provision vessel are not yet gone. I have taken every possible step to expedite them.

You will please to put Mr Charles Pinckney on his parole to go immediately to *Eddisto* Island and on no account to pass through Charlestown — to report his arrival on Eddisto Island to the Commissary of Prisoners. I likewise desire you will inform Mr Parker and Captain Lescome [*sic*] that I am much surprized they should presume to come to George Town without having sent a flag of truce to desire permission, that it is very fortunate for them that you detained them there, for, had they come on to Charlestown on so frivolous a pretext, I should certainly have sent them both on board of the prison ship. You will order them to return with their flag to North Carolina by whatever route you think most proper for them.

---

[12] *16th*: a slip of the pen. The reference should be to the 17th.

[13] *that*: the meaning is 'if'. See p 108, note 12.

I am, sir,
Your most obedient and faithful servant

[CORNWALLIS]

Cornwallis to Wemyss, 23rd July 1780   *78(40): C*

Charlestown
23rd July 1780

Major Wemyss
63rd Regiment

Sir

I saw Colonel Ball yesterday, who consented to give up his command of militia on the east side of Santee, altho' I own he appeared more mortified at it than I expected. I desired him to make his resignation known to you, which he promised to do. If he should be slow in doing it, you may proceed in your arrangements on my notification of it to you, as above all things I would wish to prevent loss of time. Major McArthur has not quitted his post on Cheraw Hill, and things on that frontier look more peaceable than they did. You will not, however, relax in your endeavours to procure good intelligence.

I am, sir,
Your most obedient humble servant

[CORNWALLIS]

Wemyss to Cornwallis, 22nd July 1780   *2(337): ALS*

George Town
July 22nd 1780

My Lord

I was honored with your Lordship's letter of the 18th last night and shall immediatly parole to the islands the most dangerous of the rebell party, and to their plantations those that are looked upon in a lesser degree criminal.

Mr Cassills is now at a plantation of his about 60 miles from this place. I have wrote to him to day and make no doubt of his coming here immediatly, when I shall inform him of your desire to see him. I will, if your Lordship pleases, delay writing to Mr Gilliard until I see Mr Cassills, as I have reason to think he is of more importance to us than I was led to believe; private quarells and resentment subsist so much, even amongst our friends, that it is a difficult matter to obtain a true character of any man. The people here are a good deal alarmed at an information they have received from North Carolina of a privateer being fitted out there to plunder the plantations on this coast. A schooner answering to her description appeared off the bar here two days ago and occasioned a good deal of apprehension, but she went away without sending any boat on shore. I am sorry to hear that a good many deserters (officers' servants) from Haddrell's Point still get away. Most of them are free Negroes and soldiers in the rebel army.

Neither galley or provision sloop is yet arrived.

I have the honor to be
Your Lordship's most obedient and most humble servant

J WEMYSS

[*Subscribed*:]

I have taken Mr Pinkney's parole to go to Edisto Island and have sent to Parker and Lesesne, who I had permitted to go to a plantation in this neighbourhood, to come to me directly, and on their arrival shall, agreable to your Lordship's desire, order them back to North Carolina by the most direct and expeditious route.

Wemyss to Cornwallis, 23rd July 1780　　　　　　　　　　*2(343): ALS*

George Town
July 23rd 1780

The Rt Hon Earl Cornwallis etc etc etc
Charlestown

My Lord

Since writing to you yesterday, I find Mr Gordon[14], a merchant here, is to be the bearer. I beg leave to say he is one of the principal people and a firm friend to Goverment. Should your Lordship wish to ask him any question relative to this part of the country, you may depend upon his information.

I have the honor to be
Your Lordship's most obedient and most humble servant

J WEMYSS

---

[14] Probably a Scot, James Gordon was one of the earliest settlers of Georgetown, where in 1736 he contributed £50 to the building costs of the parish church. A prominent merchant there by the onset of the revolution, he took little part in public affairs. Now, in 1780, he would soon accept the lt colonelcy in Robert Gray's Pee Dee Regiment of the royal militia, but as the tide turned, he would resign his commission in August 1781 and remain as a private citizen in Charlestown. His property was confiscated in January 1782 by act of the revolutionary assembly at Jacksonborough, but was restored to him two years later subject to an amercement of twelve per cent. (Rogers Jr, *Georgetown County*, *passim*; Clark, *Loyalists in the Southern Campaign*, i, 187)

Cornwallis to Wemyss, 26th July 1780   78(50): C

Charlestown
26th July 1780

Major Wemyss
63rd Regiment
George Town

Sir

Your letters were delivered to me by Mr Gordon, who seems to think that no time should be lost in establishing the militia. I therefore desire you will set about it immediately and not send Mr Cassils to me. Mr Gordon is of opinion that under him there will be no difficulty in finding proper officers. He spoke well of Gaillard. You will use your discretion about him and probably consult Mr Cassils. If you should find it necessary to ask him to decline the lt colonelcy, you will of course do it in the civilest manner possible. I mentioned to Commodore Henry the apprehensions of the inhabitants of George Town about the privateer schooner. He told me that he had ordered the *Keppel* brig to look into the entrance of Wyniaw from time to time and will take every measure in his power for their security. (By the bye he has not much in his power at present.) The galley and provision sloop have, I suppose, been delayed by the late bad weather. I have at last put a stop to the escape of the prisoners from this town. I do not know what can be done about the officers' servants at Hetherell's Point. It has already been declared to the officers that the servants who desert should not be replaced from the barracks.

I am, sir,
Your most obedient humble servant

[CORNWALLIS]

Wemyss to Cornwallis, 25th July 1780   2(366): ALS

George Town
July 25th 1780

My Lord

I was honored with your letter of the 23rd last night and shall proceed in embodying the militia as soon as Mr Cassillis arrives here, which I expect will be tomorrow or next day, altho I should not have heard from Colonel Ball by that time, as the necessity of such a measure appears more and more urgent every day. The messenger I sent to Colonel Mills was on his return stopt and searched about 50 miles from hence and threatned with death on the supposition only of his being employ'd on His Majesty's Service. It gives me pain to think that I should, by giving an opinion, occasion any mortification to Colonel Ball. I hope your Lordship will attribute my doing so to no other cause but the publick good.

I find that Captain Ardesoiff has wrote to some people here to dispose of some rice and corn meal that had been landed (out of the vessels he took here) and stored up in different places, on the supposition that they were once part of the cargoes of those vessels, altho landed long before his arrival. As I cannot see the propriety of such a claim, I have desired his agent to let those articles remain where they are at present untill I shall receive your directions. That gentleman has made a most successfull expedition against this place without grasping at every thing. There is still some inconsiderable quantitys of rice, the publick rebell property dispersed thro the country, which I shall direct to be taken care of, and submit it to your Lordship whether the detachment under my command may by your indulgence look upon it as their prize or not.

I have the honor to be with the greatest respect
Your Lordship's most obedient and most humble servant

J WEMYSS

Wemyss to Cornwallis, 25th July 1780   2(364): ALS

George Town
July 25th 1780

The Rt Hon Earl Cornwallis etc etc etc
Charlestown

My Lord

The bearer hereof, Mr Abrahams, in company with a Mr Sheftell[15] are just arrived here from Virginia. They went away from Charlestown, before we landed, to avoid bearing arms and are now on their return to Charlestown. I will referr you to them for information. By their accounts my situation is by no means safe, as they positively say a body of at least 500 horse are coming to plunder this town. I shall pay every attention to this information and shall wait with impatience for your Lordship's orders. They say the rebell party will not be ready sooner than a fortnight or three weeks.

I am, my Lord,
Your most obedient and most humble servant

J WEMYSS

---

[15] Neither Abrahams nor Sheftall has been positively identified. Abrahams, for example, may have been Joseph, who was a businessman in Charlestown, or Emanuel (c. 1760-1802), who served in Captain Richard Lushington's company of the Charlestown revolutionary militia in 1778. (Moss, *SC Patriots*, 2) Sheftall may have been related to Mordecai Sheftall (1735-1797), possibly his brother Levi. Mordecai was formerly Commissary General of Georgia's revolutionary militia and had been captured at Savannah in December 1778. (Heitman, *Historical Register*, 492) Lately a prisoner in Antigua, he had been paroled in June and was now heading for Philadelphia. His wife Francis ('Fannie'), a native of Charlestown, was presently residing there with most of their children. Levi, for his part, had the distinction of being named both in the Georgia Disqualifying Act 1780 passed by the royal assembly and in the Georgia Banishment and Confiscation Act 1782 passed by the revolutionary assembly.

Cornwallis to Wemyss, 28th July 1780 78(52): C

Charles Town
28th July 1780

Major Wemyss
63rd Regiment
George Town

Sir

I examined the two persons you sent to me who came in from Virginia. They did not appear at all intelligent, mentioned many things which could not be true, and exaggerated the force of the rebels in all parts to a most ridiculous amount. I therefore can give no credit to what they say of an intended attack of George Town by a body of cavalry, as even that is founded on the most vague hearsay and they did not come within one hundred miles of the country where they pretend this cavalry is to come from. I do not, however, wish to put you off your guard. You will do every thing in your power to procure intelligence and take care not to be surprized. I think your detachment, properly posted, would beat a large body of militia horse. It would be hurtfull to the service to leave George Town in a hurry, but if you have certain intelligence of a very superior force coming against you, it is better to come away than to be beat or taken.

In regard to what you mention about the rice in your letter of the 25th, I am no friend to army prize money but think it likely to produce the most pernicious consequences. I therefore cannot consent to your detachment's appropriating any part of prize goods for their own use, except provisions for their present consumption or any necessaries that they might find in a store and put into their knapsacks; nor indeed do I believe that any part of the troops have seized any thing for their own use, except in the manner I mentioned, since we have been in this province — I am very sure they have not by my consent.

It is not worth while disputing with Captain Ardesoif's agent about the articles you mention. It will be referred to the commanding officer of the navy how far his seizures will be deemed of a private or a publick nature; but the affair of prize money is not so dangerous in their service as in ours, where it would be impossible to detach, except by the roster, without doing a real injury to the person not employed.

I am etc

[CORNWALLIS]

[*Subscribed*:]

On the most melancholy representation of the distress of Colonel Herriot's family I have given him leave to visit them and to be absent fourteen days from the place to which he was paroled.[16]

Cornwallis to Wemyss, 28th July 1780   78(54): C

Charles Town
28th July 1780

Major Wemyss
63rd Regiment

Sir

Since I wrote this morning I have received advice that Rutherford with the militia is advanced to *Rocky River Pedee* and that it is supposed de Kalb is advancing to Salisbury. Lord Rawdon informs me that McArthur is removed from Cheraw Hill to the east branch of Lynches Creek, partly to have the corps more conpact and partly on account of the unhealthiness of the situation on Pedee. Altho' all this is at a great distance from you, still it is a reason for your being very attentive to get good intelligence and for your expediting as much as possible the business of the militia.

I am etc

[CORNWALLIS]

Wemyss to Cornwallis, 28th July 1780   2(377): ALS

George Town
Friday evening
28th July 1780

My Lord

I think it my duty to loose no time in acquainting you that Colonel Mills of the Cheraw militia is just now arrived here. He tells me that on Sunday last the 71st Regiment fell back towards Cambden, that on Monday their sick (upwards of 60) embarked in boats to come to this place. On Tuesday a party of militia from North Carolina in conjunction with several of Colonel Mills' people, who had just before taken the oaths of allegiance, intercepted and took

---

[16] Robert Heriot (1739-1792) was a Scot who had arrived in Georgetown in 1759 via Holland and Jamaica. Besides setting himself up as a merchant there, he married Mary Ouldfield in 1761, who ten years earlier had inherited several plantations and seventy-three slaves. Siding with the nascent revolutionaries in 1775, he became a member of the Committee for Prince George responsible for enforcing the association subversive of the royal government. In the spring of 1776, as a captain in the revolutionary militia, he marched with his company to Haddrell's Point in order to assist in repulsing the expected British assault on Charlestown. By 1780 a colonel of militia, he had recently entered into a parole at Camden requiring him to repair to the sea islands. He would take no further part in the war. (Rogers Jr, *Georgetown County*, 61n, 115, 118, 124; PRO 30/11/2(233))

the whole party prisoners with a Lieutenant Nairn[17] and the surgeon. The number of the rebells was betwixt two and three hundred. Colonel Mills was pursued by different partys untill he got within a few miles of this place. By all accounts Mr Cassillis is likewise taken. In short, the whole country is in confusion and uproar. All the friends of Goverment have been plundered of their Negroes and of every thing they have worth taking. The rebells have a guard at a ferry about 40 miles from here and by that means stop very much the intelligence I otherwise would have. From the first information I got of a probability of having a visit from those gentry I have taken every method of securing myself in case of a sudden attack. I now think myself perfectly secure in that particular and will be answerable for the safety of my detachment against any number for ten or twelve days, providing they come without cannon. As this country is now circumstanced, I think my remaining here untill things are a litle more settled would have a better appearance than withdrawing in a hurry, but of this your Lordship is a better judge. Neither galley or sloop are yet arrived.

I have the honor to be
Your Lordship's most obedient and most humble servant

J WEMYSS

Cornwallis to Wemyss, 30th and 31st July 1780　　　　　　　　78(61): C

Charlestown
July 30th 1780

Major Wemyss
63rd Regiment
Georgetown

Sir

I received this morning your letter of the 28th, which gave me very great concern. I cannot conceive how McArthur could have been so off his guard about his sick. I dare say Colonel Mills has rather seen things in the blackest light. However, there can be no hopes of peace and quiet untill we can advance, nor can you in the present situation of things do any good towards forming a militia at Georgetown. I cannot therefore approve of your making any longer stay there. Your coming directly back here would certainly be disgracefull and for a time at least would be attended with the worst of consequences in that part of the country. It would likewise endanger our water communication with Camden, on which our whole preparation for acting depends. I therefore think that you should march with much secrecy from Georgetown and take your route up the Black River. If you could surprise any rebel militia, it would have the best effect. If not, I should hope you and Colonel Mills might assemble a part of his militia and with their assistance seize and bring off some of the most

---

[17] Wemyss is referring to either John Nairne or William Nairne, both of whom had been commissioned lieutenants in the 1st Battalion, 71st (Highland) Regiment, the first on 27th November 1775, the second on the day after. (*Army Lists*)

violent and dangerous people in the country. The being in possession of their persons would be of the greatest service to our friends. I should then wish that you moved up the Black River, keeping it on your right, and took post for a few days at the *bridge* or *ferry* (I am not sure which it is) that is nearest to Gaillard's house, who will probably be able to assist you with intelligence and some militia. He will likewise be able to inform you of the state of the stores at Cooke's and how far the navigation is secure. I am well aware that you must not stay long in a place, especially on the Black River, which is a very sickly country, but I would have you keep moving by short and easy marches, paying the greatest attention the whole time to getting intelligence and guarding against a surprise, untill you arrive at the High Hills of Santee, where I would have you take post on any convenient spot you may chuse. I have written to Lord Rawdon to send some Provincials to meet you there, and to order a part of Colonel Moore's militia to be embodied, and put themselves under your command. I shall order the remainder of the 63rd to join you there, and when we are ready to move, you shall join the army. You will regulate your march by what you hear in the country and by the state of our boats on Santee, which are of such consequence to us that we must risk a great deal for their preservation. It is entirely owing to the perverseness of the elements that the galley and sloop are not at Georgetown. They went from hence long since – ten days at least. I cannot think that you will be distressed for flour or rice; cattle you will get in plenty; rum will be the difficulty. If you cannot get any at Georgetown and hear nothing of the sloop, of whose arrival I despair whilst this weather lasts, you must send a trusty express to Gaillard at Murray's Ferry and inclose an order to the commissary at Cooke's Landing to deliver a puncheon of rum for the use of your detachment. Gaillard will forward your order thither and get the rum down to Murray's Ferry, from whence he can send it to you when you are posted on the nearest part of the Black River to that ferry. Harrison's new corps is reported to me to be nearly compleat. They have been in the country about Linches Creek and, I should apprehend, must have kept the militia quiet in those parts. They are ordered to Camden to receive arms and cloathing, but I do not believe they are moved yet.

You must be sensible that in the execution of this plan much must be left to your discretion. You must act from circumstances and intelligence. You must even if necessary pass the Santee, but I would not have you do that unless you are well convinced that your danger is imminent. At all events I must recommend it to you to put a good face on things and talk big, threaten the plunderers with the most severe retaliation, promise indemnification as far as possible to our friends out of their effects, and try to give spirits to our cause. You have only militia to oppose you, who are often daring and troublesome in attack, always timid and panick struck when attacked. I should therefore on all occasions in your situation act offensively, and if any party of them, no matter how numerous, take post within a possibility of a night's march from you, let their position be what it will, it will be safest to attack them. Let me hear from you when you leave Georgetown, and as often as possible afterwards, and leave the best advice to the galley and sloop in case they do not get to Georgetown before you go. It will probably be to come back again.

Give out that you expect great reinforcements from hence; that a thousand men are to join you to march to the Pedee and are already on their way; that we can now spare them on account of the arrival of some troops from Savannah and some that came in the last fleet from New York. To save your *credit* some invalids are arrived from thence and a Hessian regiment from Georgia. I shall trouble you no more but with my most sincere good wishes for your success, and am

Your most obedient and most humble servant

[CORNWALLIS]

[*Subscribed*:]

From what I recollect of the country between Black River and Santee I doubt whether there is a continued road on the west bank of Black River. If not, you understand the general idea of the move being to cover the Santee. You may certainly take post for a few days on the passage of it that I mentioned; and if you cannot march on the west bank of it, you will pursue whatever route you think most eligible and agreeable to the considerations, and best suited to the purposes, which I have so fully explained.

July 31st

Lt Colonel Tarleton is going to Camden with a detachment of the Legion and sets out this evening. I have directed him to pass at Lenew's Ferry and proceed up the Santee. He is informed fully of the state of things in those parts and will take any steps in his power to contribute to the security of your movement and to intimidate the enemy. You will take care to represent this detachment in the most formidable light.

I shall order the remainder of the 63rd Regiment to march on the 5th or 6th from hence and shall direct the commanding officer to remain at Nelson's Ferry on this side the river untill he hears from you. The violent and continued storm prevented my sending the officer off last night; I hope the boat will be able to get over this day.

Wemyss to Cornwallis, 29th July 1780   *2(389): ALS*

George Town
July 29th 1780

My Lord

Finding that an inhabitant of this town who I think I may trust is going to Charlestown, I take that opportunity of giving your Lordship every information I can collect of the movements of the rebels. I cannot learn that any body of them are in motion on the frontiers, but that the 71st Regiment, being orded to fall back from Cheraw Hill, gave an opening to a party of North Carolina militia, who had before formed a scheme of plundering, to overrun a considerable part of the country which by that means was left defenceless. In their route they were joined by a good many in this province. They have effectualy broke up the militia both of the upper and lower district. Great part of Colonel Mills's officers are prisoners. It is remarkable that most of the leaders of this party are either militia officers who [were] on parole or men who had taken the oaths of allegiance. As such infamous practises are contrary to every rule in war, I submit it to your Lordship whether it would not be proper to seize and confine a certain number of the principal people we have on parole and to inform the rebels of the reasons for our doing so, assuring them that, unless those fellows who have broken the paroles are not delivered up with the prisoners they have taken, they will not be released. By this means Mr Cassillis and several other respectable people might return to us, and as the rebell commanding officer must disscourage such behaviour, a stop would in some measure be put to such a breach of faith in future.

I am sorry to say that our men are falling down very fast. The weather for some time has been rainy and variable. Our complaints are all intermitting fevers. I have several people in the country, one in North Carolina. I expect to hear from them [in] two or three days. Should their information be of consequence, I will communicate it to you by express.

I have the honor to be
Your Lordship's most obedient and most humble servant

J WEMYSS

Wemyss to Cornwallis, 31st July 1780   2(395): ALS

George Town
July 31st 1780

My Lord

I was honored with two letters from your Lordship of the 28th instant. Since my last I have received no material information. The militia that took Colonel Cassillis and the officers of Colonel Mills's regiment still continue to hunt out and plunder every friend of Goverment, and as that kind of business is profitable, their numbers of course are daily increasing. The people here are exceedingly alarmed and their fears are increased by the false reports that are constantly coming in from the country. A man came here to day from the Cheraws and said that General Casswell was there with a body of militia and that General Gates with a large body of cavalry and infantry had marched from Manson's Court House (a place about the same distance from Cambden as Cheraw Hill but a good deal higher up) on Sunday sennight, which was the day the 71st left the Cheraws, with an intention to get betwixt them and Cambden. Altho I do not believe this report, it has still a great weight with the people.

I shall take evry method of procuring the best intelligence. Our barracks are so well secured that I am not at all apprehensive of being forced and far less, I hope, of being surprised. This unlucky convulsion has put it out of my power to put in execution your Lordship's commands in regard to the militia. Should those banditti be even dispersed soon, it will require a good deal of time to bring things to their former situation.

I hope your Lordship will believe that it is very far from my thoughts to appropriate any publick rebell stores to the use of the detachment unless precedents had in some measure authorised it. At any rate it will be a pity to leave this place without having them secured for the use of Goverment.

I am sorry to say that the officer commanding the *Keppell* brig has not shown that attention either to his duty or character which might be expected. His vessell is gone to sea, and himself and a small boat's crew are still in this neighbourhood. When he came first here, he got drunk and in the grossest manner insulted both me and every officer of the detachment. By this I mean only to observe that he is not a very fit person to be trusted in any active or critical situation.

I have the honor to be with much esteem
Your Lordship's most obedient and most humble servant

J WEMYSS

Wemyss to Cornwallis, 2nd August 1780   63(7): ALS

George Town
August 2nd 1780

My Lord

I had the honor of receiving your letter last night by Lieutenant Birmingham[18]. Your directions I understand perfectly and shall endeavour to put them in execution without loss of time. I must be under the necessity of remaining here untill I can get my sick embarked for Charlestown. A sloop belonging to Mr Gordon is expected immediatly, in which I will put them, and shall march the instant they sail. Three men died yesterday of fevers and 30 are sick. I hope the weather will clear up before we move. If the storms of wind and rain which we have had for these ten days past continue, our march will be very troublesome and tedious. My route is so much out of Colonel Mills's way that he says he cannot be of any use to me in raising the militia. Gaillard perhaps may. As I can get rum here, it will be no consequence whether the galley and sloop arrive here before I leave this or not. I hope your Lordship will approve of my leaving the galley here for a little time. She will afford some protection to the few friends we have, who's situation without her would I think be very disagreeable.

If on the march I find that any body of militia is near, I shall certainly act as your Lordship desires, which perfectly agrees with my own ideas. I wish I may be fortunate enough in having an opportunity of falling in with them. I shall not fail in acquainting your Lordship of my leaving Georgetown and shall endeavour to send you all the intelligence from time to time I can possibly colect, and in every other particular shall make it my study to fullfill the whole of your instructions.

I am with much esteem
Your Lordship's most obedient and most humble servant

J WEMYSS

---

[18] On 15th August 1775 John Birmingham had been commissioned an ensign in the 63rd Regiment, being promoted to lieutenant in the regiment on 7th October 1777. (*Army Lists*)

[*Subscribed:*]

August 2nd, 5 o'clock evening

Since I wrote your Lordship in the morning, the heavy rain that has fallen this day has prevented Mr Birmingham from setting out till just now. About two hours ago a party of rebells have carried off a Mr Stritt[19], a very firm friend to Goverment, from his house about 6 miles from hence. I am likewise informed that the country thro' which I must pass to get to the Santee is intirely under water, so much so as to render a march thro' it totaly impracticable.

You may depend upon it I shall loose no time in marching whenever that obstruction is removed.

JW

Wemyss to Cornwallis, 4th August 1780 63(17): ALS

George Town
August 4th 1780

My Lord

You will receve this from Mr Stewart, the clergyman of this place, who judges it necessary for his safety to remove from hence. With him is a Doctor Fyfe[20], who for the same reason is obliged to leave his plantation in this neighbourhood. He has lived a long time in this part of the country and is well acquainted with the people. His character is a valuable one and his principals have been uniformly loyal.

---

[19] Although Wemyss clearly writes 'Stritt', he is in all probability referring to William Stitt (?-1784), an Irishman who lived at what is now Keithfield plantation a short distance north of Georgetown. It lies on the north-eastern bank of the Black River just above its confluence with the Pee Dee. (Michael E Stevens and Christine M Allen, ed, *Journals of the House of Representatives, 1789-1790* (*The State Records of South Carolina*) (South Carolina Department of Archives and History, 1984), 78-9; Alberta Morel Lachicotte, *Georgetown Rice Plantations* (The State Commercial Printing Co, 1955), 94; Colonial Plats (South Carolina Archives), xi, 345; T W Lipscomb to the editor, 23rd February 2005)

[20] Charles Fyffe was a Scottish physician who had migrated from Dundee to Georgetown in 1748. As the years went by, he proceeded to draw substantial income from his medical practice, from the post of naval officer for the port, and from planting on lands brought by his wife to their marriage. One of the earliest members of the Charlestown Library Society, he became a steward of Georgetown's Winyah Indigo Society when it was incorporated in 1757. Not only did it disseminate advice on the planting of indigo but it also provided a library, a school, and a forum for convivial and intellectual conversation. Fyffe himself had a library of 700 books. Like most Scots of his neighbourhood, he was a loyalist by inclination and openly sided with the Crown in 1780. A year later he would be appointed surgeon in charge of the Refugee Hospital in Charlestown, being paid at the rate of seven shillings per day. For his loyalty his property would be confiscated by act of the revolutionary assembly at Jacksonborough, but, apart from his town lots and movable property, it would be restored to him subject to an amercement of twelve per cent. Banished by the revolutionaries, he sailed to England on the evacuation of Charlestown but was permitted to return to South Carolina two years later. Afraid to live on his Pee Dee plantation, he remained at Charlestown. (Rogers Jr, *Georgetown County, passim*; Lambert, *SC Loyalists*, 229; Clark, *Loyalists in the Southern Campaign*, i, 533-5)

It is with great uneasiness I am obliged to report to your Lordship the unhealthiness of my detachment. Within these three days 6 men have died of putrid fevers. 4 serjeants and 28 men are now ill, eighteen of whom I have this day sent to Charlestown by water, and have by that opportunity wrote to you in case Mr Stewart should be stopt on the road, which I have some apprehensions of. They are fully informed of every thing that is going on here; therefore will referr your Lordship to them for information. I am obliged to continue here untill the water subsides, which now covers the whole country. Even people who I had sent out for intelligence on horse back have been obliged to return. As I apprehend the communication betwixt this and Charlestown will soon be dangerous for an express, I do not mean to write again to your Lordship untill I get near to Galliard's. You may therefore suppose that I will march from hence in four or 5 days at farthest if the weather permits. Should any thing happen to prevent me from moving, I will endeavour to let you know. If 15 or 20 cavalry could be sent to me, they would be of infinite service. If your Lordship should think it proper to send them, they might get here before I march, or if that appears uncertain, they might join me by Leneau's Ferry.

I have the honor to be
Your Lordship's most obedient and most humble servant

J WEMYSS

Wemyss to Cornwallis, 8th August 1780   63(23): ALS

George Town
8th August 1780

My Lord

I have the pleasure to acquaint you that the galley and provision vessel arrived here last night. My sick I have put on board a small vessel and will leave them in charge of the galley as I shall march to morrow morning. I have ordered all the vessels here to fall down the river this day and have desired the officer commanding the galley to carry them with him to New York.

From the same motives of humanity which led your Lordship to give Colonel Herriot leave to come here to see his family, I am induced to intercede for an addition to his leave. His daughter died yesterday, his son, it is imagined, will not live, and his wife is taken very ill in consequence of her distress on their account. In this situation I hope you will not think I have acted improperly in permitting him to remain here untill he shall receive your farther directions.

I understand that Lieutenant Birmingham of the 63rd Regiment has been applying to your Lordship for permission to go to New York in order to solicit the Commander in Chief's leave to go to Ireland. That gentleman came here a few days ago with your letter but never mentioned a wish of that kind to me as he well knew I would not consent. The regiment has but 7 subalterns, including him, to do the duty, none of whom I fancy your Lordship will think can be spared. May I beg therefore, if Major Stewart has been ridiculous enough to apply for him, that you will be good enough to refuse his request. I look upon Mr Birmingham's behaviour in this affair to have been very improper by secretely trying to get away from his regiment without my knowledge and taking the advantage of my absence to do so. The militia, altho collected in some numbers, are, I think, tolerably quiet. I expect litle or no anoyance from them on my march. I shall write to your Lordship as soon as I get near to Galliard's.

Believe me to be with much respect
Your Lordship's most obedient and most humble servant

J WEMYSS

CHAPTER 16

Correspondence with Savannah and St Augustine

1 - Between Cornwallis and Clarke

Cornwallis to Clarke, 2nd July 1780 *78(1): C*

Charlestown
2nd July 1780

Lt Colonel Clarke commanding in Georgia

Dear Sir

I hardly knew for certain that you was gone to Savannah untill my arrival here on the 25th of last month. I am heartily glad for the publick service that you have that command. I wish for your sake the place was more agreeable.

I have put the engineers both in Georgia and Florida under the command of Moncrief, who talks of making you a visit soon. I am told a fort is building at Savannah besides the work at Tybee. I own I should have thought the latter fully sufficient for the present security of the province. However, if the fort is in great forwardness, I consent to the finishing of it if you desire it. If it is not much advanced, I must in justice to our *suffering country* beg that a stop may be put to it. Whilst Carolina was in rebellion, Georgia was an object to a foreign enemy. The case is now altered and you can have nothing serious to apprehend from France and Spain. I have been at infinite pains to form regulations for South Carolina and shall have by the end of next month a militia of at least 8,000 men from which all rebels are excluded.

Our greatest force of militia is at Orangeburgh and about Ninety Six, which renders the upper part of Georgia perfectly secure.

The corps now gone to Augusta is a very improper one. Messrs Brown and Wright think more of kidnapping recruits than of the publick service and have already done as much mischief. I shall instantly order both these corps to return to Savannah and in lieu of them shall take from the town for the Back Country service Cruger's and Allen's battalions. I do not desire you to send away the latter 'till the other corps are return'd, but I must desire that Lt Colonel Cruger's battalion may march immediately to Augusta as I mean that he should take the command of the troops stationed there and at Ninety Six. I wish him to set out as soon as he conveniently can for Ninety Six, where Lt Colonel Balfour, after fully explaining the situation of that country to him, will invest him with the command. I have not the honour of being much acquainted with Lt Colonel Cruger, but from the character I have universally heard of him I am convinced it will greatly contribute to the good of His Majesty's Service that he should command in that very important district, upon the management of which the quiet of the two provinces greatly depends. I write this in a hurry, having only just heard that the fleet was to sail tomorrow. You shall hear from me again soon and I will endeavour to establish a regular correspondence between us. I shall depend on you for supplying the posts of Augusta and Ninety Six with rum and salt and I will take care to send you from hence any thing you may want.

I am, dear sir,
Your most obedient and faithfull servant

[CORNWALLIS]

Clarke to Cornwallis, 23rd June 1780

2(187): ALS

Savannah
June 23rd 1780

My Lord

In obedience to Sir Henry Clinton's commands I sent a detachment of about three hundred men to Augusta under the orders of Lt Colonel Brown, who had directions to co-operate with Colonel Balfour as soon as he could inform himself of his situation, which he has not yet been able to do. The remains of two or three of the regiments belonging to this and the province of Carolina have surrendered themselves on the same terms given to the people in Charles Town, and I understand the inhabitants of the country seem well inclined to do whatever is required of them. There is a report that Major Furguson is near Ninety Six and Colonel Innes at the forks of Saluda and Broad River, but Colonel Brown had not heard from either of them when he wrote. Want of instructions, owing to the multiplicity of business in which the Commander in Chief was engaged when I left Charles Town, lays me under some difficulties. I should therefore think myself obliged to your Lordship for any that may occur to you as necessary.

Although I have the honor to live on the best terms with Sir James Wright and a thorough good understanding subsists between the civil and military, I have lately been a little embarrassed by some people (who came from Carolina to ask for protections under the sanction of the proclamation) being apprehended by the civil power on a charge of treason and committed to gaol. These people have applied to me as commanding the King's troops to intercede in their behalf, which I have done from an apprehension that this mode of proceeding might militate against the Commander in Chief's intentions. Some people also who were made prisoners in Charles Town and came here under the sanction of military passes have been arrested and confined, particularly a Mr Houston, from whom I received the enclosed letter, which I transmit in order that your Lordship may from your knowledge of the reasons make the proper allowance for his not returning according to his promise. I have studiously avoided every interference with matters in which the civil power was concerned in order to prevent jealousy or misunderstandings, and I should not have troubled your Lordship on this subject but from an apprehension that hereafter it might possibly be conceived I had acted improperly by tacitly allowing a prisoner to suffer from any other authority whilst under the protection of his Excellency the Commander in Chief.

I have the honor to remain with great respect, my Lord,
Your Lordship's most obedient and most faithful humble servant

ALURED CLARKE[1]

PS

Since writing my letter I have mentioned to Sir James Wright my intention of sending Mr Houston's [case] to your Lordship, who requested I would also send the Attorney General's remarks on it in order to prevent any impression being left with you to the disadvantage of that gentleman.

I have begged of Major Prevost[2] to explain more fully my motives for giving your Lordship the trouble of perusing these letters, as some excuse for my having done so.

---

[1] Lt Colonel of the 7th Regiment (Royal Fusiliers), Alured Clarke (*c.* 1745-1832) was now to serve on secondment as the commanding officer of troops in Georgia and East Florida. According to an adversary, 'This excellent officer and perfect gentleman', to whose name 'no act of inhumanity or of oppression was ever attached,.. gained the good will of the Americans by the gentleness of his government... and by the protection afforded to property when they [*the British troops*] finally retired on the evacuation of Savannah.' After the war he would be appointed Lt Governor of Jamaica and then of Quebec, take part in reducing the Dutch colony at the Cape of Good Hope, and serve as Commander-in-Chief in India. He died a field marshal and Knight of the Bath at Llangollen vicarage, Denbighshire. (Garden, *Anecdotes* (1st series), 264; *DNB*)

[2] A staff officer, Major Augustine Prevost (1748-?) was a Deputy Inspector General of Provincial Forces under Alexander Innes and by now had served two years on the Provincial establishment. Born in Switzerland, he was no doubt related to Major General Augustine Prevost (see p 64, note 36). At the close of the war he was placed on the Provincial half-pay list. (WO 65/164(6) and WO 65/165(15) (National Archives, Kew))

Enclosure (1)
Houstoun to Clarke, 21st June 1780   *2(177): ALS*

                                                                Savannah
                                                                June 21st 1780
Sir

It is with difficulty I prevail upon myself to trouble you upon this occasion, but having made use of every expedient in my power without effect to obtain from the civil authority that justice which I think myself intitled to, I am now under the necessity of stating my case to you as commanding officer of this garrison and claiming that protection due to me as a prisoner.

I hold a commission as physician and surgeon to the hospitals of the United States and was in Charles Town at the time of the surrender of that place to His Brittanick Majesty, and gave my parole to Sir Henry Clinton and afterwards obtain'd permission from General Leslie (who commanded in Charles Town) to come to this place. Notwithstanding which, I was arrested by order of the Chief Justice for treason a very few hours after my arrival and have been detained in close confinement for ten days past. And as I cannot think myself accountable to the Chief Justice for any supposed crimes of treason, while a prisoner, and in the service of the United States, I think it very unjust that I should be prevented from returning to Charles Town agreeable to my parole. Was there any information of a private nature against me I should not expect to be protected by my parole, but as the only information which appears against me is assisting in the American hospitals during the time this town was besieged, I think my case must appear to every unprejudiced person cruel and unprecedented.

A general court has met since my confinement, and I then made applycation to the Attorney General and inform'd him that I was ready to appear and answer to any crimes of a private nature that might be alledged against me, which he refused, and since that I have offer'd security to appear at the next court, which I am told will be in December, and then to answer to any charges he may have against me. This has likewise been refused me. From these circumstances it appears very clearly that it is the intention of the Attorney General to confine me untill the meeting of the court unless he is prevented. In this situation I hold it my duty to apply to you for redress and flatter myself you will not permit your prisoner to be insulted and confined without cause contrary to the articles of capitulation enter'd into and ratifyed by the commanding officers of the two armies before the surrender of Charles Town.

I am, sir,
Your obedient servant

JAMES HOUSTOUN[3]

---

[3] James Houstoun was a younger brother of Sir Patrick Houstoun (see p 283, note 71) and had been a surgeon in the Continental service since 1778. (*DGB*; Heitman, *Historical Register*) He would be included in the Georgia Disqualifying Act passed by the royal assembly on 1st July. He died on 17th September 1793. (Edith Duncan Johnston, *The Houstouns of Georgia* (University of Georgia Press, 1950), 309)

Enclosure (2)
Robertson to Wright, 22nd June 1780 2(1): ALS

Savannah
22nd January[4] 1780

His Excellency Sir James Wright Bt etc etc

May it please your Excellency

I have been favored with the perusal of a letter of yesterday from Mr James Houstoun to Colonel Clark, commanding the garrison here, complaining of cruel unprecedented treatment.

My office giving me an opportunity of being fully acquainted with Mr Houstoun's case, and being also privy to many of the circumstances he alludes to, your Excellency will take the following relation.

Mr Houstoun and two other gentlemen — against whom were several informations for treasonable acts committed before the reduction of this province to His Majesty's army, and since, during the invasion of this town by the French and rebels — appearing openly here, where the civil government is established, were apprehended and carried before the Chief Justice, and to the best of my knowledge six or seven informations were read charging Mr Houstoun with being active in rebellion expressly, which charges he made very light of and insinuated he had done nothing he was either afraid or ashamed of, and in the course of this business said he was ready to give in bail to answer the charges. The Chief Justice told him these offences were not bailable but desired to hear what I as Attorney General had to say on the occasion. I observed that I did not conceive myself at liberty to give any consent to take bail, but that I thought there would be no impropriety in committing them to a private house under the care of special keepers if they would propose a house agreeable to themselves. Some difficulty arose about getting a house of sufficient accommodation for them, when, for their convenience, it was consented they should go to several houses on producing two discreet persons to be sworn in their special keepers. This was done and Mr Houstoun was committed to the house of Mr Mossman[5], the residence of his own wife and mother in law and place of resort of his most particular friends, and to that house and lot he has been ever since and now is confined. I think it was on the Saturday evening they were confined. The Court of Sessions began the Tuesday following, and from the time of his commitment to the present I do not recollect to have exchanged one word with him on the cause of his confinement. Neither did he in person or by any message at any time, while the Grand Jury were sitting, inform me that he was desirous to be brought to trial, and had he done so, I believe it would not have been in my power to have complied with his request, several of the persons, witnesses of his conduct during the siege, living so great a distance from town that

---

[4] *January*: a slip of the pen. The month was June.

[5] On the reestablishment in Georgia of civil government under the Crown James Mossman had been appointed to HM Council there, a body which acted partly as the upper house of the legislature and partly as a privy council advising the Governor. (Sabine, *Biographical Sketches*, ii, 110)

they could not be got to court in time. Another circumstance: I understood they all wished to have an opportunity to solicit the Commander in Chief for a pardon and meant to return to their former allegiance. Two of this party, I understand, resolved to return to their former allegiance and have requested the State oaths may be tendered them. When that disposition was certainly known and request made for that purpose, they were indulged and bailed to give them an opportunity to procure if possible their pardons before the next sessions, and they are now at large upon bail. One of them has already taken the oaths; the other means to do it this day.

But Mr Houstoun shows no such disposition. On the contrary, I am informed is sullen and obstinate in his aversion to the British Government, yet he expects the same favor with the others. During the court a friend of his asked me if he might not be bailed – it was after one of the others was bailed. I answered him: let Mr Houstoun do as the other had done, he would have the same indulgence. His friend said he believed he would. I then told him the court breaking up would be no hindrance as that business might be done at chambers on any day. A gentleman of the law since mentioned the matter to me. I made nearly the same observation and added that I thought it a very material circumstance to know whether Mr Houstoun meant to return to his former allegiance or not. Yesterday another gentleman of the profession also mentioned his case to me. I answered: let him do as the others had done, he was intitled to the same indulgence. It was mentioned his situation was somewhat different from the others, being in the Continental Service; he did not know whether his resignation from that service would be accepted of; and that he must needs go to Charles Town before he could determine anything. I then went so far as to add: let him acquaint the Governor by petition that he means voluntarily to return to his former allegiance, that his peculiar situation requires his presence in Charles Town before he can give the testimony of it the others have done, and that he meant to settle his business and take the earliest opportunity of taking the oaths. That, I said, possibly might procure him the indulgence of being bailed. But it seems all this will not do. I leave your Excellency therefore to judge how far the treatment of this man is either cruel or unprecedented, how far he can be said to be insulted and confined without cause, and how far I have shown any intention to detain him longer in confinement than the duty of my office and respect to His Majesty's Government requires.

I have the honor to be
Your Excellency's most obedient humble servant

JAMES ROBERTSON[6]
Attorney General

---

[6] A solicitor in Chancery at Savannah, James Robertson (1751-1818) had been appointed Attorney General of Georgia when civil government under the Crown was re-established there in July 1779. Ex officio he became a Member of HM Council. During his term he also served as a commissioner of claims as well as being on the board for seizing the property of active opponents to the Crown. With the loss of Georgia his estate would be confiscated by the revolutionaries and he would remove to the Virgin Islands, where he served many years as Chief Justice. He died there at Tortola. (Sabine, *Biographical Sketches*, ii, 220)

Cornwallis to Clarke, 4th July 1780   78(5): C

Charles Town
July 4th 1780

Lt Colonel Clarke commanding His Majesty's forces in Georgia

Dear Sir

I yesterday received the favour of your letter by Major Prevost. I likewise hear from him with great concern that the troops in Georgia are very sickly. I shewed your letter, and the papers relative to Dr Houston, to Mr Simpson, who agrees entirely with me in opinion that the detaining a prisoner of war on parole to bring him to tryal for treason at Savannah is highly improper and unwarrantable. He will write his sentiments on that head to Sir James Wright. I likewise beg that you will inform his Excellency that I think Dr Houston ought to be immediately sent back to Charlestown. I am informed that Lt Colonel Brown is raising some cavalry to be added to his corps. If this is true, I beg you will put an immediate stop to it. I send by this opportunity a duplicate of the letter I wrote by the *Hydra*, and am, sir, with great regard

Your most obedient and faithfull servant

[CORNWALLIS]

[*Subscribed*:]

As we are now thoroughly masters of South Carolina, and the militia of every district either is already arrayed or is put in the way of being so, the frontier of Georgia towards Carolina must be in the most perfect security. I cannot therefore see the necessity of a post at Ebenezer or indeed at any sickly part of the Savannah River. It appears to me that the only necessary posts are Savannah and Augusta, and I trust you will not sacrifice the health of the troops to the groundless terrors of the inhabitants.

Cornwallis to Clarke, 17th July 1780   78(24): C

Charlestown
17th July 1780

Lt Colonel Clarke

Dear Sir

General Paterson is in so bad a state of health that it was absolutely necessary for him to remove to some more temperate climate. He is therefore going immediately to New York.

The command of the troops devolves on Colonel Westerhagen[7], but as it is impossible for a foreigner to manage the very complicated civil business of this place, I have sent for Balfour and shall make him Commandant of the town, in which station I think he will be very usefull, having been much accustomed to business. As my situation is very precarious and that[8] I may perhaps be at a very great distance from hence, you will correspond with Balfour on common occurrences.

I think it for the good of His Majesty's Service that you should have the command of the troops in East Florida as well as Georgia. By the last accounts from Pensacola I think there is great reason to apprehend its falling soon into the hands of the Spaniards. East Florida will then become an important frontier and is very likely to be the next object of Spain. On the contrary, whilst we keep possession of South Carolina in force, nothing in my opinion is to be apprehended for Georgia. I shall therefore submit it to you whether, after Pensacola has fallen, you might not think St Augustine the properest place for your principal residence. I should likewise be of opinion that it would be proper to alter the disposition of some of the troops. The 60th Regiment is by all accounts very bad and very little to be depended on, being chiefly composed of deserters and prisoners. Perhaps, if the loss of Pensacola should happen, you may think it best to bring that corps to Georgia and place the Regiment of Wissenbach with some weak Provincial corps at St Augustine. Moncrief is going to visit Savannah and St Augustine. If it should be convenient to you to accompany him to the latter place, you will be able to form a better judgement of this business. I shall notify to both the Governors and to the commanding officer of the troops at St Augustine that the King's forces in both provinces are put under your command.

I have received a letter from Sir James Wright, which I answer by this opportunity[9], relative to an establishment of cavalry and an account of pay for some militia horse that he embodyed during the siege of Charlestown. I would have the account, which is inconsiderable, paid, but I cannot allow of any establishment of cavalry for Georgia whilst it is protected on all sides from a foreign enemy. If some horse are necessary for the interior government of the province, he must embody some militia, but as civil government is established, some mode must be fallen upon to defray that expence without coming upon the military chest, which is not capable of answering too violent demands.

[CORNWALLIS]

---

[7] Max von Westerhagen had been appointed Colonel of the Regiment von Dittfurth on 8th May 1777 and been involved with it and Browne's corps in occupying the redoubts on Fenwick's Point and at Linning's house during the siege of Charlestown. He was now commanding the three Hessian regiments forming part of the garrison of the town. Soon after being appointed Commandant, Balfour was to remark to Cornwallis, 'I find Westerhaguern the most manigable, decent German I ever knew. We go on well, and am sure must continue so.' (WO 65/164(20) (National Archives, Kew); Bernhard A Uhlendorf ed, *The Siege of Charleston* (University of Michigan Press, 1938), 69; *The Cornwallis Papers*)

[8] *that*: the meaning is 'as'. See p 108, note 12.

[9] For the exchange of letters, see pp 344-7.

Clarke to Cornwallis, 10th July 1780   *2(258): ALS*

Savannah
July 10th 1780

Lt General Earl Cornwallis etc etc etc

My Lord

Lieutenant Winter[10] arrived on the seventh with the transports from Charles Town, by whom I was honoured with your Lordship's letter, in obedience to which I have directed Lt Colonel Cruger to repair to Ninety Six and ordered his battalion to march for Augusta immediately, where Lt Colonel Allen's shall follow according to your desire. As the corps already there does not seem intirely to your satisfaction, I must in justice to myself say, had it been left to me, it would have been differently composed, but the Commander in Chief having directed me to invest Lt Colonel Brown with the command of the detachment, there was no alternative as to the other part of it, Major Wright's being the only corps commanded by an officer junior to him.

I suppose the variety of business in which Sir Henry Clinton was involved when I left Charles Town occasioned his referring me to General Prevost for such instructions as were necessary to my guidance in this command, but on my application to him I was informed that he had not received any himself, consequently had none to give me. I mention this as an excuse for troubling your Lordship on subjects which you might otherwise reasonably suppose there was no occasion to occupy your time about.

I have ventured to advance two hundred pounds, which was immediately wanted, to pay for some articles bought here and sent up to Augusta with a variety of other presents for the Indians at the desire of Lt Colonel Brown, Super Intendant of those affairs, who has applied to me for money on account of his department, but as the demands were likely to be of some magnitude, I did not feel myself authorised to answer them unless I should receive pointed instructions from your Lordship so to do, which, however, I do not expect, as it is impossible that I can in my present situation be a competent judge of this matter, not knowing the services on which it may be necessary the Indians should be employed.

The Governor has likewise applied to me for the militia pay during the time of their being embodied. The sum is not very considerable, but as I had not any directions whatever about it, I have requested that Sir James Wright would let it lay over 'till Sir Henry Clinton's answer should arrive, to whom we both wrote, but as he sail'd immediately on the receipt of our letters, I think it possible that it may escape his recollection, therefore request I may be guided by your Lordship's directions.

---

[10] John Winter had been commissioned a lieutenant in the Royal Navy on 19th April 1774. He did not rise in the service, perhaps because he was badly wounded when acting as Agent for Transports at Wilmington in early 1781. (Syrett and DiNardo ed, *The Commissioned Sea Officers*; *The Cornwallis Papers*)

Immediately on General Prevost's going from hence, I wrote to the Commander in Chief and explained to him the situation of this place, which was stript of every thing on General Paterson's marching into Carolina. This occasioned some delay in the movement to Augusta, as it was necessary to wait 'till waggons could be procured, which being done with some difficulty, we are now tolerably well off as to them, and I hope we shall have a sufficientcy of boats in a short time to supply the posts at Augusta and Ninety Six with ease agreeable to your Lordship's desire, for 'though the navigation upwards is very tedious, being on an average a passage of more than three weeks, I think by making a small depot at the former we shall prevent any inconvenience in future.

The works at Cockspur are finished and I have ordered Lieutenant Dunford[11] to furnish me with plans of them and the fort at this place for your Lordship's information. The last is considerably large, and although I can't help saying that in my opinion so expensive a work was not necessary, I think there has been already too much money laid out, and it is too far advanced, for prudence now to interfere with any propriety, the whole frame being finished, great part of it filled, the embrasseurs and platforms wanting only the planks nailing on, and a brick arched magazine in great forwardness. For the present a scarcity of boards occasions some little stop, and as no great additional expence will be incurred by going on slowly, I will wait the determination of Moncrief's better judgement in these matters, as from your Lordship's letter I may expect him very soon. I understand from Lieutenant Dunford that General Prevost gave him orders for constructing this fort, and it was considerably more than half finished when I arrived here. Lt Colonel Brown sent a plan of a work which he wished to make at Augusta. It was large and must have been attended with great expence. I gave a short negative to this proposition and ordered him on no account to throw up any thing of the kind (except upon an emergency) unless he received directions from you to that effect.

I have daily applications from the masters of Negroes who left them under the sanction of Sir Henry Clinton's proclamation on that subject[12]. The arguments used by the masters are that they have conformed and become good subjects. Those of the Negroes: the proclamation above mentioned and, most of them add, the having served in the defence of Savannah and on many other occasions, and the apprehensions they are under of being treated with cruelty in consequence of it if they go back. I cannot help remarking to your Lordship that, however policy may interfere in favor of the masters, an attention to justice and good

---

[11] Born at Fordingbridge, Hampshire, Andrew Durnford (1744-1798) was commissioned an ensign in the Corps of Engineers on 28th July 1769. The following year he was appointed to superintend the demolition of the fortifications and canal at Dunkirk in accordance with the Treaty of 1763. Quitting the town in 1774, he was posted to Plymouth and promoted to lieutenant on 6th March 1775. Sometime in 1776 he sailed for North America and was now the resident engineer at Savannah, where, in conjunction with Simon Fraser, he had been concurrently acting as a deputy quartermaster general since the end of May. From 1785 to 1787 he would serve at Chatham before going out as a captain to Bermuda in 1788 to supervise its fortification. By June 1793, when he was appointed the first Mayor of the town of St George, he had been promoted to major. He died in Bermuda. His father Elias also served in the Corps of Engineers, attaining the rank of colonel, and members of the extended Durnford family would follow in their footsteps down the years. (*Notes and Queries*, i, 3rd series (25), 21st June 1862, 492; *Army Lists*)

[12] The proclamation had been issued at Philipsburg, New York, on 30th June 1779. Among other things, it promised any slaves leaving enemy masters and taking refuge within the British lines full security to pursue there any occupation they wished. It forbad anyone from selling or claiming them. (Benjamin Quarles, *The Negro in the American Revolution* (University of North Carolina Press, 1961), 113)

faith must plead strongly in behalf of the Negroes, many of whom, having certificates of service performed, come to me to protect them from the violence of some of the most notorious offenders that Carolina has produced. I must apologize for this digression, in which I am sensible of having taken a very great liberty, as my business was merely to enquire what mode was adopted at Charles Town that I might regulate my decision in these matters accordingly.

I am well persuaded of the trouble your Lordship has had in regulating the affairs of the Back Country, but from the state they are in at present we have every reason to hope your toil will be rewarded by the assistance of a militia from which (if a less politick mode had been pursued) we should have had too much cause to apprehend trouble and distress.

I received a letter from Lt Colonel Balfour a few days ago requesting a supply of rum and salt, which I have wrote him word shall be forwarded with all possible expedition, and in the mean time Colonel Brown can assist him with some which was sent up for the use of the Indians by his deputy at this place. Balfour likewise talks of some necessary works and says he has written to you concerning them.

In consequence of the representations of General Prevost and the Governor, Sir Henry Clinton told me he had consented to some cavalry being raised for the defence of this province, and on my arrival I found that some steps had been taken towards putting it in execution. The plan intended was to mount two companies of the King's Rangers, for which purpose General Prevost ordered Lieutenant Dunford (acting Deputy Quarter Master General) to purchase horses, who has got a few, and the appointments for them are daily expected from Europe. I mention this circumstance to your Lordship lest you should not have heard any thing about it, and that you may have an opportunity of giving me such directions relative to it as you think proper previous to any material steps being taken towards the accomplishment of the design.

Finding the posts at Ebenezer and Abercorn extremely prejudicial to the health of the troops, I have withdrawn them, and also removed the regiments into town that were encamped near the lines from an apprehension that the intense heat of the sun etc contributed greatly to increase sickness, which I am sorry to inform your Lordship prevails very much amongst us. It is beyond any thing you can conceive. The thermometer in the shade was this day ninety eight.

I have the honor to remain with great respect, my Lord,
Your Lordship's most obedient and most faithful humble servant

ALURED CLARKE
Lt Colonel

Clarke to Cornwallis, 11th July 1780   *2(271): ALS*

Savannah
July 11th 1780

Lt General Earl Cornwallis etc etc etc

My Lord

After having wrote my letter of yesterday's date, I was honored with your Lordship's of the fourth and am happy in having anticipated your wishes in withdrawing the posts of Ebenezer and Abercorn, which I did from a conviction that nothing was to be apprehended in that quarter, although interested individuals represented it otherwise.

Your directions relative to the cavalry shall be complied with, and my conjectures that you had not heard of the intention and might not approve of the execution occasion'd my writing to you on the subject.

I conclude you have sent orders for Lt Colonel Brown's and Major Wright's corps's to return to Savannah, but lest any mistake should happen I shall repeat your wishes by Lt Colonel Cruger, who sets off tomorrow with his battalion, and as their march will be tedious, I have directed him to make what expedition he can to Augusta, and I fancy he will be there by Sunday next. If I may be allowed to judge from a very short acquaintance, I am convinced your Lordship will not be disappointed in your expectations from this gentleman, who will be greatly assisted by the zeal and good sense of Lt Colonel Allen and the harmony that subsists between them.

Sir James Wright seems rather tenacious of the post at Augusta and was under some apprehensions of its not being considered of sufficient consequence, but I have eased his mind in this point by assuring him that you are as sensible of its importance to this province and Carolina as he can possibly be and that you have expressed yourself so to me.

There is a district in the back part of this country called the Ceeded Lands, the inhabitants of which are a numerous, ill disposed, hardy people, and by the accounts I have received they don't seem thoroughly inclined to submit. They are commanded by one Dooley, who I don't yet find has surrendered himself, although he has been daily expected at Augusta for that purpose. As the situation of these people is such as to give trouble if an opportunity should offer, I will mention the circumstance particularly to Lt Colonel Cruger, though I suppose Balfour will not let it escape his observation.

On speaking to the Governor about Mr Houston, he told me that he would consult the Chief Justice and Attorney General, as transactions of this nature did not lay with him. I hinted, with submission, that I thought if it could be done away without any further difficulties, it would be so much the better. The matter is not yet terminated owing to the gentlemen above mentioned being fully occupied at present, but Sir James Wright has just sent me word that he is pretty sure it will be settled agreeable to your desire, which (if any fresh obstacles should arise) I shall endeavour to accomplish by every means in my power, and I will inform your Lordship of the issue by the very earliest opportunity.

I am to request your Lordship will authorise me to give an order for the payment of the bat and forage money, which has not yet been received by the troops in this province and of which the extreme dearness of every article makes them stand in great need.

I have the honor to remain with the utmost respect, my Lord,
Your Lordship's most obedient and most faithful humble servant

ALURED CLARKE

Clarke to Cornwallis, 13th July 1780　　　　　　　　　　　　　　　　*2(287): ALS*

Savannah
July 13th 1780

Lt General Earl Cornwallis etc etc etc

My Lord

By a vessel just arrived from Providence I have received the enclosed letter[13]. Governor Maxwell seems anxious about its having a safe and speedy conveyance to Charles Town. I have therefore sent it to Tybee in hopes it will be in time to go by the *Hydra*. The enclosed abstract is from a letter that came by the same opportunity, and though I don't know what credit is to be given to it, I have taken the liberty to send it for your Lordship's perusal. I also transmit the memorial of a Mr Young, the merits of which I have enquired into, and, finding the facts as stated to be true, must request to have your Lordship's directions concerning it. The militia in question served without pay.

I have the honor to remain with the utmost respect, my Lord,
Your Lordship's most obedient and most faithful humble servant

ALURED CLARKE

Enclosure (1)
Information from New Providence,　　　　　　　　　　　　　　　　*2(288): C*
　　the Bahamas, undated

Extract of a Letter from Providence

We have reason to imagine Jamaica is besieg'd, as we hear by a vessel just arrived in seven days from St Kitts that Admiral Rowley[14] had taken and sent into Barbadoes (which

---

[13] *the enclosed letter*: not extant.

[14] *Rowley*: a reference to Rodney. The intelligence was unfounded.

he took to leeward of that port) twenty five transports with troops, being part of a large fleet from Spain destin'd for Jamaica.

Enclosure (2)
Yonge to Clarke, undated   *2(248): DS*

GEORGIA

      To the Hon Lt Colonel Clark
      Commander in Chief of His Majesty's forces in Georgia

The memorial of Philip Yonge of Savannah humbly sheweth

That your memorialist, immediately after the French and rebels had retreated from before the lines of Savannah, went out, with a party of militia he had the honor to command during the siege, to make reprisals on the enemy.

That on or about the eighth day of November last past in the inlet of Ossabaw he fell in with, surprized and took a certain schooner or vessel belonging to some one of the inhabitants or vassals of the French King.

That as soon as the enemy perceived your memorialist making preparations to board her, they immediately evacuated her and took to their boats.

That amongst other things taken on board the said vessel there were five brass field pieces, a large quantity of shot, field carriages etc.

That your memorialist, immediately after the capture aforesaid, made known to General Prevost the different articles taken on board the said vessel, upon which the General requested your memorialist would dispose of the guns, shott and carriages to the commanding officer of the artillery for the use of His Majesty's Service and that he would see him amply satisfyed for the same.

Your memorialist, agreeable to General Prevost's orders, delivered the guns, shott and field carriages to the commanding officer of the Royal Artillery and took a receipt for the same.

That under the assurances your memorialist had from General Prevost of being amply paid for the same, had advanced diverse sums of money to the men under his command, who were aiding and assisting in the capture aforesaid, as part of their prize money arrising from the sales of the said vessel and other articles on board her.

Your memorialist therefore humbly prays your Honor will be pleased to take the case under your consideration and grant him such redress in the premisses as to your justice and wisdom shall seem meet.

And your memorialist will ever pray.

PHILIP YONGE[15]

Cornwallis to Clarke, 24th July 1780

78(42): C

Charlestown
July 24th 1780

Lt Colonel Clarke or officer commanding at Savannah

Sir

As I am informed by Lt Colonel Balfour that Lt Colonel Browne's corps cannot conveniently be spared from Augusta before the arrival of Lt Colonel Allen's corps, you will be pleased to order Lt Colonel Allen's corps to march to Augusta immediately.

I am, sir,
Your most obedient and most humble servant

[CORNWALLIS]

Clarke to Cornwallis, 23rd July 1780

2(349): ALS

Savannah
July 23rd 1780

Earl Cornwallis etc etc etc

My Lord

Major Moncrief arrived here last night, by whom I was honored with your Lordship's letter of the 17th, and in consequence of it I have determined on accompanying him to Augustine, hoping that by the information I shall receive from him on the spot I may be able to form a plan which will terminate in credit to the garrison and service to the publick in case a fortunate attack on Pensacola should induce the Spaniards to appear before that place, in which event I shall certainly make it my quarters immediately.

Captain Hughes of the 60th Regiment, who will have the honor of delivering this to your Lordship, arrived here from St Augustine on the 21st. He informs me that they had not three weeks' provisions left for the garrison, and I am sorry to say it is not in my power to assist

---

[15] Philip Yonge (1753-1782) was a son of Henry Yonge, who had served for more than thirty years as Surveyor General of Georgia and Member of HM Council. When Henry was banished by the revolutionaries, he and Philip purchased a vessel in 1778 to take them to the Bahamas, but they were taken on passage by a British privateer and carried to St Augustine, where Henry died the same year. With the reestablishment of civil government under the Crown in 1779, Philip succeeded his father as Surveyor General of Georgia but received a salary of only £50 per year. On his death he left a wife and four young children, on behalf of whom claims were later presented to the royal commision for property confiscated by the revolutionaries. (Coldham, *Loyalist Claims*, 542-4; Sabine, *Biographical Sketches*, ii, 600)

them very materially from hence, not having sufficient of beef and pork for the troops in this province for more than five weeks. However, I have written to Major Glasier to say, if a supply does not reach him in time from Charles Town (for which purpose the Deputy Commissary General here has wrote twice), I will order him all that can be spared from hence on his sending a proper vessel for it, as we have not any thing of the kind here.

I must beg leave to observe there should not be less than three months' provisions constantly in store at St Augustine and am to request that your Lordship will give such orders as may prevent a deficiency in this very material article in future, for, in the present critical situation of affairs, very fatal consequences may ensue.

At the desire of Lt Governor Graham I enclose the copy of a certificate given to Francis Paris[16], approved of and in part paid by General Prevost. The man is extremely well spoken of; therefore wish to have your Lordship's directions concerning the matter.

Major Moncrief joining me in opinion that the fort at this place should be finished, I will take care that it shall be done as soon as possible.

I shall have great pleasure in corresponding with Balfour as Commandant of Charles Town, being convinced that it will be a pleasant situation for him and that your Lordship will receive every assistance you expect from his having been conversant with business of that nature.

The very kind manner in which your Lordship communicates your intentions and wishes to me cannot but interest me extremely in the success of every thing that you are anxious about and demands my most grateful acknowledgements, and I flatter myself that in the prosecution of them I shall be so fortunate as to evince how sincerely anxious I am to merit your good opinion, than which I should not esteem any thing higher in my professional line, nor could any thing add more to the happiness of, my Lord,

Your Lordship's most obedient and most faithful humble servant

ALURED CLARKE

PS

Sir James Wright just now called on me. He seems reconciled to the non-establishment of the cavalry by the reasons set forth in your Lordship's letter, but says he has some other demands on the score of militia besides those contained in the account he sent you. These also must be trifling. Therefore, if they appear proper, I shall pay the whole on my return from Augustine.

§ - §

---

[16] *copy of a certificate..*: not extant. Paris was a supplier of beef and cattle. (Clark, *Loyalists in the Southern Campaign*, i, 560, 562)

2 - Between Cornwallis and Sir James Wright

Wright to Cornwallis, 3rd July 1780   2(237): ALS

Savanah in Georgia
the 3rd of July 1780

Earl Cornwallis
Commander in Chief of His Majesty's troops etc etc etc

My Lord

I receiv'd your Lordship's very polite message by Mr Graham and most heartily congratulate you on the success of His Majesty's arms in South Carolina and on your safe return to Charles Town, and I trust the generality of the inhabitants have with sincerity and cordiality returned to their allegiance and will again become good and loyal subjects and usefull members of the community.

I must now beg leave to acquaint your Lordship that on the 6th of April I wrote to Sir Henry Clinton on the then state of affairs here and requested that his Excellency would be pleased to give orders for embodying a corps of horse of at least 150 for the particular service and protection of this province. This I wrote to Lord George Germain about in November last, and by his Lordship's answer to me it was approved of and saddles and accoutrements shipt accordingly, but the vessel was unfortunately taken, and afterwards retaken and carried into Bermudas, from whence I hope we may yet get 'em.

Soon after, Mr Graham went to Carolina and I desired him to apply to Sir Henry Clinton on the matter I had wrote about and to endeavour to get it brought to a point, and Mr Graham wrote me on the 29th of April by Sir Henry Clinton's direction that his Excellency said till the business at Charles Town was finished he could give no assistance of the kind I wanted, but hoped that the reduction of the town would in its consequences give us peace and security in Georgia; however, he was extremely willing and desirous to comply with my wishes and desired him to acquaint me that, upon my making application to General Prevost, whatever number of horse shou'd be deemed necessary for this service would be employed and paid if they could be raised in the province, and proper officers got who wou'd not make a job of it[17], and would effectually do the duty, and that his Excellency hoped the multiplicity of business he had on his hands would be a sufficient apology for not writing to me himself. Mr Graham also then wrote me that he mentioned to Sir Henry Clinton that employing some partys of the militia might be a temporary expedient in the mean time till the horse could be raised, but as they are in general persons who have suffered much by the rebellion, and poor and indigent, they would expect to be paid, to which his Excellency was pleased to say that he had no objection to doing it, and that whatever partys I might think necessary and proper to employ should be paid and subsisted while on actual service.

With respect to the corps of horse, I believe General Prevost gave some directions to

---

[17] *make a job of it*: turn the office to private advantage.

Colonel Brown of the King's Rangers, but what he has done in it I can't say; and in consequence of what the Commander in Chief directed Mr Graham to write me about the militia, I embodyed three small corps of about 24 each. They could not get horses for them all, but I think there was about 40 horse and the rest foot. Two of these have been since reduced and discharged. The other is still doing duty with some regulars at the post at Ebenezer. And when they applied to me for payment, I mentioned it to Colonel Clarke, who told me the Commander in Chief had not given him any instructions on that head. Therefore I did not press the matter but paid the first party out of my own pocket, which amounted to £35-16-7½ sterling.

I must therefore request your Lordship will be pleased to favour me with your directions: what I am to do, and how this expence is to be paid. On the 2nd of June last I wrote to Sir Henry Clinton on this matter but believe he was embark'd before my letter reached him, and, now I am on this subject, it leads me to represent to your Lordship the necessity of establishing a post at Augusta.

Augusta, my Lord, is a healthey, pleasant and very plentifull part of this province. It is the key, as it were, or has the command of all the Back Country or Parts of this province and what is called the Ceded Lands, and at Augusta the rebels here who were not reduced by Colonel Campbell, and others who revolted, collected themselves together and continued the farce of their mock government and committed inroads and devastations from thence all through the country within a few miles of Savanah, notwithstanding the military force which General Prevost had here, and this so lately as till since the reduction of Charles Town.

Augusta, my Lord, I have always during my stay in England and since my return here represented to the Ministry as a place where a post is absolutely necessary, and without which an opening will be given to rekindle the flame of rebellion in this province, and without which Georgia will not be at peace and quietness and the loyal inhabitants will be always lyable to be plundered and disturbed by rebels and banditti. I presume, my Lord, about 250 may be a sufficient force for that place, but of this your Lordship is the best judge.

If your Lordship will permit me to give my opinion with respect to the security of this province, it is, in a few words, a post at Augusta of such number as may be thought proper, likewise another at Savanah, with a body of 150 horse to be a moving army to scout about and scour the country; and with this trifling force I think His Majesty's authority may be effectually supported, peace and good government take place, and every remains of the spirit of rebellion totally crushed, but I cannot undertake to answer for these things without such military assistance.

I have the honor to be with perfect esteem, my Lord,
Your Lordship's most obedient humble servant

JA WRIGHT[18]

---

[18] Born in London, Sir James Wright Bt (1716-1785) had been taken while young to South Carolina, where his father served for many years as Chief Justice. A barrister by profession, James acted as Attorney General of South Carolina and then as its Agent in London before being appointed Lt Governor of Georgia in 1760 and Governor

Cornwallis to Wright, 18th July 1780   *78(30): C*

Charlestown
18th July 1780

His Excellency Sir James Wright Bt etc etc etc

Sir

I received the favour of your Excellency's letter of the 3rd of this month, which I should have answered sooner had an opportunity offered of sending to Savannah.

I beg your Excellency to believe that whilst I have the honour to command His Majesty's forces in the southern provinces, I shall pay the greatest attention to the security and protection of Georgia, but the situation of Georgia is greatly altered since the application which your Excellency made to Sir Henry Clinton. At that time the King's troops occupied no part of South Carolina but Charlestown Neck, the whole civil government of the province was in the hands of the rebels, and considerable bodies of troops were in arms against us on the Santee and at Ninety Six. Whilst affairs were thus circumstanced in South Carolina, there can be no doubt but the cavalry for which your Excellency applied to Sir Henry Clinton was very necessary to preserve the province of Georgia from the incursions of plundering parties of the enemy; but now the whole province of South Carolina has submitted, we have a considerable army at Camden, a post at Ninety Six and one at Augusta, the militia is every where either settled or in a way of being speedily so, there are not above three or four regiments out of about twenty (and those in the most interior districts) to which the officers are not appointed, and the lists of the men begun to be taken. No officer is admitted into this militia who is not a man of approved loyalty, and they are positively directed to receive no men into their corps in whose fidelity they cannot place confidence. They are directed, as soon as their militia is formed, to disarm in the strictest manner all the inhabitants of their respective districts whom it has not been thought adviseable to admit into the militia.

I must now declare my opinion to your Excellency that so long as we are in possession of the whole power and force of South Carolina, the province of Georgia has the most ample and satisfactory protection by my maintaining a post at Savannah and another at Augusta, nor can I think myself justifiable in incurring any further expence on the army account for the

---

two years later. He held office until January 1776, when, with his authority entirely subverted, he fled the province and retired to England. On the recovery of Savannah he returned to Georgia and resumed the office of Governor in June 1779. When the town was besieged later in the same year, he is said to have cast the deciding vote against capitulation in the Council of War. With the reinstatement in South Carolina of government under the Crown, he would eloquently make the case for reinforcing Georgia to maintain order there, but for the most part his pleas would fall on deaf ears. When Savannah was evacuated in the summer of 1782, he returned to England, having been subjected to banishment and confiscation by the Georgia revolutionary assembly. The following year he became Chairman of the Board of American Loyalists in prosecution of their claims for compensation. He himself received a pension of £500 per year, having lost property worth £30,000. He died in Fludyer Street, Westminster, and is buried in the north cloister of Westminster Abbey. (*DNB*; *The New Georgia Encyclopedia*; The Georgia Banishment and Confiscation Act 1782)

protection of Georgia. If the country is infested with robbers and that[19] patroles of horse are necessary on that account, I should apprehend that they can only be considered as assistants to the police and that the charge of them must be an affair of the province.

I have directed Colonel Clarke to order the sum, which your Excellency advanced to the militia that was embodied, to be paid immediately as the province at that time was by no means protected by the King's troops.

I have given orders to Colonel Clarke to take the command of His Majesty's forces in East Florida as well as Georgia, and as I have great reliance on his judgement and discretion, I have no doubt but he will, as circumstances occur, make such arrangements as will best tend to promote the general good of His Majesty's Service.

I have the honour to be
Your Excellency's most obedient and most humble servant

[CORNWALLIS]

Wright to Cornwallis, 9th July 1780 2(256): ALS

Savanah
the 9th of July 1780

The Earl of Cornwallis etc etc etc

My Lord

On the 3rd instant I had the honor to write your Lordship a letter and on the 7th I received your Lordship's of the 17th of May[20] from Huger's Bridge in South Carolina, forwarded to me by Colonel Balfour at 96, who I should have been extremely happy to have seen here and given every possible assistance to. I have had the pleasure of being acquainted with the colonel and know he has great merit. This province, my Lord, has already felt the good effects of the reduction of South Carolina, and, since Colonel Brown has taken post at Augusta, the Back Country people in general, who had stood out in rebellion, have petitioned to be received and restored to the King's peace and protection, and every thing seems to promise well except on the Ceded Lands, where I am informed they hang back a little in expectation that the troops are to be ordered away from Augusta; but, my Lord, give me leave to repeat again that a post at Augusta is *absolutely necessary*, and without which there can be no security or safety here, but the seeds of faction and rebellion will probably take place again, and the soil there and in that neighbourhood is very fertile.

---

[19] *that*: the meaning is 'if'. See p 108, note 12.

[20] *your Lordship's..*: no extant copy.

In my former letter, my Lord, I omitted to mention Sunbury and Dartmouth. Sunbury is a seaport town about 42 miles to the southward of Savanah and in a part of the province where the people settled in that neighbourhood are chiefly from New England and of Oliverian[21] principles and from whence they sent the first delegate to the Congress at Philadelphia in the year 1774 or 5; and as it's probable many of them will return these again, I conceive a military command there of about 50 men wou'd keep all the southern parts of this province in due subjection.

Dartmouth is about 60 miles above Augusta in a fork or point of land between the River Dart and Savanah River, and about 2 miles higher up than Fort Charlot on the Carolina side of Savanah River, and I believe about 30 miles cross to 96 in Carolina. The lands at and about Dartmouth are exceedingly good and it is a healthy, pleasant country. I was there in the year 1773 and am very well informed there is not now less than 8 or 900 effective men on the Ceded Lands where Dartmouth is, and I presume a post there of 100 men may be very proper and submit it to your Lordship's better judgment whether or how far these things may be necessary or not.

I have this moment been informed that your Lordship has been pleased to order Colonel Brown and my son's corps from Augusta to Savanah and to be replaced by Colonel Cruger's and Colonel Allen's corps. I am extremely sorry, my Lord, that this has happened, as my son has been happy enough to be particularly well liked by the country people and might have been very usefull there and, I think, wou'd soon fill his regiment, whereas, if he comes to Savanah, I am afraid it will be a good while; and if it cou'd be so, my Lord, I should be very glad he might remain in the country at Augusta or at Dartmouth.

I must request the favour of your Lordship to let me know what number of His Majesty's troops are intended to be left in this province and trust your Lordship will not weaken the military force too soon or too much, for altho the flame of rebellion is pretty well extinguished at present, yet it may revive and break out again if we are not very circumspect.

My Lord, at the importunity of, and in compassion to, a number of very poor distressed families, I beg leave to inclose your Lordship a copy of a petition which they delivered to me a few days ago. They say they can prove the content to be true. However, my Lord, I don't send it by way of complaint against any person, but in a charitable view and to request your Lordship will be good enough to inform me whether, if they can prove their losses or damages, there is any fund or mode by which they can receive any assistance or satisfaction.

I have the honor to be with perfect esteem, my Lord,
Your Lordship's most obedient humble servant

JA WRIGHT

---

[21] *Oliverian*: Cromwellian.

Enclosure
Petition from inhabitants of Ebenezer, undated   *2(221): C*

To his Excellency Sir James Wright Baronet, Captain General, Governor and Commander in Chief in and over His Majesty's Province of Georgia, and the Honorable Gentlemen of His Majesty's Council

The petition of the subscribers, inhabitants of the town and district of Ebenezer, humbly sheweth

That your petitioners have constantly approved themselves good and loyal subjects to the Crown of Great Britain during the late unhappy usurpation, and on that account have always been looked upon as inimical by the opposite party and suffered fines, imprisonments, daily insults, and innumerable illconveniences.

That, however, shortly after the happy reduction of this province, little or no difference was made between your petitioners and their persecutors, but they were equally bereft of their substance and plundered even by the troops from whom they hoped to be rescued from their oppression.

That, besides, by repeated inroads of the rebels they have been plundered of great part of their Negroes, horses, cattle, carriages etc, and most of what remained of the latter was killed or taken from them by the King's troops, who, moreover, during their stay among them destroyed the greatest part of their houses, gardens and fences, by which means, and their frequent service on guards and patroles, their planting business has been almost totally obstructed.

That by the late invasion from Carolina[22] the crops of your petitioners were mostly spoiled and destroyed, by which calamity, just happening at the time of harvest, they were reduced to the greatest want of the necessaries of life and brought to a starving condition.

That your petitioners might easily produce sufficient vouchers of the several losses each individual of them has suffered if it were required, but forbear doing it at this time for fear of becoming tedious and also because they conceive that your Excellency and the Honorable Council are in a great measure already acquainted therewith.

That particularly their church, their minister's and school houses, and their public mills have been greatly damaged and nothing left in their hands to repair them.

That several families among them of old infirm people, helpless women and children are reduced to such poverty and distress that they must infallibly sink under them unless some relief can be found for them, your petitioners themselves being unable to afford any.

That another grievance your petitioners labour under is that they have had their cattle, horses, waggons, boats etc (such as had escaped other casualties) taken from them by

---

[22] *the late invasion..*: Benjamin Lincoln's march in September 1779 to join the French in besieging Savannah.

authority, for which, though some have receipts, they do not know who to apply to to recover the money, and though others have been paid, the price they were allowed was so trifling that, considering the want they stood in of the things themselves, it was mere loss to them.

That, finally, the loss of last year's crop, the loss of their Negroes, horses, cattle and other effects, the ruinous condition of their houses and public buildings, the destruction of their gardens and fences, and the inability to which they are reduced will, your petitioners humbly hope, intitle them to your commiseration.

They therefore submit their distressful case to your Excellency's and the Honorable Council's consideration, nothing doubting but you will grant them such relief as in your wisdom and goodness you shall judge their condition may require.

And your petitioners shall, as in duty bound, ever pray.

CHRISTOPHER FREDRIK TRIEBNER	GODHILF G S SCHMIDT
JOHN CHRISTOPHER BUNTZ	JACOB MEYERS (his X mark)
WIDDOW BUNTZ	JOHN [RANTZ?]
CHRISTOPHER CRAMER	JACOB BÜHLER
ANDREW GNANN (his X mark)	And several others

[*Subscribed*:]

Besides, the Widow Rothenberg with one child lost upwards of £100 worth, the Widow Maurer with five children lost a horse and twenty head of cattle, the Widow Kieffer, with five children, left in want of everything, the Widow Bohrman with one child — her house was taken for the use of the commissary and the out houses, fences and every thing about the house destroyed. The family of the Reverend Mr Lembke (deceased) had their house taken for barracks, their cattle killed, and every thing about the house destroyed. The Widow Mohr with a grandchild was several times plundered. In short, the distressful situation of these last mentioned families calls for immediate assistance and relief.

Cornwallis to Wright, 24th July 1780   78(46): C

Charlestown
24th July 1780

His Excellency Sir James Wright etc etc etc

Sir

I received by Lieutenant Winter of the navy the favour of your Excellency's letter of the 9th instant. You will find most of the material parts fully explained by the letter which I had the honour to send to you by Major Moncrief and which I hope will perfectly convince you that I have paid the utmost attention to the security of Georgia. The propriety of a post at Sunbury will of course be referred to Lt Colonel Clarke, to whom I have given the command of the troops in Georgia and East Florida; the care of the Ceded Lands and Dartmouth to that of the commanding officer at 96. I am sorry to find that my ordering Colonel Browne's and Major Wright's corps to Savannah to be replaced in the Back Country by Lt Colonel Cruger's and Allen's is disagreeable to your Excellency, but as I think it for the good of His Majesty's Service, I cannot apprehend that I should be justifiable in altering this disposition. Lt Colonel Brown's and Major Wright's corps, and, I am sorry to say, especially the latter, are composed almost entirely of rebel prisoners. Most of those which they took out of the prison ships in Georgia having deserted back to the enemy armed and cloathed, they have presumed to disobey a positive order of the Commander in Chief's and, altho' they have already experienced the bad consequences of it to the King's Service, have carried off a very considerable number of the Continental prisoners of war from this place. It has likewise been reported to me that those two corps have been making use of all the most vexatious tricks of recruiting in the Back Country, which occasioned great disgust amongst the inhabitants and made them afraid of having any intercourse with His Majesty's troops. From the consideration of the abovementioned reasons and the desire of moving the battalions of Cruger and Allen, who have been long kept in disagreeable quarters, I find myself under the necessity of adhering to my order. The melancholy representation which your Excellency has made to me of the condition and sufferings of many of the inhabitants of Georgia excites my compassion to the greatest degree, but I do not at present know of any means in my power to alleviate their distresses.

I have the honour to be
Your Excellency's most obedient humble servant

[CORNWALLIS]

Wright to Cornwallis, 28th July 1780 2(375): ALS

Savanah in Georgia
the 28th of July 1780

Earl Cornwallis
Commander in Chief of His Majesty's forces in the Southern Provinces etc etc etc

My Lord

Your Lordship's letter of the 18th I had the honor to receive on the 23rd instant and have no kind of doubt but your Lordship will give proper attention to the security and protection of the province of Georgia, and I am perfectly sensible of the difference in the situation of affairs just now and at the time of my application to Sir Henry Clinton. The difference is truly great and, from the account your Lordship gives me, the present prospect is very pleasing to what it was then; and the posts your Lordship has established, and other steps taken and regulations made, to reduce the whole province of South Carolina to His Majesty's obedience and to crush the spirit of rebellion are very judicious and do your Lordship great honor and I hope will answer every purpose etc wished for. The regulations your Lordship has thought necessary to introduce amongst the militia in South Carolina we cannot enforce in this province, for, the King having been graciously pleased to reestablish His civil government here, the laws regulating the militia must operate and be the guide in that respect unless they are taken into pay, when I presume they might be put on a different footing and made more usefull in keeping good order and preventing any cabals or attempts to promote sedition and rebellion. And the posts at Savanah and Augusta being 140 miles distant from each other gives great opportunitys to ill disposed people, and altho the return of the inhabitants to their allegiance may seem to be cordial and sincere, yet, my Lord, I conceive they are not to be trusted for some time. I am extremely sorry to differ in the least with your Lordship in opinion on this matter, but I must continue to think that the distance of 140 miles is very great and may in some measure make a corps of horse necessary for a while, altho, from the reasons your Lordship is pleased to give, I presume, with the several posts at Savanah, Sunbury, Augusta and Dartmouth, a single troop of 50 horse might answer every purpose — but that the expence of this can be defrayed by the province, my Lord, is an impossible thing. This province in its prosperity never could pay into the Treasury above £2,500 sterling per annum, which was then look'd upon as a very heavy tax; and now, my Lord, when it will not for some time make a fourth part of the annual produce which it used to make, when at least three fourths of the province is broke up and destroyed, when the people have been harassed and torn to pieces and distressed on all hands and many totally ruined, how, my Lord, is it possible for people in such a situation to pay taxes to raise troops for the purposes I have mentioned, were they ever so well disposed and willing?

However, I can only represent matters, and which I conceive my duty to His Majesty and to the people here compels me to do to your Lordship.

There are other sums due, my Lord, besides that which I paid, for, as I wrote your Lordship, I had by Sir Henry Clinton's *express approbation* embody'd three small partys of militia, all which accounts I shall lay before Colonel Clarke. I observe the orders your Lordship has been pleased to give Colonel Clarke relative to the forces in East Florida, which power I conceive to be extremely well placed, having the highest opinion of that gentleman's good sense and discretion, and have not the least doubt but he will do every thing in his power for the general good of His Majesty's Service.

I have the honor to be with perfect esteem, my Lord,
Your Lordship's most obedient humble servant

JA WRIGHT

PS

May I presume, my Lord, to recommend Mr Daniel Horry[23] as a gentleman who I am persuaded did not enter into the rebellion from principle or the original design of many but

---

[23] Wright may be referring to Daniel Horry (*c.* 1730-?) of South Carolina, who had served as an officer in the revolutionary service and may have lived in Wright's family in Charlestown before Wright left there to become Agent for the colony in London. If so, he would soon take protection, swearing allegiance to the Crown, and in January 1782 be amerced for his sin by act of the South Carolina revolutionary assembly. (Heitman, *Historical Register*, 301; Alden, *The South in the Rev*, 327n; McCrady, *SC in the Rev 1780-1783*, 587)

who I have very good reason to believe was led into it by his connections. He lived in my family several years, and, as far as may be consistent with your Lordship's wise plan, if any indulgence is granted him, I really think he will not abuse it.

I have this moment been informed that the generality of the inhabitants on the Ceded Lands have delivered up their arms and I have received a petition, by the direction of about 400 of them, to be received and restored to His Majesty's peace and protection.

Wright to Cornwallis, 31st July 1780   *2(397): ALS*

Savanah in Georgia
the 31st of July 1780

Earl Cornwallis
Commander in Chief of His Majesty's forces in the Southern Provinces etc etc etc

My Lord

Since writing my last of the 28th instant I have been honored with your Lordship's letter of the 24th and am perfectly convinced that your Lordship will pay every attention to the security of Georgia and for His Majesty's Service in general.

It gives me much concern to find such heavy charges against my son's corps. All I shall presume to say is that possibly your Lordship may have been misinformed and am certain that your Lordship's innate benevolence and candour will prevent your entertaining any prejudice or unfavourable opinion till, according to that golden maxim, you *hear the other party*.

I have the honor to be with perfect esteem, my Lord,
Your Lordship's most obedient humble servant

JA WRIGHT

§ - §

3 - Between Cornwallis and Tonyn or Glasier

Cornwallis to Glasier, 18th July 1780 78(26): C

Charlestown
18th July 1780

To the officer commanding His Majesty's troops at St Augustine

Sir

I have appointed Lt Colonel Clarke to command His Majesty's forces in East Florida as well as Georgia. I desire therefore that you will please to report on all occasions to Lt Colonel Clarke and obey any orders you may receive from him.

I am, sir,
Your most obedient and most humble servant

[CORNWALLIS]

Cornwallis to Tonyn, 18th July 1780 78(28): C

Charlestown
18th July 1780

His Excellency Patrick Tonyn Esq etc etc etc

Dear Sir

I have been so much employed in the Back Country that I have not had time to notify to you sooner my being appointed by Sir Henry Clinton to command His Majesty's forces in the southern provinces. Altho' this occasions our being nearer neighbours, I fear it is not likely that it will procure me the pleasure of an interview with you. However, it is a satisfaction to me to be connected in business with an old friend.

As soon as the troops in this province are prepared to act, it is probable that I shall be removed to a considerable distance so as to make correspondence slow and perhaps uncertain; and if any misfortune should happen at Pensacola (an event I think not improbable), the affairs of East Florida will require a serious attention. I have therefore thought it for the advantage of His Majesty's Service to appoint Lt Colonel Clarke to command the troops in East Florida as well as Georgia, and as he is an officer of discretion and judgement, I have no doubt but he will make such arrangements as will tend to secure the two provinces and to promote the good of the service. He will, I believe, make you a visit at Augustine with Major Moncrief, who is commanding engineer for the Southern District.

I have the honour to be, dear sir,
Your most obedient and faithfull servant

[CORNWALLIS]

Glasier to Cornwallis, 14th July 1780   2(292): LS

St Augustine
14th July 1780

Lord Cornwallis

Captain Hughs of the 3rd Battalion, 60th Regiment, who has my leave to go to Charlestown on some regimental affairs, will have the honor to deliver this to your Lordship with the contingent account of the garrison for the last six months. I also take the liberty to inclose the account of batt and forage money. And I must beg leave to inform your Lordship that I sett out from Savannah with the 60th Regiment the 23rd December for this place. Our rout was what is called the Inland Passage. The voyage might have been performed in ten days had the season been as favorable as usual in this country, but [from] the extreme cold and boisterousness of the weather (which was never known before in these parts) it was the 2nd of February before we arrived here. The officers as well as the men lost almost all their baggage, and our provisions and rum falling short by twelve days, we suffered more than during the whole of the summer campaign. I mention this circumstance to your Lordship in hopes of removing every objection to our receiving the batt and forage with the rest of the army.

The vouchers for the contingent account I have kept by me as directed by Major General Prevost. I never had any publick moneys in my hands but have been obligded to advance my own, without which the King's Service could not have been carried on.

Captain Hughs can well inform your Lordship respecting our situation and answer such questions as you may please to ask concerning this place.

I have the honor to be, my Lord,
Your Lordship's most obedient and most humble servant

B GLASIER[24]
Major, 60th Regiment

---

[24] Beamsly Glasier was a long-standing officer who had become a captain in the army on 16th June 1760. Entering the 60th (or Royal American) Regiment four and a half years later, he had been promoted to major in the 4th Battalion on 23rd September 1775. In command of a detachment comprising elements of the 2nd, 3rd and 4th Battalions, he had taken a courageous part in withstanding the assault on Savannah on 9th October 1779. He would soon be notified of his promotion to lt colonel of his own battalion effective from 6th May 1780. (*Army Lists*; *The Cornwallis Papers*; Lossing, *Pictorial Field-Book*, ii, 532; Boatner, *Encyclopedia*, 986; WO 65/164(13) (National Archives, Kew))

Enclosure (1)
Account of contingent expenses 2(229): DS

Account of Contingent Expences incurred for the use of the Troops and Garrison of St Augustine and its Dependencies from 15th January to 30th June 1780 By order of Major Beamsly Glasier, 60th Regiment

Date when paid	Nº of vouchers	To whom paid and for what service	Sums (£ s d)
1780			
January 15th	1	To John Clubb for hire of self and 2 Negroes with a boat to bring forward a schooner with baggage	1. 8. 6
25th	2	To Henry Myers, freight for stores and baggage of the 60th Regiment from Savannah to St John's River	26. 2. 0
29th	3	To Charles Hall for self and 4 Negroes with a boat to search for fresh beef for the sick of the 60th Regiment	3. 16. 0
February 12th	4	To James Wallace, freight of a schooner from St Augustine to St John's River with the sick and baggage of the 16th Regiment and for bringing from thence the sick of the 60th Regiment	32. 5. 0
15th	5	To Charles Hall, his account of fresh beef supplied the pioneers with Captain Bloxham as per receipt	21. 5. 0
21st	6	To Quarter Master Wright, his expences from St John's to St Augustine and back again on the business of the garrison	3. 16. 0
March 31st	7	To Charles Delap, his account of stationary	9. 5. 0
May 1st	8	To ditto for Richard Williamson's account of fresh beef supplied the families of the pilots on St John's	12. 8. 0
2nd	9	To ditto for Adam Tunno's account for pilotage of Negroe Caesar, 43 days @ 4/8 per day	10. 0. 8
4th	10	To William Moss for hire of a cart and 4 horses to bring stores from St John's to St Augustine, 10 days @ 9/6	4. 15. 0

June 15th	11	To Francis Levett's account for hire of a sloop from Savannah to St Augustine with stores, baggage etc of the 60th Regiment as per aggreement with the Deputy Quarter Master General and certified by Major General Prevost	89. 2. 0
30th	12	To Charles Shirreff, his pay as Fort Adjutant from 1st January to 30th June 1780 including 183 days @ 4/- per day, charged in this account by an order from the Secretary at War	36. 12. 0
		To expresses from and to the out posts on St John's River, at Mattanzes and Musquittos at sundry times	8. 12. 0
			259. 7. 2

B GLASIER
Major
60th Regiment

Enclosure (2)
Account for forage, baggage and bat money

2(230): DS

Return for 200 Days' Forage, Baggage and Batt Money for the 60th Regiment Commencing 1st January 1780

	Nº of Rations	Forage (£ s d)	Baggage etc (£ s d)	Batt (£ s d)	Amount (£ s d)
2nd Battalion					
1 captain commanding	7	35. 0. 0	7. 10. 0	10. 0. 0	52. 10. 0
1 company	2	10. 0. 0	-	10. 0. 0	20. 0. 0
1 more	2	10. 0. 0	-	10. 0. 0	20. 0. 0
1 subaltern	1	5. 0. 0	3. 15. 0	-	8. 15. 0
2 more	2	10. 0. 0	7. 10. 0	-	17. 10. 0
1 surgeon and chest £10	2	10. 0. 0	5. 0. 0	-	25. 0. 0
3rd Battalion					
1 captain commanding	7	35. 0. 0	7. 10. 0	10. 0. 0	52. 10. 0

1 captain and company	5	25. 0. 0	7. 10. 0	10. 0. 0	42. 10. 0
1 company	2	10. 0. 0	-	10. 0. 0	20. 0. 0
3 more	6	30. 0. 0	-	30. 0. 0	60. 0. 0
1 subaltern	1	5. 0. 0	3. 15. 0	-	8. 15. 0
5 more	5	25. 0. 0	19. 5. 0	-	44. 5. 0
1 mate	2	10. 0. 0	3. 15. 0	-	13. 15. 0
1 chaplain	1	5. 0. 0	5. 0. 0	-	10. 0. 0
4th Battalion					
1 major commanding	9	45. 0. 0	7. 10. 0	10. 0. 0	62. 10. 0
1 captain	5	25. 0. 0	7. 10. 0	10. 0. 0	42. 10. 0
3 more	15	75. 0. 0	22. 10. 0	30. 0. 0	127. 10. 0
1 company	2	10. 0. 0	-	10. 0. 0	20. 0. 0
1 subaltern	1	5. 0. 0	3. 15. 0	-	8. 15. 0
10 more	10	50. 0. 0	37. 10. 0	-	87. 10. 0
1 adjutant	1	5. 0. 0	5. 0. 0	-	10. 0. 0
1 surgeon and chest £10	2	10. 0. 0	5. 0. 0	-	25. 0. 0
1 mate	2	10. 0. 0	3. 15. 0	-	13. 15. 0
TOTAL	92	460. 0. 0	162. 0. 0	150. 0. 0	793. 0. 0

B GLASIER
Major
60th Regiment

Enclosure (3)
List of officers in 60th Regiment   *2(231):* **D**

Officers: Rank and Names

2nd Battalion

Captain Wickham, commanding

Subalterns: Davis, Schodde, Levett

Surgeon Clark

3rd Battalion

Captain Hughes, commanding

Captain Breley

Subalterns: Lieutenants Lockell, Hesselberg, Floyer

　　　　　　Ensigns Eberhard, Bradstreet, Hewlett

Staff: Surgeon's Mate Kemp

　　　　　　Chaplain Forbes

4th Battalion

Major Glasier, commanding

Captains: Murray, Burrard, Erskine, De Montrond

Subalterns: Lieutenants Britenbach, Porbeck, Kersley, Boniface
　　　　　　(1st Battalion:) Lieutenants Campbell, Vaniper

　　　　　　Ensigns Sinclair, Manning, Fatio, Clark, Cartwright

Adjutant McKenzie

Surgeon Henderson

Mate Wright

Cornwallis to Glasier, 3rd August 1780 — 79(4): C

Charlestown
August 3rd 1780

Major Glazier
60th Regiment

Sir

　　I received your letter of the 14th July by Captain Hughes and shall give orders that the forage money for the garrison of St Augustine and your contingent account shall be paid. I have dispatched the provisions as soon as the weather would permit and a convoy could be procured. For the future you will please to give in all accounts, and apply on all business relative to the troops in East Florida, to Lt Colonel Clarke.

I am, sir,
Your most obedient and most humble servant

[CORNWALLIS]

Cornwallis to Tonyn, 3rd August 1780   79(6): C

Charles Town
August 3rd 1780

His Excellency Governour Tonyn

Dear Sir

I received the favour of your letter of the 12th of last month[25]. I had just before written to you by Major Moncrief. I have only now to thank you for your attention to me in giving me an account of the state of persons and things in the province of East Florida. You may depend upon my never giving my consent that such men as you describe should be employed in any of the publick departments. I have sent some provisions, of which I am told the garrison of St Augustine is in great want and which I hope will arrive in time.

I have the honour to be etc

[CORNWALLIS]

§ - §

---

[25] *your letter..*: not extant.

CHAPTER 17

Miscellaneous letters etc

1 - From sundry British officers

Graham to Ross, 22nd June 1780 *2(175): ALS*

Holemans in Amelia Township
22nd June 1780

Captain Ross
Aid de camp
Charles Town

Dear Sir

I have the pleasure to inform you that the company of this district met this day agreeable to their intentions and I must say by much the finest I have yet seen and in apearance most unanimous in their loyalty.

The bearer, George Roy[1], a member of Turkey Hill company, has a young boy a prisoner in town, who was inveigheled away from his parents. He is gone to interceed with his Lordship for permission for the boy to come home with him and will be answerable for his appearance when he is called for. The company wish it if it is consistant.

---

[1] According to land records held by the South Carolina Department of Archives and History, George Roy owned land in Amelia Township. (T W Lipscomb to the editor, 3rd March 2005)

I have the honor to be
Yours etc

COLIN GRAHAM

[*Subscribed*:]

A number of the prisoners taken in town have made their escape and under the cloak of country people have got protection. Pray, are the militia to secure them or are they to wink at the deception?

CG

Graham to Cornwallis, 28th June 1780 2(206): ALS

Orangeburgh
28th June 1780

My Lord

Agreeable to your Lordship's directions I have waited upon Mr Fisher the moment I heard of his being arrived from town, and communicated to him your Lordship's intentions of giving him the command of the militia of this district.

He informs me that some new regulations were on the carpet and only waited your Lordship's approbation to be put in execution, that if your Lordship approved of the plan, he was already engaged in the civil branch, but that if the original plan of the militia was to be adhered to, he was ready to give every assistance in his power, and looks on himself obliged to your Lordship for the honor and confidence reposed in him.

In the mean time he will give every aid in his power to forward the service and I shall not take any step in appointing a field officer till I have your Lordship's further instructions on that head.

At my request he is to have the gaol of this place repaired, and will endeavour to find a gaoler, the former being run away, having been guilty of mall practices.

All the companies of this district have now assembled except the one lately Captain Tate's[2]. I hope they will follow the example of the others soon.

---

[2] Of Irish descent on his father's side and of English on his mother's, Samuel Tate (?-*c*. 1798) was born and raised on the Santee near Vance's Ferry in Orangeburg District. A captain in the revolutionary militia, he would now serve in Sumter's Brigade, being confused with William Tate, who was Sumter's major of brigade (see vol II, p 342, note 40). He died at the old homestead near Vance's Ferry. (Draper, *King's Mountain*, 465)

As there are so few gentlemen to be found in many of the present divisions or districts for battalions in whom confidence enough can be reposed to entitle them to be field officers, I humbly think, my Lord, if the division was made agreeable to the old course of the circuits, it would remedie the present inconvenience in a great degree, as there would be fewer regiments and a larger space of country to find the proper officers. The number of men might be the same.

I have the honor to be with great respect, my Lord,
Your Lordship's most obedient and most humble servant

COLIN GRAHAM

Turnbull to Cornwallis, 6th July 1780   2(250): ALS

Rocky Mount
July 6th 1780

The Earl of Cornwallis

My Lord

The last time I had the honor of writing your Lordship our affairs in this quarter were in a very prosperous way, and had it not been for that weak silly man Moore, who led a parcell of those poor innocent devils of North Carolina into a scrape, we should have been now in perfect peace and quietness on this frontier.

Moore's defeat made me march, some days sooner than I intended, up amongst my good friends the Bounty Irish. I wish I cou'd say something in their favor. I believe them to be the worst of the Creation, and nothing will bring them to reason but severity. Numbers had left their plantations, and severall have run of since I was amongst them, after submitting and embodying.

Captain Kinloch brought a reinforcement of the Legion to Major Brown's Cross Roads, where I was encamped. I added a pretty large body of militia and mounted men of our regiment, which made a respectable detachment, and in order that Kinloch should have a full scope I did not tye him down by written orders. He marched about twelve miles and received some intelligence which I found afterwards was none of the best, viz, that the rebels were thirteen hundred strong and that they were at a great distance. He returned and complain'd so much of the heat of the weather and the tiredness of their horses that I let him go down and sent home the militia to reap their crops, which was losing for want of reapers. They were not two days gone when the rebels begun to be saucey and encamped on the east side the Cataba River about four miles from the Old Nation Ford to the amount of about six hundred commanded by Colonel Sumpter and threatned death and destruction to us all. I conceived they wanted that I shou'd move back to Rocky Mount, and indeed they effected it by sending a party of forty men down as low as George Wade's mill on the east side the river within ten miles of Rocky Mount, which number was given me to the amount of five hundred.

I now find Major Mecan has marched against them, and if he will only remain as long at the Waxhaws as I have done here, I really believe we shou'd feel the good effects of it. Those Mecklenburgh, Roan, and my friends the Irish above are perhaps the greatest skum of the Creation. English lenity is thrown away when there is not virtue to meet it half way. If some of them could be catched who have submitted and run off and join'd the rebels, an example on the spot of immediate death and confiscation of property might perhaps make them submitt.

I am now to thank your Lordship for the attention you have had for this little corps. In about a couple of months they will be so ragged that I shou'd be very happy that the service might permitt our being moved to town. I should then embrace your Lordship's generous offer to make a short visit to Mrs Turnbull and either bring her or quit the army. The bearer of this, Lieutenant Peterson, was appointed to Major Sheridan's company[3], which is to be raised. I now send him to his assisstance.

I am with much esteem
Your Lordship's most faithfull humble servant

GEO TURNBULL

McArthur to Cornwallis, 29th July 1780   2(383): ALS

Camden
July 29th 1780

The Rt Hon Lt General Earl Cornwallis
Charlestown

My Lord

The regiment being withdrawn a few days ago to Linches Creek, I have come here for recovery of my health, having been some time ill of a fever that does not intermitt. I think it my duty to represent to your Lordship that the 71st Regiment has not been setled with since the 25th of October 1778 owing to the commissarys not giving in their demands for provisions, though Lt Colonel McDonald and myself frequently demanded these accounts of them, but I apprehend nothing but a positive order from your Lordship will procure them, which I hope you will think proper to issue with a menace that, if they are not immediately given in, they will not be paid. If our men were not the most patient creatures of any, they would before now have broke out, and as it is, we frequently overhear conversations among them on this subject reflecting on their officers for not doing them justice. This is to all the officers very distressing and will lose to us the confidence of our men. 'Tis only your Lordship can relieve us from this disagreable situation.

---

[3] Henry Sheridan (1751-?) was an Irishman who had seen several years' service in the British Army before entering the Provincial line. Appointed major in the New York Volunteers on 20th August 1778, he would serve with the regiment until its disbandment at the close of the war, when he was placed on the Provincial half-pay list. (Treasury 64/23(1), WO 65/164(31), and WO 65/165(2) (National Archives, Kew))

I have the honor to be with great respect, my Lord,
Your Lordship's most obedient humble servant

ARCH^D McARTHUR

[*Subscribed*:]

Lieutenant Murchison[4] sets off this day and will wait on your Lordship for an order for a vessell to bring our cloathing and baggage from Savannah.

Tarleton to Cornwallis, 5th August 1780   63(19): ALS

Lenew's Ferry
August 5th 1780

Earl Cornwallis etc etc etc
Charles Town

My Lord

I have the honor to inform you of my reaching this place this morning. The incessant rains having rais'd the water and destroyed the small bridges render'd the journey hitherto tedious.

Colonel Ball is here. His militia are not *numerous*. He will, I believe, be able to furnish me with about 25 young men to assist in allaying this commotion near Black River and intermediate to Lenew's and Murray's Ferrys. They likewise will be able to point out the instruments of disaffection.

I cannot ascertain whether Major Wemyss is marched from George Town. I shall if possible communicate with him. For that purpose I shall dispatch a man to him this afternoon.

The country, my Lord, I found *scared*. I prais'd the militia, tho' not large, for their alacrity in turning out.

They talk'd of the enemy crossing to this side the Santee. Their fears multiplied their dangers. A man is just come in who informs me that they lye in bodies of 30 and 40. Many of the insurgents, having taken certificates and paroles, don't deserve lenity. None shall they experience. I have promis'd the young men who chuse to assist me in this expedition the plunder of the leaders of the faction. If warfare allows me, I shall give these disturbers of the peace no quarter. If humanity obliges me to spare their lives, I shall convey them close prisoners to Camden. Fire and confiscation must take place on their effects etc. I must discriminate with severity.

---

[4] Magnus Murchieson had been commissioned an ensign in the 2nd Battalion, 71st (Highland) Regiment, on 3rd August 1778. He was promoted to lieutenant in his battalion on 18th October 1779. (*Army Lists*)

I shall cross the ferry to morrow, my Lord, and make use of every exertion and precaution in my power. I send all my baggage to Nelson's under the escort of the old militia on this side.

My Lord, I have the honor to be with the greatest respect
Your Lordship's devoted servant

BANASTRE TARLETON

[*Endorsed*:]

To press horses on the road.

B TARLETON
Lt Colonel Commandant, British Legion

McKinnon to Cornwallis, 9th August 1780   63(28): LS

Neilson's Ferry
9th August 1780

My Lord

I have the honour to inform you that I got here last night with the detachment of the 63rd Regiment, having remained in the neighbourhood of Cooke's as long as it was possible to be able to fullfill your Lordship's intention of being here in the time prescribed.

I have sent a party across the river and dispatched several messengers to Major Wemyss, of whose motions I have yet learnt nothing with certainty, but expect this day to have an answer to a letter I sent him from Cooke's by a trusty person of Gaillard's procuring.

There are but two small boats at Cooke['s] and no stores of any sort. The last loaded boat left it on Sunday and passed here yesterday.

The militia of the upper district met yesterday at Martin's Tavern and Captain Ball ordered a party of them to take post at Cooke's to day. While this party remains, things would be safe there, and there is now a quantity of rum and salt at the Corner that might be sent on there if your Lordship thought proper.

I hear of nothing stirring near us on the opposite side of the river.

I have the honour to be, my Lord,
Your Lordship's most obedient humble servant

JN McKINNON

McKinnon to Cornwallis, 11th August 1780   *63(32): LS*

Neilson's Ferry
11th August 1780
2 o'clock

My Lord

I am this moment honoured with your letter of yesterday[5] and shall immediately set the detachment in motion and observe your Lordship's further instructions.

I have sent five different people to Major Wemyss with letters — *of no consequence.* Some of them I hope will get safe and expect to hear from him to day.

The militia from St James and St Stephens's who were with Colonel Tarleton returned yesterday and found every thing quiet on the road from Cambden.

On the return of the boats to day the overseer informed me of a plan that had been concerted between a Mr Hoy[6] and the rebels on t'other side of the river for their destruction on their return. I have taken the liberty of sending a party for this man and his accusers and shall carry them forward till I have time to inquire into the affair and report to your Lordship. He was overseer to the plantation of a Major Irwing[7].

As the rising below is quashed, and as the boats were at hand and parties of ours upon the river, I had ordered every thing to be loaded and ready to set out for Cooke's, which I shall now countermand and let them proceed to McCord's, as this side of the river is the safest and the roads best.

I have the honor to be, my Lord,
Your Lordship's most obedient humble servant

JN McKINNON

§ - §

---

[5] *your letter..*: no extant copy.

[6] Perhaps James Hoy, who had served in the revolutionary militia in 1779 and would do so again in 1781 and 1782. (Moss, *SC Patriots*)

[7] Given the variety of spellings and misspellings of proper names, Irwing has not been positively identified. He may have been Alexander Irving, who was serving as a major in the royal militia at Georgetown when the place was attacked by Marion and Lee on 25th January 1781. If so, he was killed by a Lieutenant Cryer of Marion's Brigade, who sometime before had received 500 lashes by his orders for attempting to take away his horse from there. (Clark, *Loyalists in the Southern Campaign*, i, 187; *The Greene Papers*, vii, 198; James, *Marion*, 91)

2 - Between Cornwallis and Governor Martin

Martin to Cornwallis, 24th July 1780 *2(356): ALS*

Camden
July 24th 1780

The Earl Cornwallis etc etc etc
Charles Town

My Lord

As Lord Rawdon has done me the honor to communicate to me what he has written to your Lordship concerning a proposition from the Scotch of forming the Highlanders of Cumberland and Anson Counties into a Provincial regiment of which they wish me to be colonel, I think it necessary, to obviate all possibility of embarrassment on my account, to assure your Lordship that if the least difficulty occurs to your mind in the case as it respects myself, I shall wish you to put your negative upon it without scruple or hesitation. In suffering the proposition to go to Lord Rawdon I acted entirely in subserviency to what I was assured were the wishes of both officers and men, and not from any impulse of my own military vanity. I think, indeed, it will not be necessary to defend myself from this imputation when it is remembered that I was many years a lt colonel in the army. I have none, I am sure, to apprehend nor any thing to fear from your Lordship but too much delicacy in what may regard myself. I am not sure, if your Lordship approves of my nomination in this instance, but that it will beget applications to you to dub me colonel of every corps that is raised in North Carolina, and I can only employ one single argument to reconcile it to your Lordship in any case, besides that of humouring the people, which is that my intention is to serve without pay, for although my finances by no means justify my refusal of any just augmentation of income, I think, considering how unprofitable a servant I have been for years past (in which I have been supported at a great expense to the publick), it would ill become me to take additional pay for the very little service it may be in my power to do and in the first moment that I am employed. And it would besides make ground for the malicious world to charge to motives of interest a compliance on my part to which I am moved by no other consideration than the wishes of the people, that are, I confess, pleasing and flattering as they bespeak a confidence and good opinion which I have the vanity to consider as no bad testimonial of my conduct in the public station I once filled in North Carolina.

Again, I conceive the people may be gratified by nomination of me to be the head of the corps in a rank or two ranks inferior to that of colonel; and for myself (as I cannot possibly arrive at a military command flattering to my ambition), if any objection hinges upon the name of colonel, I resign myself to your Lordship to be stiled as you shall please and think corresponding with the desires of the North Carolinians.

The amendment[8] of Lord Rawdon's health may assure your Lordship of all things going well in this quarter, for I am warranted to say, as I firmly believe, that your Lordship has in him, while his health endures, a substitute competent to every thing. He has done me the honor to overrate infinitely to your Lordship my humble attempts to satisfy the North Carolinians of your Lordship's intentions to succour them as speedily as possible. Their sufferings I do believe to be insupportable, and they plead pitiously, in excuse of the poor people's impatience. No particular intelligence has been received from North Carolina lately.

I have the honor to be with the most perfect respect and devotion, my Lord,
Your Lordship's most obedient and faithfull servant

JO MARTIN

[*Subscribed*:]

I beg leave to congratulate your Lordship on the loss of the late Commandant of Charles Town.

Martin to Cornwallis, 28th July 1780   *2(379): ALS*

Camden
July 28th 1780

The Earl Cornwallis etc etc etc
Charlestown

By favor of Colonel Rugely

My Lord

In proof of my readiness to obey your Lordship's commands upon all occasions, I had the honor to send you last night a very clumsy specimen of my unskillfulness in law instruments in form and shape of a proclamation[9]. I am very sensible that it proclaims my shame as a Civil Governor who ought to be better versed in such legal knowledge. Your Lordship knows, however, that Provincial Governors have not been always chosen in our country for the fitness and competence of talents, and therefore will not be surprised to find me as ignorant as many of my brethren in office or more so. In charity, your Lordship will be pleased in my excuse, I hope, to consider (with as much stress as may be laid upon the circumstance) that I was not educated to civil business, and that disaster and misfortune alone reduced me to the necessity of embracing a line in the publick service in which I am found so wanting and unqualified. That I may not, however, appear even below my real low level,

---

[8] *amendment*: used in the archaic sense of 'improvement'.

[9] *a very clumsy specimen..*: not extant. It dealt with the sequestration of estates and Cruden's appointment as commissioner.

I am to beg your Lordship's permission to correct some grammatical errata I find I was guilty of in yesterday's miserable performance, which consist in the omission of the words *and collected* after *seized* in its first place in the proclamation and the terms *and collect* after the word *hold* in that part where the Commissioner's appointment is declared, being the best relatives I could employ as to the direction concerning debts, which, I am of opinion with Lord Rawdon, will be found but a scanty and unproductive fund. After this trivial amendment I consign my abortion to your Lordship's mercy, wishing as its best fate that it may be employed to light a candle and be never more seen or heard of. I am sure no phoenix will rise from its ashes, nor indeed do I apprehend such phenomenon will attend the exit of Mr Simpson's work, whose law terms I have cautiously and, most likely, improperly avoided, but I feared to betray my ignorance more egregiously by the misuse of them.

To the daily moanings and groans of the North Carolinians I administer all the comfort I am able, your Lordship may be assured, and I fail not to impress upon them in the strongest manner your Lordship's sense of, and feelings for, their sufferings and to certify to them your resolution to give them relief as speedily as possible. The condition of the people of Anson County, who have for the most part taken the oath of allegiance as militia men before Major McArthur, must flee the country on his falling back to his present ground, as will the inhabitants, I dare say, of the Cheraw District, but these are temporary grievances without remedy.

I have the honor to be with all possible acknowledgment of your Lordship's goodness and condescension towards me, and with the utmost respect, my Lord,
Your Lordship's most faithfull and most obliged and obedient servant

JO MARTIN

PS

As it is a quere in your Lordship's memoranda how the commissioner is to be paid, I submit to your consideration whether a certain *per centage* on the value of property committed to his guardianship will not be the best mode.

Friday evening

Dixon[10] is just returned, having been sick and fearing to be arrested by that cause until the foe should overtake him. Ten days have passed since he left Deep River. De Kalb, he says, was then in motion upwards on Deep River and, he supposes, intended taking post at the Cross Roads. I am sorry to report to your Lordship that Dixon was able to communicate with no person in whom he could confide to maintain a correspondence with us. He represents the people to be harrassed out of their lives and so intimidated that they are afraid to undertake any business that may expose them to the malignity of their persecutors, who

---

[10] On the one hand, Dixon may have been Josiah Dixon (or Dickson), a corporal in the Royal North Carolina Regiment. If so, he was to take part in the winter campaign, remain at Wilmington as part of Captain John Wormley's company, and then in 1782 be posted with the company to the Quarter House near Charlestown. (Clark, *Loyalists in the Southern Campaign*, i, 376, 403, 404) On the other hand, he may have been the Captain Dickson to whom Rawdon refers in his letter of 12th July, p 200.

hold them watched on every side with the most vigilant jealousy. There is a certain Stephen Williams, a carpenter in the service of the Chief Engineer, a native of North Carolina of very good character, whom it may be proper for your Lordship to send up here as I am told he is capable of being very serviceable.

Cornwallis to Martin, 1st August 1780   79(1): C

Charles Town
August 1st 1780

His Excellency Governour Martin

Dear Sir

I received yesterday your letter of the 24th. I am much pleased with the offer of the Highlanders and with the esteem and attachment which they profess for the person whom they propose for their commander. From the friendship and confidence in which we have lived, you will not, I am sure, suspect me of thinking any military rank too high for you, but the business of Provincial rank has occasioned so much uneasiness in this army that I do not think it proper for me on many accounts to give that of colonel. You have relieved my distress by offering in the kindest and handsomest manner to accept the command of the corps with an inferior title. I shall therefore beg of you to be their chief as lt colonel commandant with a lt colonel under you. I should have approved very much of Mr Cruden, had I not determined to employ him in the other important business. It will be necessary to explain to the men, when they are engaged, that they are to serve in either of the Carolinas or Virginia. I am much obliged to you and Lord Rawdon for your proclamations. They are in most respects exactly what I should wish, and upon their foundation I hope to form a very compleat one. I hope to leave this place next week and to see his Lordship and you well at Camden.

I am etc

[CORNWALLIS]

§ - §

3 - From Simpson

Simpson to Cornwallis, 22nd July 1780
2(339): LS

Charles Town
July 22nd 1780

The Rt Hon Earl Cornwallis

My Lord

    I take the liberty humbly to represent to your Lordship that several applications have been made at the Secretary's Office to have wills proven for warrants to appraise the estates of persons who are deceased and the other bussiness which is incident to the Court of Ordinary; and as the death of witnesses may render a delay in these matters of the utmost consequence to individuals, and as it may prove a great security to the estates of orphans and minors as well as detect and prevent frauds and irregularities which may be attempted by fictitious claims being hereafter made to property by persons who in fact are not interested therein, and, whilst it gives a confidence and security to the honest executor, will deter those who might incline to be otherwise from fraudulent practices, I humbly beg leave to submit to your Lordship whether it will not be proper to permit the usual bussiness cognizable by the Ordinary to be transacted in the manner heretofore accustomed, and the more especially as it doth not appear that the least inconvenience or detriment can arise therefrom.

I am with great regard
Your Lordship's most faithfull and most obedient humble servant

JA SIMPSON

Simpson to Cornwallis, 30th July 1780
2(393): LS

Charles Town
July 30th 1780

Rt Hon Earl Cornwallis

My Lord

    On my receiving information that the records and other publick papers belonging to this province were thrown together in great disorder at the State House, I went thither this morning in order to view the condition they were in and found they were all taken doun from the places where they were used to be deposited and promiscuously thrown into casks and boxes in such a manner that, unless some imediate care is taken for their preservation, many of them will unavoidably be destroy'd.

As the revenue of the Crown as well as all the private property in the country and the interests of many British subjects may be much prejudiced by such an event, I have thought it my duty to represent to your Lordship the condition in which I found them that, if you should judge it proper, some fit persons may be authorized to receive them into their charge and to take due care for their future preservation.

I have the honor to be with due regard
Your Lordship's most faithfull and obedient humble servant

JA SIMPSON

§ - §

4 - Other papers

Moultrie to Cornwallis, 29th June 1780　　　　　　　　　　　　　　　　*2(214): ALS*

Charles Town
June 29th 1780

My Lord

I have the honor to inform your Lordship that Doctor Houston, a Continental officer and prisoner of war upon parole to his Excellency Sir Henry Clinton, is now detained in Georgia on a charge of treason. Three evidences appear against him, who, to support this charge, swear they saw him in the American camp when that place was besieged, aiding and assisting the French and Americans. My Lord, I look upon it my duty to require his discharge from his Excellency Sir James Wright and that he may be permitted to return to the hospital in Charles Town, where he is much wanted. I am therefore to request your Lordship will allow me to write to Georgia for that purpose.

I have the honor to be, my Lord,
Your Lordship's most obedient and very humble servant

WILL^M MOULTRIE[11], Brigadier General

---

[11] William Moultrie (1730-1805) was the son of a Scottish physician who had migrated to Charlestown shortly before or shortly after William's birth. Acquiring a large estate in St John's Berkeley, William became proficient in military affairs from the time of his service as a Provincial captain in the Cherokee War. Having served several years in the Commons House of Assembly, he was from 1775 to 1780 a member successively of the two Provincial Congresses and of the Legislative Council and Senate, but these duties were incidental to his involvement in the military line. In 1775 he was elected colonel of the 2nd regiment raised by the first Provincial Congress and in June of the following year commanded at Fort Sullivan, which was later named after him following the repulse of the British fleet. Although his courage and judgement were vindicated, his preparations for the engagement offered some ground for the criticism that he was too easy-going and careless. The next September his regiment

Return of Continental prisoners of war, 27th July 1780 2(345): DS

Return of the Continental Prisoners of War to July 23rd inclusive

	In Charles Town	Sent to Hadril's Point	Officers gone out of this province and servants	Officers exchanged	Per lists in office	Total
Muster'd at barracks	1028	-	-	-	-	1028
Officers	9	258	9	4	-	280
Servants	6	260	9	-	-	275
Quarter Master's Department	36	-	-	-	-	36
Engineer's Department	22	-	-	-	-	22
Commissary of Stores' Department	14	-	-	-	-	14
Artillery Department	10	-	-	-	-	10
Taylors at work for British Legion	7	-	-	-	-	7
On prison ship	25	-	-	-	-	25
In hospital	401	-	-	-	-	401
On parole or protection	-	-	-	-	28	28
Enlisted or gone on board ships	-	-	-	-	187	187
Deserted	-	6	-	-	50	56
Dead	-	-	-	-	233	233
Total	1558	524	18	4	498	2602

LEWIS DE ROSSET[12], Commissary, Prisoners   Charles Town, July 27th 1780

---

was transferred to the Continental line and he himself was shortly afterwards promoted to brigadier general on the Continental establishment. As such he commanded a force largely of militia which in February 1779 defeated a party of British troops at Beaufort, and when in the following May Prevost marched on Charlestown, he saved the town by a rapid and skilful retreat followed by a determined stand against surrender. Having fortunately escaped death in the siege of Charlestown, when a cannon ball struck the bed from which he had just risen, he was now the officer commanding the revolutionary prisoners of war at Haddrell's Point. He would be exchanged in June 1781 under the cartel with Greene and, sailing for Philadelphia, would take no further active part in the war. In later life he would serve two terms as Governor of South Carolina before publishing his memoirs, a valuable source for the revolutionary history of South Carolina and Georgia. His brother John was a loyalist who was Lt Governor of East Florida. (Johnson, *Traditions*, 232; *DAB*; *Appletons*'; Drayton, *Memoirs*, ii, 311; McCrady, *SC in the Rev 1775-1780*, passim; Garden, *Anecdotes* (1st series), 11; Moultrie, *Memoirs*, ii, 200)

[12] From 1752 until the revolution the Hon Lewis Henry De Rosset had been a Member of HM Council in North Carolina, a body which acted both as the upper house of the legislature and as a privy council advising the Governor in the exercise of his functions. He had at times held other civil offices such as Receiver General of the King's Quit Rent and served in a military capacity under Tryon and Waddell. According to DeMond, 'He had been one of North Carolina's most useful and prominent citizens and was held in respect and confidence by the common

NB: Two sick officers and their servants I believe are included in the Hospital List.

Kalb to Cornwallis, 16th July 1780[13] 2(313): ALS

Head Quarters of the American Southern Army
July 16th 1780

His Excellency the Rt Hon Lord Cornwallis
Lt General etc

My Lord

The Virginian prisoners of war in your power being distressed for various articles of clothing, I confidently apply to you to obtain a passport for a State vessel to go to Charlestown with baggage for the captive officers, clothing for the soldiers and some articles of refreshment for all, the passport to mention the vessel to return safe. I do not doubt but your Excellency will please to grant the same and direct it to me.

Would your Lordship please also to grant the request of Miss Betsy Phile as mentioned in my inclosed letter to her[14]. I should consider it as a personal and very particular favor.

With due respect I have the honor to be
Your Excellency's most obedient and very humble servant

BARON DE KALB
Major General Commanding etc

---

people as well as by the Governor.' Now a commissary general of prisoners, he would retire after the war to England, where in 1783 he was active in supporting the claims of North Carolina loyalists for their losses. He himself claimed £10,153 and was awarded £2,695. (DeMond, *Loyalists in NC*, 56-7, 204, 252; WO 65/164(7) (National Archives, Kew))

[13] This letter was enclosed with Rawdon's of 24th July to Cornwallis, p 219.

[14] There is no copy of Kalb's letter to Elizabeth Phile, who was the daughter of Dr Frederick Phile, a physician in Philadelphia. Before the British occupation of the city Dr Phile and his wife had befriended a certain Colonel White of Georgia and a person who was claimed by White to be his wife but who was in fact his mistress. The Philes agreed to allow the childless couple to raise twelve years old Elizabeth as their own, but soon after White and his mistress had returned with her to Georgia, Dr Phile was shocked to learn that White's actual wife was living in New York. When in consequence he sought to arrange the return of his daughter, he was rebuffed not only by the couple but also by Elizabeth herself, who had the effrontery to claim that White and his mistress were her real parents. Unwilling to travel to Georgia because of his service in a Continental hospital in Pennsylvania, Dr Phile turned in 1778 for help to his old friend Kalb, whom he had known since the latter's first visit to North America ten years earlier. Kalb in turn wrote to Henry Laurens, who promised that, on receiving written and signed instructions from Phile, he would transmit them to his friends to the southward in the expectation that they would be enabled to enlist the aid of government. Now, two years later, the matter remained unresolved, leading Kalb to seek to facilitate the passage of Elizabeth to the north by land. As will be seen from Cornwallis's reply, she appeared to favour proceeding there by sea. (Kalb to Henry Laurens, 16th April 1778 (The Henry Laurens Papers, South Carolina Historical Society, Charleston SC); Henry Laurens to Kalb, 22nd April 1778 (Paul H Smith ed, *Letters of Delegates to Congress 1774-1789* (Library of Congress, 1976-2000), ix, 471; T W Lipscomb to the editor, 14th March 2005)

Cornwallis to Kalb, 6th August 1780 79(17): ACS

Charlestown
August 6th 1780

Major General Baron de Kalb etc etc etc

Sir

About the time that I received your letter of the 16th of July, an application of the same nature was made to me by Brigadier General Woodford[15]. In consequence of your request and his, I have order'd a passport to be given to Captain Blackwell of the Virginian troops[16] for four months, and the commanding officer of the navy has sent by him another passeport, for a vessel to return from Virginia with the necessaries and refreshments wanted by the officers and soldiers.

I sent immediately your letter to Miss Betsy Phile and inclose to you her answer[17]. I beg leave to assure you that if she had preferred going by land, I should have been glad to have shewn my disposition to oblige you by contributing every thing in my power to the convenience of her journey.

I am, sir, with due respect
Your most obedient and most humble servant

CORNWALLIS

---

[15] William Woodford (1734-1780) was the son of an Englishman who had settled in Caroline County, Virginia. William had served as a commissioned officer in the Provincial forces during the Seven Years' War and as a Justice of the Peace for Caroline County during the colonial era. In 1775, as colonel of a Virginia revolutionary regiment, he opposed the forces of Lord Dunmore, the royal Governor, compelling him in December to take refuge aboard ship. In February 1776 he was appointed to the colonelcy of the 2nd Virginia Continental Regiment and one year later was promoted to brigadier general in the Continental line. He subsequently fought at Brandywine, where he was wounded in the hand, and at Germantown and Monmouth before serving in New Jersey. On 13th December 1779 Washington ordered him to proceed with 700 men to the aid of Charlestown, where he arrived on 7th April, having made a march of 500 miles in 28 days. Now a prisoner, he would be permitted by Balfour to go to New York for the recovery of his health, but would die there on 13th November, being buried in Old Trinity Church Yard. (*DAB*; *Appletons'*; McCrady, *SC in the Rev 1775-1780*, 458)

[16] Blackwell was either Captain John E Blackwell (?-1808) or Captain Joseph Blackwell (?-1823), both of whom were serving in Virginia Continental Regiments and had been taken prisoner at Charlestown. (Heitman, *Historical Register*, 105)

[17] *her answer*: no copy.

Simons to Cornwallis, 11th August 1780 63(36): ALS

Friday, August 11th 1780

To the Rt Hon Earl of Cornwallis

My Lord

Hearing that your Lordship is on the road and to stop in this neighbourhood, I have presumed to address your Lordship on a subject which I much fear I have been too troublesome on already, but from your Lordship's well known humanity I hope the sircumstances which I shall relate will be such as will in some measure plead my excuse for troubling you on your journey. I have already represented to your Lordship the situation of my family, added to which the small pox is broke out among them, and I expect in a few days to have the most melancholy prospect before me that can possibly be presented. I have but one female in my plantation that has had this disorder, and four fifths of the whole of my family of blacks and whites are yet to take it. The season of the year being so far advanced makes me fear it will prove fatal to many, particularly to Mrs Simons, whose situation wou'd be dangerous to take it in any season. I have therefore to entreat your Lordship's further indulgence to remain on my plantation to render that assistance to my family which nature and humanity requires, as I have every reson to beleive that I shall, at the time limitted to go down, leave my family in a situation truly distressing. My indisposition compels me to make my application in this way, not being able to do it in person.

I have the honor to be, my Lord,
Your Lordship's most obedient and humble servant

KEAT^G SIMONS[18]

[*Endorsed:*]

Granted.

§ - §

---

[18] Keating Simons (1753-1834) was writing to Cornwallis from Lewisfield plantation, an estate of some 1,000 acres which lay on the western bank of the Cooper River in St John Berkeley Parish. He had gained it by marriage to Sarah Lewis in 1774. Having in the following year served as an ensign in the royal militia, he had by 1780 been elected twice to the South Carolina revolutionary legislature, a circumstance which had now required him to enter into a parole consigning him to the sea islands. He, his wife and at least two of his three children would survive the outbreak of small pox on his plantation, where he would remain until the summer of 1781. With the tide of events then flowing in favour of the revolutionaries, he would go off to join Marion as a brigade major. After the war he continued the factorage firm established by his father, served briefly in the legislature, and attended the conventions of 1788 and 1790, the first dealing with the ratification of the federal constitution (which he voted against) and the second involving the adoption of a revised constitution for South Carolina. Otherwise he played a mostly minor role in public affairs, culminating by 1832 in his chairmanship of a committee in support of state rights. At his death he left 178 slaves at Lewisfield, where he was buried, and 22 slaves at his three-storey residence on Orange Street in Charleston. (Bailey and Cooper, *SC House of Representaives*,iii, 650-2; McCrady, *SC in the Rev 1775-1780*, 893; Moss, *SC Patriots*, 865; Rogers Jr, *Georgetown County*, 241; Gregorie, *Sumter*, 32n, 210)

Index[1]

Abandoned plantations, appropriation or destruction of by the British, 141
Abrahams, ——, 317n-8
Actions —
    near Bratton's plantation, 150, 170, 201-2, 207, 250, 253;
    near Cedar Spring, 150, 302-3;
    involving William R Davie, 224n;
    at Earle's Ford, 150, 211, 253-5;
    involving Georgians, 251, 253;
    at Hanging Rock, 150, 179;
    at Hill's iron works, 143;
    at Lenud's Ferry, 52;
    at Ramsour's Mill, 153, 162, 182, 184-5, 188-9, 238-9, 245, 248, 253, 363;
    at Rocky Mount, 150, 176, 223-5;
    at the Waxhaws, 35, 52-3
Adamson, William, 202n, 207, 213-4, 218-9
Address to become British subjects, 67n-71
Address to the inhabitants of Charlotte, 129-130
Allen, Isaac, 152, 178, 256, 259n, 260, 269, 336, 339, 342
Allen, Levi and Ethan, 195n
American riflemen, skill of, 154
Ancrum, George, 86n
André, John, 100n, 119, 165, 171
Arbuthnot, Marriot, 4, 7n, 10-12, 14-16, 18, 22, 61-2, 66-7, 125, 166, 169, 173-5, 177, 179-180, 195
Ardesoif, John Plummer, 306n, 309, 317-8
Armand and his corps, 45n
Augusta —
    field works at, 245, 273;
    importance of post at, 339, 345;
    navigation of Savannah River to, 152-3, 284, 337;
    seat of the Indian trade etc, 152, 238, 272

Back Country, The —
    definition of, 32;
    disaffected men of influence in, 34, 40, 78-80;
    its fauna, flora, and terrain, 32;
    imminent pacification of, 243;
    lines of conduct towards proposed by Balfour, 239;
    loyalism in, 35, 111-2;
    its possession central to British strategy, 152, 256;
    settlers in, 33-5
Balfour, Nisbet, 12, 26, 32, 35n-7n, 44, 48, 60, 72-98, 106-7, 110-3, 118, 120, 161, 171, 178, 195, 198, 206, 209-213, 215, 226-7, 235-256, 260, 265-9, 273-5, 290-1, 293, 300-2, 329, 333, 335, 338-9, 343-7, 352
Ball Sr, Elias, 51n-2, 306-7, 313-4, 316, 365
Barrow, Thomas, 276n
Beames, James, 144n
Beard, Jonas, 90n, 112, 295
Benson, George, 172n
Birmingham, John, 324n-7
Black, Peter, 265n
Blackwell, John E and Joseph, 376n
Bostwick, Chesley, 278n
Bowie, John, 97n, 115, 240
Bowyer, Henry, 35
Bradshaw, J Smith, 16n
Brandon, Thomas, 295n
Branson, Eli, 186n
Bratton, William, 139n, 201, 223
'Breaking up' of loyalist habitations: see 'Plundering by banditti or revolutionaries'
British diversion in the Chesapeake, 173-4, 177, 179
British etc officers, character of, 221-2
British strategy, 3-4, 56-7, 61-2, 67-8, 152, 159, 162-3, 166, 169, 173, 177, 179, 191, 205, 215, 226-7 —
    whether to pursue a policy of lenity or severity, 155-6, 365
British superiority at sea, 4, 173
British troops convicted of desertion, 165
Brodrick, The Hon Henry, 22n
Brown, Thomas, 92, 153, 178, 237-241, 243-5, 249, 251, 256, 270, 271n-5, 277-284, 329, 334, 336-8, 345, 348 —
    his past involvement in the war and the events leading up to it, 278-281
Bryan, Samuel (see also 'North Carolina loyalists'), 153, 168n, 190, 192, 203, 211, 218-9
Buford, Abraham, 35, 52n

---

[1] The letter 'n' after the number of a page indicates the presence there of biographical or identifying information, whether in a footnote or, in the case of an introductory chapter, in the body of the text.

Camden, 31-2, 195
Cameron, Allan, 202n
Campbell, Archibald, 280n, 345
Campbell, Charles, 227n, 258, 264
Campbell, John, 167n, 281, 284
Campbell, Lord William, 279n
Cantey, Charles, 144n
Captured troops —
    enlistment of, 185, 192-3, 244-5, 276-7, 282, 351;
    escape of, 165, 189, 192, 218, 222, 315, 362;
    exchange of, 213-4, 218
Carden, John, 183n, 208, 223-4
Cary, James, 229, 245n
Cassells, James, 307n, 313-4, 316, 320, 323
Caswell, The Hon Richard, 60n, 136-7, 149, 157, 168, 170, 179, 186-7, 192, 196-7, 200, 204, 206, 211, 224, 312, 323
Caswell, William, 136n
Catawba nation, 128n-9, 139, 253
Cavalry —
    nature and effect of, 205;
    importance of, 227
Ceded Lands, 258, 345 —
    definition of, 257n;
    proposed removal of disaffected men of influence, 283;
    resort of fugitives from justice, 272;
    settlers delivering up arms etc, 353;
    settlers hardy, numerous and ill disposed, 152, 260, 267, 283, 339, 347
Chapman, Thomas, 225n
Charlestown —
    arrangement of, 162;
    confused state of public business at, 121, 170, 205, 213;
    Court of Ordinary at, 272;
    difficulty of its communication with Camden, 153-4, 216, 227;
    garrison of, 215-6;
    magazine, blowing up of, 57n, 296;
    public records at the State House, 272-3;
Cheney, Baily, 286n
Cheraw Hill, 131n
Chesnut, John, 218n
Civil and commercial affairs of SC, regulation of by the British, 157, 168, 179n, 248
Clark, Elijah, 150, 257n-8, 303
Clarke, ——, 211
Clarke, Alured, 178, 245, 328-9, 330n-343, 345, 352 —
    avoids interference with civil power, 330;
    commanding in Georgia, 328;
    to command also in East Florida, 167, 335, 347, 354
Clary, Daniel, 257, 260, 264n-5
Climate (*see also* 'Diseases'), intense heat and sickliness of, 157, 169, 171, 177, 179, 209, 214-5, 218, 225-7, 244, 304-5, 319, 321, 323-4, 326, 334, 338, 363
Clinton, Sir Henry, KB —
    biographical info, 5-6n;
    his part in the siege of Charlestown, 3-7, 9-22;
    his appointment of Cornwallis to command in the Southern Department, 31;
    his appointment of Balfour to command a corps cooperating with Cornwallis, 48;
    his appointment of Ferguson as Inspector of Militia, 48, 58;
    on the friendly disposition of SC's inhabitants, 54, 56, 60-1;
    his instructions on the discharge of Cornwallis's command, 53, 56-65, 68, 173, 175;
    his and the Commissioners' proclamations: *see* 'Proclamations';
    ready to reinforce Cornwallis's move to the Back Country, 45, 48;
    his proposed diversion in the Chesapeake, 174
Cole, ——, 224n
Commissaries, British, 63, 65, 91, 134, 164-5, 175, 183, 193-4, 212, 271, 294, 301, 321, 364
Commissioners of roads, appointment of, 192, 245
Contingent expenses at Ninety Six, 256
Convalescents, employment of, 221, 254
Cornwallis, Charles, Earl —
    his appointment as GOC in the Southern Department, 31, 63;
    his appointment of Balfour as Commandant of Charlestown, 171, 178, 209, 215, 227, 250, 335;
    his appointment of Rawdon to command at Camden and his instructions on the tactics to be pursued there, 134, 191, 198, 205-6, 209;
    his assignment of discretionary powers to subordinate officers, 88, 141, 244, 247;
    his attention to civil and commercial matters, 179, 205;
    biographical info, 5n-6;
    his carrying the war into North Carolina, 55, 119, 162-3, 166, 169, 177, 191, 198, 205-6, 215, 371;
    his command during the siege of Charlestown, 5-7, 9-22;
    on the communication between Charlestown and Camden, 216, 221-2,

226-7, 320-2;
his disposition of the corps dispatched to occupy Ninety Six, 87, 98, 177;
his disposition of the rest of the troops, 161, 177-8, 215-6, 227, 244-5, 247, 250, 256, 267, 269, 320, 322, 329, 342;
his employment of artillery, 210, 222;
his expediting supplies to Camden, 210, 212, 230;
his formation or regulation of the royal militia, 82, 87-9, 102, 109, 123-4, 134, 141, 160, 168-9, 185-6, 245, 247, 251, 301, 313-4, 316, 328-9;
his humanity, 318-9, 376-7;
on the importance of holding the Back Country, 256;
his inability to reinforce Pensacola, 167;
on incipient unrest, 175-7;
his march to occupy Camden, 31, 47, 50-3;
on the need for cavalry, 227;
his policy toward the disaffected not on parole, 123-4, 160, 244, 305;
his policy toward East Florida, 167-8, 335, 354;
his policy toward Georgia, 168, 328-9, 334-5, 346-7, 350-1;
his policy on the granting and effect of paroles or protection, 83, 109, 122-4, 130, 160-1, 191, 305, 313;
his policy, inappropriate, of lenity and conciliation, 155-6;
his policy toward native Americans, 245, 275;
his policy toward violent persecutors of loyalists, 109, 123-4, 130, 305;
on privateers infesting Charlestown bar, 180;
on prize money, 318;
his reasons for punishing insurgents east of the Wateree and Santee, 226-7;
his request for a diversion in the Chesapeake, 177;
on seizing persons for retaliation, 192;
on the sufficiency of his troops, 43-4, 51, 163, 175, 215;
his way of complying with, and criticism of, the proclamations of Clinton and the Commissioners, 83, 88, 109, 124, 130, 141, 159, 161;
his unfitness to command, 156
Cornwallis, The Hon William, 186n
Crackers, 34n
Cruden, John, 219n, 222, 371
Cruger, John Harris, 92, 152n, 178, 210, 244, 247, 249, 250, 254, 256-265, 258n, 267, 269, 270, 329, 336, 339
Cunningham, John, 242n
Cunningham, Robert, 117n-9, 169, 246-7, 252, 256, 301-2

Dansey, William Collins, 47n, 50, 72-3
Dawkins, George, 110n, 269
De Peyster, Abraham, 249n, 255, 300-1
De Peyster, Frederick, 104n, 300
Deputy judge advocate, warrant for, 59-60
De Rosset, The Hon Lewis Henry, 374n
Detachments —
    danger in distant, 191, 198, 206;
    none for New York, 215
Dickson, ———, 200, 370n
Disaffection —
    and removal of almost all men of influence outside Charlestown, 78-80, 83;
    in the neighbourhood of Augusta, 254;
    about Black River, 230;
    in former militia regiments, 91, 293, 295-6;
    of Georgetown District, 304, 310;
    from Nelson's Ferry to the Congarees, 78, 80, 266;
    in the neighbourhood of Ninety Six, 266;
    north of Rocky Mount, 194;
    from the Saluda to the Indian lands, 239
Disarming and otherwise dealing with the disaffected, 82, 85, 87, 122-4, 160-1, 239, 244, 251, 259, 293, 296, 298, 305, 310, 313-4
Diseases prevalent in the Carolinas and Georgia (*see also* 'Climate'), 157, 179, 218, 304-5, 323-4, 326, 364, 377
Dixon, ———, 370n
Dooly, John, capitulation of etc, 270n-1, 329, 339
Dowd, Connor, 136
Doyle, John, 185n, 203, 215
Drayton, William Henry, 279n
Dunlap, James, 74n, 101, 150, 211, 253-5, 302-3
Dunworth, Peter, 266n
Durnford, Andrew, 337n-8

East Florida, 167-8, 280, 335, 342-3, 354, 360
Earle, Baylis, 255
Ebenezer, petition from, 348-351
Edghill, Thomas, 289n, 290
Ellison, Robert, 144n
Elphinstone, The Hon George Keith, 16n, 18
Emissaries —
    noms de guerre, 48-9n;
    sent into the interior of SC, 93-5, 97n, 194;
    sent into NC, 133, 136, 194

Enemy strategy, 157, 168-9
England, Richard, 172n, 215

False calm in SC and Georgia, 39, 54-6, 60-1, 85, 89, 152, 329
Ferguson, Patrick, 4, 7, 15, 37n-8n, 48, 53-4, 58, 72-4, 77, 81, 85, 90, 99-109, 150, 161-2, 178, 189, 202, 237, 242, 245-7, 249, 251-2, 257-8, 269, 285-303, 329
Fisher, John, 80n, 151, 362
Flags of truce, 217-8, 220
Fletcher, Duncan, 300n
Floyd, Matthew, 142n, 151, 184, 293
Fort Rutledge (Seneca), 89n-90, 93, 238, 271, 274-5
    capitulation of, 96-7;
    demolition of, 245, 260n
Fraser, Hugh, Henry David, and William, 239n
Fraser, James, 25n
Fraser, Thomas, 243n, 245
French expeditionary forces, 173, 245
Fyffe, Charles, 325n

Gaillard, Theodore, 51n, 313-4, 316, 321, 324, 326, 366
Gàlvez, Don Bernado de (*biographical note*, III, 305), 164, 273, 282
Garden, Benjamin, capitulation of, 272n
Garrett, Patrick, 211n
Gates, Horatio, 176n, 177, 229 —
    his becoming GOC in the Southern Department, 157, 224;
    his march on Camden, 157, 179, 180, 231-2, 323
Georgetown —
    occupation of by the British, 150, 215, 304-327;
    post there secure against attack, 323;
    withdrawal from if real danger arises, 306, 311, 318;
    abandonment of, 320-2, 324, 326;
    disposition and petition of principal inhabitants, 304, 306-8, 310, 313, 324
Georgia (*see also* 'Augusta' and 'Ceded Lands') —
    delay in occupying Augusta, 337;
    disloyalty of settlers, 243;
    The Disqualifying Act 1780, 283n;
    effect of war on, 352;
    frontier towards SC in perfect security, 334;
    of no object to a foreign enemy, 168, 328, 335;
    posts necessary only at Savannah and Augusta, 334, 339;
    security of, 345-8, 351-2;
    no cavalry permitted other than militia horse, 335, 339, 343-5, 347, 352;
    payment of militia for previous service, 336, 343-5, 347, 352
Germain, Lord George, 281, 344
Gibbs, Thomas, 208n
Gist, Mordecai, 230n
Glasier, Beamsly, 343, 354, 355n-360
Goodwin, Robert, 91n, 112-3, 144n, 246, 295
Gordon, ——, 166n
Gordon, Hugh Mackay, 167n
Gordon, James, 315n-6, 324
Graham, Colin, 81n, 82, 85, 87, 90, 98, 161, 177-8, 206, 249, 361-3
Graham, John, 164n, 241, 343-5
Graham, William, 303n
Gratton, William, 175n
Graves, Thomas (*biographical note*, V, 146), 166, 173, 216
Gray, Robert, 135n
Gregory, Benjamin, 119n, 120

Hamilton, John, 55n, 162, 185-6, 193, 245
Hammond, Samuel, capitulation of etc, 236n-8, 240, 244, 270, 292-3, 295, 329
Hanger, The Hon George, 14, 33-4, 38n-9n, 58, 78, 83-4, 154, 178
Harper, Daniel and Sarah Dickey, 217n-8
Harrison, Charles, 197n
Harrison, John, (*see also* 'Regiments or corps, British American'), 133-4, 136, 149, 161n, 219
Hayes, John McNamara, 65n, 171
Heatly, William, 80n, 90, 295
Henderson, John, 144n
Henry, John, 59n, 125, 165-6, 169, 173, 179, 180, 316
Heriot, Robert, 144n, 318n-9n, 326
Heriot & Tucker, 306, 309n, 310
Hicks, George, 132n
Hill, West, 204n, 206-7
Hill, William, 142n
Hill's iron works, 140-3
Horry, Daniel, 352n-3
Hospitals or surgeons —
    at Charlestown, 65, 170, 373;
    regimental, 207-8, 251-2, 254, 320
Houstoun, James, 330-1n, 332-4, 339, 373
Houstoun, Sir Patrick, Bt, 283n
Howe, Robert, 280n
Howe, Sir William, 275n, 281
Hoy, James, 367n
Huck, Christian, 139n, 142-3, 150, 170, 176, 182, 201, 206-7
Huger, Daniel, 145n, 200
Hughes, ——, 342, 355
Hunt, Cosby, 201n, 207

Incipient unrest, 168-170, 175-8, 193, 199, 201-2, 221, 253-5, 292, 301-3, 320
Indian line, The old, 112n, 266
Innes, Alexander, 17n, 20, 47, 76, 82, 84-5, 89-90, 110-120, 161, 206, 209-210, 212, 235, 237, 240, 250, 258, 265-270, 329
Inspectors of refugees, 63, 164
Irvin, Alexander, 218n
Irwing, ——, 367n

Johnson, ——, 134-5n
Johnson, Sir William, Bt, 281n
Johnston, Andrew, 281n-2
Justices of the Peace, appointment of, 248

Kalb, Johann, 149, 157, 163n, 168, 170, 176, 187, 191, 194, 197, 200, 204-6, 208, 210, 211, 214-5, 217-220, 224, 230, 292, 319, 370, 375-6
Kershaw, Ely, 137n, 144n
Kershaw, Joseph, 31-2, 137n, 144n, 183
King, Charles, 75n
Kinloch, David, 114n, 183, 187-9, 194-5, 201, 203, 224-5, 229, 363
Kirkland, Moses, 236n, 252, 260
Knecht, Anthony, 212n
Knowles, John, 63n
Knyphausen, Freiherr Wilhelm von, 126n, 172

Lacey, ——, 194n
Lacey Jr, Edward, 188n-9, 191
La Motte Piquet, 186n
Laurens, Henry, 279n
Lee's Legion, 44n
Legge, William, Earl of Dartmouth, 281n
Legget, John, 205n
Leonard, David, John, and Thomas, 129n
Lesesne, Thomas, 311-2n, 313, 315
Leslie, The Hon Alexander (*biographical info*, III, 3-4), 331
Lewis, ——, 202
Lightner, Michael, 250n
Lincoln, Benjamin, 4, 5, 22, 349n
Lisle, John, 176n
Lord, Andrew, 86n
Love, David, 136n
Low Country, The —
    heavy storms and severe flooding of, 154, 226, 230, 321-2, 324-6, 365;
    description of, 150n
Lutwidge, Skeffington, 180n

MacDonald, Alexander, 178n, 364
Macleod, John, 210n
Malmedy, François Lellorquis, Marquis de, 19n
Majors of brigade, 175

Manley, John, 47n, 172
Manson, Daniel, 21n, 221
Martin, Josiah, 66n, 119, 192, 200, 205, 210, 211, 214, 219, 222, 227, 268-371
Mason, Charles, 131n, 136
Maxwell, Andrew, 252n, 265-6
Maxwell, John Robert (*identifying note*, III, 437), 340
McArthur, Archibald, 87n, 130-7, 149, 150-1, 161, 168, 170, 176-8, 183, 187, 190, 192, 194, 196, 199, 200, 203-5, 209, 211, 214, 216, 218, 223, 226, 267, 305, 314, 319, 320, 364-5, 370
McBean, Alexander, 135n
McClure, James, 201n
McClure, John, 201n
McCra(w), Alexander, 136n
McCra(w), Duncan, 136n
McCrea, ——, 186
McCulloch, Kenneth, 229n
McDowell, Charles (*biographical note*, II, 109), 150
McFarlane, William, 300n, 303
McGregor, John, 202n, 207
McIntosh, Alexander, 132n
McIntosh, Roderick ('Rory'), 64n
McKenny (McKinny), Timothy, 264n
McKinnon, John, 127n, 210, 221, 366-7
McLaurin, Euan, 252n, 254, 265-7
McLeane, ——, 66n
McNeil, Daniel, 185n, 193
McWilliams, ——, 189, 192
Mecan, Thomas, 190n, 194, 199, 223, 364
Meek, William, 260n
Mews, James, 186n
Middleton, Henry, 76n
Middleton, Robert, capitulation of, 272n, 329
Militia, character of, 321
Militia, revolutionary —
    Georgia, 150, 251, 253-5, 257-8, 266, 293, 301-3;
    North Carolina, 35, 149, 150, 157, 162, 168, 176, 179, 186-7, 196-7, 200, 208, 211, 214, 217, 224, 253-5, 257-8, 266-7, 293, 301-3, 319, 320, 322-3, 327;
    Overmountain, 150, 257-8, 266, 293, 301-3;
    South Carolina, 35, 150, 168, 187, 194, 200, 213, 219, 223, 229, 231, 248, 253, 301-2, 322-3, 327, 363;
    Virginia, 149, 157, 168, 186-7, 197
Militia, royal, 37, 40 —
    adoption of catchment areas demarcated by the revolutionaries, 122, 160, 287;
    adoption of pre-war catchment areas, 363;
    admission of disaffected and 'Quiet' men, 151, 177, 296-9;

Militia, royal (*continued*)
    blank warrant appointing colonels, 89;
    Bryan's corps: *see* 'North Carolina loyalists';
    characterised as light troops, 169;
    colonels to act also as Justices of the Peace, 88-9, 160;
    defections, 151, 176-7, 195, 293, 319, 320, 322-3;
    disposition, numbers, and support from regulars, 169, 224, 292-3, 303;
    failure to raise battalion in Georgetown District, 150, 323;
    field officers, want of principal persons to appoint as, 34, 40, 78-80, 112, 133, 140, 185-6, 236, 242, 249, 363;
    fragility of, 150-1, 169-170, 177, 179, 182, 207, 211, 253-5, 365;
    gratuities or other rewards for, 294-5, 301;
    instructions not to insult or molest the disaffected not in arms, 298;
    plan for regulating etc, 122-4;
    preparations for forming, 73, 76-7, 79-83, 85, 87-8, 90-1, 100-109, 112-3, 132-6, 140-3, 157, 160-2, 168, 237, 239, 242, 245-9, 251-2, 285-291, 295-9, 305-7, 313, 316, 352, 361-2;
    punishments for misbehaving, plundering, or quitting when on service, 294-5;
    any form of regularity, difficulty in imposing, 293;
    regulation of in Georgia, 274;
    shortage of arms, ammunition etc for, 208, 249, 251, 258, 293, 295-6, 301, 303, 306, 311;
    slow in turning out, 258;
    subsistence or pay of, 290, 293-4, 301;
    supply of waggons, horses etc for, 294;
    utility, or otherwise, of, 37, 77, 87, 90-1, 100, 107, 160, 169, 178, 237, 246, 252, 253-5, 328-9, 338, 346, 361;
    when embodied, 170, 177-8, 184, 189, 190, 195, 201-3, 211, 217, 224, 229, 242, 248-9, 253-5, 257, 260, 265, 267, 269, 301-3, 363, 365-7

Miller, ——, 137
Mills, Ambrose, 116n, 118-9, 242
Mills, William Henry, 132n, 134-6, 151, 177, 196-7, 226, 229, 305, 307, 311, 313, 316, 319, 320, 322-4
Misrepresentation of British policy, 40, 139
Moncrief, James, 58n, 64, 328, 335, 337, 342-3, 354, 360
Moore, James, 97n, 115
Moore, James, 229n, 231, 321

Moore, John, 162n, 182, 184-5, 188-9, 193, 202, 237, 245, 363
Moore, Philip, 164n
Mossman, James, 332n
Motte, Isaac, 27n
Motte, Jacob, 76n
Moultrie, The Hon John, 309n
Moultrie, William, 36, 373n
Murchieson, Magnus, 365n
Murphy, John, 84n, 112, 118

Nairne, John and William, 320n
Native Americans (*see also* 'Catawba nation'), 238, 245, 271-5, 278, 281-2, 336, 338
Neel, Andrew, 176n, 223
Newton, William, 57, 63
Ninety Six (village), 32, 76n, 87, 238-9 —
    field works at, 245, 291-2
Nooth, John Mervin, 171n
North Carolina —
    cattle killed by enemy or driven across Cape Fear River, 187;
    deception as to British point of entry, 198, 215;
    effect of climate on British operations there, 169;
    enemy forces there, 136-7, 140-2, 149, 162-3, 186-7, 194, 196-7, 211;
    exertions of revolutionary Government there to raise more troops, 168;
    harvest awaited there before British entry, 55, 162;
    want of provisions there, 55;
    wheat harvested or fit to reap there, 177, 187, 301
North Carolina loyalists —
    in arms, 60, 162, 182, 184-5;
    defeated at Ramsour's Mill, 153, 162, 182, 184-5, 188-9;
    general uprising of, British conditional consent to, 203, 206;
    instructed to gather harvest and remain quiet till British entry, 55, 119, 129, 162, 187, 192, 203, 213;
    numerous, 162;
    repression and maltreatment of by revolutionaries, 153, 168, 177, 186, 203, 211, 369-371;
    Samuel Bryan's corps (NC refugees), 153, 168, 177, 190-2, 199, 204, 218, 224, 226, 229;
    Scots Highlanders to form a Provincial regiment, 177, 219-222, 368, 371

Obman, Jacob Daniel, 276n
O'Neaill, Henry, 118n
O'Neale, ——, 136
Orangeburg District, loyalty of, 106-9
Orangeburg village —
    fort, courthouse and jail at, 107;
    strategic location of, 107
Osborn(e), ——, 214n, 217
Overmountain settlers, 238, 271, 273, 281

Palmer, ——, 135n
Paris, Francis, 343n
Parker, William, 311n-3, 315
Paroles —
    arrest in Georgia for treason of persons subject to, 330-3;
    cancelled partly by proclamation of 3rd June, 40, 88, 109, 130, 161;
    confining to sea islands or other places, 75, 91, 122-4, 160-1, 191, 249-250, 252, 266, 305, 307, 310, 313-4, 377;
    distinction between common and other paroles, 122n;
    form of as respects sea islands, 144-5;
    indiscriminate issue of, 75-6, 85, 132;
    non-observance of, 40, 79, 193, 322;
    substituted for protection, 83, 85, 122, 252;
    substituted for those initially granted, 85, 122
Paterson, James, 49n, 107, 121-7, 162, 164-5, 169, 171, 205n, 209, 250, 334, 337, 369
Patrick, Henry, 91n
Pattinson, Thomas, 84n, 90, 109, 215, 222-3, 226-7
Patton, Robert, 139n, 188-9, 191
Paymaster —
    at Charlestown, 57, 63, 166n;
    at New York, 178;
    for troops in the field, 178
Peacocke, George, 90n
Pearis, Richard, 89n-90, 92-7, 118
Pendleton, Henry, 165n
Persecution, violent, of loyalists, seizure or imprisonment for, 107, 109, 123, 240, 247, 305, 320-1
Peterson, Robert, 199n, 364
Phile, Elizabeth ('Betsy'), 375n-6
Pickens, Andrew, 79n, 240, 292-3, 295
Pinckney, Charles, 311n, 313, 315
Plundering —
    by banditti, 129, 132, 218, 267, 270, 272;
    by loyalists, the Royal Navy, and British or British American troops, 40, 82, 86, 116, 118, 151, 244, 285-6, 317-8, 349, 365;
    by revolutionaries, 142, 151, 177, 211, 229, 248, 254-5, 267, 269, 271, 315-6, 320, 323, 345, 349
Porterfield, Charles, 163n, 168
Potts, John, 303
Prevost, Augustine, 64n, 336-8, 341, 344, 355
Prevost, Augustine, 330n, 334
Prince's Fort —
    abandonment of by the British, 150, 211, 255;
    location of, 255n
Pringle, John Julius, 196n-7
Privateers, enemy, 180
Proclamations —
    of 22nd May, 49-50;
    of 1st June, 83n, 88, 124, 130, 141, 159, 161;
    of 3rd June, 40, 88n, 130, 141, 159, 161, 174, 183, 193-4;
    by Cornwallis, 179n, 181, 369-371
Propaganda, revolutionary, 40
Property (not provisions), appropriation of enemy's (*see also* 'Stores and other supplies'), 124, 131, 134, 136, 151, 183, 247, 323
Protection (involving oath of allegiance) —
    applicants for charged with treason in Georgia, 330;
    entering into by the disaffected or escaped prisoners, 80, 83, 362;
    indiscriminate granting of, 80, 83, 122, 135;
    no further granting of, 122;
    paroles substituted for, 83, 85, 122;
    violation of, 40, 176, 253, 292-3, 319, 322
Provisions (*see also* 'Stores and other supplies') —
    acquisition or supply of, 74-5, 79, 81, 83, 86, 111, 124, 134-7, 140-1, 151, 188, 190, 226, 240, 244, 273, 290, 293-4, 301, 316-8, 321, 323-4, 326, 342-3, 349-350, 360, 364, 366;
    payment or non-payment for, 65, 164, 175;
    receipts for, 86, 140-1, 164;
    shortage of in the Back Country, 111-2, 129
Pulaski's Legion, 133n

Ramsay, David, 36
Randall, John Bond, 276n
Rapley, Richard, 97n, 115, 240
Rawdon, Francis, Lord, 5, 31-2, 40, 51, 75, 98, 128-130, 134, 137, 140, 142, 149, 151n-2n, 153, 157, 168-9, 170, 179, 182-234, 237, 256, 269, 277, 305, 319, 321, 368-9, 371
    tactics pursued by at Camden, 194, 198-200, 204-5, 208-9, 224, 228, 231-2

Recruitment of British American troops —
    irregularities in, 105n, 243, 245, 282, 329, 351;
    by American Volunteers, 299, 300;
    by British Legion, SC Royalist Regiment, and Volunteers of Ireland, 300;
    by De Lancey's 1st Battalion, 256;
    by Georgia Loyalists, 276-8, 282, 351;
    by King's Rangers, 278, 282, 334, 351

Rees, David, 97n, 114

Reeves, Daniel and Green, 112n

Regiments or corps, British —
    7th (Royal Fusiliers), 32, 61, 84-5, 87, 90, 98, 161, 215, 223, 237, 244;
    16th, 177, 227;
    17th Light Dragoons, 45, 58, 165;
    23rd (Royal Welch Fusiliers), 12, 16, 50, 161, 177, 179, 190-1, 229;
    33rd, 4, 9n, 62, 161, 177, 179, 203, 223;
    42nd, 45, 48, 51;
    60th (Royal American Regiment), 167-8, 335;
    63rd, 61, 150, 177-8, 215-6, 227, 366-7;
    64th, 4, 16, 17, 61;
    71st, 61, 133, 137, 149, 161, 170, 176-7, 179, 183, 194, 200, 204-5, 209, 214, 216, 218, 221, 225, 227-9, 267, 319, 320, 323, 364-5;
    Grenadiers, 21;
    Light infantry, 18, 21, 32, 45, 48, 51, 81, 84-5, 90, 98, 161, 177, 228, 236, 249, 253, 258-260;
    Royal Artillery, 63, 161, 177

Regiments or corps, British American —
    American Volunteers (Ferguson's corps), 4, 32, 61, 79, 84-5, 90, 98, 161, 211, 236-7, 246-9, 253, 303;
    British Legion, 4, 18, 24, 35, 47, 50, 52-3, 140-1, 161, 169, 170, 176-9, 182-3, 190-1, 194, 201, 203, 206, 214, 217-8, 224, 227, 229, 231, 363;
    De Lancey's 1st Battalion (Cruger's corps), 178, 244-5, 247, 249, 256, 258, 260, 329, 336, 339, 348, 351;
    Georgia Loyalists (Wright's corps), 92n, 238, 243-4, 282, 329, 336, 339, 348, 351;
    Harrison's corps, 132, 137, 160-1, 177, 204, 215, 226, 321;
    King's Rangers (Brown's corps), 153, 178, 238, 243-5, 254, 256, 274, 278, 282, 329, 336, 339, 342, 348, 351;
    New Jersey Volunteers, 3rd Battalion (Allen's corps), 178, 245, 256, 259, 260, 329, 336, 342, 348, 351;
    New York Volunteers, 10, 18, 21, 61, 138, 141, 161, 170, 176-7, 183, 201-2, 215, 218, 223-4, 227, 229, 232, 244, 363-4;
    Prince of Wales's American Regiment (Browne's corps), 32, 81, 84-5, 87, 90, 161, 177, 179, 215-6, 224, 228-9, 237, 244, 248, 253;
    Queen's Rangers, 10, 56;
    Royal North Carolina Regiment (Hamilton's corps), 161, 177, 229;
    South Carolina Royalist Regiment (Innes's corps), 10, 17, 18, 84-5, 98, 178, 206, 209-210, 212, 235-6, 240, 243, 247, 249, 254, 256, 258, 260, 265-9;
    Volunteers of Ireland, 10, 61, 161, 177, 179, 190, 203, 223, 229;
    failed attempts to enlist new levies, 169, 240, 243, 245-7, 249, 252, 256

Regiments or corps, Continental, 149, 163, 168, 176, 187, 197, 200

Regiments or corps, Hessian —
    von Dittfurth, 61;
    Jäger Corps, 56;
    von Trümbach, 125;
    von Wissenbach, 167, 335;
    Grenadiers, 56

Reisinger, Fecht, 113-5n

Retaliation, policy of —
    by the British, 192;
    by the revolutionaries, 193

Returns —
    of arms etc at Ninety Six taken from the enemy, 241-2;
    of Continental prisoners of war, 374;
    of garrison at Camden, 233-4;
    of garrison at Ninety Six, 260, 262;
    of military stores sent from Fort Rutledge to Ninety Six, 263

Revolutionaries, active —
    flight of principal etc, 136, 139, 143;
    intimidation or punishment of, 153-4, 155-6, 217, 226-7, 321-2

Richardson Jr, Richard, 144n

Robertson, James, 125-6n

Robertson, James, 330-3n

Rodney, Sir George Brydges, 11n

Ross, Alexander, 73n, 129, 137, 194, 198, 203, 213-4, 218

Rowe, Samuel, 106n

Roy, George, 361n

Royal Navy, 166, 169, 216 —
    Ships: *Beaumont*, 167; *Blonde*, 12; *Halifax*, 175; *Hydra*, 334, 340; *Keppel*, 316, 324; *Loyalist*, 309; *Providence*, 166, 180; *Raleigh*, 12; *Richmond*, 12; *Sandwich*, 12, 17, 166, 169